Early Childhood Education Today

NINTH EDITION

Early Childhood
Education Today

George S. Morrison

University of North Texas

Upper Saddle River, New Jersey
Columbus, Ohio

Library of Congress Cataloging-in-Publication Data

Morrison, George S.

    Early childhood education today / George S. Morrison.—9th ed.

      p. cm.

    Includes bibliographical references and index.

    ISBN 0-13-111798-X

      1. Early childhood education—United States. I. Title

    LB1139.25M66 2004

    372.21—dc21

                                  2003051261

Vice President and Executive Publisher: Jeffery W. Johnston
Publisher: Kevin M. Davis
Associate Editor: Christina M. Tawney
Editorial Assistant: Autumn Crisp
Production Editor: Linda Hillis Bayma
Production Coordination: Elm Street Publishing Services, Inc.
Design Coordinator: Diane C. Lorenzo
Photo Coordinator: Kathleen Kirtland
Cover Designer: Keith Van Norman
Cover image: Corbis
Production Manager: Laura Messerly
Director of Marketing: Ann Castel Davis
Marketing Manager: Amy June
Marketing Coordinator: Tyra Poole

This book was set in Berkeley Book by Carlisle Communications, Ltd. It was printed and bound by Von Hoffman Press, Inc. The cover was printed by The Lehigh Press, Inc.

Photo credits appear on page 579, which constitutes a continuation of the copyright page.

Pearson Prentice Hall™ is a trademark of Pearson Education, Inc.
Pearson® is a registered trademark of Pearson plc
Prentice Hall® is a registered trademark of Pearson Education, Inc.
Merrill® is a registered trademark of Pearson Education, Inc.

Pearson Education Ltd.
Pearson Education Singapore Pte. Ltd.
Pearson Education Canada, Ltd.
Pearson Education—Japan

Pearson Education Australia Pty. Limited
Pearson Education North Asia Ltd.
Pearson Educación de Mexico, S.A. de C.V.
Pearson Education Malaysia Pte. Ltd.

10 9 8 7 6 5 4
ISBN: 0-13-111798-X

For Betty Jane—who has made many sacrifices,
all in the name of deepest love

About the Author

George S. Morrison, Ed.D., shown here with children at the University of North Texas Child Development Laboratory, is professor and the Velma E. Schmidt Endowed Chair in early childhood education at the University of North Texas. Dr. Morrison's accomplishments include a Distinguished Academic Service Award from the Pennsylvania Department of Education, an Outstanding Alumni Award from the University of Pittsburgh School of Education, and Outstanding Service and Teaching Awards from Florida International University.

Dr. Morrison is the author of many books on early childhood education, child development, curriculum, and teacher education, including *Fundamentals of Early Childhood Education,* Third Edition, and *Teaching in America,* Third Edition.

His professional affiliations include the National Association for the Education of Young Children, the Society for Research in Child Development, the Association for Supervision and Curriculum Development, the American Educational Research Association, the Association of Teacher Educators, the Council for Exceptional Children, the International Reading Association, and the Southern Early Childhood Association.

Dr. Morrison's professional interests include the application of research to early childhood programs, teacher education, and international education. Dr. Morrison and his associates have developed *Success for Life,* a research-based curriculum and program for children from birth to six years of age.

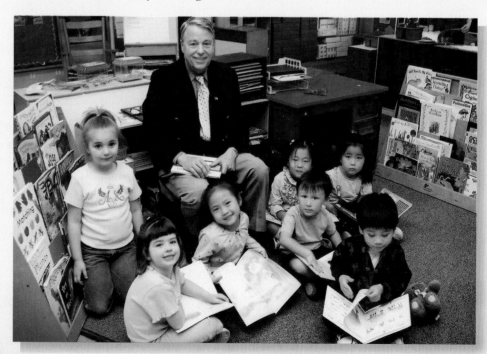

Preface

T his is my ninth preface to *Early Childhood Education Today.* I always begin with words of encouragement and challenge, and this edition is no exception. This is an exciting time to be in the field of early childhood education. In fact, I can think of only one other time during my career when there was so much excitement and challenge: 1965, with the implementation of Head Start. The excitement and possibility in the air at that time are similar to those of today because of the current emphasis on school readiness, early literacy, reading, and brain developmental research, and because of a renewed interest in the importance of the early years. Early childhood is indeed in the public spotlight!

As a result, the field of early childhood education is rapidly changing, as we will discuss in each of the seventeen chapters of this book. These changes bring with them both possibilities and challenges. The possibilities are endless for you as an early childhood education professional to participate in the restructuring and remaking of the early childhood profession. The challenges involved in remaking and reforming the profession will involve collaboration, hard work, and constant dedication to bringing to fruition the bright promise of a high-quality education for all children. An important question is: Will you take full advantage of these possibilities and challenges and help all young children get the knowledge and skills they need to succeed in school and life?

I believe that how you and I respond to the opportunities we have in front of us will determine how long the current interest in early childhood education lasts. You and other early childhood professionals must be creative in responding to the opportunities for teaching young children and in providing the support that they and their families need.

GOALS OF THE TEXT

The primary goal of *Early Childhood Education Today,* Ninth Edition, is to help you keep up to date and on the cutting edge of your profession; to help you meet the challenges of educating young children; and to help you be the best early childhood professional you can be. This edition gives you the knowledge, skills, and insights necessary to confidently and appropriately assume your goal of being a leader in educating children, parents, and families.

I wrote *Early Childhood Education Today* to provide all those who work with young children a learning text that is practical and based upon current ideas about what teaching young children is like today. Seven core themes are integrated throughout the text and provide a framework for reading, study, and professional development:

- *Professionalism in Practice.* What does it mean to be a practicing early childhood professional today? This text answers this question and helps you become a high-quality professional. Chapter 1, "You and Early Childhood Education: What Does It Mean To Be a Professional?" discusses in detail the many dimensions of professionalism. In addition, two core attributes of professional practice, collaboration and advocacy, are highlighted throughout the text. The "Voice from the Field" and "Program in Action" accounts that appear in every chapter illustrate how early childhood teachers are dedicated to helping children learn, grow, and develop to their full potential and to helping parents, families, and communities build strong educational programs. As you read about how these teachers put professionalism into practice, you will be inspired to proclaim, "I also teach young children."

- *Theory to Practice.* This text helps you understand how teachers and programs translate theories of learning and educating young children into practice. The "Voice from the Field" and "Program in Action" sections provide real-life insights into how teachers in programs across the United States endeavor to apply early childhood theories to their everyday practices. You will read firsthand about professional colleagues who make theories come alive in concrete ways that truly help children succeed in school and life.

- *Diversity.* The United States is a nation of diverse people, and this diversity is reflected in every early childhood classroom and program. You and your colleagues must have the knowledge and sensitivity to teach all students well, and you must understand how culture and language influence teaching and learning. In addition to two full chapters on diversity (chapter 15, "Multiculturalism: Education for Living in a Diverse Society," and chapter 16, "Children with Special Needs: Appropriate Education for All"), every other chapter of this edition emphasizes the theme of diversity through narrative examples and program descriptions. The theme of diversity is further emphasized by the inclusion in every chapter of a "Diversity Tie-In." These features focus on issues of diversity, promote reflection, and encourage you to consider ways to provide for the diverse needs of all the children you will teach.

- *Family-Centered, Community-Based Practice.* To effectively meet children's needs, you and other early childhood professionals must collaborate with families and communities. Today, teaching is not a solitary endeavor in which one seeks to practice the art and craft of early childhood education in isolation from colleagues and others in the school and community. Successful partnerships at all levels are essential for effective teaching and learning. In addition to a chapter on this important topic (chapter 17, "Parent, Family, and Community Involvement: Cooperation and Collaboration"), every other chapter provides examples of successful partnerships and their influences on teaching and learning.

- *Timeliness.* This ninth edition is a book for the twenty-first century. The information it contains is timely and reflective of the very latest trends and research. Every chapter has been thoroughly revised to reflect the changes in the field. I take great pride in ensuring that you and other readers will be well versed in the current state of early childhood education after reading this text. *Early Childhood Education Today* is a contemporary text, revised and designed for contemporary times.

- *Developmentally Appropriate Practice.* The theme running throughout this text, developmentally appropriate practice, is the foundation for all that early childhood professionals do. It is important, therefore, that you as an early childhood professional understand developmentally appropriate practice and become familiar with how to implement it in your teaching. It is also especially important with all the reforms and changes occurring in the field that you keep before you the goal of ensuring that all you do is appropriate for all children and their families. Appendix B reprints the NAEYC Guidelines for Developmentally Appropriate Practice in Early Childhood Programs, and every chapter provides examples and illustrations of how to apply developmentally appropriate practice.

- *Technology Applied to Teaching and Learning.* Technological and information literacy is essential for living and working in contemporary society. This ninth edition provides the information and skills you and your colleagues need to integrate technology effectively into the curriculum and use new teaching and learning styles enabled by technology. In addition to chapter 13, "Technology and Young Children: Education for the Information Age," margin notes direct you to related information on the Companion Website for this textbook, located at http://www.prenhall.com/morrison. Websites are also integrated into the content of every chapter. Additionally, included at the end of each chapter is a "Linking to Learning" section that provides an annotated list of websites. In this way, you and others are supported in using the Internet and new technologies as sources of professional growth and development.

ORGANIZATION AND COVERAGE OF THE TEXT

Early Childhood Education Today, Ninth Edition, provides a thorough introduction to the field of early childhood education in a straightforward and engaging style. The book analyzes current issues and ideas and applies practical, developmentally appropriate strategies and models to the practice of early childhood education. This edition has been extensively revised to reflect current changes in society, research, and the practice of early childhood education. The text is comprehensive in its approach to the profession and is organized into five sections:

- Part 1, "Early Childhood Education and Professional Development," begins with a chapter on professional development. This chapter has been extensively revised and is designed to place professional practice at the heart of being a good teacher. Chapter 1 helps you engage in professional, ethical practice and sets the tone for what being an early childhood professional is all about. Chapter content encourages you to use professional practice as the compass for all you do. Chapter 2 provides the context of change and reform that are sweeping across early childhood education today. You will gain insight into contemporary educational issues and understand how public policy issues and political agendas shape them into contemporary practices and programs. Chapter 3 is devoted to providing the knowledge and skills necessary to effectively observe and assess children's learning and development. Increasingly, assessment is playing a major role in directing instruction and as a means for ensuring that all children achieve mandated state and district standards. This chapter provides practical guidelines for observing and authentically assessing young children, shows how to most effectively observe and assess, and explains how to apply the results of observation and assessment to your early childhood practice.
- Part 2, "Foundations: History and Theories," provides a historical overview of the field of early childhood education and descriptions of the theories, ideas, and practices that form the basis of early childhood education. The two chapters in this section also show how the past influences the present and how the major theories of Montessori, Piaget, and Vygotsky influence programs for young children today. Chapter 4 traces the history of the field from Martin Luther through Friedrich Froebel up to modern influences on early childhood educational practice. Chapter 5 discusses the importance of learning theories and illustrates how they are used and applied in early childhood classrooms and programs.
- Part 3, "Programs and Services for Children and Families," includes three chapters that illustrate how theories and public policy are transformed into practice in child care, preschools, federal programs, and public schools. Chapter 6 illustrates how Montessori, High Scope, and Reggio Emilia function and operate. Chapter 7, "Child Care: Meeting the Needs of Children, Parents, and Families," is new to this edition. There is a growing movement to professionalize child care, to ensure that it is of the highest quality and that programs and practices are in alignment with current ideas and concepts. Chapter 8, "The Federal Government: Supporting Children's Success," is also new to this edition. Head Start has changed the field of early childhood

education, and current changes occurring in Head Start promise to further influence early education and practice. Child care and Head Start provide many opportunities for professionals through which they can participate in making life better for children and families.

- Part 4, "The New World of Early Childhood Education," begins with chapter 9, devoted to a discussion of the growth, development, and education of infants and toddlers. Chapter 10 focuses on the preschool years and outlines some of the tremendous changes that are occurring in how we care for and educate young children. Chapter 11 looks at the kindergarten year and forthrightly addresses the educational practices of this formative year. Chapter 12 looks at education in grades 1 to 3 and examines how changing practices influence teaching and learning. Taken as a whole, these chapters provide a comprehensive overview and discussion of children's development and how to implement developmentally appropriate practices beginning at birth and continuing through age 8.

- Part 5, "Meeting the Special Needs of Young Children," begins with chapter 13 and a discussion of technology and young children. Technology is an important part of the information age; it is imperative that young children learn to use it and that you and other professionals use it to support your teaching and all children's learning. How to guide children's behavior is also an important topic in early childhood education today. Chapter 14 suggests ideas for guiding children and helping them be responsible for their own behavior. These ideas will enable you to confidently manage classrooms and other early childhood settings. Chapters 15 and 16 address issues of multiculturalism, diversity, and children's special needs. These two chapters help you meet children's special needs in developmentally appropriate and authentic ways. Chapter 17 stresses the importance of cooperation and collaboration with family and community citizens. This chapter helps you learn how to develop partnerships and confidently interact with parents, families, and communities to provide the best education for all children.

Appendix A, "NAEYC Code of Ethical Conduct," a position statement of the National Association for the Education of Young Children, provides the basis for teaching in an ethical and professional manner, and Appendix B, "NAEYC Guidelines for Developmentally Appropriate Practice in Early Childhood Programs," helps ensure that you teach and develop programs so they meet the developmental and educational needs of children in ways that are appropriate to them as individuals.

SPECIAL FEATURES

- *Programs in Action.* One of the hallmarks of this edition of *Early Childhood Education Today* is its practical nature and its ability to translate theory into practice. "Program in Action" features in every chapter enable you to experience actual programs designed for children in early childhood programs and classrooms throughout the United States. I can think of no better way for you to understand what early childhood education in practice is like than to learn about real programs in action. These examples of schools, programs, classrooms, and teachers enable you to explore the best practices of early childhood education and see up close what teaching is like. They also offer special opportunities to spotlight current topics such as early education, family literacy, multiage and bilingual classrooms, technology applied to learning, gifted education, inclusion, and early intervention. This approach enables you to make the transition from thinking about being a teacher to becoming a competent professional.

- *Voices from the Field.* I believe it is important for the teacher's voice to be heard in and throughout *Early Childhood Education Today,* Ninth Edition. "Voice from the Field" features provide practicing teachers the opportunity to explain to you their philosophies, beliefs, and program practices. These teachers mentor you as they relate how they practice early childhood education. Among the contributors are teachers who have received "Teacher of the Year" honors and recognition for outstanding teaching by *USA Today.*

- *Diversity Tie-Ins.* America is a nation of diverse peoples, and this diversity is reflected in the classrooms of today. It is imperative that you honor, respect, and provide for the needs of all children who come to you to learn regardless of their culture, socioeconomic background, gender, or race. It is also important that you reflect on how to integrate topics of multiculturalism and diversity into your teaching and other program activities. The "Diversity Tie-In" in every chapter helps you achieve this goal. It is designed to introduce you to topics and issues of diversity you might not have thought about and to encourage you to address them in ways you might not have considered.

- *Portraits of Children.* When reading a text about children, it is sometimes easy to take children for granted or to think about them in the abstract. The "Portraits" found in chapters 9, 10, 11, 12, and 16 are designed to ensure that we discuss how to teach young children while reading and thinking about actual children. The "Portraits of Children" are just that: snapshots of children from all cultures and backgrounds, attending real programs across the United States. The portraits of each child include developmental information across four domains: physical, social/emotional, cognitive, and adaptive or self-help. Accompanying questions challenge you to think about how you would provide for these children's educational and social needs if you were their teacher or caregiver.

- *Lesson Plans.* Planning for teaching and learning will constitute an important dimension of your role as a professional. This is especially true today, when there is a major emphasis on ensuring that children will learn important knowledge and skills mandated in state standards. It is helpful to "look over the shoulder" of experienced teachers and observe how they plan for instruction. This is exactly what the lesson plans are designed to do. Award-winning teachers share with you their ideas about how they plan to ensure that their children will learn important knowledge and skills.

- *Margin Notes.* Keeping track of important key terms is always a concern associated with reading and studying. Key terms and concepts are defined as they are presented and are also placed in page margins. In this way, they are immediately available for your reflection and review. In addition, the margin notes maximize your time of study and review and assist with the retention of essential knowledge.

- *Video Viewpoints.* Integrated throughout this edition are feature boxes that ask you to respond to questions requiring reflective thought and decision making. These "Video Viewpoints" are linked to the video segments in the ABC News/Prentice Hall video library. The segments and the "Video Viewpoint" activities address current issues in early childhood education, help connect theory to practice, and bring to life important topics relating to young children and families. The topics and their locations are provided on page xxv.

- *Integrated Technology.* Web resources and URLs are integrated throughout the text of each chapter, and margin notes cue students to additional resources that can be found on the Companion Website for this text, located at http://www.prenhall.com/morrison. These links will help enrich and extend your learning. In addition, at the end of each chapter there is a "Linking to Learning" section that provides a list of annotated Web addresses for further research, study, and reflection.

- *New Chapter on Child Care.* Users of the eighth edition suggested the inclusion of a chapter devoted to the diverse and important field of child care, including before- and after-school programs. Chapter 7, "Child Care: Meeting the Needs of Children, Parents, and Families," responds to this user need and fosters a discussion of the many kinds of child care and the challenges facing professionals as they endeavor to provide the nation's children and families with high-quality care and education. The addition of this chapter facilitates your understanding of the field of child care and aids in developing plans for how best to meet the child care needs of America's children and families.

- *New Chapter on Federal and State Early Childhood Programs.* Again, responding to the recommendations of professors and students, chapter 8, "The Federal Government: Supporting Children's Success," provides a comprehensive view of the powerful roles the federal and state governments are playing in determining what young children will learn and how they will be taught. This chapter brings together the major federally supported programs of early childhood education that are used today, including Head Start, Early Head Start, Even Start, and Title I.

- *Portraits of Children.* These features in chapters 9, 10, 11, 12, and 16 provide a reality dimension to chapter content and discussion. In addition, they remind the reader that in all of our discussions we are talking about real children with individual characteristics. Also, the portraits enable you to apply chapter content to the characteristics of children with diverse backgrounds. In this sense, the portraits are "virtual children" available for observation and discussion with accompanying questions acting as a stimulus for reflection on implications for care and education.

- *Diversity Tie-Ins.* A focus on and discussions of topics of diversity and their associated issues are a hallmark of this ninth edition. In today's early childhood programs and classrooms, it is very common to find children from many cultures, races, and socio-economic backgrounds. This ninth edition prepares you to teach young children from diverse backgrounds. In addition to the diversity topics in chapter content and the "Portraits of Children," every chapter has a "Diversity Tie-In," designed to encourage you to look at diversity with new eyes, to rethink previously held views, and to develop new ways of teaching and relating to children and families of all backgrounds.

- *Lesson Plans.* Master teachers know how to teach and use planning to encourage and support student learning. Planning for teaching in the form of lesson plans helps good teachers become outstanding teachers. Throughout this ninth edition, award-winning teachers share their lesson plans with you. These lesson plans enable you to learn how to plan and gain skills essential to the art and craft of teaching.

- *Margin Notes.* This ninth edition supports study and retention of critical concepts, terms, and definitions. Margin notes reinforce important chapter content and call attention to what is important. The margin notes also aid in review and study and serve as an authoritative guide for reflection and thinking.

- *Continuing Emphasis on Professional Practice.* Chapter 1 is once again entirely devoted to professional practice and sets the tone and context for the entire text. By beginning with professional practice, students understand the importance of the early childhood educator's role in shaping the future. They also recognize that their own professional development is an ongoing responsibility and a necessary part of helping children grow and develop as happily and successfully as possible.

SUPPLEMENTS TO THE TEXT

The supplements package for the ninth edition has also been thoroughly revised and upgraded with some exciting new ancillaries:

- *Instructor's Manual.* The Instructor's Manual provides professors with a variety of useful resources, including chapter overviews, teaching strategies, and ideas for classroom activities, discussions, and assessment that will assist them in using this text. The manual also includes a comprehensive print test bank containing both multiple-choice and essay questions.
- *Computerized Test Bank Software.* The computerized test bank software gives instructors electronic access to the test questions printed in the Instructor's Manual, allowing them to create and customize exams on their computers. The software can help professors manage their courses and gain insight into their students' progress and performance. Computerized test bank software is available in both Macintosh and PC/Windows versions.
- *ABC News/Prentice Hall Video Library.* Available free to instructors, *Current Issues in Early Childhood Education, volumes 1 and 2,* contain a total of eleven video segments. Video segments cover a variety of topics and vary in length for maximum instructional flexibility. The "Video Viewpoint" feature boxes in the chapters can be used to link the segments to the text and to promote thoughtful classroom discussion of current issues in early childhood education.
- *Companion Website.* Located at http://www.prenhall.com/morrison, the Companion Website for this text includes a wealth of resources for both students and professors. The Syllabus Manager™ enables professors to create and maintain the class syllabus on-line while also allowing the student access to the syllabus at any time on the Internet. Focus Questions help students review chapter content. Students can test their knowledge by taking interactive Self-Tests—multiple-choice quizzes that provide immediate feedback with a percentage score and correct answers—or responding to essay questions that can be submitted to instructors or study partners via e-mail. The "Linking to Learning" module contains hot links to all the websites mentioned in the margins of the text and assists students in using the Web to do additional research on chapter topics and key issues. The "Programs in Action" module provides hot links to many of the Web pages of the "Program in Action" features in the text and extends students' learning via Web-based activities. The "Diversity Tie-Ins" module provides additional articles and web-based activities designed to enhance student understanding of the diverse needs of children in early childhood classrooms today. The glossary helps students familiarize themselves with the key vocabulary. The message board feature encourages student interaction outside the classroom. The Professional Development Checklist will help students monitor their progress toward becoming accomplished early childhood educators. Finally, the Resources module links to Merrill Education's early childhood education resources supersite.
- *Student Study Guide.* The Student Study Guide provides students with additional opportunities to review chapter content and helps them learn and study more effectively. The study guide leads readers through each chapter and helps them identify key concepts and information. Each chapter of the guide contains a number of helpful review resources, including a self-check quiz.

ACKNOWLEDGMENTS

In the course of my teaching, service, and consulting, I meet and talk with many professionals who are deeply dedicated to doing their best for young children and their families. I am always touched, heartened, and encouraged by the openness, honesty, and unselfish sharing of ideas that characterize these professional colleagues. I thank all the individuals who contributed to "Voice from the Field," "Program in Action," and other program descriptions. They are all credited for their contributions, and I am very thankful they agreed to share with you and me the personal accounts of their lives, their children's lives, and their programs.

I am also very grateful to reviewers Barbara Barton, Three Rivers Community College; Eugene Geist, Ohio University; Marian Marion, University of Wisconsin, Stout; Theresa Slusser, Passaic County Community College; and Professor Emerita Sue C. Wortham, University of Texas at San Antonio, for their very important and helpful feedback. The reviewers challenged me to rethink content and made suggestions for inclusion of new ideas. Many of the changes in this ninth edition are the result of their suggestions.

My editors at Merrill/Prentice Hall continue to be the best in the industry. It was a pleasure to work once again with my editor, Kevin Davis. I appreciate all of Kevin's ideas and efforts that make *Early Childhood Education Today* the leader in the field. Linda Bayma, production editor, is patient, persistent, and helpful. I love the way she works with me! I also greatly appreciate her attention to detail. Linda always smooths out the bumps of the production process. Heather Johnson of Elm Street Publishing Services was efficient, patient, pleasant, and helpful. Together, Kevin, Linda, and Heather have made this ninth edition one of exceptional quality.

Discover the Companion Website Accompanying This Book

THE PRENTICE HALL COMPANION WEBSITE: A VIRTUAL LEARNING ENVIRONMENT

Technology is a constantly growing and changing aspect of our field that is creating a need for content and resources. To address this emerging need, Prentice Hall has developed an online learning environment for students and professors alike—Companion Websites—to support our textbooks.

In creating a Companion Website, our goal is to build on and enhance what the textbook already offers. For this reason, the content for each user-friendly website is organized by chapter and provides the professor and student with a variety of meaningful resources.

FOR THE PROFESSOR

Every Companion Website integrates **Syllabus Manager**™, an online syllabus creation and management utility.

- **Syllabus Manager**™ provides you, the instructor, with an easy, step-by-step process to create and revise syllabi, with direct links into Companion Website and other online content without having to learn HTML.
- Students may logon to your syllabus during any study session. All they need to know is the web address for the Companion Website and the password you've assigned to your syllabus.
- After you have created a syllabus using **Syllabus Manager**™, students may enter the syllabus for their course section from any point in the Companion Website.
- Clicking on a date, the student is shown the list of activities for the assignment. The activities for each assignment are linked directly to actual content, saving time for students.

- Adding assignments consists of clicking on the desired due date, then filling in the details of the assignment—name of the assignment, instructions, and whether it is a one-time or repeating assignment.
- In addition, links to other activities can be created easily. If the activity is online, a URL can be entered in the space provided, and it will be linked automatically in the final syllabus.
- Your completed syllabus is hosted on our servers, allowing convenient updates from any computer on the Internet. Changes you make to your syllabus are immediately available to your students at their next login.

FOR THE STUDENT

Common Companion Website features for students include:

- **Chapter Objectives**—Outline key concepts from the text.
- **Interactive Self-quizzes**—Complete with hints and automatic grading that provide immediate feedback for students.

    After students submit their answers for the interactive self-quizzes, the Companion Website **Results Reporter** computes a percentage grade, provides a graphic representation of how many questions were answered correctly and incorrectly, and gives a question-by-question analysis of the quiz. Students are given the option to send their quiz to up to four email addresses (professor, teaching assistant, study partner, etc.).

- **Web Destinations**—Links to www sites that relate to chapter content.
- **Message Board**—Virtual bulletin board to post or respond to questions or comments from a national audience.

To take advantage of the many available resources, please visit the *Early Childhood Education Today,* Ninth Edition, Companion Website at

www.prenhall.com/morrison

Brief Contents

Contents

Chapter 10

The Preschool Years: Getting Ready for School and Life   268

Chapter 11

Kindergarten Education: Learning All You Need to Know   304

Chapter 12

The Early Elementary Grades: Preparation for Lifelong Success   338

Part 5

Meeting the Special Needs of Young Children   371

Chapter 13

Technology and Young Children: Education for the Information Age   372

Chapter 14

Guiding Children: Helping Children Become Responsible   404

Chapter 15

Multiculturalism: Education for Living in a Diverse Society   432

Chapter 16

Children with Special Needs: Appropriate Education for All   462

Chapter 17

Parent, Family, and Community Involvement: Cooperation and Collaboration   506

Appendix A

NAEYC Code of Ethical Conduct   539

Appendix B

NAEYC Guidelines for Developmentally Appropriate Practice in Early Childhood Programs   545

NOTE: Every effort has been made to provide accurate and current Internet information in this book. However, the Internet and information posted on it are constantly changing, and it is inevitable that some of the Internet addresses listed in this textbook will change.

Special Features

Voices from the Field

Diversity Tie-Ins

Educator Learning Center:
An Invaluable Online Resource

Merrill Education and the Association for Supervision and Curriculum Development (ASCD) invite you to take advantage of a new online resource, one that provides access to the top research and proven strategies associated with ASCD and Merrill—the Educator Learning Center. At **www.EducatorLearningCenter.com** you will find resources that will enhance your students' understanding of course topics and of current educational issues, in addition to being invaluable for further research.

HOW THE EDUCATOR LEARNING CENTER WILL HELP YOUR STUDENTS BECOME BETTER TEACHERS

With the combined resources of Merrill Education and ASCD, you and your students will find a wealth of tools and materials to better prepare them for the classroom.

RESEARCH

- More than 600 articles from the ASCD journal *Educational Leadership* discuss everyday issues faced by practicing teachers.
- A direct link on the site to Research Navigator™ gives students access to many of the leading education journals, as well as extensive content detailing the research process.
- Excerpts from Merrill Education texts give your students insights on important topics of instructional methods, diverse populations, assessment, classroom management, technology, and refining classroom practice.

CLASSROOM PRACTICE

- Hundreds of lesson plans and teaching strategies are categorized by content area and age range.
- Case studies and classroom video footage provide virtual field experience for student reflection.
- Computer simulations and other electronic tools keep your students abreast of today's classrooms and current technologies.

LOOK INTO THE VALUE OF EDUCATOR LEARNING CENTER YOURSELF

Preview the value of this educational environment by visiting **www.EducatorLearningCenter.com** and clicking on "Demo." For a free 4-month subscription to the Educator Learning Center in conjunction with this text, simply contact your Merrill/Prentice Hall sales representative.

Part 1
Early Childhood Education and Professional Development

Chapter 1

Whatever you decide to do with your hours in the classroom, use your talents to make it a beautiful and rewarding time for your students.

CHRISTA PEHRSON AND VICKI SHEFFLER,
2002 USA TODAY'S FIRST TEAM TEACHERS

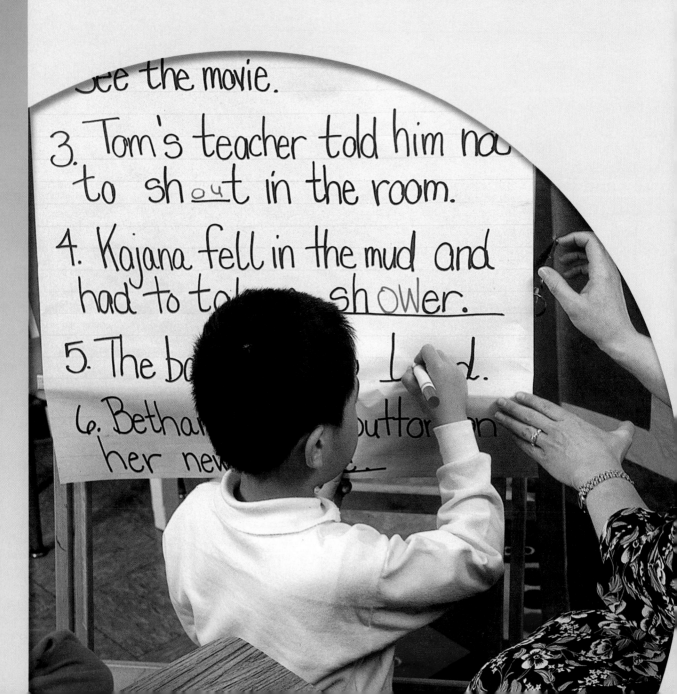

You and Early Childhood Education

What Does It Mean to Be a Professional?

Focus Questions

- Who is an early childhood professional?

- What can you do to demonstrate the personal, educational, professional practice, and public dimensions of professionalism?

- How can you prepare for a career in early childhood education?

- What does the future hold for you as an early childhood professional?

This is an exciting time to be practicing the art of providing the best possible curricula and programs for young children. Early childhood education has changed more in the last five years than in the previous fifty years, and more new directions are in store. Why is early childhood education undergoing dramatic transformation and reform? First, there has been a tremendous increase in scientific knowledge about young children and how they learn. This new knowledge encourages professionals to view young children in different ways and realize they are more capable and eager to learn at a very young age. Second, educators have developed research-based programs and curricula that enable children to learn literally from the beginning of life.

Combined, these and other changes are dramatically altering our views of how young children learn and how teachers teach. As a result, the field of early childhood education is entering a new era, and it requires professionals who are up to date and willing to adapt so that all children will learn and succeed in school and life. To paraphrase an old saying, new times demand new professionals.

The public increasingly recognizes the importance of children's early years in learning and development. Today, more than ever, the public and politicians are interested in improving the quality of education and teaching. As a result, you and other early childhood professionals have a wonderful opportunity to develop new and better programs and to advocate for best practices. You can be a leader in helping the early childhood profession make the American dream a reality for all children. Being the best professional you can will enable you to be a partner in making teaching a high-quality profession.

YOU—THE EARLY CHILDHOOD PROFESSIONAL

You are preparing to be an early childhood professional, to teach children from birth to age eight. You are going to work with families and the community to bring a high quality of education and services to all children. How

To review the chapter focus questions online, go to the Companion Website at **http://www. prenhall.com/morrison** and select chapter 1.

Early childhood professional
An educator who successfully teaches all children, promotes high personal standards, and continually expands his or her skills and knowledge.

To check your understanding of this chapter with the online Study Guide, go to the Companion Website at **http://www. prenhall.com/morrison**, select chapter 1, then choose the Study Guide module.

would you explain the term **early childhood professional** to others? What does *professional* mean?

An early childhood professional has the personal characteristics, knowledge, and skills necessary to teach and conduct programs so that all children learn, as well as the ability to inform the public about children's and family issues. Professionals are those who promote high standards for themselves, their colleagues, and their students—they are continually improving and expanding their skills and knowledge. A professional is a multidimensional person.

THE FOUR DIMENSIONS OF PROFESSIONALISM

Being a professional goes beyond degrees and experiences. Professionalism has four integrated dimensions, all of which are important: personal characteristics, educational attainment, professional practice, and public presentation (see Figure 1.1). Each of these dimensions plays a powerful role in determining who and what a professional is and how professionals implement practice in early childhood classrooms. Let's review each of these dimensions and see how you can apply them to your professional practice.

THE PERSONAL DIMENSION

I am sure you have heard the saying, "Who you are speaks so loud I can't hear what you say." This is why the personal dimension of professionalism is so important. It includes all the qualities, attitudes, and behaviors you demonstrate as a professional. These include character traits, emotional qualities, and physical and mental health.

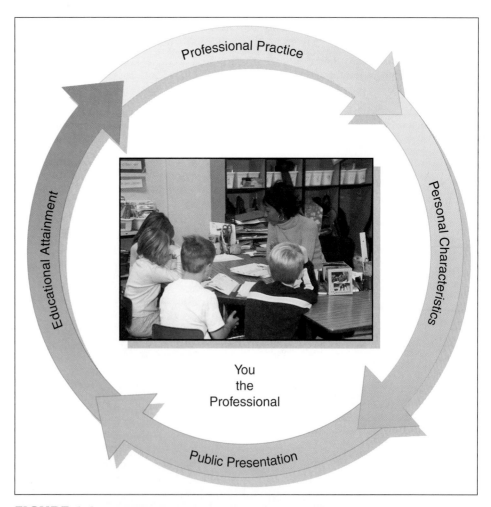

FIGURE 1.1 The Four Dimensions of Professionalism

Character Traits.   Ethical behavior—having high morals and values—is one very important quality of your personal character. Professional teachers conduct their practices in ways that are legally and ethically proper. Professionals want to do what is right in their relationship with students, colleagues, and parents. They base their knowledge on a code of professional ethics. Many professions, such as medicine and law, have unified and universal codes of ethics that govern practice. Although the teaching profession lacks such a code, professional organizations, such as the **National Association for the Education of Young Children (NAEYC),** have developed codes of ethics that help inform and guide professional practice. You can review the NAEYC Code of Ethical Conduct in Appendix A.

Civility is a second important personal characteristic. It includes compassion, patience, and acts of kindness and helpfulness. An example of civil behavior is mannerly and courteous interaction with children, parents and families, colleagues, and others.

In addition, early childhood professionals should demonstrate the following character traits: courtesy, dedication, respect, enthusiasm, honesty, intelligence, and motivation. Home and early school experiences are critical for developing these character qualities. So if we want these qualities in our future professionals, we need to promote them now, in our teaching of young children.

Emotional Qualities.   Some emotional qualities that are critical to being a successful early childhood professional are love and respect for children, understanding of children and their families, compassion, empathy, friendliness, kindness, sensitivity, trust, tolerance, warmth, and caring.

For the early childhood professional, caring is the most important of these emotional qualities. Professionals care about children. They accept and respect all children and their cultural and socioeconomic backgrounds. As a professional, you will work in classrooms, programs, and other settings where things do not always go smoothly—for example, children do not always learn ably and well, and they are not always clean and free from illness and hunger. Children's and their parents' backgrounds and ways of life will not always be the same as yours. Caring means you will lose sleep trying to find a way to help a child learn to read, and that you will spend long hours planning and gathering materials. Caring also means you will not leave your intelligence, enthusiasm, or talents at home but will bring them into the center, classroom, administration offices, boards of directors' meetings, and wherever you can make a difference in the lives of children and their families.

Physical Health.   Being healthy and fit are important parts of professional practice. When you are healthy, you can do your best and be your best. When you practice good health habits, such as eating a well-balanced diet and staying physically fit, you also set a good example for your students. Wellness and healthy living are vital for the energy, enthusiasm, and stamina that teaching requires and demands.

National Association for the Education of Young Children (NAEYC)   An organization of early childhood educators and others dedicated to improving the quality of programs for children from birth through the third grade.

 For more information about NAEYC and other similar organizations, go to the Companion Website at **http://www. prenhall.com/morrison**, select chapter 1, then choose the Linking to Learning module to connect to their home pages.

Early childhood professionals are often role models for the children they teach. Therefore, if we want children to be caring, kind, tolerant, and sensitive individuals, the adults in their lives should model those behaviors.

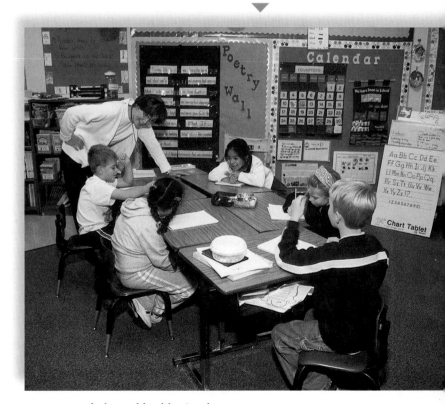

Mental Health.   Good mental health is as important as good physical health. Good mental health includes having a positive outlook on life, the profession, and the future. Having good mental health enables professionals to instill in children good mental health habits.

Some of these characteristics are optimism, attentiveness, self-confidence, and self-respect. If you have good mental health, you continue to try and try again, and you and believe the glass is half full rather than half empty.

THE EDUCATIONAL DIMENSION

The educational dimension of professionalism involves having essential knowledge regarding the profession and professional practice. This includes knowing the history of the profession and the ethics of the profession, understanding the ways children develop and learn, and keeping up to date on public issues that influence early childhood and the profession.

A major challenge facing all areas of the early childhood profession is the training and certification of those who care for and teach young children. Training and certification requirements vary from state to state, but more states are tightening personnel standards for child care, preschool, kindergarten, and primary personnel. Many states have mandatory training requirements that individuals must meet before being certified. The curriculum of these training programs frequently specifies mandatory inclusion of topics. For example in North Carolina, a lead teacher in a child care program must be at least eighteen years of age and have at least a North Carolina Early Childhood Credential or its equivalent. To receive the North Carolina Early Childhood Credential, teachers must have two early childhood curriculum credit courses—six quarter hour credits or four semester hour credits. Courses include the following topics:

- Becoming an early childhood professional
- Understanding the young child—growth and development
- Understanding the young child—individuality, family, and culture
- Developmentally appropriate practices
- Positive guidance
- Health and safety

Many states have career ladders that specify the requirements for progressing from one level of professionalism to the next. Figure 1.2 illustrates the career pathway for early childhood professionals in Oklahoma.

Degree Programs

Associate Degree Programs.   Many community colleges provide training in early childhood education that qualifies recipients to be child care aides, primary child care providers, and assistant teachers. For example, Miami-Dade Community College in Miami, Florida, offers a two-year associate's degree in early childhood education. Courses in the program include child development, early childhood education, children's literature, art and music for young children, and health and emergency care. Access the school's Web site at http://www3.mdcc.edu to review the entire program of study.

Baccalaureate Programs.   Four-year colleges provide programs that result in early childhood teacher certification. The ages and grades to which the certification applies vary from state to state. Some states have separate certification for prekindergarten programs and nursery schools; in other states, these certifications are "add-ons" to elementary (K–6, 1–6, 1–4) certification.

Master's Degree Programs.   Depending on the state, individuals may gain initial early childhood certification at the master's level. Many colleges and universities offer master's-level programs for people who want to qualify as program directors or assistant directors or may want to pursue a career in teaching.

The CDA National Credentialing Program.   At the national level, the Child Development Associate (CDA) National Credentialing Program offers early childhood professionals the opportunity to develop and demonstrate competencies for meeting the needs of young children. A CDA is one who is "able to meet the specific needs of children and who, with parents and other adults, works to nurture children's physical, social, emotional, and intellectual growth in a child development framework."[1]

The CDA program is a major national effort to evaluate and improve the skills of caregivers in center-based preschool settings, center-based infant/toddler settings, family day care homes, home visitor settings, and programs that have specific goals for bilingual children. The CDA National Credentialing Program is operated by the Council for Early Childhood Professional Recognition, which offers two options for obtaining the CDA credential. One option, the CDA Professional Preparation Program-P3, allows candidates to work in postsecondary institutions as part of the credentialing process. The second option is the direct assessment method, which is designed for candidates who have child care work experience in combination with some early childhood education training.

A candidate for the CDA credential in any setting must be eighteen years old or older and hold a high school diploma or equivalent. To obtain the CDA national credential, candidates under the direct assessment option must meet these additional eligibility requirements:

FIGURE 1.2 Early Childhood Practitioner's Professional Pathway for Oklahoma

Core Level

These positions require minimum education and training depending on the position

TRADITIONAL

- Child Care Teaching Assistant
- Family Child Care Home Provider
- Head Start Teacher Assistant
- Nanny
- Foster Parent
- Church Nursery Attendant
- Related positions which involve working with children in settings other than a child care center, family child care home, Head Start, or public school program.

RELATED

Positions may require specialized pre-service training.

- Children's Storyteller, Art Instructor, or Puppeteer
- Recreation Center Assistant
- Salesperson in toy, clothing, or bookstore
- School Crossing Guard
- Children's Party Caterer
- Restaurant Helper for birthday parties
- Van or Transportation Driver

- Children's Art Museum Guide
- Receptionist in pediatrician's office
- Camp Counselor
- Special Needs Child Care Aide
- Live-in Caregiver
- Respite Caregiver
- Cook's Aide, Assistant Cook, Camp Cook, Head Start or Child Care Center Cook

Credential Level

- Head Start Teacher
- Child Care Teacher

- Family Child Care Home Provider
- Nanny

- Child Care Center Director
- Home Visitor
- Nursing Home Aide/Worker

Associate Level

TRADITIONAL

- Head Start Teacher
- Child Care teacher
- Family Child Care Home Provider
- Nanny
- Child Care Center Director
- School-Age Provider
- Early Intervention/Special Needs Program
- Para-Teacher/Aide

RELATED

In addition to those listed at the core level:

- Family and Human Services Worker
- LPN—specialized nurse training
- Entertainer for children at theme restaurants and parks
- Social Service Aide
- Playground Helper

- Physical Therapy Assistant
- Nursing Home Aide/Worker/Technician
- Faith Community Coordinators for families and children

FIGURE 1.2   Early Childhood Practitioner's Professional Pathway for Oklahoma—*Continued*

Baccalaureate Level

TRADITIONAL

- Early Childhood Teacher in public school, Head Start, or child care settings
- Special Education teacher
- Family Child Care Home Provider
- Nanny
- Administrator in Head Start program
- Child Care Center Director/Owner/Coordinator
- Child Care Center Director in the armed services
- Parents as Teacher's Facilitator
- Director of school-age (out-of-school time) program

RELATED

Some positions will require additional coursework at the baccalaureate level which will be in a field other than early childhood:

- Child Advocate/Lobbyist
- Recreation Director/Worker/Leader
- Web Master
- Journalist/Author Publisher/Illustrator of children's books
- Children's Librarian
- Retail Manager of children's toy or book stores
- Licensing Worker
- Human Resource Personnel in industry
- Music Teacher, Musician/Entertainer for children

- Recreation Camp Director
- Camp Counselor/Scouts Camp Ranger
- Resource and Referral Trainer/Data Analyst/Referral Specialist/Child Care Food Program Consultant
- Childbirth Educator
- Gymnastic or Dance Teacher
- Pediatric Nurse Aide
- Child and Parenting Practitioner
- Producer of Children's television shows and commercials
- Faith Community Coordinator and Educator

Advanced degrees—M.S., M.A., Ph.D., Ed.D., J.D., M.D., R.N.

TRADITIONAL

- Occupational Child Care Instructor at technology centers
- Teacher Educator at a two-year college or four-year university
- Teacher/Administrator/Special Educator in a public or private elementary school—certification required
- Instructor/Curriculum Specialist in the armed services
- Child Development Specialist
- Child Guidance Specialist
- Researcher/Writer

RELATED

- Social worker
- Child Advocate/Lobbyist
- Librarian
- Pediatric Therapist—occupational and physical
- Human Resources Personnel in industry
- Child Life Specialist in a hospital
- Speech and Hearing Pathologist—Health Department, public/private school, private practice, university teaching
- Early Childhood Consultant
- Entertainer/Musician/Song Writer for Children
- Author and Illustrator of children's books
- Physician/Pediatrician
- Pedodonist (works only with children)
- Dietitian
- Counselor
- Child Psychologist

- Psychiatrist
- Dietetic Assistant
- Recreation Supervisor
- Children's Policy Specialist
- Dental Hygienist
- Scouting Director
- Child Care Center or Playground/Recreation Center Designer
- Probation Officer
- 4-H Agent or County Extension Director
- Adoption Specialist
- Child Care Resource and Referral Director
- "Friend of the Court" Counselor
- Psychometrist
- Attorney with primary focus on children
- Religious Educator
- Certified Child and Parenting Specialist
- Family Mediator

Source: Reprinted with permission from the Center for Early Childhood Professional Development, College of Continuing Education, University of Oklahoma, 2000.

- 480 hours of experience working with children within the past five years
- 120 clock hours of training with at least ten hours in each of eight CDA training areas, with an emphasis in either infant/toddler or preschool concerns:
  - Health and safety
  - Physical and intellectual development
  - Social and emotional development
  - Relationships with families
  - Program operation
  - Professionalism
  - Observing and recording children's behavior
  - Child growth and development

The candidate must then demonstrate competence in the six CDA competency areas (see Table 1.1).

TABLE 1.1   CDA Competency Goals and Functional Areas

CDA Competency Goals	Functional Areas
I. To establish and maintain a safe, healthy learning environment	1. *Safe:* Candidate provides a safe environment to prevent and reduce injuries. 2. *Healthy:* Candidate promotes good health and nutrition and provides an environment that contributes to the prevention of illness. 3. *Learning environment:* Candidate uses space, relationships, materials, and routines as resources for constructing an interesting, secure, and enjoyable environment that encourages play, exploration, and learning.
II. To advance physical and intellectual competence	4. *Physical:* Candidate provides a variety of equipment, activities, and opportunities to promote intellectual competence. 5. *Cognitive:* Candidate provides activities and opportunities that encourage curiosity, exploration, and problem solving appropriate to the development levels and learning styles of children. 6. *Communication:* Candidate actively communicates with children and provides opportunities and support for children to understand, acquire, and use verbal and nonverbal means of communicating thoughts and feelings. 7. *Creative:* Candidate provides opportunities that stimulate children to play with sound, rhythm, language, materials, space, and ideas in individual ways and to express their creative abilities.
III. To support social and emotional development and to provide positive guidance	8. *Self:* Candidate provides physical and emotional security for each child and helps each child to know, accept, and take pride in himself or herself and to develop a sense of independence. 9. *Social:* Candidate helps each child feel accepted in the group, helps children learn to communicate and get along with others, and encourages feelings of empathy and mutual respect among children and adults. 10. *Guidance:* Candidate provides a supportive environment in which children can begin to learn and practice appropriate and acceptable behaviors as individuals and as a group.
IV. To establish positive and productive relationships with families	11. *Families:* Candidate maintains an open, friendly, and cooperative relationship with each child's family, encourages their involvement in the program, and supports the child's relationship with his or her family.
V. To ensure a well-run, purposeful program responsive to participant needs	12. *Program management:* Candidate is a manager who uses all available resources to ensure an effective operation. The candidate is a competent organizer, planner, record keeper, needs communicator, and a cooperative coworker.
VI. To maintain a commitment to professionalism	13. *Professionalism:* Candidate makes decisions based on knowledge of early childhood theories and practices; promotes quality in child care services; and takes advantage of opportunities to improve competence, both for personal and professional growth and for the benefit of children and families.

Source: The Council for Professional Recognition, *Essentials for Child Development Associates Working with Young Children* (Washington, DC: Author, 1991), p. 415. Used by permission.

The CDA Professional Preparation Program. To obtain credentialing by means of the CDA Professional Preparation Program, the candidate must meet the two general eligibility requirements of age and education and must also identify an advisor to work with during the year of study, which is made up of three phases: fieldwork, coursework, and final evaluation.

Fieldwork involves study of the council's model curriculum, *Essentials for Child Development Associates Working with Young Children*. This curriculum includes the six competency areas listed in Table 1.1. In the second phase, coursework, the candidate participates in seminars offered in community colleges and other postsecondary institutions. These seminars are designed to supplement the model curriculum and are administered by a seminar instructor. The third phase is the final evaluation, which takes place in the candidate's work setting or field placement.

The results of all three phases are sent to the council office for review and determination of whether the candidate has successfully completed all aspects of the CDA Professional Preparation Program. To date, more than 115,000 persons have been awarded the CDA credential.

For additional information, you may visit the Council for Professional Recognition online at http://www.cdacouncil.org/.

Early childhood educators are professionals who—in addition to teaching and caring for children—plan, assess, report, collaborate with colleagues and families, and behave in ethical ways.

THE PROFESSIONAL DIMENSION

Professional practice involves doing what professionals do—teaching and caring for children, working with parents and families, collaborating with community partners, and assuming all the other roles and responsibilities involved in the profession. This dimension includes knowing children; developing a philosophy of education; planning; assessing; reporting; reflecting and thinking; teaching; collaborating with parents, families, and community partners; engaging in ethical practice; and seeking continued professional development opportunities.

Knowing Children. **Child development** is the foundation of early childhood professional practice. Child development knowledge enables you to know how children grow and develop across all developmental levels—the cognitive, linguistic, social, emotional, and physical, which help make children the unique individuals they are. Quality professionals really know the children they teach and care for. Knowledge of individual children, combined with knowledge of child growth and development, enables you to provide care and education that is appropriate for every child. Such knowledge is essential for understanding how to conduct developmentally appropriate practice, which is the recommended teaching practice of the profession. I will discuss developmentally appropriate practice in more detail in chapters 9, 10, 11 and 12.

For more information about becoming an early childhood professional, go to the Companion Website at **http://www. prenhall. com/morrison**, select any chapter, then choose Topic 1 of the ECE Supersite module.

Child development The sum total of the physical, intellectual, social, emotional, and behavioral changes that occur in children from the moment of conception to adulthood.

Developing a Philosophy of Education.   Professional practice includes teaching with and from a **philosophy of education,** which acts as a guidepost to help you base your teaching on what you believe about children.

A philosophy of education is a set of beliefs about how children develop and learn and what and how they should be taught. Your philosophy of education is based on your philosophy of life. What you believe about yourself, about others, and about life infuses and determines your philosophy of education. Knowing what others believe is important and useful, for it can help you clarify what you believe, but, when all is said and done, *you* have to decide what you believe. Moment by moment, day by day, what you believe influences what you will teach and how you will teach it.

A philosophy of life and education is more than an opinion. A personal philosophy is based on core values and beliefs. Core values of life relate to your beliefs about the nature of life, the purpose of life, your role and calling in life, and your relationship and responsibilities to others. Core beliefs and values about education and teaching include what you believe about the nature of children and the purpose of education, about the role of teachers, and what you think is worth knowing.

Your philosophy of education will guide and direct your daily teaching. Your beliefs about how children learn best will determine whether you individualize instruction or try to teach the same thing in the same way to everyone. Your philosophy will determine whether you help children do things for themselves or whether you do things for them.

As you read through and study this book, make notes and reflect about your developing philosophy of education. The following headings will help get you started:

- I believe the purposes of education are . . .
- I believe that children learn best when they are taught under certain conditions and in certain ways. Some of these are . . .
- The curriculum of any classroom should include certain "basics" that contribute to children's social, emotional, intellectual, and physical development. These basics include . . .
- Children learn best in an environment that promotes learning. Features of a good learning environment are . . .
- All children have certain needs that must be met if they are to grow and learn at their best. Some of these basic needs are . . .
- I would meet these needs by . . .
- A teacher should have certain qualities and behave in certain ways. Qualities I think important for teaching are . . .

Once you have determined your philosophy of education, write it down, and have other people read it. This helps you clarify your ideas and redefine your thoughts, because your philosophy should be understandable to others (although they do not necessarily have to agree with you).

Talk with successful teachers and other educators. The accounts of teachers and others in the "Voice from the Field" feature throughout this text are evidence that a philosophy can help you be an above-average teacher. Talking with others exposes you to different points of view and stimulates your thinking.

Finally, evaluate your philosophy against this checklist:

- Does my philosophy accurately relate my beliefs about teaching? Have I been honest with myself?
- Is it understandable to me and others?
- Does it provide practical guidance for teaching?
- Are my ideas consistent with one another?
- Does what I believe make good sense?

Philosophy of education
Beliefs about children's development, learning, and how best to teach them.

10 Tips for Being a Professional

1. *I am honest and trustworthy.* I present myself to all constituents (students, parents, administration, and the community) in such a way that they know I can be depended on. I am ethical and have integrity so that I never misrepresent the profession, my school, or my district.

2. *I am fair and strive diligently not to discriminate.* I respect and attempt to celebrate the diversity of all cultures represented in our school. My practice is guided by the values of equality, tolerance, and respect for others.

3. *I respect the privacy of others.* I gather personal information for the specific purpose of informing my practice. This personal information is not used for purposes that might harm or compromise the trust of the student and family.

4. *I honor confidentiality.* I discuss my students' progress, behavior, attitudes, and family circumstances with the support personnel who need the information for the sole purpose of helping me design programs to support my students intellectually, physically, socially, and emotionally. My discussions take place in the proper manner, context, and setting—not in the school halls or in the teacher's lounge.

5. *I acquire and maintain professional competence.* My most important obligation is to achieve quality. I am aware of my students' needs, interests, and abilities. I determine the best ways to impart concepts to my students and thus, employ multiple paths to learning. I understand the standards for appropriate levels of competence, and strive to achieve these standards. I participate in independent study, attend seminars, conferences, and/or courses and am involved in professional organizations. I collaborate with families, the community, and my colleagues.

6. *I know and respect existing laws pertaining to my profession.* I obey existing local, state, and national laws that are established on an ethical basis. I obey the policies and procedures of my school and district.

7. *I honor contracts, agreements, and assigned responsibilities.* I honor my commitment to provide quality instruction, even when this commitment requires me to use my personal resources, expend extra energy, and work hours that extend past the school day and year. I accept personal accountability for professional work. I am a contributing member of my school community, even when the assigned duties or voluntary tasks do not directly affect my classroom and/or students.

8. *I improve public understanding of teaching and the profession.* I willingly share knowledge with the public by encouraging understanding of the educational process and the methods utilized in my classroom. I wholeheartedly counter any false views related to the profession, my school, and my district. I seek opportunities to speak with policy makers and the community about the importance of supporting education.

9. *I communicate effectively.* My spoken communication is intelligible and suited to the audience. My written communication is free of spelling and grammatical errors. I make provisions for children and parents who have differing levels of understanding and use of the English language.

10. *I am cognizant of my appearance.* I dress appropriately for each situation, but always in a manner that represents the profession in a positive light. As a role model for students, I am purposefully neat in my attire.

Contributed by Carole D. Moyer, National Board Certified Teacher, Early Childhood Coordinator, Shepard Center, Columbus, Ohio.

- Have I been comprehensive, stating my beliefs about (1) how children learn, (2) what children should be taught, (3) how children should be taught, (4) the conditions under which children learn best, and (5) what qualities make up a good teacher?

Planning. Planning is also an essential part of practicing the art and craft of teaching. Planning consists of setting goals for children and selecting and developing activities to help you achieve your teaching goals. Without planning you can't be a good teacher. Planning will help ensure that all children will learn, which is one of the most important and meaningful challenges you will face as an early childhood professional. You may have heard it said that all children can learn. What is important is believing that all children *will* learn and acting on this basic belief. Some essential steps in the planning process are as follows:

1. State what your children will learn and be able to do. These objectives can come from a number of sources. Currently, all fifty states have developed standards regarding what students should know and be able to do in kindergarten through grade three. Standards for preschool education are commonplace. Program goals represent a second source of objectives. These goals are carefully thought out by staff and families and provide direction for what and how children will learn.
2. Select developmentally appropriate activities and materials and ones that are based on children's interests.
3. Decide how much time to allocate to an activity.
4. Decide how to assess activities and the things that children have learned.

Assessing. Assessment is the process of gathering information about children's behavior and achievement and, on the basis of this data, making decisions about how to meet children's needs. Chapter 3, "Observing and Assessing Young Children," provides you with practical skills and ideas for how to conduct developmentally appropriate assessment.

Reporting. Reporting to parents and others in an understandable and meaningful way serves several purposes. First, it answers every parent's question, "How is my child doing?" Second, information about children's achievement helps you, as a professional, be accountable to the public in fulfilling your role of helping children learn and be successful. Chapters 9 through 12 and 17 provide specific ideas and examples for reporting children's progress to parents and others.

Reflecting and Thinking. A professional is always thinking about and reflecting on what he/she has done, is doing, and will do. A good guideline for thinking and reflecting is this: Think before you teach, think while you are teaching, and think after you teach. This constant cycle of *reflective practice* will help you be a good professional and will help your children learn.

Teaching. If you asked most teachers what they do, they would tell you they have a job description that requires them to wear many hats and that their jobs are never done. Teachers' responsibilities and tasks are many and varied. Teaching involves making decisions about what and how to teach, planning for teaching, engaging students in learning activities, managing learning environments, assessing student behavior and achievement, reporting to parents and others, collaborating with colleagues and community partners, and engaging in ongoing professional development. You might feel a little overwhelmed. However, you will have a lot of help and support on your journey to becoming a good teacher. Your teacher preparation program, your instructors, participating classroom teachers, and this textbook will help you learn how to meet the many responsibilities of becoming a good teacher.

Planning Thinking about what to teach, how to teach, how to assess what is taught; includes selecting activities, deciding on a time allotment, creating the learning environment, considering the needs of individual children, and preparing assessment.

Assessment Making decisions on the needs of students by gathering information about their progress and behavior.

Reporting The process of providing information to parents gathered by means of observation, assessment, and children's work products.

VOICE FROM THE FIELD

10 Ways to Advocate for Children and Families

Advocacy is the act of engaging in strategies designed to improve the circumstances of children and families. Advocates move beyond their day-to-day classroom or program professional responsibilities and work collaboratively to help others.

Children and families today need adults who understand their needs and to work to improve the health, education, and well-being of all young children. Early childhood professionals are in a unique position to both know and understand children and their needs, and to make a difference in the lives of children. The National Association for the Education of Young Children (NAEYC) views advocacy for children and families as a professional responsibility of all early childhood professionals.

There are many ways for early childhood professionals to actively work to make a difference in the lives of young children. Early childhood professionals must become actively engaged in advocacy activities in order to change policies and procedures that negatively affect children. The following ten steps to advocacy are ways that early childhood professionals can practice advocacy for children and families.

1. *Learn about the developmental needs of young children.* Study child growth and development and early education.

   For example, join your local NAEYC affiliate organization or another group that focuses on the needs of young children and families and study their publications.

2. *Participate in activities that support children and families.* Help others in your community that work to make a difference for children and families.

   For example, make donations to organizations that support children and families, volunteer your time at a local event that supports children, and/or become a participant in local organizations that support children and families.

3. *Investigate the issues that face children and families today.* Read the news and become informed about issues that face children and families today.

   For example, subscribe to an e-mail newsletter sent from a group that supports children and families. News updates are automatically sent on current

Collaborating with Parents, Families, and Community Partners. Parents, families, and the community are essential partners in the process of schooling. Knowing how to effectively collaborate with these key partners will serve you well throughout your career. Chapter 17, "Parent, Family, and Community Involvement: Cooperation and Collaboration," will help you learn more about this important topic.

Family education and support is an important role of the early childhood professional. Children's learning begins and continues within the context of the family unit, whatever that family unit may be. Learning how to comfortably and confidently work with parents is as essential as teaching children.

Ethical conduct Responsible behavior toward students and parents that allows you to be considered a professional.

Engaging in Ethical Practice. **Ethical conduct**—the exercise of responsible behavior with children, families, colleagues, and community members—enables you to confidently engage in exemplary professional practice. A professional is an ethical person. As previously indicated, the profession of early childhood education has a set of ethical standards to guide

issues related to children and families. Share the news with colleagues, family, and friends.

4. *Talk to others about the issues facing children and families.* Identify a specific concern you have for children and families and talk to others about the issue.

   For example, if you are concerned about the number of children who do not have adequate health care, learn the facts about the issue in your community and talk to people you know about ways to solve the problem in your community. Begin with your own circle of influence: your colleagues, friends, family members, and other social groups in which you are a member.

5. *Seek opportunities to share your knowledge of young children.* Inform others about the needs of young children by talking to others and speaking with groups.

   For example, volunteer to meet with a group of parents at a local child care program to help them learn to share storybooks with their young children, or meet with a local civic group that maintains the community park to discuss securing appropriate equipment for younger children.

6. *Share your knowledge of the issues.* Inform others about the issues that face children in your community, your state, or at the national level through letters, telephone calls, personal meetings, or letters to the local newspaper.

   For example, if you are concerned about adequate health care for children, contact your local school officials to share your concerns and find out what can be done in the schools to inform parents about services available. Write a letter to the editor describing the number of children in your community who do not have adequate health care.

7. *Identify leaders in a position to make the desired changes.* Learn who the leaders are that represent you in local, state, and national government. Identify the leaders of local schools, health organizations, and so on that have the authority to make changes for children and families.

   For example, identify the members of the local school board and find out who represents you on the board. When issues arise, contact that person to express your concerns and offer solutions.

8. *Communicate with legislators and other leaders.* Learn the appropriate way to communicate with legislators and other leaders. Identify the steps to follow when meeting with your elected representatives.

   For example, find out how to track legislation and call or e-mail your state senator to express your support for pending health care legislation.

9. *Enlist the support of others.* Contact others to help you disseminate information about an issue.

   For example, enlist the help of your local school PTA in a letter writing effort to inform town leaders about the need for safety improvements at the local playground.

10. *Be persistent. Change takes time!* There are many ways to advocate for children and families.

   Identify an issue you are passionate about and find a way to make a difference!

Contributed by Mary Nelle Brunson, Assistant Chair, Elementary Education, Stephen F. Austin State University.

your thinking and behavior. NAEYC has developed a Code of Ethical Conduct (see Appendix A) and a Statement of Commitment. Following is the Statement of Commitment:

As an individual who works with young children, I commit myself to furthering the values of early childhood education as they are reflected in the NAEYC Code of Ethical Conduct. To the best of my ability I will:

Ensure that programs for young children are based on current knowledge of child development and early childhood education.

Respect and support families in their task of nurturing children.

Respect colleagues in early childhood education and support them in maintaining the NAEYC Code of Ethical Conduct.

Serve as an advocate for children, their families, and their teachers in community and society.

Advocacy

A View from the Front

Tim is in kindergarten. Every day the teacher goes over the alphabet with the class. Every day Tim sits listlessly while the other students work on learning the name of the letter of the day. Tim would rather be reading the book in his backpack. He's been reading for more than a year now, and he long ago mastered his ABCs. But learning the alphabet is what children his age are expected to do in kindergarten. He'd really like to go to the library, but his teacher says that kindergarteners only use the books in the room. So Tim spends large parts of each day bored and wishing he could be anywhere else. Tim remembers that he was really proud on the first day of school because he didn't have to go to child care anymore. Now he thinks school is stupid.

Lisa is in first grade. Last year school was fun. Her class played games, learned letters and numbers, painted, and took naps every afternoon. This year her teacher doesn't let students move around the room whenever they want. Now she sits at a desk and does worksheets. The kids in her class also read aloud every day from the books on the back shelf. If you do a good job, you get to move up to a harder book with new stories. Most of Lisa's class has already moved up several levels. Lisa has been reading the same book since the first day of school. Even though the teacher tells them not to, when Lisa reads, the kids laugh because she talks so slowly. She doesn't like to read aloud in class

anymore. Sometimes when the other students read aloud to the class she kicks her feet under her desk and looks out the window. Most of the time she just does worksheets.

This is Michelle's first year as a lead teacher. Last year she was an assistant teacher at St. Francis Day Care. Then she took a job with the Community Early Childhood Center. She is in charge of eighteen three-year-olds from 7:30 to 3:30 every day. She loves each of her students and wishes she could spend more time with each of them during the day. But there is simply too much to do. She knows that a few of her children are developing more slowly than others. She works hard to spend a little extra time each day with these children. She has spoken with the parents of each of the children to let them know about the kids' development. One father got very angry with Michelle for claiming that his son was having more difficulty mastering early language skills than most of the boy's peers. Now Michelle is afraid to offer the boy any extra attention to help him develop his language skills because she doesn't want to alienate his parents. She worries about this little boy and wishes she could do more.

What do these stories have in common? They all involve people in need of advocacy. We all learn to advocate for ourselves. Whether it's getting a piece of candy from a parent when you were a child or asking for a raise at work, we all make arguments to those in a position to give us

Maintain high standards of professional conduct.

Recognize how personal values, opinions, and biases can affect professional judgment.

Be open to new ideas and be willing to learn from the suggestions of others.

Continue to learn, grow, and contribute as a professional.

Honor the ideals and principles of the NAEYC Code of Ethical Conduct.[2]

You can also review NAEYC's Code of Ethical Conduct on-line (http://www.naeyc.org/resources/position_statements/pseth98.htm) and begin now to incorporate professional ethical practices into your interactions with children and colleagues.

what we want. But advocating on behalf of others is a skill to which few teachers give much thought. Yet, as these stories illustrate, many students need an advocate.

As a teacher, you will have the opportunity to help identify and teach students with a variety of educational needs. You might need to advocate for a gifted child like Tim, who needs approval for time to work independently, more advanced material, and an opportunity to work with the schools gifted teacher. Or you might need to work on behalf of a child like Lisa, who needs access to individual assessment and instruction. In each of these cases, your school will likely have administrative procedures in place to determine who will receive these limited services.

Your willingness to be an advocate for your students will play a large role in who is identified and served. Both Tim and Lisa are at risk for developing poor motivation and self-esteem. Lisa is already falling behind her peers in reading achievement. This is an outlook that might deepen over time if not addressed now. Your ability to advocate for students like Tim and Lisa may well affect the course of their education and the rest of their lives.

The good news is that you already have greater advocacy skills than you realize. Good teachers effectively synthesize and present information every day. These are also the skills an advocate uses. Furthermore, you are not alone. You can tap into the experience of other teachers, administrators, parents, and professionals. You will be a professional educator with access to organizations and other teacher resources to help make you an effective advocate for your students, your school, and your profession.

In my private practice as an independent educational diagnostician and advocate, I have found my greatest allies are often caring teachers. You will be a trusted figure in your students' lives. As a teacher, you can offer information and insight that can make you a powerful advocate for your students and a valued colleague to the volunteer or professional advocate. Volunteer advocates are often parents who have had experience advocating for their own children and have chosen to advocate for others as well. Some professionals such as psychologists, social workers, or former teachers also serve as independent advocates. Finally, some are attorneys who have chosen to use their legal skills as advocates for children. As a teacher, you should consider yourself part of the advocacy team for each of your students.

What about Michelle, our frustrated early childhood teacher? She is in a position to advocate for herself as well as her students. How, you ask? She could work to educate the parents of her at-risk students about developmental delays by talking with them individually, offering to talk to a group of interested parents, or at a school open house. She could seek out a sympathetic senior teacher at the center and ask how he or she handled a similar situation, and then use an already proven solution. She could ask the center director to spend some time in her classroom to observe the children firsthand. Perhaps she could seek out the assistance of a special education professional who is on staff or works as a consultant with the center. Michelle needs to meet the needs of her students not only for their sake, but for her own credibility as a teacher as well. Advocating for these students means also advocating for status as an educator.

Advocacy need not be confrontational. It is usually not very effective to yell and insult people unless you are trying to make them angry. To be persuasive, keep your cool, plan your strategy, and make good use of your resources. Most importantly, prepare.

Making an advocacy plan is similar to forming a lesson plan. Prioritize the information you need to communicate, and then decide the most effective way of presenting your message. Remember, no argument is more convincing than accurate information effectively communicated. And, after all, isn't that just good teaching?

Contributed by J. Abram Doane, Northwestern Learning Consultants, Chicago, Illinois.

Seeking Ongoing Professional Development Opportunities.   When, if ever, do you become a "finished" professional? It makes the most sense to say that you are always in the process of becoming a professional. A professional is never a "finished" product; you will always be involved in a process of studying, learning, changing, and becoming more professional. Teachers of the Year and others who share with you their philosophies and beliefs are always in the process of becoming more professional.

Becoming a professional means you will participate in training and education beyond the minimum needed for your current position. You will also want to consider your career objectives and the qualifications you might need for positions of increasing responsibility.

 To monitor your progress toward professionalism using the online version of the Professional Development Checklist, go to the Companion Website at **http://www.prenhall.com/ morrison**, select any chapter, then choose the Resources module.

Advocacy The act of engaging in strategies designed to improve the circumstances of children and families. Advocates move beyond their day-to-day classroom or program professional responsibilities and work collaboratively to help others.

THE PUBLIC DIMENSION

The fourth dimension of professional practice is the public dimension. This dimension includes advocacy, articulation, and representation.

Advocacy.   Advocacy is the act of pleading the causes of children and families to the profession and the public. There is no shortage of issues to advocate for in the lives of children and families. Some of the issues that are in need of strong advocates involve quality programs, abuse and neglect prevention, children living in poverty, good housing, and health. Some things you can to do advocate include the following:

- Join an early childhood professional organization such as the National Association for the Education of Young Children, the Association for Childhood Education International (ACEI), and the Southern Early Childhood Association (SECA). These organizations have student and local affiliates. They are very active in advocating for young children, and you can serve on a committee or be involved in some other way. Contact information on these and other professional organizations can be found at the end of this chapter.
- Organize an advocacy group in your program or as a part of your class. Select a critical issue to study, and develop strategies for increasing public awareness about this issue.

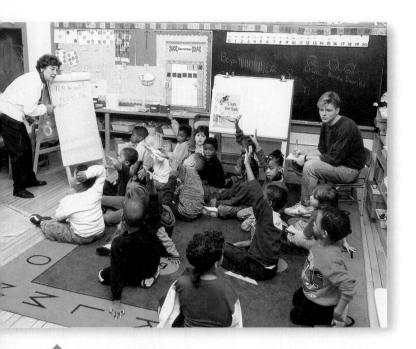

A professional is never a "finished" product. Collaborating with other professionals who share your philosophies is an excellent way to continue your professional development. What are some other ways?

Communicating with Others.   Being articulate about what you do and what the profession does and speaking to parents and the public is essential for helping children and families be successful. Early childhood professionals must be knowledgeable and informed about the profession and the issues it faces. At the same time, they have to be able to discuss these issues with the public, the media, families, and others in the community.

Representation.   Representation is the process of acting in the best possible ways on behalf of children and families. It involves being a role model for what a professional is and stands for, including how you dress, how you groom, and how you talk and act. It is important for professionals to make a good impression. We cannot practice our profession well or expect and receive the respect of parents and the public if we don't always put our best foot forward. How we look and how we behave does make a difference. And like it or not, first impressions count with many people. How we appear to others often sets the tone for interpersonal interactions. So, you should always look your best, do your best, and be your best.

These, then, are the four dimensions of professionalism—personal, educational, professional, and public. If you add these dimensions to whom and what you are now, you should be able to represent yourself and the profession very well. You can enhance your professional development by completing the Professional Development Checklist shown in Figure 1.3 now.

WHY DIVERSITY TIE-INS?

In each chapter of this book, there is a Diversity Tie-In feature (see p. 20). Perhaps you are wondering why. These Diversity Tie-Ins are designed to do the following:

To complete an activity related to the topic within the Diversity Tie-In, go to the Companion Website at **http://www. prenhall.com/morrison**, select chapter 1, then choose the Diversity Tie-In module.

- Help you become a better person and a teacher who has a wide and deep understanding of the diverse backgrounds of the children you teach.
- Enable you to teach all students regardless of their cultural, ethnic, or socioeconomic background.
- Provide you with learning ideas that support all children's intellectual, social, personal, and cultural development regardless of cultural background, socioeconomic status, and gender.
- Help you apply multicultural knowledge and information to your teaching. Every day you will want to explore the opportunities the curriculum provides for you to incorporate multicultural ideas and information.
- Enable you and your children to live happily and productively in a multicultural world.

HOW CAN YOU PREPARE YOURSELF FOR A CAREER IN EARLY CHILDHOOD EDUCATION?

A career as an early childhood professional can be greatly rewarding. Figure 1.3, your Professional Development Action Plan, outlines some important things you can do to make your career happy and productive for yourself and the children and families with whom you work. Review Figure 1.3 now. In each dimension, reflect on each item and consider how you can apply it to your professional growth.

We have considered many dimensions concerning what is involved in being an early childhood professional. At this point you may be wondering how to continue your journey of professionalism. This journey is like any other journey. It beings with a well-defined plan and first steps—one of

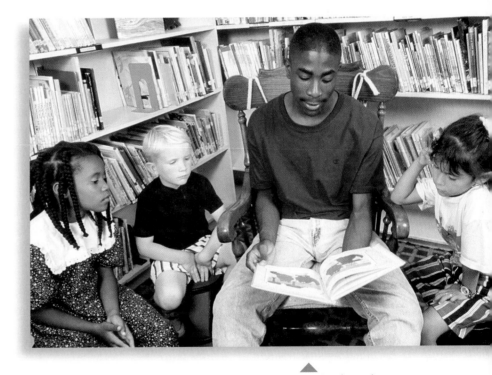

Honestly analyze your feelings and attitudes toward working with young children. Not everyone has the skills or temperament required for effective teaching of young children.

which can be to complete Figure 1.4. After you assess where you are in your journey toward professionalism, use the suggestions provided to develop a plan and a time line for achieving your professional goals for the coming year.

7 Tips for Teaching Respect and Tolerance

When I asked my class if anyone had seen the ball that was on my desk and my students said, "A bilingual took it," I knew we had a problem. My third graders were prejudiced against a group of Spanish-speaking children who they didn't know and had very little contact with. Here are some tips for teaching respect and tolerance that I used to bring the groups together.

1. *Start a conversation.* Ask an open-ended question. For instance, I asked my third graders, "What does bilingual mean?" Most kids had no idea. Some thought it meant "from Mexico" or "not too smart." Now I knew the first place to start was using our language arts skills to explore the actual definition of bilingual.

2. *Focus on what kids value.* Would you like someone just because you were told to? Kids must earn their peers' respect. So think about what kids value. Kids who can play sports or instruments well gain instant respect. Therefore, take every opportunity to showcase students' talents. Have schoolwide talent shows, poetry readings, events at recess, or impromptu moments if the kids are willing. For instance, one student said she played "America the Beautiful," a song that we were discussing in social studies. When the music room was free, we went in and listened to her. Another student who told me she danced in salsa style brought in a tape the next day and showed us some moves. The kids and I were wildly impressed!

3. *Seeing is believing.* Discuss whatever talents and special knowledge your students have, but go one step further. Have children give the class some visual examples of talents, such as a lesson in speed-skating, a finished model ship, playing a song on the harmonica, and so forth. Many children have special talents! Let them share them with others.

4. *Use history and current events.* Will Smith, Michael Jordan, and Jennifer Lopez make people forget race and color. Find historical and current people who are part of an ethnic group to stand as "cool" models. A well-liked student from the targeted group can help bridge a gap between groups. For instance, my students were pleasantly surprised when a popular kid in our class realized and announced, "I'm bilingual!"

5. *Put everyone in the same shoes.* If differences are languages, teach a class, or hand out papers in another language. If the differences are cultural, give a "quiz" on a cultural event from the minority group's culture. Discuss with your students how it feels to be confused by language and culture.

6. *Focus on the same.* Use the curriculum to give kids opportunities to discuss universal "kid" problems that illustrate how alike we are. For instance, in social studies discuss parental rules, or annoying siblings. Use math to talk allowances and bedtimes.

7. *Be a scout.* Constantly be on the lookout for special talents and knowledge from your students. Students might not realize that making tamales or tuning pianos are unique things. Use the curriculum to ask questions: Has anyone visited Puerto Rico? Does anyone speak two languages or three? Does anyone go to school on Saturdays? You and your students will be amazed at how interesting your class is.

One caution: When students see an individual getting accolades, they might attempt to do or say anything to also get attention. To avoid this, discuss with the class that there are two ways to get noticed. One is to do bad things. The class will laugh when you remind them that everyone looks at the toddler who screams at a restaurant. Doing something exceptional or unique is another way. When their "funny" comments die down, they will agree that the second way is the best.

The best way for any two people to get along is to spend time together and build respect and trust naturally. Therefore, students interacting all day long in little ways will slowly learn to tolerate and appreciate differences. You might even be rewarded by seeing lasting friendships forged.

Contributed by Rebecca Leo, Enders-Salk Elementary, Schaumburg, Illinois.

FIGURE 1.3 Your Professional Development Action Plan

Dimension 1: The Personal

✓ Examine your willingness to dedicate yourself to teaching.

✓ Analyze your attitudes and feelings toward children.

✓ Examine whether your teaching philosophy mirrors your philosophy for life.

✓ Allow your ideas about your life to guide your classroom practice.

Dimension 2: The Educational

✓ Learn what is involved in teaching.

✓ Ask yourself, "Am I willing to work hard?"

✓ Develop a philosophy of education and teaching.

✓ Visit early childhood programs.

✓ Talk with childhood professionals.

✓ Enroll in continuing education classes.

✓ Attend professional meetings and conferences.

✓ Read!

✓ Realize that learning is a lifelong process.

✓ Keep up to date with changing issues, changing children, and a changing knowledge base.

✓ Good electives in college are keyboarding, first aid, audiovisual aids and media, behavior modification/management, special education, creative writing, and arts and crafts.

Dimension 3: The Professional

✓ Ask yourself, "Would I be happier in another field, or do I really want to work with young children?"

✓ Test your attitudes toward children as you interact with them.

✓ Do not fall into the trap of believing that certain children cannot learn because of their cultural or socioeconomic background.

✓ Realize that all children have the right to be taught by a professional who believes in them.

✓ Use core requirements as a means to explore new and fascinating relationships to education.

✓ Remember, the good professional does not settle for the mediocre!

Dimension 4: The Public

✓ Branch out from public school settings—explore church schools, child care programs, private and nonprofit agencies, and babysitting as venues to broaden and expand your knowledge of children.

✓ Be willing to adjust to changing circumstances and conditions.

✓ Consider and explore the possibilities for you and your children to get involved in new things.

FIGURE 1.4 Assess Your Professional Development

Read each of the fifteen desired professional outcomes listed below. Give yourself a 3 if you have fully accomplished the outcome, a 2 if you are making satisfactory progress toward meeting the outcome, and a 1 if you are just getting started on meeting the desired outcome.

Scoring Criteria

3   Full accomplishment

2   Good progress

1   Need to get started

Desired Professional Outcome	My Rating
1. I have thought about and written my philosophy of teaching and caring for young children.	
2. I have a professional career plan for the next year that includes goals and objectives I will endeavor to meet as a professional.	
3. I engage in study and training programs to improve my knowledge and competence related to teaching and caring for young children.	
4. I am a teachable person.	
5. I have worked or am working on a degree or credential to enhance my personal life and my life as a professional.	
6. I try to improve myself as a person by engaging in a personal program of self-development.	
7. I practice in my own life and model for others good moral habits and ethical behavior. I encourage others to act ethically.	
8. I act professionally and encourage others to do the same.	
9. I place the best interests of children, parents, and the profession first in decisions about what constitutes quality teaching and care giving.	
10. I know about and am familiar with my profession's history, terminology, issues, contemporary development, and trends.	
11. I consciously and consistently find ways to apply concepts and knowledge about what is best for children to my teaching and care giving.	
12. I belong to a professional organization and participate in professional activities such as celebrations, study groups, committees, and conventions.	
13. I am an advocate for and on behalf of my profession and the needs and rights of children and families.	
14. I involve parents in my program and help and encourage parents in their roles as children's primary caregivers and teachers.	
15. I seek the advice of and cooperate with other professionals and professional groups in my work with young children, parents, and families.	
TOTAL POINTS	

Score Results

40–45   You are already an accomplished professional. You can work on refining your skills. You can be a strong advocate and mentor for others to help them with their careers.

39–30   You have accomplished a lot and are growing in your professional development. You are ready to take the next steps to assume a more active professional role.

29–0   You are ready to build a foundation of professionalism and to develop plans for being a professional. Seek out accomplished professionals for mentorship and coaching.

WHAT DOES THE FUTURE HOLD FOR EARLY CHILDHOOD PROFESSIONALS?

It is always risky to predict what the future holds for you as an early childhood professional. You now know some of the many changes occurring in the field. If the past is any indication, and I think it is, we can predict the following:

- *Rapid change.* The field of early childhood education will undergo rapid and dramatic change. Old ways of doing things will be challenged by new ideas and methods. This means that you will have to adapt as the field changes. And, you will have to continually transform your thinking as new ways make old habits obsolete.

- *Increased use of technology.* Technology will play an increasingly important and prominent role in how you teach, what you teach, and how children learn. In Chapter 13, "Technology and Young Children: Education in the Information Age," we discuss in depth the role of technology in early childhood programs and your role in using technology in teaching and learning.

- *Politicalization of early childhood education.* Politics have always influenced education in one way or another. However, in the years to come, politics and politicians will play an even greater role in determining what children are taught and how they are taught. This means that advocacy will be a major dimension of your professional practice and that you will be involved in the political process in many ways.

- *Increased emphasis on young children.* The public and politicians are recognizing the critical importance that early years play in children's school and life success. As a result, educators are developing programs for young children and their parents in efforts to help them gain the knowledge and skills that will lead to school and learning readiness. Early childhood will continue to be a time of interest, attention, and action.

- *Acceleration of early childhood teacher education and training.* As the field of early childhood changes, so does the knowledge and skills associated with it. This means that constant and continuous education will play a central role in your professional development. Many teachers spend as much time educating themselves and being educated as they spend on teaching their children. Changes that the future holds for the field of early childhood education and for you as a professional are not to be feared but are to be welcomed and embraced. This is a wonderful and exciting time to be in the field of early childhood education. A bright future awaits you and your children.

REDISCOVERING THE ROLE OF TODAY'S EARLY CHILDHOOD PROFESSIONAL

New occasions demand new duties. Nowhere is this more accurate than in the early childhood education profession. As this field changes, so, too, does your role as an early childhood professional. These rapid transformations require constant study and preparation on your part to keep up to date. In fact, the role of the early childhood professional today is radically different from what it was even two or three years ago. Although the dimensions of professionalism and the characteristics of the high-quality professional remain the same, responsibilities, expectations, and roles have changed. Let's examine some of these new roles of the contemporary early childhood professional, which are *not* so new as they are rediscovered and reemphasized.

- *Teacher as instructional leader.* Teachers have always been responsible for classroom and program instruction, but this role is now reemphasized and given a much more prominent place in what early childhood teachers do, such as planning for what children will learn, guiding and teaching so that children learn, assessing what children learn, and arranging the classroom environment so that children learn.

 To take an online self-test on this chapter's contents, go to the Companion Website at **http://www. prenhall.com/morrison**, select Chapter 1, then choose the Self-Test module.

 For additional Internet resources or to complete an online activity for this chapter, go to the Companion Website at **http://www. prenhall.com/morrison**, select Chapter 1, then choose the Linking to Learning or Making Connections module.

- *Intentional teaching of state, district, and program goals and standards.* Intentional teaching occurs when instructors teach for a purpose, are clear about what they teach, and teach so that children learn specific knowledge and skills. In this context, teachers spend more time during the day actually teaching and make a conscious effort to be more involved in each child's learning process. This process of intentional teaching can and should occur in a child-centered approach. In addition, it occurs for only specified times and purposes throughout the school day.

- *Performance-based accountability for learning.* Teachers today are far more accountable for children's learning. Previously, the emphasis was on the process of schooling. Teachers were able to explain their role as "I taught Mario how to. . . . " Today the emphasis is on, "What did Mario learn?" and "Did Mario learn what he needs to know and do in order to perform at or above grade level?"

- *Teaching of literacy and reading.* Although the teaching of reading has always been a responsibility of early childhood professionals, this role has been expanded. Today, every early childhood teacher is now a teacher of literacy and reading, subjects necessary in all content areas, including math and science.

- *Increased emphasis on assessing what children learn and using the results of assessment to plan for teaching and learning assessment and planning have become a more essential part of the teaching-learning process.*

- *A new meaning of child-centered education.* Early childhood professionals have always advocated child-centered education and approaches. This is certainly true today. Everything we discuss in this book is based on the child being the center of the teaching and learning processes. Unfortunately, not all teachers have practiced child-centered approaches, nor have they made children's learning a high priority. This is changing. Included in the child-centered approach are the ideas that children can learn at high levels of achievement; that children are eager to learn; and that they are capable of learning more than many people thought they could. So a new concept of child-centeredness embraces the whole child in all dimensions: social, emotional, physical, linguistic, and cognitive.

As the field of early childhood continues to change, the details of your role as an early childhood professional will continue to be refined. You will want to devote the time and energy necessary to keep yourself in the forefront of your field—make this time one of exciting rediscovery!

ACTIVITIES FOR FURTHER ENRICHMENT

APPLICATIONS

1. Recall the teachers who had a great influence on you. Which of their characteristics do you plan to imitate?

2. Put your philosophy of education in writing, and share it with others. Have them critique it for comprehensiveness, clarity, and meaning. How do you feel about the changes they suggested?

3. Metaphors are an effective way of expressing meanings and ideas. They are also a good way to think about yourself, your beliefs, and teaching. For example, some of the metaphors my students have identified for themselves are teacher as leader, coach, and facilitator. Add to this list and then identify one metaphor that best describes your metaphor for teaching at this time. Use these and other metaphors to help you develop your philosophy of education.

FIELD EXPERIENCES

1. Attend local meetings of an early childhood professional organization in your area, such as NAEYC or ACEI. What issues are local professional groups addressing? How are the groups meeting the needs of their members? Of children and families? Would you join the organizations you visited?

2. Many local school districts elect and honor their teachers of the year. Contact these teachers and have them share with you the ideas and attitudes that caused their colleagues to elect them as a teacher of the year. Plan for how you will integrate these qualities into your professional development plan.

RESEARCH

1. Interview preschool and kindergarten teachers about topics for in-service training they think would contribute to their professional development.

2. Interview five early childhood professionals to determine what they think constitutes professionalism and how professions can be more involved in increasing professionalism.

3. Interview professionals about careers that relate to children and parents. How did they come to their jobs? Is there evidence that they planned for these careers? Do you think you would enjoy an alternative career in education? Why?

4. Interview teachers in various programs and agencies to determine their core beliefs about teaching and the essentials of being a professional. Make a list of these core beliefs and reflect on them as you continue to consider your philosophy of education.

READINGS FOR FURTHER ENRICHMENT

Catron, C. E., and Allen, J. *Early Childhood Curriculum: A Creative Play Model*, 2nd ed. Upper Saddle River, NJ: Merrill/Prentice Hall, 1999.

This comprehensive guide provides information on planning programs with a play-based, developmental curriculum for children from birth to five years of age and covers basic principles and current research in early childhood curricula.

Devries, R. *Developing Constructivist Early Childhood Curriculum: Practical Principles and Activities.* New York: Teachers College Press, 2002.

Provides a constructivist interpretation of developmentally appropriate curriculum in early childhood education. Provides the theoretical rationale and practical advice for conducting specific activities in the classroom. Descriptive vignettes are used to show how children's reasoning and teacher interventions are transformed in the course of extended experience with a physical phenomenon or group game.

Henniger, M. L. *Teaching Young Children: An Introduction.* Upper Saddle River, NJ: Merrill/Prentice Hall, 1999.

This coverage of child development—which includes discussions about guiding young children, working families, and celebrating diversity—will help teachers facilitate all aspects of the birth-to-eight-year-old child's growth.

Paciorek, K. M., and Munro, J. H., editors. *Early Childhood Education 2002–2003.* New York: McGraw Hill College Division, 2002.

One in a series of more than seventy-five volumes, each designed to provide convenient, inexpensive access to a wide range of current, carefully selected articles from some of the most respected magazines, newspapers, and journals published today.

Saracho, O. N., and Spodek, B., editors. *Contemporary Perspectives on Early Childhood Curriculum.* Greenwich, CT: Information Age Publishing Inc, 2002.

Presents different conceptions and perspectives on early childhood curriculum. The way scholars define curriculum may continue to be elusive, but the approach in curriculum development is consistent. Curriculum developers establish goals, develop experiences, designate content, and evaluate experiences and outcomes.

Schiller, P. B., and Phipps, P. *The Daily Curriculum for Early Childhood: Over 1,200 Easy Activities to Support Multiple Intelligences and Learning Styles.* Beltsville, MD: Gryphon House, 2002.

A complete plan for every learning style for three- to six-year-olds. Organized by theme, it includes a morning circle and end-of-day reflection, and different activities for each learning center.

Seefeldt, C. *The Early Childhood Curriculum: Current Findings in Theory and Practice,* 3rd ed. New York: Teachers College Press, 1999.

Includes chapters on inclusion and the multicultural world of the early childhood classroom, an overview of current developments in the field, and coverage of teaching strategies. This information will enable educators to make decisions about what curriculum content is appropriate for young children.

White, S. C., and Coleman, T. M. *Early Childhood Education: Building a Philosophy for Teaching.* Upper Saddle River, NJ: Merrill/Prentice Hall, 2000.

Discusses early childhood issues within the context of society, family, and classroom approaches that influence the care and education of children from birth through age eight to help teachers build their teaching philosophy. It is designed to help students develop a professional identity and gain confidence in their ability to respond to the educational needs of young children in contemporary society.

Wiles, J. W. *Curriculum Essentials: A Resource for Educators.* Boston: Allyn & Bacon, 1999.

Contains compilations of important dates and events, definitions of curriculum, names to know in curriculum study, and an introduction to the philosophies and theories influencing curriculum involvement.

Wiseman, D., Cooner, D., and Knight, S. *Becoming a Teacher in a Field-Based Setting.* Stamford, CT: Wadsworth, 2001.

This text offers a traditional framework for a methods or education course, while adding the field-based component. Portfolio assessment is explained in the text and illustrated by various activities.

LINKING TO LEARNING

RELATED WEB SITES

Wheelock College Institute for Leadership and Career Initiatives
http://institute.wheelock.edu

The center's technical assistance, training delivery, research, and information dissemination activities are designed to help education institutions bring about systematic change to replace the currently fragmented training system with one that meets the needs of families, children, and the field.

Center for Early Childhood Leadership
http://www2.nl.edu/twal

The center's activities encompass four areas: improving the knowledge of early childhood program directors, technical assistance to improve program quality, research on professional development issues, and public awareness of the role early childhood directors play in providing services for children and families.

Child Development Policy Institute
http://www.cdpi.net

Advocacy group that lobbies on behalf of children in child care settings.

Children's Rights Council
http://www.gocrc.com

The Children's Rights Council focuses on work with individuals, parents, children, families, and communities to develop and strengthen the family as the building block of society.

Council for Early Childhood Professional Recognition
http://www.cdacouncil.org

Offers a nationally recognized, competency-based Child Development Associate credential that provides training, assessment, and certification of child care professionals. Bilingual specialization also available.

Early Childhood Education Online
http://www.ume.maine.edu/eceol-l/

This Web site exists to promote and facilitate information management and exchange and to serve as a resource and benefit for all children, their families, and all people who help them grow and learn.

Early Childhood Education Web Guide
http://www.ecewebguide.com

The Early Childhood Education Web Guide provides childcare professionals with the most up-to-date Internet resources. The sites on this guide are checked on a weekly basis to ensure their reliability and integrity.

ERIC Clearinghouse on Elementary and Early Childhood Education
http://ericeece.org

Provides information to parents and educators on all subjects and grade levels, publishes free biannual newsletters, and sponsors a parent question answering service (E-mail: askeric @ ericir.syr.edu) and electronic discussion groups.

National Association for the Education of Young Children
http://www.naeyc.org

Publishes brochures, posters, videotapes, books, and journals discussing teaching and program ideas, ways to improve parent–teacher relations, and resources for students about safety, language arts, and learning. National, state, and local affiliate groups offer training opportunities.

National Center for Early Development and Learning
http://www.fpg.unc.edu/~ncedl/

Research at the National Center for Early Development and Learning (NCEDL) focuses on enhancing the cognitive, social, and emotional development of children from birth through age eight.

National Resource Center for Family Centered Practice
http://www.uiowa.edu/~nrcfcp/index.html

The National Resource Center for Family Centered Practice provides technical assistance, staff training, research and evaluation, and information on family-based programs and issues to public and private human services agencies in states, counties, and communities across the United States.

The Child Care Circle
http://www.thechildcarecircle.com/index.html

Connecting daycare, preschool, and early childhood education professionals together on the Web.

Teacher Information Network
http://www.teacher.com

With listings of organizations, resources, sites, and governmental departments, TIN is a one-stop gateway to all the resources a teacher could want on the Web. Chat with other teachers, sign up for free e-mail, or just keep abreast of the latest teaching trends, all at TIN.

ELECTRONIC JOURNALS RELATED TO EARLY CHILDHOOD EDUCATION

Children's Advocate
http://www.4children.org/childadv.htm

A bimonthly newsmagazine published by the Action Alliance for Children that covers California, national, and international policy issues affecting children. Highlights from the current issue and selected articles from past issues are available on the Web site.

Early Childhood News
http://www.earlychildhoodnews.com

> *A journal on professional development in early childhood education, Early Childhood News is a valuable resource for anyone interested in the field of educating the leaders of tomorrow and the learners of today.*

Clearinghouse on Elementary and Early Childhood Education
http://ericeece.org

> *Provides information for educators, parents, and families interested in the development, education, and care of children.*

The Future of Children
http://www.futureofchildren.org

> *The Future of Children is an online child advocacy journal published three times a year by The David and Lucile Packard Foundation. Has online articles on issues pertaining to the health and well being of children in our nation.*

Instructor Magazine
http://teacher.scholastic.com/products/instructor.htm

> *Practical ideas for the classroom and information on teachers' professional development.*

Teacher Magazine
http://www.teachermagazine.org

> *Addresses issues from preschool through grade twelve.*

PROFESSIONAL ORGANIZATION CONTACTS

The following agencies are devoted to improving professional practice. Contact them for information about their programs, position statements, and professional and child advocacy initiatives.

Association for Childhood Education International (ACEI)
17904 Georgia Ave., Suite 215
Olnoy, MD 20832
(301) 570-2111 or (800) 423-3563; fax (301) 570-2212
Contact: Gina Hoagland, Public Relations Manager
E-mail: aceihq@aol.com
http://www.udel.edu/bateman/acei

National Association for the Education of Young Children (NAEYC)
1509 16th St. NW
Washington, DC 20036
(202) 232-8777 or (800) 424-2640; fax (202) 328-1846
Contact: Pat Spahr, Information Services Director
E-mail: naeyc@naeyc.org
http://www.naeyc.org

National Association of Elementary School Principals (NAESP)
1615 Duke St.
Alexandria, VA 22314
(703) 684-3345 or (800) 386-2377
Contact: Gail Gross, Deputy Executive Director
E-mail: naesp@naesp.org
http://www.naesp.org

National Early Childhood Technical Assistance Center (NECTAC)
Campus Box 8040, UNC-CH
Chapel Hill, NC 27599
(919) 962-2001; fax (919) 966-7463

Contact: Joan Dunaher, Associate Director of Information Resources
E-mail: Joan-Dunaher@unc.edu
http://www.nectac.org

Southern Early Childhood Association (SECA)
P.O. Box 55930
Little Rock, AR 72215
(800) 305-7322; fax (501) 227-5297
E-mail:seca@arstotle.net
http://www.seca50.org

ENDNOTES

[1] Phillips, Carol Brunson. *Field Advisor's Guide for the CDA Professional Preparation Program* (Washington, DC: Council for Early Childhood Professional Recognition, 1991), 2.

[2] Feeney, S. and Kipnis, K. *Code of Ethical Conduct and Statement of Commitment* (Washington, DC: National Association for the Education of Young Children). Copyright © 1997 by NAEYC. Reprinted by permission.

Chapter 2

I think education is the single most important issue in our country. If we can get that one thing right, if we can make sure every single child gets a great education, it will solve a lot of our other problems.

FIRST LADY LAURA BUSH

Early Childhood Education Today
Public Policy and Current Issues

Focus Questions

- How are p
  and current issues
  changing early
  childhood education?

- How do social,
  political, economic,
  and educational
  issues influence and
  change child rearing,
  early childhood
  education, and
  teaching?

- What are some
  implications that
  contemporary issues
  have for curriculum,
  teaching, and the life
  outcomes of children
  and families?

- How can early
  childhood programs
  and teachers help
  solve contemporary
  social problems?

I n this chapter we discuss public policy and current issues as they influence early childhood education. Public policy consists of all the plans that local, state, and national government and nongovernment organizations (NGOs) have for implementing their goals. Public policy as applied to early childhood education includes all of the goals agencies have relating to the care and education of young children.

At the national level, the federal government's policy of having all children read on grade level by grade three affects state and local education policy and influences the literacy experiences you will provide for young children. The Children's Defense Fund (CDF) is an example of a national NGO that develops and implements public policy on behalf of children and families. (The Companion Web site provides additional information about CDF).

Some states have policies designed to ensure that all children will enter school ready to learn. These policies put into place programs to improve children's health and enhance their abilities to learn. You might be involved in some of these school readiness programs. At the local level, public schools have developed policies regarding the admittance and education of three- and four-year-old children. More school districts are hiring preschool teachers, and you might be one of them.

PUBLIC POLICY AND CURRENT ISSUES

Agencies develop **public policy** in response to critical societal issues. Public policy, in turn, frequently creates public issues. The federal government's policy on standards and testing creates issues about testing and young children. Today, children and families face many issues that dramatically place at risk their educations and life outcomes.

These issues affect how you, as a professional, provide for children's development, education, and care. They influence every dimension of practice from how we teach children to read, to the health care we provide, to the quality of their teachers. We cannot ignore these issues or pretend they do not exist. We must be part of the solution to making it possible for all children to achieve their full potential. Education is very political, and politicians look to early childhood professionals to help develop educational solutions to social problems.

To review the chapter focus questions online, go to the Companion Website at **http://www. prenhall.com/morrison** and select chapter 2.

Public policy All the plans that local, state, and national government and nongovernment organizations have for implementing their goals.

 To check your understanding of this chapter with the online Study Guide, go to the Companion Website at **http://www. prenhall. com/morrison**, select chapter 3, then choose the Study Guide module.

 For more information about families and early childhood education, go to the Companion Website at **http://www.prenhall. com/morrison**, select any chapter, then choose Topic 10 of the ECE Supersite module.

FIGURE 2.1   Early Childhood in the News

Newspapers are full of articles relating to children and family news. Here are just a few representative headlines that show the enormous range of topics. A good way to keep informed about such issues is to read daily newspapers.

- "Growing Up Too Fat: Kids Suffer Adult Ailments as More Become Dangerously Obese" (*San Francisco Chronicle*)
- "AMA Puts Doctors on Lookout for Bullying" (*Chicago Sun-Times*)
- "Special Ed Gender Gap Stirs Worry: Some Say Boys Singled Out for Wrong Reasons" (*Boston Globe*)
- "School Violence Hits Lower Grades" (*USA Today*)
- "States May Get Bigger Role in Head Start" (*Los Angeles Times*)
- "Testing Expands to Kids in Head Start" (*Los Angeles Times*)

Daily newspapers provide ample evidence of critical issues and the nation's interest in young children. Figure 2.1 shows recent newspaper headlines that call attention to young children, parents, families, and child service agencies.

CHANGING FAMILIES

Families are in a continual state of change as a result of social issues and changing times. The definition of what a family is varies as society changes. Consider the following ways families are changing in the twenty-first century:

1. *Structure.* Families now include arrangements other than the traditional nuclear family:
   - Single-parent families, headed by mothers or fathers
   - Stepfamilies, including individuals related by either marriage or adoption
   - Heterosexual, gay, or lesbian partners living together as families
   - Extended families, which may include grandparents, uncles, aunts, other relatives, and individuals not related by kinship
2. *Roles.* As families change, so do the parenting roles of parents, family members, and others. For example:
   - More parents work and have less time for their children and family affairs.
   - Working parents must combine roles of both parents and employees. The number of hats that parents wear increase as families change.
   - Others such as grandparents and non–family members must learn new parenting roles.
3. *Responsibilities.* As families change, many parents are not able to provide or cannot afford to pay for adequate and necessary care for their children. Some parents find that buffering their children from social ills such as drugs, violence, and delinquency is more than they can handle. Also, some parents are consumed by problems of their own and have little time or attention for their children.

As families continue to change, you and other early childhood professionals must develop creative ways to provide services to children and families of all kinds.

Families and Early Childhood.   A primary goal of early childhood education is to meet children's needs in culturally and developmentally appropriate ways. Early childhood professionals agree that a good way to meet the needs of children is through their families, whatever that family unit may be. Review Figure 2.2, which shows methods and benefits

Early childhood education professionals provide:

- Parenting education
- Literacy programs
- Counseling programs
- Referrels to community agencies
- Assistance with problems of daily living

Family and child outcomes and effects:

- Less family and child stress
- Healthier families and children
- More involvement of families in their children's education
- Increased children's achievement
- A better quality of life for children and families
- Reduced child abuse and neglect

To complete an activity related to the topic in the Diversity Tie-in below, go to the Companion Website at **http://www.prenhall. com/morrison**, select chapter 2, then choose the Diversity Tie-in module.

FIGURE 2.2   A Model for Meeting the Needs of Children and Families

DIVERSITY TIE-IN

Children and Families Learning Together

It is now official. Recently released Census Bureau figures show that Hispanics (defined by the census Bureau as individuals of Spanish speaking ancestry) have surpassed African Americans as the nation's largest minority group (U.S. Census Bureau http://www.census.gov/Press-Release/www/2003/cb03-16.html). Hispanics, who now number 37 million, account for 13 percent of the population. This increase, due to higher birth rates and immigration, has tremendous implications for schools and communities all across the country.

Many schools such as Sidney Lanier in Dallas operate family centers designed to assure that parents have the support they need to help their children succeed in school and life. The majority of the parents at Sidney Lanier don't come from the 50 states with names that most of us are familiar with. They come from the Mexican states of Tabasco, Coahuila, Guerrero, Guanajuato, and San Luis Potosi. And they come with a strong respect for teachers and education. They want to be involved in the life of the school. According to Elizabeth Gonzalez, a community liaison, 131 parents serve as volunteers. In addition, many of the parents take English classes at night at the school. For parent Rosa Perez, the motive for volunteering is all about the American Dream. "In Mexico we didn't even have books. Here my kids can have careers. I want them to have the things I didn't have . . . I want them to get ahead and I'm going to do everything I can to see they do."*

The thing about the Parent Center at Sidney Lanier is that it is not unusual. More than likely, you will teach immigrant and minority children and you will be involved in many ways with their parents. Here are some things you can do now to prepare you for teaching minority children:

- Volunteer in schools, childcare centers, and other programs that serve minority children.
- Visit agencies in your city or other cities that provide services to minority children and families.
- If your professional training includes field experiences and teaching, request an assignment in schools serving minority children.

In addition, Chapter 15 and the Diversity Tie-In feature in each chapter will give you insight and guidance for teaching diverse populations.

---

*Terrazas, Beatriz. "Hands, Hearts and High Hopes." *Dallas Morning News* (January 26, 2003) p. 10F.

PROGRAM IN ACTION

Toyota Families in Schools Program

The year 2001 marked the anniversary of the ten-year partnership between Toyota and the National Center for Family Literacy. This partnership has allowed family literacy services to be established in twenty-three major cities throughout the United States. More than 6,000 parents have made better lives for themselves and their children through their enrollment in the Toyota Families for Learning (TFFL) programs and the Toyota Families in Schools (TFS) programs. The success of the 15 original sites created in 1991 resulted in TFFL programs expanding into 111 sites throughout 20 cities in 2001.

The Toyota Families in Schools program is a collaboration between the National Center for Family Literacy (NCFL) and local school districts across the country. The program goal is to increase achievement of at-risk children from ages five to twelve, bringing these students and their parents together to learn in the elementary school setting

In a typical TFS program, parents learn skills in various academic areas while their children participate in their own classroom education. Specific times are designated for children and their parents to work together in the child's classroom, which allows the parents to observe their child's learning firsthand. NCFL has found that parents who spend time with their children in the classroom become more comfortable in the school environment and more confident in their ability to support their children's efforts to learn.

Source: Toyota Families in Schools Program; available at http://www.toyota.com/html/about/community_care/education/family_school_program.html

To complete a Program in Action activity, visit the Companion Website at **http://www.prenhall.com/morrison**, select chapter 2, then choose the Program in Action module.

of educating children and families. Providing for children's needs through and within the family system makes sense for a number of reasons.

First, the family system has the primary responsibility for meeting many children's needs. So, helping families function means that everyone stands to benefit. Helping people in a family unit—mother, father, grandparents, and others—function better helps them and their children.

Second, professionals frequently need to address family problems and issues first in order to help children effectively. For example, helping parents gain access to adequate, affordable health care means that the whole family, including children, will be healthier. When children are healthy, they achieve better.

Third, early childhood professionals can do many things concurrently with children and their families that benefit both. Literacy is a good example. Early childhood professionals are taking a family approach to helping children, their parents, and other family members learn how to read, write, speak, and listen. Teaching parents to read helps them understand the importance of supporting and promoting their children in the learning and teaching process.

Fourth, addressing the needs of children and their families as a whole (known as the holistic approach to education and the delivery of services) enables early childhood professionals and others to address a range of social concerns simultaneously. Programs that provide education and support for literacy, health care, nutrition, healthy living, abuse prevention, AIDS education, and parenting are examples of this family-centered approach. A major trend in early childhood education is that professionals will expand the family-centered approach to providing for the needs of children and families.

Working Parents. More and more families find that both parents must work to make ends meet. An increasing percentage of mothers with children under six are currently employed (nearly 60 percent in 2002; see Figure 2.3), which creates a greater need for early childhood programs. This demand brings a beneficial recognition to early childhood programs and encourages early childhood professionals to meet parents' needs.

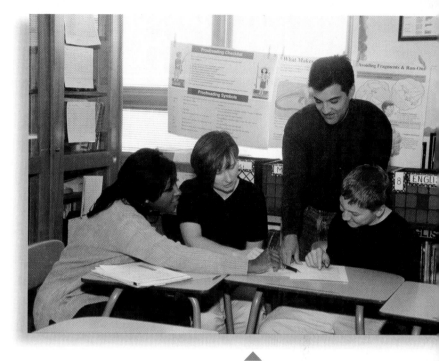

Affluent Families. Many parents with middle- and upper-level incomes are willing to invest money in early education for their children. They look for nursery schools and preschool programs they feel will give their children a good start in life. Montessori schools and franchised operations such as Bright Horizons, Kindercare, and La Petite Academy have benefited in the process. Private preschool education is a booming business. Some parents of three- and four-year-olds spend almost as much in tuition to send their children to good preschools as parents of eighteen-year-olds do to send their children to state-supported universities.

For example, Crème de la Crème, a series of premium-quality child care and preschool programs, charges $389 a month for their part-time (three-day or half day) programs and $1,134 a month for their full-time programs.

When families are involved in their children's education, everyone benefits. What are some culturally appropriate ways you can reach out to the families of the children in your care?

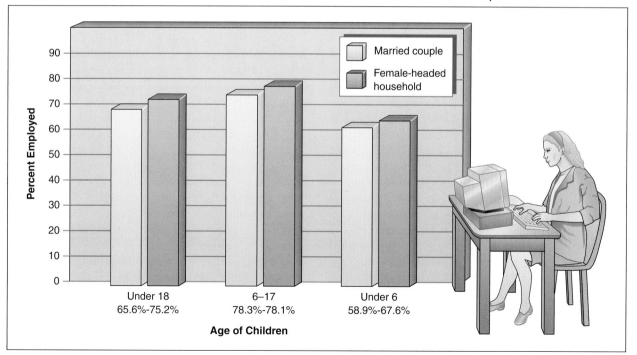

Under 18
65.6%-75.2%

6–17
78.3%-78.1%

Under 6
58.9%-67.6%

Age of Children

Percent Employed

Married couple
Female-headed household

FIGURE 2.3 **Mothers in the Workforce**

Source: U.S. Census Bureau, *Current Population Survey,* 2002.

Effort Creates Ability

We wish to be recognized as ordinary people who do extraordinary things to help each of our students meet with successes and celebrations in the classroom and in life.

Four years ago, Vicki Sheffler, an elementary school teacher in Greensburg, Pennsylvania, since 1974, met her match. She teamed up with colleague Christa Pehrson, a veteran teacher of thirteen years, to team teach a first grade classroom and later a first-to-second grade team looping classroom at Amos K. Hutchinson Elementary School.

When I (Vicki Sheffler) was a child attending elementary school in the late fifties and early sixties, I attended a neighborhood school. Everyone walked to school, and most of the teachers lived in the same neighborhood. There was one teacher in particular, that every child admired; and that was a sixth grade teacher, Mrs. Cassetta. My brother was in her class three years earlier, and every day, when walking home from school he would share the most wonderful stories about her classroom. I vividly remember walking by her home numerous times, in hopes that she would be on her porch or in her yard. When she would spot me, she would call out, "Hi there, Joey's sister. I'm saving a desk for you!" Oh, how my heart would flutter when she spoke those words! Well, she held true to her word, and when I was in sixth grade, she did save a seat for me! Every day in her classroom was an exciting and delightful adventure. Back in those days, the classroom teacher did it all: physical education, librarian, music, and art. The only break during her school day was an hour at lunchtime, when the school children walked home for lunch. Never once did she raise her voice in anger, never once did she belittle or embarrass a child, and never once did she show indifference to our classroom. She was the living expression of kindness: kindness in her eyes, kindness in her face, and kindness in her smile. Each and every day brought new discoveries and explorations. When each of us think back on our education, we don't remember the methods of teaching, but we remember our teachers; the ones who inspired us, the ones who took special interest in us, the ones who motivated us to do our best, and the ones who encouraged us to dream bigger dreams. I often think back to that year and recall the wonder I felt in her presence. I knew my calling when I finished sixth grade. I wanted to be a teacher, just like Mrs. Cassetta. I can't imagine what I would have missed had she not been my teacher. I keep a photograph of her on my desk, and each time I look at it, I smile, and remember. . . .

When I (Christa Pehrson) reminisce about my school days, I think about the wonderful memories of classrooms and teachers that have touched my life. These memories shower my heart with assurance and resolve that I have chosen a profession that gives me, every day, the unique opportunity to improve every tomorrow.

Mrs. Schmiggle was my first grade teacher, and oh, what a teacher she was! Young, energetic, and vibrant, her smile would brighten the gloomiest day, and she always had enough kind words to travel around the room and back again! I could hardly wait to get to school each day. She instilled in me the love and excitement of learning.

Miss Ridinger was my algebra teacher. I was always amazed at the way in which she changed my entire outlook about a subject that was so hard for me to understand. For you see, I had convinced myself that I could never get through a year of algebra, but Miss Ridinger had alternate plans for me. She taught me never to give up on myself. She found a way to see the good and bring out the best in me, in spite of the circumstances. She instilled in me the power of perseverance.

Mr. Wilson was my track and field coach. Although he was never my teacher, he became, in a way, my mentor. He had a reputation as being the most difficult teacher in my junior high school, yet all of the students wanted to get into his class. His rather nontraditional teaching methods and use of active participation in the classroom sparked an interest in the entire student body and I realized the impact that one teacher could have on a student. I never enjoyed running and I never placed in any of the meets, so why was I a member of the track and field team year after year? Mr. Wilson! He instilled in me the power of sheer determination.

When I became a teacher, I wanted to be a Mrs. Schmiggle, a Miss Ridinger, and a Mr. Wilson all packaged into one unique teacher, ME! I knew that just like each of them, I could make a difference, one student at a time.

Then, there is my father, George Daryl Kelvington. My father's profession was a teacher and wrestling coach. I witnessed, first-hand, the impact he had not only on his students, but especially on the young men that he coached. He would frequently bring home wrestlers to feed them a healthy meal, or help them with assignments and projects. He became their extended family. One of his wrestlers actually lived with us for two years. Because he was African-American, many of my friends and neighbors shunned us. My father instilled in me the value of the individual.

It was through these experiences that I learned many life lessons. All children need to feel loved, to have someone who cares about them, someone who is willing to bring out the best in them, and to help them reach their full potential.

Albert Einstein once said, "It is the supreme art of the teacher to awaken joy in creative expression and knowledge." Our team classroom is a creative and innovative classroom because as teachers, we live by and teach by the creed, "effort creates ability." Our beliefs about learning and daily practice are clearly focused. We teach our students in the ways in which we would want our own children to be taught. Each and every day, we are willing to go above and beyond what is required to help children meet with successes and celebrations. We promote student engagement, ownership and understanding through active participation. We know that children learn best when they are immersed in situations that have meaning for them and when there is no fear of failure. Our classroom provides each student with a wide selection of hands-on activities using kinesthetic, visual, and auditory learning styles to make learning interesting and meaningful. Differentiated instruction, tiered learning, cooperative learning, learning centers, and cluster grouping help us to achieve our goals. Community members, school board members, parents, and high school and college students have become companions in learning as they tutor students in all subject areas. Thematic units, guest speakers, in-class programs, and field trips are directly correlated to our curricula. Our community service projects promote and foster kindness, compassion, and the importance of contributing to the world around them.

It has often been said that one's first impression is a lasting impression. We want that first impression to be a love of learning, and respect and kindness toward others and the community. To achieve that goal, we must become role models for life-long learning. We must be willing to "think outside of the box," and to realize that there is so much more to learning than what is found in a child's desk. Keep in mind that when you become a teacher, you also become a counselor, a mediator, an advisor, a nurse, a lawyer, a manager, and a friend. You will do more by lunchtime, than most have ever seen! As a teacher, you will have the ability to make memories that will leave lasting impressions. "Your students are the vehicles. Some will be teachers themselves. They will carry your gifts away. Your kind words, your pure passions, and your guiding light will be passed out by them like bread to the hungry. They will take your humble light and set off diamonds in the sky. There will be fireworks in the future. People will gasp at their dazzling display, delight in their shimmering brilliance—all ablaze from your one tiny spark. Oh no, dear teacher. It doesn't stop here."*

Always remember that teachers can be some of the best encouragers in the world. Just a few simple words can make the difference between victory and defeat. "I'm so very proud of you!" "You're the best!" "You can do it." Watch your students' faces brighten, their backs straighten, their attitudes change, and their work habits improve all because you have given them words of encouragement.

A recent calculation stated that the average cost to raise a child from birth to age eighteen is $160,140. That amount translates to $24.37 a day, or a little more than $1.00 an hour. Now, some may look at these numbers and wonder whether the return is worth the investment. But as a teacher, you will realize that the rewards are priceless. You will accept the challenge enthusiastically because you will realize that you are nurturing and teaching a very unique individual. You will understand that your investment in the teaching of your students has helped to shape the future. Now, wouldn't you agree that a dollar an hour is worth every penny!

To promote a sense of community within our own classroom, we recite two pledges, and a learning cheer in addition to our Pledge of Allegiance.

Our first pledge is our "September 11th Pledge":
  Every day, in every way,
  I will show kindness to others.
  Our next pledge is our "Helping Hands Pledge":
  "I am only one, but still I am one.
  I cannot do everything, but still I can do something.
  And because I cannot do everything,
  I will not refuse to do the something that I can do."

Our last recitation is our "Learning Cheer":
  L - Listen to others.
  E - Expect to learn each day.
  A - Act kindly towards others.
  R - Remember the class rules.
  N - Never give up on yourself.
  1,2,3. . . First Grade's Cool!

---

*Loveless, C., & McKee, M. (1999). *Hugs for Teachers*. West Monroe, LA: Howard Publishing Co. pp. 72–73.
Contributed by Christa Pehrson and Vicki Sheffler, Amos K. Hutchinson Elementary School, Greensburg, PA, 2002 *USA Today's* First Team Teachers.

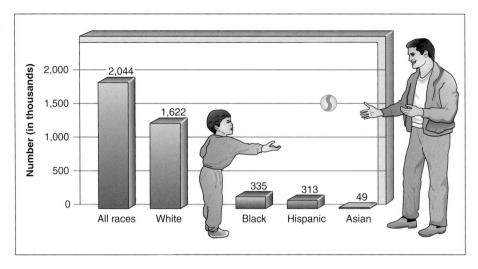

FIGURE 2.4 **Single-Parent Families Headed by Fathers Among Certain Races**
Source: U.S. Census Bureau, *Current Population Survey,* 2001.

Fathers. Fathers are rediscovering the joys of parenting and working with young children. Not only have many fathers rediscovered parenting and child rearing, but early childhood education has discovered fathers! Men are playing an active role in providing basic care, love, and nurturance to their children. The definition of *fatherhood* has changed; a father is no longer stereotypically unemotional, detached from everyday responsibilities of child care, authoritarian, and a disciplinarian. Fathers no longer isolate themselves from child rearing because they are male. Men are more concerned about their role of fatherhood and their participation in family events before, during, and after the birth of their children. Fathers want to be involved in the whole process of child rearing. Because so many men feel unprepared for fatherhood, agencies such as hospitals and community colleges are providing courses and seminars to introduce fathers to the joys, rewards, and responsibilities of fathering.

Fathers no longer quietly acquiesce to giving up custody of their children in a divorce. Men are becoming single parents through adoption and surrogate childbearing. (Figure 2.4 shows the number of single-parent families headed by fathers among certain races.) Also, increasing in number are stay-at-home dads. Estimates of the number of fathers who stay home with their children are as high as two million. Fathers are also receiving some of the employment benefits that have traditionally gone only to women, such as paternity leaves, flexible work schedules, and sick leave for family illness. In addition more agencies are involved in promoting the roles of fathers. For example, the Family Resource Coalition of America (FRCA) suggests ten ways to support fathers. These are listed in Figure 2.5.

Single Parents. The number of one-parent families, male and female, continues to increase. Certain ethnic groups are disproportionately represented in single-parent families. Figures 2.4 and 2.6 illustrate these trends. These increases are attributable to several factors. First, pregnancy rates are higher among lower socioeconomic groups. Second, teenage pregnancy rates in poor white, Hispanic, and African American populations are sometimes higher because of lower education levels, economic constraints, and fewer life opportunities.

People become single parents for a number of reasons. Half of all marriages end in divorce; some people choose single parenthood; and some, such as many teenagers, become single parents by default. In addition, liberalized adoption procedures, artificial insemination, surrogate childbearing, and increasing public support for single parents make this lifestyle an attractive option for some people. The reality is that more women are having children without marrying.

FIGURE 2.5 10 Ways Your Program Can Support Fathers Year-Round

Fathers play an important role in children's lives, and it is important for you to consider how you can involve them in your program. These ten ideas will help you do that.

1. Hold a father's fair with booths where fathers can bring their kids and brush up on diaper changing, hair braiding, teaching kids how to skate or ride a bike, and so on.

2. Throw a father–child picnic. Post fliers inviting the whole community.

3. Sponsor father-of-the-year awards. Honor fathers who have overcome obstacles in their lives and the lives of their families, or fathers who embody the principles of family support.

4. Have an event for noncustodial fathers and their kids. A day of games or an evening of pizza and movies can allow noncustodial dads with visitation rights—who might not be used to spending time with their children—to do so in a supportive environment.

5. Recruit fathers. Go door-to-door with fliers on your program's support and activities for fathers and families.

6. Offer a dads' support group. Many fathers—particularly teen fathers—feel isolated and unsure about their skills as parents and providers.

7. Support noncustodial fathers and their families. Provide counseling, referrals, and tip sheets to help fathers provide nurturing support for their children, covering issues such as paternity establishment, child support, and visitation rights.

8. Make men visible. Recruit men as staff members or volunteers.

9. Involve fathers in program decisions. Make sure fathers are represented on your parent advisory group.

10. Create a mentor program. Train participants in your program to provide one-on-one support to new fathers and fathers seeking to strengthen relationships with their children.

Source: Family Resource Coalition of America. *10 Ways Your Program Can Support Fathers Year-Round.* Available at http://www.famlit.org/momentum/mtmaug.html#fathers

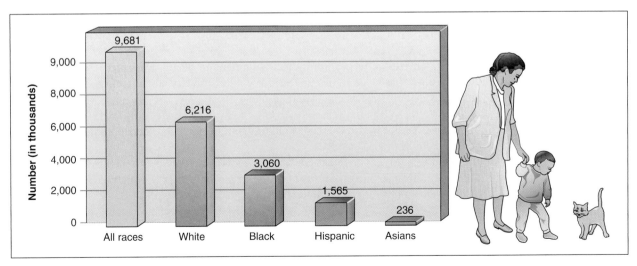

FIGURE 2.6 Single-Parent Families Headed by Mothers Among Certain Races

Source: U.S. Census Bureau, *Current Population Survey,* 2001.

Children Growing Up Without Fathers

Living in homes without fathers is a reality that affects the lives of growing numbers of children in the United States. In 25 percent of American households, mothers are raising 40 million children alone. These are children that may never see or have contact with their biological fathers.

important for children? What are some critical behaviors that fathers role model for their children? In what ways do fathers make a critical difference in the lives of children? Why is it important for mothers and fathers to tell their children "I love you"?

REFLECTIVE DISCUSSION QUESTIONS

Why are we as a society so concerned about the absence of fathers in children's formative years? From your own background and experiences, what are some consequences for children being reared in homes without fathers? What does research show are some outcomes for children who are reared in homes without fathers? Why is having two parents in the home

REFLECTIVE DECISION MAKING

What can you as an early childhood professional do to make a difference in the lives of the children and their mothers living in homes without fathers? Make a list of community-based services that would be of help to families without fathers? How could you as an early childhood professional link children and their mothers to community-based services?

No matter how people become single parents, the extent of single parenthood has tremendous implications for early childhood professionals. In response to growing single parenthood, early childhood programs are developing curricula to help children and their single parents. In addition to needing assistance with child care, single parents frequently seek help in child rearing, especially in regard to parenting practices. Early childhood professionals are often asked to conduct seminars to help parents gain these skills. Additionally, the increasing number of children living in single-parent families challenges early childhood professionals to find ways to help children grow up within this context. How well early childhood professionals meet the needs of single parents can make a difference in how successful single parents are in providing for the needs of children and other family members.

Teenage Parents. Teenage pregnancies continue to be a societal problem, although the teen birthrate has fallen in recent years. The following facts about teenage pregnancy dramatically demonstrate its extent and effects:[1]

- In 2001, for women aged fifteen through nineteen, there were 45.9 births per 1,000, down from 62.1 in 1991.
- As a group, Latino teenagers have the highest birthrate, with 92.4 births per 1,000.
- Among states, Texas has the highest birthrate for teenagers, with 68.5 births per 1,000. New Hampshire has the lowest birthrate for teenagers with 21.0 births per 1,000.

Concerned legislators, public policy developers, and national leaders view teenage pregnancy as loss of human potential. They worry about the demand for public health and welfare services and an increased number of school dropouts. From an early childhood point of view, teenage pregnancies create greater demand for infant and toddler child care and programs to help teenagers learn how to be good parents. The staff of an early childhood program must often provide nurturance for both children and parents, because the parents themselves may not be emotionally mature. Emotional maturity is necessary for parents to engage in a giving relationship with children. Early childhood professionals must nurture and help teenage parents who lack parenting skills.

CHILDREN'S SOCIAL AND ECONOMIC STATUS

A major goal of all early childhood programs is to provide for the safety and well-being of children. A complementary goal is to help parents and other family members provide for the education and well-being of themselves and their children. It is almost a given in early childhood education that poor health and unhealthy living conditions are major contributors to poor school achievement and life outcomes. A number of social issues facing children today put their chances for learning and success at risk.

POVERTY

Society and early childhood professionals know that **poverty** has serious negative consequences for children and families. Approximately 40 percent of the poor population is made up of children, even though only one-quarter of the population as a whole is children. More than 18 percent of children under six—over four million children—live in poverty.

For children living in single-parent homes with female heads of household, poverty is a greater risk. Almost one-half of these children (48.9 percent) live in poverty. Approximately 12 percent of African-American children under the age of six live in poverty; this figure climbs to 55 percent in single-mother households. Poverty rates for Hispanic-American children under the age of six are 20.5 percent overall and about 56 percent for those in single-mother homes.[2]

Living in poverty means you and your family don't have the income that allows you to purchase adequate health care, housing, food, clothing, and education services (see Figure 2.7). In 2003, poverty for a nonfarm family of four meant an income of less than $18,400. The federal government annually revises its poverty guidelines, which are the basis for distribution of federal aid to schools and student eligibility for academic services such as Head

Poverty The condition where an individual or family does not make sufficient income to support a minimum standard of living.

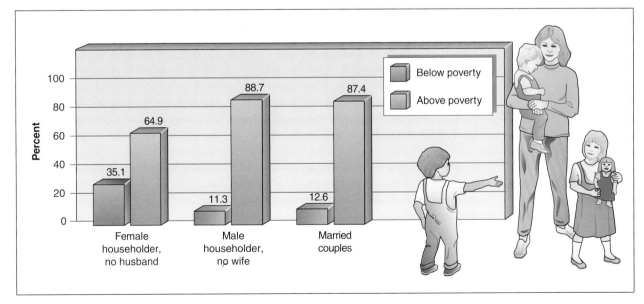

FIGURE 2.7   Families with Children Living in Poverty, 2001

Source: U.S. Department of Labor, *Employment Characteristics of Families Summary*, 2001.

**TABLE 2.1   Ten Areas
with Highest Percentage of
People in Poverty, 2001**

State	Population in Poverty
1. New Mexico	17.7%
2. Arkansas	17.1
3. Mississippi	17.1
4. Louisiana	16.7
4. Washington, D.C.	16.7
6. West Virginia	15.6
7. Texas	15.2
8. Oklahoma	15.0
9. Alabama	14.6
10. New York	14.0

Source: U.S. Census Bureau, *Current Population Survey,* 2002.

For more information about children's health and well-being, go to the Companion Website at **http://www.prenhall.com/morrison**, select chapter 2, then choose the Linking to Learning module to connect to the American Public Health Association site.

Start, Title I (a program that provides additional help in math and reading), and free and reduced-price school breakfasts and lunches.

Children and youth have no control over the social, economic, and family conditions that contribute to the conditions of poverty. Living in a rural community and in a rural southern state increases the likelihood that families will live in poverty. Cities with the highest school-age poverty rate are in the South and East. As Table 2.1 illustrates, eight of the ten states with the highest school-age poverty rates are in the South. In Mississippi, one-third of all children are poor, nearly twice the national average.[3]

Also, living in the inner city means that the chances of being poor are higher. Increases in rural and urban poverty lead to decreases in wealth and support for education. This means that, as a whole, children living in poverty will attend schools that have fewer resources and poorer facilities.

The effects of poverty are detrimental to students' achievement and life prospects. For example, children and youth from low-income families are often older than others in their grade level, move more slowly through the educational system, are more likely to drop out, and are less likely to find work.[4] Poor children are more likely to be retained in school, and students who have repeated one or more grades are more likely to become school dropouts.[5] Poverty affects students' health prospects as well. For example, more than one-half of all children who lack insured health care come from poor families.[6]

Children in poverty are more likely to have emotional and behavioral problems and are less likely than others to be "highly engaged" in school.[7] Also, parents of low-income families are less likely to help their children complete homework assignments.

HOUSING

A major study of the effects of poor and substandard housing on children reveals the following.[8]

- More than 4.5 million children live in families that spend at least half of their income in rent.
- Almost 1.5 million apartments affordable to poor families have been lost over the last two years.
- 187 children die each year in house fires caused by faulty electrical equipment, particularly heaters.
- 21,000 children have stunted growth caused by health problems related to a lack of stable housing.
- 10,000 children between the ages of four and nine are hospitalized for asthma attacks each year because of cockroach infestation at home.

- 2.5 million collective IQ points are lost among children ages one to five from lead poisoning. This impaired intellectual functioning will affect children for the rest of their lives. Virtually all these children are poisoned at home.

WELLNESS AND HEALTHY LIVING

As you know, when you feel good, life goes much better. The same is true for children and their families. One major goal of all early childhood programs is to provide for the safety and well-being of children. A second goal is to help parents and other family members provide for the well-being of themselves and their children. Poor health and unhealthy living conditions are major contributors to poor school achievement and life outcomes. A number of health issues facing children today put their chances for learning and success at risk. Lack of sufficient exercise and poor nutrition are often cited as two reasons for young children's poor health status.

Illnesses. When you think of children's illnesses, you probably think of measles, chicken pox, and strep throat. Actually, asthma, lead poisoning, and obesity are the three leading childhood diseases.

Asthma. Asthma, a chronic inflammatory disorder of the airways characterized by breathlessness, wheezing, coughing, and chest tightness, is the most common chronic childhood illness in the United States. According to the Centers for Disease Control and Prevention (CDC), an estimated 5 million children suffered from asthma in 2000. Asthma is caused in part by poor air quality, dust, mold, animal fur and dander, allergens from cockroaches and rodents' feces, and strong fumes. Many of these causes are found in poor and low-quality housing. You will want to reduce asthma-causing conditions in your early childhood programs and work with parents to reduce the causes of asthma in their homes. To reduce the causes of asthma in your school environment, you can prohibit smoking around children, keep the environment clean and free of mold, reduce or eliminate carpeting, have children sleep on mats or cots, and work with parents to ensure that their children are getting appropriate asthma medication.

Lead Poisoning. Lead poisoning is also a serious childhood disease. The CDC estimates that approximately 1 million children under the age of six have elevated blood lead levels. These children are at risk for lower IQs, short attention spans, reading and learning disabilities, hyperactivity, and behavioral problems. The major source of lead poisoning is from old lead-based paint that still exists in many homes and apartments. Other sources of lead are from car batteries and dust and dirt from lead-polluted soil. Approximately 80 percent of homes built before 1978 have lead-based paint in them. Since then, lead has not been used in paint. Lead enters the body through inhalation and ingestion. Young children are especially vulnerable because they put many things in their mouths, chew on windowsills, and crawl on floors. The Grace Hill Neighborhood Health Centers in St. Louis has dealt with this issue by treating children for lead poisoning and sending health coaches into homes of children with high levels of lead. These health workers cover peeling windowsills and provide vacuum cleaners with high-efficiency filters.

Obesity. Today's generation of young children is often referred to as the *Supersize Generation.* Many contend that one of the reasons children are overweight is because of the tendency to order "supersize" burgers, fries, and soft drinks at fast-food restaurants. The percentage of children who are overweight has more than doubled in the last three decades.

Poverty and substandard housing can adversely affect the health and well-being of children. Since children from such environments often have difficulties in school, the role of the early childhood educator in their lives is an especially important one.

What can you, as an early childhood professional, do to help children and parents win the obesity war?

- *Provide parents with information about nutrition.* For example, send home copies of the Food Guide Pyramid for Young Children (Figure 2.8) and other nutritional information.
- *Counsel parents to pull the plug on the television.* TV watching is associated with obesity because children are more likely to snack on fattening foods while they watch. Also,

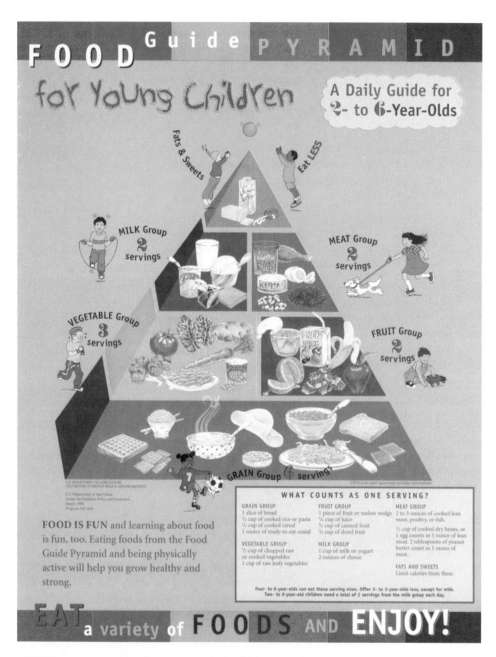

FIGURE 2.8 The Food Guide Pyramid for Young Children

What children eat or don't eat plays a major role in how they learn, grow, and develop, and whether they respond to classroom activities with lethargy or energy. How can you use this food pyramid to help ensure that children eat well?

Source: U.S. Department of Agriculture, http://www.usda.gov/cnpp/KidsPyra/LtlPyrBW.pdf

children who watch a lot of television tend to be less physically active, and inactivity promotes weight gain.

- *When cooking with children, talk about foods and their nutritional value.* Cooking activities are also a good way to eat and talk about new foods.
- *Integrate literacy and nutritional activities.* For example, reading and discussing labels is a good way to encourage children to be aware of and think about nutritional information.
- *Encourage exercise.* Provide opportunities for physical exercise and physical activities in your program.
- *Encourage breakfast.* If your school or program does not provide breakfast for children, be an advocate for starting it. Providing school breakfasts can be both a nutritional and an educational program.

You can do a lot to promote children's health. Do not blame the parents. Work with them to enable them and their children to lead healthy lives. Continuing the theme of wellness and health living, the following Video Viewpoint, "They Are What They Eat," looks at how marketing and advertising influences the food preferences and eating habits of young children. Think about some ways that you can help children eat better and healthier.

VIDEO VIEWPOINT

They Are What They Eat

Children are not born with a taste for high-fat foods. It is a learned behavior. But, often, children are not given better choices. When children are let loose in a supermarket to make their own choices, parents are often appalled at what their children do not know about good nutrition—and at food manufacturers who do not necessarily offer the healthiest choices in their kid-attractive packages.

REFLECTIVE DISCUSSION QUESTIONS

Why do you think that when given the opportunity, children select high-calorie, high-fat foods rather than healthy foods? Why do you think manufacturers produce and sell foods with higher-fat content for children than adults? How are children's cartoons and cartoon characters used to market children's foods? How does television advertising steer children toward bad food choices? What are some reasons that children are eating more unhealthy foods? What is your reaction to this comment: "There are no good or bad

foods; eaten in moderation, any food is part of a well-balanced diet"?

REFLECTIVE DECISION MAKING

Visit a local supermarket and read the fat, salt, and sugar content for foods marketed specifically for children. Make a list of the top fat, salt, and sugar foods for children. How can you work with parents to help them provide good nutritional meals for their children and other family members? What can you do in preschool and other early childhood settings to help children learn good nutritional practices? Conduct a survey of the foods that young children eat during the day. How many total grams of fat do you estimate they eat during a typical day? How does this compare with the 50 or 60 grams of fat recommended by nutritionists? Give specific examples of how manufacturers use food to promote and sell a particular product. What could you do as an early childhood educator to get children to eat more fruits and vegetables rather than fatty snacks?

RESEARCH AND EARLY CHILDHOOD EDUCATION

Although researchers have been contributing to brain research for approximately twenty-five years, public interest in the application of this research to early childhood education has recently intensified. Ongoing media coverage of brain research and its implications for early childhood education is one factor contributing to this interest.

What specifically does brain research tell us about early childhood experiences? In may cases it affirms what early childhood educators have always intuitively known. Good parental care, warm and loving attachments, and positive age-appropriate stimulation from birth onward make a tremendous difference in children's cognitive development for a lifetime.

Brain research also tells us a great deal regarding stimulation and the development of specific areas of the brain. For example, brain research suggests that listening to music and learning to play musical instruments at very early ages stimulate the brain areas associated with mathematics and spatial reasoning. Brain research also suggests that gross motor activities and physical education should be included in a child's daily schedule throughout the elementary years. Regrettably, school systems often cut programs such as physical education and music in times of budget crisis, even though research shows that these programs are essential to a child's complete cognitive development.

Early childhood curricula are being developed based on the findings of research, and these programs strive to apply research findings in a practical way. For example, Zero to Three focuses on infants, toddlers, and families and is dedicated to promoting the healthy development of America's babies and young children. Zero to Three believes that a child's first three years are crucial for developing intellectual, emotional, and social skills. If these skills are not developed, the child's lifelong potential may be hampered. The organization supports professionals, parents, and policymakers and strives to increase public awareness, inspire leaders, and foster professional excellence through training, always emphasizing the first three years of a child's life. Visit the Zero to Three Web site at www.zerotothree.org.

Research is influencing our ideas about how children learn, how to teach them, and what they should learn. As a result, there is a major shift in basic educational premises concerning what children can achieve. Early childhood professionals have arrived at the following conclusions about young children:

1. *The period of most rapid intellectual growth occurs before age eight.* The extent to which children will become intelligent, based on those things by which we measure intelligence and school achievement, is determined long before many children enter school. The notion of promoting cognitive development implies that children benefit from enriched home environments that are conducive to learning and early school-like experiences, especially for children from environments that place them at risk of not developing their full potential.

2. *Children are not born with fixed intelligences.* This outdated concept fails to do justice to children's tremendous capacity for learning and change. In addition, evidence supports developmental intelligence. The extent to which individual intelligence develops depends on many variables, such as experiences, child-rearing practices, economic factors, nutrition, and the quality of prenatal and postnatal environments. Inherited genetic characteristics set a broad framework within which intelligence will develop. Heredity sets the limits, while environment determines the extent to which individuals achieve these limits.

3. *Children reared in homes that are not intellectually stimulating may also lag intellectually behind their counterparts reared in more advantaged environments.* Implications concerning the home environment are obvious. Experience shows that children who lack an environment that promotes learning opportunities may be at risk throughout life. On the other hand, homes that offer intellectual stimulation tend to produce children who do well in school.

4. *Good parental care, warm and loving attachments, and positive, age-appropriate stimulation from birth onward make a difference in children's overall development for a lifetime.*[9] Even during the fetal stage, the kind of nourishment and care a child receives affects neural development (i.e., the development of brain nerve cells). The majority of recent research shows that much of a child's learning capacity is developed during the earliest years.

5. *Positive interactions with caring adults stimulate children's brains profoundly in terms of establishing new synaptic connections and strengthening existing ones.* For example, cuddling and signing to infants and toddlers stimulate brain connections and lay the foundation for learning throughout life. Those connections used over time become permanent, and those that are not used wither and become dormant. If a child receives little stimulation during the early months and years, synapses will not develop, and the brain will have fewer cellular connections. Increasingly, researchers are showing how early stimulation sets the stage for future cognitive processes. In addition, positive emotional interactions, formations of secure attachments, and effective regulation of temperament and emotionality lay the foundation for healthy emotional development. Temperament-related genetic predispositions, early experiences, and learned behaviors greatly influence learning, processes of development, and the way one interacts with his environment over the life span.

6. *Early experiences during critical/sensitive periods and windows of opportunity are so powerful that they can completely change the way a person develops.*[10] Research suggests that the right input at the right time is crucial for a child to fully develop his cognitive potential. Neurobiologists are still trying to understand exactly which kinds of experiences or sensory input wire the brain in particular ways. Research conducted in the area of visual perception suggests that the circuit for vision has a neuron growth spurt at two to four months of age, thus helping the child begin to notice the shape of objects, or the visual gestalt.[11] This neuron growth spurt peaks at eight months, when connections are established between these neurons, suggesting the importance of providing appropriate visual stimuli to establish connections in the brain's visual processing region.

PUBLIC POLICY AND EARLY CHILDHOOD EDUCATION

At no time in U.S. history has there been so much interest and involvement by early childhood professionals in the development of public policy. Public policy includes such things as laws, position statements of professional organizations, and court decisions. Public policies affect and influence the lives of children, parents, families, and professionals working in the field. Public policies determine at what ages children can enter school, what immunizations are required before children enter any program, how child care programs operate, and how to provide appropriate care and education for children with special needs.

For more information about public policy and early childhood education, go to the Companion Website at **http://www.prenhall. com/morrison**, select chapter 2, then choose the Linking to Learning module to connect to the Early Childhood Care and Development site.

STRESS AND VIOLENCE

Dramatic changes are occurring in contemporary society. Life is becoming more fast-paced, and more demands are placed on parents, families, and children. As a result, children today are surrounded by stressful situations in homes, child care, and schools. Much of the stress children experience comes from issues we have discussed—poverty, poor housing, poor nutrition, and unhealthy living. Violence and the threat of violence is another stress in children's lives and one that endangers their well being and life outcomes.

Social issues have public policy implications for young children, families, and early childhood professionals. On Tuesday, April 20, 1999, two Columbine High School students walked into their high school in Littleton, Colorado, and engaged in a terrorism spree that left twelve high school students and one adult dead and another twenty students suffering from various gunshot wounds. Then they committed suicide.

On Tuesday, October 8, 2002, a sniper shot and wounded a thirteen-year-old boy outside a suburban Washington, D.C., middle school. Critically wounded, the boy was the eighth victim of the two men (one not yet an adult) who methodically used sniper attacks to kill strangers. Increasing acts of violence such as these lead to proposals for how to provide violence-free homes and educational environments; how to teach children to get along nonviolently with others; and how to reduce violence on television, the movies, and in video games.

Reducing violence on television, for example, in turn leads to discussions and proposals for ways to limit children's television viewing. Such proposals include "pulling the plug" on television; using the V-chip, which enables parents to block out programs with violent content; boycotting companies whose advertisements support programs with violent content; and limiting violence shown during prime-time viewing hours for children. Early childhood professionals play important roles in these and other debates and decision-making processes. Advocacy is a critical role of the professional. You can play a major role in reducing violence by being an advocate for reducing the media violence that negatively influences children's lives.

Programs to prevent and curb bullying are another example of how educators are combating the effects of violence on children. Although in the past the bullying has been dismissed as "normal" or "kid's play," this is no longer the case, because bullying is related to school and other violence. Bullying includes teasing, slapping, hitting, pushing, unwanted touching, taking personal belongings, name calling, and making sexual comments and insults about looks, behavior, and culture. Now, schools are starting to fight back against bullies and bullying.

Readiness includes general health and physical growth, such as being well rested and fed and properly immunized. How does children's health status affect their readiness for learning?

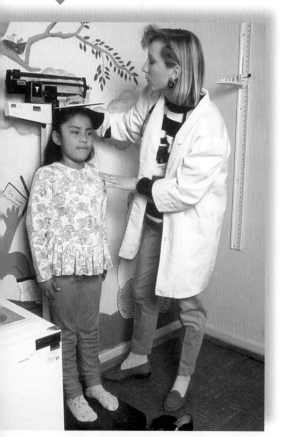

POLITICS AND EARLY CHILDHOOD EDUCATION

The more that the issue of early childhood is in the news, the more it generates public interest and attention; this is part of the political context of early childhood education. Whatever else can be said about education, one point holds true: education is political. Politicians and politics exert a powerful influence in determining what is taught, how it is taught, to whom it is taught, and by whom it is taught. Early childhood education is no exception.

FEDERAL AND STATE INVOLVEMENT IN EARLY CHILDHOOD PROGRAMS

Over the past decade there has been increased federal and state funding of early childhood programs. This trend will continue for a couple of reasons. First, politicians and the public recognize that the early years are the foundation for future learning. Second, spending money on children in the early years is more cost effective than trying to solve problems in the teenage years.

As a result, all the states are taking a lead in developing programs for young children, stimulated by these budgetary changes. As federal dollars shift to other programs, states are responding by initiating programs of their own, funded from both federal allocations and other sources, including lottery monies and increased taxes on commodities and consumer goods such as cigarettes.

The Florida Department of Education, for example, has an office dedicated to early intervention and school readiness. One of its programs is

Florida First Start, a home–school partnership designed to give children at risk of future school failure the best possible start in life and to support parents in their role as their children's first teachers. Emphasis is on enabling families to enhance their children's intellectual, physical, language, and social development by involving parents in their children's education during the critical first three years of life. Through early parent education and support services, the program lays the foundation for later learning and future school success, while fostering effective parent–school relationships. Further information is available on the Internet at http://elementarypgms.brevard.k12.f1.us/florida_1st_start.htm.

In addition, instead of giving monies directly to specific programs, many federal dollars are consolidated into what are known as **block grants**—sums of money given to states to provide services according to broad general guidelines. In essence, the states, not the federal government, control the way the money is spent and the nature of the programs funded. As targeted federal support for early education becomes subject to different methods of funding, it may well be that states will finance replacement, alternative, and substitute programs.

Block grants Sums of money given to states to provide services according to broad, general guidelines.

EXPANDED FEDERAL SUPPORT FOR EARLY CHILDHOOD EDUCATION

At the same time states are exerting control over education, so is the federal government. One of the dramatic changes occurring in society is the expanded role of the federal government in the reform of public education. President George W. Bush made education reform a major part of his election campaign. We are currently witnessing more federal dollars allocated for specific early education initiatives than ever before. For example, the Bush administration through increased federal funding wants to reform Head Start by making it more academic to emphasize the development of early literacy skills. The critics of federal support for such programs argue that the federal government should not allocate dollars for specific, targeted programs. However, the number and size of federal allocations for reform initiatives will continue.

How to reform education so that all children will be able to read on grade level and how to close the achievement gap between rich and poor, the haves and have nots, are now two of the top priorities on the national education agenda. The No Child Left Behind Act (Public Law 107–110) and other federal initiatives have focused the national attention on developing educational and social programs to serve young children and families. Two areas in particular, reading and school readiness, are now major federal priorities in helping assure that all children succeed in school and life. The Early Reading First programs established in the No Child Left Behind Act provide grants to school districts and preschool programs for the development of model programs to support school readiness of preschool programs and to promote children's understanding of letters, letter sounds, and the blending of sounds and words. We discuss the application of the No Child Left Behind Act to classroom practices in chapters 8 ("Federal Programs"), 10 ("The Preschool Years"), 11 ("Kindergarten"), and 12 ("The Early Elementary Grades").

PUBLIC SCHOOLS AND EARLY EDUCATION

Traditionally, the majority of preschool programs were operated by private agencies or agencies supported wholly or in part by federal funds to help the poor, the unemployed, working parents, and disadvantaged children. But times have changed. Parents from all socioeconomic levels exert great pressure on public school officials and state legislatures to sponsor and fund additional preschool and early childhood programs. Increasingly, preschools are providing a full range of services for children and families with an emphasis on providing for the whole child.

Another trend involves preschool programs conducted in the public schools. Currently, California, Florida, New York, North Carolina, and Texas support preschools; nationwide, about 500,000 preschool children are enrolled in public school programs. As preschool programs admit more three- and four-year-olds nationwide, opportunities for teachers of young children will grow.

The spread of preschools reflects changing family patterns, especially the rise in single-parent families and families with two adult wage earners. Demand for preschools also relates to their use in early childhood intervention programs and to the popular belief that three- and four-year-old children are ready, willing, and able to learn.

Parents lobby for public support of early childhood education for a number of reasons. First, because working parents cannot find quality child care for their children, they believe the public schools hold the solution to child care needs. Second, the persistent belief that children are a nation's greatest wealth makes it seem sensible to provide services to avoid future school and learning problems. Third, many people believe that early public schooling, especially for children from low-income families, is necessary if the United States is to promote equal opportunity for all. They argue that low-income children begin school already far behind their more fortunate middle-class counterparts and that the best way to keep them from falling hopelessly behind is for them to begin school earlier. Fourth, some parents cannot afford quality child care. They believe preschools, furnished at the public's expense, are a reasonable, cost-efficient way to meet child care needs. A fifth reason relates to the growing federal role in early education programs. The federal government provides money for preschool programs based in part on research that supports the importance of early literacy learning as a basis for successful reading. Of course early literacy is not the only thing that young children need to know and do, but it is certainly a major federal emphasis.

The alignment of the public schools with early childhood programs is becoming increasingly popular. Some think it makes sense to put the responsibility for educating and caring for the nation's children under the sponsorship of one agency—the public schools. For their part, public school teachers and the unions that represent them are anxious to bring early childhood programs within the structure of the public school system.

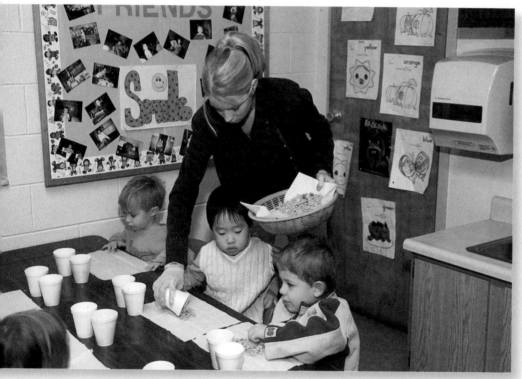

Early public schooling is a reality for growing numbers of the nation's children. What societal changes are contributing to this trend toward early public schooling?

It seems inevitable that the presence of the public schools in early childhood education will continue to expand. Given that so many public schools offer programs for three- and four-year-olds, can programs for infants and toddlers be far behind?

HOT TOPICS IN EARLY CHILDHOOD EDUCATION

The issues facing early childhood education today are many, varied, and have considerable consequences, both positive and negative, for young children. The following are hot topics that we will discuss throughout this book in order to help you be on the cutting edge of your professional practice.

- *Early literacy and reading.* Professionals regard providing children with the foundation for literacy as one of the key factors supporting their school success.
- *The politicalization of early childhood education.* There has been a dramatic increase in state and federal involvement in the education of young children. For example, the federal government is using Head Start as a means and model for reforming all of early childhood education. This federalization will likely continue and expand.
- *Emphasis on the use of early childhood programs to promote and support children's readiness for school and learning.* Increasingly, there is a recognition that if children are ready to learn when they enter school, they are more likely to succeed.
- *The increasing use of tests and testing to measure achievement and school performance in the early years.* Increasing numbers of parents, professionals, and early childhood critics are advocating for less of an emphasis on *high-stakes testing* in the early years.
- *Safety and security.* Increasingly in these violent times, parents, the public, and professionals are seeking ways to keep children safe and secure in the learning process.

This is a great time for early childhood education and a wonderful time to be a teacher of young children. Early childhood education has changed more in the last five years than in the previous fifty. These changes and the issues that accompany them provide many opportunities for you to become more professional, and they enable all children to learn the knowledge and skills necessary for success in school and life.

To take an online self-test on this chapter's contents, go to the Companion Website at **http://www. prenhall.com/morrison**, select chapter 2, then choose the Self-Test module.

For additional Internet resources or to complete an online activity for this chapter, go to the Companion Website at **http://www. prenhall.com/morrison**, select chapter 2, then choose the Linking to Learning or Making Connections module.

ACTIVITIES FOR FURTHER ENRICHMENT

APPLICATIONS

1. The daily newspapers are an excellent way to keep up-to-date with what is happening in the field of early childhood education. Many of these articles relate directly to issues of curriculum, practice, and public policy. For example, "Testing Expands to Kids in Head Start," an article in the February 6, 2003 *Los Angeles Times,* discusses the federal government's plan to test all Head Start children. Not everyone agrees this is a good idea and the proposal is generating a lot of discussion. In what ways do you agree or disagree with this proposal? Find other examples of education issues covered in the media.
2. Interview single parents and determine what effects and influences they think single parenting has on children. In what ways is single parenting stressful to parents and children? How can early childhood programs support and help single parents? Search for and review research relating to this topic. How does the research agree or disagree with what parents report?
3. Some children in local preschools and child care centers have experienced their parents' divorce, abuse, and other types of stress. What types of problems do early childhood professionals face as they help children whose lives have been affected by these situations?

FIELD EXPERIENCES

1. Visit corporations and businesses in your area and determine what they are doing to support education and family programs.
2. List at least five social, political, and economic conditions of modern society and explain how these conditions influence how people view, treat, and care for the very young.
3. List at least five significant contributions you believe good early childhood education programs can make in the lives of young children.

RESEARCH

1. Contact agencies that provide services to single parents, teenage parents, and families in need. How do these programs influence early childhood education programs in your local community?

2. Investigate the types of preschool programs available in your community. Who may attend them? How are they financed? What percentage of the children who attend have mothers working outside the home?

3. Over a period of several weeks or a month, collect articles from newspapers and magazines relating to infants, toddlers, and preschoolers and categorize them by topic (child abuse, nutrition, etc.). What topics were given the most coverage? Why? What topics or trends are emerging in early education, according to this media coverage? Do you agree with everything you read? Can you find instances in which information or advice may be inaccurate, inappropriate, or contradictory?

READINGS FOR FURTHER ENRICHMENT

Arce, E. *Early Childhood Education: Perspective Series.* Boston: Houghton Mifflin, 1999.

This collection of articles gives the reader an authentic view of children's cultures, languages, and abilities. It examines issues regarding individual differences, policies that enhance the child, and societal changes that impact early childhood education.

Levine, J. *New Expectations: Community Strategies for Responsible Fatherhood.* New York: Fatherhood Project, 1999.

This latest release from the Fatherhood Project promotes a new way of thinking and acting to promote responsible fatherhood, including a jargon-free review of research, state-of-the-art review of community-based strategies, tips from leading practitioners, and a guide to more than three hundred programs nationwide and to one hundred of the most useful publications.

Levine, J., and Pittinsky, T. *Working Fathers: New Strategies for Balancing Work and Family.* New York: Harvest Books, 1998.

In this text, parenting expert James A. Levine, director of the Fatherhood Project at the Families and Work Institute, and Todd L. Pittinsky of the Harvard Business School present a groundbreaking examination of the work–family dilemma and offer a proven and effective game plan to help fathers as well as mothers, employees as well as managers, succeed in managing the competing demands of home and work.

Moss, P., and Petrie, P. L. *From Children's Services to Children's Spaces: Public Policy, Children and Childhood.* New York: RoutledgeFalmer, 2002.

This book explores these apparent contradictions and complexities through a critique of the concept of "children's services," from the researcher in this field of study.

Wright, K., and Stegelin, D. A. *Building School and Community Partnerships Through Parent Involvement,* 2nd edition. Upper Saddle River, NJ: Merrill/Prentice Hall, 2003.

This profiles today's American families and examines the special relationships among them, their children's schools, and their communities. Through an ecological systems approach, the authors explore the family as a child's first teacher.

LINKING TO LEARNING

American Public Health Association
http://www.apha.org

Publishes material on topics including chemical toxicology, communicable diseases, natural disasters, food safety, breast-feeding, mental health, and nutrition.

Annie E. Casey Foundation
http://www.aecf.org

A friendly, newly updated resource, this Web site presents the latest information on issues affecting America's disadvantaged children.

Children Now
http://www.childrennow.org

Children Now works to translate the nation's commitment to children and families into action to improve conditions for all children. Recognized nationally for its policy expertise and up-to-date information on the status of children.

Early Childhood Care and Development
http://www.ecdgroup.com

An international, interagency group dedicated to improving the condition of young children at risk by keeping them on the agenda of policymakers, funders, and program developers.

National Center for Family Literacy
http://www.famlit.org

Advances and supports family literacy services through programming, training, research, advocacy, and dissemination of information about family literacy.

Stand for Children Action Center
http://www.stand.org

Establishes a process that enables and encourages people to become volunteers, defenders, and advocates for children. The center offers a toll-free 800 number, Web site, and monthly updates that feature success stories.

ENDNOTES

[1]U.S. Department of Health and Human Services, *Births to Teenagers in the United States, 1940–2000*. [On-line]. Available: http://www.cdc.gov/nchs/releases/02news/precare.htm

[2]U.S. Census Bureau, *Current Population Survey*, 2002.

[3]Ibid.

[4]National Center for Education Statistics, *The Condition of Education 2002* (Washington, DC: U.S. Department of Education, 2002).

[5]Ibid.

[6]U.S. General Accounting Office, *Health Insurance: Characteristics and Trends in the Uninsured Population*. [Online]. Available at http://www.gao.gov/new.items/d01507t.pdf.

[7]Ehrle, J. and Moore, K. *Snapshots of America's Families. Children's Environment and Behavior: Behavioral and Emotional Problems in Children* (Washington, DC: Urban Institute, 1999). [On-line]. Available at: http://newfederalism.urban.org/nsaf/children_c6.html.

[8]Boston Medical Center and Children's Hospital, *Not Safe at Home: How America's Housing Crisis Threatens Our Children* (Boston: Author, February 1998). [On-line]. Available at: http://www.bmc.org/program/doc4kids/index.html.

[9]National Institute of Child Health and Development, *The NICHD Study of Early Child Care* (Washington, DC: Author, 1999). [On-line]. Available at: http://www.nih.gov/nichd/publications/news/early-child/Early_Child_Care.htm.

[10]Chugani, H. "Functional Brain Reorganization in Children," *Brain and Development* 18 (1996): 347–356.

[11] Lamb, M. and Campos, J. *Development in Infancy* (New York: Random House, 1982).

Chapter 3

The only way to be sure of whether or not every child is learning is to test regularly and to show everybody, especially the parents, the results of the tests.

PRESIDENT GEORGE W. BUSH

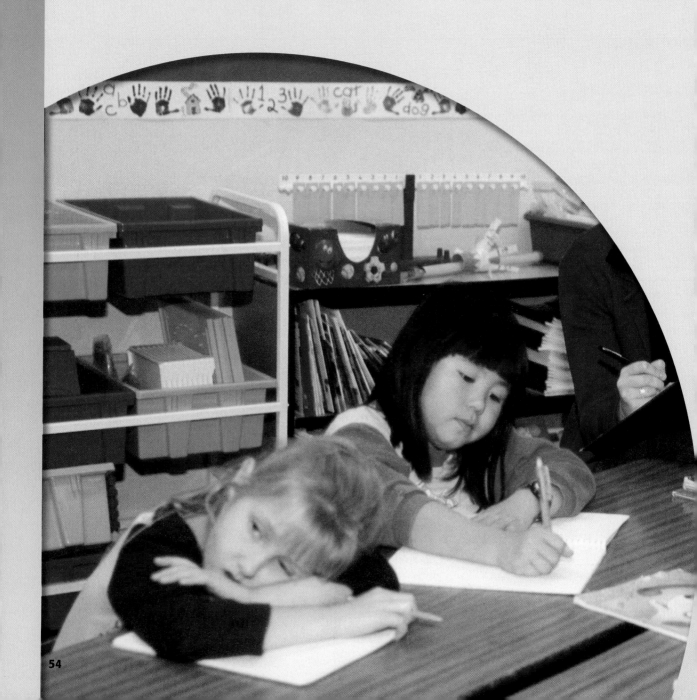

Observing and Assessing Young Children

Effective Teaching Through Appropriate Evaluation

Focus Questions

- What is assessment, and why is it important?

- Why is it important for you to know how to assess?

- What are the purposes and uses of assessment and observation?

- What are some major ways to assess children's development, learning, and behavior?

- What issues are involved in assessment?

Kindergarten teacher Jesse Jones wants to make sure that Amanda knows the initial beginning sounds that he has taught the class the last two weeks. First grade teacher Mindy McArthur wants to see how many words on the class word wall César is familiar with. Third grade teacher José Gonzalez wants to know if his class can apply what they're learning to real-life situations. Decisions, decisions, decisions.

The minutes, hours, and days are filled with assessment decisions. Questions abound: "What is Jeremy ready for now?" "What can I tell Maria's parents about her language development?" "The activity I used in the large group time yesterday didn't seem to work well. What could I have done differently?" Appropriate assessment can help you find the answers to these and many other questions relating to how to teach and what is best for children in all areas of development.

WHAT IS ASSESSMENT?

Much of children's lives are subject to and influenced by your assessment and the assessment of others. As an early childhood professional, assessment will influence your professional life and will be a vital tool of your professional practice. Assessment well done is one of your most important responsibilities, and it can benefit your children's learning.

Assessment is the process of collecting information about children's development, learning, health, behavior, academic progress, need for special services, and attainment. Figure 3.1 outlines the purposes of assessment.

Assessment occurs primarily through the following processes: observation, administration of commercial and teacher-made tests, and examination of students' products. You will probably use all three of these assessment procedures in your teaching. Keep in mind that all assessment procedures should help you inform your instruction so you can provide the best for all children. Your goal is to help children be successful.

To review the chapter focus questions online, go to the Companion Website at **http://www. prenhall.com/morrison** and select chapter 3.

Assessment The process of collecting information about children's development, learning, health, behavior, academic process, need for special services, and attainment.

 To check your understanding of this chapter with the online Study Guide, go to the Companion Website at **http://www. prenhall.com/morrison**, select chapter 3, then choose the Study Guide module.

FIGURE 3.1 Purposes of Assessment

Purposes of Assessment As It Relates To:

Children

- Identify what children know
- Identify children's special needs
- Determine appropriate placement
- Select appropriate curricula to meet children's individual needs
- Refer children and, as appropriate, their families for additional services to programs and agencies

Families

- Help determine effectiveness of child's program

Early Childhood Professionals

- Make policy decisions regarding what is and what is not appropriate for children
- Determine how well and to what extent programs and services children receive are beneficial and appropriate

Early Childhood Programs

- Make lesson and activity plans
- Select materials
- Make decisions about how to implement learning activities
- Report to parents and families about children's developmental status and achievement
- Improve teaching–learning process

The Public

- Inform the public regarding children's achievement
- Provide information relating to students' schoolwide achievements
- Provide a basis for public policy (e.g., legislation, recommendations, and statements)

You will be involved in many kinds of assessment of young children. You will serve on committees in which you will be asked to make decisions about assessment. In addition, parents and the public will ask your advice and opinion about assessment and what is best for young children. These general principles will help you in these professional involvements.

WHAT IS APPROPRIATE ASSESSMENT?

Today, early childhood professionals do their best to use assessment in appropriate ways—that is, to support children's learning. On the other hand, assessment and the results of assessment are often used inappropriately. One such example is the use of **high-stakes assessment testing** to make life-changing decisions about children. Two examples are noteworthy. In some cases, children are either admitted or not admitted to kindergarten or first grade based on the outcome of a test. In other cases, decisions about whether to promote children are based on the results of a national standardized test.

With so much emphasis on tests, it is understandable that the issue of testing and assessment raises many concerns on the part of parents and professionals. Critics maintain that the standardized testing movement reduces teaching and learning to the lowest common denominator—teaching children what they need to know to get the right answers. Many early childhood professionals believe that standardized tests do not measure children's thinking, problem-solving ability, creativity, or responsibility for their own learning. Furthermore, critics believe that group-administered, objectively scored, skills-focused

 For more information about the uses and abuses of assessment, go to the Companion Website at **http://www.prenhall.com/morrison**, select chapter 3, then choose the Linking to Learning module to connect to the Pathways to School Improvements site.

High-stakes assessment testing An assessment test used to either admit children into programs or promote children from one grade to the next.

FIGURE 3.2 General Principles of Formal Assessment of Young Children

The following general principles should guide both policies and practices for the formal assessment of young children:

- **Assessment should bring about benefits for children.**
  Gathering accurate information from young children is difficult and potentially stressful. Assessments must have a clear benefit—either in direct services to the child or in improved quality of educational programs.

- **Assessments should be tailored to a specific purpose and should be reliable, valid, and fair for that purpose.**
  Assessments designed for one purpose are not necessarily valid if used for other purposes. In the past, many of the abuses of testing with young children have occurred because of misuse. The recommendations in the sections that follow are tailored to specific assessment purposes.

- **Assessment policies should be designed recognizing that reliability and validity of assessments increase with children's age.**
  The younger the child, the more difficult it is to obtain reliable and valid assessment data. It is particularly difficult to assess children's cognitive abilities accurately before age six. Because of problems with reliability and validity, some types of assessment should be postponed until children are older, while other types of assessment can be pursued, but only with necessary safeguards.

- **Assessment should be age-appropriate in both content and the method of data collection.**
  Assessments of young children should address the full range of early learning and development, including physical well-being and motor development; social and emotional development; approaches toward learning; language development; and cognition and general knowledge. Methods of assessment should recognize that children need familiar contexts to be able to demonstrate their abilities. Abstract paper-and-pencil tasks may make it especially difficult for young children to show what they know.

- **Assessment should be linguistically appropriate, recognizing that to some extent all assessments are measures of language.**
  Regardless of whether an assessment is intended to measure early reading skills, knowledge of color names, or learning potential, assessment results are easily confounded by language proficiency, especially for children who come from home backgrounds with limited exposure to English, for whom the assessment would essentially be an assessment of their English proficiency. Each child's first- and second-language development should be taken into account when determining appropriate assessment methods and in interpreting the meaning of assessment results.

- **Parents should be a valued source of assessment information, as well as an audience for assessment.**
  Because of the fallibility of direct measures of young children, assessments should include multiple sources of evidence, especially reports from parents and teachers. Assessment results should be shared with parents as part of an ongoing process that involves parents in their child's education.

Source: The National Education Goals Panel, "Principles and Recommendations for Early Childhood Assessments," (December 14, 1998), pp. 5–6.

---

tests—which dominate much of U.S. education—do not support (indeed, may undermine) many of the curricular reforms taking place today. Figure 3.2 identifies general principles of formal assessment of young children.

WHAT IS AUTHENTIC ASSESSMENT?

Authentic assessment, also referred to as *performance-based assessment,* is conducted through activities that require children to demonstrate what they know and are able to do. Meaningless facts and isolated information are considered unauthentic. Authentic assessment has the following traits:

- *It assesses children on the basis of their actual work.* Work samples—often in a portfolio—exhibitions, performances, learning logs, journals, projects, presentations, experiments, and teacher observations are essential components of authentic assessment.

Authentic assessment
Assessment conducted through activities that require children to demonstrate what they know and are able to do; also referred to as *performance-based assessment.*

For more information about authentic assessment, go to the Companion Website at **http://www. prenhall.com/morrison**, select chapter 3, then choose the Linking to Learning module to connect to the Assessment and Standards on the Website.

- *It provides for ongoing assessment over the entire school year.* Children's performance and achievement are continuously assessed, not just at the end of a grading period or at the end of the year through a standardized achievement test.
- *It is curriculum embedded.* Children are assessed on what they are actually doing in and through the curriculum.
- *It is a cooperative and collaborative process involving children, teachers, and in many cases parents.* This is an attempt to move away from teacher-focused assessment and to make assessment more child centered.
- *It is intended to help professionals and parents learn more about children.* All areas—social-emotional, language, cognitive, and physical—are assessed. The whole child is evaluated rather than a narrow set of skills. In this sense, it is child centered and humane.
- *It assesses what individual children are able to do.* Authentic assessment evaluates what they as individuals are learning, as opposed to comparing one child with another or children with children, as is so often the case.
- *It makes assessment part of the learning process.* For example, one third grader, as part of a project on the community, visited the recycling center. She made a presentation to the class in which she used the overhead projector to illustrate her major points, displayed a poster board with pictures she had taken of the center, and presented several graphs to show which products were recycled most. In this way, she was able to demonstrate a broader range of what she had learned.

Portfolio   A compilation of children's work samples, products, and teacher observations collected over time.

Today many teachers use **portfolios**—a compilation of children's work samples, products, and teacher observations collected over time—as a basis for authentic assessment. Decisions about what to put in portfolios vary, but examples include written work, artwork, audiotapes, pictures, models, and other materials that attest to what children are able to do. Some teachers let children put their best work in their portfolios; others decide with children what will be included; still others decide for themselves what to include. Portfolios are very useful, especially during parent–teacher conferences. Such a portfolio includes your notes about achievement, teacher- and child-made checklists, artwork samples, photographs, journals, and other documentation.

In addition, some teachers are using technology to develop digital portfolios. These can stand alone or supplement the traditional portfolio. Digital portfolios include books and journals that children keep on computers and then illustrate with digital cameras. An important point to remember, and one often overlooked, is that portfolios are only one part of children's assessment.

ASSESSMENT FOR SCHOOL READINESS

For more information about assessment of young children, go to the Companion Website at **http://www.prenhall.com/morrison**, select any chapter, then choose Topic 7 of the ECE Supersite module.

Because of federal mandates and state laws, many school districts assess children in some manner before or at the time of their entrance into school. Table 3.1 shows formal methods for assessment.

Some type of screening occurs at the time of kindergarten entrance to evaluate learning readiness. Unfortunately, children are often classified on the basis of how well they perform on these early screenings. When assessment is appropriate and the results are used to design developmentally appropriate instruction, it is valuable and worthwhile.

SCREENING PROCESSES

Screening measures   Any assessment that gives a broad picture of what children know and are able to do, their physical health, and their emotional status.

Screening measures give school personnel a broad picture of what children know and are able to do, as well as their physical and emotional status. As gross indicators of children's abilities, screening procedures provide much useful information for decisions about placement for initial instruction, referral to other agencies, and additional testing that may be

TABLE 3.1 Formal Assessment Measures Used in Early Childhood

Assessment Instrument	Age/Grade Level	Purpose
Battelle Developmental Inventory	Birth to age 8	Assesses key developmental skills in children up to age 8.
Boehm Test of Basic Concepts-Revised	Kindergarten to Grade 2	Assesses children's mastery of basic concepts that are fundamental to understanding verbal instruction and necessary for early school achievement.
BRIGANCE® Diagnostic Inventory of Basic Skills	Kindergarten to Grade 6	Assesses basic readiness and academic skills, measures and records performance, and serves as an aid in individualizing instruction.
Child Observation Record (COR)	Ages 2.2 to 6	Helps teachers and caregivers determine the developmental status of young children.
Denver Developmental Screening Test-Revised	1 month to age 6	Identifies infants and preschool children with serious developmental delays.
Developmental Indicators for the Assessment of Learning-Revised (DIAL–R)	Ages 2 to 6	Identifies children who may have special educational needs.
Peabody Individual Achievement Test	Kindergarten to Grade 12	Provides wide-range assessment in the content areas of general information, reading recognition, reading comprehension, mathematics, spelling, and written expression.
Peabody Picture Vocabulary Test-Revised	Ages 2½ to 40	Tests hearing vocabulary; available in two forms.
Stanford-Binet Intelligence Scale	Ages 2 to 17	Measures verbal reasoning, quantitative reasoning, abstract/visual reasoning, and short-term memory.
Wechsler Intelligence Scale for Children-Revised	Ages 6 to 16	Shows a specific pattern of strengths and weaknesses (based on three IQ scores) to indicate how well the child is able to learn and whether there are any specific learning disabilities.
Wechsler Preschool and Primary Scale of Intelligence	Ages 4 to 6	Measures intelligence of children ages 4 to 6½ years.

Sources: ERIC/AE Test Locator, *http://ericae.net/testcol.htm;* What Tests Would the School Psychologist Use?, *http://www.ehhs.cmich.edu/~mnesset/tests.html.*

necessary to pinpoint a learning or health problem. Many school districts conduct a comprehensive screening program in the spring for children who will enter kindergarten in the fall, which can involve the following:

- Gathering information from parents about their children's health, learning patterns, learning achievements, personal habits, and special problems
- Conducting a health screening, including a physical examination, a health history, and a blood sample for analysis
- Conducting vision, hearing, and speech screening
- Collecting and analyzing data from former programs and teachers, such as preschools and child care programs
- Administering a cognitive and/or behavioral screening instrument

Comprehensive screening programs are conducted in one day or over several days. Data for each child are usually evaluated by a team of professionals who make instructional placement recommendations and, when appropriate, advise additional testing and make referrals to other agencies for assistance.

The Uneven Playing Field of Assessment

We readily acknowledge that all children come to school as individuals and with different backgrounds. On the other hand, we can quickly forget issues of individuality and differences in culture, ethnicity, home language, age, home and community environment, maternal and paternal psychological well-being, and socioeconomic background when we assess children. Children simply do not come to the assessment or testing situation with an equal background for having the same chances for success. Let's consider some of the ways their backgrounds and the testing conditions influence their approaches to and performance on assessment measures:

- Was the test given to a non-English speaking child developed for English speaking children? If so, how will this influence the outcome for the non-English speaking child? In other words, is the test linguistically appropriate for the children with whom it is being used?
- Is the teacher or other person who administers a test to a non-English-speaking child fluent in the child's language? If the answer is "no," what are some ways that this would influence how well a child responds? For example, many teachers learn Classical Spanish, the kind spoken in Spain. However, many Spanish speaking children and their families speak the Spanish of Mexico, Central and South America, or a dialect of the languages spoken in these and other Spanish speaking countries.

- Are the tests administered to a particular age group developed for that age group? With the trend to test even younger children, tests are being used for children younger than those for whom they were developed.
- Can testing procedures be adapted to meet the special needs of different cultures and age groups? For example, are young children allowed to take breaks? If a test takes 50 minutes to an hour to administer, this is much too long for many young children to attend to a testing situation. Can the test be administered in a few sections over a period of time?
- How do children's socioeconomic status influence their achievement and test performances? For example, children who live in families with high incomes score better on achievement tests and have fewer behavior problems than do children from low socioeconomic households. This link of socioeconomic status to achievement means that we have to provide poor children high quality preschool programs designed to help them "catch-up" with their more advantaged peers if we expect them to do well on assessments of any kind.*

---

*Yeung, W. Jean, Linver, Miriam R., & Brooks-Gunn, Jeanne. (November/December 2002). How Money Matters for Young Children's Development: Parental Investment and Family Processes. *Child Development* 73(6), pp.1861–1879.

To complete an activity related to the topic above, go to the Companion Website at **http://www. prenhall.com/morrison**, select chapter 3, then choose the Diversity Tie-In module.

SCREENING INSTRUMENTS AND OBSERVATION RECORDS

Screening instruments provide information for grouping and planning instructional strategies. Most can be administered by people who do not have specialized training in test administration. Parent volunteers often help administer screening instruments, many of which can be administered in about thirty minutes.

BRIGANCE® K and 1 Screen. BRIGANCE® K and 1 screen is an evaluation for use in kindergarten and grade one. The kindergarten pupil data sheet for the BRIGANCE® K and 1 screen shows the skills, behaviors, and concepts evaluated in the kindergarten portion of the screening instrument (Figure 3.3).

FIGURE 3.3 A Completed Kindergarten Pupil Data Sheet from BRIGANCE® K and 1 Screen

A. Student's Name _Colin Killoran_

Parents/Guardian _Kristin Killoran_

Address _310 Locke Street_

	Year	Month	Day
Date of Screening	2002	6	15
Birth date	97	1	10
Age	5	5	5

School/Program _Vinal School_

Teacher _Leslie Feingold_

Assessor _Dennis Dowd_

B. Basic Screening Assessments

Page	Assessment Number	Skill (Circle the skill for each correct response and make notes as appropriate.)	C. Scoring — Number of Correct Responses	Point Value	Student's Score
3	1A	**Personal Data Response:** Verbally gives: ① first name ② full name ③ age 4. address (street or mailing) 5. birth date (month and day)	3×	2 points each	6/10
4 & 5	2A	**Color Recognition:** ① red ② blue ③ green ④ yellow ⑤ orange 6. purple 7. brown ⑧ black ⑨ pink 10. gray	8×	1 point	8/10
6	3A	**Picture Vocabulary:** Recognizes and names pictures of: ① dog ② cat ③ key ④ girl ⑤ boy ⑥ airplane ⑦ apple ⑧ leaf 9. cup 10. car	8×	1 point each	8/10
7	4A	**Visual Discrimination—Forms and Uppercase Letters:** Visually discriminates which one of four symbols is different: ①○ ②□ ③○ ④⑤ ⑤○ 7. I ⑧P 9.V 10. X	7×	1 point each	7/10
8	5A	**Visual-Motor Skills:** Copies: ① — ②○ +③ ④□ 5. △	4×	2 points ea.	8/10
9 & 10	6A	**Gross-Motor Skills:** ① Hops two hops on one foot. ③ Stands on one foot for five seconds. ⑤ Stands on one foot momentarily with eyes closed. ② Hops two hops on the other foot. ④ Stands on the other foot momentarily. ⑥ Stands on the other foot for five seconds. ⑦ Walks forward heel-to-toe four steps. ⑨ Stands on one foot momentarily with eyes closed. 8. Walks backward toe-to-heel four steps. 10. Stands on the other foot momentarily with eyes closed	8×	1 pt. ea.	8/10
11	7A	**Rote Counting:** Counts by rote to: (Circle all numbers prior to the first error.) ① ② ③ ④ ⑤ ⑥ 7 8 9 10	6×	.5 point each	3/5
12	8A	**Identifies Body Parts:** Identifies by pointing to or touching: ① chin ② fingernails ③ heels ④ ankles ⑤ jaw ⑥ shoulders ⑦ elbows 8. hips ⑨ wrists 10. waist	8×	.5 point each	4/5
13 & 14	9A	**Follows Verbal Directions:** Listens to, remembers, and follows: ① one-step direction 2. two-step direction	1×	2.5 points each	2.5/5
15	10A	**Numeral Comprehension:** Matches quantity with numerals: ② ① ④ ③ 5	4×	2 points ea.	8/10
16	11A	**Prints Personal Data:** ⓟ Prints first name) Reversals: Yes___ No___	1×	5 points	5/5
17	12A	**Syntax and Fluency:** ① Speech is understandable. ② Speaks in complete sentences.	2×	5 points ea.	10/10
		Total Score:			77.5/100

D. Observations

1. Handedness: Right _✓_ Left___ Uncertain___
2. Grasps pencil with: Fist___ Finges___ Uncertain _✓_
3. Hearing appeared to be normal: (See p. vii) Yes___ No _✓_ Uncertain___
4. Vision appeared to be normal: (See p. vii) Yes___ No___ Uncertain___
5. Record other observations on another sheet

E. Recommendations:

Ask nurse to check hearing. Below cutoff (<92).

Factor score 13.5 below at-risk guideline (<18).

Presence of risk factors. Rescreen in 6–9 months.

Source: From BRIGANCE® K and 1 Screen (© 1991). Curriculum Associates, Inc. BRIGANCE® is a registered trademark of Curriculum Associates®, Inc. Used by permission. http://www.curricassoc.com.

61

DIAL-R. The DIAL-R (Developmental Indicators for the Assessment of Learning-Revised) is an instrument designed for screening large numbers of prekindergarten children. Requiring approximately twenty-five to thirty minutes to administer, it involves individual observation for motor skills, concepts, and language skills. The screening team consists of a coordinator, an operator for each of the skills areas screened, and aides or volunteers to register parents and children.

The High/Scope Child Observation Record. The High/Scope Child Observation Record (COR) for ages two and a half to six is used by teachers and other observers to assess young children's development by observing their typical classroom activities.[1] The COR measures young children's progress in all facets of their development, whether or not the teacher is using the High/Scope curriculum. The High/Scope COR assesses the full variety of processes of young children's development of initiative, social relations, creative representation, music and movement, language and literacy, and logic and mathematics. It is not limited, as typical tests are, to language and mathematics questions to which there is only one right answer.

WHAT IS OBSERVATION?

Observation is one of the most widely used methods of assessment. Table 3.2 provides information and guidelines on observation and other informal methods of assessment.

> There is only one basis for observation: children must be free to express themselves and thus reveal those needs and attitudes that would otherwise remain hidden or repressed in an environment that did not permit them to act spontaneously. An observer obviously needs something to observe; and if he must be trained to be able to see and recognize the truth, he must also have at his disposal children placed in such an environment that they can manifest their natural traits.[2]

Professionals recognize that children are more than what is measured by any particular test. Observation is an "authentic" means of learning about children—what they know and are able to do, especially as it occurs in more naturalistic settings such as classrooms, child care centers, playgrounds, and homes. Observation is the intentional, systematic act of looking at the behavior of a child or children in a particular setting, program, or situation. Observation is sometimes referred to as *kid-watching* and is an excellent way to find out about children's behaviors and learning.

PURPOSES OF OBSERVATION

Observation is designed to gather information on which to base decisions, make recommendations, develop curriculum, plan activities and learning strategies, and assess children's growth, development, and learning. For example, when professionals and parents sometimes look at children, they do not really see or concern themselves with what the children are doing or why, as long as they are safe and orderly. However, the significance and importance of critical behaviors go undetected if observation is done casually and is limited to "unsystematic looking."

Many school districts conduct a comprehensive screening for children entering kindergarten, which may include tests of vision, hearing, and speech.

Observation The intentional, systematic act of looking at the behavior of a child or children in a particular setting, program, or situation.

TABLE 3.2 Informal Methods for Assessment

Method	Purpose	Guidelines
Observation Kid watching—looking at children in a systematic way	Enables teachers to identify children's behaviors, document performance, and make decisions.	Plan for observation and be clear about the purposes of the observation.
Authentic Is performance-based and is based on real-life activities	Helps determine if children are applying what they have learned to real-life situations (e.g., making change).	Make sure that what is assessed relates to real-life events, that the learner is involved in doing something, and that instruction has been provided prior to assessment.
Anecdotal Record Brief narrative account of an event or behavior	Provides insight into a particular reason for behavior and provides a basis for planning a specific teaching strategy.	Record only what is observed or heard; should deal with the facts and should include the setting (e.g., where the behavior occurs) and what was said and done.
Running Record Focuses on a sequence of events that occurs over time	Helps obtain a more detailed insight into behavior over a period of time.	Maintain objectivity and try to include as much detail as possible.
Event Sampling Focuses on a particular behavior during a particular event (e.g., behavior at lunchtime, behavior on the playground, behavior in a reading group)	Helps identify behaviors during a particular event over time.	Identify a target behavior to be observed during particular times (e.g., fighting during transition activities).
Time Sampling Record particular events or behaviors at specific time intervals (e.g., five minutes, ten minutes)	Helps identify when a particular child demonstrates a particular behavior. Helps answer the question, "Does the child do something all the time or just at certain times and events?"	Observe only during the time period specified.
Rating Scale Contains a list for a set of behaviors	Enables teachers to record data when they are observed.	Select the type of rating scale that is appropriate for what is rated. Make sure that key descriptors and the rating scale are appropriate for what is being observed.
Checklist A list of behaviors identifying what children can and cannot do	Enables teachers to easily observe and check off what children know and are able to do.	Make sure that the checklist includes behaviors that are important for the program and for learning (e.g., counts from 1 to 10, hops on one foot).
Work Sample Collections of children's work that demonstrate what they know and are able to do	Provides a concrete example of learning; it can show growth and achievement over time.	Make sure that work samples demonstrate what children know and are able to do. Let children help select what items they want to use as examples of their learning.
Portfolio Collections of children's work samples	Provides documentation of a child's achievement in specific areas over time. It can include test scores, writing work samples, videotapes, etc.	A portfolio is not a dumpster but a thoughtful collection of materials that documents learning over time.
Interview Engaging children in discussion through questions	Children can be asked to explain behavior, work samples, or particular answers.	Ask questions at all levels of Bloom's taxonomy (see Chapter 12) in order to gain insight into children's learning at all levels.

Evaluating the
Learning Process

I have used student portfolios to evaluate my kindergarten students for fifteen years. Over time, however, I have redefined their purpose and identified several criteria to make more effective use of portfolios. I believe that the value of student portfolios is to provide a record of each student's process of learning and therefore collect student work based on the following criteria:

- Portfolio entries reflect a student's cognitive, social, emotional, and physical development.
- They provide a visual record of a student's process of learning over time.
- They encourage input from students, teachers, and parents.

My students and I together select the work samples. Each portfolio also includes a parent questionnaire, parent responses to conferences, individual assessment profiles, and anecdotal records. Because the volume of materials that can accumulate in a portfolio can become overwhelming, I use a table of contents in the format of a checklist stapled in-

side the folder, which makes it easy to examine the contents and determine at a glance what data I have to make wise instructional decisions and what information I still need.

The success of student portfolios as an evaluation tool depends on the appropriate assessment of individual students and accurate, conscientious documentation of student growth.

APPROPRIATE ASSESSMENT

Appropriate assessment is aligned to curriculum that reflects the local, state, and national standards. Additionally, appropriate assessment informs instruction. It is the process of observing, recording, and documenting the work children do and how they do it. In my classroom, assessments are ongoing and occur as children perform daily classroom routines and participate in group time, share time, center time, and recess. I note which activities the children choose, how long they work on specific activities, and their process for completing activities. I observe students' learning styles, interest levels, skill lev-

The purposes of observation, then, are these:

- *To determine the cognitive, linguistic, social, emotional, and physical development of children.* Using a developmental checklist is one way professionals can systematically observe and chart the development of children. Figure 3.4 (see p. 69) shows a checklist for emergent literacy.
- *To identify children's interests and learning styles.* Today, teachers are very interested in developing learning activities, materials, and classroom centers based on children's interests, preferences, and learning styles.
- *To plan.* The professional practice of teaching requires planning on a daily, ongoing basis. Observation provides useful, authentic, and solid information that enables teachers to intentionally plan for activities rather than to make decisions with little or no information.
- *To meet the needs of individual children.* Meeting the needs of individual children is an important part of teaching and learning. For example, a child may be advanced cognitively but overly aggressive and lacking the social skills necessary to play cooperatively and interact with others. Through observation, a teacher can gather information to develop a plan for helping him learn how to play with others.
- *To determine progress.* Systematic observation, over time, provides a rich, valuable, and informative source of information about how individuals and groups of children are progressing in their learning and behavior.

els, coping techniques, strategies for decision making and problem solving, and interactions with other children. Observations, however, have little value unless they are accurately documented.

ACCURATE DOCUMENTATION

To manage documentation more accurately and efficiently, I have developed or adapted a variety of forms to make systematic assessments. Throughout the year, I use these assessment tools to systematically record information on individual children in each area of their development. I use a symbol to date the occurrence of behaviors and describe and document skill proficiency as appropriate. Emphasis is on what each child can do, and each child's progress is compared with his or her prior work. When I review these individual assessments I am able to quickly detect areas of growth.

SYMBOL SYSTEM

+ = Progress is noted
√ = Needs more time and/or experience
* = See comments

In addition to the individual student profiles, I have also developed several class evaluation forms that allow me flexibility in recording observations quickly yet accurately. These forms are especially useful in planning group and/or individual instruction, and they provide additional documentation that supports the individual assessment records. For example, I make anecdotal records (on Post-It notes) of unanticipated events or behaviors, a child's social interactions, and problem-solving strategies. I transfer these Post-Its to a class grid so I can determine at a glance

which children I have observed. The anecdotal records, along with the individual assessment profiles, become a part of each student's portfolio to be used for instructional planning and communicating with parents.

Throughout the year, samples of students' work are dated and included in the portfolios. Quarterly work samples that I select include some that illustrate abilities with cutting activities, writing numbers (each child decides how far he or she can write), writing letters of the alphabet, and any words or stories a child can write independently (using either invented or conventional spelling). The children select samples of artwork and creative writing (e.g., journal entries, letters or drawings they have done for parents).

USE OF INFORMATION

I use the information from student portfolios to plan classroom instruction for individuals and groups, to identify children who may need special help, and to confer with parents and colleagues. During conferences, I share with parents the student's assessment profile for the different areas of development, and together we examine samples of the child's work that support the assessment. Even though progress is visually obvious, I can also point out less obvious progress as we view the samples. I give conference response forms to parents and ask for comments or suggestions for additional portfolio entries. Using the portfolio, I am satisfied that I have gleaned an accurate assessment of and appreciation for each child's total development.

Contributed by Linda Sholar, Sangre Ridge Elementary School, Stillwater, Oklahoma.

- *To provide information to parents.* Professionals report to and conference with parents on an ongoing basis. Observational information adds to other information they have, such as test results and child work samples, and provides a fuller and more complete picture of individual children.
- *To provide self-insight.* Observational information can help professionals learn more about themselves and what to do to help children.

ADVANTAGES OF INTENTIONAL, SYSTEMATIC OBSERVATION

There are a number of advantages to gathering data through observation:

- *It enables professionals to collect information about children that they might not otherwise gather through other sources.* A great deal of the consequences, causes, and reactions to children's behavior can be assessed only through observation. Observation enables you to gather data that cannot be assessed by formal, standardized tests; questioning; and parent and child interviews.
- *Observation is ideally suited to learning more about children in play settings.* Observation affords you the opportunity to note a child's social behavior in a play group and discern

Observing Will

Welcome to Ms. Liz's classroom. Will is the child you will be observing. He is the energetic, young boy dressed in overalls and a yellow shirt. You are encouraged to learn as much as you can about Will, his peers, his teacher (Ms. Liz), and the classroom. Before you focus on individual photographs, observe the classroom in general. Reflect on the following questions:

- What general statements would you make regarding classroom arrangement, organization, materials, and equipment? Based on your observation, what recommendations would you make if this was your classroom? Would you arrange your classroom differently?
- Based on your observation of the children's involvement with materials and their peers, what can you say about their development, social competence, and play behavior? How do the children and Ms. Liz get along?
- Do the children in the classroom feel comfortable taking risks, working together, and expressing emotions?
- Do you think Ms. Liz operates a child-centered classroom? How does your observation support your answer?
- Do you think the children spend more time participating in hands-on experiences or teacher-related experiences?
- Can Ms. Liz's classroom be characterized as an active learning environment? How and why?
- What can you infer regarding gender equity and the way boys and girls are treated in Ms. Liz's classroom?
- List five things children learn from large-motor activities. How does outdoor play support children's learning?

P-1

Literacy development is important in early childhood programs. In P-1, what is Ms. Liz doing to support the children's literacy development? What can you infer from the children's behavior regarding their literacy development? Note in P-2 how Ms. Liz supports Will's autonomy and "what he can do for himself." Based on your observation of P-3, what are five things Will knows about reading?

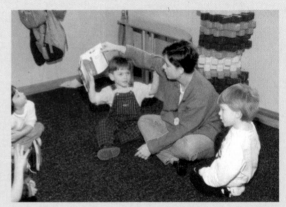

P-2

What do you notice about the behavior of Will's peers? What does their behavior indicate to you?

P-3

PERSONAL REFLECTION.

Focus once again on P-2. Do you agree with Ms. Liz allowing Will to take the picture book from her? Would you have allowed Will to read the book to the other children? What can Ms. Liz do to involve the other children in Will's retelling of the story?

In P-4 you see Will and his friend Ryan building a tall tower. What can you tell about Will's willingness to engage in cooperative play with other children? What can you infer from Will's behavior and facial expression about the activity? Observe how the top of the red tower is falling on the child behind Will.

P-4

PERSONAL REFLECTION.

Would you allow Will and his peers to build their tower as high as they are building it? Why or why not?

In P-5, observe how Will responds to the accident of the falling tower. What does Will's behavior tell you? What can you tell about Ms. Liz's behavior? What can you say about the behavior of Ryan (the child in the background behind Ms. Liz)?

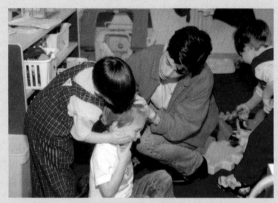

P-5

PERSONAL REFLECTION.

As a classroom teacher, how would you handle a situation in which a child was injured, though not seriously?

PERSONAL REFLECTION.

How would you categorize Will and Megan's play behavior in P-6? Based on your observation, what are some things that Will and Megan are learning? Are the materials appropriate for them to use?

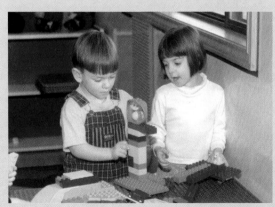

P-6

Observe Will's determination and physical effort in P-7. What are some things you can learn through observation in the outdoors? What developmental skills is Will enhancing through his outdoor play?

P-7

P-8

PERSONAL REFLECTION.

What are some outdoor activities that you would include in your early childhood program? How would you provide for Will's safety and the safety of all children in outdoor play? What are some inferences you can make about outdoor safety?

In the parent–teacher conference depicted in P-8, observe Will's facial expression and body language. What do they tell you? Does Will's mother seem supportive of him?

PERSONAL REFLECTION.

Will is participating in the conference between Will's mother and Ms. Liz. Do you think he should be involved in the parent–teacher conference? Why or why not? Do you think Ms. Liz and Will's mother value Will's participation? What are the pros and cons of Will participating in the conference?

Thanks to Director Vicki Yun, Ms. Liz, Will Sims, and the children of LaPetite Academy in Dublin, Ohio. Photos by Anthony Magnacca/Merrill.

Observing is an excellent way to find out about a child's behavior and how well he is learning. What do you think this teacher can learn about this child from watching him complete the puzzle?

how cooperatively he or she interacts with peers. Observing a child at play gives professionals a wealth of information about developmental levels, social skills, and what the child is or is not learning in play settings.

- *Observation allows you to learn a lot about children's prosocial behavior and peer interactions.* It can help you plan for appropriate and inclusive activities to promote the social growth of young children. Additionally, your observations can serve as the basis for developing multicultural activities to benefit all children.
- *Observation of children's abilities provides a basis for the assessment of what they are developmentally able to do.* Many learning skills are developed sequentially, such as the refinement of large-motor skills before small-motor skills. Through observation, professionals can determine whether children's abilities are within a normal range of growth and development.
- *Observation is useful to assess children's performance over time.* Documentation of daily, weekly, and monthly observations of children's behav-

FIGURE 3.4 Emergent Literacy Behaviors Checklist

Name:	Age	Observed	Not Observed
demonstrates visual acuity			
demonstrates hearing acuity			
Print Concepts			
recognizes left-to-right sequencing			
recognizes top, down directionality			
asks what print says			
connects meaning between two objects, pictures			
models reading out loud			
models adult silent reading (newspapers, books, etc.)			
recognizes that print has different meanings (informational, entertainment, etc.)			
Comprehension Behaviors			
follows oral directions			
draws correct pictures from oral directions			
recognizes story sequence in pictures			
interprets pictures			
sees links in story ideas			
links personal experiences with text (story, title)			
logically reasons story plot/conclusions			
sees patterns in similar stories			
Writing Behaviors			
makes meaningful scribbles (attempts to make letter-like shapes)			
draws recursive scribbles (rows of cursive-like writing)			
makes strings of "letters"			
uses one or more consonants to represent words			
uses inventive spellings			

Use this checklist to assess and date the student's progress as an emergent reader and writer.

iors and learning provides a database for the cumulative evaluation of each child's achievement and development.

- *Observation helps you provide concrete information for use in reporting to and conferencing with parents.* Increasingly, reports to parents about children involve professionals' observations and children's work samples so parents and educators can collaborate to determine how to help children develop cognitively, socially, emotionally, and physically.

In summary, intentional observation is a useful, informative, and powerful means for informing and guiding teaching and for helping ensure the learning of all children.

To complete a Program in Action activity, visit the Companion Website at **http://www. prenhall.com/morrison**, select chapter 3, then choose the Program in Action module.

STEPS FOR CONDUCTING OBSERVATIONS

The steps involved in the process of systematic, purposeful observation are listed in Figure 3.5. They include the following:

▲
Observing children at play enables teachers to learn about their developmental levels, social skills, and peer interactions. How might teachers use this information to plan future play-based activities?

Interpretation   Forming a conclusion based on observational and assessment data with the intent of planning and improving teaching and learning.

Implementation   Committing to a certain action based on interpretations of the observational data.

Step 1: Plan for Observation.   Planning is an important part of the observation process. Everything you do regarding observation should be planned in advance of the observation. A good guide to follow in planning is to ask the questions *who, what, where, when,* and *how.*

Setting goals for observation is an important part of the planning process. Goals allow you to reflect on why you want to observe and thus direct your efforts to what you will observe. Stating a goal focuses your attention on the purpose of your observation. Goals, for example, that direct your attention to the effectiveness of your efforts in providing an inclusive classroom or program, and in fully including an exceptional child into the classroom might read like this:

Goal 1: To determine what modifications might be necessary in the classroom to facilitate access to all parts of the classroom for Dana in her wheelchair.

Goal 2: To assess the development of prosocial behavioral characteristics that other children display to Dana while interacting in the classroom.

Step 2: Conduct the Observation.   While conducting your observation, it is imperative that you be objective, specific, and as thorough as possible (see Figure 3.6). For example, during your observation of Dana and her peers you notice that there is not enough room for Dana to manipulate her wheelchair past the easel and shelf where the crayons are kept. None of her peers noticed that Dana could not reach the crayons and so did not help her get them. Dana had to ask one of the children to get the crayons for her.

Step 3: Interpret the Data.   All observations can and should result in some kind of interpretation. **Interpretation** serves several important functions. First, it puts your observations into perspective—that is, in relation to what you already know and do not know about events and the behaviors of your children. Second, interpretation helps you make sense of what you have observed and enables you to use your professional knowledge to interpret what you have seen. Third, interpretation has the potential to make you learn to anticipate representative behavior indicative of normal growth and development under given conditions, and to recognize what might not be representative of appropriate growth, development, and learning for each child. Fourth, interpretation forms the foundation for the implementation, necessary adaptations, or modifications in a program or curriculum. In this observation, you can note that Dana's only exceptionality is that she is physically disabled. Her growth in other areas is normal, and she displays excellent social skills in that she is accepted by others, knows when to ask for help, and is able to ask for help. When Dana asks for help, she receives it.

Step 4: Implement a Plan.   The **implementation** phase means that you commit to do something with the results or the "findings" of your observation. For example, although Dana's behavior in your observation was appropriate, many of the children can benefit from activities designed to help them recognize and respond to the needs of others. The physical environment of the classroom as well requires some modification in the rearrangement

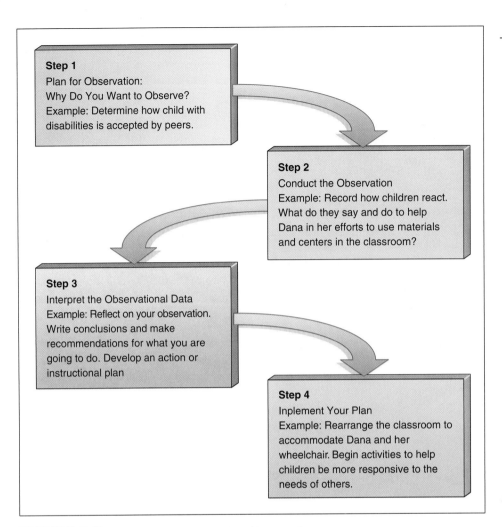

FIGURE 3.5 Four Steps for Effective Observation

FIGURE 3.6 Methods of Collecting Observation Data

- Write on self-sticking notes to record information. These notes are easily transferred to student files and folders.

- Wear a small pocket apron (a carpenter's apron available at hardware stores works well) to carry self-sticking notes, small tablets, markers, etc.

- Take photographs of children's accomplishments. You have heard that a picture is worth a thousand words and this is often true. For example, Martha Pratt at Bright Horizons Family Solutions uses a camera to record infant's milestones. In addition, digital camera images are easily manipulated and transferred to student files.

- Use a clipboard to hold the checklist and other forms to record data as you observe.

- Use technology whenever possible to record data. For example, a laptop loaded with student files makes it easier to record, store, and manage data. In addition video cameras are a good way to capture certain events and activities.

One of your major responsibilities during observation is to manage the collection of observation information. How to record and store it is another responsibility. These ideas will help you do both of these tasks.

of movable furniture to make it more accessible for Dana. Also, implementation means you report to parents or others. Implementing—that is, doing something with the results of your observations—is the most important part of the process.

USING AN OBSERVATIONAL GUIDE

Observation should help inform professionals and guide their teaching of young children. A sample observation form you can use is shown in Figure 3.7. You can also check other resources to develop more specific observation guides you could use as checklists to track developmental behaviors with individual children.

REPORTING TO AND COMMUNICATING WITH PARENTS

Part of your responsibility as a professional is to report to parents about the growth, development, and achievement of their children. Some view reporting to parents as a bother and wish it was something they did not have to do. Nonetheless, reporting to and communicating with parents is one of the most important jobs of the early childhood professional. The following guidelines will help you meet this important responsibility of reporting your assessment information to parents:

- *Be honest and realistic with parents.* Too often, we do not want to hurt parents' feelings. We want to sugarcoat what we are reporting. However, parents need your honest assessments about their children and what they know, are able to do, and will be able to do.
- *Communicate to parents so they can understand.* What we communicate to parents must make sense to them. They have to understand what we are saying. Reporting to parents often has to be a combination of written (in their language) and oral communication.

FIGURE 3.7 A Sample Observation Guide

Teacher's Name: Vicki Yung

Child's Name: Emily Chin

Date: 9-26-04

Time: 10:15 a.m.

Location: Classroom Reading Center

Purpose of Observing:

Prediction or Expectations of Findings:

Significant Events During Observation:

Reflective Analysis of Significant Events:

Plan for Using Observation Information:

- *Provide parents with ideas and information that will help them help their children learn.* Remember that you and parents are partners in helping children be successful in school and life.

WHAT ARE CRITICAL ASSESSMENT ISSUES?

As with almost everything we talk about in this book, issues surround essential questions about what is appropriate and inappropriate practice, and what is best for children and families. Assessment is no different regarding critical issues.

ASSESSMENT AND ACCOUNTABILITY

There is a tremendous emphasis on testing and the use of tests to measure achievement for comparing children, programs, school districts, and countries. This emphasis will continue

for a number of reasons. First, the public, including politicians and legislatures, sees assessment as a means of making schools and teachers accountable for teaching the nation's children. Second, assessment is seen as playing a critical role in improving education. The view is that assessment results can be used as a guide for determining how the curriculum and instructional practices can be used to increase achievement. Therefore, as long as there is a public desire to improve teaching and achievement, we will continue to see an emphasis on assessment for accountability purposes.

GOOD START, GROW SMART

For example, the Good Start, Grow Smart early childhood initiative in the No Child Left Behind Act (see also Chapter 8, Federal Programs and Early Education) calls for an accountability system to assure that every Head Start center assesses standards of learning in early language and numeracy skills. This type of accountability for assessing and assuring young children's achievement will spread to all preschool programs.

HIGH-STAKES TESTING

We have previously talked about high-stakes testing. This kind of testing occurs when standardized tests are used to make important and often life-influencing decisions about children. Standardized tests have specific and standardized content, administration and scoring procedures, and norms for interpreting scores. High-stakes outcomes include decisions about whether to admit children into programs (e.g., kindergarten) and whether to retain or promote children. Generally, the early childhood profession is opposed to high-stakes testing for children through grade three. However, as part of the accountability movement, many politicians and school administrators view high-stakes testing as a means of making

Report your assessment findings accurately and honestly to the parents of your students. How might such communication build trust?

For more information about assessment issues that relate to young children, go to the Companion Website at **http://www. prenhall.com/morrison**, select chapter 3, then choose the Linking to Learning module to connect to the National Education Goals Panel site.

Kindergarten Assessment— Current Practices

For some time now, Federal mandates, state laws, and individual school districts have required assessments for all students. The recent phenomenon is now requiring assessments for kindergarteners, not as a screening tool before entrance to kindergarten, as has been done in many school districts, but as a way for teachers to be accountable to districts, to the parents, and to align these assessments to the new learning standards. Many school systems have adopted assessments to meet the new standards for kindergarten. For many professionals, assessments are the driving force behind instruction.

Assessments are used to:

- plan for individual and group instruction
- identify at-risk students and students with special needs
- define what each child knows specifically, for example: How many upper and lower case letters can she recognize?
- discern phonemic awareness skills such as knowledge of rhyming words.

- plan for appropriate group placement for small instructional grouping during literacy and math instruction
- assist in implementing kindergarten programs and individual lesson plans
- inform parents of their children's progress

For some practioners, developmentally appropriate practice is no longer part of early childhood education. Based on my 30 plus years of experience, I am convinced that there needs to be a healthy balance between formal assessment through tests, and informal assessment through teacher observation and parent feedback. Together, formal and informal assessment comprise a balanced evaluative approach.

Communication with parents via conferences and report cards is a critical part of the teaching process. Report cards, which align with curriculum standards and the assessments, clearly present valuable data to parents. An easy checklist for skill development such as P (progressing satisfactorily), I (in progress), and N (not yet observed or introduced) is helpful. A written narrative describing a

To take an online self-test on this chapter's contents, go to the Companion Website at **http://www. prenhall.com/morrison**, select chapter 3, then choose the Self-Test module.

For additional Internet resources or to complete an online activity for this chapter, go to the Companion Website at **http://www. prenhall.com/morrison**, select chapter 3, then choose the Linking to Learning or Making Connections module.

sure that children learn and that promotions are based on achievement. Many school critics maintain that in the pre-K and primary grades there is too much social promotion—that is, passing children from grade to grade merely to enable students to keep pace with their age peers.

As an early childhood professional, part of your responsibility is to be an advocate for the appropriate use of assessment. You will make ongoing, daily decisions about how best to assess your children and how best to use the results of assessment.

Some states are tying teacher salaries to student achievement. This process is called "pay for performance." Denver, Colorado, city schools were the first in the nation to tie student performance to teacher pay.[3] Many school districts allow their teachers to receive extra compensation or bonuses if their schools meet certain student achievement goals. These programs will increase in other states and school districts across the country. Such plans are based on measuring student achievement with standard tests, and this means more testing for all students at all ages.

TEST BIAS

Many contend that the way many school district testing programs, as they are currently structured, do not allow all children to show what they are able to do. There are many gen-

student's social and emotional growth and development, work habits, mastery of literacy, and math objectives is necessary to tie in the checklist with an overview of the whole child to get an accurate picture of the student. Conferencing with parents is especially important in kindergarten. Developmental and social issues that clarify a student's performance more effectively than a mere checklist or letter grade can be addressed in conversation. The narrative portion of the report card is beneficial because it provides parents an opportunity to know how their child performs in the classroom. I always encourage parents to contact me with questions as follow up. In some cases I follow up with a parent meeting, or parent meeting with other colleagues, if I have concerns such as speech articulation, emotional issues, or personal family problems. Many of these issues may have a very strong impact on a child's ability to learn. Indeed, assessments and conferencing are vital components of sound teaching practice today.

Standards and assessments are integral parts of the instructional framework and kindergarten curriculum of most school systems. Assessments are used to guide instruction. When used in isolation, such as isolated skills testing, their value is limited. However, when used as part of a classroom lesson, they can be very effective. For example, looking at a writing sample with a writing rubric for kindergarten is a very explicit and valid form of assessment that it is helpful to the students. They can gain a beginning understanding of what is expected in a clear and concise manner. For example, a kindergarten writing rubric could be one like this:

*I wrote my name the kindergarten way using capital and lower case letters.
**I made a picture, which matches my words (the text).
***I used a capital letter at the beginning of each sentence and a period at the end of each sentence.
****I used my best handwriting with spaces between words.

Teachers have always used observation and portfolios of student work to assure that students are meeting stated goals and receiving the appropriate content and concepts presented. Assessments provide the teacher with valuable information about differentiation for individual student instruction, for reporting student progress to parents, and to use as a kindergarteners' self evaluation tool. I have used the writing rubric above as a kindergartener's self-evaluative measure.

Kindergarten rubrics allow children to know what is generally expected of them and help them complete a specific piece of work. By adapting the rubric for writing, the child's progress is acknowledged. As the circumstances change, the rubrics may become more specific, more challenging, and include higher expectations.

Assessment measures individual differences in students. Students who are at risk, English language learners (ELL), specials needs students, gifted students, and average students all must be educated and assessment is another tool to measure a student's ability and skill. It is clearly a vital component of the kindergarten instructional program today. As we continue to acquire more research, the assessment process will undergo modifications. Productive assessment strategies will benefit everyone—students, teachers, administrators, and parents—as we all share in this collaborative effort to educate our youngest learners.

Contributed by Sandy Reiss, Early Childhood Educator, Olney, Maryland.

der and ethnic biases in test performance. What is needed are testing programs that include different ways of testing children so that all students are able to demonstrate what they know and are able to do.

HOW YOUNG IS TOO YOUNG?

As I mentioned above, the federal government is currently in the process of testing all of the Head Start children to determine if they have achieved the knowledge and skills specified in the Head Start Performance Standards (see Chapter 8). They will be the first children as young as four-years-old who will be tested on such a large scale. The federal government has contracted with Westat, a national test maker, for $1.8 million to develop the test. Testing children at such young ages is a major issue of this testing initiative. Some early childhood professionals believe that four and five-year-old children are too young to be subjected to such testing.

CONCLUSION

Today there is a great deal of emphasis on accountability. Teachers are asked to be accountable to parents, legislators, and the public. Providing for and conducting developmentally appropriate assessment of young children and their programs is one of the best ways that you can be accountable for what you do. Conducting appropriate assessment not only enables you to be accountable to parents and the public, but also enables you to be accountable to young children. You have accepted a sacred trust and have dedicated your life to helping children learn and develop. Effective assessment practices will help you achieve this goal.

ACTIVITIES FOR FURTHER ENRICHMENT

APPLICATIONS

1. Create a developmental checklist similar to that shown in Figure 3.4. Watch an early childhood classroom and determine how effective you are at observing some aspect of children's development and learning.
2. Observe a particular child during play or other activity. Before your observation make sure you follow the steps for conducting observations reviewed in this chapter. Use the information you gathered to plan a learning activity for the child. As you plan, determine what information you need that you didn't gather through observation. When you observe again, what will you do differently?
3. Observe a program that is providing services for children with disabilities. Your purpose is to determine what accommodations need to be made for them.

FIELD EXPERIENCES

1. Interview several kindergarten and primary teachers and ask them for ideas and guidelines for how to assess with portfolios. Which ideas can you use?
2. Review the contents of several children's portfolios. How are they similar and different? What do the contents tell you about the children?

RESEARCH

1. Frequently there are articles in newspapers and magazines about assessment and testing. Over a two-week period, review these sources and determine what assessment and evaluation issues are "in the news." Put these materials in your portfolio or teaching file.
2. Visit pre-k–3 programs in several different school districts. Make a list of the various ways they assess and the instruments and procedures they use. Compare them with the ones identified in this chapter. How and for what purposes are the tests used? What conclusions can you draw from the information you gathered?

READINGS FOR FURTHER ENRICHMENT

Anderson, L. W. *Classroom Assessment: Enhancing the Quality of Teacher Decision Making.* Mahwah, NJ: Lawrence Erlbaum, Associates Inc., 2002.

Discusses assessing achievement using selection and short-answer tasks, extended response and performance tasks, classroom behavior and student effort, and interpreting assessment results.

Chase, C. *Contemporary Assessment for Educators.* New York: Longman, 1999.

This text focuses on providing a basic foundation of knowledge about assessment with strong applications to real classroom settings. Designed specifically to guide teachers in the creation and management of classroom assessment and to assist them in interpreting and understanding published assessment results.

Chudowsy, N., Glaser, R., and Pellegrino, J. W. *Knowing What Students Know: The Science and Design of Educational Assessment.* Washington, DC: National Academy Press, 2001.

Explains how expanding knowledge in the scientific fields of human learning and educational measurement can form the foundations of an improved approach to assessment. Suggests ways that the targets of assessment—what students know and how well they know it—as well as the methods used to make inferences about student learning can be made more valid and instructionally useful. Principles for designing and using these new kinds of assessments are presented, and examples are used to illustrate the principles. Implications for policy, practice, and research are also explored.

Gredler, M. *Classroom Assessment and Learning.* New York: Longman, 1999.

The book redirects assessment—whether quantitatively or qualitatively based—back to the classroom. Students will benefit by learning how assessment models can be constructed and used to guide teacher decision making and student learning. Emphasizes the role assessment plays in stimulating cognitive advancement.

Puckett, M., and Black, J. *Authentic Assessment of the Young Child: Celebrating Development and Learning,* 2nd ed. Upper Saddle River, NJ: Merrill/Prentice Hall, 2000.

While retaining its strong emphasis on child growth and development, this edition has been expanded to include new information on learner-centered approaches. This text is based on the idea that teaching, learning, and assessment are parts of a single ongoing process that provides meaningful, authentic learning experiences for children.

LINKING TO LEARNING

ARCNet
http://arc.missouri.edu/index.html

The Web site created for anyone interested in the world of assessment.

National Education Goals Panel
http://www.negp.gov/

Provides a variety of early childhood reports, including "Reconsidering Children's Early Development and Learning," "Getting a Good Start in School," "Ready Schools," "Principles and Recommendations for Early Childhood Assessments," and "Trends in Early Childhood Assessment Policies and Practices."

Pathways to School Improvement on the Web
http://www.ncrel.org/sdrs/areas/issues/students/earlycld/ea500.htm

A Web site containing information on current issues, including assessment of the progress and attainments of young children three to eight years of age and the uses and abuse of assessment.

ENDNOTES

[1] High/Scope Educational Research Foundation, *High/Scope Child Observation Record (COR) for Ages 2½ to 6* (Ypsilanti, MI: Author, 1992).

[2] Montessori, M. *The Discovery of the Child* (New York: Ballantine Books, 1980), 46.

[3] Bradley, Ann. "Denver Teachers to Pilot Pay-for-Performance Plan," *Education Week* (September 22, 1999), 5.

Part 2

Foundations: History and Theories

Chapter 4

Few will have the greatness to bend history itself; but each of us can work to change a small portion of events, and in the total; of all those acts will be written the history of this generation.

ROBERT F. KENNEDY

The Past and the Present

Prologue to the Future

Focus Questions

- Why is it important for you to have an appreciation for the ideas, professional accomplishments, and contributions of great educators?

- What are the basic beliefs of the following people who have influenced early childhood education: Luther, Comenius, Locke, Rousseau, Pestalozzi, Owen, Froebel, Dewey, Maslow, Erikson, Gardner, and Hirsch?

- How have the beliefs and ideas of great educators influenced early childhood programs?

- How is contemporary education influenced by historical events?

WHY IS THE PAST IMPORTANT?

By reading of the hopes, ideas, and accomplishments of people whom our profession judges famous, we realize that today's ideas are built on those of the past. There are at least five reasons to know about the ideas and theories of great educators who have influenced the field of early childhood education.

REBIRTH OF IDEAS

Old ideas and theories have a way of being reborn. Good ideas and practices persist over time and tend to be recycled through educational thought and practices in ten- to twenty-year periods. For example, many practices popular in the 1970s—using phonics to teach reading; family grouping and multifamily grouping; child-centered education; and active learning—are now popular again in the first decade of the twenty-first century.

Old ideas and practices seldom get recycled exactly in their previous form. They are changed and modified as necessary for contemporary society and situations. Knowing about these former ideas and practices helps us recognize them when they do come around again. Most important, this knowledge enables you to be an active participant in the recycling process of applying good practices of previous years to contemporary practice. You can more fully appreciate this recycling if you understand the roots of the early education profession.

BUILD THE DREAM—AGAIN

Many ideas of famous educators are still dreams, despite the advances we attribute to modern education. In this regard, we are the inheritors of the ideas of a long line of early childhood educators. We should acknowledge this inheritance and use it as a base to build meaningful teaching careers and lives for children and their families. We have an obligation to have bright visions for children and build on the dreams of others. You are both a builder of dreams and an implementer of dreams.

 To review the chapter focus questions online, go to the Companion Website at **http://www.prenhall.com/morrison** and select chapter 4.

To check your understanding of this chapter with the online Study Guide, go to the Companion Website at **http://www.prenhall.com/morrison,** select chapter 4, then choose the Study Guide module.

IMPLEMENT CURRENT PRACTICE

Ideas expressed by early educators will help you better understand how to implement current teaching strategies, whatever they may be. For instance, Rousseau, Froebel, and Montessori all believed children should be taught with dignity and respect. This attitude toward children is essential to an understanding of good educational practice and contributes to good teaching and quality programs. Any program you are involved in should include respect—among many other attributes—as one of its core values.

EMPOWER PROFESSIONALS

Theories about how young children grow, develop, and learn decisively shape educational and child-rearing practices. Some parents and teachers may not realize, however, what assumptions form the foundations of their daily practices. Studying the beliefs of the great educators helps parents, you, and other early childhood educators clarify what to do and gives insight into behavior and practice. In this sense, knowing about theories liberates the uninformed from ignorance and empowers professionals and parents. As a consequence, those who understand the theories are able to implement developmentally appropriate practices with confidence.

INSPIRE PROFESSIONALS

Exploring, analyzing, and discovering the roots of early childhood education helps inspire professionals. Recurring rediscovery forces people to contrast current practices with what others have advocated. Examining sources of beliefs helps clarify modern practice, and reading and studying others' ideas make us rethink our own beliefs and positions. In this regard, the history of the great educators and their beliefs helps keep us current. When you pause long enough to listen to what they have to say, you frequently find a new insight or idea that will motivate you to continue your quest to be the best you can be.

HISTORICAL FIGURES AND THEIR INFLUENCE ON EARLY CHILDHOOD EDUCATION

MARTIN LUTHER

Although the primary impact of the Protestant Reformation was religious, other far-reaching effects were secular. Two of these effects involved universal education and literacy, both topics very much in the forefront of educational practice today.

In Europe, the sixteenth century was a time of great social, religious, and economic upheaval, partly because of the Renaissance and partly because of the Reformation. Great emphasis was placed on formal schooling to teach children how to read, the impetus for which is generally attributed to Martin Luther (1483–1546) and the Reformation he spurred.

The question of what to teach is an issue in any educational endeavor. Does society create schools and then decide what to teach, or do the needs of society determine what schools it will establish to meet desired goals? This is a question early childhood professionals wrestle with today. In the case of European education of that time, Luther emphasized the necessity of establishing schools to teach children to read. Simply stated, Luther replaced the authority of the hierarchy of the Catholic Church with the authority of the Bible. Believing that individuals were free to work out their own salvation through the Scriptures meant that people had to learn to read the Bible in their native tongue.

For links to many of Martin Luther's writings online, go to the Companion Website at **http://www.prenhall.com/morrison,** select chapter 4, then choose the Linking to Learning module to connect to the Martin Luther site.

This concept marked the real beginning of teaching and learning in people's native language, or vernacular, as opposed to Latin, the official language of the Catholic Church. Before the Reformation, only the wealthy and those preparing for a religious vocation learned to read and write Latin. Luther translated the Bible into German. Other translations followed, finally making the Bible available to people in their own language. In this way, the Protestant Reformation encouraged and supported popular universal education.

Luther also believed the family was the most important institution in the education of children. To this end, he encouraged parents to provide religious instruction and vocational education in the home. Throughout his life Luther remained a champion of education, writing letters and treatises and preaching sermons on the subject.

Out of the Reformation evolved other religious denominations, all interested in preserving the faith through education and schooling. Today, many churches, synagogues, and mosques operate child care and preK–12 programs. A growing number of parents want early childhood programs that support their religious values, beliefs, and culture. They look for and find such programs operated by religious organizations.

JOHN AMOS COMENIUS

John Amos Comenius (1592–1670) was born in Moravia, a former province of the Czech Republic, and became a Moravian minister. He spent his life serving as a bishop, teaching school, and writing textbooks. Of his many writings, those that have received the most attention are *The Great Didactic* and the **Orbis Pictus** ("The World in Pictures"), considered the first picture book for children.

Comenius believed that humans are born in the image of God. Therefore, each individual has an obligation and duty to be educated to the fullest extent of one's abilities so as to fulfill this godlike image. Since so much depends on education, then, as far as Comenius was concerned, it should begin in the early years.

> It is the nature of everything that comes into being, that while tender it is easily bent and formed, but that, when it has grown hard, it is not easy to alter. Wax, when soft, can be easily fashioned and shaped; when hard it cracks readily. A young plant can be planted, transplanted, pruned, and bent this way or that. When it has become a tree these processes are impossible.[1]

Comenius also believed that education should follow the order of nature, which implies a timetable for growth and learning. Early childhood professionals must observe this pattern to avoid forcing learning before children are ready. Comenius also thought that learning is best achieved when the senses are involved and that sensory education forms the basis for all learning.

Comenius said that the golden rule of teaching should be to place everything before the senses—for example, that children should not be taught the names of objects apart from the objects themselves or pictures of the objects. *Orbis Pictus* helped children learn the names of things and concepts, as they appeared during Comenius's time, through pictures and words. Comenius's emphasis on the concrete and the sensory is a pedagogical principle early childhood professionals still try to grasp fully and implement. Many contemporary programs stress sensory learning, and several early childhood materials promote learning through the senses.

A broad view of Comenius's total concept of education is evident by examining some of his principles of teaching:

Following in the footsteps of nature we find that the process of education will be easy

   i. If it begins early, before the mind is corrupted.
  ii. If the mind be duly prepared to receive it.
 iii. If it proceeds from the general to the particular.
 iv. And from what is easy to what is more difficult.

Orbis Pictus The first picture book for children; written by John Amos Comenius.

For more information about how John Amos Comenius contributed to the "invention of childhood," go to the Companion Website at **http://www.prenhall.com/morrison**, select chapter 4, then choose the Linking to Learning module to connect to a *Life* magazine article honoring John Amos Comenius.

v. If the pupil be not overburdened by too many subjects.

vi. And if progress be slow in every case.

vii. If the intellect be forced to nothing to which its natural bent does not incline it, in accordance with its age and with the right method.

viii. If everything be taught through the medium of the senses.

ix. And if the use of everything taught be continually kept in view.

x. If everything be taught according to one and the same method.

These, I say, are the principles to be adopted if education is to be easy and pleasant.[2]

Comenius's two most significant contributions to today's education are books with illustrations and the emphasis on sensory training found in many early childhood programs. We take the former for granted and naturally assume that the latter is a necessary basis for learning.

JOHN LOCKE

Blank tablet (white paper)
The belief that at birth the mind is blank and that experience creates the mind.

The English philosopher John Locke (1632–1704) popularized the *tabula rasa,* or **blank tablet,** view of children. More precisely, Locke developed the theory of and laid the foundation for environmentalism—the belief that the environment, not innate characteristics, determines what children will become. The extent of Locke's influence on modern early childhood education and practice is probably unappreciated by many who daily implement practices based on his theories.

Locke's assumption in regard to human learning and nature was that there are no innate ideas. This belief gave rise to his theory of the mind as a blank tablet, or "white paper." As Locke explains,

For links to important works by John Locke, go to the Companion Website at **http://www.prenhall.com/morrison,** select chapter 4, then choose the Linking to Learning module to connect to the John Locke site.

Let us suppose the mind to be, as we say, white paper void of all characters, without ideas. How comes it to be furnished? Whence comes it by that vast store which the busy and boundless fancy of man has painted on it with an almost endless variety? Whence has it all the materials of reason and knowledge? To this I answer, in one word, from experience; in that all our knowledge is founded, and from that it ultimately derives itself.[3]

For Locke, then, environment forms the mind. The implications of this belief are clearly reflected in modern educational practice. The notion of the primacy of environmental influences is particularly evident in programs that encourage and promote early education as a means of overcoming or compensating for a poor or disadvantaged environment. Based partly on the idea that all children are born with the same general capacity for mental development and learning, these programs also assume that differences in learning, achievement, and behavior are attributable to environmental factors such as home and family conditions, socioeconomic context, early education, and experiences. Programs of early schooling, especially the current move for public schooling for three- and four-year-olds, work on the premise that "disadvantaged" children fail to have the experiences of their "more advantaged" counterparts. In fact, it is not uncommon to provide public funding for early schooling for those who are considered disadvantaged and to design such programs especially for them.

Because Locke believed that experiences determine the nature of the individual, sensory training became a prominent feature in the application of his theory to education. Locke exerted considerable influence on others, particularly Maria Montessori, who developed her system of early education based on sensory training.

For more information about Jean-Jacques Rousseau, go to the Companion Website at **http://www.prenhall.com/morrison,** select chapter 4, then choose the Linking to Learning module to connect to the Jean-Jacques Rousseau site.

JEAN-JACQUES ROUSSEAU

Jean-Jacques Rousseau (1712–1778) is best remembered by educators for his book *Émile,* in which he raises a hypothetical child from birth to adolescence. Rousseau's theories were radical for his time. The opening lines of *Émile* set the tone not only for Rousseau's educational views but many of his political ideas as well: "God makes all things good; man meddles with them and they become evil."[4]

Rousseau advocated a return to nature and an approach to educating children called **naturalism.** To Rousseau, naturalism meant abandoning society's artificiality and pretentiousness. A naturalistic education permits growth without undue interference or restrictions. Rousseau would probably argue against such modern practices as dress codes, compulsory attendance, minimum basic skills, frequent and standardized testing, and ability grouping, on the grounds that they are "unnatural."

There is some tendency in American education to emphasize naturalism. For example, family grouping seeks to create a more natural family-like atmosphere in schools and classrooms, literacy programs emphasize literature from the natural environment (e.g., using menus to show children how reading is important in their everyday lives), and conflict resolution programs teach children how to get along with others.

According to Rousseau, natural education promotes and encourages qualities such as happiness, spontaneity, and the inquisitiveness associated with childhood. In his method, parents and teachers allow children to develop according to their natural abilities, do not interfere with development by forcing education, and tend not to overprotect children from the corrupting influences of society. Rousseau felt that Émile's education occurred through three sources: nature, people, and things. He elaborates:

> All that we lack at birth and need when grown up is given us by education. This education comes to us from nature, from men, or from things. The internal development of our faculties and organs is the education of nature. . . . It is not enough merely to keep children alive. They should learn to bear the blows of fortune; to meet either wealth or poverty, to live if need be in the frosts of Iceland or on the sweltering rock of Malta.[5]

Rousseau believed, however, that although parents and others have control over education that comes from social and sensory experiences, they have no control over natural growth. In essence, this is the idea of unfolding, in which the nature of children—what they are to be—unfolds as a result of maturation according to their innate timetables. We should observe the child's growth and provide experiences at appropriate times. Some educators interpret this as a laissez-faire, or "let alone," approach to parenting and education.

Educational historians point to Rousseau as dividing the historic and modern periods of education. Rousseau established a way of thinking about the young child that is reflected in innovators of educational practice such as Pestalozzi and Froebel. His concept of natural unfolding echoes Comenius's concept of naturalness and appears in current programs that stress promoting children's readiness as a factor in learning. Piaget's developmental stages also reinforce Rousseau's thinking about the importance of natural development. Educational practices that provide an environment in which children can become autonomous and self-regulating have a basis in his philosophy. The common element in all the approaches that advocate educating in a free, natural environment is the view of children as essentially good and capable of great achievement. It is the responsibility of early childhood professionals and parents to apply appropriate educational strategies at the right time, enabling all children to reach their full potential.

Émile Jean-Jacques Rousseau's famous book that outlines his ideas about how children should be reared.

Naturalism Education that follows the natural development of children; does not force the education process on them.

Rousseau maintained that a natural education encourages qualities such as happiness, spontaneity, and inquisitiveness. What should parents and teachers do to provide experiences where children can develop their natural abilities?

For more information about Johann Heinrich Pestalozzi, go to the Companion Website at **http://www. prenhall.com/morrison,** select chapter 4, then choose the Linking to Learning module to connect to the Johann Heinrich Pestalozzi site.

JOHANN HEINRICH PESTALOZZI

Johann Heinrich Pestalozzi (1746–1827) was so impressed by Rousseau's back-to-nature concepts that he purchased a farm and, in 1774, started a school called Neuhof. There Pestalozzi developed his ideas of the integration of home life, vocational education, and education for reading and writing.

Pestalozzi spent many years writing about his educational ideas and practices in such writings as *Leonard* and *Gertrude*. He became well known as a writer and educator, spending his later years developing and perfecting his ideas at various schools throughout Europe.

Rousseau's influence is most apparent in Pestalozzi's belief that education should follow the child's nature. His dedication to this concept is demonstrated by his rearing his only son, Jean-Jacques, using *Émile* as a guide. His methods were based on harmonizing nature and educational practices:

> And what is this method? It is a method which simply follows the path of Nature, or, in other words, which leads the child slowly, and by his own efforts, from sense-impressions to abstract ideas. Another advantage of this method is that it does not unduly exalt the master, inasmuch as he never appears as a superior being, but, like kindly Nature, lives and works with the children, his equals, seeming rather to learn with them than to teach them with authority.[6]

Unfortunately, Pestalozzi did not have much success rearing his son according to Rousseau's tenets, as evidenced by Jean-Jacques's inability to read and write by age twelve. This may be due to either his physical condition (he was thought to have epilepsy) or Pestalozzi's inability to translate Rousseau's abstract ideas into practice. Pestalozzi was able, however, to refine his own pedagogical ideas as a result of the process.

Probably the most important lesson from Pestalozzi's experience is that in the process of education, early childhood professionals cannot rely solely on children's own initiatives and expect them to learn all they need to know. For example, although some children do teach themselves to read, parents and others have created the climate and conditions for that beginning reading process. To expect that children will be or can be responsible for learning basic skills and appropriate social behaviors by themselves is simply asking too much.

Pestalozzi believed all education is based on sensory impressions and that through the proper sensory experiences, children can achieve their natural potential. This belief led to "object lessons." As the name implies, Pestalozzi thought the best way to learn many concepts was through manipulatives, such as counting, measuring, feeling, and touching. Pestalozzi believed the best teachers were those who taught children, not subjects. He also believed in multiage grouping. Pestalozzi anticipated by about 175 years the many family-centered programs of today that help parents teach their young children in the home. He believed mothers could best teach their children, and he wrote two books—*How Gertrude Teaches Her Children* and *Book for Mothers*—detailing procedures to do this. He felt that "the time is drawing near when methods of teaching will be so simplified that each mother will be able not only to teach her children without help, but continue her own education at the same time."[7]

For a bibliography of writings by Robert Owen, go to the Companion Website at **http://www. prenhall.com/morrison,** select chapter 4, then choose the Linking to Learning module to connect to the Robert Owen site.

ROBERT OWEN

Quite often, people who affect the course of educational thought and practice are also visionaries in political and social affairs. Robert Owen (1771–1858) was no exception. Owen's influences on education resulted from his entrepreneurial activities associated with New Lanark, Scotland, a model mill town he managed. Owen was an environmentalist; that is, he believed that the environment in which children are reared is the main factor contributing to their beliefs, behavior, and achievement. Consequently, he maintained that society and persons acting in the best interests of society can shape children's individual characters. He also was a Utopian, believing that by controlling the circumstances and consequent outcomes of child rearing, it was possible to build a new and perhaps more perfect society. Such a deterministic view of child rearing and education pushes free will to the background and makes environmental conditions the dominant force in directing and determining human behavior. As Owen explained it:

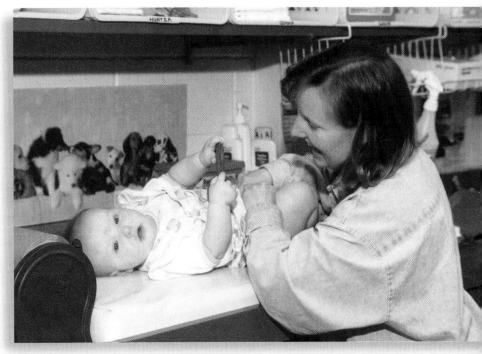

> Any character, from the best to the worst, from the most ignorant to the most enlightened may be given to any community, even to the world at large, by the application of proper means; which means are to a great extent at the command and under the control of those who have influence in the affairs of men.[8]

Owen believed that good traits were instilled at an early age and that children's behavior was influenced primarily by the environment. Thus, in Owen, we see influences of both Locke's blank tablet and Rousseau's ideas of innate goodness and naturalism.

To implement his beliefs, Owen opened an infant school in 1816 at New Lanark designed to provide care for about a hundred children ages eighteen months to ten years while their parents worked in his cotton mills. This led to the opening of the first infant school in London in 1818. Part of Owen's motivation for opening the infant schools was to get the children away from their uneducated parents. Owen opened a night school for his workers to provide them an education and transform them into "rational beings."

Although we tend to think that early education for children from low-income families began with Head Start in 1965, Owen's infant school came more than a hundred years before! Owen also had Utopian ideas regarding communal living and practice. In 1824, he purchased the village of New Harmony, Indiana, for a grand experiment in communal living. Part of the community included a center for a hundred infants. The New Harmony experiment failed, but Owen's legacy lived on in the infant schools of England. These eventually developed into kindergartens, influenced by European educators.

Several things about Owen's efforts and accomplishments are noteworthy. First, his infant school preceded Froebel's kindergarten by about a quarter of a century. Second, Owen's ideas and practices influenced educators as to the importance of early education and the relationship between education and societal improvements, an idea much in vogue in current educational practice. In addition, early childhood professionals and other professionals today, not unlike Owen, seek through education to reform society and provide a better world for all humankind.

▲
Robert Owen believed that infant schools were an ideal way to provide for the needs of young children while their families worked. What are some issues facing early childhood professionals today as they try to provide quality infant care for working parents?

For a bibliography and biography of Friedrich Wilhelm Froebel, go to the Companion Website at **http:// www. prenhall.com/ morrison,** select chapter 4, then choose the Linking to Learning module to connect to the Friedrich Wilhelm Froebel site.

FRIEDRICH WILHELM FROEBEL

Friedrich Wilhelm Froebel (1782–1852) devoted his life to developing a system for educating young children. While Pestalozzi, his contemporary with whom he studied and worked, advocated a system for teaching, Froebel developed a curriculum and educational methodology. In the process, Froebel earned the distinction "father of the kindergarten." As a result of his close relationship with Pestalozzi and his reading the works of Rousseau, Froebel decided to open a school and put his ideas into practice.

Froebel's primary contributions to educational thought and practice are in the areas of learning, curriculum, methodology, and teacher training. His concept of children and how they learn is based in part on the idea of unfolding, held by Comenius and Pestalozzi before him. The educator's role, whether parent or teacher, is to observe this natural unfolding and provide activities that will enable children to learn what they are ready to learn when they are ready to learn. The teacher's role is to help children develop their inherent qualities for learning. In this sense, the teacher is a designer of experiences and activities.

Consistent with his idea of unfolding, comparable to the process of a flower blooming from a bud, Froebel compared the child to a seed that is planted, germinates, brings forth a new shoot, and grows from a young, tender plant to a mature, fruit-producing one. He likened the role of educator to that of gardener. In his **kindergarten,** or *garden of children,* he envisioned children being educated in close harmony with their own nature and the nature of the universe. Children unfold their uniqueness in play, and it is in the area of unfolding and learning through play that Froebel makes one of his greatest contributions to the early childhood curriculum.

Kindergarten The name Friedrich Froebel gave to his system for education of children 3 through 6; means "garden of children."

> Play is the purest, most spiritual activity of man at this stage, and, at the same time, typical of human life as a whole—of the inner hidden natural life in man and all things. It gives, therefore, joy, freedom, contentment, inner and outer rest, peace with the world. It holds the sources of all that is good. A child that plays thoroughly, with self-active determination, persevering until physical fatigue forbids, will surely be a thorough, determined man, capable of self-sacrifice for the promotion of the welfare of himself and others. Is not the most beautiful expression of child-life at this time a playing child?— a child wholly absorbed in his play?— a child that has fallen asleep while so absorbed?
>
> As already indicated, play at this time is not trivial, it is highly serious and of deep significance. Cultivate and foster it, O mother; protect and guard it, O father! To the calm, keen vision of one who truly knows human nature, the spontaneous play of the child discloses the future inner life of the man.
>
> The plays of childhood are the germinal leaves of all later life; for the whole man is developed and shown in these, in his tenderest dispositions, in his innermost tendencies.[9]

Froebel knew from experience, however, that unstructured play represented a potential danger and that it was quite likely, as Pestalozzi learned with his son Jean-Jacques, that a child left to his own devices may not learn much. Without guidance, direction, and a prepared environment in which to learn, there was a real possibility that little or the wrong kind of learning would occur.

According to Froebel, the teacher is responsible for guidance and direction so children can become creative, contributing members of society. To achieve this end, Froebel developed a systematic, planned curriculum for the education of young children. Its bases were "gifts," "occupations," songs he composed, and educational games.

"Gifts" were objects for children to handle and explore with the teachers' supervision and guidance. The children form impressions about the shapes and materials relating to mathematics, design (symmetry), and their own life experiences. Froebel himself only named the first six materials as "Gifts." His followers have since included other materials that Froebel used in his own kindergarten. Currently, there are ten sets of learning materials, or "Gifts," designed to help children learn through play and manipulation. The first six **Gifts** are meant to represent solid forms, Gift 7 represents surfaces, Gift 8 represents line, Gift 9 represents the point, and Gift 10 completes the cycle with the use of point and line to represent the framework of solid forms.

Gifts Ten sets of learning materials designed to help children learn through play and manipulation.

FIGURE 4.1 **Froebel's gifts were designed for children to play with as a means of promoting learning.**
This concept of learning through play remains one of the basic principles of early childhood practice. Froebel's second gift, the cube, cylinder, and sphere, is his most well-known gift.
Source: Uncle Goose Toys. Available through www.froebelUSA.com

The objects that make up the second gift—consisting of a cube, a cylinder, and a sphere—were suspended in such a way that the children could examine their different properties by rotating, spinning, and touching. The second gift is shown in Figure 4.1. The sphere, because of its symmetry, had only one loop hole by which it was to be suspended. But the cube and cylinder had multiple loop holes, so the children could suspend the solids in different ways and examine the complexity of these seemingly simple shapes.

A significant idea behind the gifts is the importance for developing minds of examining things around them in a freely structured manner. It is not difficult to imagine a three- or four-year-old playing with the wooden solids and learning from their play.[10] Figure 4.2 identifies all the ten gifts.

In addition to his Gifts, Froebel also used **occupations,** or craft activities, such as drawing, paper weaving, folding paper, modeling with clay, and sewing. These activities were intended as extensions of the Gift play in which children could create and explore different materials. The difference between an Occupation and a Gift is that a Gift can resume its original form while an Occupation has been permanently altered.

Occupations Materials designed to engage children in learning activities.

Froebel is called the father of the kindergarten because he devoted his life to developing both a program for young children and a system of training for kindergarten teachers. Many of the concepts and activities of the gifts and occupations are similar to activities that many kindergarten and other early childhood programs provide.

Froebel's recognition of the importance of learning through play is reinforced by contemporary early childhood professionals who plan and structure their programs around play activities. Other features of Froebel's kindergarten that remain are the play circle (where children sit in a circle for learning) and songs that are sung to reinforce concepts taught with gifts and occupations. Froebel was the first educator to develop a planned, systematic program for educating young children. He also was the first to encourage young, unmarried women to become teachers, a break with tradition that caused Froebel no small amount of criticism and was one reason his methods encountered opposition. The Voice From the Field on page 91 provides more information about Froebel's kindergarten and efforts to revive his ideas.

MARIA MONTESSORI

Maria Montessori (1870–1952) devoted her life to developing a system for educating young children. Her system has influenced virtually all subsequent early childhood programs. A

FIGURE 4.2 Froebel's Gifts

First Gift:
Six colored balls of soft yarn or wool

Second Gift:
Wooden sphere, cylinder, and cube

Third Gift:
Eight cubes, presented together as a cube ($2 \times 2 \times 2$)

Fourth Gift:
Eight rectangular pieces ($1/2 \times 1 \times 2$), presented as a cube

Fifth Gift:
Twenty-one cubes, six half-cubes (triangular prisms), and twelve quarter cubes (triangular prisms)

Sixth Gift:
Twenty-four rectangular pieces, six columns ($1/2 \times 1/2 \times 2$), and twelve caps ($1 \times 1 \times 1/2$)

Seventh Gift:
Parquetry tablets derived from the surfaces of the solid Gifts including squares, equilateral triangles, right triangles, and obtuse triangles

Eighth Gift:
Straight sticks of wood, plastic, or metal in various lengths plus rings and half-rings of various diameters made from wood, plastic, or metal

Ninth Gift:
Small points in various colors made of plastic, paper, or wood

Tenth Gift:
Materials that utilize rods and connectors, similar to Tinkertoys

Source: Scott Bultman, Froebel Foundation USA, http://www.froebelfoundation.org

precocious young woman who thought of undertaking either mathematics or engineering as a career, she instead chose medicine. Despite the obstacles to entering a field traditionally closed to women, she became the first woman in Italy to earn a medical degree. Following this achievement, she was appointed assistant instructor in the psychiatric clinic of the University of Rome. At that time, it was customary not to distinguish between children with mental retardation and those who were mentally ill, and her work brought her into contact with mentally retarded children who had been committed to insane asylums. Although Montessori's first intention was to study children's diseases, she

The Froebel Kindergarten Today

The Froebel Kindergarten, more than any other method, was responsible for popularizing early childhood education throughout the world. Froebel created the morning circle, the sand table, the use of paper-folding to teach mathematics, the use of block play, the concept of the prepared environment, and the idea of play-based, child-centered education. His method proposes to educate the whole child through activities (and nature study) that support his view that humans are creative beings.

His work was extremely advanced, anticipating the development of neurology and child psychology, as well as new developments in the fields of mathematics and physics. Today, Froebel's claim that the highest period of brain development is between birth and age three does not seem as far-fetched as it did 170 years ago.

However, in the early 1900s, several factors—including anti-German sentiment and a desire to create a more factory-like approach to education—precipitated a rapid decline of the Froebel Kindergarten method. Froebel's philosophy was labeled as "romantic." His ideas continued to influence educators but much of the power and true intention of Froebel's work was lost through misuse of his materials and methods.

While Froebel wrote mostly in philosophical terms, he put his ideas into practice in his own schools. Froebel kindergarten teachers were highly trained observers of children—the world's first child development specialists. However, many popular books about the Froebel Kindergarten from that era were largely "how to" or recipe-like curriculum guides that were sometimes misunderstood.

Because of the lack of modern analysis of Froebel's work and the reliance on outdated and badly translated texts, the Froebel Foundation USA was established in 2001 as a 501(c)(3) non-profit organization. The mission of the organization is to preserve the history of the Froebel kindergarten and promote the educational philosophy of Friedrich Froebel to the world at large. The Froebel Foundation USA maintains a large library and archive of books, periodicals, and ephemera dating from the mid-1800s to the present day. The organization reprints some of this historic material and publishes new books, CD-ROMs, videos, and a quarterly newsletter, *The Kindergarten Messenger.*

The Foundation has sponsored a new Froebel school in Grand Rapids, Michigan. Beginning a true Froebel Kindergarten in 2003, the Froebel Education Center is building a new school facility on 18 acres, set to open in August 2004. The school will educate 150 children from 12 weeks to 7 years of age throughout the calendar year. This will be a model/laboratory school for the purpose of training teachers and educating parents in the methods of the Froebel Kindergarten.

There is a small but growing Froebel Kindergarten movement worldwide. South Korea, Japan, Canada, Finland, and the UK all have active Froebel centers. The Froebel Foundation USA works closely with other archives and programs around the world. For more information please visit www.froebelfoundation.org.

soon became interested in educational solutions for problems such as deafness, paralysis, and "idiocy."

At that time she said, "I differed from my colleagues in that I instinctively felt that mental deficiency was more of an educational than medical problem."[11] Montessori became interested in the work of Edouard Seguin, a pioneer in the development of an educational system for children with mental retardation, and of Jean Itard, who developed an educational system for individuals who were both deaf and mute. Montessori credits Itard and

For more information
about how Maria
Montessori's ideas
apply to certain age
groups, go to the
Companion Website at **http://
www.prenhall.com/morrison**,
select chapter 4, then choose the
Linking to Learning module to
connect to the Maria Montessori
School and Teacher Training
Center site.

**Children's House (Casa dei
Bambini)** Montessori's first
school especially designed to
implement her ideas.

Seguin with inspiring her to continue her studies with children who were mentally retarded. She wrote of her initial efforts at educating children:

> I succeeded in teaching a number of the idiots from the asylums both to read and
> to write so well that I was able to present them at a public school for an examina-
> tion together with normal children. And they passed the examination successfully.[12]

This was a remarkable achievement, which aroused interest in both Montessori and her
methods. Montessori, however, was already considering something else:

> While everyone else was admiring the progress made by my defective charges, I was
> trying to discover the reasons which could have reduced the healthy, happy pupils
> of the ordinary schools to such a low state that in the intelligence test they were on
> the level with my own unfortunate pupils.[13]

While continuing to study and prepare herself for the task of educating children,
Montessori came upon the opportunity quite by chance to perfect her methods and implement them with nondisabled school-age children. In 1906 she was invited by the director
general of the Roman Association for Good Building to organize schools for young children
of families who occupied the tenement houses constructed by the association. In the first
school, named the Casa dei Bambini, or **Children's House**, she tested her ideas and gained
insights into children and teaching that led to the perfection of her system.

Montessori was profoundly religious, and a religious undertone is reflected throughout
her work. She often quoted from the Bible to support her points. For example, at the dedication ceremonies of the first Children's House, she read from Isaiah 60:1–5 and ended by
saying, "Perhaps, this Children's House can become a new Jerusalem, which, if it is spread
out among the abandoned people of the world, can bring a new light to education."[14] Her
religious dedication to the fundamental sacredness and uniqueness of every child and subsequent grounding of educational processes in a religious conviction undoubtedly account
for some of her remarkable achievements as a person and educator. Thus, her system functions well for those who are willing to dedicate themselves to teaching as if it were a religious vocation. We discuss Montessori's system in detail in chapter 6.

JOHN DEWEY

John Dewey (1859–1952) represents a truly American influence on U.S. education. Through
his positions as professor of philosophy at the University of Chicago and Columbia University, his extensive writing, and the educational practices of his many followers, Dewey did
more than any other person to redirect the course of education in the United States.

Dewey's theory of schooling, usually called **progressivism**, emphasizes children and
their interests rather than subject matter. From this child-centered emphasis comes the
terms *child-centered curriculum* and *child-centered school*. The progressive education philosophy also maintains that schools should be concerned with preparing children for the realities of today rather than some vague future time. As expressed by Dewey in *My
Pedagogical Creed*, "Education, therefore, is a process of living and not a preparation for future living."[15] Thus, out of daily life should come the activities in which children learn
about life and the skills necessary for living.

What is included in Dewey's concept of children's interests? "Not some one thing," he
explained, "it is a name for the fact that a course of action, an occupation, or pursuit absorbs
the powers of an individual in a thorough-going way."[16] In a classroom based on Dewey's
ideas, children are involved with physical activities, utilization of things, intellectual pur-
suits, and social interaction. Physical activities include running, jumping, and being actively
involved with materials. In this phase the child begins the process of education and develops other interest areas that form the basis for doing and learning. The growing child learns

Progressivisim Dewey's
theory of education that emphasizes the importance of focusing
on the needs and interests of
children rather than teachers.

For more information
about John Dewey, go
to the Companion
Website at **http://
www.prenhall.com/
morrison**, select chapter 4,
then choose the Linking to
Learning module to connect to
the Center for Dewey Studies
site.

to use tools and materials to construct things. Dewey felt that an ideal expression for this interest was daily living activities, or occupations such as cooking and carpentry.

To promote an interest in the intellectual—solving problems, discovering new things, and figuring out how things work—children are given opportunities for inquiry and discovery. Dewey also believed that social interest, referring to interactions with people, was encouraged in a democratically run classroom.

Although Dewey believed the curriculum should be built on the interests of children, he also felt it was the teacher's responsibility to plan for and capitalize on opportunities to integrate or weave traditional subject matter through and around the fabric of these interests. Dewey describes a school based on his ideas:

> All of the schools . . . as compared with traditional schools [exhibit] a common emphasis upon respect for individuality and for increased freedom; a common disposition to build upon the nature and experience of the boys and girls that come to them, instead of imposing from without external subject-matter standards. They all display a certain atmosphere of informality, because experience has proved that formalization is hostile to genuine mental activity and to sincere emotional expression and growth. Emphasis upon activity as distinct from passivity is one of the common factors.[17]

Teachers who integrate subjects, use thematic units, and encourage problem-solving activities and critical thinking are philosophically indebted to Dewey.

There has been much misinterpretation and criticism of the progressive movement and of Dewey's ideas, especially by those who favor a traditional approach that emphasizes the basic subjects and skills. Actually, Dewey was not opposed to teaching basic skills or topics. He did believe, however, that traditional educational strategies imposed knowledge on children, whereas their interests should be a springboard for involvement with skills and subject matter.

JEAN PIAGET

Jean Piaget (1896–1980) studied in Paris, where he worked with Theodore Simon at the Alfred Binet laboratory, standardizing tests of reasoning for use with children. (Binet and Simon developed a scale for measuring intelligence.) This experience provided the foundation for Piaget's clinical method of interviewing, used in studying children's intellectual development. As Piaget recalls, "Thus I engaged my subjects in conversations patterned after psychiatric questioning, with the aim of discovering something about the reasoning process underlying their right, but especially their wrong, answers."[18] The emphasis on this method helps explain why some developers of a Piaget-based early childhood curriculum encourage the teacher's use of questioning procedures to promote thinking.

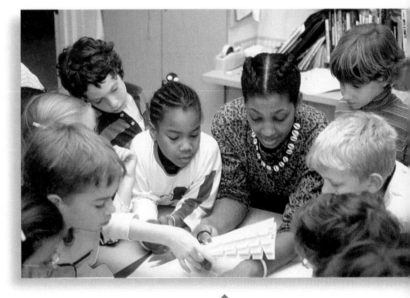

Piaget concluded that children's thinking is not "wrong" but qualitatively different from adult thought. Can you give two examples of how children's thinking is different from adult thinking?

Following his work with children in Paris, which established the direction of his life work, Piaget became associated with the Institute J. J. Rousseau in Geneva and began studying intellectual development. Piaget's own three children played a major role in his studies, and many of his consequent insights about children's intellectual development are based on his observations and work with them. Using his own children in his studies caused some to criticize his findings. His theory, however, is based on not only his research

The City and Country School Today

The City & Country School, founded by Caroline Pratt in 1914, is an example of a progressive school that continues to educate children using the curriculum structure that was set forth over eighty years ago: "giving children experiences and materials that will fit their stage of development and have inherent in them unlimited opportunities for learning." Pratt, a teacher, sought to provide a school environment that suited the way children learn best—by doing.

BASIC, OPEN-ENDED MATERIALS

The younger groups (ages two through seven) use basic, open-ended materials to reconstruct what they are learning about the world and organize their information and thinking in meaningful ways. Materials such as blocks, clay, water, paint, and wood are chosen because of their simplicity, flexibility, and the challenging possibilities that they offer. The blocks, developed by Pratt, are the mainspring of the curriculum today as they were in the early days of the school. It is City & Country School's belief that an early childhood curriculum based on open-ended materials fosters independence, motivation, and interest, all essential components of learning.

THE JOBS PROGRAM

The Lower School curriculum provides a firm foundation for the more formal academic skills that children must master in later years. The Jobs Program was developed to play the central role in groups aged eight through thirteen. Each group has a specific job to perform related to the school's functioning as an integrated community. These jobs provide both a natural impetus for perfecting skills in reading, writing, spelling, and mathematics and a relevant framework for the exploration of social studies and the arts.

Beyond their work with blocks and jobs, children at City & Country are given opportunities to experience art, music, dramatics, foreign languages, science, computer, and woodworking, often integrated with their classroom work.

Located in the Greenwich Village district of New York City on 13th Street, the school currently has an enrollment of 250 students between the ages of two and thirteen. It continues to exemplify child-centered education.

Contributed by Kate Turley, principal of the City & Country School.

To complete a Program in Action activity, visit the Companion Website at **http://www.prenhall.com/ morrison**, select chapter 4, then choose the Program in Action module.

For more information about Jean Piaget, go to the Companion Website at **http:// www.prenhall.com/ morrison**, select chapter 4, then choose the Linking to Learning module to connect to the Jean Piaget Society site.

but also literally hundreds of other studies involving thousands of children. Piaget came to these conclusions about early childhood education:

- Children play an active role in their own cognitive development.
- Mental and physical activity are important for children's cognitive development.
- Experiences constitute the raw materials children use to develop mental structures.
- Children develop cognitively through interaction with and adaptation to the environment.
- Development is a continuous process.
- Development results from maturation and the transactions or interactions between children and the physical and social environments.

Piaget also popularized the age–stage approach to cognitive development and influenced others to apply the theory to other processes such as moral, language, and social development. He encouraged and inspired many psychologists and educators to develop

DIVERSITY TIE-IN

Then and Now:
The Evolution of American Indian Education

Then: The Carlisle (PA) Indian School, 1879

The Carlisle Indian School was founded in 1879 with the intention of assimilating American Indian children into the white, Protestant culture.

- A U.S. Army officer ran the school.
- Children were not allowed to speak in their native tongue.
- Children learned trades in the mornings and academics in the afternoon.
- Boys wore uniforms, while girls wore Victorian-style dresses; moccasins were not allowed.

Now: Current BIA Operated Schools

The Bureau of Indian Affair's (BIA) education mission is to "provide quality education for lifelong learning." Schools are empowered under a policy of Indian self-determination.

- Tribes operate the majority of programs.
- Schools attempt to preserve the native language.
- Schools' curricula focus on literacy and math.
- Knowledge of native culture is encouraged.

- How has the federal government's philosophy of American Indian education changed over time?
- What are the symbolic implications of the Carlisle Indian School's dress policies?
- Do the dress and appearance policies of schools that you are familiar with respect diverse cultures? Which school dress codes might conflict with cultural practices?
- American Indians have a rich story-telling heritage. How can this be incorporated into to-

day's classroom to promote the BIA's goal of literacy?
- Why is learning a tribal language important for American Indians?

Sources: Landis, B. Carlisle Indian Industrial School History [Online]. Available at *http://home.epix.net/~landis/histry.html*

Bureau of Indian Affairs, Office of Indian Education Programs [Online]. Available at *http://www.oiep.bia.edu/*.

educational curricula and programs utilizing his ideas and promoted interest in the study of young children's cognitive development that has in turn contributed to the interest in infant development and education. We discuss Piagetian education in detail in chapter 5.

In America, in 1879, the Carlisle (PA) Indian School was established. The Diversity Tie-In compares attitudes toward American Indian education then and now.

LEV VYGOTSKY

Lev Vygotsky (1896–1934), a contemporary of Piaget, increasingly inspires the practices of early childhood professionals. Vygotsky's sociocultural theory of development is particularly useful in describing children's mental, language, and social development. His theory also has many implications for how children's play promotes language and social development. We discuss his theory and application to teaching and learning in chapter 5.

To complete an activity related to the above topic, go to the Companion Website at **http://www.prenhall.com/morrison**, select chapter 4, then choose the Diversity Tie-In module.

For a bibliography of additional readings about Lev Vygotsky, go to the Companion Website at **http://www.prenhall.com/morrison**, select chapter 4, then choose the Linking to Learning module to connect to the Lev Vygotsky site.

For more information about Abraham Maslow's concept of self-actualization, go to the Companion Website at **http://www. prenhall.com/morrison**, select chapter 4, then choose the Linking to Learning module to connect to the Abraham Maslow site.

According to Gardner's theory of multiple intelligences, children demonstrate many types of intelligences. How would you apply his theory in the early childhood environment?

▼

ABRAHAM MASLOW

Abraham Maslow (1890–1970) developed a theory of motivation based on the satisfaction of needs. Maslow identified self-actualization, or self-fulfillment, as the highest need, but maintained that self-actualization cannot be achieved until certain basic needs are met. These basic needs include life essentials, such as food, safety, and security; belongingness and love; achievement and prestige; and aesthetic needs. We discuss Maslow's *hierarchy of needs* in greater detail in chapter 5, and show how meeting basic needs in appropriate ways is essential for development.

ERIK ERIKSON

Erik H. Erikson (1902–1994) developed an influential theory of *psychosocial development*. Cognitive development occurs hand in hand with social development; you cannot separate the two. This is why Erikson's theory is so important. According to Erikson, children's personalities and social skills grow and develop within the context of society and in response to society's demands, expectations, values, and social institutions, such as families, schools, and other child care programs. As part of his education, Erikson studied Freudian theory with Anna Freud, Sigmund's daughter, and participated in Montessori teacher training. For Erikson, psychosocial development is largely the successful identity with parents, family, and society. Adults, especially parents and teachers, are principal components of these environments and therefore play a powerful role in helping or hindering children in their personality and cognitive development. For example, school-age children must deal with demands to learn new skills or risk a sense of incompetence—a crisis of "industry versus inferiority." We discuss Erikson's theory in more detail in chapter 5 and relate his psychosocial theory to care and education.

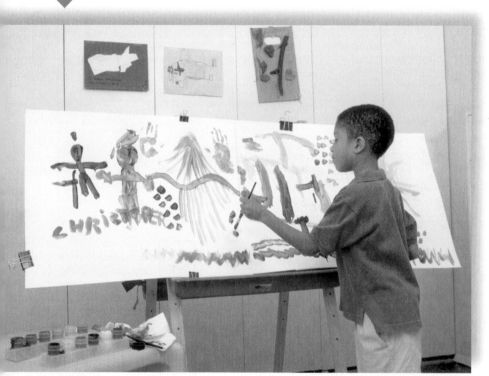

HOWARD GARDNER

Howard Gardner (b. 1943) is well known in educational circles for his theory of multiple intelligences, which maintains that instead of a single intelligence, there are actually nine. I discuss these nine in chapter 5. Gardner and his colleagues at Harvard's Project Zero (http://www.pz.harvard.edu) have been working on the design of performance-based assessments, education for understanding, and the use of multiple intelligences to achieve more personalized curriculum, instruction, and assessment.

For more information about Howard Gardner's ideas, go to the Companion Website at **http://www. prenhall.com/morrison**, select any chapter, then choose Topic 3 of the ECE Supersite module.

E. D. HIRSCH

E. D. Hirsch Jr. (b. 1928), professor of English at the University of Virginia, is the contemporary articulator and proponent of an *essentialist curriculum*. Hirsch outlined his essentialist position in his manifesto, *Cultural Literacy: What Every American Needs to Know.* Cultural literacy, according to Hirsch, consists of those things that constitute the "common core" of a literate citizenry and that form the basis of American civilization. In other words, everyone should be culturally literate. Others who support cultural literacy include William Bennett, former U.S. Secretary of Education and author of the popular *Book of Virtues.*

Hirsch believes the lack of a cultural literacy curriculum contributes to children's general failure and poor school performance. He maintains, for example, that one reason children don't read with comprehension and understanding is because they have a limited cultural background—what Hirsch calls "cultural currency"— necessary to understand what they read. Hirsch argues, for example, that if a second-grader never heard of Alice, as in *Alice's Adventures in Wonderland,* how can we expect the student to comprehend elements of a story that refer to Alice? Hirsch proposes that one solution is to teach students, beginning in kindergarten (indeed, even before, in the home), the names, dates, and events that constitute the core, the foundation of "our national cultural heritage."

You can consult E. D. Hirsch's *Dictionary of Cultural Literacy: What Every American Needs to Know* for an A–Z description of what this essentialist thinks is important. Additionally, review Hirsch's *First Dictionary of Cultural Knowledge: What Our Children Need to Know.* This revised second edition offers the common core of knowledge children should have by the end of grade school.

Hirsch has established the Core Knowledge Foundation as a means of promoting a core essentialist curriculum. Many school districts and individual schools are teaching a core knowledge curriculum based on Hirsch's ideas. Although Hirsch's revised benchmarks of cultural literacy include new books and topics that have a more multicultural perspective, he and his followers are criticized for Eurocentric views in which American cultural diversity is not acknowledged.

For essentialists, the teacher's role includes the following:

- *Imparting knowledge.* Although it is a teacher's role to impart knowledge, it is the students' job to learn—whether or not they feel like it or like what they are learning.
- *Initiating and promoting learning.* In other words, the classroom is teacher directed, not student centered. The teacher is responsible for motivating students to learn and for maintaining the appropriate discipline for learning. Emphasis is placed on having students learn the basics they need for success in life.
- *Engaging in teacher-directed activities characterized by discipline and teacher authority.*

Figure 4.3 shows a Core Knowledge® curriculum sequence for the preschool. The Program in Action on page 99 describes the first Core Knowledge School.

FROM LUTHER TO THE PRESENT: BASIC CONCEPTS ESSENTIAL TO GOOD EDUCATIONAL PRACTICES

It is possible for us to identify basic ideas and practices developed over the years that are essential for professionals to practice as they work with children and families. As you read the following basic concepts, consider how you can apply them to your teaching.

AS THEY RELATE TO CHILDREN

- Everyone needs to learn how to read and write.
- Children learn best when they use all their senses.
- All children are capable of being educated.
- All children should be educated to the fullest extent of their abilities.

For more information about how young children learn, go to the Companion Website at **http://www. prenhall.com/morrison**, select any chapter, then choose Topic 3 of the ECE Supersite module.

FIGURE 4.3 **Core Knowledge® Preschool Sequence at a Glance**

MOVEMENT AND COORDINATION

I.   Physical Attention and Relaxation
II. Gross Motor Skills
III. Eye-Hand and Eye-Foot Coordination
IV. Group Games
V.   Creative Movement and Expression

AUTONOMY AND SOCIAL SKILLS

I.   Sense of Self and Personal Responsibility
II. Working in a Group Setting

WORK HABITS

I.   Memory Skills
II. Following Directions
III. Task Persistence and Completion

LANGUAGE

I.   Oral Language
II. Nursery Rhymes, Poems, Fingerplays and Songs
III. Storybook Reading and Storytelling
IV. Emerging Literacy Skills

MATHEMATICS

I.   Patterns and Classification
II. Geometry
III. Measurement
IV   Numbers and Number Sense
V.   Addition and Subtraction with Concrete Objects
VI. Money

ORIENTATION IN TIME AND SPACE

I.   Vocabulary
II. Measures of Time: Time
III. Passage of Time (Past, Present, and Future)

MEASURES OF TIME AND SPACE

I.   Vocabulary
II. Actual Represented Space
III. Simple Maps
IV. Basic Geographical Concepts

SCIENCE

I.   Human Characteristics, Needs, and Development
II. Animal Characteristics, Needs, and Development
III. Plant Characteristics, Needs, and Development
IV. Physical Elements (Water, Air, Light)
V.   Tools

MUSIC

I.   Attention to Differences in Sound
II. Imitate and Produce Sounds
III. Listen and Sing
IV. Listen and Move

VISUAL ARTS

I.   Attention to Visual Detail
II. Creating Art (Printing, Painting, Drawing, Collage, Sculpture)
III. Looking At and Talking About Art

This Core Knowledge® curriculum sequence is an example of essentialist beliefs applied to the preschool. Do you support an essential approach to educating young children? Is this sequence of "core knowledge" one that you would use in your preschool?

Source: Core Knowledge® [Online]. Core Knowledge® Preschool: *Preschool Sequence* At a Glance. Available at http://www.coreknowledge.org/CKproto2/Preschool/PreKGlance.htm.

- Education should begin early in life. Today, especially, there is an increased emphasis on beginning education at birth.
- Children should not be forced to learn but should be appropriately taught what they are ready to learn and should be prepared for the next stage of learning.
- Learning activities should be interesting and meaningful.
- Social interactions with teachers and peers are a necessary part of development.
- All children have many ways of knowing, learning, and relating to the world.

AS THEY RELATE TO TEACHERS

- Teachers must show love and respect for all children.
- Teachers should be dedicated to the teaching profession.

A Core Knowledge School

Three Oaks Elementary School, located in Fort Myers, Florida, is proud to be the Nation's First Core Knowledge School. Our mission is to provide a fair and excellent education for all students. Dr. E. D. Hirsch's basic premise that "knowledge builds on knowledge" and that "all youngsters must have access to a body of critical content which provides a firm foundation for later learning" has resulted in a program of studies for our students that is exciting, hands-on, and very rewarding!

Core Knowledge is a solid, specific, and shared curriculum, which helps children to establish strong foundations of knowledge grade by grade. The Core Knowledge sequences are a detailed outline of specific content in Language Arts, Mathematics, Science, History, Geography, and the Fine Arts. This, combined with skills instruction, gives all of our students the opportunity to experience success. It also arouses in them a love of knowledge and a strong desire to learn even more. The sequenced curriculum also serves to eliminate gaps and repetitions of study that students often encounter in school.

Students at Three Oaks learn from teams of teachers who plan units of study around the Core Knowledge® topics. Teachers at every grade level are knowledgeable of the complete sequence and are aware of the topics taught at each grade level. When students arrive in music, art, physical education, the library, or the computer lab they quickly discover that all of their teachers know what they are learning about in class and see these themes continued in the special areas. This builds a school community with strong bonds and feelings of belonging for students and staff, and contributes to a high level of achievement for all.

Contributed by Luanne Sutton, Curriculum/Technology Specialist, Three Oaks Elementary, Fort Meyers, Florida.

- Good teaching is based on a theory, a philosophy, goals, and objectives.
- Children's learning is enhanced through the use of concrete materials.
- Teaching should move from the concrete to the abstract.
- Observation is a key means for determining children's needs.
- Teaching should be a planned, systematic process.
- Teaching should be child centered rather than adult or subject centered.
- Teaching should be based on children's interests.
- Teachers should collaborate with children as a means of promoting development.
- Teachers should plan so they incorporate all types of intelligence in their planning and activities.

AS THEY RELATE TO PARENTS

- The family is an important institution in children's education and development. The family lays the foundation for all future education and learning.
- Parents are their children's primary educators. However, parents need help, education, and support to achieve this goal.
- Parents must guide and direct young children's learning.
- Parents should be involved in any educational program designed for their children.
- Everyone should have knowledge of and training for child rearing.
- Parents and other family members are collaborators in children's learning.
- Parents must encourage and support their children's many interests and their unique ways of learning.

To complete a Program in Action activity, visit the Companion Website at **http://www. prenhall.com/morrison**, select chapter 4, then choose the Program in Action module.

VIEWS OF CHILDREN THROUGH THE AGES

How you and others view children determines how you and they teach and rear them and how society responds to their needs. As you read here about how people and society view children, try to clarify and change, when appropriate, what you believe. Also, identify social, environmental, and political factors that tend to support each particular view. Sometimes, of course, views overlap, so it is possible to synthesize ideas from several perspectives into a particular personal view of children.

MINIATURE ADULTS

Miniature adults Belief that children are similar to adults and should be treated as such.

Childhood has not always been considered a distinct period of life. During medieval times, the notion of childhood did not exist; little distinction was made between children and adults. The concept of children as **miniature adults** was logical for the time and conditions of medieval Europe. Economic conditions did not allow for a long childhood dependency. The only characteristics that separated children from adults were size and age. Children were expected to act as adults in every way, and they did so.

In many respects, today is no different. Children are still viewed and treated as adults. Concern is growing that childhood as we knew or remember it is disappearing. Children are viewed as pseudoadults; they even dress like adults, in designer clothes and expensive footwear designed especially for them. Some believe that childhood is not only endangered but already gone. Others fear that, even when allowed a childhood, children are forced to grow up too fast, too soon.

Reasons for society increasingly viewing children as adults are many and varied. Some contend that with more parents in the workforce, home and family life are more work centered than child centered. Children are given more responsibility at younger ages for their care, the care of siblings, and for household work. Also, children are being introduced to the adult world at earlier ages. Children attend R-rated movies, view adult programs on television, and encounter media violence at earlier ages. In many instances the boundaries between childhood and adulthood are blurred, if not altogether eliminated.

Childhood and children are endangered in another way. In many countries of Latin America, Africa, and Asia, children are, of necessity, expected to be economically productive. They are members of the adult working world at age four, five, or six. The United Nations Educational, Scientific, and Cultural Organization (UNESCO) estimates that 250 million children around the world work and live in city streets. In many countries children are involved in war as active participants and casualties. In the United States, as in many urban areas, children participate in gang-related and other activities as though they were adults. Almost daily, newspapers show these children dead or wounded and waiting for help.

In the United States, where child labor laws protect children from the world of adult work and exploitation, some people advocate allowing children to enter the workplace at earlier ages and for lower wages. In some rural settings, young children still have economic value. Approximately one million migrant children annually pick crops and help their parents earn a livelihood. At the other end of the spectrum, child actors and models engage in highly profitable, and what some call glamorous, careers.

Encouraging children to act like adults and hurrying them toward adulthood causes conflicts between capabilities and expectations, particularly when early childhood professionals demand adultlike behavior from children and set unrealistic expectations. Problems associated with learning, behavior, and social skills can occur when children are constantly presented with tasks and activities that are developmentally inappropriate for them.

Child as sinful View that children are basically sinful and need supervision and control, and they should be taught to be obedient.

THE CHILD AS SINFUL

Based primarily on the religious belief in original sin, the view of the **child as sinful** was widely accepted in the fourteenth through eighteenth centuries, particularly in colonial

North America during the Puritan era of the sixteenth and seventeenth centuries. Misbehavior was a sign of this inherent sin. Those who sought to correct misbehavior emphasized forcing children to behave and using corporal punishment whenever "necessary." Misbehavior was taken as proof of the devil's influence, and "beating the devil out" of the child was an acceptable solution.

This view of inherent sinfulness persists, manifested in the belief that children need to be controlled through rigid supervision and insistence on unquestioning obedience to and respect for adults. Educational institutions are perceived as places where children can be taught "right" behavior. The number of private and parochial or religious schools that emphasize respect, obedience, and correct behavior is growing because of parents' hopes of rearing children who are less susceptible to the temptations of crime, drugs, and declining moral values. Also, many Christian religious conservatives advocate a "biblical" approach to child rearing, encouraging parents to raise their children to obey them. Disobedience is viewed as sinful, and obedience is promoted, in part through strict discipline. With the emphasis on conservative child rearing many parents are turning to biblically based approaches to child rearing.

BLANK TABLETS

Earlier we discussed that John Locke believed that children were born into the world as *tabula rasae,* or blank tablets. After extensive observations, Locke concluded, "There is not the least appearance of any settled ideas at all in them; especially of ideas answering the terms which make up those universal propositions that are esteemed innate principles."[19] He believed that children's experiences, through sensory impressions, determined what they learned and, consequently, what they became. The blank tablet view presupposes no innate genetic code or inborn traits; that is, children are born with no predisposition toward any behavior except what is characteristic of human beings. The sum of what a child becomes depends on the nature and quality of experience; in other words, environment is the primary determinant.

The blank tablet view has several implications for teaching and child rearing. If children are seen as empty vessels to be filled, the teacher's job is to fill them—to present knowledge without regard to needs, interests, or readiness for learning. What is important is that children learn what is taught. Children become what adults make of them.

This view de-emphasizes individual differences and assumes that as children are exposed to the same environmental influences, they will tend to behave and even think the same. This concept is the basis for many educational beliefs and practices in socialist countries. Children begin schooling early, often at six weeks of age, and are taught a standard curriculum that promotes a common political consciousness. They are expected to behave in ways that are consistent with and appropriate to how a citizen of the state should behave.

GROWING PLANTS

A perennially popular view of children, that dates back to Froebel, likens them to **growing plants,** with teachers and parents acting as gardeners. Classrooms and homes are greenhouses in which children grow and mature in harmony with their natural growth patterns. A consequence of growth and maturing is that children unfold, much as a flower blooms under the proper conditions. In other words, what children become results from natural growth and a nurturing environment. Two key ingredients of this natural unfolding are play and readiness. The content and process of learning are included in play, and materials and activities are designed to promote play.

Children become ready for learning through motivation and play. This concept prompts teaching subjects and skills when children reach the point at which they can benefit from appropriate instruction. Lack of readiness to learn indicates that the child has not sufficiently matured; the natural process of unfolding has not occurred.

Growing plants View of children popularized by Froebel that equates children to plants and teachers and parents to gardeners.

VOICE FROM THE FIELD

The Kingdom of Amos K. Hutchinson Elementary School

Once upon a time, in the kingdom of Amos K. Hutchinson Elementary School there lived two teachers—Mrs. Sheffler and Mrs. Pehrson.

Now, these two teachers were master gardeners, and their students were their garden. In the hearts of their students they tenderly and lovingly planted their seeds. They planted seeds in the garden to help their students become better readers. They planted seeds in the garden to help their students become better mathematicians. They planted seeds in the garden to help their students become more knowledgeable in health, social studies, and science. They planted seeds in the garden to help their students maintain good work habits and social skills.

But they wanted their garden to produce more than academic blooms. They wanted their garden to be special and unique. And so they planted in their garden seeds that would teach their students to make good choices and be good friends. They planted seeds in their garden that would teach their students to obey their parents, their teachers, and those in authority. They planted seeds in their garden that would teach their students to be good citizens and show patriotism toward their country. They planted seeds in their garden that would teach their stu-

dents to show respect for people, animals, and the environment. They planted seeds in their garden that would teach their students to speak and act in kindness. They planted seeds in their garden that would teach their students to follow the Golden Rule. They planted seeds in their garden that would produce community service volunteers.

At times, their garden struggled through periods of drought, and the teachers carefully watered their tender sprouts. They staked their sprouts so that they would grow straight and reach for the light. They weeded, hoed, and fertilized the soil, and they celebrated at the sight of continuous growth.

Their gardens produced a harvest that was more bountiful than the teachers could ever imagine! The fruits of their labor had brought them many, many, blessings and they were pleased; for they realized that when a garden grows, something beautiful happens each and every day.

And all was well in their kingdom.

Contributed by Christa Pehrson and Vicki Sheffler, Amos K. Hutchinson Elementary School, Greensburg, Pennsylvania, 2002 *USA Today's* First Team Teachers.

Belief in this concept is evident in certain social and educational policies, such as proposals to raise the age requirements for entry into kindergarten and first grade so that children have more time to mature and get ready for school. Many people also believe each child's maturation occurs in accordance with an innate timetable, that there is a "best time" for learning specific tasks. They feel it is important to allow time for children's inner tendencies to develop, and that teachers and parents should not "force" learning. This maturation process is as important as, if not more important than, children's experiences. Many contemporary programs operate on the unfolding concept, whether or not it is explicitly stated.

Evidence for the widespread view of children as growing plants is poignantly illustrated by Christa Pehrson and Vicki Sheffler, two of *USA Today's* All USA First Team Teachers. Their Voice from the Field sincerely conveys the powerful metaphor of teacher as gardener and children as growing plants.

PROPERTY

The view that children are **property** has persisted throughout history. Its foundation is that children are the property of their parents or institutions. This view is justified in part by the idea that, as creators of children, parents have a right to them and their labors. Children are, in a real sense, the property of their parents. Parents have broad authority and jurisdiction over their children. Interestingly, few laws interfere with the right of parents to control their children's lives, although this situation is changing somewhat as children are given more rights and the rights they have are protected.

Property Belief that children are literally the property of their parents.

Laws (although difficult to enforce) protect children from physical and emotional abuse. Where there are compulsory attendance laws, parents must send their children to school. Generally, however, parents have a free hand in dealing with their children. Legislatures and courts are reluctant to interfere in what is considered a sacrosanct parent–child relationship. A recent and widely publicized Supreme Court decision, *Troxel v. Granville,* reaffirmed this right and declared that parents have a "fundamental right to make decisions concerning the care, custody, and control" of their children.[20] Parents are generally free to exercise full authority over their children. Within certain broad limits, most parents feel their children are theirs to do with as they please. Parents who embrace this view see themselves as their children's decision makers and may place their own best interests above those of their children.

INVESTMENTS IN THE FUTURE

Closely associated with the notion of children as property is the view that children represent future wealth or potential for parents and a nation. Since medieval times, people have viewed child rearing as an investment in the future. Many parents assume (not always consciously) that, when they are no longer able to work or must retire, their children will provide for them. Consequently, having children becomes a means to an end. Seeing that children are clothed and fed ensures their future economic contribution to their parents.

This view of **children as investments,** particularly in their parents' future, is being dramatically played out in contemporary society. More middle-age adults are becoming "parents" to their own aging and ill parents. This group, known as the *sandwich generation,* also is taking care of their grandchildren, because their own children have surrendered responsibility for child rearing as a result of divorce, death, abandonment, or other circumstances. (see chapter 17). Many of these middle-age parents who thought they were investing in their future through their children might not have any investment at all.

Children as investments View that investing in the care and education of children reaps future benefits for parents and society.

Over the last several decades, some U.S. social policies have been based on the view that children are future investments for society in general. Many programs are built on the underlying assumption that preventing problems in childhood leads to more productive adulthood. An extension of this attitude is that preventing a problem is less expensive than curing one. Some local educational programs thus emphasize identifying the problems of children and their families early, to take preventive rather than remedial action. As professionals, we also know that besides being more expensive, remediation is not as effective as prevention.

Particularly during the 1960s, many federal programs were based on the idea of conserving one of the country's greatest resources—its children. Head Start, Follow Through, and child welfare programs are products of this view, which has resulted in a "human capital," or "investment," rationale for child care and other services.

The public believes a primary goal of education is to develop children who will be productive and will help protect the nation against foreign competition. Therefore, the early education of young children in "good" programs is seen as one way to strengthen the United States economically. Thus, the country's best defense against outside economic forces is a well-educated, economically productive population. From this perspective, then, investing in children is seen as an investment in the country. Also, the view that children are our greatest wealth implies that we cannot and should not waste this potential.

Some believe, however, that this perspective of children as an investment in the future fails to consider children's intrinsic human worth. Trying to make a nation stronger through its children tends to emphasize national priorities over individuals. Also, solving a nation's problems is not and should not be viewed primarily as a "children's" problem.

CHILDREN AS PERSONS WITH RIGHTS

Persons with rights   View that children have certain basic rights of their own.

A contemporary legal and humanistic view recognizes children as **persons with rights** of their own. While children are often still treated as economic commodities and individuals who need protection, their rights are beginning to be defined, promoted, and defended. Since children are not organized into political groups, others must act as their advocates. Courts and social service agencies are becoming particular defenders.

The U.N. Convention on the Rights of the Child, a human rights treaty, went into effect on September 2, 1990, after ratification by more than twenty nations. It has the status of a legally binding treaty for all nations that sign it. The United States did not sign the treaty.

The convention contains fifty-four articles, and the highlights are printed in Figure 4.4. The articles convey a very strong view of the child as a family member and individual. You will note that the convention combines political, civil, economic, and cultural rights. In this sense, the convention acknowledges that health and economic well-being are also essential to political freedoms and rights. In addition, by extending rights to individual children, the convention challenges the view of children as property.

Although children of the world are gaining more rights, societal attitudes toward children's rights are often still ambivalent. Some children's rights supporters believe children need advocates to act on their behalf. They maintain that children are politically disenfranchised, economically disadvantaged, the personal property of their parents, vulnerable to abuse and exploitation because of their lack of experience, and have passive legal status. On the other hand, many people, including some parents, feel they should be allowed to raise their children as they think best, free of interference from children's rights advocates.

Rights are being extended to children in ways that would not have been thought possible even ten years ago. Particularly in the area of fetal rights, parents are encountering conflicts between their rights and the lives of their unborn children. Many states require places that sell liquor to post a sign reading, "Warning: Drinking alcoholic beverages during pregnancy can cause birth defects." Major controversies are arising between the right of the unborn and the rights of pregnant women. Such questions as "What rights of the pregnant woman supersede those of her unborn child?" and "Does the government or other agency have the right to intervene in a woman's life on behalf of her unborn child?" are not easy to answer.

The debate regarding children's rights will continue as the rights of children become further defined and clarified through the judicial system. The rights of all children will be examined, and more special interest groups will join the trend to gain even more rights for children.

A review of the ways we see children leads to some intriguing questions. In this generation, are parents and professionals as child centered as they should be? Are early childhood professionals interested in helping children receive the best so they can realize their best? What we know we should do and what we do are often two different things. Public and social policies often supersede our interest in children. Wars, national defense, and economics sometimes take precedence over questions of what is best for children.

To take an online self-test on this chapter's contents, go to the Companion Website at **http://www. prenhall.com/morrison,** select chapter 4, then choose the Self-Test module.

CHILD-CENTERED EDUCATION

As early childhood professionals and the public increasingly view children as persons with rights, educators are implementing more child-centered approaches. Our discussion of the rights of children fits in nicely with the topic of child-centered education. *Child-centered* is a widely used term that is often misunderstood by many. This uncertainty about its use and meaning can lead to heated debates and misinterpretation of instructional practices. It will be

FIGURE 4.4 Highlights of the United Nations Convention on the Rights of the Child

- Every child has the inherent right to life, and States shall ensure, to the maximum, child survival and development.
- Every child has the right to a name and a nationality from birth.
- When courts, welfare institutions or administrative authorities deal with children, the child's best interests shall be a primary consideration. The child's opinions shall be given careful consideration.
- States shall ensure that each child enjoys full rights without discrimination or distinctions of any kind.
- Children should not be separated from their parents, unless by competent authorities for their well-being.
- States should facilitate reunification of families by permitting them to travel into, or out of, their territories.
- Parents have the primary responsibility for a child's upbringing, but States shall provide them with appropriate assistance and develop childcare institutions.
- States shall protect children from physical or mental harm and neglect, including sexual abuse or exploitation.
- States shall provide parentless children with suitable alternative care. The adoption process shall be carefully regulated and international agreements should be sought to provide safeguards and assure legal validity if and when adoptive parents intend to move the child from his or her country of birth.
- Disabled children shall have the right to special treatment, education and care.
- The child is entitled to the highest attainable standard of health. States shall ensure that health care is provided to all children, placing emphasis on preventative measures, health education and reduction of infant mortality.

- Primary education shall be free and compulsory; discipline in schools should respect the child's dignity. Education should prepare the child for life in a spirit of understanding, peace and tolerance.
- Children shall have time to rest and play and equal opportunities for cultural and artistic activities.
- States shall protect the child from economic exploitation and work that may interfere with education or be harmful to health and well being.
- States shall protect children from the illegal use of drugs and involvement in drug production or trafficking.
- All efforts shall be made to eliminate the abduction and trafficking of children.
- Capital punishment or life imprisonment shall not be imposed for crimes committed before the age of eighteen.
- Children in detention should be separated from adults; they must not be tortured or suffer cruel and degrading treatment.
- No child under fifteen should take any part in hostilities; children exposed to armed conflict shall receive special protection.
- Children of minority and indigenous populations shall freely enjoy their own culture, religion and language.
- Children who have suffered maltreatment, neglect or detention should receive appropriate treatment for recovery and rehabilitation.
- Children involved in infringements of the penal law shall be treated in a way that promotes their sense of dignity and worth and that aims at reintegrating them into society.
- States should make the rights in the Convention widely known to both adults and children.

Source: United Nations, Convention on the Rights of the Child *(New York: United Nations Department of Public Information, 1993), pp. 4–8. Reprint 4717–May 1993–20M. Publication Source DPI/1101, United Nations. Available online at: http://www.unhchr.ch/html/menu2/6/crc/treaties/crc.htm*

helpful to keep these guiding principles about child-centered education in mind as you work with children, parents, and colleagues:

- All children have a right to an education that helps them grow and develop to their fullest. This basic premise is at the heart of our understanding of child-centered education. Therefore, daily interactions with children should be based on the fundamental question, "Am I teaching and supporting all children in their growth and development across all domains—social, emotional, physical, linguistic, and intellectual?"
- Every child is a unique and special individual person. As such, we have to teach individual children and be respectful of and account for this individual uniqueness.

- Children are active participants in their education and development. This means that they should be mentally involved and physically active in learning what they need to know and do.
- Children's ideas, preferences, learning styles, and interests are considered in the planning for and implementation of instructional practices.

Child-centered education has been an important foundation of early childhood education since the time of Froebel. As a professional, you will want to make your teaching and practice child centered. In addition, you will want to advocate for the inherent right of every child to a child-centered education. The field of early childhood education has always been to a greater or lesser degree child-centered, and today it is becoming more so. This reemphasis on child-centered education is occurring for a number of reasons. First, society in general is much more interested in the whole child and efforts to address all of children's needs, not just their academic needs. As a result, there is much more concern for encouraging children to be healthy and lead healthy lifestyles. Consequently, interest in providing children with medical immunizations and seeing that all children are fully immunized by age two has received a lot of attention. Programs to help children be free of drugs are common in early childhood and primary programs. Concern for the welfare of children in all areas of their growth and development is evident.

Child-centered approaches are evident in such pedagogical practices as cooperative learning (see chapter 12); having children make choices about what they will learn and how; transition programs that help children move easily from program to program, grade to grade, and agency to agency; and concern for children's health, safety, and nutrition.

All great educators have believed in the basic goodness of all children. The teacher is to provide the environment for this goodness to manifest itself. A central theme that the teachings of Luther, Comenius, Pestalozzi, Froebel, Montessori, and Dewey speak to us across the years is that we must do our work as educators well, and we must really care about those for whom we have been called to serve. This indeed is the essence of child-centered education.

For additional Internet resources or to complete an online activity for this chapter, go to the Companion Website at **http://www. prenhall.com/morrison**, select chapter 4, then choose the Linking to Learning or Making Connections module.

ACTIVITIES FOR FURTHER ENRICHMENT

APPLICATIONS

1. Reflect on your experiences in elementary school. What experiences were most meaningful? Why? What teachers do you remember best? Why?
2. Interview the parents of children who attend a private or alternative preschool, kindergarten, or elementary school. What are their reasons for sending their children to these schools? Do you agree or disagree with their reasons?
3. To what extent do religious beliefs determine educational practice? Give specific examples from your own experiences and from current accounts in newspapers and other media.
4. Reflect about how your philosophy of education has been or is being influenced by the ideas and contributions of great educators. Which of the ideas has influenced you the most? What ideas of yours have been most challenged by what you read in this chapter?

FIELD EXPERIENCES

1. Visit early childhood programs in your area. Observe to determine how they apply basic ideas of people you studied in this chapter.
2. As you visit schools, classrooms, and agencies, keep a journal in which you identify the philosophy or theory you think underlies the curriculum, teaching methods, and approach to learning. Reflect on your observations and consider the implications for your professional practice.
3. Develop an observation guideline based on Gardner's intelligences. Observe children and provide specific examples that demonstrate individual specific intelligences. Use Figure 5.9, page 131, as a guide.

RESEARCH

1. Research journals, newspapers, the Internet, and other sources to determine how people, agencies, and legislation are influencing early childhood education. Do you think these influences will be long-lasting? Why? Why not?

2. A clipping file of newspaper, journal, and magazine articles relating to education is a great way to observe philosophies and theories in action. Many articles will critique how the schools are or are not implementing a certain reform or practice. As you read and review these articles, identify the ideas and philosophies that are influencing a particular point of view.

3. You have just been assigned to write a brief historical summary of the major ideas for the key educational pioneers you read about in this chapter. You are limited to fifty words for each person and are to write as though you were the person. For example:

    Locke: "At birth the mind is a blank slate and experiences are important for making impressions on the mind. I believe learning occurs best through the senses. A proper education begins early in life and hands-on experiences are an important part of education."

READINGS FOR FURTHER ENRICHMENT

Brosterman, N. *Inventing Kindergarten.* New York: Harry N. Adams, 1997.

A comprehensive book about the original kindergarten, a revolutionary educational program invented in the 1830s by German educator Friedrich Froebel. It reconstructs the most successful system ever devised for teaching young children about art, design, math, and natural history. The book also includes an exploration of the origins of modern art in the early childhood experiences of some of its greatest creators.

Dewey, John. *Experience and Education,* Reprint Edition. New York: Collier, 1998.

Dewey's comparison of traditional and progressive education. Provides a good insight into what Dewey believed schools should be like.

Fogarty, R., and Bellanca, J. *Multiple Intelligences: A Collection.* Boston: Allyn and Bacon, 1998.

Contains research and writing about Howard Gardner's multiple intelligences theory. Students will find that the articles explore practical applications of the theory and provide supporting evidence that teaching to the multiple intelligences is effective with all learners.

Hymes, J. L., Jr. *Twenty Years in Review: A Look at 1971–1990.* Washington, DC: National Association for the Education of Young Children, 1991.

A treasure trove of detail about recent history in early childhood education. Each chapter chronicles a year's history.

Montore, Will S. *Comenius and the Beginnings of Educational Reform,* 19th ed. New Hampshire: Ayer, 2000.

The author traces the reform movement in education before and up to Comenius, who was responsible for the movement's most significant contributions. He also talks about the life of Comenius and his educational writings.

Murphy, Daniel. *Comenius: A Critical Reassessment of His Life and Work.* Dublin: Irish Academy Press, 1995.

Murphy reexamines the principles of Comenius's pedagogic philosophy, giving particular attention to the learner-centered methods of teaching, which constitute his main legacy to world education.

Wolfe, J. *Learning from the Past: Historical Voices in Early Childhood Education.* Mayerthorpe, Alberta, Canada: Piney Branch Press, 2000.

Beginning with Plato, this book examines early childhood education through eleven historical figures, ending with Lucy Sprague Mitchell in the 1900s. Each chapter provides a detailed description of a particular era. Background information about each educator emphasizes their work in early childhood education. Illustrations, questions, and available resources are included.

Martin Luther
http://www.iclnet.org/pub/resources/text/wittenberg/wittenberg-home.html
Links to many of Luther's writings on-line.

Jean-Jacques Rousseau
http://www.infed.org/thinkers/et-rous.htm
Contains a brief statement by Rousseau on education, as well as a few links to other Rousseau sites.

Jean Heinrich Pestalozzi
http://www.infed.org/thinkers/et-pest.htm
From the same site as the above concerning Rousseau, a similar page about Pestalozzi.

Robert Owen
http://www.infed.org/thinkers/et-owen.htm
A bibliography of writings by Robert Owen.

Friedrich Wilhelm Froebel
http://www.infed.org/thinkers/et-froeb.htm
Biography and bibliography of the father of the kindergarten.

John Dewey
http://www.siu.edu/~deweyctr/
The Center for Dewey Studies is housed at the University of Southern Illinois at Carbondale, and its Website offers online documents about Dewey, numerous links, and instructions for joining the John Dewey Internet mailing list.

John Amos Comenius
http://www.mala.bc.ca/~mcneil/comenius1.htm
A list of links to various sites on Comenius and his work.

John Locke
http://www.utm.edu/research/iep/l/locke.htm
The Internet Encyclopedia of Philosophy's entry on John Locke, including his writings and a list of sources.

Maria Montessori
http://www.montessori.org/mariawho.htm
A historical perspective concerning her life and her works.

Lev Vygotsky
http://www.marxists.org/archive/vygotsky/
The Vygotsky Internet Archive, with biographical and philosophical information.

Abraham Maslow
http://www.ship.edu/~cgboeree/maslow.html
About Maslow's personality theories and the man himself.

Jean Piaget
http://www.piaget.org/
The Jean Piaget Society's Web site is an excellent source of information regarding publications and conferences about the work and theories of Piaget.

Erikson Tutorial Home Page
http://facultyweb.cortland.edu/~andersmd/erik/welcome.html
An introduction to and summary of Erik Erikson's eight stages of psychosocial development.

Howard Gardner
http://www.pz.harvard.edu/PIs/HG.htm
A biography of Howard Gardner as well as his work on Harvard's Project Zero.

[1] Comenius, John Amos. *The Great Didactic of John Amos Comenius,* ed. and trans. M. W. Keating (New York: Russell & Russell, 1967), 58.

[2] Ibid., 127.

[3] Locke, John. *An Essay Concerning Human Understanding,* ed. Peter H. Nidditch (Oxford: Oxford University Press, 1975), 104.

[4] Rousseau, Jean-Jacques. *Émile; Or, Education,* trans. Barbara Foxley (New York: Dutton, Everyman's Library, 1933), 5.

[5] Rousseau, Jean-Jacques. *Émile; Or, Education,* ed. and trans. William Boyd (New York: Teachers College Press, by arrangement with Heinemann, London, 1962), 11–15.

[6] DeGuimps, Roger. *Pestalozzi: His Life and Work* (New York: Appleton, 1890), 205.

[7] Ibid., 196.

[8] Bamford, S. *Passages in the Life of a Radical* (London: London Simpkin Marshall, 1844), n.p.

[9] Froebel, Friedrich. *The Education of Man,* trans. M. W. Hailman (New York: Appleton, 1887), 55.

[10] Froebel gifts and blocks, http://www.geocities.com/Athens/Forum/7905/fblgaben.html, 1999.

[11] Montessori, Maria. *The Discovery of the Child,* trans. M. J. Costelloe (Notre Dame, IN: Fides, 1967), 22.

[12] Montessori, Maria. *The Montessori Method,* trans. Anne E. George (Cambridge, MA: Bentley, 1967), 38.

[13] Montessori, *The Discovery of the Child,* 28.

[14] Ibid., 37.

[15] Archambault, Reginald D. ed., *John Dewey on Education—Selected Writings* (New York: Random House, 1964), 430.

[16] Suzzallo, Henry, ed., *John Dewey's Interest and Effort in Education* (Boston: Houghton Mifflin, 1913), 65.

[17] Archambault, *John Dewey on Education,* 170–171.

[18] Boring, Edwin G. ed., *A History of Psychology in Autobiography,* vol. 4 (Worcester, MA: Clark University Press, 1952; New York: Russell & Russell, 1968), 244.

[19] Locke, John. *An Essay Concerning Human Understanding* (New York: Dover, 1999), 92–93.

[20] Vygotsky, L. S. *Mind in Society* (Cambridge, MA: Harvard University Press, 1978), 244.

Chapter 5

Children's minds, if planted in fertile soil, will grow quite naturally on their own.

JEAN PIAGET

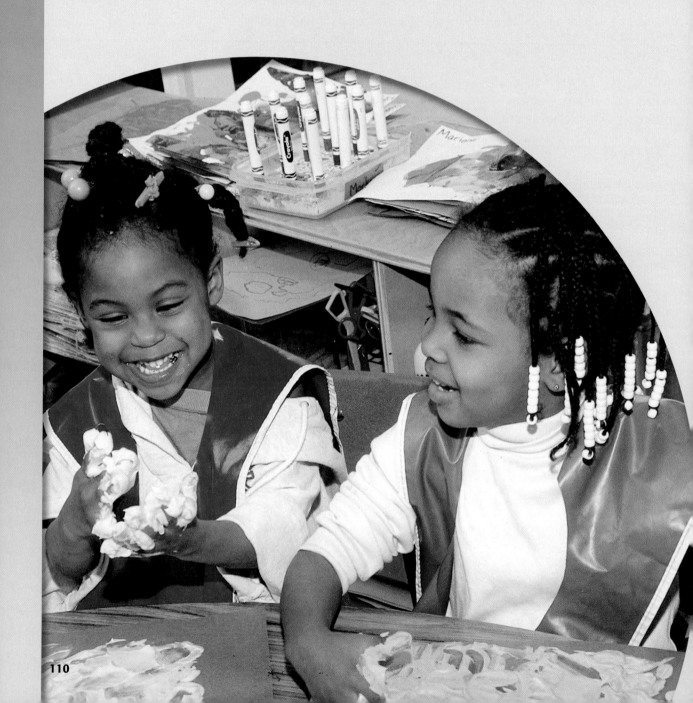

Theories Applied to Teaching and Learning
Foundations for Practice

Focus Questions

- What are theories of behavior and learning and why are they important?

- What are the major features and common beliefs of the theories of Piaget, Vygotsky, Maslow, Freud, Erikson, and Gardner?

- How can you use theories of learning in your professional practice?

In this chapter I discuss the pioneering work of theorists who have also contributed to our knowledge and our understanding of how children learn, grow, and develop. In addition, they have laid the foundation for the practice of constructivism, the theory according to which children literally construct their knowledge of the world and level of cognitive functioning. These constructivist theorists include Jean Piaget, Lev Vygotsky, and Howard Gardner. Table 5.1 lists some of these educators' contributions to constructivism. In addition, I discuss the psychosocial theory of Erik Erikson, the brain needs theory of Abraham Maslow, and the cultural context theory of Urie Bronfenbrenner.

Jean Piaget was interested in how humans learn and develop intellectually, beginning at birth and continuing across the life span. He devoted his life to conducting experiments, observing children (including his own), and developing and writing about his theory, the *cognitive theory* approach to learning. Piaget has enriched our knowledge about children's thinking, and his influence on early childhood education continues to be significant. Many programs base their curricula squarely on Piaget's theory about how children learn.

THEORIES OF LEARNING AND DEVELOPMENT

LEARNING

Reflect for a minute on your learning. How do you learn? How do children learn? We take learning for granted and frequently don't pay much attention to *how* learning occurs. But your answer to how children learn will play a major role in the curriculum you select for them and how you teach them. Think for a moment about how you would define *learning* and what learning means to you. For some, the ability to learn is a sign of intelligence. For others, it means the grades children bring home on their report cards. For many parents, learning is the answer to "What did you learn in school today?"

To review the chapter focus questions online, go to the Companion Website at **http://www. prenhall. com/morrison**, and select chapter 5.

To check your understanding of this chapter with the online Study Guide, go to the Companion Website at **http://www. prenhall.com/morrison**, select chapter 5, then choose the Study Guide module.

TABLE 5.1   **Contributors to Theories of Learning and Development**

Contributor	Contributions to Curriculum and Teaching
Jean Piaget (1896–1980)	• Learning involves discovery. • Manipulating objects promotes learning. • Interactions with people, places, and things lead to development of intellect and knowledge.
Lev Vygotsky (1896–1934)	• Learning is social and occurs through personal interactions. • More competent individuals help students scaffold learning. • Group work promotes learning.
Howard Gardner (b. 1943)	• Intelligence is multidimensional. • Human potential is the ability to solve problems. • There are many ways of knowing and expressing knowledge.

Learning   Cognitive and behavioral changes that result from experiences.

However, for our purposes, **learning** refers to the cognitive and behavioral changes that result from experiences, and the experiences that make up the curriculum are at the core of the learning process. So the experiences you provide for children should be based on a theory or theories of how children learn.

How will you know if and what children are learning? You can determine if learning occurs in a number of ways: by observing what each child is doing; by noting how he or she is interacting with other children; by interpreting the results on achievement tests; and by reading stories children have written. I discussed these and other methods for observation and assessment of learning in chapter 3.

THEORIES

Theory   A set of explanations for how children develop and learn.

A **theory** consists of statements and assumptions about relationships, principles, and data designed to explain and predict a phenomenon. In our case, a theory is a set of explanations used to explain how children learn. For example, many professionals use Piaget's theory of learning as a basis for curriculum and practice. His theory is very influential and is applied to many early childhood programs, including those discussed in chapter 6. In fact, Piaget's theory is used more often than any other theory to explain children's thinking and learning and as a basis for program development.

Learning theories such as Piaget's are important for several reasons. First, they help us think about how children learn. Thinking about and understanding how children learn makes it easier for you and others to plan and teach. Second, theories enable you to explain to others, especially parents, how learning occurs and what you and they can expect of children. Explaining children's learning to parents when you are explaining it based on a theory of learning—Piaget's, Montessori's, or other theories—is easier and makes more sense than not having a theory on which to base your explanations. Third, theories enable you to evaluate children's learning because you have a basis on which to evaluate; for example, when you observe, you know what you are observing and why. Fourth, theories provide you with guidance in developing programs for children that support and enhance their learning. Read how a teacher of the year uses Piaget's theory to guide her teaching in the Voice from the Field box on the following page.

For more information about Jean Piaget, go to the Companion Website at **http:// www.prenhall.com/ morrison**, select chapter 5, then choose the Linking to Learning module to connect to several sites about Jean Piaget.

PIAGET'S THEORY OF LEARNING

Piaget's theory is about cognitive development, which seeks to explain how individuals perceive, think, understand, and learn. His theory is basically a logicomathematical theory; that is, cognitive development is perceived as consisting primarily of logical and mathematical abilities. Review chapter 4 for background on Piaget's life.

Generally, the term *intelligence* suggests intelligence quotient, or IQ—that which is measured on an intelligence test. This is not what Piaget meant by intelligence; rather, *in-*

Philosophy of Teaching
Marta Galindo, 2002 Texas Teacher of the Year

The most important traits a teacher should cultivate in students are independence, confidence, hard work, perseverance, respect, empathy, fun, and a desire to learn. A teacher must learn to listen to the children for they can be great teachers, too. Part of being a good teacher also involves understanding children because so many times they are misunderstood. My goal is to inspire them to succeed at any task, no matter how small, for tomorrow they will understand and thank me for getting them there. Parents are the child's first and most important teachers. The seed has been planted. It is my job to guide them and help them accomplish their educational goals. Working alongside parents helps to promote a child's academic and emotional growth. Regardless of a child's home environment, it is my responsibility to communicate with the child and cul-

tivate the above traits that will help lead to the child's goals, desires, and overall accomplishments in life.

As I work on my lesson plans, it is necessary for me to be cognizant of the growth and development of the children. I match the curriculum in instructional activities to the development and characteristics of the needs of the student through hands on experiences. I make learning fun and memorable, which is one of my known traits as a teacher. Every lesson allows me to incorporate the traits I value and feel are important for children. Through these experiences students will search for meaning, learn to appreciate the uncertainty, and always seek answers in a responsible way using their acquired knowledge. Being a believer in Piaget's Cognitive Theory, I am able to identify, interpret, and appreciate student responses.

telligence is the cognitive, or mental, process by which children acquire knowledge; hence, *intelligence* is "to know." It is synonymous with *thinking* in that it involves the use of mental operations developed as a result of acting mentally and physically in and on the environment. Active involvement is basic to Piaget's cognitive theory; through direct experiences with the physical world, children develop intelligence. In addition, intelligence develops over time, and children are intrinsically motivated to develop intelligence.

Piaget conceived of intelligence as having a biological basis; that is, all organisms, including humans, adapt to their environments. You are probably familiar with the process of physical adaptation, in which an individual, stimulated by environmental factors, reacts and adjusts to that environment; this adjustment results in physical changes. Piaget applied the concept of adaptation to the mental level, using it to explain how intellectual development occurs as a result of children's encounters with parents, teachers, siblings, peers, and the environment. The result is cognitive development.

For more information about constructivism, go to the Companion Website at **http://www.prenhall.com/morrison**, select chapter 5, then choose the Linking to Learning module to connect to several sites about constructivism.

CONSTRUCTIVISM AND COGNITIVE DEVELOPMENT

Piaget's theory is a *constructivist* view of development. **Constructivism**

> is defined in terms of the individual's organizing, structuring and restructuring of experience—an ongoing lifelong process—in accordance with existing schemes of thought. In turn, these very schemes become modified and enriched in the course of interaction with the physical and social world.[1]

Children continuously organize, structure, and restructure experiences in relation to existing schemes of thought. As a result, children build their own intelligence.

Constructivism   Theory that emphasizes the active role of children in developing their understanding and learning.

In explaining the role of constructivism, Constance Kamii, a leading Piaget scholar, states, "Constructivism refers to the fact that knowledge is built by an active child from the inside rather than being transmitted from the outside through the senses."[2] Review now Figure 5.1, which lists the key concepts of constructivism.

ACTIVE LEARNING

Active learning as both a concept and a process is an inherent part of constructivism. As a concept, active learning means that children construct knowledge through physical and mental activity. As a process, active learning means that children are actively involved with a variety of manipulative materials in problem-setting and problem-solving activities. The majority of early childhood professionals support active learning as the preferred practice in early childhood programs.

Think for a minute what would happen if you gave six-month-old Emily some blocks. What would she try to do with them? More than likely, she would put them in her mouth. She wants to eat the blocks. On the other hand, if you gave blocks to Emily's three-year-old sister Madeleine, she would try to stack them. Both Emily and Madeleine want to be actively involved with things and people as active learners. This active involvement comes naturally for them.

COGNITIVE DEVELOPMENT AND ADAPTATION

According to Piaget, the adaptive process at the intellectual level operates much the same as at the physical level. The newborn's intelligence is expressed through reflexive motor actions

▲ One of Piaget's tenets is that children think differently at different stages of cognitive development. How would this affect the way you design learning experiences for children?

Active learning The view that by being physically and mentally engaged in learning activities, children develop knowledge and learn.

FIGURE 5.1   **Basic Concepts of Constructivism**

- Children construct their own knowledge. They play the major role in their own cognitive development.
- Children better understand when they construct for themselves than when they are told the answers to problems.
- Mental and physical activity is crucial for construction of knowledge. Knowledge is built step-by-step through active involvement—that is, through exploring objects in their environment and through problem solving and interacting with others.
- Children construct knowledge best in the context of—out of—experiences that are of interest and meaningful to them.
- Autonomy is preferred to obedience.
- Cognitive development is a continuous process. It begins at birth and continues across the life span.

As you review these basic premises of constructivism, reflect about how you can apply them to your care and education of young children. Which of these do you think is most important? Why?

such as sucking, grasping, head turning, and swallowing. Through the process of adaptation to the environment via these reflexive actions, the young child's intelligence is developed.[3]

Through this interaction with the environment, children organize sensations and experiences. Obviously, therefore, the quality of the environment and the nature of children's experiences play a major role in the development of intelligence. For example, Zachary, with various and differing objects available to grasp and suck, and many opportunities for this behavior, will develop differentiated sucking organizations (and therefore an intelligence) quite different from that of Gary, who has nothing to suck but a pacifier.

SCHEMES

Piaget used the term **schemes** to refer to units of knowledge that children develop through the adaptation process. (In reality, children develop many schemes.) Newborns have only reflexive actions. By using reflexive actions such as sucking (remember what Emily did with the blocks you gave her) and grasping, children begin to build their concept and understanding of the world.

In the process of developing new schemes, Piaget ascribed primary importance to physical activity, which is important for developing such schemes. Physical activity leads to mental stimulus, which in turn leads to mental activity. Thus, it is not possible to draw a clear line between physical activity and mental activity in infancy and early childhood. Settings should provide for active learning by enabling children to explore and interact with people and objects. Early childhood professionals' understanding of this key concept helps explain their arranging infant and toddler settings so children can be active. It also helps explain the growth of programs that encourage and provide active learning for all children.

Piaget believed that the opportunity to be physically and mentally involved in learning is necessary to mental development in the early years. What are some examples of how children's active involvement contributes to their learning?

Schemes Mental systems of knowledge categories.

LEARNING AS THE ADAPTATION OF MENTAL CONSTRUCTS

Assimilation.   Piaget believed that adaptation is an active process composed of two interrelated processes, assimilation and accommodation. **Assimilation** is the taking in of sensory data through experiences and impressions and incorporating this information into existing knowledge of people and objects already created as a result of previous experiences.[4] Through assimilation, children use old methods or experiences to understand and make sense of new information and experiences. Emily used assimilation when she put the block in her mouth and sucked on it. The block was fine for sucking, but not for eating.

Assimilation   The process of fitting new information into existing schemes.

Accommodation.   **Accommodation** is the process by which individuals change their way of thinking, behaving, and believing to come into accord with reality. Accommodation involves changing old methods and adjusting to new situations. Whereas Emily tried to eat the blocks, Madeleine didn't want to eat them but wanted to stack them. This is accommodation. Robbie, who is familiar with kittens and cats because he has several cats at home, may, upon seeing a dog for the first time, call it a kitty. He has assimilated dog into his organization of kitty. However, Robbie must change (accommodate) his model of what constitutes "kittyness" to exclude dogs. He does this by starting to construct or build a scheme for dog and thus what "dogness" represents.[5]

The twin processes of assimilation and accommodation, viewed as an integrated, functioning whole, constitute *adaptation*.

Accommodation   Changing or altering existing schemes or creating new ones in response to new information.

Equilibrium A balance between existing schemes developed through assimilation and intake of new information through accommodation.

Equilibrium. Equilibrium is another aspect of Piaget's theory of intelligence. **Equilibrium** is a balance between assimilation and accommodation. Children cannot assimilate new data without to some degree changing their way of thinking or acting to fit those new data. A balance is needed between the two. Diagrammed, the role of equilibrium in the constructivist process looks something like that in Figure 5.2.

Upon receiving new sensory and experiential data, children assimilate, or fit, these data into their already existing knowledge (scheme) of reality and the world. If the new data can be immediately assimilated, then equilibrium occurs. If unable to assimilate the data, children try to accommodate and change their way of thinking, acting, and perceiving to account for the new data and restore the equilibrium to the intellectual system.

Rejection of new information is common if what children are trying to assimilate and accommodate is radically different from their past experiences and the data they have received. This partially accounts for Piaget's insistence that new experiences must have some connection or relationship to previous experiences. Child care and classroom experiences should build on previous life and school experiences.

STAGES OF INTELLECTUAL DEVELOPMENT

Figure 5.3 summarizes Piaget's developmental stages and provides examples of stage-related characteristics. Piaget contended that developmental stages are the same for all children, including the atypical child, and that all children progress through each stage in the same order. The ages are only approximate and should not be considered fixed. The sequence of growth through the developmental stages does not vary; the ages at which progression occurs do vary.

Sensorimotor stage The stage during which children learn through the sense and motor activities.

Sensorimotor Stage. The sensorimotor stage is the first of Piaget's stages of cognitive development. During the period from birth to about two years, children use senses and motor reflexes to build knowledge of the world. They use their eyes to see, mouths to suck, and hands to grasp. When a child uses primarily reflexive actions to develop intellectually, he or she is in the **sensorimotor stage.** Reflexive actions help children construct a mental scheme of what is suckable and what is not (what can fit into the mouth and what cannot) and what sensations (warm and cold) occur by sucking. Children also use the grasping re-

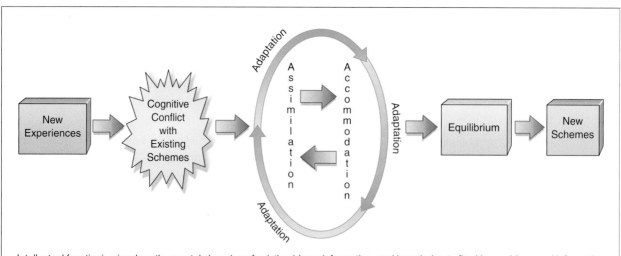

Intellectual functioning involves the mental changing of existing ideas, information, and knowledge to fit with new ideas and information as a result of experiences with people, places, and things.

FIGURE 5.2 **The Constructivist Process**

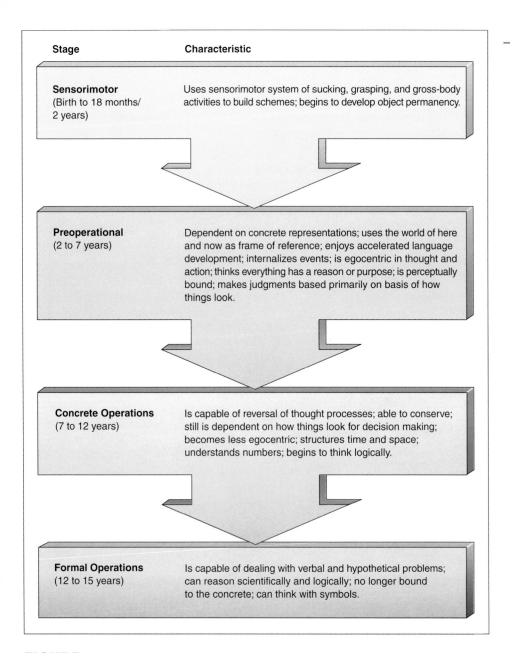

FIGURE 5.3 **Piaget's Stages of Cognitive Development**

flex in much the same way to build schemes of what can and cannot be grasped. Through these innate sensory and reflexive actions, they continue to develop an increasingly complex, unique, and individualized hierarchy of schemes. What children are to become physically and intellectually is related to these sensorimotor functions and interactions.

The sensorimotor period has these major characteristics:

- Dependency on and use of innate reflexive actions
- Initial development of object permanency, the idea that objects can exist without being seen, heard, or touched
- Egocentricity, whereby children see themselves as the center of the world and believe events are caused by them

• Dependence on concrete representations (things) rather than symbols (words, pictures) for information
• By the end of the second year, less reliance on sensorimotor reflexive actions; beginning use of symbols for things that are not present

(We will discuss intellectual development in infants, toddlers, preschoolers, and primary grade children in more detail in later chapters.)

Preoperational stage The stage of cognitive development in which young children develop knowledge using symbolic thinking.

Preoperational Stage.   The **preoperational stage**, the second stage of cognitive development, begins at age two and ends at approximately seven years. Preoperational children are different from sensorimotor children in these ways:

• Language development begins to accelerate rapidly.
• There is less dependence on sensorimotor action.
• These children have an increased ability to internalize events and think by using representational symbols such as words in place of things.

Preoperational children continue to be egocentric, expressing ideas and basing perceptions mainly on how they perceive or see things. Children learn to use symbols such as words or mental images to solve problems and think about things and people who are not present. How things look to preoperational children is the foundation for several other stage-related characteristics. First, when children look at an object that has multiple characteristics, such as a long, round, yellow pencil, they will "see" whichever of those qualities first catches their eye. Preoperational children's knowledge is based mainly on what they are able to see, simply because they do not yet have operational intelligence or the ability to think using mental images.

Piaget believed that, developmentally, after children are capable of making one-to-one correspondence and classifying and ordering objects, they are ready for higher-level thinking activities such as those that involve numeration and time and spatial relationships.

Second, the absence of operations makes it impossible for preoperational children to *conserve,* or determine that the quantity of an object does not change simply because some transformation occurs in its physical appearance. For example, show preoperational children two identical rows of checkers (see Figure 5.4). Ask whether each row has the same number of checkers. The children should answer affirmatively. Next, space out the checkers in each row, and ask whether the two rows still have the same number of checkers. They might insist that more checkers are in one row "because it's longer." Children base their judgment on what they can see—namely, the spatial extension of one row beyond the other row. This example also illustrates that preoperational children are not able to *reverse* thought or action, which requires mentally putting the row back to its original length.

Preoperational children believe and act as though everything happens for a specific reason or purpose. This explains children's constant and recurring questions about why things happen and how things work.

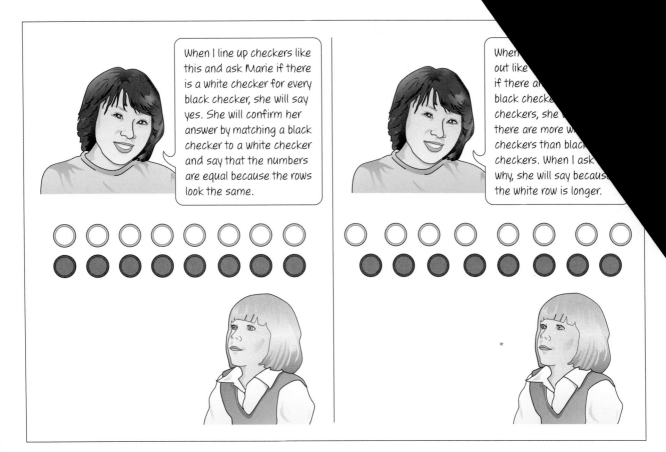

FIGURE 5.4 The Absence of Operations

It is impossible for preoperational children to determine that the quantity of a group of objects does not change because some changes occur in how the objects look. Try this checker experiment with several children and see how they are thinking and making sense of their world based on how things look to them.

Preoperational children also believe everyone thinks as they think and acts as they do for the same reasons. Preoperational children have a hard time putting themselves in another's place, and it is difficult for them to be sympathetic and empathetic.

How preoperational children talk reflects their egocentrism. For example, in explaining about his dog that ran away, Matt might say something like this: "And we couldn't find him . . . and my dad he looked . . . and we were glad." Matt assumes you have the same point of view he does and know the whole story. The details are missing for you, not for Matt. Young children's egocentrism also helps explain why they tend to talk at each other rather than with each other. This dialogue between two children playing at a day care center reveals egocentrism:

Jessica: My Mommy's going to take me shopping.
Ashley: I'm going to dress this doll.
Jessica: If I'm good I'm going to get an ice cream cone.
Ashley: I'm going to put this dress on her.

The point is that egocentrism is a fact of cognitive development in the early childhood years. Our inability always to see clearly someone else's point of view is evidence that egocentrism in one form or another is part of the cognitive process across the life span.

For more information about child development, go to the Companion Website at **http://www. prenhall.com/morrison**, select any chapter, then choose Topic 2 of the ECE Supersite module.

Concrete Operations Stage. **Concrete operations** is the third stage of Piaget's cognitive development plan. Piaget defined an operation as an action that can be carried out in thought as well as executed materially and that is mentally and physically reversible.

Children in the *concrete operations stage,* from about age seven to about age twelve, begin to use mental images and symbols during the thinking process and can reverse operations. Teachers can encourage the development of mental processes during this stage through the use of concrete or real objects when talking about and explaining concepts.

Concrete operational children begin to develop the ability to understand that change involving physical appearances does not necessarily change quality or quantity. They also begin to reverse thought processes, by going back over and "undoing" a mental action just accomplished. Other mental operations children are capable of during this stage are these:

- One-to-one correspondence
- Classification of objects, events, and time according to certain characteristics
- Classification involving multiple properties of objects
- Class inclusion operations
- Complementary classes

Observation serves as a basis for assessing children's abilities, achievements, and stage of cognitive development. What do you think this teacher can learn about the child she is observing?

Concrete operations   The mental stage of development in which children's mental tasks are tied to concrete objects.

Formal operations   The stage of cognitive development involving the development of knowledge through diplomatic reasoning.

The concrete stage does not represent a period into which children suddenly emerge, after having been preoperational. The process of development from stage to stage is gradual and continual and occurs over a period of time as a result of maturation and experiences. No simple sets of exercises will cause children to move up the developmental ladder. Rather, ongoing developmentally appropriate activities lead to conceptual understanding.

Formal Operations Stage.   The second part of operational intelligence is **formal operations,** which is the fourth and final stage of cognitive development. The *formal operations stage* begins at about twelve years of age and extends to about fifteen years. Children become capable of dealing with increasingly complex verbal and hypothetical problems and are less dependent on concrete objects to solve problems. Thinking ranges over a wide time span that includes past, present, and future. Children develop the ability to reason scientifically and logically, and they can think with all the processes and power of adults. How a child thinks is thus pretty well established by age fifteen, although adolescents do not stop developing new schemes.

Piaget came to these conclusions about early childhood education:

- Children play an active role in their own cognitive development.
- Mental and physical activity are important for cognitive development.
- Experiences constitute the raw materials necessary to develop mental structures.
- Children develop cognitively through interaction with and adaptation to the environment.

- Development is a continuous process.
- Development results from maturation and the transactions, or interactions, between children and the physical and social environments.

Early childhood professionals use these tenets to guide their planning and teaching. The "New City School" Program in Action feature on page 125 is one example of a program based on the constructivist theory.

LEV VYGOTSKY AND SOCIOCULTURAL THEORY

Lev Vygotsky (1896–1934), a contemporary of Piaget, increasingly inspires the practices of early childhood professionals. Vygotsky's theory of development is particularly useful in describing children's mental, language, and social development. His theory also has many implications of how children's play promotes language and social development.

Vygotsky believed that children's mental, language, and social development is supported and enhanced by others through social interaction. This view is opposite from the Piagetian perspective, in which children are much more solitary developers of their own intelligence and language. For Vygotsky, development is supported by social interaction. "Learning awakens a variety of developmental processes that are able to operate only when the child is interacting with people in his environment and in collaboration with his peers. Once these processes are internalized, they become part of the child's independent developmental achievement."[6] Vygotksy further believed that children seek out adults for social interaction beginning at birth; development occurs through these interactions.

For early childhood professionals, one of Vygotsky's most important concepts is that of the **zone of proximal development**, which he defines as follows:

> The area of development into which a child can be led in the course of interaction with a more competent partner, either adult or peer. [It] is not some clear-cut space that exists independently of joint activity itself. Rather, it is the difference between what the child can accomplish independently and what he or she can achieve in conjunction with another, more competent person. The zone is thus created in the course of social interaction.[7]

To summarize, the zone of proximal development (ZPD) represents the range of tasks that children cannot do independently but can do when helped by a more competent person—teacher, adult, or another child. Tasks below the ZPD, children can learn independently. Tasks, concepts, ideas, and information above the ZPD, children are not yet able to learn, even with help. Figure 5.5 illustrates the ZPD.

In addition, Vygotsky believed that learning and development constitute a dynamic and interactive process:

> Learning is not development; however, properly organized learning results in mental development and sets in motion a variety of developmental processes that would be impossible apart from learning. Thus, learning is a necessary part and universal aspect of the process of developing culturally organized, specifically human, psychological functions.[8]

In other words, learning drives development; the experiences children have influence their development. This is why it is important for teachers and parents to provide high-quality learning experiences for children.

Intersubjectivity is a second Vygotskian concept. Intersubjectivity is based on the idea that "individuals come to a task, problem, or conversation with their own subjective ways

Zone of proximal development Encompasses the range of tasks that are too difficult to master alone but that can be learned with guidance and assistance.

Tasks or activities that the child can accomplish with assistance, guidance, and direction

Tasks or activities that the child can complete independently

FIGURE 5.5 The Zone of Proximal Development
In the zone of proximal development (ZPD), children can achieve with the help of a more competent person. Think about some of the ways you and other more competent persons such as peers, siblings, and parents can help children master certain tasks.

of making sense of it. If they then discuss their differing viewpoints, shared understanding may be attained. . . . In other words, in the course of communication participants may arrive at some mutually agreed-upon, or intersubjective, understanding."[9]

Vygotsky also believed communication or dialogue between teacher and child is very important and literally becomes a means for helping children *scaffold,* or develop new concepts and think their way to higher level concepts. **Scaffolding** is assistance of some kind that enables children to complete tasks they cannot complete independently. Figure 5.6 shows an example of a teacher providing instructional assistance of scaffolding with a child during a literacy lesson. When adults "assist" toddlers in learning to walk they are scaffolding from not being able to walk to being able to walk.

The idea of intersubjectivity is similar to Piaget's theory that disequilibrium sets the stage for assimilation and accommodation, and consequently, new schemes develop. Furthermore, Vygotsky believed that as a result of teacher–child collaboration, the child uses concepts learned in the collaborative process to solve problems when the teacher is not present. As Vygotsky said, the child "continues to act in collaboration even though the teacher is not standing near him. . . . This help—this aspect of collaboration—is invisibly present. It is continued in what looks from the outside like the child's independent solution of the problem."[10] According to Vygotsky, social interactions and collaboration are essential ingredients in the processes of learning and development.

Many current practices such as cooperative learning, joint problem solving, coaching, collaboration, mentoring, and other forms of assisted learning are based on Vygotsky's theory of development and learning.

Scaffolding The process of providing different levels of support, guidance, or direction during the course of an activity.

122

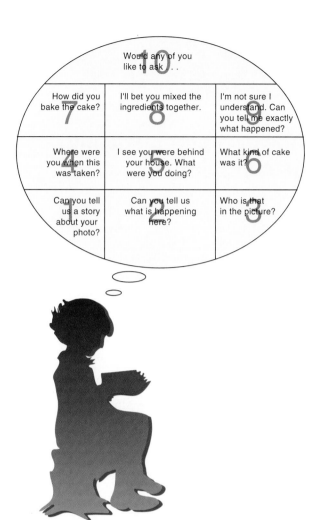

FIGURE 5.6 The Scaffolding Process: Scaffolding Children's Language Development

Assistance in the zone of proximal development (ZPD) is called scaffolding and is a major component of teaching. Through scaffolding, the teacher guides and supports children's language learning by building on what they are already able to do, moving them to a higher level of language use. Read the above script from left to right starting at the lower left. Take a few minutes to write a scaffolding script based on a favorite children's book.

Source: Text from *Implementing the Pre-kindergarten Guidelines for Language and Early Literacy—Part I: Language Development* (2001). Austin, TX: Texas Education Agency. Used with permission from the University of Texas, Texas Center for Reading and Language Arts and the Texas Education Agency.

ABRAHAM MASLOW AND SELF-ACTUALIZATION THEORY

Abraham Maslow (1890–1970) developed a theory of motivation called *self-actualization* based on the satisfaction of human needs. Maslow identified self-actualization, or self-fulfillment, as the highest human need. However, he said, children and adults don't achieve self-actualization until basic needs are satisfied. These basic needs include life essentials such as food, safety, and security; belongingness and love; achievement and prestige; and aesthetic needs. Everyone has these basic needs regardless of sexual orientation, race, gender, socioeconomic status, or age. Satisfaction of basic needs is essential for individuals to function well and to achieve all they are capable of achieving. We know that

Representations of Culturally and Linguistically Diverse Students in Special Education

The figure below shows the percentage of enrollment in special education for Hispanic and African-American children in relation to the general population. As you can see, on the one hand, African-American children are overrepresented in the mental retardation, serious emotional disturbances, and specific learning disabilities. At the same time, they are underrepresented in the gifted and talented. Hispanics are somewhat over-represented in specific learning disability and underrepresented in all other categories.

There has been and continues to be an ongoing discussion and debate about the disproportionate representation of culturally and linguistically diverse students in special and gifted education programs. How are we to explain these over and underrepresentations? Some things we need to consider are these:

- Some districts and schools with predominately African-American and Hispanic populations may not have the classroom support services necessary to adequately provide for children in the mainstream school setting.

- Teachers and administrators may not have a full cultural understanding about how minority children develop and learn.
- In some states and school districts, children are not eligible for dual special education services. For example, children who are receiving linguistic services (bilingual education) may not be eligible for special education. This would help to account for why Hispanic children are underrepresented in special education and gifted programs. All educators need to make positive and proactive initiatives to eliminate over and underrepresentation issues. The Arlington, Virginia, public schools are implementing these remedies for over and under representation:
- Examining assessment practices with a focus on non-biased assessments
- Recruiting qualified teachers
- Developing a special education intervention checklist for general education teachers
- Expanding mental health services for students and their families prior to referral to special education

The 22nd Annual Report to Congress on the Implementation of the Individuals with Disabilities Act revealed that African-American youth, ages 6 through 21, account for 14.8 percent of the general population and 20.2 percent of the special education population.

Students with Special Needs by Ethnicity in Relation to the General Population

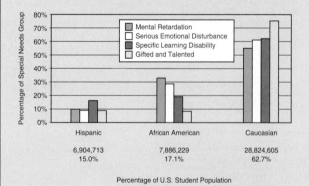

Percentage of U.S. Student Population

Sources: U.S. Department of Education, Office for Civil Rights (1998). OCR Elementary and Secondary School Survey. OCR Reports [Online]. Available at http://205.207.175.80/ocrpublic/ wds_list98p.asp.
U.S. Census Bureau, Census 2000 Summary File 1, Matrices P3, P4, PCT4, PCT5, PCT8, and PCT11 [Online]. Available at http://factfinder.census.gov/servlet/QTTable?_ts=62957369460.
Crawley, A. L. (2002). *Arlington public schools reducing number of African–American students in special education programs.* The Citizen, Summer 2002 [Online]. Available at http://www.co.arlington.va.us/cmo/citizen_summer_2002/sed_programs.htm.

New City School

You don't have to be in early childhood education very long to hear a teacher say, "That boy is just soooo active." Indeed, this statement often has a "well, what can you do" tone to it. At New City School, an independent school in St. Louis with students three years old through 6th grade, both the tone and the words are different even though we certainly have lots of active boys. Our statement, "That's a very b-k [Bodily-Kinesthetic] kid," reflects our focus on Howard Gardner's Multiple Intelligences. We develop curriculum and look at children (and adults!) from the belief that there are at least eight intelligences: Bodily-Kinesthetic, Spatial, Logical-Mathematical, Musical, Linguistic, Naturalistic, Intra-Personal, and Inter-Personal. We believe children (and adults!) have strengths in all of these areas. We work to support children's growth in using their strengths and in understanding their particular strengths and those of others.

When New City teachers and administrators started working with Howard Gardner's Multiple Intelligences model about fourteen years ago, we quickly agreed that our preschool program had the fewest changes to make in order to reflect the Multiple Intelligences. Indeed, preschool programs in general with their use of centers and choice time have traditionally given children many opportunities to explore and create. Puzzle areas and art centers offer spatial choices; pretending provides many interpersonal options; games and manipulatives offer logical-mathematical, spatial, and inter-personal choices; the list is long.

How then has our preschool program changed? Two changes come quickly to mind. First, we now have a framework with which to plan centers and assessment. Our preschool teachers use the Multiple Intelligences framework in planning centers and activities, checking themselves to make sure that children have opportunities to use and develop their various intelligences. Remember that b-k kid we talked about in the beginning? Rather than thinking about "containing him" with rules and time-outs, New City teachers plan centers making sure that there are bodily-kinesthetic activities available during choice time, not just at recess. Do we suddenly have an instant gym connected to our classroom? Definitely not! But, teachers now use adjacent halls and even classroom space for activities such as hopscotch, scooter boards, basketball, jump ropes and the like. Once children do activities, teachers provide parents and colleagues with assessment information using the Multiple Intelligence framework. Parents receive information about their children through multiple-page progress reports and portfolio nights; here again, the Multiple Intelligences focus is used in showing the children's work and sharing their progress. So, the parents of that child with strong Bodily-Kinesthetic Intelligence learn that their child often chooses b-k related activities and that teachers use that bodily-kinesthetic strength in helping the child learn other things. Thus, that child might practice counting while jumping rope or shooting baskets or learn letters by throwing bean bags at alphabet squares.

Second, we put a strong emphasis on the Personal Intelligences, Intra-Personal, knowing yourself, and Inter-Personal, knowing how to work and play with others. Believing strongly that these talents can be developed just as a musical or linguistic talent, New City teachers have developed activities and assessment techniques to support growth in the Personal Intelligences. In our 4/5s classrooms, for example, teachers regularly schedule "Buddy Days" during choice time. On a Buddy Day, children are paired up by the teachers and must then work together to choose activities for the morning. Teachers model, problem solve, comfort and support children as they learn to express their interests and accept the interests of their partners. Over the school year, these children learn to listen, negotiate, delay gratification and solve problems with a variety of peers. Parents recognize the importance we place on the Personals when they read our Progress Reports, where the first page is devoted entirely to the Personal Intelligences with assessment topics ranging from teamwork and appreciation for diversity to motivation and problem solving.

The Multiple Intelligences framework has allowed us to further develop an early childhood program where all of the Intelligences of the children are appreciated.

Contributed by Barbara James Thomson, New City School, 5209 Waterman Ave., St. Louis, Missouri (314) 361–6411.

To complete an activity related to the topic in the box on page 124, go to the Companion Website at **http://www.prenhall.com/morrison**, select chapter 5, then choose the Diversity Tie-In module.

To complete a Program in Action activity, visit the Companion Website at **http://www.prenhall.com/morrison**, select chapter 5, then choose the Program in Action module.

Hierarchy of needs

Maslow's theory that basic needs must be satisfied before higher-level needs can be satisfied.

without air, water, or food, a child would die. We also know from basic brain research that water is essential for the proper functioning of the brain. Many teachers encourage their children to drink water as a means of ensuring that their brains have enough water to function well. The same applies to food. We know that when children are hungry, they perform poorly in school. Children who begin school without eating breakfast don't achieve as well as they should and experience difficulty concentrating on their school activities. This explains why many early childhood programs provide children with breakfast, lunch, and snacks throughout the day.

Safety and security needs play an important role in children's lives. When children think that their teachers do not like them or are fearful of what their teachers say and how they treat them, they are deprived of a basic need. As a consequence, they do not do well in school, and they become fearful in their relationships with others. In addition, classrooms that have routines and predictability provide children with a sense of safety and security.

Children need to be loved and feel that they "belong" within their home and school in order to thrive and develop. All children have affectional needs that teachers can satisfy through smiles, hugs, eye contact, and nearness. For example, in my work with three- and four-year-old children, many want to sit close to me and want me to put my arms around them. They seek love and look to their teachers and me to satisfy this basic need.

Recognition and approval are self-esteem needs that relate to success and accomplishment. Children who are independent and responsible, and who achieve, will have high self-esteem. Today, many educators are concerned about how to enhance children's self-esteem. A key way to achieve this goal is through increasing achievement.

Children like and appreciate beauty. They like to be in classrooms and homes that are physically attractive and pleasant. As an early childhood professional, you can satisfy aesthetic needs by being well-dressed and providing a classroom that is pleasant to be in by including plants and flowers, art, and music.

When children have the basic needs met, they become self-actualized. They have a sense of satisfaction, are enthusiastic, and are eager to learn. They want to engage in activities that will lead to higher levels of learning. Figure 5.7 depicts Maslow's **hierarchy of needs.** As you review and reflect on this hierarchy, identify ways you can help children meet each of them.

ERIK ERIKSON

Erik H. Erikson (1902–1994) developed his theory of psychosocial development based on the premise that cognitive and social development occur hand in hand and cannot be separated. According to Erikson, children's personalities and social skills grow and develop within the context of society and in response to society's demands, expectations, values, and social institutions such as families, schools, and child care programs. Adults, especially parents and teachers, are key parts of these environments and therefore play a powerful role in helping or hindering children in their personality and cognitive development. For example, school-age children must deal with demands to learn new skills or risk a sense of incompetence, or a crisis of *industry*—the ability to do, be involved, be competent, and achieve—versus *inferiority*—marked by failure and feelings of incompetence. Many of the cases of school violence in the news today are caused in part by children who feel inferior and unappreciated and who lack the social skills for getting along with their classmates. Figure 5.8 outlines the stages of psychosocial development according to Erikson, while the Video Viewpoint (see p. 130) discusses emotional IQ.

HOWARD GARDNER

Howard Gardner (b. 1943) has played an important role in helping educators rethink the concepts of intelligence. Rather than relying on a single definition of intelligence, Gardner's philosophy of multiple intelligences suggests that people can be "smart" in many ways.

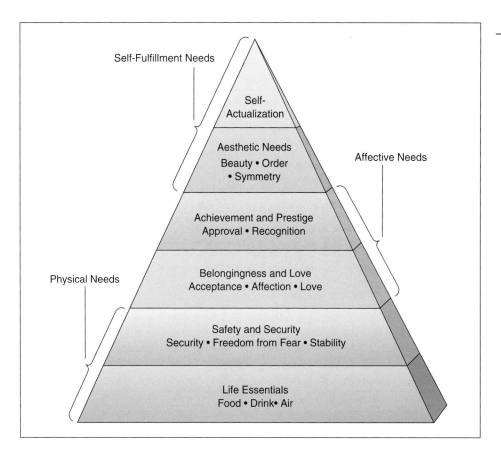

FIGURE 5.7 Hierarchy of Needs

Source: Maslow's hierarchy of needs data from *Motivation and Personality,* 3rd ed. by Abraham H. Maslow. Revised by Robert Frager et al. Copyright © 1954, 1987 by Harper & Row, Publishers, Inc. Copyright © 1970 by Abraham H. Maslow. Reprinted by permission of Addison-Wesley Educational Publishers, Inc.

Gardner has identified nine intelligences: visual spatial, verbal/linguistic, mathematical/logical, bodily/kinesthetic, musical/rhythmic, intrapersonal, interpersonal, naturalistic, and existentialist. Gardner's view of intelligence and its multiple components has influenced and will undoubtedly continue to influence educational thought and practice. Review Figure 5.9 to learn more about these nine intelligences and their implications for teaching and learning.

URIE BRONFENBRENNER AND ECOLOGICAL THEORY

Urie Bronfenbrenner's (b. 1917) ecological theory looks at a children's development within the context of systems of relationships that form their environment. There are five inter-relating environmental systems—the microsystem, the mesosystem, the exosystem, the macrosystem, and the chronosystem. Figure 5.10 shows a model of these environmental systems and how each influences development. Each system influences and is influenced by the other.

The **microsystem** encompasses the environments of parents, family, peers, child care, schools, neighborhood, religious groups, parks, and so forth. The child acts on each of these and is influenced by them and influences them. For example, four-year-old April might have a physical disability that her child care program accommodates by making the

Microsystem The environmental setting in which children spend a lot of their time. Children in child care spend about thirty-three hours a week there.

127

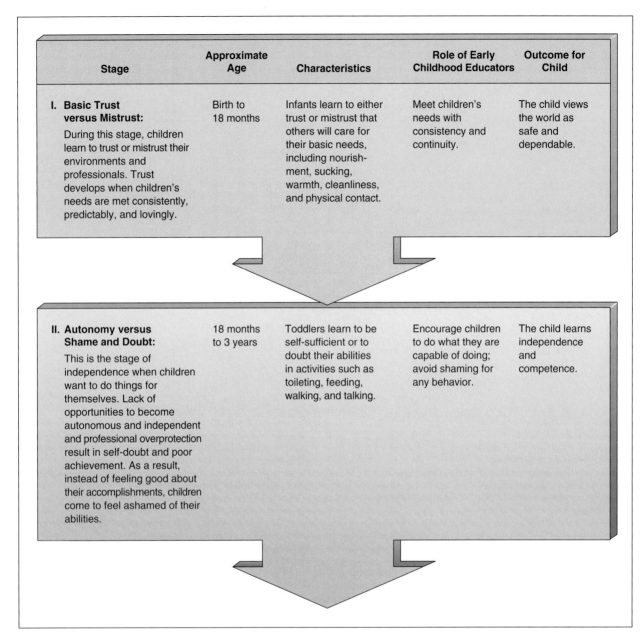

Stage	Approximate Age	Characteristics	Role of Early Childhood Educators	Outcome for Child
I. Basic Trust versus Mistrust: During this stage, children learn to trust or mistrust their environments and professionals. Trust develops when children's needs are met consistently, predictably, and lovingly.	Birth to 18 months	Infants learn to either trust or mistrust that others will care for their basic needs, including nourishment, sucking, warmth, cleanliness, and physical contact.	Meet children's needs with consistency and continuity.	The child views the world as safe and dependable.
II. Autonomy versus Shame and Doubt: This is the stage of independence when children want to do things for themselves. Lack of opportunities to become autonomous and independent and professional overprotection result in self-doubt and poor achievement. As a result, instead of feeling good about their accomplishments, children come to feel ashamed of their abilities.	18 months to 3 years	Toddlers learn to be self-sufficient or to doubt their abilities in activities such as toileting, feeding, walking, and talking.	Encourage children to do what they are capable of doing; avoid shaming for any behavior.	The child learns independence and competence.

FIGURE 5.8 Erikson's Stages of Psychological Development in Early Childhood

classroom more accessible. Or, five-year-old Mack's aggressive behavior prompts his teacher to initiate a program of bibliotherapy.

The **mesosystem** encompasses linkages or interactions between microsystems. Interactions and influences there relate to all of the environmental influences in the microsystem. For example, the family's support of or lack of attention to literacy will influence the child's school performance. Likewise, the school support for family literacy will influence the extent to which families value literacy.

The **exosystem** is the environmental system that encompasses those events in which children do not have direct interaction but which nonetheless influence them. For example, when school boards enact a policy that ends social promotion, this can and will influence children's

Mesosystem Links or interactions between microsystems.

Exosystems Environments or settings in which children do not play an active role but that nonetheless influence their development.

Stage	Approximate Age	Characteristics	Role of Early Childhood Educators	Outcome for Child
III. Initiative versus Guilt: During the preschool years children need opportunity to respond with initiative to activities and tasks, which gives them a sense of purposefulness and accomplishment. Erikson believes children can feel guilty when they are discouraged or prohibited from initiating activities and are overly restricted in attempts to do things on their own.	3–5 years	Children are learning and want to undertake many adultlike activities, sometimes overstepping the limits set by parents and thus feeling guilty.	Encourage children to engage in many activities; provide environments in which children can explore; promote language development.	The child is able to undertake a task, be active and involved.
IV. Industry versus Inferiority: In this period, children display an industrious attitude and want to be productive. They want to build things, discover, manipulate objects, and find out how things work. Productivity is important during this stage. They also want recognition for their productivity, and adult response to children's efforts and accomplishments helps develop a positive self-concept. Feelings of inferiority result when children are criticized, belittled, or have few opportunities for productivity.	5–8 years	Children actively and busily learn to be competent and productive or feel inferior and unable to do things well.	Help children win recognition by producing things; recognition results from achievement and success.	The child has feelings of self-worth and industry.

FIGURE 5.8 continued

development. When the family's workplace mandates increased work time (e.g., a 10-hour workday), this may decrease parent–child involvement, which influences development.

The **macrosystem** encompasses the culture, customs, and values of society in general. For example, contemporary societal violence and media violence influence children's development. Many children are becoming more violent, and many children are fearful of and threatened by violence.

The **chronosystem** includes environmental influences over time and how they impact development and behavior. For example, today's children are technologically adept and are comfortable with the use of technology in education and entertainment. We have already referred to how the large-scale entry of mothers into the workforce has changed family life.

Macrosystem The broader culture in which children live (e.g., democracy, individual freedom, religious freedom, and so forth).

Chronosystem The environmental contexts and events that influence children over their lifetimes, such as living in a technological age.

Emotional IQ

Researchers are now saying that the verbal intelligence of young children is not the only indicator of future success. Determining the emotional intelligence of people—including their reactions when they are angry, their ability to read others' nonverbal cues, and their self-control—may better identify individuals who can adapt to societal pressures and the demands of the workplace. Parents and early childhood professionals can play a role in helping children develop healthy emotional attitudes.

REFLECTIVE DISCUSSION QUESTIONS

Write down several examples of emotional intelligence. Give some examples of your personal emotional intelligence and how you manifest such emotions. How would you explain emotional intelligence to a parent? Why is impulse control so important in children's lives?

REFLECTIVE DECISION MAKING

How can you as an early childhood professional teach students about a healthy emotional intelligence? Give some examples of how you can role-play to demonstrate such emotions. What social skills can you help students learn to increase their emotional intelligence? What can you do to help children develop impulse control? Why is impulse control so important for success in life? What are some consequences of not being able to delay gratification and not being able to exercise impulse control? As an early childhood professional, how can you help children control their anger? Make a list of children's books and other materials that you could use to help children "read other children's emotions." What are some things that you can do to be your students' emotional tutor?

THEORIES RECONSIDERED

Like all things designed to advance our knowledge and understanding of children, theories must stand the tests of time, criticism, and review. Theories are subject to the scrutiny, testing, and evaluation of professionals. This is the way theories are accepted, rejected, modified, and refined. Researchers have conducted thousands of studies to test the validity of the theories we have discussed. The following discussion will help you put the theories we discussed in perspective as you prepare to apply them to your teaching.

A powerful advantage of Piaget's theory is that it is an elegant explanation of four stages of cognitive development. It enables us to clearly track cognitive development through the four stages from birth to adolescence. Second, with each stage Piaget and others describe what children are and are not able to do. Third, Piaget's four stages offer a somewhat complete description of cognitive development from birth through adulthood. For over half a century, Piaget's theory has provided professionals and researchers with a theory on which to develop curricula and guide program development.

On the other hand, there are a number of things you must consider in applying Piaget's theory. First, Piaget seems to have underestimated the ages at which children can perform certain mental operations. In fact, it appears that he underestimated the intellectual abilities of all children, but particularly younger children. Children can understand more than Piaget believed, based on the problems and tasks he gave them to perform. For example, children in the preoperational stage can perform tasks he assigned to the concrete operations stage. Additionally, recent advances in infant research suggest that infants have more cognitive tools than Piaget or others thought (more about this in the last section of the chapter).

Second, Piaget's emphasis on a unidimensional view of intelligence as consisting primarily of logicomathematical knowledge and skills tends to de-emphasize other views. Pro-

Visual/Spatial	Children who learn best visually and who organize things spatially. They like to see what you are talking about in order to understand. They enjoy charts, graphs, maps, tables, illustrations, art, puzzles, costumes—anything eye catching.
Verbal/Linguistic	Children who demonstrate strength in the language arts: speaking, writing, reading, listening. These students have always been successful in traditional classrooms because their intelligence lends itself to traditional teaching.
Mathematical/Logical	Children who display an aptitude for numbers, reasoning, and problem solving. This is the other half of children who typically do well in traditional classrooms where teaching is logically sequenced and students are asked to conform.
Bodily/Kinesthetic	Children who experience learning best through activity: games, movement, hands-on tasks, building. These children were often labeled "overly active" in traditional classrooms where they were told to sit and be still!
Musical/Rhythmic	Children who learn well through songs, patterns, rhythms, instruments, and musical expression. It is easy to overlook children with this intelligence in traditional education.
Intrapersonal	Children who are especially in touch with their own feelings, values, and ideas. They may tend to be more reserved, but they are actually quite intuitive about what they learn and how it relates to themselves.
Interpersonal	Children who are noticeably people oriented and outgoing, and do their learning cooperatively in groups or with a partner. These children may have typically been identified as "talkative" or "too concerned about being social" in a traditional setting.
Naturalist	Children who love the outdoors, animals, and field trips. More than this, though, these students love to pick up on subtle differences in meaning. The traditional classroom has not been accommodating to these children.
Existentialist	Children who learn in the context of where humankind stands in the "big picture" of existence. They ask "Why are we here?" and "What is our role in the world?" This intelligence is seen in the discipline of philosophy.

FIGURE 5.9 Gardner's Nine Intelligences

Howard Gardner has identified these nine intelligences. They help teachers understand how children learn differently and how to teach children according to their varying intelligences.

Source: Reprinted with permission from Walter McKenzie, *Multiple Intelligences Overview.* http://surfaquarium.com/im.htm

fessionals now recognize other definitions of intelligence and how it develops, such as Howard Gardner's multiple intelligences. You must consider varying definitions of *intelligence* when designing curricula and activities for children.

Third, Piaget's theory emphasizes that individual children are literally responsible for developing their own intelligence. In this regard, he likened children to "little scientists,"

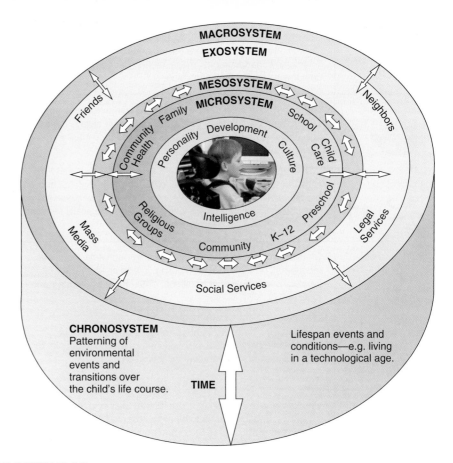

FIGURE 5.10 **Ecological Influences on Development**

As you can see, there are many influences on children's development. Currently there is a lot of interest in how these influences shape children's lives and what parents and educators can do to enhance positive influences and minimize or eliminate negative environmental influences and negative social interactions.

engaged in a solitary process of intellectual development. With his emphasis on the role of the individual child, Piaget's approach to cognitive development tends to downplay the role of social interactions and the contributions of others to this process. On the other hand, Lev Vygotsky believed that people play a major role in children's cognitive development and that children are not alone in their development of mental schemes. For Vygotsky, children develop knowledge, attitudes, and ideas through interactions with more capable others—parents, teachers, and peers. Early childhood professionals' embracing of Vygotsky's ideas helps explain the popularity of many social-based learning processes such as cooperative learning, multiage grouping, child–teacher collaboration, and peer-assisted teaching.

Fourth, one characteristic of children's language and cognitive development is that children talk to themselves. Perhaps you have observed a four-year-old busily engrossed in putting a puzzle together and heard her say, "Which piece comes next?" Piaget called this self-directed talk *egocentric speech* and believed it furnished additional evidence of children's egocentrism, that children are more preoccupied with their own needs and concerns rather than the views of others.

Vygotsky believed that children's private speech plays an important role in cognitive development. He thought that children communicate with themselves to guide their behavior and thinking. As children develop, their audible private speech becomes silent inner speech and continues to serve the important functions of helping to solve problems and guide behavior. By being attentive to children's private speech, professionals can ask questions that will help children think and solve problems. Additionally, learning environments that permit children to be verbally active while solving problems support their cognitive development.

Erikson's theory of psychosocial development is likewise popular with teachers and schools who work with children. It provides a helpful way to look at children's social development and to consider how children's identity needs change over developmental time. In addition, when teachers and parents endeavor to meet children's psychosocial needs, their achievement is encouraged and supported.

Bronfenbrenner's ecological theory is popular in that it provides teachers a systematic way to examine how they and others influence children's development and learning. In addition, Bronfenbrenner encourages professionals and others to consider children's lives in more than one sitting or environment. What happens in classrooms affects children at home and vice versa. Indeed, it is good to remember that your actions as an early childhood professional will affect children in their different environments.

To take an online self-test on this chapter's contents, go to the Companion Website at **http://www.prenhall.com/morrison**, select chapter 5, then choose the Self-Test module.

NEW DIRECTIONS IN COGNITIVE DEVELOPMENT

As with most theories, new research and discoveries lead to modification and new directions. Since Piaget did his groundbreaking work, several advances have occurred that influence how we view children's cognitive development. First are the ongoing discoveries about genetic influences on cognitive development. These developments show, for example, that the genetic influences on verbal development were not as clearly established in Piaget's time as they are today. When I discuss infant language development in chapter 9, I will address this process in more detail.

Second, research in infant development clearly shows that infants possess a great many more cognitive skills than previously thought and that they are very actively involved in learning. For example, shortly after birth, neonates can discriminate and imitate happy, sad, and surprised facial expressions, indicating an innate ability to compare the sensory information of a visually perceived expression with the feedback of the movements involved in matching that expression. The developmental significance of such ability may be that it is the starting point of infant psychological development.[11]

For additional Internet resources or to complete an online activity for this chapter, go to the Companion Website at **http://www.prenhall.com/morrison**, select chapter 5, then choose the Linking to Learning or Making Connections module.

ACTIVITIES FOR FURTHER ENRICHMENT

APPLICATIONS

1. Now is a good time to review the philosophy you developed after reading chapter 1. How do your beliefs fit in with the theories presented in this chapter?
2. Compare Piaget's theory with another theory, such as Montessori's. How are they similar and different?
3. List five concepts or ideas about Piaget's theory that you consider most significant for how to teach and rear young children. Explain how learning about Piaget's beliefs and methods may be influencing your philosophy of teaching.
4. For each of the theories presented in this chapter, explain how you could apply some portion of it to your work with young children.

FIELD EXPERIENCES

1. Constructivists believe that one of the main functions of teachers is to create a climate for learning. Interview early childhood teachers and ask them what they believe are important elements or features of classrooms that support learning. From this teacher data, develop a list of characteristics that you will use in your classroom. Place this list in your portfolio or learning file.

2. In a constructivist classroom, children's autonomy and initiative are accepted. Observe classrooms and give examples of how teachers are encouraging or discouraging initiative and autonomy in their classrooms. Based on your observations, develop plans for how you will support these two important factors in promoting learning.
3. Visit early childhood classrooms and observe to determine which theories or theory you see being implemented.

RESEARCH

1. Observe three children—one six months old, one two years old, and one four years old. Note in each child's activities what you consider typical of behavior for that age. Can you find examples of behaviors that correspond to one of Piaget's stages?
2. Observe a child between birth and eighteen months. Can you cite any concrete evidence, such as specific actions or incidents, to support how the child is developing schemes of the world through sensorimotor actions?
3. Use the Links to Learning provided here to find out more information on each of the theories we discussed.

READINGS FOR FURTHER ENRICHMENT

Brooks, J., and Brooks, M. *In Search of Understanding: The Case for Constructivist Classrooms.* Alexandria, VA: Association for Supervision & Curriculum Development, 1999.

Builds a case for the development of classrooms where students construct deep understandings of important concepts. Presents new images for educational settings: student engagement, interaction, reflection, and construction.

Gardner, H. *Intelligence Reframed: Multiple Intelligences for the 21st Century.* Basic Books, 2000.

A revisitation and elaboration of Multiple Intelligence theory, Gardner details the modern history of intelligence and the development of MI, responds to the myths about multiple intelligences, and handles FAQs about the theory and its application. He also restates his ideal educational plan, which would emphasize deep understanding of iconic subjects following from a variety of instructional approaches.

Martin, D. *Elementary Science Methods: A Constructivism Approach.* Belmont, CA: Wadsworth, 2000.

This text's unique constructivist approach guides students in learning by doing. Geared to teachers of preschool through sixth grade students, it represents the cutting edge of elementary science teaching with up-to-date investigations into contemporary topics.

Oldfather, P., and West, J. *Learning Through Children's Eyes: Social Constructivism and the Desire to Learn.* Washington, DC: American Psychological Association, 1999.

The authors of this book show how teachers who take a social constructivist stance may enhance motivation and meaningful learning. The book illustrates the power of this theory by taking an interactive approach that includes discussion questions and case studies. Ideal for teacher education courses, professional development workshops, and independent use.

LINKING TO LEARNING

Building an Understanding of Constructivism
http://www.sedl.org/scimath/compass/v01n03/understand.html

A description of the basic tenets of constructivism and a list of resources.

Multidisciplinary/Cognitive Skills
http://www.ed.gov/pubs/EPTW/eptw10

This gopher site contains a complete list of projects on cognitive skills development approved by the U.S. Department of Education. (The Web address is case sensitive.)

Computers, Teachers, Peers
http://www.clp.berkeley.edu/CLP.html

This project at the University of California at Berkeley presents information on project-based learning, technology-supported scaffolding, and descriptions of activities and applications.

Constructivism and the Five Es
http://www.miamisci.org/ph/lpintro5e.html

    A description of constructivism and the "five Es"—Engage, Explore, Explain, Elaborate, and Evaluate.

Resources for the Constructivist Educator
http://www.users.interport.net/~roots/act/ACT1.html

    Web site for The Association for Constructivist Teaching, which provides a rich, problem-solving arena that encourages the learner's investigation, invention, and inference. Its mission is to enhance the growth of all educators and students through identification and dissemination of effective constructivist practices in both the professional cultures of teachers and the learning environment of children.

Essays on Constructivism and Education
http://towson.edu/csme/mctp/Essays.html

    A collection of essays compiled by the Maryland Collaborative for Teacher Preparation.

High/Scope Educational Research Foundation
http://www.highscope.org/

    An independent nonprofit research, development, training, and public advocacy organization whose mission is to improve the life chances of children and youth by promoting high-quality educational programs. Activities include training teachers and administrators, conducting research projects on the effectiveness of educational programs, developing curricula for programs, and publishing books, videos, and other tools for educators and researchers.

Jean Piaget and Genetic Epistemology
http://www.gwu.edu/~tip/piaget.html

    Detailed description of Piaget's theories concerning genetic epistemology. Site contains a QuickTime video clip of Piaget discussing this topic.

Critique of Piaget's Genetic Epistemology
http://hubcap.clemson.edu/~campber/piaget.html

    This website includes an extensive bibliography of Jean Piaget's life and works, as well as a critique and discussion of his chief ideas. This document is well cited, and provides the reader with a valuable resource from which to gain information about the noted psychologist.

ENDNOTES

[1] Brodzinsky, David M. and Sigel,Irving E., and Golinkoff, Roberta M. "New Dimensions in Piagetian Theory and Research: An Integrative Perspective," in *New Directions in Piagetian Theory and Practice*, ed. Irving E. Sigel, David M. Brodzinsky, and Roberta M. Golinkoff (Hillsdale, NJ: Erlbaum, 1981), 5.

[2] Kamii, Constance. "Application of Piaget's Theory to Education: The Preoperational Level," in *New Directions in Piagetian Theory and Practice*, ed. Irving E. Sigel, David M. Brodzinsky, and Roberta M. Golinkoff (Hillsdale, NJ: Erlbaum, 1981), 234.

[3] Spencer Pulaski, Mary Ann. *Understanding Piaget* (New York: Harper and Row, 1980), 9.

[4] Richmond,P. G., *An Introduction to Piaget* (New York: Basic Books, 1970), 68.

[5] Ibid.

[6] Vygotsky, L. S., *Mind in Society* (Cambridge, MA: Harvard University Press, 1978), 244.

[7] Tudge, Jonathan R. H., "Processes and Consequences of Peer Collaboration: A Vygotskian Analysis," *Child Development* 63 (1992), 1365.

[8] Ibid.

[9] Vygotsky, *Mind in Society*, 90.

[10] Tudge, "Processes and Consequences," 1365.

[11] Meltzoff, A. and Moore, K. M. "Resolving the Debate About Early Imitation," *Reader in Developmental Psychology* (1999): 151–155.

Part 3

Programs and Services for Children and Families

Chapter 6

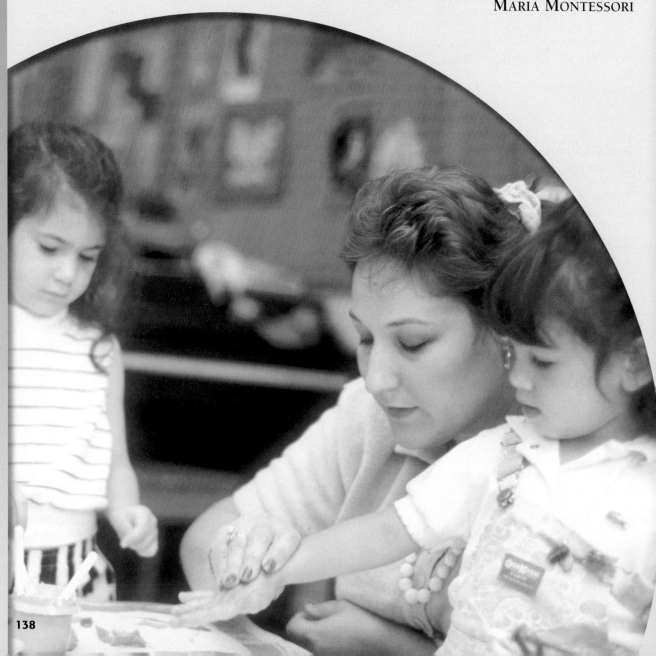

If education is always to be conceived along the same antiquated lines of a mere transmission of knowledge, there is little to be hoped from it. . . . For what is the use of transmitting knowledge if the individual's total development lags behind?

And so we discovered that education is not something which the teacher does, but that it is a natural process which develops spontaneously in the human being.

MARIA MONTESSORI

Early Childhood Programs
Applying Theories to Practice

Focus Questions

- Why is there a need for high-quality early childhood education programs?

- What are the basic features of high-quality early childhood education programs?

- What are the unique characteristics and strengths of early childhood education programs?

- How can you apply features of early childhood programs to your professional practice?

Parents want their children to attend high-quality programs that will provide them with a good start in life. They want to know that their children are being well cared for and educated. Parents want their children to get along with others, be happy, and learn. How to best meet these legitimate parental expectations is one of the ongoing challenges of early childhood professionals.

THE GROWING DEMAND FOR QUALITY EARLY CHILDHOOD PROGRAMS

The National Association for the Education of Young Children (NAEYC), the nation's largest organization of early childhood educators, accredits 7,600 early childhood programs serving almost 700,000 children. An additional 8,000 programs are in the process of being accredited. These programs are only a fraction of the total number of early childhood programs in the United States. Think for a minute about what goes on in these and other programs from day to day. For some children, teachers and staff have developed well-thought-out and articulated programs that provide for their growth and development across all the developmental domains—cognitive, linguistic, emotional, social, and physical. In other programs, children are not so fortunate. Their days are filled with aimless activities that fail to meet their academic and developmental needs.

With the national spotlight on the importance of the early years, the public is demanding more from early childhood professionals and their programs. On the one hand, the public is willing to invest more heavily in early childhood programs, but on the other hand, it is demanding that the early childhood profession and individual programs respond by providing meaningful programs. The public demands these things from early childhood professionals:

- *Programs that will help ensure children's early academic and school success.* The public believes that too many children are being left out and left behind.

To review the chapter focus questions online, go to the Companion Website at **http://www. prenhall.com/morrison** and select chapter 6.

- *The inclusion of early literacy and reading readiness activities in programs and curricula that will enable children to read on grade level in grades one, two, and three.* Literacy is the key to much of school and life success, and school success begins in preschool and before.
- *Environments that will help children develop the social and behavioral skills necessary to help them lead civilized and nonviolent lives.* In the wake of daily news headlines about shooting and assaults by younger and younger children, the public wants early childhood programs to assume an ever-growing responsibility for helping get children off to a nonviolent start in life.

Model early childhood program An exemplary approach to early childhood education that serves as a guide to best practices.

To check your understanding of this chapter with the online Study Guide, go to the Companion Website at **http://www.prenhall.com/morrison**, select chapter 6, then choose the Study Guide module.

As a result of these public demands, there is a growing and critical need for programs that teachers and others can adopt and use. In this chapter we examine and discuss some of the more notable programs for use in early childhood settings. As you read about and reflect on each of these, think about their strengths and weaknesses and the ways each tries to best meet the needs of children and families. One thing is certain: We cannot conduct business as usual. The public will demand more of us than that. The public will hold you and your colleagues accountable for programs that at a minimum meet the needs mentioned earlier. Pause for a minute and review Table 6.1, which outlines the **model early childhood programs** discussed in this chapter.

Let's now look at three highly regarded and widely adopted model programs: Montessori, High/Scope and Reggio Emilia. There is a good probability that you will be associated in some way as a teacher, parent, or advisory board member with one of these programs. In any event, you will want to be informed about their main features and operating principles.

PRINCIPLES OF THE MONTESSORI METHOD

Montessori method A system of early childhood education founded on the ideas and practices of Maria Montessori.

The following basic principles are a synthesis of Montessori ideas and practices. They fairly and accurately represent how Montessori educators implement the Montessori method in many kinds of programs across the United States. Figure 6.1 illustrates five basic principles of the **Montessori method**.

TABLE 6.1 Models of Early Childhood Education: Similarities and Differences

Program	Main Features	Theoretical Basis
Montessori	• Prepared environment supports, invites, and enables learning. • Children educate themselves—self-directed learning. • Sensory materials invite and promote learning. • Set curriculum regarding what children should learn—Montessorians try to stay as close to Montessori's ideas as possible. • Grouping is multiage. • Students learn by manipulative materials and working with others. • Learning takes place through the senses.	• Montessori's beliefs about children
High Scope	• Plan–do–review teaching–learning cycle. • Emergent curriculum—curriculum is not established in advance. • Children help determine curriculum. • Key experiences guide the curriculum in promoting children's active learning.	• Piagetian • Constructivist • Dewey
Reggio Emilia	• Emergent curriculum—curriculum is not established in advance. • Curriculum is based on children's interests and experiences. • Project-oriented curriculum. • Thousand Languages of Children—symbolic representation of work and learning. • Learning is active. • *Atelierista* (teachers are trained in the arts). • *Atelier* (art/design studio).	• Piagetian • Constructivist • Vygotskian • Dewey

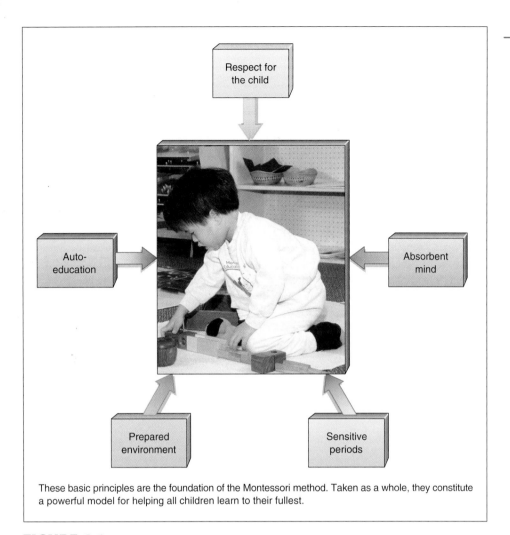

These basic principles are the foundation of the Montessori method. Taken as a whole, they constitute a powerful model for helping all children learn to their fullest.

FIGURE 6.1 **Basic Montessori Principles**

RESPECT FOR THE CHILD

Respect for the child is the cornerstone on which all other Montessori principles rest. As Montessori said:

> As a rule, however, we do not respect children. We try to force them to follow us without regard to their special needs. We are overbearing with them, and above all, rude; and then we expect them to be submissive and well-behaved, knowing all the time how strong is their instinct of imitation and how touching their faith in and admiration of us. They will imitate us in any case. Let us treat them, therefore, with all the kindness which we would wish to help to develop in them.[1]

Because each child is unique, education should be individualized, as Montessori stated, "There exists only one real biological manifestation: the living individual; and toward single individuals, one by one observed, education must direct itself."[2]

Educators and parents show respect for children in many ways. Helping children do things and learn for themselves, for example, encourages and promotes independence. At the same time, it also demonstrates a basic respect for their needs as individuals to be independent and self-regulating. When children have choices, they are able to develop the skills and abilities necessary for effective learning, autonomy, and positive self-esteem. (The theme of respect for children resurfaces in our discussion of guiding behavior in chapter 14.)

THE ABSORBENT MIND

Montessori believed that children educate themselves: "It may be said that we acquire knowledge by using our minds; but the child absorbs knowledge directly into his psychic life. Simply by continuing to live, the child learns to speak his native tongue."[3] This is the concept of the **absorbent mind**.

There are unconscious and conscious stages in the development of the absorbent mind. From birth to three years, the unconscious absorbent mind develops the senses used for seeing, hearing, tasting, smelling, and touching. The child literally absorbs everything.

From three to six years, the conscious absorbent mind selects sensory impressions from the environment and further develops the senses. In this phase children are selective in that they refine what they know. For example, children in the unconscious stage merely see and absorb an array of colors without distinguishing among them; however, from three on, they develop the ability to distinguish, match, and grade colors.

Montessori wanted us to understand that children cannot help but learn. Simply by living, children learn from their environment. Children are born to learn, and they are remarkable learning systems. Children learn because they are thinking beings. What they learn depends greatly on the people in their environment, what those people say and do, and how they react. In addition, available experiences and materials also help determine the type and quality of learning—and thus the type and quality of the individual.

Early childhood professionals are reemphasizing the idea that children are born into the world learning and with constant readiness and ability to learn. We will discuss these concepts further in chapter 9.

SENSITIVE PERIODS

Montessori believed there are **sensitive periods** when children are more susceptible to certain behaviors and can learn specific skills more easily:

A sensitive period refers to a special sensibility which a creature acquires in its infantile state, while it is still in a process of evolution. It is a transient disposition and limited to the acquisition of a particular trait. Once this trait or characteristic has been acquired, the special sensibility disappears. . . .[4]

The secret of using sensitive periods in teaching is to recognize them when they occur. Although all children experience the same sensitive periods (e.g., a sensitive period for writing), the sequence and timing vary for each child. Therefore, it becomes the role of the teacher or the parent to detect times of sensitivity and provide the setting for optimum fulfillment. Observation thus becomes crucial for teachers and parents. Indeed, many educators believe that information gained by observation of children's achievement and behavior is more accurate than that acquired through the use of tests. Refer to chapter 3 to learn how to do this through guidelines for observing children.

THE PREPARED ENVIRONMENT

Montessori believed that children learn best in a **prepared environment**, the purpose of which is to make children independent of adults. It is a place in which children can *do things for themselves*. The prepared environment also makes learning materials and experiences available to children in an orderly format. The ideal classrooms Montessori described are

Absorbent mind The idea that the minds of young children are receptive to and capable of learning. The child learns unconsciously by taking in information from the environment.

Sensitive period In imprinting, this is a relatively brief time during which learning is most likely to occur. Also called the critical period.

Prepared environment A classroom or other space that is arranged and organized to support learning in general and/or special knowledge and skills.

really what educators advocate when they talk about child-centered education and active learning. Freedom is the essential characteristic of the prepared environment. Since children within the environment are free to explore materials of their own choosing, they absorb what they find there.

AUTOEDUCATION

Montessori referred to the concept that children are capable of educating themselves as **autoeducation** (also known as self-education). Children who are actively involved in a prepared environment and exercising freedom of choice literally educate themselves. Through the principle of autoeducation, Montessori focuses our attention on this human capability. The art of teaching includes preparing the environment so that children, by participating in it, educate themselves.

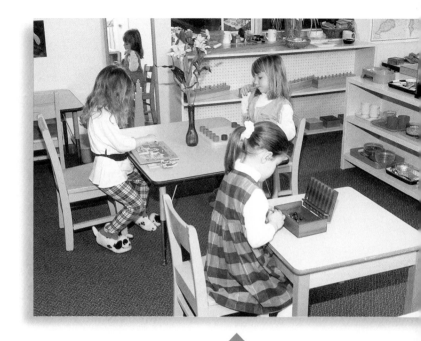

THE TEACHER'S ROLE

Montessori believed that "it is necessary for the teacher to guide the child without letting him feel her presence too much, so that she may be always ready to supply the desired help, but may never be the obstacle between the child and his experience."[5]

The Montessori teacher should demonstrate certain behaviors to implement the principles of this child-centered approach, listed below and shown in Figure 6.2.

1. *Make children the center of learning.* As Montessori said, "The teacher's task is not to talk, but to prepare and arrange a series of motives for cultural activity in a special environment made for the child."[6]
2. *Encourage children to learn* by providing freedom for them in the prepared environment.
3. *Observe children* so as to prepare the best possible environment, recognizing sensitive periods and diverting inappropriate behavior to meaningful tasks.
4. *Prepare the learning environment* by ensuring that the learning materials are provided in an orderly format and that the materials provide for the appropriate experiences for all the children.
5. *Respect each child* and model ongoing respect for all children and their work.
6. *Introduce learning materials,* demonstrate learning materials, and support children's learning. The teacher introduces learning materials after observing each child.

HOW DOES THE MONTESSORI METHOD WORK?

In a prepared environment, materials and activities provide for three basic areas of child involvement: practical life or motor education, sensory materials for training the senses, and academic materials for teaching writing, reading, and mathematics. All these activities are taught according to a prescribed procedure.

PRACTICAL LIFE

The prepared environment emphasizes basic, everyday motor activities, such as walking from place to place in an orderly manner, carrying objects such as trays and chairs, greeting a visitor, learning self-care skills, and other **practical life** activities. For example, the

A Montessori environment is characterized by orderliness. The low shelving gives children ready access to materials to encourage their use. Why is it important to prepare such an organized environment?

Autoeducation The idea that children teach themselves through appropriate materials and activities.

For more information about the Montessori Curriculum model, go to the Companion Website at **http:// www.prenhall.com/morrison**, select chapter 6, then choose the Linking to Learning module to connect to a variety of Montessori sites.

Practical life Montessori activities that teach skills related to everyday living.

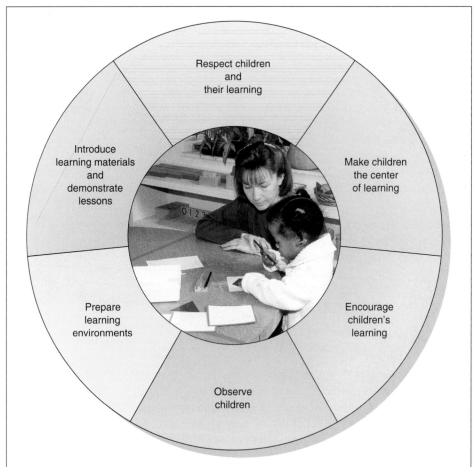

These six essential roles of the Montessori teacher make child-centered, high-quality education a reality. These roles practiced by highly skilled teachers help distinguish the Montessori approach from other programs.

FIGURE 6.2   Teacher's Role in a Montessori Classroom

While these roles are especially prescribed for Montessori teachers, they are applicable to all teachers. You can use these essential roles to help you become a good teacher regardless of the type of program or curriculum you have in your classroom.

dressing frames are designed to perfect the motor skills involved in buttoning, zipping, lacing, buckling, and tying. The philosophy for activities such as these is to make children independent of the adult and develop concentration.

Practical life activities are taught through four different types of exercises. *Care of the person* involves activities such as using the dressing frames, polishing shoes, and washing hands. *Care of the environment* includes dusting, polishing a table, and raking leaves. *Social relations* include lessons in grace and courtesy. The fourth type of exercise involves *analysis and control of movement* and includes locomotor activities such as walking and balancing.

Sensory materials
Montessori learning materials designed to promote learning through the senses and to train the senses for learning.

SENSORY MATERIALS

The following **sensory materials** are among those found in a typical Montessori classroom (the learning purpose appears in parentheses):

144

- *Pink tower* (visual discrimination of dimension)—ten wood cubes of the same shape and texture, all pink, the largest of which is ten centimeters cubed. Each succeeding block is one centimeter smaller. Children build a tower beginning with the largest block.

- *Brown stairs* (visual discrimination of width and height)—ten blocks of wood, all brown, differing in height and width. Children arrange the blocks next to each other from thickest to thinnest so the blocks resemble a staircase.

- *Red rods* (visual discrimination of length)—ten rod-shaped pieces of wood, all red, of identical size but differing in lengths from ten centimeters to one meter. The child arranges the rods next to each other from largest to smallest.

- *Cylinder blocks* (visual discrimination of size)—four individual wood blocks that have holes of various sizes; one block deals with height, one with diameter, and two with the relationship of both variables. Children remove the cylinders in random order, then match each cylinder to the correct hole.

▲ Practical life activities help children learn about and practice everyday activities. Children enjoy doing practical, useful activities. Why do you think this is?

- *Smelling jars* (olfactory discrimination)—two identical sets of white, opaque glass jars with removable tops through which the child cannot see but through which odors can pass. The teacher places various substances, such as herbs, in the jars, and the child matches the jars according to the smells.

- *Baric tablets* (discrimination of weight)—sets of rectangular pieces of wood that vary according to weight. There are three sets—light, medium, and heavy—which children match according to the weight of the tablets.

- *Color tablets* (discrimination of color and education of the chromatic sense)—two identical sets of small, rectangular pieces of wood used for matching color or shading.

- *Sound boxes* (auditory discrimination)—two identical sets of cylinders filled with various materials, such as salt and rice. Children match the cylinders according to the sound the fillings make.

- *Tonal bells* (sound and pitch)—two sets of eight bells, alike in shape and size but different in color; one set is white, the other brown. The child matches the bells by tone.

- *Cloth swatches* (sense of touch)—two identical swatches of cloth. Children identify them according to touch, first without a blindfold but later using a blindfold.

- *Temperature jugs or thermic bottles* (thermic sense and ability to distinguish between temperatures)—small metal jugs filled with water of varying temperatures. Children match jugs of the same temperature.

Materials for training and developing the senses have these characteristics:

- *Control of error.* Materials are designed so that children can see if they make a mistake; for example, if a child does not build the blocks of the pink tower in their proper order, she does not achieve a tower effect.

- *Isolation of a single quality.* Materials are designed so that other variables are held constant except for the isolated quality or qualities. Therefore, all blocks of the pink tower are pink because size, not color, is the isolated quality.
- *Active involvement.* Materials encourage active involvement rather than the more passive process of looking.
- *Attractiveness.* Materials are attractive, with colors and proportions that appeal to children.

One purpose of Montessori sensory materials is to train children's senses to focus on some obvious, particular quality; for example, with the red rods, the quality is length; with pink tower cubes, size; and with bells, musical pitch. Montessori felt it is necessary to help children discriminate among the many stimuli they receive. Accordingly, the sensory materials help make children more aware of the capacity of their bodies to receive, interpret, and make use of stimuli. In this sense, the Montessori sensory materials are labeled didactic, designed to instruct.

Second, Montessori thought that perception and the ability to observe details were crucial to reading. The sensory materials help sharpen children's powers of observation and visual discrimination as readiness for learning to read.

A third purpose of the sensory materials is to increase children's ability to think, a process that depends on the ability to distinguish, classify, and organize. Children constantly face decisions about sensory materials: which block comes next, which color matches the other, which shape goes where. These are not decisions the teacher makes, nor are they decisions children arrive at by guessing; rather, they are decisions made by the intellectual process of observation and selection based on knowledge gathered through the senses.

Finally, all the sensory activities are not ends in themselves. Their purpose is to prepare children for the occurrence of the sensitive periods for writing and reading. In this sense, all activities are preliminary steps in the writing–reading process.

▲
This child is learning visual relationships and improving her visual motor skills while working on a physical, land-water geographic activity. Montessori believed that it is important for children to learn geographical concepts as basis for learning about their world.

ACADEMIC MATERIALS FOR WRITING, READING, AND MATHEMATICS

The third area of Montessori materials is academic; specifically, items for writing, reading, and mathematics. Exercises are presented in a sequence that encourages writing before reading. Reading is therefore an outgrowth of writing. Both processes, however, are introduced so gradually that children are never aware they are learning to write and read until one day they realize they are writing and reading. Describing this phenomenon, Montessori said that children "burst spontaneously" into writing and reading. Montessori anticipated contemporary practices, such as the whole language approach, in integrating writing and reading and in maintaining that through writing children learn to read.

Montessori believed that many children were ready for writing at four years of age. Consequently, a child who enters a Montessori system at age three has done most of the sensory exercises by the time he is four. It is not uncommon to see four- and five-year-olds in a Montessori classroom writing and reading. Figure 6.3 shows an example of children's writing.

Following are examples of Montessori materials that lay the foundation for and promote writing and reading:

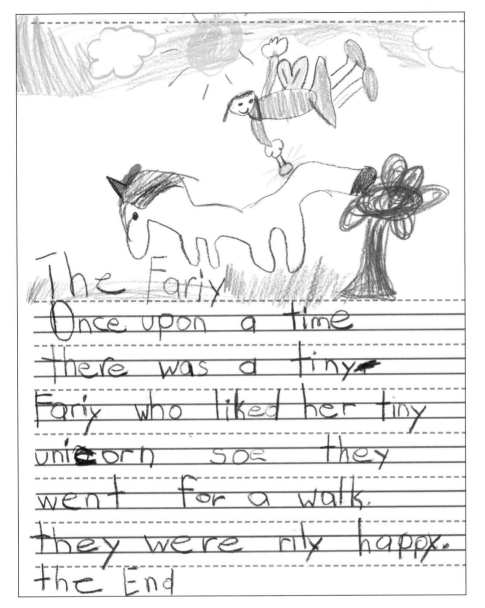

FIGURE 6.3 Writing Sample by Montessori Student Ella Rivas-Chacon

- *Ten geometric forms and colored pencils.* These introduce children to the coordination necessary for writing. After selecting a geometric inset, children trace it on paper and fill in the outline with a colored pencil of their choosing.
- *Sandpaper letters.* Each letter of the alphabet is outlined in sandpaper on a card, with vowels in blue and consonants in red. Children see the shape, feel the shape, and hear the sound of the letter, which the teacher repeats when introducing it.
- *Movable alphabet, with individual letters.* Children learn to put together familiar words.
- *Command cards.* These are a set of red cards with a single action word printed on each card. Children read the word on the card and do what the word tells them to do (e.g., run, jump).

Reading First—and Always!

Students in the K/1 classroom at University Primary School begin their day reading a daily sign-in question that is intended to provoke a thoughtful response. For example, "Have you ever eaten the flowers of a plant?" or "Do you think a van is more like a car or a bus?" These questions are related to the topic of the project investigations under study and are intended to engage children in discussing their different views during their whole group meeting later in the morning.

Opportunities for children to express themselves abound at University Primary School. In addition to an hour of systematic literacy instruction, authentic and meaningful opportunities to read and write occur throughout their day in the course of the children's regular activities.

Providing students with meaningful topics to read and write about is a major key to the successful integration of literacy skills into a curriculum that incorporates project investigations. The project approach involves students in conducting in-depth investigations of worthy real world topics (Katz & Chard, 2000). Learning becomes meaningful for students as they pursue answers to their own questions.

In the beginning of the project (Phase 1), students recall and share their previous experiences related to the topic through stories, pictures, and representations. By labeling pictures and writing stories, students utilize phonemic awareness and phonetics by identifying the individual sounds and writing the letters to match the sounds.

During Phase 2, the investigative phase, students write questions, predictions, hypotheses, and collect data. Data collection involves doing fieldwork, making observational drawings, recording findings, constructing representations, analyzing data, and placing the data in a variety of graphic organizers. Students develop surveys and write stories of their experiences, thank you letters, and captions for their drawings or photographs. Throughout this phase, students have authentic contexts to spell, write words, and build their vocabulary.

In whole group time, students listen to stories and informational texts read aloud to them about the topic. They also read secondary sources to help answer their questions and compare what they read with what the experts shared. By comparing what they knew with what they have learned from the secondary sources, they develop their analytical thinking and comprehension skills. They become more fluent readers and writers by using their skills to answer their own questions.

Phase 3 is the culmination and sharing of the project with parents and families. Students reflect on their new understandings and choose to represent what they have learned by making charts, displays, reports, PowerPoint presentations, or plays to share with their families. Some students share their stories orally in "Readers Theatre."

The five reading components articulated in the *No Child Left Behind Act,* phonemic awareness, phonics, fluency, vocabulary, and comprehension, are taught throughout the students' day within the context of project investigations and during small group direct literacy instruction. Direct instruction includes a whole group meeting where the teacher reads books aloud (shared reading) for specific purposes. The teacher may choose to highlight specific authors or illustrators. She might choose stories that focus on rhyming words or specific patterns of phonemes. Following the shared reading time, students engage in writing activities related to the story they heard. These activities may include literature extensions that encourage students to write creatively. They may write a different ending to the story they heard or write a related story from a different point of view. Students may also write their own stories using the *principles of writer's workshop* where students learn to edit and extend their language skills. The teacher may also introduce extended mini-lessons on authors' tools of writing such as alliteration, similes, metaphors, or syllabic rhythms. After their noon recess, students choose books to read quietly while the teacher provides individual guided reading. Students conclude their silent reading with approximately ten minutes to engage in "buddy reading." During the buddy reading time, students talk about what they have just read with their "buddy" and read favorite excerpts of their books to their buddy. This collaboration reinforces comprehension skills and instills the love of literature that motivates all children to read. At University Primary School, students are always improving and using their literacy skills!

Katz, L. G., & Chard, S.C. (2000). *Engaging children's minds: The project approach.* (2nd ed.). Norwood, NJ: Ablex Publishing Corporation.

Contributed by Nancy B. Hertzog, Ph.D. Assistant Professor, Department of Special Education and Director, University Primary School and Marjorie M. Klein, Head Teacher, K/1.

The following are examples of materials for mathematics:

- *Number rods.* A set of red and blue rods varying in length from ten centimeters to one meter, representing the quantities one through ten. With the help of the teacher, children are introduced to counting.
- *Sandpaper numerals.* Each number from one to nine is outlined in sandpaper on a card. Children see, touch, and hear the numbers. They eventually match number rods and sandpaper numerals. Children also have the opportunity to discover mathematical facts through the use of these numerals.
- *Golden beads.* A concrete material for the decimal system. The single bead represents one unit. A bar made up of ten units in a row represents a ten; ten of the ten bars form a square representing one hundred; and ten hundred squares form the cube representing one thousand.

Montessori recognized the importance of reading and writing and her materials support these essential life activities. All high-quality programs assure that children gain the essential language and literacy skills necessary for success. It is appropriate, then, that the Voice from the Field on the following page underscores the importance of reading.

MONTESSORI AS AN EDUCATIONAL SYSTEM

MONTESSORI AND THE PUBLIC SCHOOLS

Patricia McGrath was the first to implement Montessori in the public schools in the United States. She taught a Montessori methods class in Philadelphia, Pennsylvania, at the Benjamin Franklin Elementary School from 1968 to 1974. Since then, Montessori programs have been implemented in many public school programs, especially preschool programs and kindergartens.

 For more information about Montessori education, go to the Companion Website at **http://www. prenhall.com/morrison**, select chapter 6, then choose the Linking to Learning module to connect to a variety of Montessori sites.

A number of reasons account for the public school popularity of Montessori. First, Montessori is one of many programs of early childhood education that the public schools have used to *restructure,* or fundamentally change, the way they educate children. This restructuring of the schools is in keeping with the reform of early childhood education.

Second, public school Montessori programs are often used at *magnet* schools. Although the basic purpose of magnet schools is to integrate schools racially, at the same time they give parents a choice about what kind of program to give their children. Magnet schools as a means of integration have enabled professionals to use federal dollars that otherwise would not be available to them. Without a doubt the availability of federal dollars has been a major factor for public school implementation of the Montessori program. If Montessori is implemented to the level it should be, the cost can be $20,000 a classroom.

Third, since Montessori developed her program for children with disabilities, some public schools see the Montessori method as an ideal inclusion of the learning needs of today's children with disabilities. Many Montessori programs practice *inclusion,* educating children with disabilities in regular education classrooms. More information about inclusion is provided in chapter 16.

The application of Montessori to the public school settings is so popular that these professionals have their own publication, the *Public School Montessorian* (published by Jola Publications, 2933 N. Second St., Minneapolis, MN 55411, http://www.jolapub.com).

The following Program in Action will help you get an up-close look at the Montessori program in action.

A Day in the Life of a Child in a Full-Day Montessori Environment

In the heart of Denver's lowest-income neighborhood, Edna Oliver Montessori Child Development Center, one of Mile High Child Care's thirteen sites, offers a quality, full-day, Montessori program for eighty-three children, eight weeks to eight years of age. A staff member from each age group served (infants: birth to 18 months, toddlers: 18 months to 30/36 months, preschoolers: 2½/3 to 6 years, and schoolagers: 5 to 8 years) is there to greet children beginning at 6:30 every morning, and another to bid children farewell at 6:00 in the evening. Some children stay the full eleven and a half hours, depending on the number of jobs the parents have and/or the shifts they work. All of the children eat breakfast, lunch, and dinner at the center five days a week, year round.

Preschool children arriving between 6:30 and 8 A.M. gather together in one of the two preschool classrooms to begin their day. Some of the first children to arrive seem as though they are still waking up, and find a soft corner or a quiet area to prepare themselves to join the group at their own pace. Others busy themselves with the tasks involved in readying the classroom for the day and seem to enjoy and take pride in their responsibilities. They turn on the calming music, open the shades covering the windows, wet all the sponges for each activity, fill the paint bucket with water, open and stir the paint in the paint jars with the paint brushes, slice two bananas into six unpeeled chunks and put them in the jar with the food preparation activity, feed the fish and gerbils and refill the water bottle in the gerbil cage, check activities to be sure they are supplied for the children's use that day, and set the table for breakfast. Some other children choose individual activities from the shelves, or find a friend to engage in an activity together. Children identify their own needs and choose appropriate experiences for themselves throughout the day; this is an integral part of the Montessori methodology.

While supervising the children's activities, the Montessori teacher greets arriving children and parents, and receives and relays pertinent messages about the children and program activities, for example, a mom who could be reached that day at a different number in case of emergency, the child who was returning from two days of illness, the field trip to the Museum the next week. At 7:00 an assistant arrives to help. Most staff work eight-hour staggered shifts to maintain adequate teacher/child ratio throughout the day; some part-time staff are hired to help in the early morning and late afternoon.

When breakfast arrives in the classroom at 7:45 A.M., the children wash their hands, sit at the set tables, and join in a community meal, chatting about their plans for the day and sharing about their home life the night before, while they serve themselves and pass the food to the next child, family style. As they finish, each child pushes his chair in, scrapes the leftovers from his dish and puts it in the bucket, sweeps up any crumbs on the table or floor, wipes his place at the table, washes his hands and brushes his teeth, and goes off to choose an activity in that classroom, or the classroom down the hall, depending on which he belongs to. It is the job of two children on a rotating basis to assure the breakfast area is completely cleaned up, and the cart of leftovers and dirty dishes is returned to the cook in the kitchen.

By 8:30 A.M., the children are all engaged in various activities; some have chosen activities they will work on by themselves and some have chosen to interact with another child or a small group of children on some activity or project. Choices vary depending on what each child has been presented, personal learning styles, individual personalities, personal preferences, activities chosen as they may be for only one person, a suggestion from an adult or another child, the need to complete an activity that was begun previously, and so forth. The teacher involves herself in giving the children lessons on the various activities, one after another, while the assistant helps the children as needed, assuring they choose and follow through on activities appropriate for their abilities.

The guideline of respect for self, others and the environment has been established for the children: they know they need to ask the teacher for a lesson on an activity they have not yet been shown; they know to return activities to the shelf, clean and ready for another child to use them; they know to take care of the materials so they will stay beautiful; they know to not disturb another child's activity unless invited by that child. They know all this because this guideline of respect is continually reinforced by the teacher, the assistant, and the children.

Following a two-and-a-half-hour individual choice activity period, the children gather together for a fifteen-minute group activity. This teacher-directed time could include singing songs, reciting poetry, movement, dance, music, a group meeting or discussion, storytelling, etc. Many of the activities planned for this time connect to the monthly theme that may be botany, or ecology, or something else depending on the majority of the children's interests at the time.

A thirty- to forty-five-minute period outdoors on the playground occurs next. The children immediately seek their favorite outdoor activities such as trikes, swings, caring for the garden, sandbox, climbing structure, basketball, chatting in the shade under the trees, playing hide-and-seek. The teacher and assistant both interact with the children as they ensure their safety and encourage the development of both gross motor and social skills. Occasionally, this time is used for nature exploration (even in the city!) or a walk around the community, which helps build understanding and relationships, a sense of connectedness with their neighborhood community.

At about 12 noon, children are approached, three to four at a time, to return inside and prepare for lunch. The first children inside wash their hands and help set up the tables, moving them together so that four to eight children sit at each, and setting out flatware, plates, glasses, napkins, pitchers of milk, serving utensils, and bowls of food at each table. As children sit at the table, they serve themselves and engage in discussions as they wait for everyone at their table to start eating together. Clean up for lunch occurs the same as breakfast. As children finish cleaning up, they each get their mat, sheet and blanket; make their bed/rest mat; get a book to look at/read; and lay down for nap.

After twenty minutes of quiet, older children who are not needing a nap are invited to choose quiet activities until the other children wake up. This is a time the children generally engage in more advanced math and language activities with one or two other children, receiving more one-on-one guidance from the adult.

As children wake up, they put their mats, sheets and blankets away, and they are free to choose their own activities. In most cases, however, these full-day children choose to follow the lead of others, whether that be watching others as they do their activities, listening to a story read by an adult, finding pieces to a 100-piece puzzle over casual conversations, listening to classical music while gazing out the window, etc. Though children of this age are quite capable of making good decisions regarding their own development and the activities that lead to that development, decisions do not come easily to them at this time of the day. Respect for their need to not direct themselves is facilitated by the teacher who has prepared this full-day environment to include opportunities for minimal participation and small group activities and prepared the schedule in such a way that this choice time in the afternoon is brief, 45 to 60 minutes in length.

At 3:45/4:00 P.M., the children again head outside to the playground. They return inside at 4:30 for dinner, in the same manner as before, a few children at a time. Following dinner, the children can again choose their own activities and/or participate in the closing of the classroom for the day. Their end-of-the-day responsibilities include cleaning the easel and brushes and closing the paints, replenishing paper and consumable supplies in the activities, sweeping the floor, emptying the trash and replacing the bag, putting children's dry art work into their folders, etc.

Staff greet parents as they come to retrieve their children between 5 and 6 P.M., and encourage the children to tell their parents about their day as they depart, giving them a specific reminder about something pertinent that occurred to them as a trigger for parent/child communication on the way home.

This account by Janet Humphryes M.A., director of education of Mile High Child Care, is based on the program and activities of the Mile High Child Care program at Edna Oliver Montessori Child Development Center in Denver, Colorado. There are six AMS (American Montessori Society)-certified directresses/teachers, and an AMI (Association Montessori International)-certified director at this center.

To complete a Program in Action activity, visit the Companion Website at **http://www. prenhall.com/morrison**, select chapter 6, then choose the Program in Action module.

MONTESSORI AND CONTEMPORARY PRACTICES

The Montessori approach supports many methods used in contemporary early childhood programs. Some of these are the following:

- *Integrated curriculum.* Montessori provides an integrated curriculum in which children are actively involved in manipulating concrete materials across the curriculum—writing, reading, science, math, geography, and the arts. The Montessori curriculum is integrated in other ways, such as across age and developmental levels. Montessori materials are age appropriate for a wide age range of children.
- *Active learning.* In Montessori classrooms, children are actively involved in their own learning, as dramatized in the Program in Action feature, "A Day in the Life of a Child in a Full-Day Montessori Environment." Manipulative materials provide for active and concrete learning.
- *Individualized instruction.* Curriculum and activities should be individualized for children. Montessori does this through individualizing learning for all children. Individualization occurs through children's interactions with the materials as they proceed at their own rates of mastery.
- *Independence.* The Montessori environment emphasizes respect for children and promotes success, both of which encourage children to be independent. Indeed, independence has always been a hallmark of Montessori.
- *Appropriate assessment.* Observation is the primary means of assessing children's progress, achievement, and behavior in a Montessori classroom. Well-trained Montessori teachers are skilled observers of children and are adept at translating their observation into appropriate ways for guiding, directing, facilitating, and channeling children's active learning.
- *Developmentally appropriate practice.* From the preceding illustrations, it is apparent that the concepts and process of developmentally appropriate curricula and practice (see chapters 9 through 12) are inherent in the Montessori method. Indeed, it may well be that some of the most developmentally appropriate practices are conducted by Montessori practitioners.

Furthermore, I suspect that quality Montessori practitioners understand, as Maria Montessori did, that children are much more capable than some early childhood education practitioners think.

FURTHER THOUGHTS

In many respects, Maria Montessori was a person for all generations, and her method is proving to be a program for all generations. Montessori contributed greatly to early childhood programs and practices. Through her method she will continue to do so. Many of her practices—such as preparing the environment, providing child-size furniture, promoting active learning and independence, and using multiage grouping—have been incorporated into many early childhood classrooms. As a result, it is easy to take her contributions, like Froebel's, for granted. We do many things in a Montessorian way without thinking too much about it.

As we have noted, today Montessori education is enjoying another rebirth, especially in the public schools' embracing of its method. What is important is that early childhood professionals adopt the best of Montessori for children of the twenty-first century. As with any practice, professionals must adopt approaches to fit the children they are teaching while remaining true to what is best in that approach. Respect for children is never out of date and should be accorded to all children regardless of culture, gender, or socioeconomic background.

We have the tremendous benefit of hindsight when it comes to evaluating and analyzing educational thought and practice. In this process we need to consider what was appropriate then and determine what is appropriate today. When appropriate, early childhood professionals need to make reasoned and appropriate changes in educational practice. This is what "growing" the profession is all about.

More information about Montessori programs and training can be obtained by writing to the following organizations:

- The American Montessori Society, 281 Park Ave. South, 6th floor, New York, NY 10010-6102; 212-358-1250. http://www.amshq.org/
- Association Montessori International (this is the oldest international Montessori organization, founded by Maria Montessori in 1929). Address inquiries to AMI/USA, 410 Alexander St., Rochester, NY 14607; 716-461-5920
- North American Montessori Teachers' Association (NAMTA), 11424 Bellflower Rd. NE, Cleveland, OH 44106; 216-421-1905. http://www.montessori-namta.org/

HIGH/SCOPE: A CONSTRUCTIVIST APPROACH

The High/Scope Educational Research Foundation is a nonprofit organization that sponsors and supports the **High/Scope** Educational Approach. The program is based on Piaget's intellectual development theory discussed in chapter 5. High/Scope provides broad, realistic educational experiences for children geared to their current stages of development to promote the constructive processes of learning necessary to broaden emerging intellectual and social skills.[7]

High/Scope An educational program for young children based on Piaget's ideas.

High/Scope is based on three fundamental principles:

1. Active participation of children in choosing, organizing, and evaluating learning activities, which are undertaken with careful teacher observation and guidance in a learning environment replete with a rich variety of materials located in various classroom learning centers
2. Regular daily planning by the teaching staff in accord with a developmentally based curriculum model and careful child observations
3. Developmentally sequenced goals and materials for children based on the High/Scope "key experiences"[8]

 For more information about High/Scope, go to the Companion Website at **http://www.prenhall.com/morrison**, select chapter 6, then choose the Linking to Learning module to connect to the High/Scope Education Research Foundation site.

BASIC PRINCIPLES AND GOALS OF THE HIGH/SCOPE APPROACH

The High/Scope program strives to

develop in children a broad range of skills, including the problem solving, interpersonal, and communication skills that are essential for successful living in a rapidly changing society. The curriculum encourages student initiative by providing children with materials, equipment, and time to pursue activities they choose. At the same time, it provides teachers with a framework for guiding children's independent activities toward sequenced learning goals.

The teacher plays a key role in instructional activities by selecting appropriate, developmentally sequenced material and by encouraging children to adopt an active problem-solving approach to learning. . . . This teacher–student interaction— teachers helping students achieve developmentally sequenced goals while also encouraging them to set many of their own goals—uniquely distinguishes the High/Scope Curriculum from direct-instruction and child-centered curricula.[9]

The High/Scope approach influences the arrangement of the classroom, the manner in which teachers interact with children, and the methods employed to assess children. The

High/Scope in Practice

The High/Scope educational approach for three- to five-year-olds is a developmental model based on the principle of active learning. The following beliefs underlie this approach:

- Children construct knowledge through their active involvement with people, materials, events, and ideas, a process that is intrinsically motivated.
- While children develop capacities in a predictable sequence, adult support contributes to children's intellectual, social, emotional, and physical development.
- Consistent adult support and respect for children's choices, thoughts, and actions strengthen the child's self-respect, feelings of responsibility, self-control, and knowledge.
- Careful observation of children's interests and intentions is a necessary step in understanding their level of development and planning and carrying out appropriate interactions with them.

In High/Scope programs these principles are implemented throughout the day, both through the structure of the daily routine and in the strategies adults use as they work with children. Staff of each program plan for the day's experiences, striving to create a balance between adult- and child-initiated activity.

As they plan activities, the staff considers five "factors of intrinsic motivation" that research indicates are essential for learning. These factors are enjoyment, interest, control, probability of success, and feelings of competence. During greeting circle and small group, staff members actively involve the children in decisions about activities and materials as a way of supporting their intrinsic motivation to learn. This emphasis on child choice continues throughout the day, even during activities initiated by adults.

A DAY AT A HIGH/SCOPE PROGRAM

Each program implements the High/Scope approach in a different way. A typical day's activities at Giving Tree School follows.

The day begins with greeting time. Children gather as the teacher begins a well-known animal finger play, and join in immediately. Then the teacher suggests that the group make a circus of animals who are moving in many ways.

High/Scope curriculum consists of the five interrelated components shown in Figure 6.4. This figure shows how active learning forms the hub of the "wheel of learning" and is supported by the key elements of the curriculum.

THE FIVE ELEMENTS OF THE HIGH/SCOPE APPROACH

Professionals who use the High/Scope curriculum must be fully committed to providing settings in which children learn actively and construct their own knowledge. Children's knowledge comes from personal interaction with ideas, direct experience with physical objects, and application of logical thinking to these experiences. The professional's role is to supply the context for these experiences, to help the child think about them logically, and, through observation, to understand the progress children are making. Professionals create the context for learning by implementing and supporting five essential elements: active learning, classroom arrangement, the daily schedule, assessment, and the curriculum (content).

Two children do not want to be animals, and the teacher suggests that these children may want to be the "audience." They get chairs and prepare to watch. Children suggest elephants, bears, and alligators as animals for the group to imitate. The children parade before the audience pretending to be animals and moving to the music. At the close of greeting time, the teacher suggests that children choose an animal to be as they move to the next activity, small-group time. During small-group time the children make "inventions" of their choice with recyclable materials a teacher has brought in and pine cones they collected the previous day.

As small-group activities are completed, planning begins. At this time, the teacher asks the younger children to indicate their plans for work time by going to get something they will use in their play. She asks the older children to draw or copy the symbols or letters that stand for the area in which they plan to play (each play area is labeled with a sign containing both a simple picture symbol and words for the area). To indicate his plan, Charlie, age three, gets a small hollow block and brings it to the teacher. "I'm going to make a train. That's all," he says. Aja, age four, brings a dress and a roll of tape. "I'm going to the playhouse to be the mommy, and then I'm going to the art area to make something with tape," she explains. Five-year-old Ashley shows the teacher her drawing of the tub table and the scoops she will use with rice at the table.

During work time, the teachers participate in children's play. Riding on Charlie's train, one teacher shows Tasha how to make the numerals 3 and 5 for train "tickets," joins two children playing a board game, and listens to Aja as she explains how she made a doll bed out of tape and a box. One teacher helps Nicholas and Charlie negotiate a conflict over a block, encouraging them by listening and asking questions until they agree on a solution.

At recall time, the children gather with the small groups they met with at planning time. Standing in a circle, each group rotates a hula hoop (one of many such facilitating techniques) through their hands as they sing a short song. When the song ends, the child nearest the tape is first to recall his or her work time experiences. Charlie tells about the train they made out of blocks. Nicholas describes the special "speed sticks" he played with. Aja shows her doll bed, and Tasha describes her "tickets." After snack, the children get their coats on and discuss what they will do outside. "Let's collect more pine cones. We can use them for food for the baby alligators"; "Let's go on the swings. I just learned how to pump"; "Let's see if we can find more bugs hiding under the rocks. They go there for winter." The teacher responds, "I'd like to help you look for bugs."

KEY EXPERIENCES

As children play, they are actively involved in solving problems and participate in many of the High/Scope "key experiences." There are fifty-eight key experiences that fall into ten categories: *social relation and initiative, language, creative representation, music, movement, classification, seriation, numbers, space,* and *time.* Teachers use the fifty-eight key experiences as guides for understanding development, planning activities, and describing the thinking and actions involved in children's play.

The High/Scope approach to learning supports developmentally appropriate, active learning experiences for each child as it encourages decision making, creative expression, problem solving, and other emerging abilities.

Contributed by Betsy Evans, The Giving Tree School, Gill, Massachusetts, and Field Consultant, High/Scope Education Research Foundation.

Active Learning. The idea that children are the source of their own learning forms the center of the High/Scope curriculum. Teachers support children's **active learning** by providing a variety of materials, making plans and reviewing activities with children, interacting with and carefully observing individual children, and leading small- and large-group active learning activities.

Classroom Arrangement. The classroom arrangement invites children to engage in personal, meaningful, educational experiences. In addition, the classroom contains five or more interest areas that encourage choice. Review Figure 6.5 to see a High/Scope room arrangement for kindergarten.

The classroom organization of materials and equipment supports the daily routine—children know where to find materials and what materials they can use. This encourages development of self-direction and independence. The floor plan in Figure 6.5 shows how room arrangement supports and implements the program's philosophy, goals, and objectives and

Active learning Involvement of the child with materials, activities, and projects in order to learn from concepts, knowledge, and skills.

To complete a Program in Action activity, visit the Companion Website at **http://www. prenhall.com/morrison**, select chapter 6, then choose the Program in Action module.

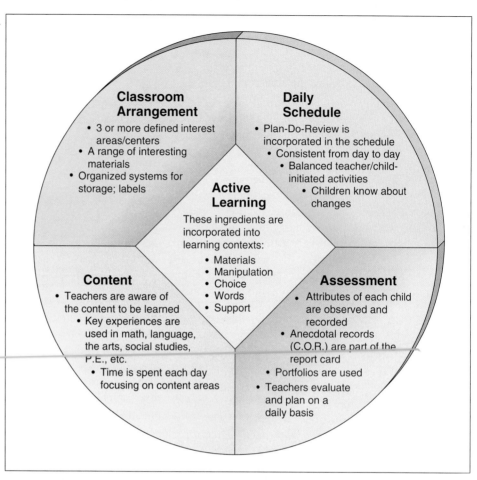

FIGURE 6.4 **High/Scope Curriculum Wheel**

Source: Used with permission of David P. Weikart, president, High/Scope Educational Research Foundation, 600 N. River St., Ypsilanti, MI 48198-2898.

how a center approach (books, blocks, computers, dramatic play, art, construction) provides space for large-group activities and individual work. In a classroom where space is at a premium, the teacher makes one area serve many difference purposes.

The teacher selects the centers and activities to use in the classroom based on several considerations:

- Interests of the children (e.g., kindergarten children are interested in blocks, housekeeping, and art)
- Opportunities for facilitating active involvement in seriation, number, time relations, classification, spatial relations, and language development
- Opportunities for reinforcing needed skills and concepts and functional use of those skills and concepts

Arranging the environment, then, is essential to implementing a program's philosophy. This is true for Montessori, for High/Scope, and for every other program.

Daily Schedule. The schedule considers developmental levels of children, incorporates a sixty- to seventy-minute plan–do–review process, provides for content areas, is as consistent throughout the day as possible, and contains a minimum number of transitions.

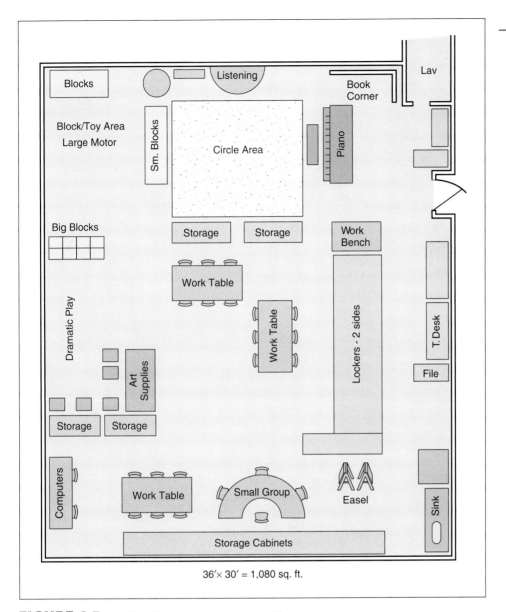

FIGURE 6.5 **A High/Scope Kindergarten Classroom Arrangement**

Source: Used with permission of David P. Weikart, president, High/Scope Educational Research Foundation, 600 N. River St., Ypsilanti, MI 48198-2898.

Assessment. Teachers keep notes about significant behaviors, changes, statements, and things that help them better understand a child's way of thinking and learning. Teachers use two mechanisms to help them collect data: the key experiences note form and a portfolio. The High/Scope Child Observation Record (see chapter 3) is also used to assess children's development.

Curriculum. The High/Scope curriculum comes from two sources: children's interests and the key experiences, which are lists of observable learning behaviors (see Figure 6.6). Basing a curriculum in part on children's interests is very constructivist and implements the philosophies of Dewey and Piaget.

A DAILY ROUTINE THAT SUPPORTS ACTIVE LEARNING

The High/Scope curriculum's daily routine is made up of a plan–do–review sequence and several additional elements. The plan–do–review sequence gives children opportunities to express intentions about their activities while keeping the teacher intimately involved in the whole process. The following five processes support the daily routine and contribute to its successful functioning.

Planning Time. **Planning time** gives children a structured, consistent chance to express their ideas to adults and to see themselves as individuals who can act on decisions. They experience the power of independence and the joy of working to be conscious of their intentions, and this supports the development of purpose and confidence.

The teacher talks with children about the plans they have made before the children carry them out. This helps children clarify their ideas and think about how to proceed. Talking with children about their plans provides an opportunity for the teacher to encourage and respond to each child's ideas, to suggest ways to strengthen the plans so they will be successful, and to understand and gauge each child's level of development and thinking style. Children and teachers benefit from these conversations and reflections. Children feel reinforced and ready to start their work, while teachers have ideas of what opportunities for extension might arise, what difficulties children might have, and where problem solving may be needed. In such a classroom, children and teachers are playing appropriate and important roles.

Notice the facial expressions of these children as they engage in active, hands-on learning with manipulative materials. Certainly this picture is worth a thousand words in conveying the power of active learning.

Planning time A time when children plan and articulate their ideas, choices, and decisions about what they will do.

Key experiences Activities that foster developmentally important skills and abilities.

Work time The period of time when children carry out their plans and are engaged in a project or activity.

Recall time The time in which children form mental pictures of their work-time experiences and discuss them with their teachers.

Key Experiences. Teachers continually encourage and support children's interests and involvement in activities, which occur within an organized environment and a consistent routine. Teachers plan from **key experience** that may broaden and strengthen children's emerging abilities. Children generate many of these experiences on their own; others require teacher guidance. Many key experiences are natural extensions of children's projects and interests. Refer again to Figure 6.4 to review key experiences for children in pre-K programs.

Work Time. This part of the plan–do–review sequence is generally the longest time period in the daily routine. The teacher's role during **work time** is to observe children to see how they gather information, interact with peers, and solve problems, and when appropriate they enter into the children's activities to encourage, extend, and set up problem-solving situations.

Cleanup Time. During cleanup time, children return materials and equipment to their labeled places and store their incomplete projects, restoring order to the classroom. All children's materials in the classroom are within reach and on open shelves. Clear labeling enables children to return all work materials to their appropriate places.

Recall Time. **Recall time**, the final phase of the plan–do–review sequence, is the time when children represent their work time experience in a variety of developmentally appropriate ways. They might recall the names of the children they involved in their plan, draw a picture of the building they made, or describe the problems they encountered. Recall strategies include drawing pictures, making models, physically demonstrating how a plan was carried out, or verbally recalling the events of work time. The teacher supports children's linking of the actual work to their original plan.

FIGURE 6.6   Key Experiences in a High/Scope Preschool Curriculum

CREATIVE REPRESENTATION

- Recognizing objects by sight, sound, touch, taste, and smell
- Imitating actions and sounds
- Relating models, pictures, and photographs to real places and things
- Pretending and role playing
- Making models out of clay, blocks, and other materials
- Drawing and painting

LANGUAGE AND LITERACY

- Talking with others about personally meaningful experiences
- Describing objects, events, and relations
- Having fun with language: listening to stories and poems, making up stories and rhymes
- Writing in various ways: drawing, scribbling, letterlike forms, invented spelling, and conventional forms
- Reading in various ways: reading storybooks, signs and symbols, one's own writing
- Dictating stories

INITIATIVE AND SOCIAL RELATIONS

- Making and expressing choices, plans, and decisions
- Solving problems encountered in play
- Taking care of one's own needs
- Expressing feelings in words
- Participating in group routines
- Being sensitive to the feelings, interests, and needs of others
- Building relationships with children and adults
- Creating and experiencing collaborative play
- Dealing with social conflict

CLASSIFICATION

- Exploring and describing similarities, differences, and the attributes of things
- Distinguishing and describing shapes
- Sorting and matching
- Using and describing something in several ways
- Holding more than one attribute in mind at a time
- Distinguishing between "some" and "all"
- Describing characteristics that something does *not* possess or what class it does *not* belong to

SERIATION

- Comparing attributes (longer/shorter, bigger/smaller)
- Arranging several things one after another in a series or pattern and describing the relationships (big/bigger/biggest, red/blue/red/blue)
- Fitting one ordered set of objects to another through trial and error (small cup—small saucer/medium cup—medium saucer/big cup—big saucer)

FIGURE 6.6 *(Continued)*

NUMBER
- Comparing the numbers of things in two sets to determine "more," "fewer," "same number"
- Arranging two sets of objects in one-to-one correspondence
- Counting objects

SPACE
- Filling and emptying
- Fitting things together and taking them apart
- Changing the shape and arrangement of objects (wrapping, twisting, stretching, stacking, enclosing)
- Observing people, places, and things from different spatial viewpoints
- Experiencing and describing positions, directions, and distances in the play space, building, and neighborhood
- Interpreting spatial relations in drawings, pictures, and photographs

TIME
- Starting and stopping an action on signal
- Experiencing and describing rates of movement
- Experiencing and comparing time intervals
- Anticipating, remembering, and describing sequences of events

Source: Nancy Altman Brickman (Ed.)(2001). Key Experiences in the Preschool Classroom, Chapter 4 (pp. 143–216) in *Supporting Young Learners 3*. Ypsilanti, MI: High/Scope Press.

This review permits children to reflect on what they did and how it was done. It brings closure to children's planning and work-time activities. Putting their ideas and experiences into words also facilitates children's language development. Most important, it enables children to represent to others their mental schemes.

ADVANTAGES

There are a number of advantages to implementing the High/Scope approach. It offers you and others a method for implementing a constructivist-based program that has its roots in Piagetian cognitive theory. Second, it is widely popular and has been extensively researched and tested. Third, there is a vast network of training and support provided by the High/Scope Foundation. You can learn more about High/Scope through its website at www.highscope.org. This will further help you decide if High/Scope is a program you would consider implementing in your classroom.

REGGIO EMILIA

Reggio Emilia, a city in northern Italy, is widely known for its approach to educating young children.[10] Founded by Loris Malaguzzi (1920–1994), **Reggio Emilia** sponsors programs for children from three months to six years of age. Certain essential beliefs and practices underlie the Reggio Emilia approach. These basic features define the Reggio approach, make it a constructivist program, and enable it to be adapted and implemented in many U.S. early childhood programs.

BELIEFS ABOUT CHILDREN AND HOW THEY LEARN

Relationships.   Education focuses on each child and is conducted in relation with the family, other children, the teachers, the environment of the school, the community, and the wider society. Each school is viewed as a system in which all these interconnected relationships are reciprocal, activated, and supported. In other words, as Vygotsky believed, chil-

Reggio Emilia   An approach to education based on the philosophy and practice that children are active constructors of their own knowledge.

 For more information about Reggio Emilia, go to the Companion Website at **http:// www.prenhall.com/ morrison,** select chapter 6, then choose the Linking to Learning module to connect to the Reggio Emilia Approach to Early Childhood Education site.

dren learn through social interactions. In addition, as Montessori indicated, the environment supports and is important to learning.

When preparing space, teachers offer the possibility for children to be with the teachers and many of the other children, or with just a few of them. Also, children can be alone when they need a little niche to stay by themselves.

Teachers are always aware, however, that children learn a great deal in exchanges with their peers, especially when they interact in small groups. Such small groups of two, three, four, or five children provide possibilities for paying attention, hearing and listening to each other, developing curiosity and interest, asking questions, and responding to them. Also, groups provide opportunities for negotiation and ongoing dynamic communication.

Time.   Reggio Emilia teachers believe that time is not set by a clock and that continuity is not interrupted by the calendar. Children's own sense of time and their personal rhythm are considered in planning and carrying out activities and projects. The full-day schedule provides sufficient time for being together among peers in an environment that is conducive to getting things done with satisfaction.

Teachers get to know the personal rhythms and learning styles of each child. This really getting to know children is possible in part because children stay with the same teachers and the same peer group for three-year cycles (infancy to three years and three years to six years).

ADULTS' ROLE

Adults play a very powerful role in children's lives. Children's well-being is connected with the well-being of parents and teachers. Children have a right to high-quality care and education that supports the development of their potentials. Adults can provide these educational necessities. Parents have rights to be involved in the life of the school, and teachers have rights to grow professionally.

The Teacher.   Teachers observe and listen closely to children to know how to plan or proceed with their work. They ask questions and discover children's ideas, hypotheses, and theories. They collaboratively discuss what they have observed and recorded, and they make flexible plans and preparations. Teachers then enter into dialogues with the children and offer them occasions for discovering and also revisiting and reflecting on experiences, since they consider learning an ongoing process. Teachers are partners with children in a continual process of research and learning.

The Atelierista.   An **atelierista**, a teacher trained in the visual arts, works closely with teachers and children in every preprimary school and makes visits to the infant–toddler centers.

Parents.   Parents are an essential component of the program, and they are included in the advisory committee that runs each school. Parents' participation is expected and supported and takes many forms: day-to-day interaction, work in the schools, discussion of educational and psychological issues, special events, excursions, and celebrations.

THE ENVIRONMENT

The infant–toddler centers and school programs are the most visible aspect of the work done by teachers and parents in Reggio Emilia. They convey many messages, of which the most immediate is that this is a place where adults have thought about the quality and the instructive power of space.

The Physical Space.   The layout of physical space, in addition to welcoming whoever enters, fosters encounters, communication, and relationships. The arrangement of structures, objects, and activities encourages choices, problem solving, and discoveries in the process of learning.

The centers and schools of Reggio Emilia are beautiful. Their beauty comes from the message the whole school conveys about children and teachers engaged together in the pleasure

For more information about the Reggio Emilia curriculum model, go to the Companion Website at **http://www.prenhall. com/morrison,** select any chapter, then choose Topic 4 of the ECE Supersite module.

Atelierista   A teacher trained in the visual arts who works with teachers and children.

Reggio Emilia

Reggio Emilia is a city in northern Italy. The excellent educational program the city offers its children, based on providing an educational environment that encourages learning, is known as the Reggio Emilia approach. Reggio Emilia sponsors infant programs for children three months to three years and programs for children three to six years.

Most of the Reggio schools can accommodate seventy-five children, with each group or class consisting of about twenty-five children with two co-teachers. Children of single parents and children with disabilities have priority in admission. The other children are admitted according to a scale of needs. Parents pay on a sliding scale based on income.

The Reggio Emilia approach is unique in that children are encouraged to learn by investigating and exploring topics that interest them. Learning is a social and cultural process that does not occur in isolation from other children, adults, and the environment. The Reggio school environment is designed to accommodate the child's developmental culture and provide a wide range of stimulating media and materials for children to express their learning, such as words, sounds and music, movement, drawing, painting, sculpting, modeling clay or wire, making collages, using puppets and disguises, photography, and more.

Reggio children typically explore topics by way of group projects. This approach fosters a sense of community, respect for diversity, and a collaborative approach to problem solving—all important aspects of learning. Two

of learning. There is attention to detail everywhere: in the color of the walls, the shape of the furniture, the arrangement of simple objects on shelves and tables. Light from the windows and doors shines through transparent collages and weavings made by children. Healthy, green plants are everywhere. Behind the shelves displaying shells or other found or made objects are mirrors that reflect the patterns that children and teachers have created.

The environment is also highly personal. For example, a series of small boxes made of white cardboard creates a grid on the wall of a school. On each box the name of a child or a teacher is printed with rubber stamp letters. These boxes are used for leaving little surprises or messages for one another. Communication is valued and favored at all levels.

The space in the centers and schools of Reggio Emilia is personal in still another way: it is full of children's own work. Everywhere there are paintings, drawings, paper sculptures, wire constructions, transparent collages coloring the light, and mobiles moving gently overhead. Such things turn up even in unexpected spaces like stairways and bathrooms. Although the work of the children is pleasing to the eye, it is not intended as decoration, but rather to show and document the competence of children, the beauty of their ideas, and the complexity of their learning processes.

co-teachers are present during the projects to guide the children and widen the range of learning. This is the way Carina Rinaldi, *pedagogista* (consultant resource person), describes a project:

> A project, which we view as sort of an adventure and research, can start through a suggestion from an adult, a child's idea, or from an event such as a snowfall or something else unexpected. But every project is based on the attention of the educators to what the children say and do as well as what they do not say and do. The adults must allow enough time for the thinking and actions of children to develop.*

The children pictured here are working on a special "Shadows" project. The exploration of shadows has great attraction for children and many implications for learning with pleasure. Children discuss their ideas and formulate hypotheses about shadows' origins and destiny. Exploration of shadows in the schools for Reggio Emilia continues to be a favorite theme for children and teachers. In this

specific episode, after exploring shadow outside (at different times of the day) and inside (with artificial light and flashlights), the teacher extends the interest of a child who has represented a little girl with a full skirt by posing a question-problem to her. She places a yellow sticker under the feet of the little girl in the drawing and asks: "If the sun were here, where would the shadow be?"

Additional resources for Reggio Emilia are available online at http://ericps.ed.uiuc.edu/eece/reggio/reglink.html.

Contributed by Lella Gandini, Northampton, Massachusetts. Photos from the city of Reggio Emilia, teachers, and children of the preprimary schools Diana and Gulliver, *Tutto ha un ombra meno le formiche* (Everything but the ant has a shadow) (City of Reggio Emilia, Italy: Department of Education Via Guido de Castello, 1990), p. 12; photos provided by Lella Gandini.
* Carina Rinaldi, "The Emergent Curriculum and Social Constructivism," in Carolyn Edwards, Lella Gandini, and George Forman, eds., *The Hundred Languages of Children* (Norwood, NJ: Ablex, 1993), 108.

The Atelier.   A special workshop or studio, called an *atelier,* is set aside and used by all the children and teachers in the school. It contains a great variety of tools and resource materials, along with records of past projects and experiences.

Atelier   A special area or studio for creating projects.

The activities and projects, however, do not take place only in the *atelier*. Smaller spaces called *mini-ateliers* are set up in each classroom. In fact, each classroom becomes an active workshop with children involved with a variety of materials and experiences that they have discussed and chosen with teachers and peers. In the view of Reggio educators, the children's use of many media is not art or a separate part of the curriculum but an inseparable, integral part of the whole cognitive/symbolic expression involved in the process of learning.

PROGRAM PRACTICES

Cooperation is the powerful mode of working that makes possible the achievement of the goals Reggio educators set for themselves. Teachers work in pairs in each classroom. They see themselves as researchers gathering information about their work with children by means of continual documentation. The strong collegial relationships that are maintained

To complete a Program in Action activity, visit the Companion Website at **http://www. prenhall.com/morrison**, select chapter 6, then choose the Program in Action module.

with teachers and staff enable them to engage in collaborative discussion and interpretation of both teachers' and children's work.

Documentation.   Transcriptions of children's remarks and discussions, photographs of their activity, and representations of their thinking and learning using many media are carefully arranged by the *atelierista*, along with the other teachers, to document the work and the process of learning. This **documentation** has many functions. First, to make parents aware of children's experience and maintain their involvement. Second, to allow teachers to understand children better and to evaluate their own work, thus promoting professional growth. Third, to facilitate communication and exchange of ideas among educators. Fourth, to make children aware that their effort is valued. And fifth, to create an archive that traces the history of the school and the pleasure of learning by many children and their teachers.

Documentation   Records of children's work including recordings, photographs, transcripts, work samples, projects, drawings, and so forth.

Curriculum and Practices.   The curriculum is not established in advance. Teachers express general goals and make hypotheses about what direction activities and projects might take. On this basis, they make appropriate preparations. Then, after observing children in action, teachers compare, discuss, and interpret together their observations and make choices that they share with the children about what to offer and how to sustain the children in their exploration and learning. In fact, the curriculum emerges in the process of each activity or project and is flexibly adjusted accordingly through this continuous dialogue among teachers and with children.

Projects provide the backbone of the children's and teachers' learning experiences. These projects are based on the strong conviction that learning by doing is of great importance and that to discuss in groups and to revisit ideas and experiences is the premier way of gaining better understanding and learning.

Ideas for projects originate in the experiences of children and teachers as they construct knowledge together. Projects can last from a few days to several months. They may start from either a chance event, an idea or a problem posed by one or more children, or an experience initiated directly by teachers.

CONSIDERATIONS

There are a number of things to keep in mind when considering the Reggio Emilia approach. First, its theoretical base rests within constructivism and shares ideas compatible with those of Piaget, Vygotsky, Dewey, Gardner, and other constructivists, and the concept or process of learning by doing. Second, there is no set curriculum. Rather, the curriculum emerges or springs from children's interests and experiences. This approach is, for many, difficult to implement and does not ensure that children will learn basic academic skills valued by contemporary American society. Third, the Reggio Emilia approach is suited to a particular culture and society. How this approach works and flourishes and meets the educational needs of children in an Italian village may not necessarily be appropriate for meeting the needs of contemporary American children. The Italian view of education is that it is the responsibility of the state, and the state provides high levels of financial support. Although education is a state function in the United States, traditionally the local community control of education is a powerful and sacrosanct part of American education. Having said all of this, a number of schools and programs are implementing the Reggio approach.

While all of the program models we have discussed in this chapter are unique, at the same time they all have certain similarities. All of them, regardless of their particular philosophical orientation, have as a primary goal the best education for all children.

To take an online self-test on this chapter's contents, go to the Companion Website at **http://www. prenhall.com/morrison**, select chapter 6, then choose the Self-Test module.

DIVERSITY TIE-IN

Saving Tribal Languages

I don't know about you, but with the exception of learning a few new words from time to time and practicing good grammar, I take my native language (English) for granted. I assume that English will be around forever. But not all speakers of native languages can say the same thing. For example, take the current situation in Washington State. "The last two fluent speakers of the Makah tribal language died last year. Only 10 people, all over the age of 65, still speak Spokane fluently. The only skilled speakers of Lushootseed are elderly and frail, and can no longer take part in their tribe's formal activities to pass on their language skills."* However, efforts are underway to save American Indian languages. In a new program, "Washington state's 28 federally recognized tribes will train and recommend to the state board people they deem to be qualified to be teachers. The state will provide a 'first peoples language/culture' certification or endorsement to those candidates, giving them equal status with teachers who are certified to teach other subjects in the public schools."† As a result, more speakers of tribal language will be in classrooms and hopefully endangered American Indian languages will

be saved. Washington's program is similar to programs in Oregon, Idaho, and Montana, which has 133 teachers with such certification. In the meantime, on the Tulalip (WA) reservation at Tulalip Elementary School, 80 children are enrolled in the Lushootseed language program.

- How would you feel if your native language was in danger of extinction?
- What does losing American Indian languages do to American Indian culture and your own? To U.S. culture?
- What are the benefits of developing programs designed to help assure that American Indian languages survive?
- Why are we are in danger of losing some American Indian languages?
- Can you think of some other ideas for how to help preserve American Indian languages?

---

* Zehr, Mary Ann. (February 5, 2003). Washington. Program Strives to Sustain Tribal Languages. *Education Week.* p. 15.
† Ibid, p.15.

As an early childhood professional, you will want to do several things now. First, begin to identify which features of the program models you can and cannot support. Second, decide which of these models and/or features of models you can embrace and incorporate into your own practice. An ongoing rule of the early childhood professional is to decide what you believe is best for children and families before you make decisions about what to teach.

As we end this chapter, there is one more thing for you to consider. All three of these programs emphasize language and literacy. But what if there were no language? Our Diversity Tie-In puts this question into a very contemporary and troubling perspective.

To complete an activity related to the above topic, go to the Companion Website at **http://www. prenhall.com/morrison**, select chapter 6, then choose the Diversity Tie-In module.

For additional Internet resources or to complete an online activity for this chapter, go to the Companion Website at **http://www. prenhall.com/morrison,** select chapter 6, then choose the Linking to Learning or Making Connections module.

ACTIVITIES FOR FURTHER ENRICHMENT

APPLICATIONS

1. Which of the programs in this chapter do you think best meets the needs of young children? What accounts for this popularity? Would you implement one of them in your program? Why?

2. Write three or four paragraphs describing how you think the programs discussed in this chapter have influenced early childhood educational practice.

3. What features of Montessori, High/Scope, and Reggio do you like best? Why? What features do you like least? Why? What features are best for children?

4. Interview a Montessori school director to learn how to go about opening a Montessori school. Determine what basic materials are needed and their cost, then tell how your particular location would determine how you would market the program.

FIELD EXPERIENCES

1. Visit various early childhood programs, including center and home programs, and discuss similarities and differences in class. Which of the programs incorporate practices from programs discussed in this chapter?

2. Compare Montessori materials with those in other kindergartens and preschool programs. Is it possible for teachers to make Montessori materials? What advantages or disadvantages would there be in making and using these materials?

3. Develop a checklist of "best practices" found in Montessori, High/Scope, and Reggio. Use your checklist to observe other programs. Tell how or how not these programs demonstrate the "best practices."

RESEARCH

1. Survey parents in your area to determine what service they desire from an early childhood program. Are most of the parents' needs being met? How is what they want in a program similar to and different from the basic program features discussed in this chapter?

2. Write to the ASM, AMI, and NAMTA for information about becoming a certified Montessori teacher. Compare the requirements for becoming a certified Montessori teacher with your university training. What are the similarities and differences?

3. Interview public and private school teachers about their understanding of the programs discussed. Do they have a good understanding of the programs? What are the most critical areas of understanding or misunderstanding? Do you think all early childhood professionals should have knowledge of the programs? Why?

READINGS FOR FURTHER ENRICHMENT

Abbot, L., and Nutbrown, C. *Experiencing Reggio Emilia: Implications for Pre-School Provisions.* Open University Press, UK 2001.

This book reflects the impressions and experiences of the Reggio Emilia approach gained by a range of early childhood educators following a study visit to the Italian region where the approach was invented. It focuses on key issues such as staffing, training, working with parents, play, learning, the culture of early childhood, and special educational needs.

Cadwell, L.B., and Rinaldi, C. *Bringing Learning to Life: A Reggio Approach to Early Childhood Education* (Early Childhood Education, 86). New York: Teachers College Press, 2002.

Addresses the fundamental principles of the Reggio approach, as they are experienced in the daily life of schools that have attained a very high level of understanding and practice. Describes real-life classrooms, including details on the flow of the day, parent participation, teacher collaboration, the importance of the environment, documenting students' work, and assessment. Features many illustrations of children's work as well as photos of "Reggio-inspired" classroom interiors and art materials.

Catron, C. E., and Allen, J. *Early Childhood Curriculum: A Creative Play Model*, 3rd ed. Upper Saddle River, NJ: Merrill/Prentice Hall, 2002.

This comprehensive guide provides information on planning programs with a play-based, developmental curriculum for children from birth to five years of age and covers basic principles and current research in early childhood curricula.

Fu, V.R., Stremmel, A.J., and Hill, L.T. *Teaching and Learning: Collaborative Exploration of the Reggio Emilia Approach.* Upper Saddle River, NJ: Merrill/Prentice Hall, 2001.

Through rich stories and examples of children's projects, this text invites readers to examine their personal learning process. It offers innovative ways to meld theory with teaching and action research while considering the professional development of each reader—pre-service, in-service, teacher educator, and teacher researcher.

Hohmann, M., et al. *Educating Young Children: Active Learning Practices for Preschool and Child Care Programs.* High/Scope Press, Ypsilanti, MI. 2002.

This book is the official manual for High/Scope curriculum. It outlines how to set up a High/Scope classroom, from setting up the learning environment to guiding adult interactions.

Spietz, H. A. *Montessori Resources: A Complete Guide to Finding Montessori Materials for Parents and Teachers.* Rossmoor, CA: American Montessori Consulting, 2002.

Contains in-depth reviews of products, information on where to buy supplies for integrated lesson planning, recommended computer software, and reviews and recommendations of foreign language products.

Stephenson, S. M., and Stephenson, J. M. *The Joyful Child: Michael Olaf's Essential Montessori for Birth to Three Years.* Arcata, CA: Michael Olaf Montessori Company, 2001.

Contains valuable information on aiding the optimum development of the child from birth to three years and is used as an overview of this age in Montessori teacher training courses and other early childhood development courses. Included is a catalogue of books and materials.

Wentworth, R. A. *Montessori for the New Millennium.* Mahawah, NJ: Lawrence Erlbaum Associates, 1999.

This book elucidates the vital aspect of Maria Montessori's life work and shows how it applies to real-life teaching situations. Montessori believed that by transforming the process of children's education she could help to transform the attitudes for the adults they will later become.

LINKING TO LEARNING

American Montessori Society
http://www.amshq.org

> *AMS serves as a national center for Montessori information, both for its members and for the general public—answering inquiries and facilitating research wherever possible. To Montessori, a child's environment was a most important element in the learning process.*

International Montessori Index
http://montessori.edu/

> *Montessori information for parents and teachers, links to Montessori school lists, conference lectures, organizations, educational materials, and other valuable sites.*

International Montessori Society
http://trust.wdn.com/ims/

> *Founded to support the effective application of Montessori principles throughout the world, the society provides a range of programs and services of the fundamental principles of (1) observation, (2) individual liberty, and (3) preparation of the environment.*

Montessori Online
http://www.montessori.org/

> *Site for the Montessori Foundation, a nonprofit organization dedicated to the advancement of Montessori education. Offers programs and resources to anyone interested in learning about Montessori education.*

Montessori Unlimited
http://www.montessori.com

> *Through this program, your child will learn the basis of Montessori—to respect oneself and one's environment. This basis, called practical life, is carried into other areas of learning, including language arts, math, and science.*

Carnegie Mellon Cyert Center for Early Childhood Education
http://www.cmu.edu/cyert-center/rea.htm

> *The Cyert Center has a strong commitment to provide quality full day, year round care and education for young children. The program is built upon deep relationships between children, parents, and educators. The Center is inspired and challenged by the infant/toddler and preschool programs in Reggio Emilia, Italy.*

ERIC Reggio Emilia Page
http://ericps.ed.uiuc.edu/eece/reggio.html

> *This section of the ERIC/EECE website contains information and resources related to the approach to early childhood education developed in the preschools of Reggio Emilia, Italy.*

The Merrill-Palmer Institute Reggio Emilia Resources
http://www.mpi.wayne.edu/resource.htm

> *A comprehensive resource listing, including information on Reggio Emilia-related conferences, and study tours, and general information on Reggio children, the Reggio Emilia educational philosophy, and contact information for the North American Reggio Network.*

ENDNOTES

[1] Montessori, Maria. *Dr. Montessori's Own Handbook* (New York: Schocken, 1965), 133.

[2] Montessori, Maria. *The Montessori Method,* trans. Anne E. George (Cambridge, MA: Bentley, 1967), 104.

[3] Montessori, Maria. *The Secret of Childhood,* trans. M. J. Costello (Notre Dame, IN: Fides, 1966), 20.

[4] Montessori, *The Secret of Childhood,* 46.

[5] Montessori, Maria, *The Absorbent Mind,* trans. Claude A. Claremont (New York: Holt, Rinehart & Winston, 1967), 25.

[6] Montessori, *Dr. Montessori's own Handbook,* 131.

[7] High/Scope Education Research Foundation, *The High/Scope K-3 Cirriculum:* An Introduction (Ypsilanti, MI: Author, 1989), 1..

[8] Ibid.

[9] Ibid., 3.

[10] This section is adapted from L. Gandini, "Foundations of the Reggio Emilia Approach," in J. Hendrick, ed., *First Steps Toward Teaching the Reggio Way* (Upper Saddle River, NJ: Merrill/Prentice Hall, 1997), 14–25.

Chapter 7

Early childhood development and education helps prepare children to learn and succeed in preschool, and access to safe, reliable child care allows parents to work and be self-sufficient.

MARIAN WRIGHT EDELMAN

Child Care

Meeting the Needs of Children, Parents, and Families

Focus Questions

- Why is there a need for child care services?

- What are the types of child care offered today?

- What constitutes quality in child care programs?

- How effective is child care in meeting the needs of children and families?

- What are significant issues surrounding child care and its use?

Maria Gloria is young a single parent with two children ages two and four. Maria works in a local convenience store for the minimum wage. "I really can't afford child care, but I have to work. A woman in an apartment three floors up from me keeps my kids and five others while I work. I give her $25 a week. It's all I can afford. I'm lucky to have someone to take care of my kids."

Charlie and Beth Shanker have jobs that pay enough for them to "get by" on their combined incomes. Charlie drops off their one-year-old daughter, Amanda, and three-year-old son, Jesse, at the "Children's Barn" child care center on his way to work. "It's not the best, but it is about what we can afford. I have to leave fifteen minutes early because the child care is out of the way. We're looking for something closer, but we haven't found it yet."

Seven-year-old Chantel Harris walks home and lets herself in to the family apartment after school each day. There is no one else at home. Her mother wishes she had more choices. "I know it isn't the best or safest thing to do. I can't afford anyone to take care of her, and the school doesn't offer any kind of programs after school. What am I to do?"

Amy Charney is a stay-at-home mom. Three mornings a week she takes her four-year-old daughter, Emily, to a Mothers' Day Out (MDO) program at a local church. "It's a great arrangement and very reasonable, in terms of cost. When Emily is in MDO I volunteer in the community, and still she and I get to do a lot of things together. The staff is great and is up to date on the latest trends, and I feel Emily is definitely getting ready for school."

Abby Belanger is an up-and-coming attorney in a prestigious law firm. She is also a single mother by choice. Abby's four-year-old daughter, Tiffany, is enrolled in a "high quality–high end" child care program. "I want Tiffany to have the best, and I can afford the best. I want her to have a good start in life so she can go to whatever schools she wants to attend. Education is important to me."

Child care arrangements such as these and others are duplicated countless times each day all across America. Think a moment about the child care arrangements you know about or are involved with. They paint a picture that

To review the chapter focus questions online, go to the Companion Website at **http://www. prenhall.com/morrison** and select chapter 7.

TABLE 7.1 Children in Different Types of Child Care Arrangements

Child care outside the home is provided in many kinds of arrangements. What implications do these data have for you as an early childhood professional?

	Number of Children (in Thousands)	Percent in Arrangement
Total children under 5	19,611	100
Nonrelative Care	6,937	35.4
• Organized Care Facility	3,933	20.1
• Day Care Center	2,273	11.6
• Nursery or Preschool	1,108	5.7
• Head Start	171	0.9
• School	582	3.0
• Other nonrelative care	3,413	17.4
• In child's home	831	4.2
• In provider's home	2,614	13.3
Family day care	1,426	7.3
Other care arrangements	1,250	6.4

Source: U.S. Census Bureau (2002). *Who's Minding the Kids? Child Care Arrangements* (Spring 2002).

combines the good, the bad, and the unavailable. Child care in America is often referred to as a "patchwork" of programs and arrangements of varying costs and quality. Unfortunately, this is the reality of child care today.

Part of your and my job as early childhood professionals is to advocate and work for high-quality child care for all children and families that is affordable, accessible, and of the highest quality. For, as we will discuss, the kind and quality of care children receive outside their homes make a big difference in their lives and the lives of parents and families. As Table 7.1 illustrates, more than 35 percent of the nation's children are in nonrelative child care.

WHAT IS CHILD CARE?

Child care Comprehensive care and education for young children outside their home.

Child care is a comprehensive out-of-home service to children and families that supplements the care and education children receive from their families. Care is supplemental in that parents delegate responsibility to caregivers for providing care and appropriate experiences in their absence. It is comprehensive in that, although it includes custodial care such as supervision, food, shelter, and other physical necessities, it goes beyond these to include educational and other activities that encourage and aid learning and are responsive to children's health, social, and psychological needs. Child care is educational in that it provides for the intellectual needs of children and helps engage them in the process of learning that begins at birth. Quality child care incorporates educational learning activities as part of the curriculum. Furthermore, child care staff work with parents to help them learn how to support children's learning in the home. A comprehensive view of child care considers the child to be a whole person; therefore, the major purpose of child care is to facilitate optimum development of the whole child including the cognitive and linguistic and support efforts to achieve this goal.

WHY IS CHILD CARE POPULAR?

 For more information about child care, go to the Companion Website at **http://www.prenhall.com/ morrison**, select chapter 7, then choose the Linking to Learning module to connect to several sites on child care.

Child care is popular and in the center of the public eye for a number of reasons. One is that recent demographic changes have created a high demand for child care. There are more dual-income families and more working single parents than ever before. For example, nearly 62 percent of mothers with children under three are employed, and it is not uncommon for mothers to return to work as early as six weeks after giving birth. More than thirty-five million employed parents with young children reported significant work–family conflict, creating a general demand for infant and young child care. The current unprecedented entry of large numbers of mothers into the workforce has greatly impacted the care and education of children in the early years. The numbers of working mothers will increase and create an even bigger demand for child care of children six weeks to the time of their entry into a public school program. One thing is certain: economic conditions and the demands of the workplace have changed the American family. At the same time, child care is now viewed as a workforce and economic development issue. However, while child care helps meet the needs of working parents and the needs of employers for a stable workforce, we should never forget that child care is for children.

Second, child care is an important part of many politicians' solutions to the nation's economic and social problems. In this regard, child care is an instrument of public policy. Child care can be used to address political and social issues. For example, child care is an essential part of work-training programs designed to get people off welfare and help them join the workforce. At the same time, many work-training programs train welfare recipients for child care jobs. So, many welfare recipients are moving from welfare to gainful employment as child care workers.

Quality child care is also seen by politicians and the public as a way of addressing many of the country's problems through early intervention in children's lives. The reasoning goes that if we provide children with quality programs and experiences early in life, we reduce the possibility that they will need costly social services later in life.

Furthermore, as we have discussed, state and federal governments are using all preschool programs, including federally and state supported child care programs, to help reform public education. There is no better example of this than the current federal early literacy initiatives. As a result, child care programs are including and emphasizing early literacy skills to an extent not seen before.

As the demand for child care increases, the challenge to you and other early childhood professionals is clear. You and the profession must participate in advocating for and creating quality child care programs that meet the needs of children and families.

PLACEMENTS IN CHILD CARE PROGRAMS

Decisions to place children in child care are personal, individual, and complex. We can say with some assurance that because parents work, they place their children in child care. But it could also be the other way around. Because child care is available, some parents choose to work. Decisions then relating to placement in child care are not necessarily straightforward but depend on many factors. Consider some of these interesting facts about child care placement:

- Three-fourths of families with working mothers use child care for children under five.
- One-third of children with nonworking mothers are placed in child care.
- Better-educated parents are more likely to place their children in child care than those who are not as well educated. Seventy-two percent of children with parents who attended some college are placed in child care, versus 42 percent of children whose parents have less than a high school diploma.
- As children grow older, their likelihood of being placed in child care increases.
- Children in the South are more likely to enter child care than children in the Northeast.
- Children who are white or Latino are less likely to be placed in child care.
- Parents are more likely to initiate child care when a child has a birthday.
- A child in a single-parent family is more likely to be placed in child care than is a child in a two-parent family.
- If a mother works during pregnancy, the likelihood of the child being placed in child care is four times higher than if the mother does not work during pregnancy.[1]

VOICE FROM THE FIELD

Children's Defense Fund

Advocating for Children at the National Level

Ensuring a voice for children in the legislative process requires a multifaceted strategy. In 2002, the Children's Defense Fund worked to spark strong interest in child care at the federal level, making it a top issue in the welfare/child care reauthorization debate through ongoing research and data collection, combined with sustained efforts with state and local advocates, policy makers, and the media.

In 2002, CDF focused on the reauthorization of the Temporary Assistance to Needy Families (TANF) Block Grant and the Child Care and Development Block Grant (CCDBG). We began our efforts in 2000 by putting in place a process to ensure that we had the necessary data on state child care assistance policies to make the case to members of Congress and others for increased investments and positive policies for child care and early education.

CDF has extensive experience working on surveys of state policies in child care and early education. Working with a group of experts, we fine-tuned an exhaustive survey form and then sent it to the individuals in each state who administer child care assistance programs. Following

up with extensive phone interviews, we drafted *A Fragile Foundation: State Child Care Assistance Policies*. The report, published in November 2001, was distributed widely to members of Congress and their staff, state policy makers, and advocates. It offered the most in-depth information available on the state of child care for low-income families. As a result, it was used widely as a basis for congressional briefings, hearings, and fact sheets.

The CDF child care team continued to update key indicators throughout the year. By the late spring, we realized that in the face of an economic downturn and budget deficits, many states were making cutbacks in their child care programs for low-income working families. It would be important to share these cutbacks with Congress as they continued to debate child care. This led to a brief report, *Low-Income Families Bear the Burden of State Child Care Cutbacks*, that was released in September 2002 after the August congressional recess.

In addition to thorough data collection, working closely with members of Congress and their staff is essential to any successful advocacy effort. This involves a

TYPES OF CHILD CARE PROGRAMS

Child care is offered in many places, by many persons and agencies that provide a variety of care and services. The options for child care are almost endless. However, regardless of the kinds of child care provided, the three issues of quality, affordability, and accessibility always are part of the child care landscape.

CHILD CARE BY FAMILY AND RELATIVES

To complete a Program in Action activity related to family child care, visit the Companion Website at **http://www. prenhall.com/morrison**, select chapter 7, then choose the Program in Action module.

Child care is frequently arranged within nuclear and extended families or with friends. Parents handle these arrangements in various ways. In some cases, children are cared for by grandparents, aunts, uncles, or other relatives. Care by grandparents has increased to 21 percent of all preschoolers. These arrangements satisfy parents' needs to have their children cared for by people with similar lifestyles and values, and such care may be less costly. On average, child care provided by relatives costs about $1.63 an hour. Also, the caregiver-to-child ratio is low, and relatives often care for ill children.[2] These types of arrangements allow

range of activities. CDF staff and others play a role in conceiving of and drafting legislation. CDF helped lay the groundwork for the child care reauthorization by drafting the Act to Leave No Child Behind, a piece of comprehensive legislation for children and families that includes provisions related to the reauthorization of both CCDBG and TANF. In addition to helping staff to draft legislation, advocates also help to plan congressional hearings. CDF staff testified at several congressional hearings using data published in *A Fragile Foundation*. Working with our extensive field network, we also arranged for two low-income parents who were on their states' waiting list for child care assistance to come to Washington and testify at congressional hearings. These parents' poignant stories put a face on the statistics representing the gaps in the child care system and helped supportive members of Congress and advocates to make the case for new investments. Good advocates are also always ready to prepare short fact sheets on key issues and to respond to questions that staff might have on issues that are being debated during the reauthorization process.

Members of Congress must also hear directly from their constituents about the need for increased child care investments in their communities. There are numerous strategies to encourage this contact. The Child Care Division at CDF sends out a weekly e-mail newsletter to more than 10,000 individuals, who forward it to countless others. In addition, CDF sends out a more general legislative action newsletter that reaches thousands more. These newsletters contain alerts that encourage constituents to contact their members of Congress at key moments throughout the congressional session.

CDF also uses targeted strategies to generate constituent activity. For example, working with our coalition we designated two days, one in March and one in May, as special days for constituents to contact their members of Congress. In addition to encouraging phone calls, we made it possible for advocates nationwide to e-mail a special message to their members of Congress directly from CDF's Web site. Throughout the year we also worked with a group of advocates in target states. These target states were selected because their senators were on key committees with the authority to make decisions about child care funding. These state advocates made a special effort to publicize child care in their states, generate media articles, distribute public service announcements about child care, and encourage their senators and representatives to visit local child care centers.

Clearly, child care and early education advocates must work on many fronts to make change. It is important to collect reasoned and thoughtful data and publish reports, as well as work directly with elected officials, encourage coalition and constituent activity around child care issues, and also engage the public through the media. However, you need not be an expert in all or any of these areas. You just need to come forward and make your voice heard. Simply convey what you know about what children and families need at every opportunity, with the resources available to you, and in a manner that suits your personal and professional situation. When many people come together to stand up for children, we can make a difference.

Contributed by Helen Blank, Director of Child Care and Development at the Children's Defense Fund, http://www.childrensdefense.org/.

children to remain in familiar environments with people they know. Child care by family members provides children with continuity and stability parents desire for their children.

FAMILY CHILD CARE

When home-based care is provided outside a child's home in a family setting, it is known as **family child care** or *family care*. In this arrangement an individual caregiver provides care and education for a small group of children in her or his home. Seven percent of children under five in child care are in family day care. Family care generally involves three types of settings: homes that are unlicensed and unregulated by a state or local agency, homes that are licensed by regulatory agencies, and homes that are licensed and associated with an administrative agency.

Both the quantity and quality of specific services provided in family homes vary from home to home and from agency to agency. However, almost 50 percent of family child care providers spend a substantial amount of their time in direct interaction with children. Read the Program in Action, "Bridges Family Child Care," to see how good family care is much more than baby-sitting.

Family child care Home-based care and education provided in a private family home. Also known as family care.

Bridges Family Child Care

Welcome to the Bridges Community! Bridges is family child care. We work to model the child care experience after our natural human experience on earth. In a time when biological families now live great distances apart, we must develop relationships that we can depend on similar to the way that families have historically depended on each other. Modeling our program after the natural human experience influences our every decision in the design of our program, such as the number of children, the quality of food, the mix of ages, and the influence of the physical child care environment. With this as our "prime directive," we have incorporated what we know as early childhood educators to create a program that encourages exploration, challenges learning, emphasizes social and emotional development, offers wholesome and nutritious food, and provides quiet, restful spaces in a homelike, ecologically sensitive environment.

Bridges Child Care is committed to families by offering ongoing communication of the child's development and family concerns; sliding-scale fees that encourage accessibility, regardless of income; and networking with others for support services such as agencies that offer parent training, social support, and special needs support. Currently one-fourth of the children enrolled are children whose parents became pregnant as teenagers. We encourage parents in their parenting skills and share with them information on what has worked successfully for other families. We also try to keep current on community support services that they may be eligible to receive.

RATIOS

Our child:adult ratios reflect our biological capabilities. We have eight children and two staff present, a similar ratio to our natural order of procreating. We believe that the low child:adult ratio is the single greatest factor in providing high-quality care. In a group setting it can be challenging to complete a learning opportunity with a child when other children may have the need for guidance at the same time. With the use of volunteers we are able to enhance our program further to offer one-on-one interactions.

ACTIVITIES

In an environment with a range of self-directed options, children are able to determine what skills they would like to develop and work on. Opportunities such as a "help yourself project/art table" encourage creativity, as well as develop fine motor skills. Our cozy book area is stocked with pillows for quiet small group or even alone time for book exploration. An indoor cotton yoga swing (that doesn't hurt when a child gets bumped by it and is too thick to strangle anyone) provides large motor development and is in constant use! A permanently set up drum and percussion circle encourages regular sessions in music and rhythm and is located near the dramatic play area for children to merge music, dance, and drama. We sing routinely, borrowing tunes from other songs and singing about what we are doing or the qualities of a child. We have a table for puzzles and games that has limited choices through regular equipment rotation. One area is reserved specifically for rotating themes such

INCLUSIVITY

Our program primarily serves children two to five years old. However, we make exceptions based on individual needs. Bridges alumni include children who are blind, autistic, have had cerebral palsy, and have had other physical differences. Currently we have a child with Down's syndrome who has been with us for five years, as well as a child who was born to a mother using crack.

THE ENVIRONMENT

Bridges Child Care is located in a ninety-plus-year-old home. We have built a "school" addition using natural, nontoxic materials and recycled materials, which was designed by architects who specialize in environmentally friendly building designs and built in a communal setting. The children's "program" for those years evolved around exploring the work that had been done after child care hours, observing some of the process during construction, and "helping" when it was appropriate. We set up some small activities, such as mixing clay and straw, so they could get a sense of the process. We also talked about what other animals use to make homes and made bird nests from straw and clay. We made pumpkin pies from our gardens' harvest as "thank you" gifts for some of the folks who had helped. We now have separate spaces for learning and playing, eating, and resting. Having ample space in a well designed child care facility is like having an extra staff person because the room works for us, in a supportive and functional way!

FAIR COMPENSATION

Bridges Family Child Care is committed to paying a living wage to the employees, which includes health care for full-time staff and paid continuing education, holidays, vacation, and personal days for all the staff. We are also asking the community to help us reach our goal in attaining the sufficient resources so that every staff member may be paid not just a living wage but a professional wage.

RESOURCES

We are continually evolving and developing our program to improve our service as well as enhance the resources. However, we feel that until public policy acknowledges that the cost of child care is a part of the cost of the greater societal infrastructure and contributes to our booming economy, the stability of child care will continue to be challenged. In Wisconsin, we have nearly an equal amount of licensed child care facilities open each year as we have closed. Can you imagine if we operated our public school systems this way?

Visit Bridges Family Child Care on the Web at http://www.bridgeschildcare.org/

as setting up a hospital scene, store, post office, and such. This area is most often set up as a response to the children's interests or experiences. We also go on field trips, four to five times per week. Each morning at breakfast we share our ideas about what we could do. After the discussion of ideas we vote to determine where we'll head out for that day. We talk about street safety, and we take many opportunities to learn about the earth, animals, business, and politics, as well as doing many large-motor activities.

SELF-CARE

As the children grow they are encouraged to wash, dress, and toilet independently. The children at Bridges are encouraged to "help themselves" more and more as their skills develop. Self-care is a process: through repetitive and consistent reminders children become responsible for themselves. Self-care is evolutionary: what is an accomplishment for one child becomes an expectation for another as their skills develop.

FOOD AND NUTRITION

In an effort to ensure that the children are receiving the best nutrients and are safe from additives, hormones, and pesticides, we make a great effort to serve mostly organic, almost exclusively vegetarian and nonprocessed food. We are able to do this mostly because we have made it a priority, looking again at our natural experience on earth, this time in regards to food. We routinely involve the children in cooking, composting, and gardening.

SOCIAL-EMOTIONAL DEVELOPMENT

At Bridges we feel that the one "job" of children in their early years is to learn how to live in the world with others. While each child differs in skill level of communication, each child is treated with great respect by the adults and is expected to treat others with respect. The conflict we deal with is a healthy part of development and is embraced at Bridges.

Text and photos contributed by Vic McMurray, Bridges Family Child Care director, Madison, Wisconsin.

INTERGENERATIONAL CHILD CARE

Intergenerational child care programs take two forms. One kind integrates children and the elderly into an early childhood and adult care facility. The elderly derive pleasure and feelings of competence from helping care for and interact with children, and young children receive attention and love from older caregivers. In today's mobile society, families often live long distances from each other, and children may be isolated from the care that grandparents can offer. Intergenerational programs blend the best of two worlds: children and the elderly both receive care and attention in a nurturing environment.

For example, the Friendship Center is an intergenerational child care facility that incorporates senior citizens into its child care programs. Read the accompanying Program in Action on The Friendship Center at Schooley's Mountain on page 182, and reflect on the benefits for children and adults.

A second type of intergenerational child care utilizes older adults, often retirees, as employees and volunteers to help care for children. Valuable and often untapped resources of skills and knowledge, older citizens have much to offer children and programs.

CENTER-BASED CHILD CARE

Center-based child care | Child care and education provided in a facility other than a home.

Center-based child care is conducted in specially constructed and/or renovated facilities in churches, YMCAs, and YWCAs, and other such facilities. Each state has its own definition of a center-based program, so you should research and become familiar with how your state defines center-based child care, as well as the other types of child care discussed in this chapter. Many center programs are comprehensive, providing a full range of services. Some are babysitting programs, while some offer less than good custodial care. Search for your state's definitions and regulations regarding child care, center care, and other kinds of care. You can access the licensure regulations for all fifty states through the website for the National Childcare Information Center: http://www.nccic.org/.

EMPLOYER-SPONSORED CHILD CARE

New responses to child care arise as more and more parents enter the workforce. The most rapidly growing segment of the workforce, in fact, is married women with children under one year of age. To meet the needs of working parents, employers are increasingly called on to provide affordable, accessible, quality child care. Corporate-supported child care is one of the fastest-growing employee benefits, as identified by the U.S. Chamber of Commerce. Employer-sponsored child care is not new. The Stride Rite Corporation started the first on-site corporate child care program in Boston in 1971.

Employer-sponsored child care has become one of the more talked-about programs in child care. In fact, on-site child care is one of the most frequently asked-for benefits by employees. Corporations supply space, equipment, and child care workers. Some corporations contract with an outside agency to provide child care service. Some also maintain a list of family day care homes and contract for spaces. They may also assist in equipping the providers' homes for child care services.

BACKUP CHILD CARE

Backup child care is a growing form of child care provided to corporate employees. For example, the O'Brien Family Center at PNC Firstside in Pittsburgh provides its employees with up to twenty days of child care a year, which they can use when their regular child care arrangements fall through, or when there is a snow day. Employees pay $15 a day for the child care services. The Center has twelve full-time staff and can care for seventy children ages 6 months to 13 years. In addition, new parents who wish to return to work in their first

PROGRAM IN ACTION

La Causa: Innovations in Child Care Practice

It is almost midnight when Lourdes Ortiz wearily steps off the bus that has brought her from her cleaning job at a downtown office building to this street corner in the oldest and poorest neighborhood in Milwaukee. The security guard buzzes her into a large building. Walking down the hall, Lourdes glances at the brightly colored children's art decorating the wall. She enters a dimly lit room. A dozen children are sleeping on cots, covered with beautiful woven Mexican blankets. As the child care teacher helps Lourdes dress her sleeping three-year-old in a snowsuit, they chat softly in Spanish. Carrying Angelina, Lourdes steps out into the frozen darkness for the walk home.

"I just can't take it anymore! Tyrone messes with everything and won't mind when I tell him to quit. The baby cries all the time. Sometimes I'm afraid I'll lose it and hurt somebody," LaKinta Greer tells Carl, while her three children noisily explore the adjacent playroom. The Crisis Nursery worker listens patiently as the exhausted, teary-eyed young mother recounts how she's been struggling to find a job to meet welfare-to-work requirements, how her boyfriend left because he was fed up with all the attention she pays to the kids, how her landlord threatens to evict them since she's two months behind in the rent. It's Sunday afternoon. Carl tells LaKinta that tomorrow he'll work on getting her some long-term help, like rent assistance, and will connect her to the agency's Family Resource Center for parenting education and support. For the short-term he invites her to leave her children here for a few days so she can get some much-needed needed rest. They will be well cared for in a homelike atmosphere by trained child care providers. Relieved, LaKinta enters the playroom to kiss her kids goodbye.

Marisol Gómez sits at a table in the P.E.A.C.E. Training Academy, laughing with two other assistant child care teachers. The three have just completed a role-play in which Marisol as "teacher" has tried to help "preschoolers" Karen and Youa resolve their conflict over a riding toy. They are amused because the teachers sounded exactly like kids fighting. Marisol worries, though, that she did not really support the "kids" in solving their problem themselves, since she suggested the solution. She motions to the instructor, who has been working with another small group. Sara, a nationally endorsed High/Scope instructor, makes some gentle suggestions, speaking in English and Spanish. On her way back to work at the end of the training session, Marisol waves to her third-grader who is walking to the gym with his classmates, and peeks in on her baby in the Infant Room.

At La Causa, Inc. quality means so much more than the basics of safety, good nutrition, and a stimulating environment for children. The name of the organization, La Causa, means "The Cause," and has its roots in the rallying cry of César Chavez' movement for civil rights and economic development for Hispanics. In 1972 two Mexican mothers opened La Causa for seventeen children in a small storefront. They wanted quality care for their children that would help them retain their own language and culture while their families were becoming part of the economic and social fabric of their adopted country. Today La Causa serves 9,000 children and parents with accessible, comprehensive services that support the development of the child within the context of family, community, and culture. La Causa's eight buildings are located around Milwaukee's oldest neighborhood. The area is populated largely by immigrant families from Puerto Rico, Mexico, and Central America. In recent years African American and Southeast Asian families have joined the mix. Some of La Causa's programs now reach out beyond the neighborhood to serve the city and county.

La Causa's programmatic centerpiece consists of three child care centers and an elementary school. While La Causa's child care facilities all serve the same neighborhood, each has a particular set of services and atmosphere that offer choices to parents. One small homey center serves only children under five years old. The largest center is open practically around the clock—from 5:30 A.M. to 1:30 A.M. This facility cares for infants, toddlers, and preschoolers, as well as children up to twelve years old before and after their day at the bilingual public school down the block. Soon this center will be open on weekends as well. A new center was recently built to house La Causa's bilingual elementary charter school, along with care for children from four weeks old through kindergarten, and a gallery of Mexican art and culture.

Working parents need easy access, convenience, support, and familiarity. La Causa's success derives from its extended hours, transportation, nutritious culturally appropriate meals, sliding fees, and acceptance of government vouchers for care. At La Causa a child can enter at four weeks old and move seamlessly through Head Start, kindergarten, and elementary school. Spanish and English speakers mingle easily in the classrooms, as both languages are spoken and valued by their teachers. La Causa's Fam-

ily Resource Center provides parenting education, a toy lending library, and other opportunities for family support. The Crisis Nursery and Social Services help families at risk to remain intact, keep their children out of the foster care system, and recover from crises.

Families appreciate being served by people who can relate to them culturally and linguistically. La Causa's staff, administration, and board largely come from the communities served, they are 61 percent Latino, 12 percent African American, 1 percent Native American and Asian, and 26 percent Euro-American. The majority of the staff is bilingual in English and Spanish. Most child care teachers and administrators are women from the surrounding neighborhood. The agency has a "grow your own" practice that fosters the development of a multicultural, bilingual staff at all levels by dedicated extraordinary resources to recruitment, training, and advancement.

The child care staff's professional and personal growth is key to La Causa's success at retaining a quality stable workforce. The P.E.A.C.E. Training Academy provides entry-level and continuing education courses to more than 2,000 child care professionals and paraprofessionals yearly. Course topics include everything from the basics of infant care to active learning techniques to working with children with autism. La Causa's educational philosophy includes a commitment to child-centered, developmentally appropriate practices, and to fostering the social and emotional skills that prevent violence. Child care personnel are provided opportunities to develop themselves as nurturers, community peacemakers, and teachers of peace through specially designed courses at the Academy. They learn how to take care of their own needs; manage stress and anger; communicate with and understand others better; resolve conflicts; feel pride in their own cultural heritage and interest in others' cultures; and unleash their

own creativity and playfulness—all so they can model and teach these skills to children.

La Causa is the first bilingual, multicultural child care center in Wisconsin accredited by the National Association for the Education of Young Children (NAEYC). It has been declared a Governor's Center of Excellence and it won a *Promesa de un Futuro Brillante* (Promise of a Brilliant Fu-

ture) Award from the National Latino Children's Institute. The attention La Causa has received is the result of the innovative ways it has found to become a "one-stop shop" in the cause of child, family, and community development.

Contributed by Fran Kaplan, MSW, EdD, Director, P.E.A.C.E. Training Academy, La Causa, Inc., Milwaukee, Wisconsin. Photos contributed by Fran Kaplan.

year receive eight weeks of free infant care.[3] At the backup child care center operated by J.P. Morgan Chase in Dallas, each employee receives twenty days of free backup childcare.[4]

In addition to sponsoring child care programs, employers can provide child care services in a number of other ways, as shown in Figure 7.1. Many corporations have child care management programs operate their child care programs for them.

To complete a Program in Action activity related to La Causa, visit the Companion Website at **http://www. prenhall.com/morrison**, select chapter 7, then choose the Program in Action module.

PROPRIETARY CHILD CARE

Some child care centers are run by corporations, businesses, and individual proprietors for the purpose of making a profit. Some for-profit centers provide custodial services and preschool and elementary programs as well. Many of these programs emphasize their educational component and appeal to middle-class families who are willing to pay for the promised services. About 35 percent of all child care centers in the United States are operated for profit, and the number is likely to grow. Child care is a $30 billion service industry, with more and more entrepreneurs realizing that there is money to be made in caring for the nation's children. For-profit child care companies are growing in number and size. Table 7.2 lists the seven largest child care management organizations.

FIGURE 7.1   How Businesses Support Child Care

- *Resource and referral services.* Corporations supply information and counseling to parents on selecting quality care and referrals to local child care providers. These services can be offered in-house (i.e., on site) or through community or national resource and referral agencies.

- *Direct aid.* Some companies provide a flat subsidy—a specific amount to their employees to help cover the cost of child care. For example, NationsBank, the largest bank in the South, pays its associates with limited incomes up to $35 per week to pay for child care.

- *Voucher systems.* Corporations give employees vouchers with which to purchase services at child care centers.

- *Vendor systems.* Corporations purchase spaces at child care centers and make them available to employees either free or at reduced rates.

- *Contributions to a child care center.* Corporations pay a subsidy to help reduce rates for employees at a particular center.

- *Parent-family leave.* Some corporations provide paid or subsidized leaves of absence for parents in lieu of specific child care services.

- *Other arrangements.* Employers can offer a flexible work schedule, so parents may need less or no child care. They may also offer maternity leave extension and paternity leaves and allow sick leave to include absence from work for a sick child.

Businesses play an increasingly popular and important role in providing resources and benefits relating to child care. Why and how do you consider business involvement to be beneficial for children and families?

PROGRAM IN ACTION

Intergenerational Child Care
A Venture into the Future

Intergenerational child care centers help promote social and emotional bonds between our very youngest and oldest populations. With an estimated population of 37 million seniors beyond the age of sixty-five and a likely doubling of that population in the next twenty years, it is easy to see why such programs could grow in importance for both generations.

We have explored the evolution and development of such a program with the Friendship Center at Schooley's Mountain, an intergenerational child care center located on the Heath Village Retirement Community campus.

FORMULATION

Many of the intergenerational programs we studied seemed to favor the idea of having children attend and participate in activities geared for nursing home–level residents. However, the Board of the Friendship Center made a conscious decision to recruit elderly residents who would stimulate the children through various experiences.

RECRUITMENT OF VOLUNTEERS

Proponents of the intergenerational concept are often overly optimistic about the level of senior participation. It is not unusual for the number of volunteers to be relatively small, for a variety of reasons.

A significant number of seniors, especially those of advanced age, are simply not physically capable of the level of activity that one-on-one interaction with small children requires. The dynamics of the senior environment are such that even those who initially have the required vigor will eventually reduce their level of participation, making a steady flow of replacement volunteers essential.

Younger seniors, especially those used to a more active lifestyle, are already involved in a number of activities and are not inclined to assume additional ones.

Those seniors who see their own children or grandchildren on a regular basis may feel less of a need to participate in child care activities.

CHILD CARE FOR CHILDREN WITH ONGOING MEDICAL NEEDS

As child care becomes more popular, it also is becoming more specialized. For most parents, balancing the demands of a job and the obligations of parenthood is manageable as long as children are healthy. But when children get sick, parents must find someone who will take care of them, or they must stay home. The National Child Care Survey data reveal that 35 percent of mothers employed outside the home reported that in the month previous to the survey their child was sick on a day they were supposed to work. Fifty-one percent of these women missed an average of 2.2 days of work per month because of sick children.[5]

Consequently, child care providers have begun to respond to parents' needs. More and more programs are providing care for children with medical needs, such as care when they have illnesses (both contagious and noncontagious) that keep them from attending other regular child care programs. Also, some children may have broken bones, which require special care and keep them from attending their programs. Some centers provide care for sick children as part of their program, and other providers are opening centers exclusively for the care of ill children. Ill children are cared for in the following ways:

- *In the home.* Child care aides go into homes to care for ill children.
- *In the hospital.* Some hospitals have programs providing for sick children.
- *In the center.* Ill child care is part of the program's services and is usually in a separate room or area.

PROGRAM DIVERSITY

The Friendship Center at Schooley's Mountain has forty-seven children who experience the warmth and love of seniors from seventy to ninety years old. The children, ranging in age from two and a half to six years, benefit immensely from their exposure to the very oldest generation.

Seniors at Heath Village offer a potpourri of programs and classes to the Friendship Center children on a regular basis. French class for prekindergartners, woodshop class on a weekly basis, and the very popular nature trail program are examples. Some Villagers visit the children at playtime and push the little ones on the playground swings, while others teach baking classes, flower arranging, or piano classes. The children learn to accept the sight of medical equipment, such as wheelchairs and oxygen tanks, while visiting the Nursing Center. Classes of children join in programming activities, such as finger painting, with the nursing center residents. In truth, the children begin to see beyond what many in society are frightened to view at all.

Evidence of the creativity of the children and the involvement of the Village residents is everywhere. The Village Men's Club gave a very special gift to the children, a handcrafted, 24- by 16-foot pirate ship christened "The Friend Ship." The same group of men worked nine months on the newest playground addition—the Heathosaur, a life-sized (16- by 4-foot) wooden dinosaur.

The key element in both projects was the camaraderie that developed among the men as they successfully built the oversized toys. What's more, these men captured the children's imagination, and the woodshop class has moved to the forefront of popularity with our preschoolers.

FURTHER BENEFITS

Unknown to us at the start of our intergenerational experiment was the profound impact the Friendship Center concept would have on the *middle* generation— namely, the parents of the Center's children. In seven years of operation, the exposure that this "sandwich generation" (and younger parents, too!) has had to the residents and the facilities at Heath Village has been enlightening to them. Many have become aware of the retirement community living style and no longer label senior housing as a "nursing home." Still others have remarked at how their children now seem to feel comfortable around grandparents and great-grandparents while at social and family reunions, a decided change brought about by the Friendship Center experience.

SUMMARY

Intergenerational child care benefits young and old alike by offering a whole new avenue of programs for residents, along with opportunities for them to share their enormous reservoir of knowledge and talent with children.

Intergenerational child care operates on the idea that the first and last of the "ages of man" should not be isolated from one another. Friendship Center children have helped the elderly residents of Heath Village to feel younger and more useful. The resident volunteers continue to help the children to develop socially and academically.

Both groups find their lives enriched.

Contributed by Patrick E. Brady, Executive Director of Heath Village Retirement Community and President of the Board of Trustees of the Friendship Center at Schooley's Mountain. Phone (908) 852-2221. *pbrady@heathvillage.com*

TABLE 7.2 Largest Child Care Management Organizations in the United States

Organization/Headquarters	Contracted Centers	Office Park Centers
Bright Horizons Family Solutions (Nashville, TN)	248	30
Children's Discovery Centers/Knowledge Beginnings (San Rafael, CA)	81	77
Childtime Learning Centers (Farmington Hills, MI)	35	17
ARAMARK Educational Resources (Golden, CO)	30	12
KinderCare Learning Centers (Portland, OR)	43	0
Mulberry Child Care Centers (Needham, MA)	15	23
La Petite Academy (Overland Park, KS)	29	0

Source: Inside Child Care: Trend Report 2000. Reprinted with permission from Child Care Information Exchange, P.O. Box 3249, Redmond, Washington 98073. (800) 221-2864.

To extend your knowledge of intergenerational child care, visit the Companion Website at **http://www. prenhall.com/morrison**, select chapter 7, then choose the Program in Action module.

Bright Horizons GlaxoSmithKline Onsite Child Center

The standards at Bright Horizons Child Center focus on two primary aspects: the quality of our child-centered programming including interaction between faculty and families, and the quality of our faculty and the conditions in which they work. Guidelines have been created to continually assess our programs to assure that they exercise developmentally appropriate practices and that the delivery of our programs and design of our surroundings remain child centered.

Developmentally appropriate standards established by the National Association for the Education of Young Children form the basis of our program's curriculum. To develop our curriculum, we not only recognize the universal patterns and milestones of child development but also work to find in each individual child his or her unique pattern of developmental capabilities, temperamental characteristics, and learning styles. The intent of our curriculum, therefore, is to provide learning activities and materials that are real, concrete, and relevant to the lives and experiences of our young children.

The teacher's role in classrooms at Bright Horizons is to provide a variety of challenging activity choices for children and then facilitate children's engagement in the activities they select. A teacher's thoughtful input at the right moment can advance a child's competence and challenge a child's thinking. Small group sizes, intensive teacher:child

To complete a Program in Action activity, visit the Companion Website at **http://www.prenhall.com/morrison**, select chapter 7, then choose the Program in Action module.

- *In a separate facility.* This facility is specifically designed, built, and staffed to provide child care as needed for sick children.
- *In a family day care.* Ill children are provided for in a family day care home.

BEFORE-SCHOOL AND AFTER-SCHOOL CARE

In many respects, public schools are logical places for before-school and after-school care. They have the administrative organization, facilities, and staff to provide such care. Many taxpayers and professionals have always believed that schools should not sit empty in the afternoons, evenings, holidays, and summers. Using resources already in place for child care makes good sense. This is why in many communities public schools are helping meet the need for after-school child care. For example, the public schools in Dade County, Florida, provide before- and after-school care for more than 25,000 students in 205 after-school centers and 3,300 students in 111 before-school centers. Special needs students are mainstreamed at 83 schools with well over 700 students in after-school care. Parents pay $15 to $30 per week depending on the per-child cost at the individual school. Because the programs are school based and managed, the costs of services vary depending on the nature and cost of each program. Services begin at dismissal and end at 6 P.M.

child development and their particular insights about young children. To facilitate better communication, Bright Horizons issues a company-wide parent survey every year to solicit input with regard to all aspects of each center's program, such as program quality, faculty quality, and the level of satisfaction with the program. The faculty is surveyed as well.

Bright Horizons established a task force to investigate the needs of families with both parents working and overall attitudes toward preschool education practices and school readiness. As a result of this undertaking, the center developed LANGUAGE WORKS!, a preschool program that is a whole language learning experience to address the key element that contributes to a child's readiness for school and lifelong learning: language proficiency. LANGUAGE WORKS! is an expansion in Bright Horizon's developmental preschool education program to help children develop a foundation of social and cognitive skills. This program also offers opportunities for more parent participation, both in the classroom and at home, in order for children to enter elementary school "ready to learn."

Visit Bright Horizons on the Web at http://www.brighthorizons.com/.

ratios, and highly qualified and trained teachers provide assurance that each child receives individual attention and develops a sense of belonging in the center. The development of self-esteem in each child is a fundamental goal. We believe that children develop a positive self-image when they are given opportunities to exercise the power of their own choices.

Essential to the Bright Horizons program is parent involvement and satisfaction. The center believes the systems created to support parent communication and involvement form the cornerstone of the Bright Horizon–Parent Partnership. The center emphasizes the important role parents play in the early learning and development of their children. As teachers of young children, staff at the center are able to share with parents aspects of their knowledge about

Bright Horizons Family Solutions (www.brighthorizons.com) is the world's leading provider of employer-sponsored child care, early education, and work/life solutions. The company operates more than 450 child care and early education centers across the United States, Europe, Canada, and the Pacific Rim. Bright Horizons serves more than 350 clients worldwide, including GlaxoSmithKline. Photos are provided by Bright Horizons.

Before- and after-school care programs play an increasingly important role in school-based programs and in the lives of children and families. Opportunities for play and exercise such as this are important in before- and after-school programs. Increasingly, however, parents want such programs to provide help with homework, opportunities for children to study, and for enrichment through extracurricular activities such as music and the arts.

According to the National Study of Before and After School Programs, about 1.7 million children in kindergarten through grade eight are enrolled in 49,500 programs.[6] The three most common sponsors of before- and after-school child care are the public schools, for-profit corporations, and nonprofit organizations. As child care grows and expands across the nation, it forces a number of critical issues. These are how to maintain and provide high-quality care for *all* children; how to provide high-quality *affordable* care for all families; and how to ensure that high-quality affordable care is *available* to all families that want and need it.

Full Service Child Care, and Then Some!

You have heard of one-stop shopping, I'm sure. The idea is to go to one store or service center and get what you need. Now the one-stop concept is coming to child care. The Little Leprechaun day care center provides a variety of services for children and their families such as free Starbucks coffee for parents; a dry-cleaning drop-off service; dance, martial arts, and foreign language classes for children; a hair stylist to provide haircuts for the children; and that is not all! The academy offers dinner to go!

The academy also offers electronic monitoring of their children. Parents can view their child through classroom cameras at anytime, over the Internet. The classroom cameras are robotic, controlled by the parents from the Web. Parents can access this service, as well as their child's schedule, account, and personal information, by logging in at the Little Leprechaun Academy's website with a user ID and password. The goal: to accommodate the schedules and special needs of busy families.[*]

Mark Ginsberg, executive director of the National Association for the Education of Young Children, said he expects more and more day-care centers around the country to offer services for the entire family. "We believe there has to be a strong partnership between schools, childcare centers, and parents," Ginsberg said. "Services like take-home meals are another step in creating one-stop shopping and would be a big help to families that are increasingly strapped for time in today's society."[†]

---

[*]Little Leprechaun Academy. Available at http://www.littleleprechaun.com/.
[†]Associated Press, "Day-care centers cater to busy families." *CNN-com* (2003). Available at http://www.cnn.com/2003/US/Midwest/01/15/daycare. gourmets.ap/index.html.

▲ Child care involves much more than merely providing physical care. All caregivers should provide children with love and affection. They should meet each child's full range of social and emotional needs.

WHAT CONSTITUTES QUALITY EDUCATION AND CARE?

Although there is much debate about quality and what it involves, we can nonetheless identify the main characteristics of quality programs that provide care and education for children and families.

DEVELOPMENTAL NEEDS

Good care and education provides for children's needs and interests at each developmental stage. For example, infants need good physical care as well as continual love and affection and sensory stimulation. Toddlers need safe surroundings and opportunities to explore. They need caregivers who support and encourage active involvement.

APPROPRIATE AND SAFE ENVIRONMENTS

At all age levels, a safe and pleasant physical setting is important. Such an area should include a safe neighborhood free from traffic and environmental hazards; a fenced play area with well-maintained equipment; child-sized equipment and facilities (toilets, sinks); and areas for displaying children's work, such as finger painting and clay models. The environment should also be attractive and pleasant. The rooms, home, or center should be clean, well lit, well ventilated, and cheerful.

Supporting Diversity in a Faith-Based Multicultural Child Care Setting

Hampton Place Baptist Church resides in the low-income region of Oak Cliff, an urban area of Dallas, Texas, composed of many minorities. The church provides child care services to primarily Hispanic, Spanish-speaking families. However, we also house a Laotian mission. Our preschool department includes approximately fifteen infants, ten toddlers, and fifteen preschoolers and serves the Hispanic and Laotian congregations. Here are some of the considerations and adjustments we have made to accommodate these different cultures:

- Greet families in a culturally sensitive manner. With Hispanic families, the father is greeted first, then the mother. Children are greeted last.
- Provide inclusive artwork. Murals include children with different skin and hair colors.
- Use linguistically appropriate materials. Books in English and Spanish are provided.
- Adjust caregiving practices according to culture. While most Hispanic infants are calmed with quick, repetitive, choppy phrases and back patting, the Laotian infants are calmed through soft, smooth talking, cradling, and gentle rocking.

- Adjust caregiver–infant interaction style appropriately. Some infants interact primarily person-to-person. Others interact through toys.
- Be aware of and respect different social preferences. While Hispanic toddlers tend to interact with peers, Laotian toddlers tend to keep to themselves and sometimes want to be left alone. A Laotian child may need to be provided with a special place of her own.
- Apply limits to cultural accommodation when necessary. Discuss compromise with parents. For example, some cultures allow infants to eat items that could be choked on. In this instance, we explain the danger the food provides to the infants in the room and ask parents to bring alternative snacks.
- Recognize that all families have their own individual cultures and be careful not to stereotype based on ethnicity.

Contributed by Amy Turcotte, Children's Director, Hampton Place Baptist Church, Oak Cliff, Texas.

CAREGIVER–CHILD RATIO

The ratio of adults to children should be sufficient to give children the individual care and attention they need. NAEYC guidelines for the ratio of caregivers to children are 1:3 or 1:4 for infants; 1:3 or 1:4 for toddlers; and 1:8 to 1:10 for preschoolers, depending on group size.

The American Public Health Association (APHA) and the American Academy of Pediatrics (AAP) recommend these ratios and standards:

- Child/staff ratios of 3:1 for children under twenty-five months, 4:1 for children twenty-five to thirty months, and 7:1 for children thirty-one to thirty-five months
- Group sizes of 6 for children under twenty-five months, 8 for children twenty-five to thirty months, and 14 for children thirty-one to thirty-five months
- Child care providers who have formal, post–high school training in child development, early childhood education, or a related field for all child-care workers at all ages

Research shows that when programs meet these recommended child–staff ratios and recommended levels of caregivers training and education, then children have better outcomes.[7]

Also, analyses of research data reveals that low-quality care for all children—regardless of whether they were in child care centers, in homes, or taken care of by

To learn more about full service childcare, visit the Companion Website at **http:// www.prenhall.com/ morrison**, select chapter 7, then choose the Program in Action module.

To complete an activity related to this topic, go to the Companion Website at **http://www. prenhall.com/morrison**, select chapter 7, then choose the Diversity Tie-In module.

PROGRAM IN ACTION

Military Child Development System

The Department of Defense (DoD) military child development system (CDS) provides services for the largest number of children on a daily basis of any employer in the United States. Military child care is provided in 800 centers in more than 300 geographic locations, both within and outside of the continental United States.

Military families face challenges that are not found in other work environments. Shifting work schedules that are often longer than the typical eight-hour day, and the requirement to be ready to deploy anywhere in the world on a moment's notice, require a child development system that is flexible in nature, yet maintains the standards exemplified by the National Association for the Education of Young Children (NAEYC), the National Association of Family Child Care (NAFCC), and the National School-Age Care Association (NSACA). Frequent family separations and the requirement to move, on average, every three years, place military families in situations not often experienced in the civilian world. For this population, finding affordable, high-quality child care is paramount, if they are to be ready to perform the mission and their jobs. It is also important to military personnel that

child care services be consistent at installations throughout the military.

DoD considers child care a workforce issue. It impacts the effectiveness and readiness of the force. There are some general statistics about the military child care environment:

- More than 1.2 million children are under the age of eighteen.
- Approximately 244,000 children are under the age of three.
- 53 percent of the active duty workforce is married.
- Two-thirds (63 percent) of young enlisted military spouses are employed or seeking employment.
- 6 percent of military members are single parents.
- 6 percent of military members are in dual-military marriages.

Four main components make up the DoD CDS: child development centers (CDC), family child care (FCC), school-age care (SAC), and resource and referral programs (R & R). Through these four areas, the DoD serves more than 200,000 children (ages six weeks to twelve years) daily. More than 48 percent of all of the care provided is for infants and toddlers. The system offers full-day, part-day,

◀ Child care providers need to provide opportunities for children to learn social and academic skills through play. What are some ways that you could provide for play opportunities to assure that children are learning important concepts and skills?

family members—is associated with poorer school readiness and poorer performance on tests of expressive and receptive language skills. In contrast, child care quality was not associated with a child's social behavior.

DEVELOPMENTALLY APPROPRIATE PROGRAMS

Programs should have written, developmentally based curricula for meeting children's needs. A program's curriculum should specify activities for children of all ages that caregivers can use to stimulate infants, provide for the growing independence of toddlers, and address the readiness and literacy skills of four- and five-year-olds. All programs should include education to meet the social, emotional, and cognitive needs of all children. Quality programs use developmentally appropriate practices to implement the curriculum and achieve their program goals.

and hourly (drop-in) child care; part-day preschool programs, before- and after-school programs for school-age children, and extended hour care including nights and weekends. Using the total number of children of military members (approximately 1.2 million), and the number of working spouses of military members, DoD needs approximately 215,000 child care spaces. Currently, DoD provides approximately 176,000 spaces.

CHILD DEVELOPMENT CENTERS (CDC)

The DoD oversees 800 CDCs at more than 300 locations and provides care for children six weeks to twelve years of age. Care is usually provided between the hours of 6:00 A.M. to 6:30 P.M. Monday to Friday. Approximately 64,000, or 38 percent of all child care spaces, are provided through CDCs. More than 99 percent of all centers are currently accredited by NAEYC.

FAMILY CHILD CARE (FCC)

Family child care (FCC) provides in-home care by certified providers. Historically, providers have had to live on base or in government-leased housing; recently, several of the services expanded this to include military families living in civilian housing. There are more than 9,000 FCC providers. These providers deliver critical services to service members on shift work, working extended hours or weekends, and for those who prefer a home-based environment for their children. In addition, FCC providers can provide care for mildly ill children, something CDCs are not set up to do.

All FCC providers go through rigorous background checks, must go through licensure, and are encouraged to achieve accreditation as determined by the NAFCC in conjunction with the DoD or other process approved by the service.

SCHOOL-AGE CARE (SAC)

School-age care (SAC) programs are offered for children (ages six to twelve years) before and after school, during holidays, and during summer vacations. The SAC programs complement, rather than duplicate, the school day. Emphasis is placed on SAC programs that meet community needs, reinforce family values, and promote the cognitive, social, emotional, and physical development of children. Currently, about 43,248 (25 percent) of the total number of spaces are provided for SAC. This area of care is currently expanding, with new initiatives being implemented at the service level to more fully meet this need. Not all SAC is provided in CDCs, much of it is provided in youth centers or other suitable facilities. In addition, new initiatives that include partnering with local schools and other off-base organizations have begun.

RESOURCE AND REFERRAL (R & R)

Local resource and referral (R & R) services augment child care systems. R & R services assist parents in finding child care when all spaces on base are full or a parent can't get the preferred child care arrangement through military provided services. Bridging the gap between those needing child care and those served by military child care services, R & R is a critical component of the system. R & R services at the local level work closely with community agencies to serve as a liaison to nonmilitary child care services. Currently, only about 5 percent of child care need is served through R & R. Efforts are being made to partner with civilian child care services in order to expand their service.

Source: Military Family Resource Center. Available at http://mfrc.calib.com/mcy/mm_cdc.htm.

FAMILY EDUCATION AND SUPPORT

Parents and other family members should know as much as possible about the program their children are enrolled in, their children's growth and development, and the curriculum program of activities. Parents need encouragement to make the program's services part of their lives, so they are not detached from it, its staff, or what happens to their children. Professionals must demonstrate to parents their competence in areas such as child development, nutrition, and planning and implementing developmentally appropriate curricula. They must also assure parents that they will maintain daily communication about the child's progress. Additionally, parents and professionals must agree on discipline and guidance procedures, and professionals and social service agencies need to guide parents about what constitutes good child rearing and appropriate discipline practices.

STAFF TRAINING AND DEVELOPMENT

All professionals should be involved in an ongoing program of training and development. The CDA program discussed in chapter 1 is a good beginning for staff members to become competent and maintain necessary skills. Program administrators should have a background and training in child development and early childhood education. Knowledge of child growth and development is essential for caregivers. Professionals need to be developmentally aware and child oriented rather than self or center oriented.

PROGRAM ACCREDITATION

To take an online self-test on this chapter's contents, go to the Companion Website at **http://www. prenhall.com/morrison**, select chapter 7, then choose the Self-Test module.

In any discussion of quality, the question invariably arises, "Who determines quality?" Fortunately NAEYC has addressed the issue of standards in its Center Accreditation Project (CAP). CAP is a national, voluntary accreditation process for child care centers, preschools, and programs that provide before- and after-school care for school-age children. Accreditation is administered through NAEYC's National Academy of Early Childhood Programs.

The criteria addressed in the accreditation project include interactions among staff and children; curriculum, staff, and parent interactions; administration, staff, and parent interactions; staff qualifications and development; staffing patterns; physical environment; health and safety; nutrition and food service; and program evaluation.[8]

THE EFFECTS OF CARE AND EDUCATION ON CHILDREN

Recent research reveals that high-quality early care and education has influences that last over a lifetime. High-quality care and education have these benefits:

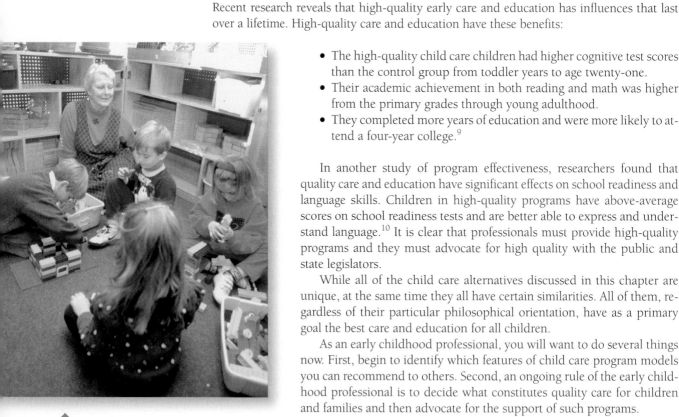

- The high-quality child care children had higher cognitive test scores than the control group from toddler years to age twenty-one.
- Their academic achievement in both reading and math was higher from the primary grades through young adulthood.
- They completed more years of education and were more likely to attend a four-year college.[9]

In another study of program effectiveness, researchers found that quality care and education have significant effects on school readiness and language skills. Children in high-quality programs have above-average scores on school readiness tests and are better able to express and understand language.[10] It is clear that professionals must provide high-quality programs and they must advocate for high quality with the public and state legislators.

While all of the child care alternatives discussed in this chapter are unique, at the same time they all have certain similarities. All of them, regardless of their particular philosophical orientation, have as a primary goal the best care and education for all children.

As an early childhood professional, you will want to do several things now. First, begin to identify which features of child care program models you can recommend to others. Second, an ongoing rule of the early childhood professional is to decide what constitutes quality care for children and families and then advocate for the support of such programs.

Observing children at play enables teachers to learn about their developmental levels, social skills, and peer interactions. How might teachers use this information to plan future play-based activities?

ACTIVITIES FOR FURTHER ENRICHMENT

APPLICATIONS

1. Invite people from child care programs, welfare departments, and social service agencies to speak to your class about child care and education. Also, determine what qualifications and training are necessary to become a child care employee.

2. Which of the child care programs discussed in this chapter do you think best meets the needs of children and families? What kind of program would you want for your child? why?

FIELD EXPERIENCES

1. Visit various child care programs, including center and home programs, and discuss similarities and differences in class. Which of the programs provides the best services? What changes or special provisions need to be made to improve the success of these kinds of programs?
2. Visit an employer-sponsored child care program and describe it to your classmates. List the pros and cons for parents and for employers of employer-sponsored child care.
3. Visit several child care programs and compare and contrast what you see. How are they similar and different? How do you account for this?

RESEARCH

1. Survey parents in your area to determine what services they desire from child care. Are most of the parents' child care needs being met? How is what they want in a child care program similar to and different from standards for quality child care discussed in this chapter?
2. Determine the legal requirements for establishing center and home child care programs in your state, city, or locality. What are the similarities and differences in regard to establishing home and center programs? What is your opinion of the guidelines? Why?
3. Link to NAEYC's Web site (www.naeyc.org) and review its Position Statement on Licensing and Public Regulation of Early Childhood Programs. Why does NAEYC believe licensing and regulation of child care are important processes?
4. Conduct a survey to learn the cost of child care services in your area. Arrange your data in a table. What conclusions can you draw?

For additional Internet resources or to complete an online activity for this chapter, go to the Companion Website at **http://www.prenhall.com/ morrison**, select chapter 7, then choose the Linking to Learning or Making Connections module.

READINGS FOR FURTHER ENRICHMENT

Bergmann, B. R., and Helburn, S. W. *America's Childcare Program*. New York: St. Martin's Press, 2002.

A look at the child care industry, identifying problems such as quality of care and the high cost, as well as needed changes, including stronger regulatory procedures on providers and suppliers of care.

Catron, C. E., and Allen, J. *Early Childhood Curriculum: A Creative Play Model*, 3rd ed. Upper Saddle River, NJ: Merrill/Prentice Hall, 2003.

This comprehensive guide provides information on planning programs with a play-based, developmental curriculum for children from birth to five years of age and covers basic principles and current research in early childhood curricula.

Curtis, A., and O'Hanagan, M. *Early Childhood Care and Education*. New York: RoutledgeFalmer, 2002.

Provides a comprehensive and up-to-date review of the key issues in the field of early childhood care and education. Included are discussions on equal opportunities and children's rights, an examination of how children learn, and the learning difficulties they may face. There is also a comparison with European perspectives on early years' care and education.

Lombadri, J. *Time to Care: Redesigning Child Care to Promote Education, Support Families, and Build Communities*. Philadelphia: Temple University Press, 2002.

Lays out seven principles that should shape our image of child care and presents detailed, well-documented discussions of the why, the what, and the how for improving child care systems. Suggests a new view of child care as a potential asset—not as a crisis or a deficit—leading to new opportunities to further the traditional American values of education, family, and quality.

LINKING TO LEARNING

Connect for Kids
http://www.connectforkids.org

> *A coalition of leaders from diverse organizations advocating for high-quality child care whose activities include education, information service, proposing possible solutions, and technical assistance to government offices.*

Child Care Bureau
http://www.acf.dhhs.gov/programs/ccb

> *Information on the Child Care and Development Block Grant, links to other Administration on Children and Families sites and other information within the Department of Health and Human Services, with links to other related child care sites.*

Electronic Policy Network
http://movingideas.org

> *A resource site, including information and links to national organizations working in child and family policy, welfare reform, health policy, and economic research.*

National Child Care Information Center
http://nccic.org

> *Sponsored by the Child Care Bureau, Administration for Children and Families, Department of Health and Human Services, this site provides a central access point for information on child care.*

National Resource Center for Health and Safety in Child Care
http://nrc.uchsc.edu

> *Funded by the Maternal and Child Health Bureau, Department of Health and Human Services, this site has the child care licensure regulations for each state. Also available are health and safety tips and full-text resources.*

Childcare.gov
http://www.childcare.gov

> *A site for parents, child care programs, and early childhood educators that brings all Federal agency resources together in one place.*

National Association for the Education of Homeless Children and Youth
http://www.naehcy.org

> *As a professional association dedicated to homeless education, NAEHCY has created guidelines, goals, and objectives that function to outline strategies for dealing with government agencies and designing effective programs to help solve problems faced by homeless children, youth, and families.*

ENDNOTES

[1] Singer, J. D., Fuller, B., Keiley, M. K., and Wolf, A. "Early Child-Care Selection: Variation by Geographic Location, Maternal Characteristics, and Family Structure," *Developmental Psychology* 34, no. 5 (1998): 1129–1144.

[2] "Relative Care: Closer Together," *Parenting* (June/July 1999), 123.

[3] Carpenter, M. "Study Finds Few Child Care Programs in Pennsylvania Offer High-quality Early Learning." *Post-Gazette*, December 3, 2002.

[4] Rivera, P. "Child Care Service Helps Firms Save." *Dallas Morning News*, December 10, 2002.

[5] Brayfield, April., Deich, Sharon., Holcomb, Pamela. *National Child Care Survey* 1990 (Washington, DC: Urban Institute Press, 1991), 355.

[6] U.S. Department of Education, National Study of Before and After School Programs. Available at http://www.ed.gov/offices/OUS/PES/esed/64&aftr.html.

[7] NICHD Early Child Care Research Network. "Child Outcomes when Child Care Center Classes Meet Recommended Standards for Quality." *American Journal of Public Health.* vol 88, No 7, 1072–1077.

[8] National Association for the Education of Young Children, *Accreditation by the National Academy of Early Childhood Programs* (Washington, DC: Author, 1991), 2.

[9] Wilgoren, Jodi. "Quality Day Care, Early, Is Tied to Achievements as an Adult," *New York Times*, 22 (October 22 1999), A16.

[10] Jacobson, Linda. "Study: High-Quality Child Care Pays Off," *Education Week* (April 28, 1999), 9.

Chapter 8

Head Start provides comprehensive services that children living in poverty need to achieve school readiness.

SARAH GREENE, CEO NATIONAL HEAD START ASSOCIATION

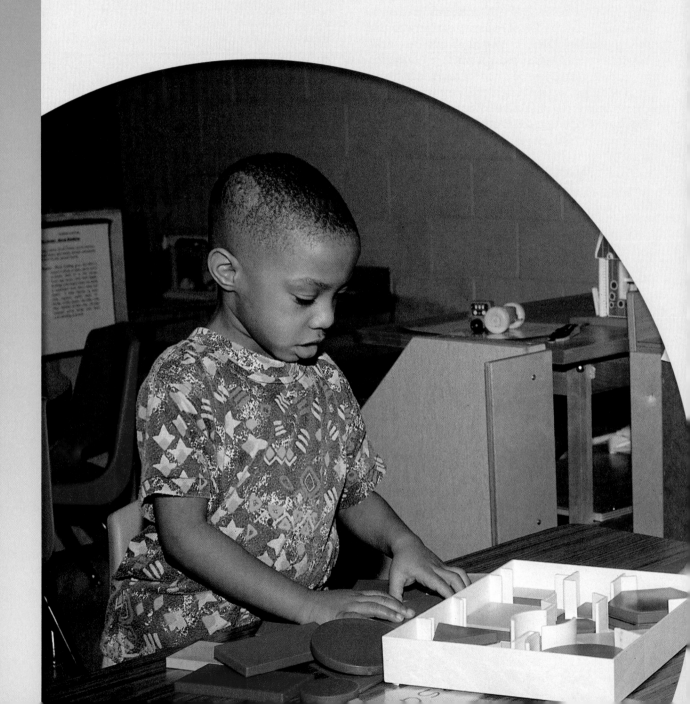

The Federal Government
Supporting Children's Success

Focus Questions

- Why are federal agencies so involved in programs that support and educate children and families?

- How are federal agencies transforming early childhood education?

- What are the essential purposes of federal programs that serve young children and their families?

- What are basic issues involved in the federal funding and control of early childhood programs?

I n chapter 2, "Early Childhood Education Today," we discussed the increasing influence of the federal and state governments in early childhood education. One of the remarkable political events of the last decade has been the use of early childhood education to achieve certain political goals and to reform all of education, including early childhood education. The reform of education was a major political campaign issue during the 2000 presidential election and in many state elections including Texas, California, and Florida. The 2002 elections were known as the "education elections" because of the public's overwhelming support in the form of constitutional amendments and local initiatives for such educational reforms as smaller class size, after-school programs, and universal preschool (more about this topic in chapter 10). There are several reasons for the phenomenal public, federal, and state interest in early childhood education:

- There is growing recognition by the public and politicians that learning begins at birth long before children enter school.
- What children learn or don't learn before they enter schools helps determine how successful they will be in school.
- Increasing numbers of working parents want their children in quality care and educational programs, as we discussed in chapter 7.
- Early childhood programs are being used to care for children whose parents are participating in work-training programs as part of welfare reform.
- Politicians and the public are dissatisfied with the growing number of children who are failing at reading and writing.
- The public genuinely cares about education and is willing to support it with higher taxes. Seventy-two percent of the American public supports current education reform efforts.[1]

For these reasons, more federal and state dollars are being poured into early childhood programs. This is a very exciting and challenging time for all early childhood professionals and the programs they teach in and administer. However, with increased federal and state funding come mandates, control, and

To review the chapter focus questions online, go to the Companion Website at **http://www. prenhall.com/morrison** and select chapter 8.

restructuring. Federal and state laws, regulations, and dollars are changing what early childhood programs look like and how they function. Federally funded programs such as Head Start and Early Head Start are leading the way in changing how the professional cares for and educates young children.

FEDERAL LEGISLATION AND EARLY CHILDHOOD

Federal legislation has had an influence on the educational process. For early childhood education, the passage of the Economic Opportunity Act of 1964, which funded Head Start, marks the contemporary beginning of federal political and financial support. As you read this chapter and become involved in the profession, you will learn that the federal and state governments are changing the field of early childhood education.

NO CHILD LEFT BEHIND ACT OF 2001 (NCLB ACT)

No Child Left Behind Act
Federal law passed in 2001 that significantly influences early childhood education.

The **No Child Left Behind Act of 2001** is intended to significantly reform K–12 education. Since its passage, it has radically and rapidly changed how America conducts its educational business. NCLB emphasizes state and district accountability, mandates state standards for what children should know and be able to do, puts in place a comprehensive program of testing in grades 3 to 12, and encourages schools to use teaching methods that have demonstrated their ability to help children learn.

The No Child Left Behind Act targets six fundamental areas: accountability, literacy, a focus on what works (scientifically based research), professional development, education technology, and parental involvement. In my opinion, because of its simplicity and condensed format, the Apple Web site, listed in the Linking to Learning section at the end of the chapter, best explains the entire concept behind the act. NCLB states that it is necessary to integrate technology into teaching and learning as a means for improving student achievement. According to the NCLB, U.S. students need to become technologically literate by the time they complete the eighth grade.

NCLB is a significant educational act and will influence what you teach and how you teach for at least the next ten years. The act also influences pre–K education because there is a major emphasis on getting children ready for school. Many federally funded programs will use guidelines and mandates in the No Child Left Behind Act to develop goals and objectives and guidelines for their own programs. In other words, all facets of programs that serve young children are influenced by the No Child Left Behind Act. You should familiarize yourself with the main features of this law. You can access more information about the NCLB Act at http://www.nclb.gov.

LITERACY AND READING FIRST

Early Head Start A federal program serving pregnant women, infants, toddlers, and their families.

Head Start A federal early childhood program serving poor children ages three to five and their families.

Another far-ranging influence of NCLB is that it puts literacy and reading first by trying to ensure that every child can read on grade level by the end of third grade. This means that efforts to provide young children with the literacy skills they need begins in **Early Head Start** and **Head Start** programs. For example, the Department of Health and Human Services (HHS) provides Head Start programs with assistance on ways in which they can better prepare children to be ready for school. Particular emphasis is placed on both child and family literacy so that Head Start children can better develop the skills they need to become lifelong readers, and parents can better develop the skills they need to both improve their own lives and to help their children become reading proficient. Head Start is investing considerable resources in early literacy, including targeting training and technical assistance resources to assure that every Head Start classroom is delivering training that promotes reading, vocabulary, and language skills.[2]

FEDERAL PROGRAMS AND EARLY EDUCATION

One of the purposes of this chapter is to help you understand the tremendous influence the federal government has on early childhood education. Every dimension of almost every educational program—public, private, and faith-based—is touched in some way by the federal government. We now discuss some of these, but I emphasize that in terms of federal influences in early childhood education, we are examining only the tip of the iceberg. Indeed, it would take an entire book to fully explore and document the role of the federal government in K–12 education. Figure 8.1 shows some of the federal programs that provide early care and education.

Head Start (children ages 3–5) and Early Head Start (children ages 0–3) are comprehensive child development programs that serve children, families, and pregnant women. These programs provide comprehensive health, nutrition, educational, and social services in order to help children achieve their full potential and succeed in school and life. They are currently programs for poor children and families. In this regard, Head Start and Early Head Start are **entitlement programs.** This means that children and families who qualify, in this case by low income, are entitled to the services. However, only about one third of eligible children and families receive these services because of the lack of funding to support full implementation.

Entitlement programs
Programs and services children and families are entitled to because they meet the eligibility criteria for the services.

▲
Federally funded programs such as Head Start are designed to provide for the full range of children's social, emotional, physical, and academic needs. Increasingly, however, federal and state supported early childhood programs are emphasizing literacy, math, and science skills. How can traditional play-based activities such as this one help children learn skills in these three areas?

HEAD START

Head Start, America's premiere preschool program, was implemented during the summer of 1965, and approximately 550,000 children in 2,500 child development centers were enrolled in the program. The first programs were designed for children entering first grade

---

FIGURE 8.1 Federal Programs That Support Early Care and Education

Department of Health and Human Services	Department of Education
• Head Start • Early Head Start • Child Care Development Funding • Temporary Assistance for Needy Families (TANF) • Block Grants to States to Support Early Care and Education	• Title I PreK and Elementary • Early Reading First • Even Start • Special Education Preschool and Infant Grants • Early Childhood Educator Professional Development Programs

Here are some of the federal programs that provide early care and education. Add to this figure as you study about and research federal influences on young children and families.

0–5 Head Start and Family Program

Our Head Start program for children and families is located in rural Macon County, North Carolina. Our program serves infant and toddler children and pregnant women. We also provide subsidized child care, developmental day care, and **wraparound services**, which are services that are layered around children and families, and are tailored to their needs. Built on a long-standing commitment to quality, our Macon Program for Progress centers are four- and five-star state rated, and are licensed and accredited by the National Association for the Education of Young Children (NAEYC).

Our program follows the Head Start Performance Standards. These standards are based on four major content areas: child health and developmental services, family and community partnerships, program design and management, and services for children with disabilities. Implementing these standards assists us in providing a holistic approach to the children and families that we serve. We provide curriculum, health, nutrition, mental health, social, and family services. We encourage parent involvement in all aspects of the child's life and assist families in moving toward self-sufficiency in their own lives.

We currently operate seven centers that serve children ages six weeks to five years. We are open year-round, eleven and a half hours a day. We maintain a low teacher–child ratio—1:4 in our infant and toddler classrooms and 1:7 in our preschool classrooms. We are a program that is committed to everyday excellence.

Contributed by Jeanne Roberts, Early Head Start Director, and Debbie Moffit, Education Coordinator, 0–5 classrooms, New Horizons Center for Children and Families, Macon County, North Carolina.

Wraparound services
Services that are layered around children and families. Services are tailored to the particular needs of individuals.

To complete a Program in Action activity, visit the Companion Website at **http://www. prenhall.com/morrison**, select chapter 8, then choose the Program in Action module.

Performance standards
Federal guidelines for Head Start and Early Head Start designed to ensure that all children and families receive high-quality services.

who had not attended kindergarten. The purpose of Head Start was literally to give children from low-income families a "head start" on their first grade experience and, hopefully, on life itself. As public schools have provided more kindergarten and preschool programs, Head Start has served younger children. Head Start is administered by the Administration for Children and Families (ACF) in the department of Health and Human Services (HHS). Figure 8.2 shows the organizational structure for Head Start and Early Head Start.

As of 2002, the National Head Start program has an annual budget of more than $6.9 billion and serves some 905,000 low-income children and families. There are 1,545 Head Start programs nationwide, with a total of nearly 19,000 centers and more than 49,000 classrooms. The average cost per child of the Head Start program is $6,633 annually. Head Start has a paid staff of 195,000 and 1,345,000 volunteers.[3] You can keep up to date on Head Start statistics by accessing the Fact Sheet online at http://www.acf.dhhs.gov/programs/opa/facts/headst.htm.

Both Head Start and Early Head Start must comply with federal **performance standards,** designed to ensure that all children and families receive high-quality services. Head Start performance standards guide program development and implementation and cover child health and developmental services, education and early childhood development, child health and safety, child nutrition, child mental health, family and community partnerships, program management, and program governance. In addition, the performance standards stress that local programs emphasize the professional development of Head Start teachers, and include reading and math readiness skills in the curriculum. Although the Head Start Bureau provides guidance on meeting the performance standards local agencies are responsible for designing programs to best meet the needs of their children and families. You

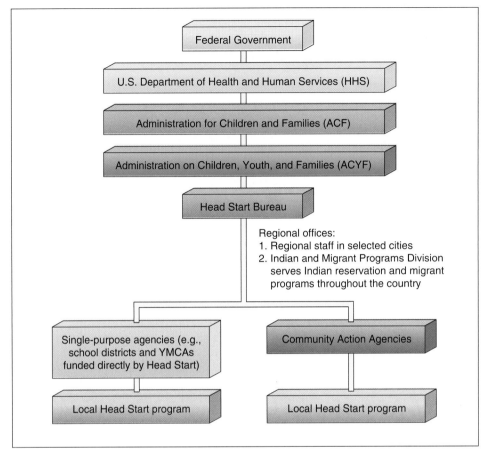

FIGURE 8.2 **Organizational Structure of Head Start/Early Head Start**

can access the performance standards for Head Start and Early Head Start at http://www.head-start.lane.or.us/administration/regulations/45CFR130x.index.html.

HEAD START OBJECTIVES

Five objectives for Head Start are defined in the program performance standards:

1. Enhance children's growth and development.
2. Strengthen families as the primary nurturers of their children.
3. Provide children with educational, health, and nutritional services.
4. Link children and their families to needed community services.
5. Ensure well-managed programs that involve parents in decision making.

During the 1999 reauthorization of Head Start, Congress mandated that Head Start programs implement standards of learning in early literacy, language, and numeracy skills. These nine standards of learning or indicators identify the following goals for children enrolled in Head Start:

- Develop phonemic, print, and numeracy awareness.
- Understand and use language to communicate for various purposes.
- Understand and use increasingly complex and varied vocabulary.
- Develop and demonstrate an appreciation of books.
- In the case of non–English-background children, progress toward acquisition of the English language.

Unique Characteristics of Native American Head Start Programs

GOVERNING BODY

The grantee and governing body for the Head Start program is the tribal council or a consortium of smaller tribes. Standards of performance are established by the federal funding agency, as well as local tribally established standards. In some cases, state standards apply to tribal programs.

Federally recognized Tribes are considered sovereign nations, so many establish their own governing policies, procedures, and codes. An example of how that impacts tribal Head Start programs is in child abuse and neglect reporting. Head Start standards apply; tribal code specifies the reporting and investigative process; and State reporting requirements apply if the tribal center is state-certified. The impact is that program policies and procedures must be written to maintain compliance with all the agency standards in order to continue funding, maintain certification, and ensure consistency in program service delivery.

The tribal government may have related programs available to indirectly support the Head Start program. Services may include facility repair and maintenance, transportation safety, emergency response, administrative services (payroll, purchasing, contracts, planning, etc.), and budget and grants management.

EARLY CHILDHOOD DEVELOPMENT

Head Start curriculum development addresses the culture and traditional practices of the tribal community. Native language may include more than one tribal language, as often multiple tribes are represented in the service area. It is necessary to determine the native languages spoken in the home and identify a native speaker in the program or request assistance from a tribal culture and heritage program employee or community member.

Native language curriculum in Head Start programs includes words to describe body parts, colors, animals, family relatives (sister, brother, grandfather, aunt, etc.), as well as common phrases and greetings. The approach will vary depending on the cultural resources of the tribe. Some programs will provide pull-out instruction, immersion classrooms, or integrate native language throughout the normal school day.

Cultural activities in the program may include traditional meal time practices; native food identification, gathering, preparation, and service; traditional social dancing; celebrations of significant tribal events; and storytelling and native arts and crafts.

HEALTH SERVICES

Head Start children who are members of federally recognized tribes or can prove Indian blood lineage are eligible to receive health care from the Indian Health Service. Health care includes physical examinations, immunizations, medical and dental care, and follow up after screenings. Referrals to specialists for special health or medical care is provided if unavailable in the out-patient clinic.

Consultation is provided to program administrators in the areas of nutrition, health policy development, and program planning. Support staff provide valuable assistance from nutritionists for menu planning, health and safety inspections from sanitarians, classroom visits from nurses, and prevention information for parents.

Contributed by Julie Quaid, Director Essential Education Department, Early Childhood Education Programs, The Confederated Tribes of Warm Springs, P.O. Box C, Warm Springs, Oregon 97761.

- Know that the letters of the alphabet are a special category of visual graphics that can be individually named.
- Recognize a word as a unit of print.
- Identify at least ten letters of the alphabet.
- Associate sounds with written words.

These nine standards of learning are being implemented by local programs. They are shown under "indicators" in Figure 8.3 and are identified by a ✩. The federal government provides Head Start support by training Head Start teachers to use the best methods of early reading and language skills instruction in order to better teach these standards.[4] These standards and others, embedded in the Head Start performance standards, are having several influences on Head Start:

- The curriculum of Head Start is more academic
- Literacy and reading is a priority
- Teachers and programs are being held more accountable for children's learning

You can review how these nine indicators of learning are included in the Head Start Child Outcomes Framework shown in Figure 8.3. This outcome framework is important for several reasons:

- It specifies learning outcomes that are essential to children's success in school and life.
- It assures that all Head Start children in all Head Start programs will have the same learning outcomes.
- It is and will continue to impact what children learn in all preschool programs, not just Head Start.

GOOD START, GROW SMART

A new early childhood initiative—**Good Start, Grow Smart**—helps state and local communities strengthen early learning for young children. This will ensure that young children are equipped with the skills they will need to start school ready to learn.

The Good Start, Grow Smart initiative addresses three major areas:

1. *Strengthening Head Start.* Through the Department of Health and Human Services, the administration will develop a new accountability system for Head Start to ensure that every Head Start center assesses standards of learning in early literacy, language, and numeracy skills.
2. *Partnering with states to improve early childhood education.* Good Start, Grow Smart proposes a stronger federal–state partnership in the delivery of quality early childhood programs. This new approach will ask states to develop quality criteria for early childhood education, including voluntary guidelines on prereading and language skills activities that align with state K–12 standards.
3. *Providing information to teachers, caregivers, and parents.* In order to close the gap between the best research and current practices in early childhood education, the Department of Education will establish a range of partnerships as part of a broad public awareness campaign targeted toward parents, early childhood educators, child care providers, and other interested parties.[5]

We will see more of these kinds of initiatives in the future.

HEAD START PROGRAM OPTIONS

Head Start and Early Head Start programs have the freedom to tailor their programs to meet the needs of the children, families, and communities they serve. Every three years, local programs conduct a community survey to determine strengths and resources and then design the program option based on these data. There are four program options: center-based, home-based, combination, and local option (text continues on page 208).

Good Start, Grow Smart
The Bush administration early childhood initiative designed to help states and local communities strengthen early learning for young children.

DOMAIN	DOMAIN ELEMENT	INDICATORS
LANGUAGE DEVELOPMENT	Listening & Understanding	◆ Demonstrates increasing ability to attend to and understand conversations, stories, songs, and poems.
		◆ Shows progress in understanding and following simple and multiple-step directions.
		☆ **Understands an increasingly complex and varied vocabulary.**
		☆ **For non-English-speaking children, progresses in listening to and understanding English.**
	Speaking & Communicating	☆ **Develops increasing abilities to understand and use language to communicate information, experiences, ideas, feelings, opinions, needs, questions and for other varied purposes.**
		◆ Progresses in abilities to initiate and respond appropriately in conversation and discussions with peers and adults.
		☆ **Uses an increasingly complex and varied spoken vocabulary.**
		◆ Progresses in clarity of pronunciation and towards speaking in sentences of increasing length and grammatical complexity.
		☆ **For non-English-speaking children, progresses in speaking English.**
LITERACY	☆Phonological Awareness	◆ Shows increasing ability to discriminate and identify sounds in spoken language.
		◆ Shows growing awareness of beginning and ending sounds of words.
		◆ Progresses in recognizing matching sounds and rhymes in familiar words, games, songs, stories and poems.
		◆ Shows growing ability to hear and discriminate separate syllables in words.
		☆ **Associates sounds with written words,** such as awareness that different words begin with the same sound.
	☆Book Knowledge & Appreciation	◆ Shows growing interest and involvement in listening to and discussing a variety of fiction and nonfiction books and poetry.
		◆ Shows growing interest in reading-related activities, such as asking to have a favorite book read; choosing to look at books; drawing pictures based on stories; asking to take books home; going to the library; and engaging in pretend-reading with other children.
		◆ Demonstrates progress in abilities to retell and dictate stories from books and experiences; to act out stories in dramatic play; and to predict what will happen next in a story.
		◆ Progresses in learning how to handle and care for books; knowing to view one page at a time in sequence from front to back; and understanding that a book has a title, author and illustrator.
	☆Print Awareness & Concepts	◆ Shows increasing awareness of print in classroom, home and community settings.
		◆ Develops growing understanding of the different functions of forms of print such as signs, letters, newspapers, lists, messages, and menus.
		◆ Demonstrates increasing awareness of concepts of print, such as that reading in English moves from top to bottom and from left to right, that speech can be written down, and that print conveys a message.
		◆ Shows progress in recognizing the association between spoken and written words by following print as it is read aloud.
		☆ **Recognizes a word as a unit of print,** or awareness that letters are grouped to form words, and that words are separated by spaces.

☆ Indicates the 4 specific Domain Elements and 9 Indicators that are legislatively mandated.

FIGURE 8.3 **Head Start Child Outcomes Framework**

DOMAIN	DOMAIN ELEMENT	INDICATORS
LITERACY (cont.)	Early Writing	◆ Develops understanding that writing is a way of communicating for a variety of purposes.
		◆ Begins to represent stories and experiences through pictures, dictation, and in play.
		◆ Experiments with a growing variety of writing tools and materials, such as pencils, crayons, and computers.
		◆ Progresses from using scribbles, shapes, or pictures to represent ideas, to using letter-like symbols, to copying or writing familiar words such as their own name.
	Alphabet Knowledge	◆ Shows progress in associating the names of letters with their shapes and sounds.
		◆ Increases in ability to notice the beginning letters in familiar words.
		☆ **Identifies at least ten letters of the alphabet, especially those in their own name.**
		☆ **Knows that letters of the alphabet are a special category of visual graphics that can be individually named.**
MATHEMATICS	☆Number & Operations	◆ Demonstrates increasing interest and awareness of numbers and counting as a means for solving problems and determining quantity.
		◆ Begins to associate number concepts, vocabulary, quantities and written numerals in meaningful ways.
		◆ Develops increasing ability to count in sequence to ten and beyond.
		◆ Begins to make use of one-to-one correspondence in counting objects and matching groups of objects.
		◆ Begins to use language to compare numbers of objects with terms such as more, less, greater than, fewer, equal to.
		◆ Develops increased abilities to combine, separate and name "how many" concrete objects.
	Geometry & Spatial Sense	◆ Begins to recognize, describe, compare, and name common shapes, their parts and attributes.
		◆ Progresses in ability to put together and take apart shapes.
		◆ Begins to be able to determine whether two shapes are the same size and shape.
		◆ Shows growth in matching, sorting, putting in a series and regrouping objects according to one or two attributes such as color, shape, or size.
		◆ Builds an increasing understanding of directionality, order and positions of objects, and words such as up, down, over, under, top, bottom, inside, outside, in front, and behind.
	Patterns & Measurement	◆ Enhances abilities to recognize, duplicate, and extend simple patterns using a variety of materials.
		◆ Shows increasing abilities to match, sort, put in a series, and regroup objects according to one or two attributes such as shape or size.
		◆ Begins to make comparisons between several objects based on a single attribute.
		◆ Shows progress in using standard and nonstandard measures for length and area of objects.
SCIENCE	Scientific Skills & Methods	◆ Begins to use senses and a variety of tools and simple measuring devices to gather information, investigate materials, and observe processes and relationships.
		◆ Develops increased ability to observe and discuss common properties, differences, and comparisons among objects and materials.
		◆ Begins to participate in simple investigations to test observations, discuss and draw conclusions, and form generalizations.
		◆ Develops growing abilities to collect, describe, and record information through a variety of means, including discussion, drawings, maps and charts.
		◆ Begins to describe and discuss predictions, explanations, and generalizations based on past experiences.

☆ **Indicates the 4 specific Domain Elements and 9 Indicators that are legislatively mandated.**

FIGURE 8.3 (Continued)

DOMAIN	DOMAIN ELEMENT	INDICATORS
SCIENCE (cont.)	Scientific Knowledge	◆ Expands knowledge of and abilities to observe, describe and discuss the natural world, materials, living things and natural processes.
		◆ Expands knowledge of and respect for their body and the environment.
		◆ Develops growing awareness of ideas and language related to attributes of time and temperature.
		◆ Shows increased awareness and beginning understanding of changes in materials and cause-effect relationships.
CREATIVE ARTS	Music	◆ Participates with increasing interest and enjoyment in a variety of music activities, including listening, singing, finger plays, games, and performances.
		◆ Experiments with a variety of musical instruments.
	Art	◆ Gains ability in using different art media and materials in a variety of ways for creative expression and representation.
		◆ Progresses in abilities to create drawings, paintings, models, and other art creations that are more detailed, creative or realistic.
		◆ Develops growing abilities to plan, work independently, and demonstrate care and persistence in a variety of art projects.
		◆ Begins to understand and share opinions about artistic products and experiences.
	Movement	◆ Expresses through movement and dancing what is felt and heard in various musical tempos and styles.
		◆ Shows growth in moving in time to different patterns of beat and rhythm in music.
	Dramatic Play	◆ Participates in a variety of dramatic play activities that become more extended and complex.
		◆ Shows growing creativity and imagination in using materials and in assuming different roles in dramatic play situations.
SOCIAL & EMOTIONAL DEVELOPMENT	Self Concept	◆ Begins to develop and express awareness of self in terms of specific abilities, characteristics and preferences.
		◆ Develops growing capacity for independence in a range of activities, routines, and tasks.
		◆ Demonstrates growing confidence in a range of abilities and expresses pride in accomplishments.
	Self Control	◆ Shows progress in expressing feelings, needs and opinions in difficult situations and conflicts without harming themselves, others, or property.
		◆ Develops growing understanding of how their actions affect others and begins to accept the consequences of their actions.
		◆ Demonstrates increasing capacity to follow rules and routines and use materials purposefully, safely, and respectfully.
	Cooperation	◆ Increases abilities to sustain interactions with peers by helping, sharing and discussion.
		◆ Shows increasing abilities to use compromise and discussion in working, playing and resolving conflicts with peers.
		◆ Develops increasing abilities to give and take in interactions; to take turns in games or using materials; and to interact without being overly submissive or directive.

FIGURE 8.3 (Continued)

DOMAIN	DOMAIN ELEMENT	INDICATORS
SOCIAL & EMOTIONAL DEVELOPMENT (cont.)	Social Relationships	◆ Demonstrates increasing comfort in talking with and accepting guidance and directions from a range of familiar adults.
		◆ Shows progress in developing friendships with peers.
		◆ Progresses in responding sympathetically to peers who are in need, upset, hurt, or angry; and in expressing empathy or caring for others.
	Knowledge of Families & Communities	◆ Develops ability to identify personal characteristics including gender and family composition.
		◆ Progresses in understanding similarities and respecting differences among people, such as genders, race, special needs, culture, language, and family structures.
		◆ Develops growing awareness of jobs and what is required to perform them.
		◆ Begins to express and understand concepts and language of geography in the contexts of their classroom, home, and community.
APPROACHES TO LEARNING	Initiative & Curiosity	◆ Chooses to participate in an increasing variety of tasks and activities.
		◆ Develops increased ability to make independent choices.
		◆ Approaches tasks and activities with increased flexibility, imagination, and inventiveness.
		◆ Grows in eagerness to learn about and discuss a growing range of topics, ideas, and tasks.
	Engagement & Persistence	◆ Grows in abilities to persist in and complete a variety of tasks, activities, projects, and experiences.
		◆ Demonstrates increasing ability to set goals and develop and follow through on plans.
		◆ Shows growing capacity to maintain concentrations over time on a task, question, set of directions or interactions, despite distractions and interruptions.
	Reasoning & Problem Solving	◆ Develops increasing ability to find more than one solution to a question, task, or problem.
		◆ Grows in recognizing and solving problems through active exploration, including trial and error, and interactions and discussions with peers and adults.
		◆ Develops increasing abilities to classify, compare and contrast objects, events, and experiences.
PHYSICAL HEALTH & DEVELOPMENT	Fine Motor Skills	◆ Develops growing strength, dexterity and control needed to use tools such as scissors, paper punch, stapler, and hammer.
		◆ Grows in hand-eye coordination in building with blocks, putting together puzzles, reproducing shapes and patterns, stringing beads, and using scissors.
		◆ Progresses in abilities to use writing, drawing and art tools including pencils, markers, chalk, paint brushes, and various types of technology.
	Gross Motor Skills	◆ Shows increasing levels of proficiency, control and balance in walking, climbing, running, jumping, hopping, skipping, marching, and galloping.
		◆ Demonstrates increasing abilities to coordinate movements in throwing, catching, kicking, bouncing balls, and using the slide and swing.
	Health Status & Practices	◆ Progresses in physical growth, strength, stamina, and flexibility.
		◆ Participates actively in games, outdoor play and other forms of exercise that enhance physical fitness.
		◆ Shows growing independence in hygiene, nutrition and personal care when eating, dressing, washing hands, brushing teeth and toileting.
		◆ Builds awareness and ability to follow basic health and safety rules such as fire safety, traffic and pedestrian safety, and responding appropriately to potentially harmful objects, substances and activities.

FIGURE 8.3 (Continued)

Source: The Administration for Children and Families, Head Start Bureau. Available at: http://www.hsnrc.org/hsnrc/CDI/COF.cfm

Higher Horizons Head Start

Higher Horizons Day Care Center, Inc. is a Head Start and Early Head Start program that provides quality early childhood development and family services for low income families who meet federal poverty guidelines. The organization supports and empowers children, parents, and staff as they grow to their fullest potential through education, information, resources, and advocacy. Higher Horizons offers consistent, comprehensive services that support the core elements of Head Start. The program recognizes that everyone has gifts and talents to offer within the diverse community. The management and staff are committed to deliver the services with pride and excellence.

THE FACILITY

The 20,000 square foot facility is housed in a former segregated elementary school in the Bailey's Crossroads/Falls Church community of Fairfax County, Virginia. The renovated, state of the art facility includes eleven classrooms and the administrative offices. The site was renovated in 1999 with a state of the art wing that includes four classrooms, a health room, a family room, a screening room, an infant observation room, and an indoor play area. The program is fully licensed by the Virginia Department of Social Services, Division of Licensing.

PROGRAM OPERATION

Higher Horizons operates a full day, full year Head Start and Early Head Start program for children from 6 weeks of age to 5 years. Early Head Start offers home and center based services for infants, toddlers and pregnant women. Full day center based services are provided for preschool age children. Class size is 17 preschoolers in the Head Start classrooms and 8 infants/toddlers in the Early Head Start classes. Children are transported daily and receive breakfast, lunch, and a snack which is prepared on-site. The twelve-hour operational day accommodates the working parent's schedules in the Washington, D.C., suburb.

FAMILIES AND CHILDREN SERVED

Higher Horizons continues its legacy of a comprehensive child and family empowerment program utilizing community resources with strong parent and community support. Children, families, and staff represented at Higher Horizons are representative of the diverse community; over forty-nine of the children speak languages other than English. Some of the many languages represented at the program include Spanish, Creole, Urdu, Somali, Cambodian, Punjabi and Vietnamese. A unique feature of this Head Start program is the wide range of languages and ethnic groups represented.

PERFORMANCE STANDARDS

Higher Horizons program is guided by Head Start Performance Standards. These standards provide the blueprint for optimal program operation. Major elements of the standards include early childhood development and health services, family and community partnerships, staffing, and program design and management. Higher Horizons involves parents and community representatives in all aspects of the program including policy, program design, and curriculum and management decisions. Shared governance is the strength for this Head Start program.

Higher Horizons provides a **seamless service** delivery in Early Head Start and Head Start. The simple concept of a single point of contact for each Head Start/Early Head Start family makes service delivery more efficient. Families are recruited from the surrounding community. A Head Start family worker is assigned to each family in order to determine eligibility for the program. Once eligibility is determined and a classroom placement is made for the child, the family receives a home visit from the classroom teacher, assistant, and family worker.

ENROLLMENT

The majority of intake for new enrollment is completed during the summer months for September enrollment in Early Head Start and Head Start. Information regarding the family and child is exchanged during the home visit; parents are given the opportunity to discuss the child's growth and development and establish a relationship with the Head Start staff. This is also an opportunity to gain valuable information pertaining to family goals during a child's enrollment in Head Start. The family worker maintains regular contact with the Head Start parent. She encourages the parent to fulfill personal goals, continue educational goals, participate in Head Start activities, and volunteer in the Head Start classroom. Referrals are made to community resources when parents need support in the area of housing, health care providers, advocacy, credit counseling, parenting skills, etc. All of this information is maintained in the agency data base and provides ongoing records of family contacts and essential family information. This information is consolidated for the Head Start program information report at the end of each program year.

THE DAY

A routine day for Head Start children at Higher Horizons may include transportation pick-up from an apartment complex located off one of the main streets that lead to Washington, D.C. Children are transported on an agency owned school bus with a driver who holds a CDL license and a bus monitor. Children are delivered to the Head Start daily with several bus runs; others are dropped off daily by parents or caregivers. Transportation is not provided to the infants and toddlers enrolled in the Early Head Start program. Children are taken directly to the classrooms by the bus monitors and classroom staff. All children are checked in and out from home to bus and from bus to the classroom. Daily bus checks are completed after each bus run. Once in the classroom, children are observed for general health concerns. Any unusual or observable concerns are reported to the Health Specialist for follow-up with the teacher and parent. Regular mental health observations are conducted by a community mental health organization. Mental health consultants meet with parents and staff regularly and are responsive to identified behavioral/mental health concerns. Children are engaged in activities throughout the day, then there is an afternoon rest period. After the rest period, children begin preparing for departure by bus or receive a snack and participate in organized activities. As the numbers of children decrease, staff members have the opportunity for individualized instruction.

MEAL TIME

Meals are served in a family style setting in each classroom. Children have the opportunity to help with food service such as table setting. Children help themselves to the food offered at breakfast, lunch, and snack. Adults in the classroom sit at each table, sharing the same food the children eat, and utilize this time to encourage the use of language and discuss both classroom and home activities.

Teachers have the opportunity to gain additional information from the children's meal time discussions. The food services staff and the registered dietitian, who is also a staff member, prepare menus. Parents participate quarterly in a Health Services Advisory Committee; they offer suggestions for the cycle menus and visit the classrooms during meal time. The menus are reflective of the diverse population served; meal adjustments are made for children with special dietary needs or food allergies. Special nutrition activities are regularly planned in each classroom.

Children have the opportunity to wash their hands before each meal and brush their teeth after each meal; the classroom staff uses these opportunities to discuss the value of good health and hygiene habits. Each classroom is equipped with a sink for handwashing and a bathroom for easy access. Two restrooms in the facility are equipped with changing tables to accommodate children who are not toilet trained or children who have transitioned from Early Head Start.

THE CURRICULUM

Learning in the Head Start classroom is based on the core values of Head Start. Higher Horizons provides a supportive learning environment for children, parents, and staff. The Education Advisory Committee developed the locally designed curriculum "Setting Our Sights." The Committee is comprised of Head Start parents, staff, community educators, public school partners, and representatives of the early childhood community. The program promotes respectful, sensitive, and proactive approaches to diversity issues. Higher Horizons' staff also respects the importance of an individual's development, including social, emotional, cognitive, and physical growth. Each child is screened for developmental, sensory, and behavioral concerns several times during the program year.

The Head Start Child Outcomes Framework (see Figure 8.3) guides Head Start staff in preschool classes with the ongoing assessment of the progress and accomplishments of children and supports the efforts to analyze and use the data on child outcomes in program self assessment and continuous program improvement. The staff use multiple sources of information to gain a valid picture of the child to individualize programming. They use the information from screenings to determine how they can best respond to each child's individual characteristics, strengths and needs.

Degreed classroom staff and experienced classroom assistants plan daily activities for the Head Start children, using the curriculum as a guide combined with a variety of curriculum resources. The program maintains a resource library for staff to keep abreast of current trends, curriculum approaches, and innovative approaches to early learning. An array of activities are planned each day which include computer learning, pre-reading, pre-writing, role-play, science and math, physical indoor and outdoor activity, creative arts, etc. The program is located in a tranquil, wooded area and daily nature walks and visits to nearby vegetable and flower gardens and parks are incorporated in the daily activities. The staff wellness activities are planned monthly to support staff. These activities provide needed information and resources in the area of exercise and diet, massage therapy, aroma therapy, women's health issues, and stress. These monthly activities support wellness in the workplace at Higher Horizons.

The Higher Horizons' "Great Ideas" inclusion model provides services to children with disabilities in a non-traditional service delivery model. Head Start Performance Standards require that at least 10% of the total number of enrollment opportunities be made available to children with disabilities. This unique model is a partnership with the local public school district. Two special education teachers and classroom assistants are housed in the Head Start facility on a full time basis; they provide direct services to children with disabilities in the Head Start classrooms. This successful model has reduced the number of transitions preschool children may have in one day and the provision of care and specialized programming is provided at the Head Start site. Head Start teachers and "Great Ideas" teachers plan regularly, meet with parents, and work collaboratively to provide individualized services to children with disabilities enrolled at Higher Horizons.

PARENT INVOLVEMENT

Parents play an active role in communicating with classroom staff. Parents are encouraged to visit the classrooms and to participate in two formal conferences and two home visits during a program year. The information gained during these staff–parent conferences enhances the adult's knowledge and understanding of the developmental progress of children in the program.

STAFF DEVELOPMENT

Staff development is central to providing high quality, comprehensive, culturally sensitive services to children and families in Early Head Start and Head Start. Head Start requires a systematic approach to staff development. Monthly professional development activities are scheduled for all Head Start staff. Higher Horizons management staff also recognizes the value of making sure new teachers have access to help on short notice, responding to new teachers' teaching strategies, or responding to a parent requiring an immediate conference. New teachers are paired with mentors who have time to observe and offer advice or a small team of teachers convenes for help on short notice. The program focus continues to enhance the quality, intentionality, and effectiveness of staff interactions with children and families though staff training activities. All staff has the opportunity to prioritize professional goals, participate in Head Start and early childhood conferences and institutes, and continue their professional growth and development.

Higher Horizons Head Start continues to focus on developing and implementing quality programs that reflect current research and best practice and to work toward promoting the Head Start goal of social competence in children. The program responds flexibly to the child, family, and community needs. There are many strong community partnerships. Higher Horizons' staff strives towards excellence in management by adapting services according to the rapidly changing social policies that impact on families with young children.

Contributed by Mary Ann Cornish, Director Higher Horizons Head Start, Fairfax, Virginia.

Seamless services Providing services for children and families at one place. Also known as one-stop service delivery.

 To complete a Program in Action activity related to Head Start, visit the Companion Website at **http://www.prenhall. com/morrison**, select chapter 8, then chooose the Program in Action module.

1. The *center-based option* delivers services to children and families using the center as the base or core. Center based programs operate either full-day or half day for 32–34 weeks a year, the minimum required by the Head Start Performance Standards, others operate full-year programs. Center staff makes periodic visits to family homes.

2. The *home-based option* uses the family home as the center for providing services. Home visitors work with the parents and children. Twice a month, children and families come to gather for field trips and classroom experiences. Today, 668 Head Start agencies and 5,200 home visitors serve more than 48,000 children and their families in the home-based option. The home-based option has these strengths:
   - Parent involvement is the very keystone of the program
   - Geographically isolated families have an invaluable opportunity to be part of a comprehensive child and family program
   - An individualized family plan is based on both a child and a family assessment
   - The family plan is facilitated by a home visitor who is an adult educator with knowledge and training related to all Head Start components
   - The program includes the entire family

3. In the *combination option* or model, programs combine the center and *home-based options.*

Size of Family Unit	Poverty Guideline
2	$11,940
3	$15,020
4	$18,100
5	$21,180
6	$24,260
7	$27,340
8	$30,420

TABLE 8.1 2002 Poverty Guidelines for the 48 Contiguous States and the District of Columbia

Source: "Annual Update of the Department of Health and Human Services Poverty Guidelines." *Federal Register 67*(31) (2002), 6931–6933.

4. The *local option*, as its name indicates, includes programs created specifically to meet unique community and family needs. For example, some Early Head Start programs provide services in family child care homes.

Head Start has always prided itself on tailoring its local programs to the children and families in the local community. In fact, this goal of meeting the needs of families and children at the local level is one of the strengths, and one that makes it popular with parents.

ELIGIBILITY FOR HEAD START SERVICES

To be eligible for Head Start Services, children must meet age and family income criteria. Head Start enrolls children ages three to five from low-income families. The income eligibility provision means that families establish eligibility on the basis of whether or not their incomes fall below the official poverty line set annually by the U.S. Department of Health and Human Services. Poverty guidelines for 2002 are shown in Table 8.1.

Ninety percent of a Head Start's enrollment has to meet the income eligibility criteria. The other 10 percent of enrollment can consist of children from families that exceed the low-income guidelines. In addition, 10 percent of a program's enrollment must include children with disabilities.

Head Start always has been and remains a program for children of poverty. Although it currently reaches a significant number of poor children, increasing federal support for Head Start will likely increase the number of poor children served. However, keep in mind that the federal government is using Head Start to reform all of early childhood education. Federal officials believe the changes they make in the Head Start curriculum, what and how teachers teach, and how Head Start operates will serve as a model for other programs as well.

EARLY HEAD START

Early Head Start (EHS) was created in 1994, and is designed to promote healthy prenatal outcomes for pregnant women; enhance the development of very young children (birth through age three); and promote healthy family functioning. Early Head Start enrolls pregnant women. When the child is born, the mother is provided family services. As with Head Start, EHS is a program for low-income families who meet federal poverty guidelines. EHS serves about 62,000 infants and toddlers with a budget of $654 million. More than 660 grantees participate in the Early Head Start program.[6] Program services include

- Quality early education both in and out of the home
- Parenting education
- Comprehensive health and mental health services, including services to women before, during, and after pregnancy
- Nutrition education
- Family support services

Head Start's entry into the field of infant and toddler care and education has achieved several things. First, it has given Head Start an opportunity to work with a long-neglected age group. Second, as the public schools have enrolled preschoolers at an accelerated rate, the infant and toddler field gives Head Start a new group to serve. Third, it has enabled Early Head Start to be a leader in the field of infant and toddler education. Without a doubt, Early Head Start has been a pioneer and catalyst in providing high-quality programs for infants and toddlers.

OTHER HEAD START PROGRAMS

In chapter 1, when we discussed the role of the early childhood professional, one of the attributes we emphasized was the willingness and ability to work with children and families who are at risk in some way. The chances are good that you will work in a federal program that is designed and funded to help those populations that are in need of special care and education. Let's look at some Head Start programs that have, as their mission, serving special populations that might not otherwise be served. The following are some of these programs. As you read about them, consider their impact on the well being of children and families.

Currently, all early childhood programs, including Head Start, emphasize the development of children's early literacy skills. Early literacy skills are seen as a key to success in school and life.

Migrant Head Start   A federal program designed to provide educational and other services to migrant children and families.

Migrant family   A family with children who engages in agriculture work and moves from one geographic location to another.

MIGRANT HEAD START

Services provided to migrant children and families are identical to those of other Head Start programs while also addressing the unique needs of migrant children and families. Furthermore, **Migrant Head Start** programs emphasize serving infants and toddlers so that they do not have to accompany their parents to the fields or be left with young siblings.

A **migrant family** is a family with children *under* the age of compulsory school attendance who changed their residence by moving from one geographic location to another, for the purpose of engaging in agricultural work. Migrant Head Start provides services tailor made to meet the unique needs of migrant families depending on where they live and what type of migrant services they provide. Home-based programs are usually located in the southern part of the United States (generally in California, Arizona, New Mexico, Texas, and Florida). They provide services to mobile migrant farm worker families. Upstream programs (generally in Washington, Idaho, Michigan, Illinois, Maine, Indiana, Wisconsin, Nebraska, and Minnesota) provide services to families as they move northward in search of agricultural work during the spring, summer, and fall months.[7]

AMERICAN INDIAN–ALASKA NATIVE HEAD START PROGRAMS

The American Indian–Alaska Native program branch of Head Start provides American Indian and Alaska Native children (birth to age five) and families with comprehensive health, education, nutritional, social, and developmental services designed to promote school readiness.

PROGRAM IN ACTION

Inclusion and Collaboration

The Head Start program of Upper Des Moines Opportunity, Inc., operates twenty-five fully inclusive preschool classrooms. We have three classrooms specific to toddlers, ages eighteen to thirty-six months. We also have twenty-two classrooms set up for children ages three to five. Our programs are designated for all children, regardless of race or disability.

Our Head Start programs take pride in the strength of our partnerships with local school districts and other local education agencies (LEAs). Because of the strength of these relationships we are able to collaborate in program design and offer natural or least restriction environments to all children.

In Early Head Start, our staff have been trained in case management of children with special needs. They have taken the lead position in coordination of services to our children and their families. These services can be provided in the home, in the classroom, or in a day care setting. Our toddler rooms are facilitated by support service staff trained in specific areas of early childhood development. We use the Child Study model to continually update staff on individual progress, concerns, and needs of our children.

Our Head Start classrooms for children ages three to five offer many opportunities for inclusion. In some centers we dually enroll children, allowing them the opportunity to spend half a day in Head Start and the other half in an early childhood special education (ECSE) classroom. We also have classrooms where Head Start teachers and ECSE teachers work side by side, allowing for full-day programming for all children in the least restrictive settings. We operate Head Start classrooms where the lead teacher has a degree in early childhood special education and associate(s) have backgrounds in early childhood; or, the lead teacher has a background in early childhood and associate(s) are qualified to work with children having special needs. All of our three- to five-year-old classrooms are facilitated by support service staff, and they, too, use the Child Study team approach to communicate the progress, needs, and concerns of all children.

Contributed by Mary Jo Madvig, Upper Des Moines Opportunity, Inc.

WILLIAM F. GOODLING EVEN START FAMILY LITERACY PROGRAM

The Even Start Family Literacy Program, first authorized in 1989, was reauthorized as part of the No Child Left Behind Act of 2001.[8] The purpose of **Even Start** is to provide low-income families with integrated literacy services for parents and their young children (birth through age seven). The purpose of the program is to break the cycle of poverty and illiteracy for low-income families. The basic premise behind Even Start's family literacy approach is that the four components of adult education, early childhood education, parenting education, and interactive literacy activities for parents and their children build on each other, and that families need to receive all four services in order to bring lasting change and improve children's school success.[9]

The National Even Start Association provides a national voice and vision for Even Start Family Literacy Programs. The NESA is committed to supporting approximately 800 sites across the United States in their efforts to provide high-quality programming for approximately one million parents and children. The NESA's mission is as follows:

- To extend learning, enrich language development, and support high levels of success for children birth to age seven and their families.

Even Start A federal program that provides literacy services for low-income families and children.

 To complete a Program in Action activity, visit the Companion Website at **http://www.prenhall.com/morrison**, select chapter 8, then choose the Program in Action module.

Alice and Robert

Alice was a seventeen-year-old junior at Southwestern High School and eight months pregnant when she was caught shoplifting. The court assigned her to home supervision and arranged for her enrollment in Friends of the Family's Early Head Start (EHS) program. Alice's sonogram indicated that the baby would be a breach birth. Alice was concerned about what to expect during labor and delivery and how to take care of the baby during the day when she would be home without any adult support. Alice says she never could meet her mother's expectations with respect to household chores *and* continue in school *and* raise a child. She was worried that there will not be enough time to spend with her boyfriend, Robert, who was twenty-two years old at the time and the baby's father. Alice confided that she had heard rumors that he had another girlfriend. Robert had quit school after the tenth grade and drifted between jobs. He was already the father of two children by other women. Alice's mother had forbidden her to continue seeing Robert because of his age and lack of employment and commitment to her daughter and, she suspected, the unborn baby.

Alice said that the EHS family support worker was helpful not only by assisting her to identify personal goals and follow through with career and family plans, but also by helping her to make and keep medical appointments, prepare to care at home for a newborn, and stay in and successfully complete school. Alice valued the help the EHS program provided to "negotiate the relationship between my mother and my boyfriend."

Alice completed her junior year at Southwestern and gave birth to a healthy baby. Over the summer, Alice and the family support worker, who visited twice a week for the first two months after the birth and weekly during the summer, focused on parenting skill development and established a few routines that helped the household run smoothly. At first, Alice had trouble with breastfeeding but eventually became comfortable with the process, and her baby nurses well. Alice initially believed that babies should not be held and soothed when they cry. But after watching several videos that the family support worker brought home for her to watch, Alice holds her baby a lot and talks to him, gazing into his eyes frequently.

Alice volunteered five hours a week in a summer day camp for elementary school-aged children while Robert watched the baby at his house. Alice no longer considers herself Robert's partner, but they have begun to team up to raise their child. Alice returned to school in the fall, where she and her baby participate in the school-based component of the Friends of the Family EHS program. Because the center-based staff provide regular, ongoing parent support services, the family support worker checks in with Alice less frequently, once or twice a month, and will continue until the baby turns four. Alice expects never again to come into contact with the juvenile justice system, although she would like to some day apply for a job with a local peer-support program that helps first-time juvenile offenders!

Contributed by Margaret E. Williams, executive director, Friends of the Family, Inc., 1001 Eastern Ave., 2nd Floor, Baltimore, Maryland 21202; Phone: 410-659-7701, ext. 121; Fax: 410-783-0814; e-mail:mwilliams@friendsofthefamily.org.

To complete a Program in Action activity, visit the Companion Website at **http://www.prenhall.com/morrison**, select chapter 8, then choose the Program in Action module.

- To break the cycle of limited literacy, underemployment, and high mobility of participating families by building literacy skills in both parents and children.
- To provide simultaneous services for families, where parents and their children learn together. This builds support for parents to succeed with their educational and employment goals, and develop habits of life-long learning for their children.
- To support families committed to education and to economic independence.[10]

MIGRANT EDUCATION EVEN START (MEES)

Migrant Even Start programs include early childhood education, parent education, and adult education and, like many other programs, services are delivered through the home, site-based instruction, or a combination of these. Migrant Even Start programs are designed to break cycles of poverty and improve the literacy of migrant families.

TITLE I PROGRAMS

The No Child Left Behind Act of 2001 reauthorized the Elementary Secondary Education Act (ESEA) of 1965. Under this reauthorization, Title I provides financial assistance through state educational agencies (SEAs) to local educational agencies (LEAs) and schools with high numbers or percentages of poor children to help ensure that all children meet challenging state academic content and student academic achievement standards.[11] In 2002, the federal government spent almost $10 billion on Title I services.

FATHERHOOD INITIATIVES

The National Fatherhood Initiative (NFI), a nonprofit organization, was founded in 1994 to lead a society-wide movement to confront the problem of father absence. NFI's mission is to improve the well-being of children by increasing the proportion of children growing up with involved, responsible, and committed fathers. The NFI works to accomplish this mission by doing the following:

- Educating and inspiring all people, especially fathers, through public awareness campaigns, research, and other resources.
- Equipping and developing leaders of national, state, and community fatherhood initiatives through curricula, training, and technical assistance.
- Engaging every sector of society through strategic alliances and partnerships.[12]

The NFI has served as a catalyst for government, state, and other agencies to be more involved in emphasizing the importance of fathers in the lives of children and families.

The Department of Health and Human Services (DHHS) has developed a special **fatherhood initiative** to support and strengthen the roles of fathers in families. This initiative is guided by the following principles:

- All fathers can be important contributors to the well-being of their children.
- Parents and partners should be involved in raising their children, even when they do not live in the same household.
- The roles fathers play in families are diverse and related to cultural and community norms.
- Men should receive the education and support necessary to prepare them for the responsibility of parenthood.
- Government can encourage and promote father involvement through its programs and through its own workforce policies.

The DHHS emphasis on the important role of fathers has, in turn, spawned a Head Start Fatherhood Initiative. It is designed to sustain fathers' involvement in their children's lives and, as a result, enhance the development of children.

The Early Head Start Research and Evaluation Project has launched research relating to the role of low-income fathers in the lives of their infants and toddlers, in their families, and in the Early Head Start programs in which they participate. The father studies fill a significant gap in knowledge by increasing understanding of how fathers and mothers, in the context of the family, influence infant and toddler development.[13]

Fatherhood initiatives
Various efforts by federal, state, and local agencies to increase and sustain fathers' involvement with their children and families.

QUILT—Quality in Linking Together: Early Education Partnerships

QUILT is the Federal Administration for Children and Families' national training and technical assistance project that supports local, state, tribal, regional, and national partnerships among Head Start, Child Care, State-funded PreK and other early education programs aimed at providing quality, full-day, year-round services.

QUILT continues to focus on three major service delivery strategies: onsite technical assistance to states, territories, tribes, and local communities; training at national, regional, and state workshops, forums, and meetings; and, development and dissemination of best practice materials and resources.

Here's what people in early education are saying about QUILT's services:

"What a difference it makes to know that I can rely on QUILT specialists—people who have lived it and done it—from the Head Start side, the child care side, and the public school side. They helped us see the possibilities." (from a Head Start State Collaboration Director)

"So often, families are forced to patch together care that involves two, three, or even four different care providers, each with a different approach, a different set of standards, and a different curriculum. QUILT helped us bring all these players together to create a common community vision—so that we can provide children and families with the quality services they deserve." (from an Executive Director of a Child Care Agency)

The QUILT Project is led by three organizations: Community Development Institute in Denver, Colorado; Education Development Center, Inc. in Newton, Massachusetts; and, the National Child Care Information Center in Vienna, Virginia. For further information visit QUILT's website at www.quilt.org.

Contributed by Grace Hardy, QUILT Project Director Community Development Institute, 9745 E. Hampden Avenue—Suite 310 Denver, Colorado 80231.

To complete a Program in Action activity, visit the Companion Website at **http://www. prenhall.com/morrison**, select chapter 8, then choose the Program in Action module.

PARTNERSHIPS AND COLLABORATION

All Head Start programs endeavor to develop and build collaborative relationships with local agencies and programs. These collaborative approaches are designed to better serve children and families and to maximize the use of resources. This account of Healthy Beginnings illustrates such collaborative services.

The Healthy Beginnings initiative provides onsite screening at licensed child care sites in seven counties in the northern Florida Panhandle. The Florida-based Early Childhood Services, Inc., administers a number of early childhood funding streams, including Head Start. Healthy Beginnings collaborated with Head Start's health and nutrition coordinator, with assistance from the Head Start Health Services Advisory Committee, to develop a coalition of health and safety providers. Health care professionals visit each licensed child care center in the seven-county area twice a year in a mobile medical van donated by two local hospitals. Only basic screenings (height, weight, health, and dental) are completed because the coalition does not have funding for the liability coverage necessary for blood screenings. (Funding comes from the local Kiwanis Club through its national initiative to provide safe and healthy beginnings to children under five).

The program is producing measurable results—approximately 20 percent of children screened for physical health problems and nearly 50 percent of those screened for dental

DIVERSITY TIE-IN

Fathers, Culture, and Infant Mental Health

Research on the fathering role provides us with some interesting data from which to begin to develop programs for fathers' positive interactions with their infants and toddlers. For example:

- Across a wide range of cultures, when fathers have access to their children, they take advantage of it.
- Physical distance between fathers and their children decreases father involvement.
- When the father's role as a breadwinner is compromised, he is less likely to be involved with his children. When such fathers are not living with their children, mothers are likely to limit their access to them.
- As mothers' economic independence increases, fathers are less likely to be involved with their children.[*]

With these as a background, here are some things for you to reflect on as a starting point to develop ways to involve fathers of all cultures in infant/toddler programs.

If fathers decrease their involvement with children when a woman is present, it makes sense to use men as home visitors to families with resident biological or social fathers. If fathers are specialists in rough-and-tumble play, recruit them to teach Early Head Start toddlers soccer and other high-energy sports. If nonresident fathers gradually distance themselves from their children because they lose their status as providers and protectors in the home, find ways to give them provider and protector roles within Early Head Start—for example, as "lifeguards" with significant responsibilities for children's safety on the playground or on excursions.[†]

---

[*]H. E. Fitzgerald and M. Montañez, "Zero to Three," *Fathers as Facilitators of Infant Mental Health: Implications for Early Head Start,* 22, no. 1 (2001), 25–28.
[†] Ibid.

---

health needs are referred for further services. The response from parents, particularly working parents who have difficulty scheduling routine health care for their children, is overwhelmingly positive.

Recommendations for expanding Healthy Beginnings include funding for staff to oversee more intensive follow-up services, maintenance of a centralized database to track children's health as they move from setting to setting, and provision of onsite immunizations and blood screenings. You can read more about Healthy Child Care America and other successful examples at http://ericps.ed.uiuc.edu/nccic/hcca/action.html.

To complete an activity related to this topic, go to the Companion Website at **http://www. prenhall.com/morrison**, select chapter 8, then choose the Diversity Tie-In module.

HEAD START RESEARCH

A question that everyone always asks is, "Do Head Start, Early Head Start, and Even Start programs work?" By *work*, people generally mean, "Do these programs deliver the services they were authorized and funded to deliver, and do these services make a difference in the lives of children and families?"

Over the last five years, the federal government has been much more aggressive in wanting to assure that the programs it funds provide results. Consequently, we have seen a tremendous increase in federal monies allocated for research of its programs and a corresponding increase in the number of research studies designed to measure the effectiveness of federally funded programs.

Title I—Helping Children Become Lifelong Learners

Title I is a federal aid program for elementary and secondary schools. The money is disbursed to school districts based on the number of low-income families in the district. The school district allocates the Title I money to those schools that have the largest percentages of low-income students based on the number of free and reduced price lunches. A Title I school uses the funds to pay for extra educational services for children, such as additional teachers, aides, materials, and professional development for the instructional staff. If a school's free and reduced price lunches total over 40% they are considered a Schoolwide Title I school. This means that the funds can then be used to benefit the entire school population

Montevallo Elementary School in Montevallo, Alabama, is a Schoolwide Title I school with low-income families totaling 55% of the school population. More importantly, they are recognized as a Distinguished Title I school. As Shelby County's nomination and subsequent applicant for this award, Montevallo had to demonstrate implementation of a quality program that was in compliance with federal requirements. To be recognized, the school had to meet certain criteria in the areas of: providing opportunity for all children to meet proficient and advanced level of performance, professional development, coordination with other programs, curriculum, and in-

struction to support achievement of high standards and partnerships among schools, parents, and communities. Achievement data were also considered and Montevallo had to provide evidence of the unusual effectiveness of the school over a three-year period.

Montevallo Elementary's success story began with a vision "that all students will grow to become lifelong learners who make a positive impact on their communities and the world in which they live." It continued with a mission of "believing that all students can learn when teachers are provided the knowledge, skills, and support they need to address individual learner needs." Montevallo Elementary School strives to ensure that our learners today are our leaders tomorrow. Our mission is our vision in action.

As a school, Montevallo believes that it is essential to provide instructional opportunities using research based methods and technologies and on-going assessment of student performance to guide the instruction. Montevallo is an Alabama Reading Initiative Demonstration site and is currently going through re-certification. Through 20 hours of job embedded inservice the teachers are observing, practicing, and reflecting on reading strategies. The goal is to improve reading instruction and increase literacy in the school. The instructional opportunities afforded to

For example, results of a seven-year national evaluation of the federal Early Head Start program shows that three-year-old children completing the program performed better in cognitive and language development than children not participating in the program. The children also developed behavior patterns that prepared them for success in school, such as engaging in tasks, paying attention, and showing less aggression. Parents in Early Head Start showed more positive parenting behavior, reported less physical punishment of their children, and did more to help their children learn at home through activities such as reading to their children.[14]

CONCERNS WITH FEDERAL EARLY CHILDHOOD EDUCATION PROGRAMS

As with all programs, Head Start has associated issues of concern. Some of the issues are inherent in what we have discussed so far. Some of these concerns are making Head Start a center of national attention.

Montevallo Elementary through funds as a Title I school include:

- Accelerated Reader—Students read books on their level and take a computerized quiz, grades K–5
- STAR Early Literacy—Diagnostic Assessment, grades K–2
- STAR Reading—Reading Assessment, grades 1–5
- Accelerated Math—Math management system, scores and grades assignments and tests, grades 1–5
- STAR Math—Math assessment, grades 3–5
- Perfect Copy—Writing Skills software, grades 1–5
- Read 180 Lab—Teacher-computer model used with fourth and fifth grade students reading below grade level.
- Reading Recovery—Serves children ranking in the bottom 20% of first grade.
- Write-To-Read Lab—Serves first grade students during first semester and kindergarten students during the second semester of the year.
- Literacy Lab—Teacher directed program for first graders focusing on phonics and word work.
- Computer Lab—First grade students participate second semester as part of their reading rotation schedule.
- Modified Block Schedule in first grade—the classroom teacher divides her class into thirds: 1/3 stay with the classroom teacher for a guided reading group, 1/3 of students attend the Write to Read Lab (first semester) and Computer Lab (second semester), and 1/3 of students participate in the Literacy Lab.

With Title I funds Montevallo is able to hire substitutes and pay for workshop registrations. It is important that teachers are given the opportunity to attend inservices and meet with grade level teams during the school day to review assessments. Substitute teachers are also used to free up the assessment team three times a year to administer the Dy-namic Indicators of Basic Early Literacy Skills assessment in grades K–3 and to allow time for all teachers to attend the four Alabama Reading Initiative re-certification modules. Ongoing professional development on technology, reading strategies, math, writing, and classroom management have been offered to Montevallo teachers using Title I funds for registrations, substitutes, and presenters.

The school has also been able to purchase technology to be used in the classrooms in addition to what the technology budget can provide. By supplying classrooms with various computers, televisions, and computer software, Montevallo teachers have access to up-to-date equipment used for instruction and assessment.

A Title I school advocates a parent involvement policy. Principal, teachers, parents, and students all sign a school compact reinforcing each person's role in the educational process. A Parent Advisory Committee is an important part of Title I Schools. The Committee meets three times a year to review the schoolwide plan, the budget, and parent-school compacts. Funds are also available for parenting groups which provide information on topics such as the No Child Left Behind Act of 2001, stages of child growth and development, state performance standards, and Shelby County School System's curriculum and instruction. Title I also provides Home-School Links, materials which the teacher sends home to help reinforce concepts learned at school.

The extra materials, supplies, staff, and professional development opportunities offered to Montevallo Elementary as a Title I Schoolwide School are only truly beneficial if translated into academic growth and progress for the students involved. Montevallo's data show yearly growth and support the fact that the extra educational services provided by being a Title I School make a difference in the lives of Montevallo school children.

Contributed by Christine M. Hoffman, Principal, Montevallo Elementary School, Montevello, Alabama.

Accountability.   Part of the federal government's efforts to reform Head Start and as a consequence, all early education programs, involves making them more accountable for how monies are spent, children's achievement, and for overall program performance. It is likely that Head Start administrators and other personnel will be challenged to enhance performance in all three of these areas. As you might expect, accountability does not come easily for some programs and agencies. However, as we have discussed, part of the changing educational climate is that the public wants to be assured that programs, especially those serving young children, achieve the goals for which they are funded.

To complete a Program in Action activity related to Title I, visit the Companion Website at **http://www.prenhall.com/morrison**, select chapter 8, then choose the Program in Action module.

Testing Head Start Children.   One of the provisions of the No Child Left Behind Act of 2001 is to test children's achievement beginning in grade three. Similar plans are underway to test Head Start children. The purpose of testing Head Start children is to determine what progress they have made throughout the year and, by extension, to determine how effective Head Start teachers are in teaching them. Needless to say, there is a great deal of con-

When children are healthy, they are much more able to benefit from Head Start and other educational programs. Head Start has been a leader in providing for young children's health needs. As a result, other programs such as public school pre-K programs are also providing for children's health needs.

troversy about testing Head Start children. However, it is likely that Head Start children will be tested. It is not clear at this time how they will be tested and what the precise content of the tests will be. What is clear is that testing young children will be part of Head Start's future, and the future of children in other early childhood programs, as well. As an early childhood professional, you will probably be involved in discussions that help assume that this process of evaluation is developmentally appropriate.

Federal Control. One of the concerns that some people have about federal legislation, regulations, and funding is that they represent an increasing encroachment of the federal government into state and local educational programs. Historically, the U.S. educational system was based on the idea that states and local communities should develop and implement educational programs and curricula. Opponents of federal control fear that this highly valued local control is an endangered species and may become extinct. It is fair to say that generally, with federal funding comes federal control in the form of regulations and guidelines.

Head Start is big business and serious business. It has what some consider to be a complex operating structure, standards, and regulations. It has a vast federal bureaucracy of personnel, regional offices, and training centers. The point is that Head Start is entrenched in the Early Childhood field and is now exerting a powerful influence on how the field functions and operates.

Many other federal and state programs touch the lives of children and influence their physical, cognitive, and social development. For example, the National School Lunch Program, a $10 billion annual federal nutrition program that provides breakfast, lunch, and snacks free or at a reduced rate to the nation's children.

The federal legislative and financial influence on early childhood education—indeed, all of education, birth through higher education—is vast and significant. You, your colleagues, and the children you teach will be under the direction of federal mandates and guidelines. What this means is that you must be aware of the influence of federal and state governments on you and your profession, and you must be willing to be politically involved in influencing legislation, as well as how legislation is implemented in programs and classrooms.

National Curriculum. The specter of a national curriculum is closely associated with the issue we have just discussed. Head Start, in particular, began and is based on "local option" initiatives. This means that local Head Start programs are responsible for developing programs for the people that they represent and serve. Currently, there is an ongoing process of erosion that is eating away at the autonomy of local programs to deliver local options with the programs.

Staff Development. Staff development plays an important role in Head Start/Even Start programs. By 2003, 50 percent of center-based staff must have an AA or BA degree. How to achieve this goal with high-quality personnel will certainly challenge administrators of

VIDEO VIEWPOINT

Parenting: The First Years Last Forever (Early Head Start)

The federally funded Early Head Start program provides children younger than three in so-called at-risk families with the brain stimulation they need to grow and prosper and provides families with the support they need to raise healthy children.

REFLECTIVE DISCUSSION QUESTIONS

Why is it that some children seem smarter and learn faster than others? What difference do you think early intervention can make in a child's life? Why do you think the government has continued to expand the Head Start program over the past four decades?

REFLECTIVE DECISION MAKING

Visit the Department of Health and Human Services Web site (http://www.acf.dhhs.gov/) to learn more about Early Head Start. What are some of Early Head Start's goals and services? Are there any Head Start or Early Head Start programs in your area where you could visit or volunteer? Are there other resources in your community you could recommend to a parent in need?

all center-based programs. Nonetheless, high-quality teachers and other staff are the heart and soul of any educational program. Every child deserves the best teacher it is possible for us to provide. One thing is for certain, upgrading the credentials of all Head Start personnel will be a top priority in the years to come.

ACTIVITIES FOR FURTHER ENRICHMENT

APPLICATIONS

1. Not everyone agrees that increases in federal spending on early childhood programs are a good idea. Identify three pros and three cons for increases in federal allocations to early childhood programs.
2. Why have fathers been so neglected in the child-rearing process and early childhood education? What are some specific things you could plan to do to involve fathers in your program?

FIELD EXPERIENCES

1. Visit a Head Start program and interview teachers regarding what they believe are the most important services that Head Start provides. Likewise, interview parents to determine what Head Start services matter most to them.
2. Visit three Head Start programs and observe their educational program. Use observation guidelines provided in chapter 3 to evaluate the educational programs. Use a scale of high, medium, and low. Then write recommendations for how you would improve each program you observed.

RESEARCH

1. Research the history of Head Start from 1965 to the present and list what you believe are the major changes that Head Start has made during this time. In addition, interview veteran Head Start teachers and ask them what they identify as the most signifi-

cant changes in Head Start over the course of their careers. An interesting project would also be to initiate an oral history of Head Start that documents significant events in Head Start by those involved in its development.

2. For each of the Head Start issues we discussed, conduct interviews that gather data about the pros and cons of each. Based on your data, make recommendations regarding each issue.

READINGS FOR FURTHER ENRICHMENT

Cravens, H. *Before Head Start: The Iowa Station and America's Children.* Chapel Hill, NC: University of North Carolina Press, 2002.

Chronicles the transformation of early childhood education. Addresses the changing role played by women and shows how a women's reform movement became a male-dominated, conservative profession.

Marcus, S. M., Oden, S., Schweinhart, L. J., Weikart, D. P., and Xie, Y. *Into Adulthood: A Study of the Effects of Head Start.* Ypsilanti, MI: High/Scope Press, 2000.

A compilation of several reports and an analysis of the information to support the effectiveness of early childhood programs.

Sissel, P. A. *Staff, Parents, and Politics in Head Start: A Case Study in Unequal Power, Knowledge, and Material Resources.* New York: Garland Publishing, 1999.

A case study of two Head Start centers that offers an analysis of the struggles over power, knowledge, and resources that surround Project Head Start.

LINKING TO LEARNING

Apple Education Web Site
http://www.apple.com/education/k12/nclba

Simply and concisely explains the No Child Left Behind Act of 2001.

Teachervision
http://www.teachervision.com/lesson-plans/lesson-10274.html

Explains how the No Child Left Behind Act *provides new flexibility for all fifty states and every local school district in America in the use of federal education funds.*

Fatherhood Initiative
http://fatherhood.hhs.gov/

This federal site presents facts, statistics, and reports in an overview of the Department of Health and Human Services' involvement and activities with the Fatherhood Initiative.

For Fathers
http://www.nhsa.org/parents/parents_father_intro.htm

National Head Start Association's Web source for the Fatherhood Initiative and male and father involvement issues, including funding, partnerships, initiative models, and resources.

Head Start Bureau
http://www2.acf.hhs.gov/programs/hsb

The Head Start Bureau is dedicated to providing comprehensive developmental services to low-income children from birth to age five and social services for their families.

Head Start Publications Management Center (HSPMC)
http://www.hskids-tmsc.org

A service of the Head Start Bureau that supports the Head Start community and families by providing informational products and services, conference and meeting support, publication distribution, and marketing and outreach efforts.

National Fatherhood Initiative
http://www.fatherhood.org
> *This nonprofit organization offers an online catalog, a listing of online resources, tips and advice for fathers, and relevant links for further information.*

National Head Start Association (NHSA)
http://www.nhsa.org
> *A nonprofit organization dedicated to meeting and addressing the concerns of the Head Start community.*

The Quality in Linking Together (QUILT) Program
http://www.quilt.org
> *A training and technical assistance initiative for early education partnerships that enhances quality and expands services for low-income children and their families.*

Understanding the Role of Low-Income Fathers
http://www.mathematica-mpr.com/3rdLevel/headstar.htm
> *Discusses research projects underway with the Early Head Start research consortium to study the role of fathers in Head Start families.*

ENDNOTES

[1] The Gallup Organization. The 33rd Annual Phi Delta Kappa/Gallup Poll of the Public's Attitudes Toward the Public Schools, 2001.

[2] Head Start: Promoting Early Childhood Development, United States Department of Health and Human Services, 2002. Available at http://www.hhs.gov/news/press/2002pres/headstart.html.

[3] 2002 Head Start Fact Sheet, 2002. Department of Health and Human Services. Available at http://www.acf.hhs.gov/programs/hsb/research/factsheets/02_hsfs.html.

[4] Good Start, Grow Smart: The Bush Administration's Early Childhood Initiative. Available at http://www.whitehouse.gov/infocus/earlychildhood/toc.html.

[5] Ibid.

[6] U.S. Department of Health and Human Services, Head Start: Promoting Early Childhood Development, 2002. Available at http://www.os.dhhs.gov/news/press/2002pres/headstart.html.

[7] http://www.acf.dhhs.gov/programs/opa/facts/headst.htm

[8] California Department of Education, William F. Goodling Even Start Family Literacy Program, 2002. Available at http://www.cde.ca.gov/iasa/es.html.

[9] U.S. Department of Education, William F. Goodling Even Start Family Literacy Program, 2002. Available at http://www.ed.gov/offices/OESE/reference/1b3.html.

[10] National Even Start Association. Available at http://www.evenstart.org.

[11] U.S. Department of Education. Title I, Part A. Available at http://www.ed.gov/offices/OESE/SASA/cepprogresp.html.

[12] National Fatherhood Initiative. Available at http://www.fatherhood.org.

[13] Fatherhood Research in the Early Head Start Research and Evaluation Project. Mathematica Policy Research Inc. Available at http://www.mathematica-mpr.com/3rdLevel/fatheroverview.htm.

[14] U.S. Department of Health and Human Services, "Study Shows Positive Results from Early Head Start Program." Available at http://www.hhs.gov/news/press/2002pres/20020603.html.

Part 4

The New World of Early Childhood Education

Chapter 9

Babies are not just cute faces but are the greatest learning machines in the universe.

Patricia Kuhl

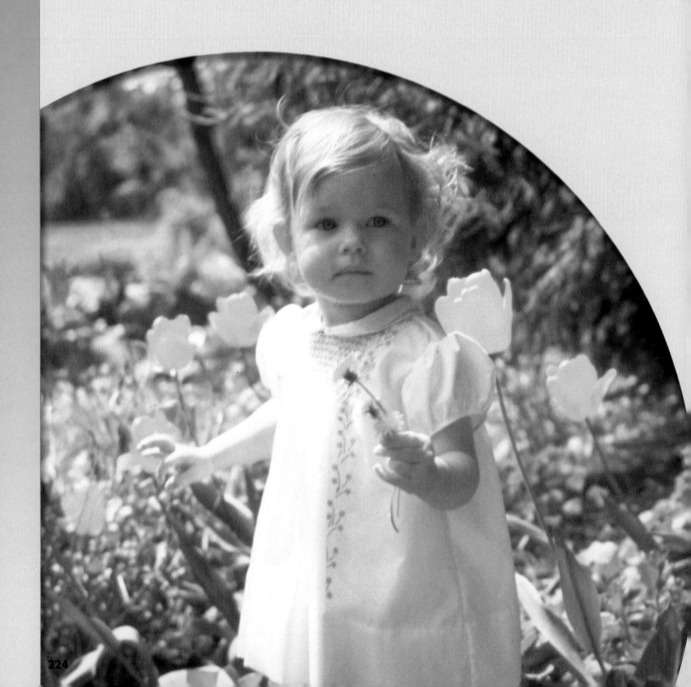

Infants and Toddlers
Foundation Years for Learning

Focus Questions

- How is research influencing the care and education of infants and toddlers?

- What are the milestones in infant and toddler development?

- How do theories of development explain infant and toddler cognitive, language, and psychosocial development?

- How can you and other professionals provide quality programs for infants and toddlers?

Interest in infant and toddler care and education is at an all-time high; it will continue at this level well into the future. The growing demand for quality infant and toddler programs stems primarily from the reasons discussed in chapter 2. It is also fueled by parents who want their children to have an early start and get off on the "right foot" so they can be successful in life and work. The popularity of early care and education is also attributable to a changing view of the very young and the discovery that infants are remarkably competent individuals. Let's examine the ways that infants' and toddlers' development and early experiences shape their lives.

WHAT ARE INFANTS AND TODDLERS LIKE?

Think for a minute about your experiences with infants. What characteristics stand out most in your mind? I know that infants never cease to amaze me! Take a few minutes to review the profiles of Spencer, Amy, Hyato, and Marisa in the Portraits of Infants and Toddlers. They are infants in programs across the country. After you have reviewed their development across the four domains, reflect on and answer the accompanying questions.

Have you ever tried to keep up with a toddler? Everyone who tries ends up exhausted at the end of the day. A typical response is, "They are into everything!" The infant and toddler years between birth and age three are full of developmental milestones and significant events. Infancy, life's first year, includes the first breath, the first smile, first thoughts, first words, and first steps. Significant developments also occur during toddlerhood, the period between one and three years. Two of the most outstanding developmental milestones are walking and rapid language development. Mobility and language are the cornerstones of autonomy that enable toddlers to become independent. These unique developmental events are significant for children as well as those who care for and teach them. How you and other early childhood professionals and parents respond to infants' first accomplishments and toddlers' quests for autonomy helps determine how children grow and master life events.

 To review the chapter focus questions online, go to the Companion Website at **http://www. prenhall.com/morrison** and select chapter 9.

PORTRAITS OF INFANTS AND TODDLERS

Spencer

Introduce yourself to Spencer, a 4-month-old Caucasian male. Spencer weighs 15 pounds and is 25 inches long. Spencer is a very alert baby. He uses his eyes, hands, and mouth to explore the world around him. Spencer enjoys attention from any adult who will play with him.

Social-Emotional	Cognitive	Motor	Adaptive (Daily Living)
Smiles when you talk to him.	"Coo"s a lot.	Is very active and alert.	Drinks breast milk and formula from a bottle.
Will listen to caregiver talk for a long time.	Chews on everything.	Tries to put things in his mouth, but misses.	Eats cereal.
Likes everyone to hold him.	Screeches when he is upset.	Rolls over in both directions.	Breastfeeds at home.
Does not prefer any. particular caregiver.	Watches everything.	Sits up with support.	
		Reaches for things.	

Amy

Introduce yourself to Amy, a 4-month-old Caucasian female. Amy weighs 14 pounds and is 24 inches long. Amy frequently expresses her happiness through smiles and babbling. She enjoys playing with bar toys, where she develops motor skills such as reaching, grasping, and kicking.

Social-Emotional	Cognitive	Motor	Adaptive (Daily Living)
Likes being talked to one-on-one by caregivers.	Likes playing on the floor with bar toys.	Kicks, waves her hands, and reaches feet and arms. toward toys.	Cries when she wants to eat.
Is "all smiles".	Full of "goo"s and "gaa"s.	Does not like being on her stomach.	Eats every four hours.
Recognizes caregiver by smiling when picked up.	Pulls on toy bar to reach toys.	Reaches with her hands.	Wakes up from nap when it is time to eat.
Does not cry when she encounters strangers.	Explores with her hands and feet.	Grasps chain links and bigger toys.	
Does not smile when strangers pick her up.			

Questions about 4-month-olds:

- What similarities exist between Spencer and Amy?
- What significant differences are there?
- What is a common theme in Spencer and Amy's cognitive development?
- What roles do toys play in Spencer and Amy's development?
- Identify three ways play can enhance and influence a child's development.
- What activities can you use to promote development in a 4-month-old?

Marisa

Introduce yourself to Marisa, a 10-month-old Hispanic female. Marisa weighs 23 pounds and is 28 inches long. Unlike Hyato, Marisa is not mobile. She prefers to lay on her back and becomes agitated when in other positions. Marisa spends the majority of her awake time observing people and toys.

Social-Emotional	Cognitive	Motor	Adaptive (Daily Living)
Does not bother anyone. Is very quiet. Gets frustrated when other babies get too close to her. Likes caregivers to talk to her.	Only likes to play with certain toys. Likes mirrors. Likes music and mobiles. Follows toys with her eyes and hands.	Sits with support. Rotates in circles on her back. Does not like to be held up in a standing position. Does not like to be on her tummy. Does not crawl.	Eats solid baby food. Drinks formula from a bottle. Engages in one activity for several minutes.

Hyato

Introduce yourself to Hyato, a 10-month-old Laotian male. Hyato weighs 19 pounds and is 28 inches long. Hyato has recently become very active and does not like being confined to a crib. He enjoys personal attention from caregivers. Hyato has a good sense of humor and prefers interacting with adults to playing with toys.

Social-Emotional	Cognitive	Motor	Adaptive (Daily Living)
Likes to play alone in his own space. Does not play with toys much. Gets frustrated easily. Likes to play with caregivers. Prefers one particular caregiver.	Spills his bottle on purpose. Makes single sounds; tries to talk. Whines for attention. Points and babbles at things.	Crawls around quickly. Pulls up on furniture. Walks with support. Picks up small pieces of food with fingers.	Drinks formula and juice from a bottle. Nibbles on crackers. Holds his own bottle.

Questions about 10-month-olds:

- What cultural factors may affect Hyato's interaction with toys and people?
- Referring to the weight chart on page (230), how might Marisa's physical characteristics influence her development?
- How might Marisa and Hyato's different cultures affect their adaptive behavior?

- Based on the descriptions provided, what similarities might exist between Marisa and Hyato's home lives?
- How might classrooms you are familiar with need to be adjusted for the Laotian and Hispanic cultures?
- Why is it important for you to be sensitive to cultural differences as you care for and teach young children?

Joseph

Introduce yourself to Joseph, a 15-month-old Honduran male. Joseph weighs 26 pounds and is 31 inches tall. He uses his hands to explore and communicate. Joseph knows many words, but is not yet speaking. He enjoys expressing himself through actions and noise.

Social-Emotional	Cognitive	Motor	Adaptive (Daily Living)
Recognizes his own name. Plays with other children. Smiles and babbles when talked to.	Tries to talk. Likes to explore and discover new things. Points to pictures when named.	Paints and scribbles. Plays with instruments musical. Picks up food with his fingers.	Drinks from a baby cup by himself. Likes to snack on crackers. Uses gestures to ask for things.

Mariafe

Introduce yourself to Mariafe, a 15-month-old Peruvian female. Mariafe weighs 24 pounds and is 30 inches tall. She speaks only Spanish. Mariafe is a bright and cheerful toddler. She is very animated and enjoys pretending and participating in activities that involve music.

Social-Emotional	Cognitive	Motor	Adaptive (Daily Living)
Gives things to an adult upon request. Laughs when you call her name and make faces at her. Makes eye contact and smiles.	Says words like "mama," "papa," and "no." Sings along with music. Likes to pretend to be different animals.	Dances and bounces up and down to music. Likes to color with crayons. Enjoys climbing up steps.	Eats solid foods. Drinks milk from a bottle. Increased resistance to naptime.

Questions about 15-month-olds:

- Do you think that culture explains some of the differences between Joseph and Mariafe in adaptive development?
- How can you accommodate the different adaptive needs of toddlers in the classroom?
- How strictly should you require Mariafe to adhere to the classroom naptime?
- How would you provide for Mariafe's resistance to naptime?

- What role, if any, has music played in Mariafe's development? What are some ways music can be used to enhance development in all four domains?
- What adjustments can be made to your classroom to encourage exploration and mobility in young toddlers?
- What are some developmental differences between Joseph and Mariafe?

Christy

Introduce yourself to Christy, a 2-year-old Caucasian female. Christy weighs 21 pounds and is 32 inches tall. Christy is a shy, yet sociable toddler. She loves attending school and playing with her classmates. Although her words are sometimes difficult to understand, Christy is already sharing stories about what she learns in class.

Social-Emotional	Cognitive	Motor	Adaptive (Daily Living)
Does not like big groups of people.	Knows the names of classmates.	Can almost do forward rolls.	Asks for help.
Laughs a lot.	Speaks in short sentences.	Likes to jump up and down.	Eats with a fork.
Prefers male adults over female.	Shares about past events.	Can catch a bouncing ball.	Helps with chores.
Has favorite playmates.			

Daniel

Introduce yourself to Daniel, a 2-year-old Hispanic male. Daniel weighs 29 pounds and is 34 inches tall. Daniel is a rambunctious toddler. He is extremely active and tends to involve himself in activities that are dangerous to him and other children. Although he is beginning to hit others, Daniel is also very affectionate and likes to help others.

Social-Emotional	Cognitive	Motor	Adaptive (Daily Living)
Is beginning to hit others a lot.	Follows simple instructions.	Likes to climb on things.	Feeds himself.
Is very quiet but playful.	Uses gestures to ask for things.	Can run around the room.	Does not like change.
Loves his big brother and sister.	Says several words.	Throws a ball and retrieves it.	Gets stuck under furniture, etc.

Questions about 2-year-olds:

- At age one, Christy was diagnosed as *failure to thrive*. Does her overall development reflect this diagnosis? Why or why not?
- What is an *enriched environment*? How can it support the development of toddlers who are developmentally at risk?
- Which of Daniel's behavioral characteristics might be dangerous in the classroom? How can you make your classroom a safe environment for active two-year-olds such as Daniel?

- Do all two-year-olds need the same level of supervision? What kinds of supervision might Daniel and Christy need?
- In what domains are Daniel and Christy most similar? In what domains are they most different? What are some activities that both toddlers can successfully engage in and learn from?

TABLE 9.1 Average Height and Weight of Infants and Toddlers

Age	Males		Females	
	Height (inches)	Weight (pounds)	Height (inches)	Weight (pounds)
Birth	20.0	8.0	19.5	7.5
3 months	24.0	13.0	23.5	12.5
6 months	26.5	17.5	25.5	16.0
9 months	28.5	20.5	27.5	19.0
1 year	30.0	23.0	29.5	21.0
1 1/2 years	32.5	27.0	33.0	24.5
2 years	34.0	28.0	34.0	26.5
2 1/2 years	36.5	30.0	36.0	28.5
3 years	37.5	31.5	37.5	30.5

Source: National Center for Health Statistics in collaboration with the National Center for Chronic Disease Prevention and Health Promotion (2000). Available at http://www.cdc.gov/growthcharts

To check your understanding of this chapter with the online Study Guide, go to the Companion Website at **http://www.prenhall.com/morrison**, select chapter 9, then choose the Study Guide module.

Understanding the major development processes that characterize the formative years of infants and toddlers will help you and other early childhood professionals fully grasp your roles as educators and nurturers. To begin, we must recognize that infants and toddlers are not the miniature adults many baby product advertisements picture them to be. Children need many years to develop fully and become independent. This period of dependency and professionals' responses to it are critical for children's development. You must constantly keep in mind that "normal" growth and development milestones are based on averages, and the "average" is the middle ground of development (for example, Table 9.1 gives average heights and weights for infants and toddlers). To assess children's progress or lack of it, you must know the milestones of different stages of development. At the same time, you must consider the whole child to assess what is "normal" for each child. You must also take into account gender, socioeconomic, cultural, and family background, including nutritional and health history, to determine what is normal for individual children. Also keep in mind that when children are provided with good nutrition, health care, and a warm, loving emotional environment, development tends toward what is "normal" for each child.

YOUNG BRAINS: A PRIMER

For the past decade, brain and child development research has been a hot national topic. This research has created a great deal of interest in the first three years of life. As a result, there has been an explosion of additional research regarding brain functioning and the ways that professionals and programs can help children get a good start in life. As we discuss these early years now, let's review some interesting facts about infant and toddler brain development and consider the implications they have for how you practice as a professional. Also review Figure 9.1, which shows the regions of the brain and their functional processes.

The brain is a fascinating and complex organ. Anatomically, the young brain is like the adult brain, except it is smaller. The average adult brain weighs approximately 3 lb. At birth, the infant's brain weighs ¾ lb.; at six months, 1½ lb.; and at two years, 2¾ lb. So you can see that during the first two years of life the brain undergoes tremendous physical growth. The brain finishes developing at age ten, when it reaches its full adult size.

At birth, the brain has 100 billion neurons, or nerve cells—all the brain cells it will ever have! That is why it is important for parents and other caregivers to play with, respond to, interact with, and talk to young children. It is through such processes that brain connections develop and learning takes place. As brain connections are repeatedly used, they become permanent. On the other hand, brain connections that are not used or used only a

For more information about brain development, go to the Companion Website at **http://www.prenhall.com/morrison,** select chapter 9, then choose the Linking to Learning module to connect to the I Am Your Child site.

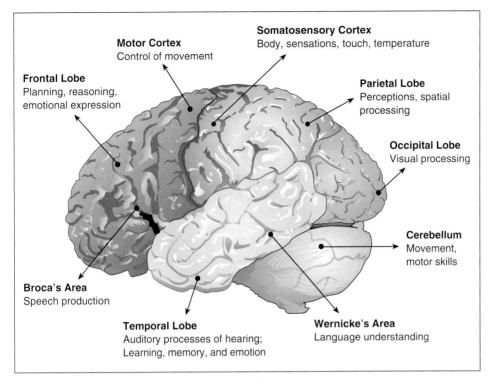

FIGURE 9.1 Brain Regions

Over the last decade, scientists and educators have spent considerable time and energy exploring the links between brain development and functions and classroom learning. Brain research provides many implications for how to develop enriched classrooms for children and for how to engage them in activities that will help them learn and develop to their optimal levels. Most important, brain research has made educators aware of the importance of providing young children with stimulating activities early in life.

little may wither away. This withering away or elimination is known as neural **shearing** or **pruning**. Consequently, a child whose parents seldom talk or read to him may have difficulty with language skills later in life. This helps explain why children who are reared in language-rich environments do well in school, while children who are not reared in such environments may be at risk for academic failure.

Also by the time of birth, these billions of neurons have formed more than 50 trillion connections, or synapses, through a process called **synaptogenesis**, the proliferation of neural connections; this process will continue to occur until the age of ten. But this is just the beginning. During the first month, the brain will form more than 1,000 trillion more synaptic connections between neurons. The forming of these connections and neural pathways is essential for brain development, and it is the experiences that children have that help form these neural connections. Experiences count. If children don't have the experiences they need to form neural connections, they may be at risk for poor developmental and behavioral outcomes. Incredibly, almost from birth, the brain begins to lose neurons.

Children need not just any experiences but the right experiences at the right times. For example, the critical period for language development is the first year of life. It is during this time that the auditory pathways for language learning are formed. Beginning at birth, an infant can distinguish the sounds of all the languages of the world. But at about six months, through the process of neuron pruning or shearing, infants lose the ability to distinguish the sounds of languages they have not heard. By twelve months, their auditory maps are pretty well in place.[1] It is literally a case of use it or lose it.

Shearing (pruning) The selective elimination of synapses.

Synaptogenesis The rapid development of neural connections.

 For more information about the importance of the first three years of life, go to the Companion Website at **http://www.prenhall. com/morrison**, select chapter 9, then choose the Linking to Learning module to connect to the Zero to Three site.

Sensitive period A period of developmental time during which certain things are learned easier than at earlier or later times.

Having the right experiences at the right time also relates to *critical periods*, developmental *windows of opportunity* or **sensitive periods** during which it is easier to learn something than it is at another time. (See Table 9.3, on page 242, which shows the progress of vocabulary development in the early years.) This is another example of how experiences influence development. An infant whose mother or other caregiver talks to her is more likely to have a larger vocabulary than an infant whose mother doesn't talk to her. Mothers who use different words and speak to their infants in complex sentences increase the infants' knowledge of words and their ability to speak in complex sentences.[2] Figure 9.2 identifies some major and critical facts about brain development in the early years.

There are several conclusions we can draw in our discussion about the brain:

- Babies are born to learn. They are remarkable learning instruments. Their brains make them so.
- Children's brain development and their ability to learn throughout life rely on the interplay between nature (genetic inheritance, controlled by 80,000 genes) and nurture (the experiences they have and the environments in which they are raised).

FIGURE 9.2   **The Importance of Brain Development in the Early Years**

- Neuroscience research findings suggest that good parental care, warm and loving attachments, and positive age-appropriate stimulation from birth onward make a difference in children's overall development for a lifetime.[1]

- Experiences during the early critical years of development are so powerful that they can greatly change the way a person develops.[2]

- Babies quickly revise their perceptions about people and the world in general based on new experiences. Their brains are less committed, or "cluttered," than adult brains, and they can revise their views of the world quite rapidly.[3]

- Auditory stimuli through word use in a particular language stimulate the formation of nerve connections. When children hear a phoneme (i.e., small unit of speech that distinguishes one sound from another) over and over, connections are being formed in the auditory cortex.[4]

- Sounds in different languages formulate different maps. Infants growing up in English-speaking homes have a different auditory map compared with those children from homes where other languages are spoken.[5]

- Eight-month-old infants have been shown to engage in long-term storage of words that occur frequently in speech after exposure to children's stories in comparison with children who had not been exposed to the stories.[6]

- Children who receive multivitamin supplements for ninety days have shown positive effects in relation to cognitive development.[7]

- Exercise supports learning. Increasing balance, spatial awareness, and motor coordination skills can enhance children's academic performance and learning.[8]

- Exposure to music has an impact on wiring the brain's neural network.[9]

Sources: [1]J. J. Newberger, "New Brain Development Research: A Wonderful Window of Opportunity to Build Public Support for Early Childhood Education," *Young Children* (February 1997), 4–9; 2H. Chugani, "Functional Brain Reorganization in Children," *Brain and Development* 18 (1996), 347–56; 3P. Kuhl, "Early Language Acquisition: The Brain Comes Prepared," *Parents as Teachers National Center* (1999); 4P. Kuhl, "Learning and Representation in Speech and Language," *Current Opinion in Neurobiology* 4 (1994), 812–22, and S. Begley, "Your Child's Brain," *Newsweek* (February 19, 1996). [Online.] Available: http://www.home.earthlink.net/~misbet/good.html 5Ibid.; 6P. W. Jusczyk and E. Hohne, "Infants' Memory for Spoken Words," *Science* 277 (1997), 1984–1986; 7D. H. Fishbein and S. E. Pease, "Diet, Nutrition, and Aggression," *Journal of Offender Rehabilitation* 21 (1995); 8R. T. Johnson, "Story Retelling in a Learning Technology Context," *Early Child Development and Care* 32 (1999), 53–58; 9A. Kemp, *The Musical Temperament* (New York: Oxford University Press, 1996).

- What happens to children early in life has a long-lasting influence on how children develop and learn.
- Critical periods influence learning positively and negatively.
- The human brain is quite "plastic." It has the ability to change in response to different kinds of experiences and environments.
- Prevention and early intervention are more beneficial than later remediation.
- The brain undergoes physiological changes in response to experiences.
- An enriched environment influences brain development. (Figure 9.5 on page 240 shows the characteristics of an enriched environment.)

NATURE AND NURTURE

Today we hear a lot about nature, heredity, and genes. All of these are the influences that we enter the world with. Nurturing involves all the environmental influences that affect and play a role in development. Which of these factors, nature (genetics) or nurture (environment) plays a larger role? This question is the focus of a never-ending debate. At this time there is no one right and true answer to the question. One reason for this is that the answer depends on many things. On the one hand, many traits are fully determined by heredity. For example, your eye color is a product of your heredity. Physical height is also largely influenced by heredity—as much as 90 percent. So we can say that many differences in individuals are due to heredity rather than to environmental factors. Certainly height can be influenced by nutrition, growth hormones, and other environmental interventions. But by and large, an individual's height is genetically determined. Other traits, such as temperament and shyness, are highly heritable.

On the other hand, nurturing—the environment in which individuals grow and develop—plays an important role in what individuals are and how they behave. For example, the years from birth to age eight are extremely important environmentally. Some environmental factors that play a major role in early development include nutrition, quality of the environment, stimulation of the brain, affectionate relationships with parents, and opportunities to learn. Think for a moment about other kinds of environmental influences—such as family, environment, school, and friends—that affect development. Now review Figure 9.2 again, regarding what research says about brain development and the early years.

VIDEO VIEWPOINT

Building Brains: The Sooner, the Better

Powerful research evidence exists that shows that the period from birth to age three is critical to a child's healthy growth and development and to later success in school and life.

REFLECTIVE DISCUSSION QUESTIONS

Some policymakers are realizing that if they spend money on early intervention in a child's first few years of life, while their brains are most changeable, the government will save money down the line on special education, foster care, and prisons. What are some of the other costs to society when children do not receive the care they need when they are young?

REFLECTIVE DECISION MAKING

What kind of interventions would most benefit the families in your neighborhood or school district? If you were to write a letter to your congressperson suggesting that your state enact early intervention legislation and programming, what would you recommend?

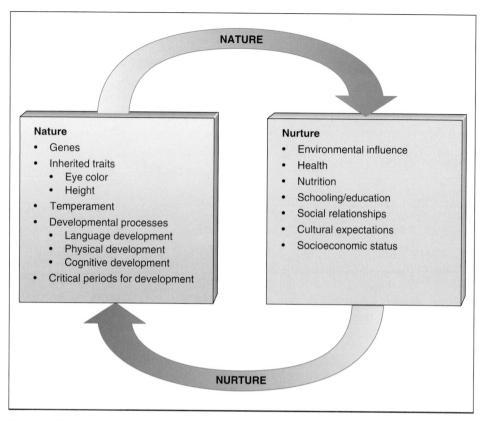

FIGURE 9.3 **Nature and Nurture: Dimensions of Development**

A decade or two ago, we believed that nature and nurture were competing entities and that one of these was dominant over the other. Today we understand that they are not competing entities; both are necessary for normal development, and it is the interaction between the two that makes us the individuals we are (see Figure 9.3).

HOW DOES MOTOR DEVELOPMENT OCCUR?

What would life be like if you couldn't walk, run, and participate in your favorite activities? Motor skills play an important part in all of life. Even more so, motor development is essential for infants and toddlers because it contributes to their intellectual and skill development. Table 9.2 lists infant and toddler motor milestones. Human motor development is governed by certain basic principles. Here are some for you to keep in mind:

- Motor development is sequential.
- Maturation of the motor system proceeds from gross (large) to fine (small) behaviors. For example, as part of her learning to reach, Maria sweeps toward an object with her whole arm. Over the course of a month, however, as a result of development and experiences, Maria's gross reaching gives way to specific reaching, and she grasps for particular objects.
- Motor development is from *cephalo* to *caudal*—from head to foot (tail). This process is known as **cephalocaudal development.** At birth, Maria's head is the most developed part of her body; she holds her head erect before she sits, and her being able to sit precedes her walking.
- Motor development proceeds from the *proximal* (midline, or central part of the body) to the *distal* (extremities), known as **proximodistal development.** Maria is able to control her arm movements before she can control her finger movements.

Cephalocaudal development
The principle that development proceeds from the head to the toes.

Proximodistal development
The principle that development proceeds from the center of the body outward.

TABLE 9.2 Infant and Toddler Motor Milestones

These age ranges indicate that children vary in the age at which they achieve major motor milestones. The important thing to observe is children's achievement of them.

Behavior	Age Range of Accomplishment
Lifts head	Birth
Arms and legs move equally	Birth
Smiles responsively	2 months
Smiles spontaneously	3 months
Rolls over	6 months
Reaches for objects	6 months
Sits without support	7 months
Pulls self to stand	10 months

Source: William K. Frankenburg, Josiah Dodde, et al. *Denver II Training Manual,* 1992. Denver Developmental Materials; PO Box 6919 Denver, CO 80206-0919. Used by permission.

Motor development plays a major role in social and behavioral expectations. For example, toilet training (also called *toilet learning* or *toilet mastery*) is a milestone of the toddler period. This process often causes a great deal of anxiety for parents, professionals, and toddlers. Many parents want to accomplish toilet training as quickly and efficiently as possible, but frustrations arise when they start too early and expect too much of children. Toilet training is largely a matter of physical readiness, and most child-rearing experts recommend waiting until children are two years old before beginning the training process.

The principle of toilet training is that parents and professionals help children develop control over an involuntary response. When an infant's bladder and bowel are full, the urethral and sphincter muscles open. The goal of toilet training is to teach children to control this involuntary reflex and use the toilet when appropriate. Training involves maturational development, timing, patience, modeling, preparing the environment, establishing a routine, and developing a partnership between the child and parents/professionals. Another necessary partnership is that between parents and professionals who are assisting in toilet training, especially when parents do not know what to do, are hesitant about approaching toilet training, or want to start the training too soon.

Motor development plays a major role in cognitive and social development. For example, learning to walk enables young children to explore their environment, which in turn contributes to cognitive development. Can you think of other examples?

HOW DOES INTELLECTUAL DEVELOPMENT OCCUR?

Reflect on the discussion of cognitive development in chapter 5, and think about how a child's development of first schemata (schemes) are sensorimotor. According to Piaget, infants do not have "thoughts of the mind." Rather, they come to know their world by actively acting on it through their senses and through motor actions. Piaget said that infants *construct* (as opposed to absorb) schemes using reflexive sensorimotor actions.

ASSIMILATION, ACCOMMODATION, AND ADAPTATION AT WORK

Infants begin life with only reflexive motor actions that they use to satisfy biological needs and their billions of neurons. In response to specific environmental conditions, they modify these reflexive actions through a process of *assimilation, accommodation,* and *adaptation.* Recall that *adaptation* is the process of building new schemes through acting directly on the environment. Adaptation consists of two processes, *assimilation* and *accommodation.* During assimilation, children adjust their already existing schemes to interpret what is going on in their environment. As a result, through accommodation, children create new schemes or modify existing schemes so they fit with the reality of their environments. Patterns of adaptive behavior initiate more activity, which leads to more adaptive behavior, which, in turn, yields more schemes. Consider sucking, for example, an innate sensorimotor scheme. Kathy turns her head to the source of nourishment, closes her lips around the nipple, sucks, and swallows. As a result of experiences and maturation, Kathy adapts or changes this basic sensorimotor scheme of sucking to include both anticipatory sucking movements and nonnutritive sucking, such as sucking a pacifier or blanket.

Children construct new schemes through the processes of assimilation and accommodation. Piaget believed that children are active constructors of intelligence through *assimilation* (taking in new experiences) and *accommodation* (changing existing schemes to fit new information), which results in *equilibrium.*

STAGES OF COGNITIVE DEVELOPMENT: SENSORIMOTOR INTELLIGENCE

Sensorimotor cognitive development consists of six stages (shown in Figure 9.4 and described in the following subsections). Let's follow Madeleine through her six stages of cognitive development.

Stage 1: Birth to One Month.   During this stage, Madeleine sucks and grasps everything. She is literally ruled by *reflexive actions.* Reflexive responses to objects are undifferentiated, and Madeleine responds the same way to everything. Sensorimotor schemes help her learn new ways of interacting with the world. New ways of interacting promote Madeleine's cognitive development.

Grasping is a primary infant sensorimotor scheme. At birth, the grasping reflex consists of closing the fingers around an object placed in the hand. Through experiences and maturation, this basic reflexive grasping action becomes coordinated with looking, opening the hand, retracting the fingers, and grasping, thus developing from a pure, reflexive action to an intentional grasping action. As Madeleine matures in response to experiences, her grasping scheme is combined with a delightful activity of grasping and releasing everything she can get her hands on!

Stage 2: One to Four Months.   The milestone of this stage is the modification of the reflexive actions of stage 1. Sensorimotor behaviors not previously present in Madeleine's repertoire of behavior begin to appear: habitual thumb sucking (indicates hand–mouth coordination), tracking moving objects with the eyes, and moving the head toward sounds (indicates the beginning of the recognition of causality). Madeleine starts to direct her own behavior rather than being totally dependent on reflexive actions.

Primary circular reactions begin during stage 2. A circular response occurs when Madeleine's actions cause her to react or when another person prompts her to try to repeat the original action. The circular reaction is similar to a stimulus–response, cause-and-effect relationship.

For more information about infant and toddler development, go to the Companion Website at **http://www.prenhall.com/morrison,** select any chapter, then choose Topic 2 of the ECE Supersite module.

Primary circular reactions
Repetitive actions that are centered on the infant's own body.

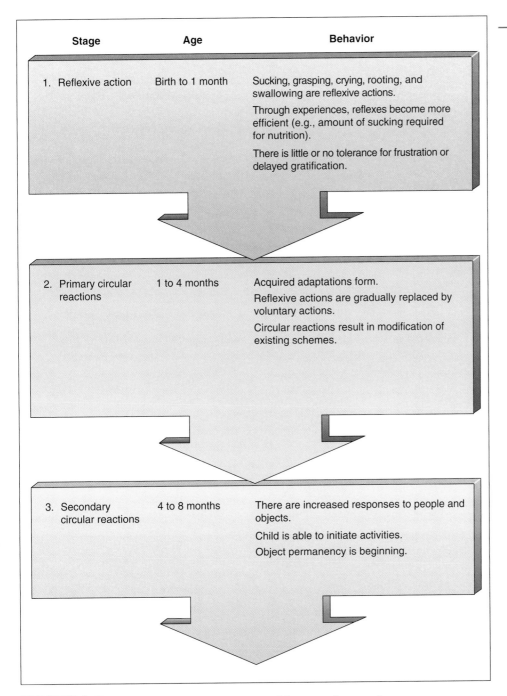

Stage	Age	Behavior
1. Reflexive action	Birth to 1 month	Sucking, grasping, crying, rooting, and swallowing are reflexive actions. Through experiences, reflexes become more efficient (e.g., amount of sucking required for nutrition). There is little or no tolerance for frustration or delayed gratification.
2. Primary circular reactions	1 to 4 months	Acquired adaptations form. Reflexive actions are gradually replaced by voluntary actions. Circular reactions result in modification of existing schemes.
3. Secondary circular reactions	4 to 8 months	There are increased responses to people and objects. Child is able to initiate activities. Object permanency is beginning.

FIGURE 9.4 **Stages of Sensorimotor Cognitive Development**

Stage 3: Four to Eight Months. Piaget called this stage of cognitive development "making interesting things last." Madeleine manipulates objects, demonstrating coordination between vision and tactile senses. She also reproduces events with the purpose of sustaining and repeating acts. The intellectual milestone of this stage is the beginning of **object permanence.** When infants in stages 1 and 2 cannot see an object, it does not exist for them—out of sight, out of mind. During later stage 3, however, awareness grows that things that are out of sight continue to exist.

Object permanence The concept that people and objects have an independent existence beyond the child's perception of them.

237

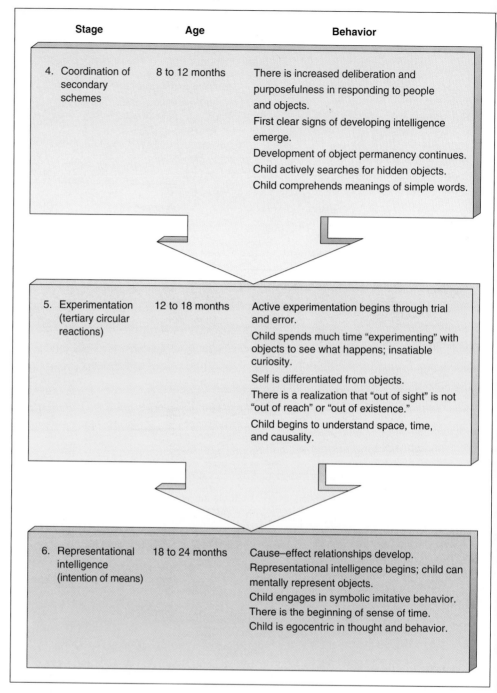

Stage	Age	Behavior
4. Coordination of secondary schemes	8 to 12 months	There is increased deliberation and purposefulness in responding to people and objects. First clear signs of developing intelligence emerge. Development of object permanency continues. Child actively searches for hidden objects. Child comprehends meanings of simple words.
5. Experimentation (tertiary circular reactions)	12 to 18 months	Active experimentation begins through trial and error. Child spends much time "experimenting" with objects to see what happens; insatiable curiosity. Self is differentiated from objects. There is a realization that "out of sight" is not "out of reach" or "out of existence." Child begins to understand space, time, and causality.
6. Representational intelligence (intention of means)	18 to 24 months	Cause–effect relationships develop. Representational intelligence begins; child can mentally represent objects. Child engages in symbolic imitative behavior. There is the beginning of sense of time. Child is egocentric in thought and behavior.

FIGURE 9.4 *(continued)*

Secondary circular reactions
Repetitive actions focused on the qualities of objects, such as their shapes, sizes, colors, and noises.

Secondary circular reactions begin during this stage. This process is characterized by Madeleine repeating an action with the purpose of getting the same response from an object or person; for example, Madeleine will repeatedly shake a rattle to repeat the sound. Repetitiveness is characteristic of all circular reactions. *Secondary* here means that the reaction is elicited from a source other than the infant. Madeleine interacts with people and objects to make interesting sights, sounds, and events happen and last. Given an object, Madeleine will use all available schemes, such as mouthing, hitting, and banging; if one of these schemes produces an interesting result, she continues to use the scheme to elicit the same response. Imitation becomes increasingly intentional as a means of prolonging interest.

Stage 4: Eight to Twelve Months. During this stage, "coordination of secondary schemes," Madeleine uses means to attain ends. She moves objects out of the way (means) to get another object (end). She begins to search for hidden objects, although not always in the places they were hidden, indicating a growing understanding of object permanence.

Stage 5: Twelve to Eighteen Months. This stage, the climax of the sensorimotor period, marks the beginning of truly intelligent behavior. Stage 5 is the stage of experimentation. Madeleine experiments with objects to solve problems, and her experimentation is characteristic of intelligence that involves **tertiary circular reactions,** in which she repeats actions and modifies behaviors over and over to see what will happen. This repetition helps develop understanding of cause-and-effect relationships and leads to the discovery of new relationships through exploration and experimentation.

Physically, stage 5 is also the beginning of the toddler stage, with the commencement of walking. Toddlers' physical mobility, combined with their growing ability and desire to experiment with objects, makes for fascinating and often frustrating child rearing. Madeleine and other toddlers are avid explorers, determined to touch, taste, and feel all they can. Although the term *terrible twos* was once used to describe this stage, professionals now recognize that there is nothing terrible about toddlers exploring their environment to develop their intelligence. What is important is that teachers, parents, and others prepare environments for exploration. As Madeleine's mom describes it, "I keep putting things up higher and higher because her arms seem to be getting longer and longer!" Novelty is interesting for its own sake, and Madeleine experiments in many different ways with a given object. For example, she will use any available item—a wood hammer, a block, a rhythm band instrument—to pound the pegs in a pound-a-peg toy.

Stage 6: Eighteen Months to Two Years. This is the stage of transition from sensorimotor to symbolic thought. It is the stage of **symbolic representation,** which occurs when Madeleine can visualize events internally and maintain mental images of objects not present. Representational thought enables Madeleine to solve problems in a sensorimotor way through experimentation and trial and error and predict cause-and-effect relationships more accurately. She also develops the ability to remember, which allows her to try out actions she sees others do. During this stage, Madeleine can "think" using mental images and memories, which enables her to engage in pretend activities. Madeleine's representational thought does not necessarily match the real world and its representations, which accounts for her ability to have other objects stand for almost anything: a wooden block is a car; a rag doll is a baby. This type of play, known as **symbolic play,** becomes more elaborate and complex in the preoperational period.

Tertiary circular reactions
Modifications that infants make in their behavior in order to explore the effects of those modifications.

Symbolic representation
The ability to use mental images to stand for something else.

Symbolic play The ability of a young child to have an object stand for something else.

All children are different, and early childhood educators must provide for the individual needs of each child. Review the Portraits of Infants and Toddlers at the beginning of the chapter and consider the individual differences found in the children

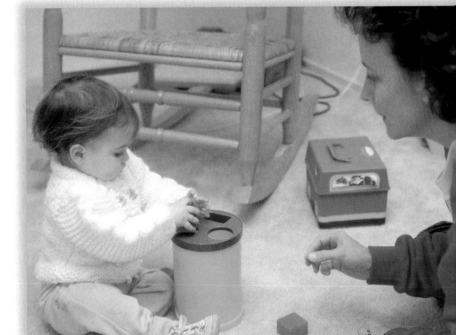

FIGURE 9.5 Characteristics of Enriched Environments for Young Children

- Includes a wide variety of materials to support all areas of development—physical, social, emotional, and linguistic
- Enables children to be actively involved
- Provides for children's basic emotional needs—safety, security, love, and emotional support
- Encourages social interactions with other children and adults
- Provides for children's physical, nutritional, and health needs
- Provides activities based on children's interests and abilities
- Enables children to learn the basic language and cognitive skills necessary for future school success

Research studies repeatedly show that children who are reared, cared for, and taught in environments that are enriched are healthier, happier, and more achievement-oriented. How would you apply these characteristics to your program?

In summary, we need to keep in mind several important concepts of infant and toddler development:

- The chronological ages associated with Piaget's stages of cognitive development are approximate. In fact, children can do things earlier than the ages Piaget assigned. You should not be preoccupied with children's ages but should focus on cognitive behavior, which gives a clearer understanding of a child's level of development. This is the true meaning of developmentally appropriate education and caregiving.
- Infants and toddlers do not "think" as adults do; they come to know their world by acting on it and need many opportunities for *active* involvement.
- Infants and toddlers are actively involved in *constructing* their own intelligence. Children's activity with people and objects stimulates them cognitively and leads to the development of mental schemata (schemes).
- Parents and early childhood professionals need to provide *environments* and *opportunities* for infants and toddlers to be actively involved. These are two important conditions for intellectual development. Reflexive actions form the basis for assimilation and accommodation, which enable cognitive structures to develop. You must ensure that infants and toddlers have experiences that support and contribute to successful intellectual construction.
- At birth, Madeleine and other infants do not know that there are objects in the world and, in this sense, have no knowledge of the external world. They do not and cannot differentiate between themselves and the external world. For all practical purposes, Madeleine *is* the world. All external objects are acted on through sucking, grasping, and looking. This acting on the world enables Madeleine to construct schemes of the world.
- The concept of *causality,* or cause and effect, does not exist at birth. Infants' and toddlers' concepts of causality begin to evolve only through acting on the environment.
- As infants and toddlers move from one stage of intellectual development to another, later stages evolve from, rather than replace, earlier ones. Schemes developed in stage 1 are incorporated and improved on by the schemes constructed in stage 2, and so forth.

Providing an enriched environment is a powerful way to promote infants' and toddlers' overall development. Figure 9.5 identifies some of the essential elements of an enriched environment.

LANGUAGE DEVELOPMENT

Language development begins at birth. Indeed, some argue it begins before birth. The first cry, the first coo, the first "da-da" and "ma-ma," the first words are auditory proof that children are participating in the process of language development. Language helps define us as human and represents one of our most remarkable intellectual accomplishments. How does the infant go from the first cry to the first word a year later? How does the toddler develop from saying one word to several hundred words a year later? Although everyone agrees that children learn language, not everyone agrees how. How does language development begin? What forces and processes prompt children to participate in one of the uniquely human endeavors? Let us examine some of the explanations.

LANGUAGE ACQUISITION

Heredity plays a role in language development in a number of ways. First, humans have the respiratory and laryngeal systems that make rapid and efficient vocal communication possible. Second, the human brain makes language possible. The left hemisphere is the center for speech and phonetic analysis and the brain's main language center. But the left hemisphere does not have the exclusive responsibility for language. The right hemisphere plays a role in our understanding of speech intonations, which enables us to distinguish between declarative, imperative, and interrogative sentences. Without these processing systems, language as we know it would be impossible. Third, heredity plays a role in language development in that some theorists believe that humans are innately endowed with the ability to produce language.

THEORIES OF LANGUAGE DEVELOPMENT

Noam Chomsky is one proponent of the theory that humans are born with the ability to acquire language. He hypothesizes that all children possess a structure or mechanism called a *language acquisition device* (LAD) that permits them to acquire language. The young child's LAD uses all the language sounds heard to process many grammatical sentences, even sentences never heard before. The child hears a particular language and processes it to form grammatical rules.

Eric Lenneberg has studied innate language acquisition in considerable detail in many different kinds of children, including the deaf. According to Lenneberg,

All the evidence suggests that the capacities for speech production and related aspects of language acquisition develop according to built-in biological schedules. They appear when the time is ripe and not until then, when a state of what I have called "resonance" exists. The child somehow becomes "excited," in phase with the environment, so that the sounds he hears and has been hearing all along suddenly acquire a peculiar prominence. The change is like the establishment of new sensitivities. He becomes aware in a new way, selecting certain parts of the total auditory input for attention, ignoring others.[3]

The idea of a sensitive period of language development makes a great deal of sense and had a particular fascination for Montessori, who believed there were two such sensitive periods. The first begins at birth and lasts until about three years. During this time, children unconsciously absorb language from the environment. The second period begins at three years and lasts until about eight years. During this time, children are active participants in their language development and learn how to use their power of communication. Milestones of language development are listed in Table 9.3.

ENVIRONMENTAL FACTORS

While the ability to acquire language has a biological basis, the content of the language—syntax, grammar, and vocabulary—is acquired from the environment, which includes parents and other people as models for language. Development depends on talk between children and adults, and between children and children. Optimal language development ultimately depends on interactions with the best possible language models. The biological process may be the same for all children, but the content of their language will differ according to environmental factors. Children left to their own devices will not learn a language as well as children reared in linguistically rich environments.

Focus on Infant Care and Development

The period from birth to age five is a most critical period of life with respect to the rate of development. Children's physical and mental growth absorbs and reflects experiences with caregivers and their surrounding environments. Opportunities for meaningful learning must be brain compatible and developmentally appropriate both in practice and expectation. Our guiding vision of quality extends beyond the realm of good care, education, health, and safety, to the child's total development, including the relationship between each child and family within the context of their culture. Our approach deals with the whole child as an integrated entity and is responsive to their needs, desires, and initiatives.

We believe the four interrelated domains of early development (body, mind, person, and brain) highlight the central accomplishments of early childhood and underscore the obligations of our caregivers. Children are active participants in their own development together with the adults who care for them. For example, it is crucial for babies to feel good about themselves and think they are learning. We are excited about the things that our babies accomplish. We praise them for pulling up, crawling, waving, smiling, and any number of small accomplishments they make during the day. Babies thrive on the attention and look to the caregivers for their approval. They learn they can make things happen and are delighted that the teacher is excited about it, too!

The environmental considerations that we use to support individual development for infants are attachments, trust, mobility, senses, language, and health/safety.

- Attachment is a necessity for development and learning to occur. Comfortable chairs and floor areas encourage one-to-one interaction with babies and encourage attachment. Small group size and low teacher–child ratios also help promote attachment as

TABLE 9.3 Language Development in Infants and Toddlers

Months of Age	Language
Birth	Crying
1½	Social smile
3	Cooing (long pure vowel sound)
5	"Ah-goo" (the transition between cooing and early babbling)
5	Razzing (child places tongue between lips and produces a "raspberry")
6½	Babbling (repetition of consonant sounds)
8	"Dada/mama" (inappropriate)
10	"Dada/mama" (appropriate)
11	One word
12	Two words
14	Three words
15	Four to six words
15	Immature jargoning (sounds like gibberish; does not include any true word)
18	Seven to twenty words
18	Mature jargoning
21	Two-word combinations
24	Fifty words
24	Two-word sentences
24	Pronouns (*I, me, you*; used inappropriately)

Source: A. J. Capute and P. J. Accardo, "Linguistic and Auditory Milestones During the First Two Years of Life," Clinical Pediatrics 17(11)(November 1978), 848. Used by permission.

teachers interpret and meet the diverse needs of each child. Each infant has a primary caregiver. The selection of a primary caregiver is not driven by assignment but, rather, how the personalities draw the children and caregivers together.

- Trust is developed by the familiarity of the environment and by association with the same small group and with the same caregiver. A trusting relationship between child and caregiver is necessary for exploration and learning to occur. Additionally, predictable and consistent routines are used to nurture and create a feeling of security.
- Mobility is encouraged by allowing babies to play freely on the floor and protecting less mobile babies with soft barriers.
- Senses are stimulated with colorful and soft, safe toys. Care is taken to prepare the environment to avoid sensory overload.
- Language development is fostered by songs and rhythm, interesting objects, views outside, pictures, and experiences in which adults talk to infants. We recognize that before babies talk they do a lot of listening. We, too, listen to the sounds that infants are hearing and observe their body language; we then talk to the infants about how they are reacting to the sounds and about what they might be thinking.
- Health and safety awareness by all staff members is habit. Protection from physical danger and biological hazards is an obligation of caregivers to the children and families that we serve. We respect infants'

knowing what they need so we provide a safe environment for their natural development. Since we include children with disabilities throughout the center, it is not unusual to have a baby with a heart monitor or other equipment. Differences in the needs of our children are embraced as a natural part of life.

SUPPORTING PARENTS AND PARENTING NEEDS

We recognize and encourage the fact that the parent is the best teacher in the child's life. Relationships are more intense with parents of infants than with other children. A deeper level of trust is involved, and teachers have a more intimate relationship with infants. It is imperative that we communicate in a collaborative manner with parents rather than take the role of the expert. Feeding schedules, for example, are completed and updated by the parent or guardian stating foods to be given, along with preferred times and amounts. A daily feeding record is kept for each child, along with times of diaper changes. Notations of a child's activities for the day are also recorded. The collaboration with parents comes with a commitment to our part to create and maintain effective communication and good relationships with parents.

Contributed by Jeanne Roberts, Early Head Start Director and Debbie Moffitt, Education Coordinator, 0–5 classrooms, New Horizons Center for Children and Families, Macon County, North Carolina.

THE SEQUENCE OF LANGUAGE DEVELOPMENT

Regardless of the theory of language development we choose to adopt as our own, the fact remains that children develop language in predictable sequences, and they don't wait for us to tell them what theory to follow in their language development. They are very pragmatic and develop language regardless of our beliefs.

Baby Signing   Think of the number of ways you use signs—gestures to communicate a need or emotion. You blow a kiss to convey affection and hold your thumb and little finger to the side of your head to signal talking on the telephone. I'm sure you can think of many other examples. Now apply this same principle to young children. Children have needs and wants and emotional feelings long before they learn to talk. There is a growing movement of teaching children to use signs and gestures to communicate desires or signify objects and conditions. Beginning at about five months, babies can learn signals that stand for something else (e.g., a tap on the mouth for food, squeezing the hand for milk).

There is not universal agreement about whether to teach babies a common set of signs or to use ones that parents and children themselves make up. Linda Acredola and Susan Goodwyn, popularizers of baby signing, identify these benefits: It reduces child and parent frustration, strengthens the parent–child bond, makes learning to talk easier, stimulates intellectual development, enhances self-esteem, and provides a window into the child's world.[4]

Baby signing   Teaching babies to use signs or gestures to communicate a need or emotion.

First Words. Although the process of language development begins at the moment of birth, parents usually don't think of language as beginning until children say their first word. In a parent education session a young mother recently said to me, "Dr. Morrison, why should I talk to her when she can't talk to me?" Professionals have a responsibility to educate parents and other family members about the imperative of early language development. Children must have good language proficiency if they are to come to school ready to learn.

The first words of children are just that, first words. What are these first words? Children talk about people—dada, papa, mama, mummie, and baby (referring to themselves); animals—dog, cat, kitty; vehicles—car, truck, boat, train; toys—ball, block, book, doll; food—juice, milk, cookie, bread, drink; body parts—eye, nose, mouth, ear; clothing and household articles—hat, shoe, spoon, clock; greeting terms—hi, bye, night-night; and a few words for actions—up, no more, off.

Holophrasic Speech. Children are remarkable communicators without words. When children have attentive parents and professionals, they develop into skilled communicators, using gestures, facial expressions, sound intonations, pointing, and reaching to make their desires known and get what they want. Pointing at an object and saying, "uh-uh-uh" is the same as saying, "I want the rattle" or "Help me get the rattle." Responsive caregivers can respond by saying, "Do you want the rattle? I'll get it for you. Here it is!" One of the attributes of an attentive caregiver is the ability to read children's signs and signals, anticipating their desires even though no words are spoken.

The ability to communicate progresses from "sign language" and sounds to the use of single words. Toddlers are skilled at using single words to name objects, to let others know what they want, and to express emotions. One word, in essence, does the work of a whole sentence. These single-word sentences are called **holophrases.**

> **Holophrase** The single words (Up!, Doll!) children use to refer to what they see, hear, and feel.

The one-word sentences children use are primarily *referential* (used primarily to label objects, such as "doll"), or *expressive* (communicating personal desires or levels of social interaction, such as "bye-bye" and "kiss"). The extent to which children use these two functions of language depends in large measure on the professional and parent. For example, children's early language use reflects their mother's verbal style. This makes sense and the lesson is this: How parents speak to their children influences how their children speak.

Symbolic Representation. Two significant developmental events occur at about the age of two. First is the development of symbolic representation. Representation occurs when something—a mental image, a word—is used to stand for something else not present. A toy may stand for a tricycle; a baby doll may represent a real person. Words become signifiers of things—ball, block, blanket.

This ability frees children from the here and now, from acting on concrete objects present only in the immediate environment. It enables their thoughts to range over the full span of time—past and present—and permits them to remember and project thoughts into the future. Concrete objects, the things themselves, need not be present for children to act on them. The ability to represent liberates the child from the present. He can imagine things as separate from himself. In this regard, mental representation literally frees the child of space and time.

The use of mental symbols also enables the child to participate in two processes that are characteristic of the early years: symbolic play and the beginning of the use of words and sentences to express meanings and make references.

Vocabulary Development. The second significant achievement that occurs at about two is the development of a fifty-word vocabulary and the use of two-word sentences. This vocabulary development and the ability to combine words mark the beginning of rapid language development. Vocabulary development plays a very powerful and significant role in school achievement and success. Research repeatedly demonstrates that children who come to school with a broad use and knowledge of words achieve better than their peers who do not have an expanded vocabulary. Adults are the major source of children's vocabularies.

Telegraphic Speech.   You have undoubtedly heard a toddler say something like "Go out" in response to a suggestion such as "Let's go outside." Perhaps you've said, "Is your juice all gone?" and the toddler responded, "All gone." These two-word sentences are called **telegraphic speech.** They are the same kind of sentences you would use if you wrote a telegram. The sentences are primarily made up of nouns and verbs. Generally, they do not have prepositions, articles, conjunctions, and auxiliary verbs.

Motherese or Parentese.   Many recent research studies have demonstrated that mothers and other caregivers talk to infants and toddlers differently than adults talk to each other. This distinctive way of adapting everyday speech to young children is called **motherese,**[5] **or parentese.** Characteristics of such speech include the following:

- The sentences are short, averaging just over four words per sentence with babies. As children become older, the length of sentences mothers use also becomes longer. Mothers' conversations with their children are short and sweet.
- The sentences are highly intelligible. When talking to their children, mothers tend not to slur or mumble their words. This may be because mothers speak slower to their children than they do to adults in normal conversation.
- The sentences are "unswervingly well formed"—that is, they are grammatical sentences.
- The sentences are mainly imperatives and questions, such as "Give Mommie the ball," and "Do you want more juice?" Since mothers can't exchange a great deal of information with their children, their utterances are such that they direct their children's actions.
- Mothers use sentences in which referents ("here," "that," "there") are used to stand for objects or people: "Here's your bottle." "That's your baby doll." "There's your doggie."
- Mothers expand or provide an adult version of their children's communication. When a child points at a baby doll on a chair, the mother may respond by saying, "Yes, the baby doll is on the chair."
- Mother's sentences involve repetitions. "The ball, bring Mommie the ball. Yes, go get the ball—the ball—go get the ball."

Grammatical Morphemes.   There is more to learning language than learning words. There is also the matter of learning grammar. Grammar is the way we change the meanings of sentences and place events and action in time: past, present, and future tense. Grammatical morphemes are the principal means for changing the meanings of sentences. A *morpheme* is the smallest unit of meaning it is possible to have in a language. A morpheme can be a word, such as "no," or an element of a word, such as "-ed." A morpheme that can stand alone, such as "child," is a *free morpheme.* A morpheme that cannot stand alone is a bound morpheme. "Kicked" consists of the free morpheme "kick" and the bound morpheme "-ed." Morphological rules include the rules governing tenses, plurals, and possessives.

The order in which children learn grammatical morphemes is well documented. The pattern of mastery is orderly and consistent. The first morpheme to be mastered is the present progressive (I drinking), followed by prepositions (in and on), plural (two dolls), past irregular (toy fell), possessive (Sally's doll), uncontractible verb (there it is), articles (a block, the doll), past regular (Eve stopped), third-person regular (he runs), uncontractible auxiliary (I am going), contractible verb (that's a doll), and contractible auxiliary (I'm going).[6]

Negatives.   If you took a vote on the toddler's favorite word, "no" would win hands down. When children begin to use negatives, they simply add "no" to the beginning of a word or sentence ("no milk"). As their "no" sentences become longer, they still put "no" first ("no put coat on"). Later, they place negatives appropriately between subject and verb ("I no want juice").

When children move beyond the use of the one-word expression "no," the expression of negation progresses through a series of meanings. The first meaning conveys nonexistence, such as "no juice" and "no hat," meaning that the juice is all gone and the hat isn't present. The next level of negation is for the rejection of something. "No go out" is the rejection of

Telegraphic speech   Two word sentences (Milk gone!) that express actions and relationships.

Motherese (parentese)   The way parents and others speak to young children in a slow, high-pitched, exaggerated way. Also includes the use of short sentences and repetitions of words and phrases.

the offer to go outside. Next, the use of "no" progresses to the denial of something the child believes to be untrue. If offered a carrot stick under the pretense it is candy, the child will reply, "No candy."[7]

By the end of the preschool years, children have developed and mastered most language patterns. The basis for language development is the early years, and no amount of later remedial training can make up for development that should have occurred during this sensitive period for language learning.

Implications for Professionals. Professionals must attune themselves to children's developing language style and abilities. As children develop in their ability to use language, professionals can "mirror" that language back, adapting their way of talking to children in accordance with their growing use of language. Communicating with children provides a rich linguistic environment for children to learn language. Language that is short, direct, and grammatically correct supports children's efforts at language development. Expanding what the child says is also helpful.

Although it seems obvious to say that children can talk about what they know, some professionals act as though what they say to children makes little difference. Professionals should provide many experiences for children so they have something to talk about. Walks, encounters with other children and adults, field trips, and vicarious experiences through reading and technology all provide children with things to talk about. The other half of the equation, of course, is that children need professionals who will talk with them and provide opportunities for conversation. Having an opportunity to talk is as important as having something to talk about.

As noted earlier, children's first words are the names of things. Parents and professionals can teach children the names of things directly ("This is a ball") or indirectly ("Tell me what this is"). They can label, putting the name of the object on the object: "chair." They can use the names of things in their conversation with children ("This is a shoe; let's put your shoe on"). Children need to know the names of things if they are going to refer to them and talk about them.

The process of language development begins at birth—perhaps even before. What are some specific things parents, teachers, and caregivers can do to promote a child's language development?

Since children's first words are words for things, and since Piaget believed children need a mental representation of an object to match a name to it, it makes sense to give children experiences with real objects to lay the foundation for knowing their names. Experiences with toys, household objects, and people provide the basis for developing mental representations to which names can then be attached. On the other hand, a child whose environment lacks opportunities for experiences with real objects will have fewer mental representations and consequently a more limited vocabulary of the names of things.

Given the biological propensity for language development and the tremendous ability of children to learn language on their own even under the most difficult circumstances, there may be a tendency for some parents to treat language development with benign neglect and not do much to assist children with language acquisition. This approach is unfortunate and does a great disservice to children. The ability of children to teach themselves language flourishes best in a cooperative and supportive environment for language development.

Success in school is determined in part by how well children know and use language. Children who know the names of things, who can express themselves well, who can talk to the teacher, who understand the language of schooling, are children who, for the most part, will do well in school and life.

A high priority for early childhood professionals is to provide programs that support and facilitate children's language development. Providing children with professionals who are well trained and sensitive and responsive to children's language development is one place to start. Another is to provide a child–staff ratio that supports language development. For example, in a recent study of the effects of reduced child–staff ratio on children's development, researchers found that in programs with ratios of 1:4 for infants and 1:6 for toddlers, language proficiency improved dramatically from when ratios were higher.[8]

Figure 9.6 provides guidelines that will help you promote children's language development.

FIGURE 9.6 Promoting Language Development

- Treat children as partners in the communication process. Many infant behaviors, such as smiling, cooing, and vocalizing, serve to initiate conversation, and professionals can be responsive to these through conversations.

- Conversations are the building blocks of language development. Attentive and caring adults are infants' and toddlers' best stimulators of cognitive and language development.

- Talk to infants in a soothing, pleasant voice, with frequent eye contact, even though they do not "talk" to you. Most mothers and professionals talk to their young children differently from the way they talk to adults. They adapt their speech so they can communicate in a distinctive way called *motherese* or *parentese*. Mothers' language interactions with their toddlers are much the same as with infants. When conversing with toddlers who are just learning language, it is a good idea to simplify verbalization—not by using "baby talk," such as "di-di" for diaper or "ba-ba" for bottle, but rather by speaking in an easily understandable way. For example, instead of saying, "We are going to take a walk around the block so you must put your coat on," you would instead say, "Let's get coats on."

- Use children's names when interacting with them, to personalize the conversation and build self-identity.

- Use a variety of means to stimulate and promote language development, including reading stories, singing songs, listening to records, and giving children many opportunities to verbally interact with adults and other children.

- Encourage children to converse and share information with other children and adults.

- Help children learn to converse in various settings by taking them to different places so they can use their language with a variety of people. This approach also gives children ideas and events for using language.

- Have children use language in different ways. Children need to know how to use language to ask questions, explain feelings and emotions, tell what they have done, and describe things.

- Give children experiences in the language of directions and commands. Many children fail in school settings not because they do not know language but because they have little or no experience in how language is used for giving and following directions. It is also important for children to understand that language can be used as a means to an end—a way of attaining a desired goal.

- Converse with children about what they are doing and how they are doing it. Children learn language through feedback—asking and answering questions and commenting about activities—which shows children that you are paying attention to them and what they are doing.

- Talk to children in the full range of adult language, including past and future tenses.

Promoting children's language development constitutes one of the major goals of the early childhood field. Providing a language-rich context that supports children's language and literacy is one of the most important things you can do as an early childhood professional.

Infant Mental Health in a Cultural Context

Currently, there is a great deal of emphasis on social relations and their influences on infant mental health. Nonetheless, we must always remember that social relationships are affected by many other processes and contexts, including culture.

Virtually all contemporary researchers agree that children's development is a highly complex process that is influenced by the interplay of nature and nurture. The influence of nurture consists of the multiple, nested, contexts in which children are reared, including home, extended family, child care settings, community, and society, each of which is embedded in the values, beliefs, and practices of a given culture. The influence of nature is deeply affected by these environments and, in turn, shapes how children respond to their experiences.*

Consequently, it is wise for us to always consider and understand children's culture as we educate and socially interact with them. For example, the Afrocentric model of development encourages us to look at the African worldview and use this as a context to reflect on ways in which African-American parents and other family members may think, feel, and act as they relate to and rear their children. Such a perspective would also be helpful to understand how African-American parents set goals and guide developmental outcomes for their infants and toddlers.

1. *Spirituality,* or belief in a supreme being or supreme powers, goes beyond religiosity to focus on the qualities of people rather than material possessions. For example, when asked what they want for their children in the future, some African-American mothers may answer "to be happy" (a spiritual goal) rather than to "graduate from college" (a material goal).
2. *Communalism* or an interpersonal orientation reflects an emphasis on group over individual goals, an emphasis on cooperation rather than competition, and people-focused versus task-focused activities. Mothers with this orientation may place a high value on young children learning to share their toys or engaging in play activities that involve other children.
3. *Harmony* refers to the importance of integrating one's life into a whole, recognizing one's interdependency with the environment, and seeking unity rather than control.

To complete an acitivity related to the topic in the Diversity Tie-In, go to the Companion Website at **http://www.prenhall. com/morrison**, select chapter 9, then choose the Diversity Tie-In module.

IMPORTANCE OF LANGUAGE

I cannot emphasize enough the importance of providing all children a language-rich environment beginning at birth. When children are not provided with quality language experiences such as those we have discussed, they run the risk of falling behind their more linguistically advantaged counterparts, as Figure 9.7 so dramatically demonstrates. In addition, once children fall behind in any area of development, efforts to catch them up or close the gap are expensive in terms of resources and time. Read carefully the caption that accompanies Figure 9.7, as it emphasizes the consequences associated with high-quality and low-quality language experiences. This information about children's language experiences supports the necessity for parents and teachers to work together to create linguistically rich experiences for children.

PSYCHOSOCIAL AND EMOTIONAL DEVELOPMENT

PSYCHOSOCIAL DEVELOPMENT

We discussed Erik Erikson's Theory of Psychosocial Development in chapter 5. Review his theory as a preparation for this discussion. The first of Erikson's psychosocial stages, Basic

4. *Expressive communication or orality,* emphasizes transmitting and receiving information orally, through rhythmic communication and call and response.
5. *Sensitivity* to emotional cues reflects the integration of feelings with cognitions, and a synthesis of the verbal and nonverbal. For example, parents may signal children to alter their behaviors with a simple gesture or look.
6. *Rhythmic* movement is expressed in gross motor behavior and reflects an interest in flexible yet patterned action.
7. *Multidimensional perception,* or *verve,* is illustrated in the preference for stimulus variety in learning (e.g., visual, auditory, tactile, motor); both parent and child value experimentation.
8. *Stylistic expressiveness* refers to the valuing of the individual's unique style, flair, or spontaneity in expressing oneself (e.g., the way one walks, talks, or wears an article of clothing), but this value is emphasized only when it facilitates group goals.
9. *Time as a social phenomenon* reflects the view that time is spiritual, not material or linear. For example, an event begins when the first person arrives and ends when the last person leaves, rather than at fixed points on a clock. There is also recognition of the linkages of present time to the past and the future.
10. *Positivity* refers to the desire to see good in all situations, no matter how bad they seem on the surface. This positive perspective is thought to stop self-defeating behavior and generate positive problem-solving activity.[†]

As you consider how you can use the ten dimensions in your professional practice, keep in mind that they might not all apply to all African-American parents. Groups within the African-American society might have differences of opinion about any or all of these. It is important for you, therefore, to work closely and individually with all of your parents as you assess their cultural beliefs about parenting and education and the implications that they have for infant and toddler mental health, care, and education.

—————————
*D. A. Phillips, and J. P. Shonkoff, *From Neurons to Neighborhoods: The Science of Early Childhood Development* (Washington, DC: National Academy Press, 2000), 23–24.
[†]S. A. Koblinsky, and S. M. Randolph, "Zero to Three," *The Sociocultural Context of Infant Mental Health in African American Families,* vol. 22., no.1 (2001), 29–38.

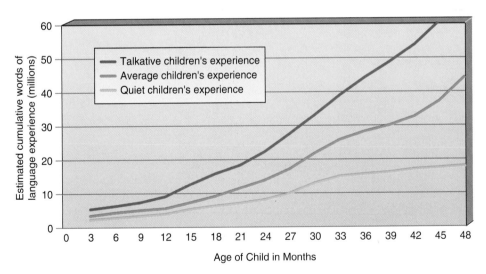

FIGURE 9.7 **Children's Language Experiences and Language Development**
The above shows the estimated cumulative number of words of children's total language experience, assuming fourteen waking hours per day, or approximately one hundred hours per week of experience time. As you reflect on the implications of this data, consider what the researchers had to say. "When we examined the children's practice, we discovered that a child's talkativeness grew rapidly until it matched that of the child's parents and then stopped increasing. In each family the child's talkativeness came to be similar to the family."

Charlie and Emma's Very, Very Good Day at the Bright Horizons Family Center

Imagine a warm, sunny, homey room—one part living room, one part playroom/laboratory for messy little scientists—and an adjacent, quiet, comfortable area for cribs and nursing moms. Small cozy spaces, pillows, a couch, places to be together with friends, places to be alone, places to use all your new motor skills, lots of good books, and abundant conversation. There are always laps, hugs, and smiles.

CHARLIE'S DAY

Twenty-two-month-old Charlie burst through the door, his dad trailing behind with eleven-month-old Emma in his arms. "Bunnies," he said excitedly to his teacher Alicia as he dumped his jacket in his cubby and climbed up next to her on the couch. They talked about his bunny sighting and waved Dad and Emma off. Alicia produced a book on bunnies, which he pored over while she greeted others.

Charlie's friends trickled in, and he and almost-preschooler Jerrod built and crashed walls with the brick blocks while waiting for breakfast. After a brief group get-together to welcome each other, sing, and talk about bunnies, new clothes, feeding the fish and the parakeet named Mr. Alejandro (don't ask), and other current events, Charlie's morning was spent experimenting with "chemistry and physics" with colored water and corks at the water table and a short visit to the infant room to spend time with Emma. He created a picture for Mom and moved around and over things, going in and out of the tent, "hiding" behind the couch, and spending forty-five minutes of wild abandon tearing about outdoors.

Of course, life has ups and downs—a bump on the knee, an unfortunate heated dispute with Jeremiah over a wagon that led to Charlie's temporary banishment from the path and redirection to the slide, enduring bossy five-year-old Ashley's proudly tying his shoe (Ashley already had the infallible air of the prom queen), and a short pout about not sitting next to Alicia at lunch. He almost re-

membered to go potty but was so busy, he didn't make it in time.

Lunch involved serious eating and silly discussions with Selena, who was teaching them some Spanish by speaking it to them, centering on, "Mi Madre takes me to." Charlie showed Nicholas how he could pour his own milk from the tiny pitcher into his cup. Then it was time for the one story and two poems they always read at nap, a successful trip to the potty, and nap. The nap recharged Charlie's batteries. Snack was ready for each child when he or she woke up, and then the group took a walk to find acorns and leaves for tomorrow's art. The rest of the afternoon was spent with Ashley and Nicholas playing with real pots, pans, and dishes. Best of all, Jerrod's 10-year-old brother read him a book on the couch after wrestling a bit with him. At 5:30 P.M. it was time to say good-bye and help Dad collect Emma.

EMMA'S DAY

What was the 352nd day of Emma's life like? After a weepy parting from Dad, she spent the day in "conversation"—great responsive language interactions. She explored the world with her mouth, nose, skin, and ears, and used her newfound skill of walking (actually, lurching about). She used the couch as a walking rail and a pull-me-up-space and had great delight using her whole body to explore the concepts of "over," "under," "around," "in," and "out" as she staggered and crawled around the room, over the footstool, under the table. She played peek-a-boo hiding in the big box. She splashed her fingers in the soapy tub of water with fourteen-month-old Keesha. She loved seeing her brother Charlie and survived his exuberant hug.

Between her three short naps, she ate lunch, lounged around with a bottle or two, and went for a buggy ride with Keesha, second favorite caregiver Tony, and two children from next door. She explored the damp grass and trees outside. Of course, Emma spent quite a bit of time being cared for by and endlessly "chatting" with her very special care-giver Kim, especially during the "prime times" of diapering and feeding. She was diapered three times with the requisite singing and tickle games and snuggled at least four or five times, reading picture books, rhyming, and having fascinating "conversations" as Kim talked about current events: the birds that they saw, the poop in her diaper, the water she drank, Charlie, and the zipper on her coat. She also watched closely as fourteen-month-old Nguyen and Tony did a fingerplay together.

Emma was busy. She "helped" Kim get the laundry out of the drier. Kim and Emma called Emma's mom to congratulate her for her new promotion. Emma cried after hearing her mom, as did her mom at the wonderful gesture, but it was still worth it. Of course she fussed quite a bit and had a fit when Keesha's dad got too close. She cried a little bit when Kim left. She also burst into tears when Dad arrived, delighted beyond words to have him back. She held him close as he discussed her day with Tony.

The relaxed but full day of Charlie and Emma left them ready to go home with enough energy to handle the rush of reuniting with mom, sharing Charlie's picture, and spending some good time together before beginning it all over again the next day.

DECONSTRUCTING THE VERY, VERY GOOD DAY

Taking what we know about the development of children and the development of families, this was an extraordinarily good day for Charlie and Emma.

Family

Emma and Charlie are developing the foundations of a relationship that will last two lifetimes. They each spend forty-five hours a week at the center. They need time together, and they get it. The family is also a strong presence: from Charlie helping Dad with Emma to his picture for Mom and Emma's phone call.

Responsive Interactions with Abundant Language

Charlie and Emma's days are filled with conversations with adults and other children. They aren't just talked to or at, questioned, or responded to. These are real give-and-takes, often initiated by a vocalization by the children. Their days are laced with books, poems, and singing.

Undivided Attention

There are a number of moments during the day when Charlie and Emma each have the undivided attention, the full human presence, of their primary caregiver—sometimes for chatting, sometimes for solace, and some-

times for helping them understand that group life has responsibilities. For that brief moment, the only thing in the world that matters is the interaction between the child and caregiver.

Exploration

Days are full of exploration inside and out, not only with toys but materials from real life and nature.

Relationships

Emma and Charlie spend the day in a community, not just a room with children just like themselves. They have relationships with older and younger children and adults throughout the center. When the beloved primary caregivers Vicki or Kim are out, it is still a secure place for them to be.

Teaching and Learning

Both Charlie and Emma learn from children and teach other children a thing or two.

Expectations

Charlie and Emma are respected as people and expected to behave appropriately. Charlie is learning social graces, and Emma is expected to fuss and cry as she navigates new waters.

Parent Partnership

Charlie and Emma's mother and father are members of the family center community and are respected as the experts on their children. The care Emma and Charlie receive is based on a thorough mutual understanding between the family and the caregivers and on ongoing communication.

Why a Very, Very Good Day?

It wasn't a great day because it wasn't smooth and care-free. There were accidents and tears, teapot tempests, and the sweet sorrow of parting from loved ones. But it was a very, very good day for Charlie and Emma because everything really important that they needed happened. We don't know whether it was a great day for all the other children. But Alicia, Selena, Tony, Kim, and all the staff work hard to try to make it great for *each* child and *each* family *every* day. When it all comes together, ain't life grand?

Contributed by Jim Greenman, Senior Vice President of Bright Horizons Family Solutions. This company operates more than 350 family centers in the United States, England, and Ireland.

To complete a Program in Action activity, visit the Companion Website at **http://www. prenhall. com/morrison**, select chapter 9, then choose the Program in Action module.

Trust vs. Basic Mistrust, begins at birth and lasts until about one-and-a-half to two years. For Erikson, basic trust means that "one has learned to rely on the sameness and continuity of the outer providers, but also that one may trust oneself and the capacity of one's organs to cope with urges."[9] The key for children developing a pattern of trust or mistrust depends on the "sensitive care of the baby's individual needs and a firm sense of personal trustworthiness within the trusted framework of their culture's life-style."[10]

Basic trust develops when children are reared, cared for, and educated in an environment of love, warmth, and support. An environment of trust also reduces the opportunity for conflict between child, parent, and caregiver.

SOCIAL BEHAVIORS

Social relationships begin at birth and are evident in the daily interactions between infants, parents, and teachers. Infants are social beings with a repertoire of behaviors they use to initiate and facilitate social interactions. *Social behaviors* are used by everyone to begin and maintain a relationship with others. Therefore, healthy social development is essential for young children. Regardless of their temperament, all infants are capable of social interactions and benefit from interactions with others.

Crying is the primary social behavior in infancy. It attracts parents or caregivers and promotes a social interaction of some type and duration, depending on the skill and awareness of the caregiver. Crying has a survival value. It alerts caregivers to the presence and needs of the infant. However, merely meeting the basic needs of infants in a perfunctory manner is not sufficient to form a firm base for social development. Parents and teachers must react to infants with enthusiasm, attentiveness, and concern for them as unique *persons.*

Imitation is another social behavior of infants. They have the ability to mimic the facial expressions and gestures of adults. When a mother sticks out her tongue at a baby, after a few repetitions, the baby will also stick out her tongue. This imitative behavior is satisfying to the infant. The mother is also pleased by this interactive game. Since the imitative behavior is pleasant for both persons, they continue to interact for the sake of interaction, which in turn promotes more social interaction. Social relations develop from social interactions.

ATTACHMENT AND RELATIONSHIPS

Bonding and *attachment* play major roles in the development of social and emotional relationships. **Bonding** is the process by which parents or teachers become emotionally attached or bonded to infants. It is the development of a close, personal, affective relationship. It is a one-way process. Some maintain that bonding occurs in the first hours or days after birth. **Attachment** is the enduring emotional tie between the infant *and* the parents and other primary caregivers. It is a two-way relationship.

Attachment behaviors serve the purpose of getting and maintaining proximity. They form the basis for the enduring relationship of attachment. Parent and teacher attachment behaviors include kissing, fondling, caressing, holding, touching, embracing, making eye contact, and looking at the face. Infant attachment behaviors include crying, sucking, making eye contact, babbling, and general body movements. Later, when the infant is developmentally able, attachment behaviors include following, clinging, and calling.

Adult speech has a special fascination for infants. Interestingly enough, given the choice between listening to music or listening to the human voice, infants prefer the human voice. This preference for the human voice plays a role in attachment by making the baby more responsive. Infants attend to language patterns they will later imitate in their process of language development. Babies move their bodies in rhythmic ways in response to the human voice. Babies' body movements and caregiver speech synchronize to each other. Adult speech triggers behavioral responses in the infant, which, in turn, stimulate responses in the adult, resulting in a "waltz" of attention and attachment. Today, the focus in studying infant social development is on the caregiver-to-infant relationship, not on the individuals as separate entities.[11]

Bonding   The parents' initial emotional tie to an infant.

Attachment   An enduring emotional tie between a parent/caregiver that endures over time.

Multiple Attachments.   Increased use of child care programs inevitably raises questions concerning infant attachment. Parents are concerned that their children will not attach to them. Worse yet, they fear that their baby will develop an attachment bond with their caregiver rather than with them. Children can and do attach to more than one person, and there can be more than one attachment at a time. Infants attach to parents as the primary teacher as well as to a surrogate, resulting in a hierarchy of attachments. The latter attachments are not of equal value. Infants show a preference for the primary caregiver, usually the mother. Parents should not only engage in attachment behaviors with their infants, they should also select child care programs that employ caregivers who understand the importance of the caregiver's role and function in attachment.

It is natural and desirable for child care workers to form attachments with infants. It is not at all uncommon for caregivers to have feelings of loss when "their" infants leave their care and go to the toddler room. One teacher said, "I've gone home many nights and cried about losing my infants to another teacher." Better by far for a teacher and infant to have a relationship that the caregiver can cry about when the attachment must physically and emotionally end than to have a caregiver indifferent to the importance of attachments and the need to let go.

High-quality child care programs help mothers maintain their primary attachments to their infants in many ways. The staff keeps parents well informed about infants' accomplishments. Parents should be allowed to "discover" and participate in infants' developmental milestones. A teacher, for example, might tell a mother that today her son showed signs of wanting to take his first step by himself. The teacher thereby allows the mother to be the first person to experience the joy of this accomplishment. The mother might then report to the center that her son took his first step at home the night before.

The Quality of Attachment.   The quality of infant–parent attachment varies according to the relationship that exists between them. A primary method of assessing the quality of parent–child attachment is the *Strange Situation*. The Strange Situation consists of observing and recording children's reactions to several events: a novel situation, separation from their mothers, reunion with their mothers, and reactions to a stranger. Based on their reactions and behaviors in these situations, children are classified into one of three groups. These groups are illustrated in Table 9.4.

The importance of knowing and recognizing different classifications of attachment is that you can inform parents and help them engage in the specific behaviors that will promote the growth of secure attachments.

Fathers and Attachment.   Fathers—and their roles as fathers in families—are a prominent part of early childhood education today. Many fathers have played important roles in child rearing and have engaged in shared and participatory parenting. Today, however, there is an increased emphasis on ways to encourage fathers to become even more involved in their families and in child rearing.

TABLE 9.4 **Individual Differences in Attachment Behaviors**

Attachment Classification	Behavioral Characteristics
Group A: Anxious-Avoidant	Avoids contact with mother after separation. Ignores attempts of mother to initiate interaction.
Group B: Secure	Presence of mother supports exploration and facilitates return to exploration after separation.
Group C: Anxious-Resistant	Resists contact with mother during reunion. Is not comforted by the presence of the mother after separation. Lack of exploration prior to separation.

Source: Mary Ainsworth et al., *Patterns of Attachment* (Hillsdale, N.J.: Erlbaum Associates, 1978).

Fathers who feed, diaper, bathe, and engage in other caregiving activities demonstrate increased attachment behaviors such as holding, talking, and looking. Early childhood educators can encourage fathers to participate in all facets of caregiving. Early childhood programs can conduct training programs that will help fathers gain the skills and confidence they need to assume their rightful places as co-parents in rearing responsible children.

TEMPERAMENT AND PERSONALITY DEVELOPMENT

Temperament A child's general style of behavior.

Children are born with individual behavioral characteristics that, when considered as a collective whole, constitute **temperament.** This temperament, what children are like, helps determine their personalities. The development of personality occurs as a result of the interplay of the particular temperament characteristics and the environment. The classic study undertaken to determine the relationship between temperament and personality development was conducted by Alexander Thomas, Stella Chess, and Herbert Birch.[12] They identified nine characteristics of temperament: level and extent of motor activity; rhythm and regularity of functions such as eating, sleeping, regulation, and wakefulness; degree of acceptance or rejection of a new person or experience; adaptability to changes in the environment; sensitivity to stimuli; intensity or energy level of responses; general mood (e.g., pleasant or cranky, friendly or unfriendly); distractibility from an activity; and attention span and persistence in an activity.

Thomas and his colleagues developed three classes or general types of children according to how these nine temperament characteristics clustered together. These types are the *easy child,* the *slow-to-warm-up child,* and the *difficult child,* as shown in Figure 9.8.

The importance of developing a match between children's temperament and the caregiver's child-rearing style cannot be overemphasized. This is particularly true in child care programs. In this sense, parenting is a process that extends beyond the natural parents to include all those who care for and provide services to infants. It is reasonable to expect that all who are part of this parenting cluster will accommodate their behavior to take infants' basic temperaments into account.

FIGURE 9.8 Children's Temperaments

What babies are like—their temperaments—help determine their personalities. Reflect on each of these three temperaments and provide examples for how temperament could affect the outcome of children's development.

Source: A. Thomas, S. Chess, and H. Birch, "The Origin of Personality," *Scientific American, 223* (August 1970), 102–109.

Easy Children

- Present few problems in care and training
- Positive mood
- Regular body functions
- Low or moderate intensity of reaction
- Adaptability and positive approach to new situations

Slow-to-warm-up

- Low activity level
- Slow to adapt
- Withdraw from new stimuli
- Negative mood
- Respond with low intensity

Difficult

- Irregular body function
- Tense reactions
- Withdraw from new stimuli
- Slow to adapt to change
- Negative mood

INFANT AND TODDLER MENTAL HEALTH

The early childhood profession has always emphasized the importance of providing for children's social and emotional development. One of the benefits of the recent research about the importance of early learning is the rediscovery that emotions and mental health play a powerful role in influencing development, especially cognitive development and learning. Think of your own emotions and how they influence your daily well being and approaches to learning. As you read this, if you are mad or angry, your attention is focused elsewhere and these words do not carry or convey the importance they could if you were happy, focused, and attentive. Now think about many of the stressful and traumatic events that affect children each day and how these have negative impacts on their lives. Consequently, there is growing attention to helping assure that all young children are reared and educated in environments that will assure their optimum mental health and well being, assuring that they will grow and develop and learn to their fullest potential. Figure 9.9 illustrates some causes for poor mental health in children; the outcomes associated with these; and some remedies available to you, early childhood professionals, community services providers, mental health experts, and others.

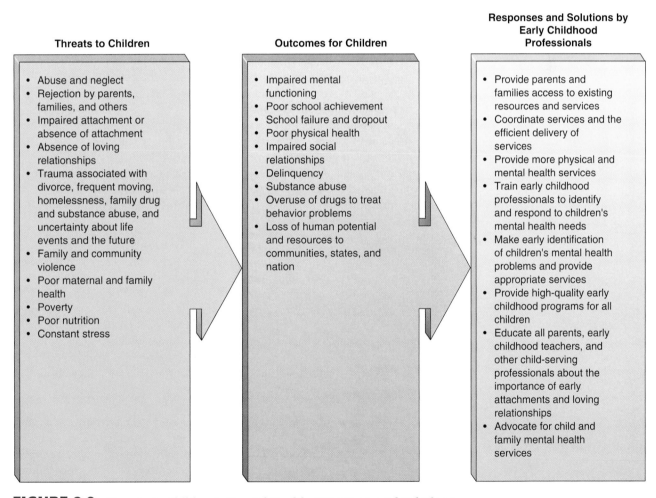

FIGURE 9.9   Threats to Children's Mental Health, Outcomes, and Solutions

With the national emphasis on infant mental health, it is important for you to be aware of the negative impact that risk factors can have on children's mental health. More important, you must take a leading role in helping to assure that all children have positive mental health outcomes.

Infant/toddler mental health
The overall health and well-being of young children in the context of family, school, and community relationships.

GROWTH OF INFANT MENTAL HEALTH MOVEMENT

The infant mental health movement represents a new direction in early childhood education. As a result, there is renewed interest in and a commitment to enhancing and supporting the mental health of infants and toddlers. While infant mental health has been an elusive concept, new efforts are underway to make it a central part of infant/toddler care and education. **Infant/toddler mental health** is the state of emotional and social competence in young children who are developing appropriately within the interrelated context of biology, relationships, and culture.[13]

There are a number of reasons for the growth of the infant mental health movement:

- There is growing realization by early childhood professionals that the life and education of children is holistic, not unidimensional. There has been a tendency in the early childhood profession to focus predominantly on a child's socioemotional development. Currently, there is a tendency to focus on a child's cognitive development. We know that we should educate children as whole beings and that we should provide them with comprehensive services that provide for physical, socioemotional, cognitive, and language needs.
- Brain research has enlightened the profession about how important relationships are in the growth and development of young children. It has demonstrated that high-quality early environments and nurturing relationships are essential for children's optimal development. For example:

  > The scientific evidence on the significant developmental impacts of early experiences, caregiving relationships, and environmental threats is incontrovertible. Virtually every aspect of early human development, from the brain's evolving circuitry to the child's capacity for empathy, is affected by the environments and experiences that are encountered in a cumulative fashion, beginning early in the prenatal period and extending throughout the early childhood years. The science of early development is also clear about the specific importance of parenting and of regular caregiving relationships more generally. The question today is not whether early experience matters, but rather how early experiences shape individual development and contribute to children's continued movement along positive pathways.[14]

- There is new and enhanced public awareness about how maternal–child relationships and caregiver–child relationships can and do affect children's mental health. For example, over the last decade, there has been renewed interest in maternal depression and the effects that maternal depression does have on children's development.
- Renewed interest in the early years has spotlighted how young children are affected by multiple risk factors in their lives, including maternal depression, abusive home environments, absence of fathers from the homes, parent and teacher stress (which influence relationships with children), and the lack of continuity of care in homes and child care programs. Figure 9.9 shows some of these risk factors, children's responses to them, and suggested interventions and outcomes.

As a result, the field of early childhood is witnessing burgeoning initiatives designed to help programs strengthen attachments between parents and children and caregivers/teachers and children, and to provide continuity of care for children from birth through grade 3. In chapter 11, we discuss *looping,* in which a teacher stays with the same children for one to three years. *Looping* is known as continuity of care for infants and toddlers. Some other methods for promoting continuity of care include screening teachers prior to hiring to determine their beliefs about the importance of relationships and how to best provide for them; having infants and toddlers and their caregivers "choose" each other to arrive at a "best fit" for each other; and providing help and support for grandparents who become the primary caregivers for infants and toddlers.

SOCIAL ENVIRONMENTS AND INFANT MENTAL HEALTH

Although there are many environments that influence children's development positively and negatively, the infant mental health movement focuses primarily on the social environment as the primary source of children's positive or negative mental health influences. This is why, today, there is a great deal of emphasis on the transactions, interactions, and relationships that exist between parents and a child. In a transactional model approach to providing for infant's mental health, emphasis is placed on developing and sustaining positive attachments and relationships between parent(s), child, and caregiver(s). For example,

Parents and other regular caregivers in children's lives are "active ingredients" of environmental influence during the early childhood period. Children grow and thrive in the context of close and dependable relationships that provide love and nurturance, security, responsive interaction, and encouragement for exploration. Without at least one such relationship, development is disrupted and the consequences can be severe and long-lasting. If provided or restored, however, a sensitive caregiving relationship can foster remarkable recovery.[15]

▲
When making decisions about child care, parents must consider five essential factors: the environment, quality professionals, staff–child ratios, the quality of care, and the curriculum.

QUALITY INFANT AND TODDLER PROGRAMS

DEVELOPMENTALLY APPROPRIATE PROGRAMS

Many issues I discuss in this book have implications for infant and toddler education. First is the issue of developmental appropriateness. All early childhood professionals who provide care for infants and toddlers—indeed, for all children—must understand and recognize this important concept, which provides a solid foundation for any program. The NAEYC defines *developmentally appropriate* as having three dimensions:

- What is known about child development and learning—knowledge of age-related human characteristics that permits general predictions within an age range about what activities, materials, interactions, or experiences will be safe, healthy, interesting, achievable, and also challenging for children;
- What is known about the strengths, interests, and needs of each individual child in the group to be able to adapt for and be responsive to inevitable individual variation; and
- Knowledge of the social and cultural contexts in which children live to ensure that learning experiences are meaningful, relevant, and respectful for the participating children and their families.[16]

Early childhood professionals must also understand the importance of providing programs for infants and toddlers that are uniquely different from programs for older children. NAEYC states the following about the necessity for unique programming for infants and toddlers:

For more information about Developmentally Appropriate Practice, go to the Companion Website at **http://www.prenhall.com/morrison**, select any chapter, then choose Topic 4 of the ECE Supersite module.

The First Three Years of Life

The Carnegie Corporation released a study of how important the first three years of life are for stimulation and nurturing and what being deprived of experiences and opportunities in those years can mean for the future of our children and our nation.

REFLECTIVE DISCUSSION QUESTIONS

Why is this such an important issue for professionals? for parents? How does poverty negatively influence children's environments and prevent them from fully developing in the early years?

REFLECTIVE DECISION MAKING

What are some things you can do to improve the quality of children's environments in the first three years of life? How can parents improve the quality of home environments? What are some things educators and parents can do to provide infants and toddlers with appropriate attention and stimulation?

Developmentally appropriate programs for children from birth to age 3 are distinctly different from all other types of programs—they are not a scaled-down version of a good program for preschool children. These program differences are determined by the unique characteristics and needs of children during the first three years:

- Changes take place far more rapidly in infancy than during any other period in life.
- During infancy, as at every other age, all areas of development—cognitive, social, emotional, and physical—are intertwined.
- Infants are totally dependent on adults to meet their needs.
- Very young children are especially vulnerable to adversity because they are less able to cope actively with discomfort and stress.

Infants and toddlers learn through their own experience, trial and error, repetition, imitation, and identification. Adults guide and encourage this learning by ensuring that the environment is safe and emotionally supportive. An appropriate program for children younger than three invites play, active exploration, and movement. It provides a broad array of stimulating experiences within a reliable framework of routines and protection from excessive stress. Relationships with people are emphasized as an essential contribution to the quality of children's experiences.[17]

Based on these dimensions, professionals must provide different programs of activities for infants and toddlers. This involves helping parents and other professionals recognize that infants, as a group, are different from toddlers and need programs, curricula, and facilities specifically designed for them. It is then necessary to design and implement developmentally appropriate curricula. The early childhood education profession is leading the way in raising consciousness about the need to match what professionals do with children to children's development as individuals. We have a long way to go in this regard, but part of the resolution will come with ongoing training of professionals in child development and curriculum planning.

Finally, it is important to match professionals with children of different ages. Not everyone is emotionally or professionally suited to provide care for infants and toddlers. Both groups need adults who can respond to their particular needs and developmental charac-

Develop a written plan based on these concepts:

1. Knowledge of child development
2. Program's philosophy and goals
3. Nature of children in program
4. Parent's beliefs, culture, and values

Develop a set of experiences:

1. Respect of individual children
2. Knowledge of individual children based on observation, screening, assessment, and parent information
3. Cultural practices
4. Materials needed

Implement curriculum:

1. Implement and adapt plans as appropriate based on needs of children.
2. Follow the lead of infants and toddlers in implementing and adjusting the curriculum to individual children and groups of children.

Evaluate curriculum:

1. Reflect on and renew the curriculum as appropriate, based on teaching and children's responses.
2. Have parents provide feedback regarding curriculum effectiveness and learning outcomes.

FIGURE 9.10 Planning and Implementing Infant/Toddler Curricula

Not everyone agrees that planning for infants and toddlers should be the linear process described here. They think that planning should be more circular; that is, planning is based on responses of child and teacher interactions. I believe planning is a combination of linear and circular processes.

teristics. Infants need especially nurturing professionals; toddlers, on the other hand, need adults who can tolerate and allow for their emerging autonomy and independence.

CURRICULA FOR INFANTS AND TODDLERS

Curricula for infants and toddlers consist of all the activities and experiences they are involved in while under the direction of professionals. Consequently, early childhood teachers plan for all activities and involvement: feeding, washing, diapering/toileting, playing, learning and having stimulating interactions, outings, being involved with others, having conversations, and providing appropriate and stimulating cognitive and language experiences. Professionals must plan the curriculum so it is developmentally appropriate. Figure 9.10 provides a process and sequence for planning infant and toddler curricula.

PROVIDING HEALTHY PROGRAMS FOR YOUNG CHILDREN

The spread of diseases in early childhood programs is a serious concern to all who care for young children. Part of the responsibility of all caregivers is to provide healthy care for all children. One of the most important things you can do to promote a healthy environment is to wash your hands properly.

Diapering is another prime vehicle for germ transmission. The spread of germs can be greatly reduced through the use of sanitary diapering techniques. It is imperative that sanitary procedures be followed while diapering children.

Montessori Under Three

"The most important period of life is not the age of University studies but the period from birth to 6 years . . . for this is the time when intelligence itself, its greatest implement, is being formed." Maria Montessori

Conceptually, the infant/toddler Montessori philosophy follows the method discussed in chapter 5, the Montessori method. It relies on the concept of profound respect for the child. A follower of Maria Montessori, Adele Costa Gnocchi, began the Assistance to Infancy program in Italy in 1947, training young girls in the knowledgeable care of the newborn. The girls would live with the families and transfer the practice of sensitive and respectful care of the infant to the parents and families of the newborn child.

Maria Montessori believed very strongly in the notion that we need to provide the most knowledgeable care to our infants because the first three years of life set the tone and foundation for all later learning.

THE INFANT PROGRAM

The teacher, environment, child dyad is crucial to the quality of any infant program but particularly to a Montessori infant program. By this I mean that a Montessori infant "community" has, as its core, a system in place to nurture the relationship of complex communication that supports the developing infant. It begins with the first visit of parents to the program. It is integral to the success of the program that parents are initially educated regarding Montessori educational philosophy. This keeps the care of the infant in a consistent pattern. The Montessori program requires that the mother and child spend at least a week transitioning in their infant. This period of time should precede the time when the mother returns to work. This is paramount to a smooth transition and separation between the child and mother. This reinforces a consistent basis regarding the care of the child between the parents and the Montessori program. Requiring the mother to spend time in the classroom provides two valuable exchanges. It provides the teacher an opportunity to observe the infant/mother pair. Through this observation the skilled teacher learns the cries of the infant

and how the mother responds to those cries. The teacher learns how the mother holds the infant and talks to her baby, and sees how this interchange of needs is met.

For the mother, having the opportunity to observe the teachers in action provides the basis for trust and good communication. It provides the very first steps in the mentoring process. The mother watches the gentle and respectful care of the other babies in the program and begins to learn by watching.

For the infant this transition time is crucial. The infant can adjust to the sounds and smells of a new environment under the safety of the mother's care. The infant is held and talked to by the teachers with the mother close by. The baby learns that in this place her needs will be met. The faces and movements of the new caregivers become more familiar and the baby has the opportunity to interact not only with the new teachers but also other babies as well. The visiting babies are also encouraged to nap in the program; this provides them with the experience of waking up in the new environment. As the babies adjust to the new environment, the mothers are encouraged to leave for short periods of time, thus allowing the babies to gradually adapt to the new environment.

Creating an environment where the infant feels comfortable and can trust the caregivers to meet her needs is very much a part of a Montessori infant program. What Montessori strives to create, is an environment where the child can maintain a calm interest in her world. The child can only do this if she feels a strong sense of security, comfort, and trust.

As stated previously, respect for the child is a crucial element in a Montessori environment. The way you talk to and touch infants shows respect. The Montessori infant teacher must take time with each infant as each activity deserves attention. It is not just a maintenance-based program where learning activities are saved for other times. Every activity is an opportunity for learning to take place. Diapering, dressing, and feeding offer opportunities for one-on-one interaction. It is also important that the teachers work "with" the children, not around them. Including the child in her care is vitally important. The Montessori infant teachers tell children what they are going to do before they do it. They also wait for infants to respond back. They do not swoop down on unsuspecting children to wipe a nose or pick them up to change a diaper. Teachers tell the infant, "I am going to pick you up." She holds her hands out and waits for the infant to respond with a smile, turn of the head, or lifted arms. Telling a child what you are going to do before you do it encourages infant participation.

The infant teachers must be able to interact in a knowledgeable and intimate way with the many different temperaments and characteristics that show themselves during the early development of the child. The knowledge base of the Montessori infant teacher includes not only child development and Montessori philosophy, but also an understanding of the variety of temperamental traits so the teacher can nurture the infant in gentleness of manner, speech, touch, and play. Because the relationship of the infant to the teacher is a vital part of the infant's development, the child is not moved to a new classroom during the first year. The infant is placed in the infant community starting at eight weeks and stays until the child is approximately eighteen months. The child is then transitioned into the toddler program slowly with many short visits with the infant's teacher along.

INFANT ENVIRONMENT AND ACTIVITIES

As educators recognize, different environments elicit different behaviors. We behave much differently in a church than we do in a sporting event. Children are also sensitive to their environments, so Montessori classrooms are set up with this sensitivity in mind. They are designed to encourage concentration, curiosity, and independence. The most noticeable difference between a Montessori environment and other high-quality child care centers is often the physical space—clean, sparse, and uncluttered. There are low shelves, mirrors, and low bars for pulling up on and a staircase with sidebars to encourage climbing. There are no high chairs, cribs, or exercise chairs for the infants. The infants are placed on the floor for complete freedom of movement. They sleep on low beds that afford them the opportunity to independently crawl into when they are tired and out of when they wake up. They are always held while given a bottle or placed in a low sling chair if they are being fed solid food.

If infants are sitting, they are placed on a tiny chair with a table. Infants are always fed one-on-one, with the baby and teacher facing each other. Natural wood materials are used when possible instead of plastic toys as we begin to teach the child an appreciation for natural beauty. Activities are carefully selected by the trained teacher and are arranged neatly on shelves, in baskets, or hung on hooks. This arrangement makes putting things away much more logical and enjoyable. The activities chosen reflect the knowledge base of the teachers and their ability to

clearly understand the developmental stage of each of the children in the program. Pictures are hung at the child's level and there are a variety of surfaces for the infant to crawl on and over. Babies are never propped up but are encouraged to move freely in the natural progression of development. The children's toys, identified as "work" in a Montessori program, are simple, clean, and carefully chosen. They are not placed on the shelves unless all the pieces are there. When people walk into an infant environment, they should get a feeling of peace and order. Because of the Montessori emphasis on adult–child relationships, adequate staffing is crucial. The ratio of teacher to child is 1:3, and often this is much lower than state laws require. This low ratio allows for close supervision and the ability of the teachers to not only observe but also keep detailed notes on each child's development. The teacher meets frequently with the parents, and formal conferences are held a minimum of four times a year. This provides a formal opportunity for the teacher and parent to further discuss the child's development and collaborate on any issues.

It is the desire of the Montessori infant program to provide a nurturing, knowledgeable, and safe environment. This is the environment that allows infants to be free to discover the beginning stages of independence, concentration, movement, self-esteem, and decision making. These are essential steps in the most formative stages of infants' development.

THE MONTESSORI TODDLER PROGRAM

It is often said that the toddler Montessori program is merely a "watered down" three- to six-year-old environment. It does share many similarities to the preschool classroom, as it takes into account the structure, routines, and organization of the Montessori preschool environment. It includes all the areas of the prepared preschool classroom including practical life activities, sensorial areas, art, math, language, and cultural studies. It incorporates the concepts of observation of the child and teaching the child by instruction, not by correcting. The environment for the toddler classroom must be sparse, with carefully chosen materials that call the child to work, concentration, and joy. A crowded or chaotic environment can cause stress and can dissipate a child's energy. The organization of the shelves, however, is also quite different from a three- to six-year-old environment. Toddlers are still in the preabsorbent stage of development, meaning they are learning from direct contact with the environment, taking in all that they see. Toddlers are often line-of-sight learners. They might be working with one activity but then see something else of interest and immediately drop what they are doing to go after the new activity. Children take in information through all of their senses without really knowing or controlling the input.

In this approach, toddlers learn the sequence of activities (i.e., we wash our hands before we eat, or we put our shoes on before we go outside). The organization of the activities on the shelves reflects this process. The toddlers are learning what Montessori referred to as the *work cycle*. That is, a child takes the activity off the shelf; the child plays with the activity and then puts the activity back on the shelf. Most toddlers can do one of these steps. There are some children who take all the work off the shelves, some who will only play with the work that is out, and some who only like to put the work away. As a child begins to move into a more cognizant stage of development, he or she begins to remember activities and where they are placed on the shelves. The toddler teacher will also complete the cycle of work for the child, modeling the desired behavior. The trained teacher will engage children just at the moment that they have finished with one work and have not quite chosen another activity. The teacher might say, for example, "Are you finished with this work? Would you like me to put it on the shelf, or would you like to do it?" Most toddlers like to do things for themselves and will readily put the work back. It does not take long for children even at this young age to begin to understand a cycle of activity. It is an amazing transformation to watch. One parent said, "I had no idea that my child was capable of this type of sequential thinking until I watched him freely choose activities and then place them back on a shelf when

he was finished, and he was only twenty-three months old." Her love and joyfulness was clearly evident.

This particular organization leads the toddler environment into an organized peaceful place where the children are allowed to freely explore.

RESPECT, COMMUNICATION, AND ROUTINES

Teachers engage in respectful communication with toddlers. The teacher always tells children what is expected before actually assisting. Children are told what the teacher wants them to do, rather than being told what not to do. For example, instead of saying, "Don't climb on the chair," the teachers says, "The chairs are for sitting; if you want to climb, you can play on the stair climber." Teachers are also trained to wait for toddlers to process the request or solve the problem on their own. Toddlers love the struggle of an activity. They enjoy dragging heavy objects across the room or working in an extremely concentrated focus on completing a puzzle. Adults, however, want to relieve the child of any struggle and will quickly jump in and help the child. This often robs the child of the wonderful feeling of accomplishment. It is part of the Montessori philosophy for the teacher to wait a moment, observing closely, to see if the child can solve the problem independently. Toddlers will give the teacher signals when they need help. Montessori toddlers are taught to ask for help when they are in need, with words or gestures. For example, if a child is struggling to sit in a chair, the teacher will not go over and pick the child up, place the child on the chair, and push the chair in. The teacher will wait to see what the child will do. Can the child solve the problem? If not, the teachers will say, for example, "Joshua, if you would like me to help you, you can say, 'Help me please.'" After many repetitions, children begin to understand how to elicit help without crying. Children are allowed the freedom to solve difficulties, and the teachers are able to discover how different children process information and learn to find solutions.

In a Montessori toddler program, it is important to have consistent routines for the children. Children need to know what is going to happen next. This knowledge helps children to feel safe and secure. The teachers have planned transitions between one activity and the next. For example, if it is time for the children to clean up and have a short circle time, the teachers will sing a song or ring a bell to signal the children that the circle time is about to begin. When this pattern is repeated many times, the children begin to understand that the bell means that we are getting ready to have a circle time. The length of time the children spend in each activity during the day can vary somewhat, but the order must remain the same. The following is an example of a Montessori toddler program schedule:

8:30–8:45 Children arrive, greetings are exchanged, and the children transition from parent to classroom.

8:45–9:45 The children are individually choosing activities throughout the classroom. The teacher is free to work with each child individually.

9:45 Bell rings or a song is sung. The children complete the work that they are doing, clean up, and come to the circle. The teacher has already put out a special rug to indicate that it is circle time.

9:45–10:00 Circle time; songs, finger plays, dance, or stories are used.

10:00–Transition time; Children are released *individually* for toileting or to wash hands for snack, or to prepare the table for eating. Toileting is also done throughout the morning as needed.

10:15–10:45 Children serve their own snack and sit at the table with the teacher. The room is peaceful, with soft music playing. Food is not just put in front of the children with the teacher standing. It is served family style with the children serving themselves. The children also learn to pour their own juice from small pitchers into small glasses. The children clean up their own dishes, scraping the food off of the dishes and placing them into bins for washing. As children finish, they go to their cubbies to begin dressing for outside play.

10:45–11:15 Outside time, or if weather does not permit, inside gross motor time; this includes singing, dance, or stories.

11:15–11:30 Children gather together to come inside, take off coats, have circle time for a story, and say good-bye.

At every point during the morning, children are involved in self-help activities. Eating, dressing, washing, and cleaning up are all part of the curriculum for a toddler. The toddlers actively participate in all the routines of the classroom, and delight in these chores is apparent in their level of concentration. The choice of activities is not as important as the level of concentration. Deep concentration can occur while stringing beads, washing a table, or just digging in the sand. The Montessori toddler environment is created to foster work. When a child begins to concentrate on an activity, that child is protected from interruption by the teacher. This protection affords the child the chance to experience focused concentration and thus balance and happiness.

Sharing activities is also something that is taught gradually. A child is allowed to work on an activity without interruption for as long as that child needs to. If another

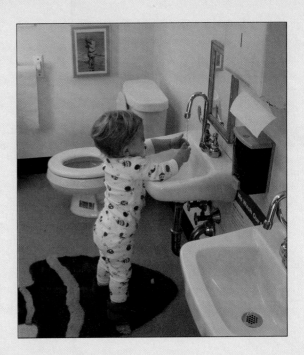

would like to work with an activity that is already being used, the child is asked by the teacher to wait until the other child is finished. The teacher then reorients the child to another activity. As the children acquire language, they are taught to ask first if they can join a child who is already engaged in an activity. What happens as the first few months of the year progress is that the children begin to respect each others' work time. You will see many times during the morning when a child, after finishing with a work, will find the child who wanted to use the activity next and tell him or her that it is that child's turn. The respectful nature of the teacher–child relationship is modeled and thus passed on in the child–child relationship. Grace and courtesy are very important lessons that are taught in this manner in the toddler programs.

The child's reasons for, and approach to, work are very different compared to an adult's. Adults carry out a task in a quick and efficient manner. A child is working to master the activity and to practice and perfect abilities. Through repetition and concentration in the activity, a toddler begins to learn independence. Independence in thought and action leads the child to intelligent choice and responsibility at all ages.

Text and photos contributed by Elizabeth Stone, Director, Infant and Toddler Program, Harborlight Montessori School, Beverly, Massachusetts.

To complete a
Program in Action
activity related to
Montessori schools,
visit the Companion
Website at **http://www.
prenhall.com/morrison**,
select chapter 9, then choose
the Program in Action module.

COMMUNITY COLLABORATION

It is difficult for many families to provide for the total health needs of their children. Because families sometimes need help in rearing healthy children, communities in which these children live should also help in this regard. Through collaboration, it is possible to make healthy living a reality for all children. In many communities around the country, the public health community has combined efforts with the early childhood community in order to create the best care for children. Healthy Child Care America is an excellent example of this community collaboration in action.

The American Academy of Pediatrics coordinates the Healthy Child Care America campaign in partnership with the U.S. Department of Health and Human Services Child Care Bureau and the Maternal and Child Health Bureau. Healthy Child Care America is based on the principle that, through partnerships, families, child care providers, and health care providers can promote the healthy development of young children in child care and increase access to preventive health services and safe physical environments for children. Linking health care providers, child care providers, and families makes good sense—for maximizing resources, for developing comprehensive and coordinated services, and, most important, for nurturing children.

Goals of Healthy Child Care America include the following:

- Safe, healthy child care environments for all children, including those with special health needs
- Up-to-date and easily accessible immunizations for children in child care
- Access to quality health, dental, and developmental screening and comprehensive follow-up for children in child care
- Health and mental health consultation, support, and education for all families, children, and child care providers
- Health, nutrition, and safety education for children in child care, their families, and child care providers[18]

BLUEPRINT FOR ACTION

The purpose of the *Blueprint for Action* part of Healthy Child Care America is to provide communities with steps they can take to either expand existing public and private services and resources or to create new services and resources that link families, health care, and child care. Communities using *Blueprint for Action* are encouraged to identify their own needs and to adapt the ten steps as needed. The steps are not prioritized; communities can determine which step(s) should be implemented. The ten steps are as follows:

1. Promote safe, healthy, and developmentally appropriate environments for all children in child care.
2. Increase immunization rates and preventive services for children in child care settings.
3. Assist families in accessing key public and private health and social service programs.
4. Promote and increase comprehensive access to health screenings.
5. Conduct health and safety education and promotion programs for children, families, and child care providers.
6. Strengthen and improve nutrition services in child care.
7. Provide training and ongoing consultation to child care providers and families in the areas of social and emotional health.
8. Expand and provide ongoing support to child care providers and families caring for children with special health needs.
9. Use child care health consultants to help develop and maintain healthy child care.
10. Assess and promote the health, training, and work environments of child care providers.[19]

There are no quick and easy solutions to the challenges that families, child care providers, and health care providers face today in providing for and ensuring the healthy development of children. It is important that these three groups work together to expand and create partnerships. *Blueprint for Action* will help communities as they set priorities and goals that will lead to healthier child care in America.

Infants and toddlers are interesting and remarkably competent individuals. The developmental and educational milestones of these years are the foundations of all that follow throughout life. All professionals must use their knowledge, understanding, energy, and talents to assure that this foundation is the best it can be.

To take an online self-test on this chapter's contents, go to the Companion Website at **http://www. prenhall.com/morrison**, select chapter 9, then choose the Self-Test module.

ACTIVITIES FOR FURTHER ENRICHMENT

APPLICATIONS

1. You have been asked to speak to a group of parents about what they can do to promote their children's language development in the first two years of life. Outline your presentation and list five specific suggestions you will make.
2. Observe children between the ages of birth and eighteen months. Identify the six stages of sensorimotor intelligence by describing the behaviors you observed. Cite specific examples of secondary and tertiary reactions. For each of the six stages, develop two activities that would be cognitively appropriate.
3. Why is motor development important in the early years? What are five activities you can include in your program to promote motor development?
4. Identify at least ten games or activities that are beneficial to the developing infant and the growing toddler. Describe the benefits of each of the games or activities you list.

FIELD EXPERIENCES

1. Visit at least two programs that provide care for infants and toddlers. Observe the curriculum to determine whether it is developmentally appropriate. What suggestions would you make for improving the curriculum? Explain what you liked most and least about the program.
2. Visit centers that care for young children of different cultures. List the differences you find. What role does culture play in how we care for and educate children?

RESEARCH

1. In addition to the qualities cited in this chapter, list and explain five other qualities you think are important for professionals caring for infants and toddlers.
2. Identify customs that are passed down to infants and toddlers as a result of the family's cultural background. How do these customs affect young children's behavior?
3. Interview professionals who care for infants and toddlers. How are their rules similar and different? Which age group would you prefer to care for? Why?

READINGS FOR FURTHER ENRICHMENT

For additional Internet resources or to complete an online activity for this chapter, go to the Companion Website at **http://www. prenhall.com/morrison**, select chapter 9, then choose the Linking to Learning or Making Connections module.

Eliot, L. *What's Going on in There?: How the Brain and Mind Develop in the First Five Years of Life.* New York: Bantam Books, 2000.

This book covers brain biology, influences, and how certain faculties are acquired and enhanced.

Golinkoff, R., and Pasek-Hirsh, K. *How Babies Talk: The Magic and Mystery of Language in the First Three Years of Life.* New York: Dutton, 1999.

The culmination of years of research, this text explains exactly how babies learn language in the first years of life. Outlines the milestones babies reach and how parents can help their babies reach them.

Herschkowitz, E. C., Herschkowitz, N., and Kagan, J. *A Good Start in Life: Understanding Your Child's Brain and Behavior.* Malden, MA: Joseph Henry Press, 2002.

This book aims to reduce the stress, compiling basic information about child development from conception to age six in one concise book. Written by a neuroscientist and an educator, there is information about the physical stages of early childhood.

Jellinek, M. *Bright Futures in Practice: Mental Health.* Washington, DC: Georgetown University Press, 2002.

A two-volume set considering the mental health of children in a developmental context, presenting information on early recognition and intervention for specific mental health problems and mental disorders, and providing a tool kit with hands on tools for health professionals and families for use in screening, care management, and health education.

Karr-Morse, R. *Ghosts from the Nursery: Tracing the Roots of Violence.* Poulsbo, WA: Grove/Atlantic, 1999.

Cutting to the heart of the alarming trend of violence committed by children, Ghosts from the Nursery *gives startling new evidence that violent behavior is fundamentally linked to abuse and neglect in the first two years of life. Makes a convincing case for the revolution in our beliefs about the care of babies.*

Kreuger, A. *Parenting Guide to Your Baby's First Year.* New York: Ballantine Books, 1999.

With its timely, in-depth advice and hands-on guidance, Parenting *magazine brings you a comprehensive, up-to-the-minute guide to the all-important first year of your baby's life.*

Shonkoff, J. P. *From Neurons to Neighborhoods: The Science of Early Childhood Development.* Washington, DC: National Academy Press, 2000.

Psychiatrists, psychologists, pediatricians, and other experts in child development reviewed research from numerous disciplines covering the period from before birth until the first day of kindergarten. Their study includes efforts to understand how early experiences affect neurological, social, and cultural aspects of development.

Warner, P. *Baby Play and Learn.* New York: Simon & Schuster, 1999.

A child development expert offers 160 specific suggestions for games and activities that will provide hours of development challenges and rewards for babies and parents.

LINKING TO LEARNING

I Am Your Child Foundation
http://www.iamyourchild.org/

A national public awareness and engagement campaign to make early childhood development a top priority for our nation, I Am Your Child has educated millions of parents and professionals about breakthrough new discoveries in the process of brain development.

KidSource OnLine for Healthcare
http://www.kidsource.com/kidsource/pages/Health.html

Health care articles, online forums, and websites concerning the proper care of young children.

Zero to Three
http://www.zerotothree.org/

Concentrates exclusively on the miraculous first years of life, the critical period when a child undergoes the greatest human growth and development. Zero to Three's mission is to develop a solid intellectual, emotional, and social foundation for young children.

About Brain Injury: A Guide to Brain Anatomy
http://www.waiting.com/brainanatomy.html

Provides areas, functions, and associated signs and symptoms of the brain.

The Brain Store
http://www.thebrainstore.com
Revolutionary discoveries suggest how we can make changes to improve education, training, and our personal lives.

Early Brain Development: What Parents and Caregivers Need to Know
http://www.educarer.org/brain.htm
Presents facts about early brain development that parents and educarers need to know.

Brain Development in Infants and Toddlers: Information for Parents and Caregivers
http://www.nccic.org/cctopics/brain.html
A resource list that provides an overview of resources available concerning the brain.

ENDNOTES

[1] Kuhl, P. *Early Language Acquisition: The Brain Comes Prepared,* Parents as Teachers National Center (1996). Available at http://www.patnc.org/neuroforum.htm.

[2] Huttenlocher, J. "Language Input and Language Growth," *Preventive Medicine: An International Devoted to Practice and Theory* 27, no. 2 (March–April 1998), 195–199.

[3] Lenneberg, Eric H. "The Biological Foundations of Language," in Mark Lester, ed., *Readings in Applied Transformational Grammar* (New York: Holt, Rinehart & Winston, 1970), 8.

[4] Acredolo, L., and Goodwyn, S. *Baby Signs: How to Talk with Your Baby before Your Baby Can Talk* (Chicago: Contemporary Books, 1996).

[5] Newport, E. L."Mother, I'd Rather Do It Myself: Some Effects and Non-effects on Maternal Speech Style," in C. E. Snow and C. A. Ferguson, eds., *Talking to Children* (Cambridge, England: Cambridge University Press, 1977), 112–129.

[6] Brown, R. *A First Language* (Cambridge, MA: Harvard University Press, 1973), 281.

[7] Bloom, L. *Language Development: Form and Function in Emerging Grammars* (Cambridge, MA: MIT Press, 1970).

[8] Portner, J. "Two Studies Link High-Quality Day Care and Child Development," *Education Week* (19 April 1995), 6.

[9] Bredekamp, Sue and Copple, Carol, eds. *Developmentally Appropriate Practice in Early Childhood Programs,* rev. ed. (Washington, DC: National Association for the Education of Young Children, 1997), 9.

[10] Erikson, Erik. *Childhood and Society,* 2nd ed. (New York: Norton, 1963 (first pub. 1950), 249).

[11] Erikson, *Childhood,* 249.

[12] Thomas, A. Chess, S. and Birch, H. "The Origin of Personality," *Scientific American* (1970), 102–109.

[13] Zeanah Jr., Charles J. "Zero to Three," *Towards a Definition of Infant Mental Health* 22, no. 1 (2001), 13–20.

[14] Phillips, D.A. and Shonkoff, J.P. *From Neurons to Neighborhoods: The Science of Early Childhood Development* (Washington, D.C.: National Academy Press, 2000), 6.

[15] Ibid. 7.

[16] Bredekamp, Sue and Copple, Carol, eds. *Developmentally Appropriate Practice in Early Childhood Programs,* rev. ed. (Washington, DC: National Association for the Education of Young Children, 1997), 9.

[17] National Association for the Education of Young Children, *Developmentally Appropriate Practice in Early Childhood Programs Serving Infants* (Washington, DC: Author, 1989), no. 547.

[18] National Child Care Information Center, "Healthy Child Care America." (May 1995). Available at http://nccic.org/hcca/abthcca.html.

[19] National Child Care Information Center, "Healthy Child Care America Blueprint for Action." (May 1995). Available at http://nccic.org/hcca/action.html.

Chapter 10

Some say the ground is uneven, and that more trees grow in the fertile ground than in the rocky ground. But look around you. Look in our urban centers. There are schools across America who face all the major challenges and still succeed. If they can do it, all of us can do it. Once we know that trees can grow in rocky ground, we have no excuse for not planting them.

—ROD PAIGE, U.S. SECRETARY OF EDUCATION

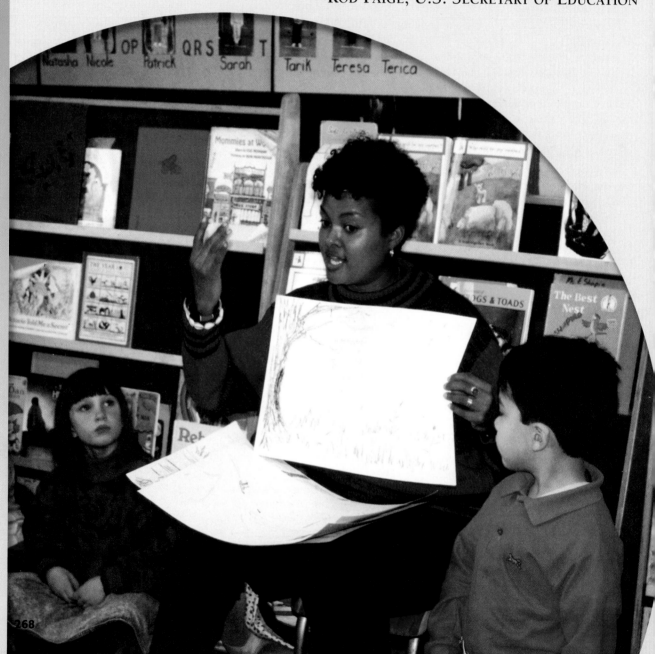

The Preschool Years

Getting Ready for School and Life

E arly childhood professionals view the events of the preschool years as the cornerstone of later learning. The road to success in school and life begins long before kindergarten or first grade. The preschool years have assumed a more important place in the process of schooling. For many children, the preschool years are the beginning of a period of at least fourteen years during which their lives will be dramatically influenced by teachers and schooling. As a result, the preschool years are playing a more important role in the education process than at any time in history. The preschool years will continue to be the focus of public attention and financial support. For example, Florida voters recently passed a state constitutional amendment that provides for universal preschool beginning in 2005.

WHAT IS PRESCHOOL?

For our purposes, preschools are programs for three- to five-year-old children, before they enter kindergarten. Today it is common for many children to be in a school of some kind beginning as early as age two or three, and child care beginning at six weeks is commonplace for children of working parents. Thirty-nine states and the District of Columbia currently invest in preschool education, whether as public preschools or as support for Head Start. Since 1997, New York has provided free early childhood education to every four-year-old whose parents want it. In Georgia, preschool programs are provided for all children. In 1999, the states spent more than $1.9 billion on preschool care and education. Preschool education continues to grow, with greater numbers of four-year-olds entering preschools. Currently, about 2.2 million three- to five-year-old children are in some kind of preschool program.

Focus Questions

- Why are the preschool years so important?

- What are the characteristics of preschoolers' growth and development?

- Why and how are preschools so popular?

- What is the role of play in children's learning?

- How and why is the preschool curriculum changing?

- What are the important issues concerning preschool programs?

To review the chapter focus questions online, go to the Companion Website at **http://www. prenhall.com/morrison**, and select chapter 10.

WHY ARE PRESCHOOLS GROWING IN POPULARITY?

To check your understanding of this chapter with the online Study Guide, go to the Companion Website at **http://www. prenhall.com/morrison**, select chapter 10, then choose the Study Guide module.

A number of reasons help explain the current popularity of preschool programs. They include the following:

- Many parents are frustrated and dissatisfied with efforts to find quality and affordable care for their children. They view public schools as the agency that can and should provide care and education for their children.
- With changing attitudes toward work and careers, more parents are in the workforce. Additionally, many parents believe it is possible to balance family and career. This in turn places a great demand on the early childhood profession to provide more programs and services, including programs for three- and four-year-olds.
- Parents, public policy planners, and researchers believe intervention programs designed to prevent such social problems as substance abuse and the incidence of school dropout work best in the early years. Research supports the effectiveness of this early intervention approach. Quality early childhood programs help prevent and reduce behavioral and social problems.
- With growing concern on the part of corporations and businesses about the quality of the American workforce, business leaders see early education as one way of developing literate workers. Many preschool programs include work-related skills and behaviors in their curriculum. For example, learning how to be responsible and trustworthy are skills that are learned early in life. Likewise, being literate has its foundations in the early years as well.
- Advocacy exists for publicly supported and financed preschools as a means of helping ensure that all children and their families, regardless of socioeconomic background, are not excluded from the known benefits of attending quality preschool programs. Given that more than 16 percent of American children live in poverty (11.6 million in 2000) and that more than 8 percent are disabled, affordable quality programs have the potential to serve as an important avenue for positive social change.[1]
- It is becoming widely understood that the foundation for learning is laid in the early years and that three- and four-year-old children are ready, willing, and able to learn.
- The National Research Council concluded in its recent study, *Eager to Learn: Educating our Preschoolers,* the last thirty years of child development research demonstrate that "two- to five-year-old children are more capable learners than had been imagined, and that their acquisition of linguistic, mathematical, and other skills relevant to school readiness is influenced (and can be improved) by their educational and developmental experiences during those years."[2]
- From birth to age five, children rapidly develop foundational capabilities on which subsequent development builds. In addition to their remarkable linguistic and cognitive gains, they exhibit dramatic progress in their emotional, social, regulatory, and moral capacities. These critical dimensions of early development are intertwined, and each requires focused attention.[3]
- Politicians see the implementation of high-quality early childhood programs as one means of supporting and reforming K–12 education.

For more information about preschools, go to the Companion Website at **http://www. prenhall.com/morrison**, select chapter 10, then choose the Linking to Learning module to connect to several preschool sites.

As preschool programs have grown in number and popularity over the last decade, they have also undergone significant changes in purposes. Previously, the predominant purposes of preschools were to help socialize children, enhance their social-emotional development, and get them ready for kindergarten or first grade. Today there is a decided move away from socialization as the primary function for preschooling. Preschools are now promoted as places to accomplish the following goals:

- Support and develop children's innate capacity for learning. The responsibility for "getting ready for school" has shifted from being primarily children's and parents' responsibilities to being a cooperative venture among child, family, home, schools, and communities. Review again the information on the importance of early learning for brain development discussed in chapter 9. The same reasons for providing early education to infants and toddlers also apply to preschool children and their curriculum.

- Use the public schools as a centralized agency to deliver services at an early age to all young children and their families.
- Deliver a full range of health, social, economic, and academic services to children and families. Family welfare is also a justification for operating preschools. In fact, increasingly, preschool education is seen as a family affair as I have and will repeatedly discuss.
- Solve or find solutions for pressing social problems. The early years are viewed as a time when interventions are most likely to have long-term positive influences. Preschool programs are seen as ways of lowering the number of dropouts, improving children's health, and preventing serious social problems such as substance abuse and violence.
- Promote early literacy and math and readiness for reading and future school achievement.
- Prepare children to read. An increasing proportion of children in U.S. schools, particularly in certain school systems, are considered learning disabled; most of the children are so identified because of reading difficulties. Failure to learn to read adequately for continued school success is especially likely among poor children, members of racial minority groups, and children whose native language is not English. Achieving educational excellence for all requires an understanding of why these disparities exist, as well as serious, informed efforts to redress them.[4]

Given the popularity of and goals for preschool, it is little wonder that the **preschool years** are playing a larger role in early childhood education and will continue to do so.

Preschool years The period from three to five years of age before children enter kindergarten during which many children attend preschool programs.

WHAT ARE PRESCHOOLERS LIKE?

Today's preschoolers are not like the children of previous decades. Many have already attended one, two, or three years of child care or nursery school. They have watched hundreds of hours of television. Many are technologically sophisticated. Many have experienced the trauma of family divorces or the psychological effects of abuse. Both collectively and individually, the experiential backgrounds of preschoolers are quite different from those of previous generations. You and other early childhood professionals must understand precisely the impact and implications of this background to effectively meet preschoolers' needs and teach them effectively and well.

We have stressed the importance of the individuality of each child while at the same time understanding them in the context of the commonalities of development for all children. Within this context of individuality of consequences and developmental commonalities, introduce yourself to four preschoolers who are similar and different in The Portraits of Preschoolers. Answer the questions that accompany the portraits and reflect about how you would meet the needs of these children if they were in your classroom.

For more information about preschoolers' development, go to the Companion Website at **http://www.prenhall.com/morrison**, select any chapter, then choose Topic 2 of the ECE Supersite module.

PHYSICAL AND MOTOR DEVELOPMENT

Understanding preschoolers' physical and motor development enables you to acknowledge why active learning is so important. To begin with, a noticeable difference between preschoolers and infants and toddlers is that preschoolers have lost most of their baby fat and taken on a leaner, lankier look. This "slimming down" and increasing motor coordination enables them to participate with more confidence in the locomotor activities so vitally

PORTRAITS OF PRESCHOOLERS

José

Introduce yourself to José, a 3-year-old Puerto Rican male. José weighs 35 pounds and is 3 feet 2 inches tall. He speaks both English and Spanish. José is an outgoing child who enjoys participating in a wide variety of activities at school. He eagerly participates in small and large group times.

Social-Emotional	Cognitive	Motor	Adaptive (Daily Living)
Gets along well with and enjoys interacting with other children. Verbally expresses emotions such as happy and sad. Prefers to play with favorite friends. Likes to help other children.	Counts from 1 to 10 in sequence. Likes to do puzzles. Repeats simple rhymes. Identifies some colors and shapes.	Uses brushes, crayons, and markers to draw. Pedals a tricycle. Likes to build with blocks.	Can put his legs into and pull up pants without help. Opens containers with simple lids without help. Drinks from a cup.

Gisselle

Introduce yourself to Gisselle, a 3-year-old Hispanic female. Gisselle weighs 44 pounds and is 3 feet 8 inches tall. She speaks only Spanish. Unlike José, Gisselle is reserved and needs encouragement to participate in large-group activities. She enjoys center time, where she interacts with a small group of friends.

Social-Emotional	Cognitive	Motor	Adaptive (Daily Living)
Is very shy and sensitive. Gets frustrated when other children get too close to her. Prefers to play with female friends. Enjoys talking with caregiver.	Is very curious and asks "why" a lot. Plays matching games with colors and shapes. Will listen to a short story and reenact it.	Enjoys painting pictures. Developing fine motor skills allow her to dress and undress baby dolls. Attempts to copy shapes and lines.	Drinks milk and water from a cup. Dresses herself for school. Uses the bathroom without assistance.

Questions about 3-year-olds:

- What cognitive skills does Gisselle have that will help her be successful in preschool?
- How will José's positive peer relations encourage success in school?
- Could Gisselle's social-emotional development be a risk factor when she enters preschool?

- Identify five developmental-related gender differences between José and Gisselle.
- What types of learning centers are developmentally appropriate for José and Gisselle?
- Teacher-child closeness plays an important role in school success. Which of these two children is more prone to a close teacher relationship? Why?

Emily

Introduce yourself to Emily, a 4-year-old Hispanic female. Emily weighs 36 pounds and is 3 feet 5 inches tall. She speaks English. Emily is a very active and assertive preschooler. She likes to be in control of things and is a leader in the classroom. Emily is eager to learn how to read and write.

Social-Emotional	Cognitive	Motor	Adaptive (Daily Living)
Pouts when upset. Looks forward to and participates in group time. Bosses other children around. Talks back to adults.	Puts 6 to 8 piece puzzles together. Identifies some letters of the alphabet. Enjoys reading books and magazines.	Would rather run than walk. Loves to dance. Likes to ride her bike. Turns somersaults. Brushes her teeth.	Has quiet time in the afternoon but does not nap for long. Can snap and unsnap clothing.

Benjamin

Introduce yourself to Benjamin, a 4-year-old Haitian male. Benjamin weighs 33 pounds and is 3 feet 3 inches tall. He speaks both Creole and English. Benjamin is very sociable and enjoys activities where he can interact with other children. He is creative and enjoys expressing himself in a variety of ways.

Social-Emotional	Cognitive	Motor	Adaptive (Daily Living)
Is interested in learning about new things. Will take turns when reminded. Controls anger when upset by clenching his fists. Is talkative; enjoys talking to teachers and peers.	Likes to sing silly songs. Likes to play alliteration games. Tells elaborate fictional stories.	Enjoys playing the piano. Uses scissors to cut on a line. Demonstrates good balance and body control. Is very active—likes to be involved in different activities.	Unzips and zips clothing. Washes hands before eating. Asks for help when needed.

Questions about 4-year-olds:

- Refer to the portraits and identify developmental changes between three- and four-year-olds.
- How can you use Benjamin's love of songs to develop preliteracy skills?
- Do you think that putting together 6 to 8 piece puzzles is developmentally appropriate for Emily's age? Should Emily be putting together puzzles with more pieces?
- Why is active learning important for children such as Benjamin?
- What developmental skills do Benjamin and Emily need to be prepared for kindergarten?
- How can you as an early childhood teacher help prepare these preschoolers for transition into kindergarten?

TABLE 10.1 Average Height and Weight of Preschoolers

Age	Males		Females	
	Height (inches)	Weight (pounds)	Height (inches)	Weight (pounds)
3 years	37.5	32.0	37.0	31.0
3 1/2 years	39.0	34.0	38.5	32.5
4 years	40.0	36.0	40.0	35.0
4 1/2 years	41.5	38.0	41.0	38.0
5 years	43.0	40.5	42.5	40.0

Source: National Center for Health Statistics in collaboration with the National Center for Chronic Disease Prevention and Health Promotion (2000). Available at http://www.cdc.gov/growthcharts

necessary during this stage of growth and development. Both girls and boys continue to grow several inches per year throughout the preschool years. Table 10.1 shows the average height and weight for preschoolers.

Preschool children are learning to use and test their bodies. It is a time for learning what they can individually do and how they can do it. Locomotion plays a large role in motor and skill development and includes activities of moving the body through space—walking, running, hopping, jumping, rolling, dancing, climbing, and leaping. Preschoolers use these activities to investigate and explore the relationships among themselves, space, and objects in space.

Preschoolers also like to participate in fine-motor activities such as drawing, coloring, painting, cutting, and pasting. Consequently, they need programs that provide action and play, supported by proper nutrition and healthy habits of plentiful rest and good hygiene.

COGNITIVE DEVELOPMENT

Preschoolers are in the preoperational stage of intelligence. As discussed in chapter 7, characteristics of the preoperational stage are that children (1) grow in their ability to use symbols, including language; (2) are not capable of operational thinking (an operation is a reversible mental action), which explains why Piaget named this stage *preoperational;* (3) center on one thought or idea, often to the exclusion of other thoughts; (4) are unable to conserve; and (5) are egocentric.

Preoperational characteristics have particular implications for you and other early childhood professionals. You can promote children's learning during the preoperational stage of development by doing the following:

- *Furnish concrete materials to help children see and experience concepts and processes.* Children learn from touching and experimenting with an actual object, as well as from pictures, stories, and videos. When you read stories about fruit and nutrition, bring in a collection of apples for children to touch, feel, smell, taste, discuss, classify, manipulate, and explore. Collections also offer children an ideal way to learn the names for things, classify, count, and describe. Also, use many opportunities to have children participate in activities using "real" things.
- *Use hands-on activities that give children opportunities for active involvement in their learning.* When you encourage children to manipulate and interact with the world around them, they begin to construct concepts about relationships, attributes, and processes. Through exploration, preoperational children begin to collect and organize data about the objects they manipulate. For example, when children engage in water play with funnels and cups, they learn about concepts such as measurement, volume, sink/float, bubbles and the prism, evaporation, and saturation.

- *Give children many and varied experiences.* Diverse activities and play environments lend themselves to teaching different skills, concepts, and processes. Children should spend time daily in both indoor and outdoor activities. Give consideration to the types of activities that facilitate large and fine motor, social, emotional, and cognitive development. For example, outdoor play activities and games such as tag, hopscotch, and jump rope enhance large motor development; fine motor activities include using scissors, stringing beads, coloring, and writing.

- *Model appropriate tasks and behaviors, because preoperational children learn to a great extent through modeling.* Children should see adults reading and writing daily. It is also helpful for children to view brief demonstrations by peers or professionals on possible ways to use materials. For example, after children have spent a lot of time in free exploration with math manipulatives, teachers and others can show children patterning techniques and strategies they may want to experiment with in their own play.

- *Provide a literacy-rich environment to stimulate interest and development of language and literacy in a meaningful context.* The physical environment should display room labeling, class stories and dictations, children's writing, and charts of familiar songs and fingerplays. There should be a variety of literature for students to read, including books, magazines, and newspapers. Paper and writing utensils should be abundant to motivate children in all kinds of writing. Daily literacy activities should include opportunities for shared, guided, and independent reading and writing; singing songs and fingerplays; and creative dramatics. Children should be read to every day.

- *Allow children periods of uninterrupted time to engage in self-chosen projects.* Children benefit more from blocks of time provided for in-depth involvement in meaningful projects than they do from frequent, brief ones.

It is essential that programs provide opportunities for children to engage in active play, both in indoor and outdoor settings. What are some things that children can learn through participation in playground activities?

LANGUAGE DEVELOPMENT

Children's language skills grow and develop rapidly during the preschool years. Vocabulary increases, and sentence length increases as children continue to master syntax and grammar. Infants and toddlers first use *holophrases,* single words that convey the meaning of a sentence. For example, a child might say "milk" to express, "I'd like some more milk, please."

At one year, infants know two or more words; by the age of two, about 275. During their second year, toddlers' language proficiency increases to include *telegraphic speech:* two- or three-word utterances acting as a sentence. "Amy go," for example, can mean that Amy wants her mother to take her for a walk in the stroller. During their third year or earlier, children add helping verbs and negatives to their vocabulary; for example, "No touch," or "I don't want milk." Sentences also become longer and more complex. During the fourth and fifth years, children use noun or subject clauses, conjunctions, and prepositions to complete their sentences.

FIGURE 10.1 Language Development and Potential Impact at Kindergarten

A report from the National Institute of Health highlights income level and language development, and their potential impacts on kindergartners:

- A child from a family **at or below the poverty line** hears **600 to 700** words per hour at 12 to 18 months old (result at kindergarten = 5,000 words).

- A child from a **middle-income** family hears **1,200 to 1,300** words per hour at 12 to 18 months old (result at kindergarten = 9,000 words).

- A child from an **upper-income** family hears **2,900 to 3,100** words per hour at 12 to 18 months old (result at kindergarten = 15,000 + words).

There is a strong correlation between vocabulary development in the early years and learning how to read and school success. Two of the most important things you can do are to promote vocabulary development with your students and work with parents on ways to promote vocabulary development in the home.

Source: Montgomery County (Maryland) Public Schools Office of Instruction and Program Development (2001 June). *Resources for Vocabulary Instruction (Draft).* (June 2001). Available at http://www.mcps.k12.md.us/curriculum/secenglish/bott_table/pdf_files/VOCAB.PDF.

During the preschool years, children's language development is diverse and comprehensive and constitutes a truly impressive range of learning. An even more impressive feature of this language acquisition is that children learn intuitively, without a great deal of instruction, the rules of language that apply to words and phrases they use. You can use many of the language practices recommended for infants and toddlers with preschoolers as well.

I cannot overemphasize the importance of language and vocabulary development. Figure 10.1 shows the dramatic effect of children's early language experiences on their later language development.

SCHOOL READINESS: WHO GETS READY FOR WHOM?

School readiness is a major national and state topic of discussions about preschool and kindergarten programs. The early childhood profession is reexamining "readiness," its many interpretations, and the various ways the concept is applied to educational practices.

For most parents, *readiness* means that their children have the knowledge and abilities necessary for success in preschool and for getting ready for kindergarten. Figure 10.2 shows what kindergarten teachers believe are important factors for kindergarten readiness. These are some of the things children should know and be able to do before coming to kindergarten. Thus, they shape, influence, and inform the preschool curriculum and the activities of preschool teachers.

Various discussions about readiness have changed the public's attitude about what it means. Readiness is no longer seen as consisting solely of a predetermined set of specific capabilities children must attain before entering preschool or kindergarten. Furthermore, the responsibility for children's early learning and development is no longer placed solely on the child or his or her parents but rather is seen as a shared responsibility among children, parents, families, early childhood professionals, communities, states, and the nation.

Proficiency Levels in Reading

1. Identifying uppercase and lowercase letters of the alphabet by name
2. Associating letters with sounds at the beginning of words
3. Associating letters with sounds at the end of words
4. Recognizing common words by sight
5. Reading words in context

Proficiency Levels in Mathematics

1. Identifying some one-digit numerals, recognizing geometric shapes, and one-to-one counting of up to ten objects
2. Reading all single-digit numerals, counting beyond ten, recognizing a sequence of patterns, and using nonstandard units of length to compare objects
3. Reading two-digit numerals, recognizing the next number in a sequence, identifying the ordinal position of an object, and solving a simple word problem
4. Solving simple addition and subtraction problems
5. Solving simple multiplication and division problems and recognizing more complex number patterns

General Knowledge

1. Establishing relationships between and among objects, events, or people
2. Making inferences and comprehend the implications of verbal and pictorial concepts

FIGURE 10.2 What Kindergarten Teachers Believe Are Important Factors for Kindergarten Readiness

Source: National Center for Education Statistics, *Special Analysis 2000—Entering Kindergarten: A Portrait of American Children When They Begin School,* 2001. Available at http://nces.ed.gov/programs/coe/2000/essay/index.asp.

Definitions and concepts of readiness vary from state to state and from community to community. North Carolina views readiness as consisting of a two-piece "puzzle" that is solved when the two pieces fit together. Figure 10.3 shows North Carolina's readiness puzzle and the components of its two pieces.

MATURATION AND READINESS

Some early childhood professionals and many parents believe that time cures all things, including a lack of readiness. They think that as time passes, children grow and develop physically and cognitively and, as a result, become ready to achieve. This belief is manifested in school admissions policies that advocate children's remaining out of school for a year if they are not ready for school as measured by a school readiness test. Assuming that the passage of time will bring about readiness is similar to the concept of unfolding, popularized by Froebel. Unfolding implies that development is inevitable and certain and that a child's optimum degree of development is determined by heredity and a biological clock. Froebel

FIGURE 10.3 The Readiness Puzzle

Ready Kids

- *Health and physical development:* Children's physical development, health status, and physical abilities.
- *Social and emotional development:* Children's feelings, ability to form relationships, ability to understand perspective and feelings of others, and skills needed to get along well in a group setting.
- *Approaches toward learning:* Curiosity, enjoyment of learning, confidence, creativity, attention to task, reflection, and interests.
- *Language development and communication:* Verbal and nonverbal skills to convey and understand others' meaning and early literacy skills.
- *Cognition and general knowledge:* Basic knowledge about the world, early mathematical skills, and basic problem-solving skills.

Ready Schools

- Knowledge of growth and development of typically and atypically developing children.
- Knowledge of the strengths, interests, and needs of each child.
- Knowledge of the social and cultural contexts in which each child and family lives.
- Ability to translate developmental knowledge into developmentally appropriate practices.

Readiness is really no puzzle in that the profession knows what children need to know and do in order to be successful in school and life. You and your colleagues must help in assuring that all children are ready for learning, which begins at birth.

Source: North Carolina School Improvement Panel, *School Readiness in North Carolina: Strategies for Defining, Measuring, and Promoting Success for All Children.* Public Schools of North Carolina, State Board of Education (2000), 5–6.

likened children to plants, and he likened parents and teachers to gardeners whose task is to nurture and care for children so they can mature according to their genetic inheritance and maturational timetable. The concept of unfolding continues to be a powerful force in early childhood education and is based on the belief that maturation is predictable, patterned, and orderly.

Parents and teachers make their greatest contribution to readiness by providing a climate in which children can grow without interference to their innate timetable and blueprint for development. The popularity of this *maturationist* view has led to a persistent sentiment that children are being hurried to grow up too soon too fast. Some critics of early education say that we should let children be children, allow them to enjoy the only childhood they will ever have, and not push them into schooling and learning.

IMPORTANT READINESS SKILLS

Keeping in mind Figure 10.3, "The Readiness Puzzle," consider the readiness skills and behaviors of language, independence, impulse control, interpersonal skills, experiential background, and physical and mental health. All of these are necessary for a successful preschool experience.

Language. Language is the most important readiness skill. Children need language skills for success in both school and life. Important language skills include receptive language, such as listening to the teacher and following directions; expressive language, demonstrated in the ability to talk fluently and articulately with teacher and peers, the ability to express oneself in the language of the school, and the ability to communicate needs and ideas; and

VIDEO VIEWPOINT

Improving Intelligence in Children

Scientists have discovered that if certain brain cells are not engaged by certain ages, the cells die off. They have also found some keys to helping children's brains to develop more fully.

REFLECTIVE DISCUSSION QUESTIONS

What are some consequences for society and for children of not providing them with the early stimulation they need to grow their brains? How does the phrase "use it or lose it" apply to children's neurological development? How early in life should parents begin to promote language development in their children?

REFLECTIVE DECISION MAKING

Make a list of things you can do to stimulate early language development. Interview a music educator regarding how exposing children to music stimulates logical thinking. What are some math games you can teach youngsters to promote higher-level thinking skills?

---

symbolic language, knowing the names of people, places, and things, words for concepts, and adjectives and prepositions. Knowledge of the letters of the alphabet is one of the most important factors in being able to learn to read. Additionally, vocabulary is essential for school success, as previously illustrated. In addition, the language skills outlined in Figure 10.4 are essential for children's literacy success.

Independence.   Independence means the ability to work alone on a task, take care of oneself, and initiate projects without always being told what to do. Independence also includes mastery of self-help skills, including but not limited to dressing skills, health skills (toileting, hand washing, using a handkerchief, and brushing teeth), and eating skills (using utensils and napkins, serving oneself, and cleaning up).

Impulse Control.   Controlling impulses includes working cooperatively with others; not hitting others or interfering with their work; developing an attention span that permits involvement in learning activities for a reasonable length of time; and being able to stay seated for a while. Children who are not able to control their impulses are frequently (and erroneously) labeled hyperactive or learning disabled.

Interpersonal Skills.   Interpersonal skills are those of getting along and working with both peers, teachers, and other adults. Asked why they want their children to attend preschool, parents frequently respond, "To learn how to get along with others." Any preschool program is an experience in group living, and children have the opportunity to interact with others to become successful in a group setting. Interpersonal skills include working cooperatively with others, learning and using basic manners, and, most important, learning how to learn from and with others.

Experiential Background.   Experiential background is important to readiness because experiences are the building blocks of knowledge, the raw materials of cognitive development. They provide the context for mental disequilibrium, which enables children to develop higher levels of thinking. Children must go places—the grocery store, library, zoo—and they must be involved in activities—creating things, painting, coloring, experimenting, discovering. Children can build only on the background of information they bring to a new experience.

Language Skill	Teacher/Parent Input	Child Outcome
Exposure to varied vocabulary	Use techniques such as definitions, synonyms, references, comparisons, and children's past experiences to help children understand meanings of words.	Knowing the "right word" is vital if one is to communicate information clearly. Large vocabularies lead to reading success.
Opportunities to be part of conversations that use extended discourse	Provide opportunities to use and hear interesting words in conversations, books, readings, play, snacks, and mealtimes.	Extended discourse is talk that develops understanding beyond the here and now, and that requires the use of several sentences to build a linguistic structure, such as in explanations, narratives, or pretend talk.
Home and classroom environments that are cognitively and linguistically stimulating	Provide books and opportunities to read and be read to.	Children are most likely to experience conversations that include comprehensible and interesting extended discourse and are rich with vocabulary when their parents obtain and read good books and when their teachers create classrooms with a curriculum that is varied and stimulating.

FIGURE 10.4 **Dimensions of Children's Experiences Related to Literacy Success**

The nature and frequency of children's language experiences matter. Be sure to provide experiences and support in all of these areas.

Source: D. K. Dickinson and P. O. Tábors, "Fostering Language and Literacy in Classrooms and Homes," *Young Children* (March 2002), 12–13.

Varied experiences are the context in which children learn words, and the number and kinds of words children know is a major predictor of later school success.

Physical and Mental/Emotional Health. Children must have good nutritional and physical habits that will enable them to participate fully in and profit from any program. They must also have positive, nurturing environments and caring professionals to help them develop a self-image for achievement. Today, more attention than ever is paid to children's physical and mental health and nutrition. Likewise, the curriculum at all levels includes activities for promoting wellness and healthy living.

Increasingly, early childhood professionals are taking into account children's emotional development as an important factor in school readiness. A major reason for this new attention to mental health is that research clearly shows that young children with aggressive and disruptive behaviors are much less likely to do well in school. There are three key reasons for this:

1. Disruptive children are tough to teach: As early as preschool, teachers provide disruptive children with less positive feedback, so that disruptive children spend less time on task and receive less instruction.

DIVERSITY TIE-IN

Supporting English Language Learners' Language and Literacy Skills

Here are some things you can do to support English language learners (ELL) in five important literacy domains. As you review and reflect on these activities teachers can do, consider how you can apply them to your classroom teaching.

What Teachers Do	What Children Learn
Alphabet Knowledge Activities that target letter recognition	To identify the letters of the alphabet
Activities that target comparing alphabets or writing systems in other languages	*That other languages have different alphabets or writing systems*
Phonological Awareness Activities that emphasize the sounds that make up words	To identify the sounds that make up English words
Activities that present the sounds of other languages to make words	*That other languages have different sounds, but all languages use sounds to make words*
Book and Print Concepts Activities that show how books look and how they work	What the contents of a book are, including where the print is and where the book starts and ends
Activities that show how books written in other languages look and how they work	*That books may look quite different, even be read in a different way, if they are written in other languages*
Vocabulary Knowledge Activities that emphasize words and their meanings	That there are lots and lots of words that are used for talking, writing, and reading
Activities that emphasize that there are words in other languages that mean the same thing as words in English	*That other languages use different words for the same object or concept*
Discourse Skills Activities that encourage telling stories, explaining how the world works, building a fantasy world using English	To use these more sophisticated oral language forms in English
Activities that demonstrate that other languages have similar forms although they may seem a bit different	*That these or similar forms exist in other languages as well*

Source: Head Start Bulletin (2002), *Enhancing Head Start Communication.* Issue 74, p. 13. Available: www.headstartinfo.org/publications/hsbulletin74/hsb74_04.htm.

2. Emotionally negative, angry children might lose opportunities to learn from their classmates as children gather to work on projects together, help each other with homework, and provide each other with support and encouragement in the classroom.
3. Children who are disliked by teachers and classmates grow to like school less, feeling less love for learning, and avoid school more often, with lower school attendance.

To complete an activity related to this topic, go to the Companion Website at **http://www.prenhall.com/morrison**, select chapter 10, then choose the Diversity Tie-In module.

There are many ways you and others can help develop children's mental/emotional health:

- Using modeling, role play, and group discussion, teachers can devote relatively small amounts of class time to instruct children on how to identify and label feelings, how to appropriately communicate with others about emotions (e.g., to use words instead of fists), and how to resolve disputes with peers.
- Because many of children's emotional problems appear to be so profoundly affected by parenting practices, many intervention programs aimed at helping adults parent more effectively may also indirectly improve children's emotional and behavioral outcomes. Specifically, many of these programs aim to improve families' provision of sensitive, responsive care, and to curtail families' use of inconsistent and harsh parenting as an indirect means of improving children's later life chances.

Readiness for life and learning begins at birth and is affected and influenced by many factors. Here are some things to keep in mind about readiness:

Readiness is never ending. Readiness is a continuum throughout life—the next life event is always just ahead, and the experiences children have today prepare them for the experiences of tomorrow.

All children are always ready for some kind of learning. Children always need experiences that will promote learning and get them ready for the next step.

Schools and professionals should promote readiness for children, not the other way around. In this regard, schools should get ready for children and offer a curriculum and climate that allows for children's inevitable differences.

Readiness is individualized. Three-, four-, and five-year-old children exhibit a range of abilities. Although we have said previously that all children are ready for learning, not all children are ready for learning the same thing at the same time.

Readiness is a function of culture. Teachers have to be sensitive to the fact that different cultures have different values regarding the purpose of school, the process of schooling, children's roles in the schooling process, and what the family's and culture's roles are in promoting readiness.

THEORIES ABOUT PLAY

The notion that children learn through play began with Froebel, who built his system of schooling on the educational value of play. As discussed in chapter 5, Froebel believed that natural unfolding (development) occurs through play. Since his time, most early childhood programs have incorporated play into their curricula or have made play a major part of the day.

Montessori viewed children's active involvement with materials and the prepared environment as the primary means through which they absorb knowledge and learn. John Dewey also advocated and supported active learning and believed that children learn through play activities based on their interests. Dewey thought, too, that children should have opportunities to engage in play associated with everyday activities (e.g., the house center, post office, grocery store, doctor's office). He felt that play helps prepare children for adult occupations. Many curriculum developers and teachers base play activities, such as a dress-up corner, around adult roles.

Piaget believed play promotes cognitive knowledge and is a means by which children construct knowledge of their world. He identified three kinds of knowledge: physical, logical-mathematical, and social. According to Piaget, through active involvement, children learn about things and the physical properties of objects; gain knowledge of the environment and their role(s) in it; and acquire logical-mathematical knowledge—numeration, seriation, classification, time, space, and number. Piaget believed that children learn social knowledge, vocabulary, labels, and proper behavior from others.

Unlike Piaget, Vygotsky viewed the social interaction that occurs through play essential to children's development. He believed that children learn through social interactions with

For more information about early childhood play, go to the Companion Website at **http://www. prenhall.com/morrison**, select any chapter, then choose Topic 5 of the ECE Supersite module.

others the language and social skills such as co-operation and collaboration that promote and enhance their cognitive development. Viewed from Vygotsky's perspective, adults' play with children is as important as children's play with their peers. Thus, play promotes cognitive development and provides a way to develop social skills.

Montessori thought of play as children's work and of the home and preschool as "workplaces" where learning occurs through play. This comparison conveys the total absorption, dedication, energy, and focus children demonstrate through their play activities. Children engage in play naturally and enjoy it; they do not select play activities because they intentionally set out to learn. Noah does not choose to put blocks in order from small to large because he wants to learn how to seriate, nor does he build an incline because he wants to learn the concept of "down" or the principles of gravity; however, the learning outcomes of this play are obvious. Children's play is full of opportunities for learning, but there is no guarantee that children will learn all they need to know when they need to know it through play.

Providing opportunities for children to choose among well-planned, varied learning activities enhances the probability that they will learn through play.

Puppets and plays provide many opportunities for children to learn and interact with others.

PURPOSES OF PLAY

Children learn many things through play. Play activities are essential for their development across all developmental domains—the physical, social, emotional, cognitive, and linguistic. Play enables children to achieve knowledge, skills, and behaviors as shown in Figure 10.5.

- Learn concepts

- Develop social skills

- Develop physical skills

- Master life situations

- Practice language processes

- Develop literacy skills

- Enhance self-esteem

- Prepare for adult life and roles (e.g., learn how to become independent, think, make decisions, cooperate/collaborate with others)

FIGURE 10.5 What Children Learn Through Play

Without the opportunity for play and an environment that supports it, children's learning is limited. Early childhood programs that provide time for play that promotes and supports learning increase and enhance children's opportunities for success in school and life.

The Value of Play

Early childhood educators have long recognized the value of play for social, emotional, and physical development. Recently, however, play has attracted greater importance as a medium for literacy development. It is now recognized that literacy develops in meaningful, functional social settings rather than as a set of abstract skills taught in formal pencil-and-paper settings.

Literacy development involves a child's active engagement in cooperation and collaboration with peers; it builds on what the child already knows with the support and guidance of others. Play provides this setting. During observation of children at play, especially in free-choice, cooperative play periods, one can note the functional uses of literacy that children incorporate into their play themes. When the environment is appropriately prepared with literacy materials in play areas, children have been observed to engage in attempted and conceptual reading and writing in collaboration with other youngsters. In similar settings lacking literacy materials, the same literacy activities did not occur.

To demonstrate how play in an appropriate setting can nurture literacy development, consider the following classroom setting in which the teacher has designed a veterinarian's office to go along with a class study on animals focusing in particular on pets.

The dramatic play area is designed with a waiting room, including chairs; a table filled with magazines, books, and pamphlets about pet care; posters about pets; office hour notices; a "No Smoking" sign; and a sign advising visitors to "Check in with the nurse when arriving." On a nurse's desk are patient forms on clipboards, a telephone, an address and telephone book, appointment cards, and a calendar. The office contains patient folders, prescription pads, white coats, masks, gloves, a toy doctor's kit, and stuffed animals for patients.

Ms. Meyers, the teacher, guides students in using the various materials in the veterinarian's office during free-play time. For example, she reminds the children to read important information they find in the waiting area, to fill

KINDS OF PLAY

Children engage in many kinds of play: social, cognitive, sociodramatic, outdoor, and rough-and-tumble.

Social Play. Much of children's play occurs with or in the presence of other children. **Social play** occurs when children play with each other in groups. Mildred Parten (children's play researcher, now deceased) developed the most comprehensive description and classification of the types of children's social play. These types of social play are shown in Figure 10.6.

Social play, as shown in Figure 10.6, supports many important functions. First, it provides the means for children to interact with others and learn many social skills. Play provides a context in which children learn how to compromise ("OK, I'll be the baby first and you can be the mommy"), learn to be flexible ("We'll do it your way first and then my way"), resolve conflicts, and continue the process of learning who they are. Children learn what skills they have, such as those relating to leadership. Second, social play provides a vehicle for practicing and developing literacy skills. Children have others with whom to practice language and learn from. Third, play helps children learn impulse control; they realize they

Social play Play of children with others and in groups.

out forms about their pets' needs, to ask the nurse for appointment times, or to have the doctor write out appropriate treatments or prescriptions. In addition to giving directions, Ms. Meyers also models behaviors by participating in the play center with the children when first introducing materials.

This play setting provided a literacy-rich environment with books and writing materials; modeled reading and writing by the teacher that children could observe and emulate; provided the opportunity to practice literacy in a real-life situation that had meaning and function; and encouraged children to interact socially by collaborating and performing meaningful reading and writing activities with peers. The following anecdotes relate the type of behavior Ms. Meyers observed in the play area.

Jessica was waiting to see the doctor. She told her stuffed animal dog, Sam, not to worry, that the doctor would not hurt him. She asked Jenny, who was waiting with her stuffed animal cat, Muffin, what the kitten's problem was. The girls agonized over the ailments of their pets. After a while they stopped talking and Jessica picked up the book *Are You My Mother?* and pretended to read to her dog. Jessica showed Sam the pictures as she read.

Preston examined Christopher's teddy bear and wrote a report in the patient's folder. He read his scribble writing out loud and said, "This teddy bear's blood pressure is twenty-nine points. He should take sixty-two pills an hour until he is better and keep warm and go to bed." At the same time he read, he showed Christopher what he had written so he could understand what to do.

When selecting settings to promote literacy in play, choose those that are familiar to children and relate them to themes currently being studied. Suggestions for literacy materials and settings to add to the dramatic play areas include the following:

- A fast-food restaurant, ice cream store, or bakery suggests menus, order pads, a cash register, specials for the day, recipes, and lists of flavors or products.
- A supermarket or local grocery store can include labeled shelves and sections, food containers, pricing labels, cash registers, telephones, shopping receipts, checkbooks, coupons, and promotional flyers.
- A post office to serve for mailing children's letters needs paper, envelopes, address books, pens, pencils, stamps, cash registers, and labeled mailboxes. A mail carrier hat and bag are important for children who deliver the mail and need to identify and read names and addresses.
- A gas station and car repair shop, designed in the block area, might have toy cars and trucks, receipts for sales, road maps for help with directions to different destinations, automotive tools and auto repair manuals for fixing cars and trucks, posters that advertise automobile equipment, and empty cans of different products typically found in service stations.

Contributed by Lesley Mandel Morrow, professor and coordinator of early childhood programs, Rutgers University.

cannot always do whatever they want. And fourth, in giving a child other children with whom to interact, social play negates isolation and helps children learn how to have the social interactions so vital to successful living.

Cognitive Play. Froebel, Montessori, and Piaget recognized the cognitive value of play. Froebel through his gifts and occupations and Montessori through her sensory materials saw children's active participation with concrete materials as a direct link to knowledge and development. Piaget's theory influences contemporary thinking about the cognitive basis for play. From a Piagetian perspective, play is literally cognitive development. Piaget described four stages of play through which children progress as they develop: functional play, symbolic play, playing games with rules, and constructive play.

1. **Functional play,** the only play that occurs during the sensorimotor period, is based on and occurs in response to muscular activities and the need to be active. Functional play is characterized by repetitions, manipulations, and self-imitation. Piaget described functional play (which he also called *practice play* and *exercise play*) this way: "The child

Functional play The only play of the sensorimotor period, involves muscular activities.

FIGURE 10.6 Types of Social Play

As you reflect on these types of social play, recall examples of them that you have observed in early childhood classrooms. Then, observe in classrooms and record specific examples of children engaged in each kind of play and their learning outcomes.

Source: Mildred Parten, "Social Play Among Preschool Children," *Journal of Abnormal and Social Psychology* 27 (1933), 243–269.

- *Unoccupied play:* The child does not play with anything or anyone; the child merely stands or sits without doing anything observable.

- *Solitary play:* Although involved in play, the child plays alone, seemingly unaware of other children.

- *Onlooker play:* The child watches and observes the play of other children; the center of interest is others' play.

- *Parallel play:* The child plays alone but in ways similar to and with toys or other materials similar to those of other children.

- *Associative play:* Children interact with each other, perhaps by asking questions or sharing materials, but do not play together.

- *Cooperative play:* Children actively play together, often as a result of organization of the teacher. (This is the least frequently witnessed play in preschools.)

sooner or later (often even during the learning period) grasps for the pleasure of grasping, swings [a suspended object] for the sake of swinging, etc. In a word, he repeats his behavior not in any further effort to learn or to investigate, but for the mere joy of mastering it and of showing off to himself his own power of subduing reality."[5]

Functional play allows children to practice and learn physical capabilities while exploring their immediate environments. Very young children are especially fond of repeating movements for the pleasure of it. They engage in sensory impressions for the joy of experiencing the functioning of their bodies. Repetition of language also is common at this level.

Symbolic play   The "let's pretend" stage of play.

2. **Symbolic play,** the second stage, is also called the "let's pretend" stage of play. During this stage, children freely display their creative and physical abilities and social awareness in a number of ways—for example, by pretending to be something else, such as an animal. Symbolic play also occurs when children pretend that one object is another—that a building block is a car, for example—and may also entail pretending to be another person—a mommy, daddy, or caregiver. As toddlers and preschoolers grow older, their symbolic play becomes more elaborate and involved.

Playing games with rules Playing within limits and rules.

3. **Playing games with rules** begins around age seven or eight. During this stage, children learn to play within rules and limits and adjust their behavior accordingly, and they can make and follow social agreements. Games with rules are common in middle childhood and adulthood.

Constructive play   Play involving the use of modules to build things.

4. **Constructive play** develops from symbolic play and represents children's adaptations to problems and their creative acts. Constructive play is characterized by children engaging in play activities to construct their knowledge of the world. They first manipulate play materials and then use these materials to create and build things (a sand castle, a block building, a grocery store) and experiment with the ways things go together.

Informal (free) play   Play in which children play in activities of interest to them.

Informal or Free Play.   Proponents of learning through spontaneous, **informal (free) play** activities maintain that learning is best when it occurs in an environment that contains materials and people with whom children can interact. Learning materials may be grouped in centers with similar equipment: a kitchen center, a dress-up center, a block center, a music and art center, a water or sand area, and a free-play center, usually with items such as tricycles, wagons, and wooden slides for promoting large-muscle development.

The atmosphere of this kind of preschool setting tends to approximate a home setting, in which learning is informal, unstructured, and unpressured. Talk and interactions with adults are spontaneous. Play and learning episodes are generally determined by the interests of the children and, to some extent, professionals, based on what they think is best for children. The expected learning outcomes are socialization, emotional development, self-control, and acclimation to a school setting.

Three problems may result from a free-play format. First, some teachers interpret it to mean that children are free to do whatever they wish with whatever materials they want to use. Second, aside from seeing that children have materials to play with, some teachers do not plan for what special play materials to have, how children will interact with the materials, or what children are to learn while playing. Third, sometimes teachers do not hold children accountable for learnings from free play. They rarely question children about concepts or point out the nature of the learning. Such teachers are seldom part of the play process. They act as disinterested bystanders, their primary goal being to see that children do not injure themselves while playing. In a quality program of free play both indoors and outside, teachers are active participants. Sometimes they observe, sometimes they play with the children, sometimes they help the children, but they never intrude or impose. Avoiding the possible pitfalls of the free-play format enables children to learn many things as they interact with interesting activities, materials, and people in their environment.

Sociodramatic (Pretend) Play. Dramatic play allows children to participate vicariously in a wide range of activities associated with family living, society, and their and others' cultural heritage. Dramatic play is generally of two kinds: *sociodramatic* and *fantasy*. **Sociodramatic play** usually involves everyday realistic activities and events, whereas **fantasy play** typically involves fairytale and superhero play. Dramatic play centers often include areas such as housekeeping, dress-up, occupations, dolls, school, and other situations that follow children's interests. A skillful professional can think of many ways to expand children's interests and then replace old centers with new ones. For example, after a visit to the police station, a housekeeping center might be replaced by an occupations center.

In sociodramatic play, children have an opportunity to express themselves, assume different roles, and interact with their peers. Sociodramatic play centers thus act as a nonsex-

Dramatic play promotes children's understanding of concepts and processes. Here, play allows children to explore their feelings and ideas about medical practitioners and medical settings.

Sociodramatic play   Play involving realistic activities and events.

Fantasy play   Play involving fantasy and superheroes.

VIDEO VIEWPOINT

Wild About Learning

The NAEYC Guidelines for Developmentally Appropriate Practice recommend that young children have ample amounts of time and proper environments in which to play, since children do a great deal of learning when they play.

REFLECTIVE DISCUSSION QUESTIONS

In what ways does play help a child's social, cognitive, emotional, and physical development? What is the role of structured play (team sport participation, music lessons, scouting, etc.) in relation to free play?

REFLECTIVE DECISION MAKING

Visit a preschool, day care center, or grade school and observe a group of children at play. What are they doing? What learning is taking place? How do the activities, the people they interact with, the objects around them, and the immediate environment affect their play? Based on your observations, what could you do as an early childhood professional to promote meaningful learning experiences through play?

ist and multicultural arena in which all children are equal. Teachers can learn a great deal about children by watching and listening to their dramatic play. For example, one teacher heard a child remark to the doll he was feeding that "you better eat all of this 'cause it's all we got in the house." After investigating, the teacher linked the family with a social service agency that helped them obtain food and assistance.

Teachers must assume a proactive role in organizing and changing dramatic play areas. They must set the stage for dramatic play and participate with children. They must also encourage those who "hang back" and are reluctant to play and involve those who may not be particularly popular with the other children. Surprisingly, because of their background and environment, some children have to be taught how to play. In other words, as in all areas of early childhood education, professionals must deal with children's dramatic play in an individual and holistic way.

Outdoor Play. Children's play outside is just as important as that inside. Children need to relieve stress and tension through play, and outdoor activities provide this opportunity; however, teachers should plan for what children will do and what equipment will be available. Outdoor play is not a chance for children to run wild.

Outdoor environments and activities promote large- and small-muscle development and body coordination as well as language development, social interaction, and creativity. Professionals should plan for a particular child or group of children to move through progressively higher skill levels of running, climbing, and throwing. The outdoor area is a learning environment, and as such, the playground should be designed according to learning objectives. Figure 10.7 shows some things you can do to make sure children with disabilities can participate in outdoor play.

Many teachers also enjoy bringing the indoor learning environment outdoors, using easels, play dough, or dramatic play props to further enhance learning opportunities. In addition, taking a group of children outdoors for story or music time, sitting in the shade of

FIGURE 10.7 Adaptation of Outdoor Play for Children with Physical Challenges

- Position a child with physical challenges so that he or she can achieve maximum range of motion, muscle control, and visual contact with materials and other children. A child might need to lie on his or her side or use a bolster to access materials and interact with other children during activities such as gardening and painting.

- Furnish specifically adapted play and recreation equipment when necessary. This might include modified swings, tricycles, and tables for independent participation in activities.

- Encourage the child to use his or her own means of getting around—whether a wheelchair, walker, or scooter—to participate in the activities and games of other children.

- Provide activities for the lower body and feet, such as foot painting, splashing in a wading pool, digging in the garden or sand, and kicking a ball, for a child with limited use of his or her hands and upper body.

- Provide activities including painting, water table, sandbox, and gardening that a child with limited use of his or her feet, legs, and lower body can do independently and successfully with his or her upper body. Always ensure correct positioning of the child's torso.

- Increase the width of balance beams and modify slippery surfaces to support better balance.

- Use softer balls (e.g., foam balls) or lightweight objects to facilitate throwing and catching when a child lacks strength and endurance.

- Use large balls (e.g., beach balls) and other large objects to make catching easier for a child who is unable to grasp smaller objects.

The benefits of outdoor play for all children are well established. The items listed provide suggestions of things you can do to assure that children with physical challenges can participate in outdoor play.
Source: L. L. Flynn and J. Kieff, "Including Everyone in Outdoor Play," *Young Children Magazine* (2002), 24–25.

a tree, brings a fresh perspective to daily group activities. As with indoor activities, provisions for outdoor play involve planning, supervising, and helping children be responsible for their behavior.

Rough-and-Tumble Play. All children, to a greater or lesser degree, engage in rough-and-tumble play. One theory of play says that children play because they are biologically programmed to do so; that is, it is part of children's (and adults') genetic heritage to engage in play activities. Indeed, there is a parallel in children's rough-and-tumble play and behaviors in the animal kingdom—for example, run-and-chase activities and "pretend" fighting. Rough-and-tumble play activities enable children to learn how to lead and follow, develop physical skills, interact with other children in different ways, and grow in their abilities to interact with children.

TEACHERS' ROLES IN PROMOTING PLAY

You and your colleagues are the key to promoting meaningful play, which promotes a basis for learning. What you do and the attitudes you have toward play determine the quality of the preschool environment and the events that occur there. You have the following responsibilities for supporting a quality play curriculum:

- Plan to implement the curriculum through play and integrate specific learning activities with play to achieve specific learning outcomes. Play activities should match children's developmental needs and be free of gender and cultural stereotypes. Teachers have to be clear about curriculum concepts and ideas they want children to learn through play.
- Provide time for learning through play. Include it in the schedule as a legitimate activity in its own right.
- Structure time for learning through play. Create both indoor and outdoor environments that encourage play and support its role in learning.
- Organize the classroom or center environment so that cooperative learning is possible and active learning occurs.
- Provide materials and equipment that are appropriate to children's developmental levels and support a nonsexist and multicultural curriculum.
- Educate assistants and parents about how to promote learning through play.
- Supervise play activities and participate in children's play. In these roles, help, show, and model when appropriate and refrain from interfering when appropriate.
- Observe children's play. Teachers can learn how children play and the learning outcomes of play to use in planning classroom activities.
- Question children about their play, discuss what children did during play, and "debrief" children about what they have learned through play.
- Provide for safety in indoor and outdoor play.

PLAY AND SAFETY

Providing a safe and healthy environment is an important part of a teachers' responsibilities and applies to the playground as well as to the inside facilities. Outdoor areas should be safe for children to play in. Usually, states and cities have regulations requiring the playground to be fenced and have a source of drinking water, a minimum number of square feet of play area for each child, and equipment that is in good repair. Careful child supervision is a cornerstone of playground safety.

Play is an important part of children's lives and the early childhood curriculum. You and others need to honor, support, and provide many opportunities for children to play.

THE NEW PRESCHOOL CURRICULUM

Standards Statements of what children should know and be able to do.

The purposes of preschool are changing dramatically. More and more, preschools are seen as places that get children ready for kindergarten. What was traditionally taught in kindergarten is now taught in the preschool. The preschool curriculum is now stressing academic skills related to reading, writing, and math as well as social skills. Increasingly, the responsibility for setting the preschool curriculum is being taken over by state departments of education through **standards,** statements of what preschoolers should know and be able to do. Preschool goals and learning standards are being set by state departments of education, and the preschool curriculum is becoming more focused on academics. For example, you can access the full text of the Texas Prekindergarten Guidelines at www.tea.state.tx.us/curriculum/eci.html. Keep in mind these key concepts as you reflect on and plan the preschool curriculum.

How do we determine an appropriate curriculum for three- and four-year-olds? Some say the curriculum should stress academic skills related to reading, writing, and math as well as social skills and getting along with others. Others say the curriculum should be based on what children will learn and do in kindergarten and first grade. Still others say that individual children should determine the curriculum according to what each knows or does not know; thus, one should start with the needs and interests of children. These have always been three conflicting learning outcomes for preschool programs.

Increasingly, however, the responsibility for setting the preschool curriculum is being taken over by state departments of education through standards and statements of what preschoolers should know and be able to do. As attention to the preschool years increases, the public believes goals should state what preschoolers should know and be able to do.

APPROPRIATE PRESCHOOL GOALS

All programs should have goals to guide activities and on which to base teaching methodologies. Without goals, it is easy to end up teaching just about anything without knowing why. Goals of individual preschools vary, but all programs should have certain essential goals. Quality preschools plan goals in these areas: social and interpersonal skills, self-help and intrapersonal skills, approaches to learning, learning how to learn and developing a love for learning, academics, thinking skills, learning readiness, language and literacy, character education, music and the arts, wellness and healthy living, and independence.

Social and Interpersonal Skills

Human beings are social, and much of learning involves social interactions.

- Learning how to get along with other children and adults and how to develop good relationships with teachers
- Learning to help others and develop caring attitudes

Self-Help and Intrapersonal Skills

Children must learn how to manage their behavior and their affairs.

- Learning how to take care of personal needs, such as dressing (tying, buttoning, zipping) and knowing what clothes to wear
- Learning eating skills (using utensils, napkins, and a cup or glass; setting a table)
- Learning health skills (how to wash and bathe, how to brush teeth)
- Learning grooming skills (combing hair, cleaning nails)

Approaches to Learning

I am sure you have heard the old saying that you can lead a horse to water but you can't make him drink. In some regard, the same is true for children. While on the one hand we talk about children always being ready and eager to learn, on the other hand, professionals understand that this readiness and eagerness to learn are not expressed equally across all preschool children. Consequently, with today's emphasis on early learning, there is also an accompanying emphasis on supporting children's motivation for learning and helping them develop positive dispositions toward learning. This is particularly true for those children who are at risk for school failure. **Approaches to learning** (also known as dispositions to learning) include

- Self-regulation of attention and behavior
- Positive social skills for developing a positive relationship with others
- Positive attitude toward learning
- Self-motivation for learning

Learning to Learn

Learning how to learn is as important as learning itself—in fact, learning depends on the acquisition of learning skills.

For more information about preschool curricula and teaching strategies, go to the Companion Website at **http://www.prenhall.com/morrison**, select any chapter, then choose Topic 6 of the ECE Supersite module.

Approaches to learning
How children react to and engage in learning and activities associated with school.

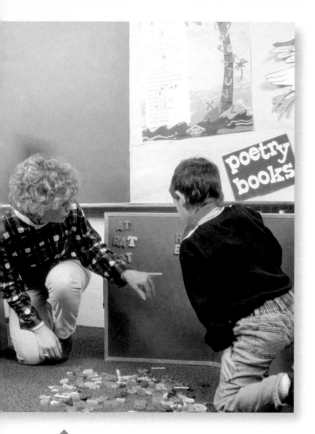

Although we want children to be involved in child-initiated and active learning, sometimes it is necessary to directly teach children certain concepts or skills. What concept or skill is this teacher directly teaching the child?

- Promoting self-help skills to help children develop good self-image and high self-esteem
- Learning about themselves, their family, and their culture
- Developing a sense of self-worth by providing experiences for success and competence
- Learning persistence, cooperation, self-control, and motivation to learn

Academics

Academics is playing a more central role in preschool curriculum.

- Learning their names, addresses, and phone numbers
- Learning of colors, sizes, shapes, and positions such as under, over, and around
- Learning of numbers and prewriting skills, shape identification, letter recognition, sounds, and rhyming

Thinking Skills

Thinking is the basis of learning and makes all kinds of learning possible.

- Developing the skills essential to constructing schemes in a Piagetian sense—classification, seriation, numeration, and knowledge of space and time concepts. These form the basis for logical-mathematical thinking.
- Learning to synthesize, analyze, and evaluate

Language and Literacy

There is a great emphasis on helping preschool children learn literacy skills. In addition to these skills, include all those that are included in this chapter.

- Provide opportunities for interaction with adults and peers as a means of developing oral language skills
- Increase vocabularies
- Learn to converse with other children and adults
- Build proficiency in language
- Develop literacy skills related to writing and reading
- Learn the letters of the alphabet
- Be familiar with a wide range of books

Character Education

Provide multiple opportunities for children to learn about and demonstrate such character traits as these. Many schools and school districts identify with parents' help the character traits they want all students to demonstrate.

- Positive mental attitude
- Persistence
- Respect for others
- Cooperation
- Honesty
- Trustworthiness
- Sensitivity

Music and the Arts

Brain research supports the use of music and the arts to support learning in all areas.

- Using a variety of materials (e.g., crayons, paint, clay, markers) to create original work
- Using different colors, surface textures, and shapes to create form and meaning

- Using art as a form of self-expression
- Participating in music activities
- Singing a variety of simple songs
- Responding to music of various tempos through movement
- Engaging in dramatic play with others

Wellness and Healthy Living

When children are not healthy, they cannot achieve their best. Helping children to learn healthy habits will help them do well in school.

- Learning the role of good nutritional practices and habits in their overall development
- Learning good nutrition habits
- Introducing children to new foods, a balanced menu, and essential nutrients

Independence

Learning skills of independence helps children have the confidence they need to achieve in school activities.

- Becoming independent by encouraging them to do things for themselves
- Learning responsibility for passing out, collecting, and organizing materials

THE DAILY SCHEDULE

What should a preschool day be like? While a daily schedule depends on many things—your philosophy, the needs of children, parents' beliefs, and state and local standards—the following descriptions illustrate what you can do on a typical preschool day.

This preschool schedule is for a whole-day program; many other program arrangements are possible. Some preschools operate half-day, morning-only programs five days a week; others operate both a morning and an afternoon session; others operate only two or three days a week. In still other programs, parents choose how many days they will send their children. Using creativity and meeting parents' needs seem to be hallmarks of effective preschool programs. However, an important trend is toward full-day and full-year programs for young children as we discussed at the beginning of the chapter.

Opening Activities.   As children enter, the teacher greets each individually. Daily personal greetings make the child feel important, build a positive attitude toward school, and provide an opportunity to practice language skills. They also give the teacher a chance to check each child's health and emotional status.

Children usually do not arrive all at one time, so the first arrivals need something to do while others are arriving. Offering free selection of activities or letting children self-select from a limited range of quiet activities (such as puzzles, pegboards, or markers to color with) are appropriate. Some teachers further organize this procedure by having children use an "assignment board" to help them make choices, limit the available choices, and practice concepts such as colors and shapes and recognition of their names. Initially, the teacher may stand beside the board when children come and tell each child what the choices are. The teacher may hand children their name tags and help them put them on the board. Later, children can find their own tags and put them up. At the first of the school year, each child's name tag can include her or his picture (use an instant camera) or a symbol or shape the child has selected.

Group Meeting/Planning.   After all children arrive, they and the teacher plan together and talk about the day ahead. This is also the time for announcements, sharing, and group songs and for children to think about what they plan to learn during the day.

Learning Centers.   After the group time, children are free to go to one of various learning centers, organized and designed to teach concepts. Table 10.2 lists types of learning centers and the concepts each is intended to teach.

TABLE 10.2 Learning Centers

Learning centers provide many useful functions. They enable children to engage in active learning and support learning in all the developmental domains. Planned well, centers enable you to meet state and district standards for what children should know and do. The concepts here are only some of many that you will select.

Center	Concepts	Center	Concepts
• Housekeeping	Classification Language skills Sociodramatic play Functions Processes	• Science	Identification of odors Functions Measure Volume
• Water/sand	Texture Volume Quantity Measure		Texture Size Relationship
• Blocks	Size Shape Length Seriation Spatial relations	• Manipulatives	Classifications Spatial relationships Shape Color Size Seriation
• Books/language	Verbalization Listening Directions How to use books Colors Size Shapes Names	• Math	Numerical comparisons (more and less) Order and sequence Quantity (how much and how many) Understanding patterns Spatial relationships Measurement of volume, length, weight Charting
• Puzzles/perceptual development	Size Shape Color Whole/part Figure/ground Spatial relations	• Literacy/Reading	Reading for pleasure Reading with others Writing Making choices (what to read, materials, etc.) Listening Vocabulary development Comprehension Book familiarity Names of authors and books Joy and fun of reading and writing
• Woodworking	Following directions Planning Whole/part		
• Art	Color Size Shape Texture Design Relationship		

Bathroom/Hand Washing. Before any activity in which food is handled, prepared, or eaten, children should wash and dry their hands.

Snacks. After center activities, a snack is usually served. It should be nutritionally sound and something the children can serve (and often prepare) themselves.

Outdoor Activity/Play/Walking. Ideally, outside play should be a time for learning new concepts and skills, not just a time to run around aimlessly. Children can practice climbing, jumping, swinging, throwing, and using body control. Teachers may incorporate walking trips and other events into outdoor play.

Increasing Expectations for Preschoolers

The world of preschool is different today than it was twenty years ago. State governments are expecting more of young children and teachers. Compare excerpts from these state preschool expectations to each other and to those of your state. What can you say about:

- Increasing expectations for young children.
- Increasing expectations for parents and families of preschoolers.
- Increasing expectations for preschool teachers.

New Jersey Department of Education
Math Expectations
http://www.state.nj.us/njded/ece/expectations/2002

- Demonstrate an understanding of number and numerical operations.
- Develop knowledge of spatial concepts (e.g., shapes and measurement).
- Understand patterns, relationships and classification.
- Develop knowledge of sequence and temporal awareness.
- Use mathematical knowledge to represent, communicate, and solve problems in their environment.

Mississippi Department of Education
Reading Expectations
http://www.mde.k12.ms.us/ACAD/ID/Curriculum/LAER/MsPreK.pdf

- Demonstrate an awareness of print.
- Construct meaning when responding to a story read or to a picture.
- Exhibit developmentally appropriate oral language for communication purposes.
- Begin to demonstrate phonemic awareness.
- Develop listening skills.

Connecticut Department of Education
Cognitive Expectations
http://www.state.ct.us/sde/deps/early/Frmwrkbench.pdf

- Demonstrate the ability to think, reason, question, and remember.
- Engage in problem solving.
- Use language to communicate, convey, and interpret meaning.
- Establish social contacts while beginning to understand the physical and social world.

Bathroom/Toileting. Bathroom/toileting times offer opportunities to teach health, self-help, and intrapersonal skills. Children should also be allowed to use the bathroom whenever necessary.

Lunch. Lunch should be a relaxing time, and the meal should be served family style, with professionals and children eating together. Children should set their own tables and deco-

To complete a Program in Action activity related to preschools today, visit the Companion Website at **http://www. prenhall. com/morrison**, select chapter 10, then choose the Program in Action module.

rate them with place mats and flowers they can make in the art center or as a special project. Children should be involved in cleaning up after meals and snacks.

Relaxation. After lunch, children should have a chance to relax, perhaps to the accompaniment of stories, records, and music. This is an ideal time to teach children breathing exercises and relaxation techniques.

Nap Time. Children who want or need to should have a chance to rest or sleep. Quiet activities should be available for those who do not need to or cannot sleep on a particular day. Under no circumstances should children be forced to sleep or lie on a cot or blanket if they cannot sleep or have outgrown their need for an afternoon nap.

Centers or Special Projects. Following nap time is a good time for center activities or special projects. (Special projects can also be conducted in the morning, and some may be more appropriate then, such as cooking something for snack or lunch.) Special projects might involve cooking, holiday activities, collecting things, work projects, art activities, and field trips.

Group Time. The day can end with a group meeting to review the day's activities. This meeting develops listening and attention skills, promotes oral communication, stresses that learning is important, and helps children evaluate their performance and behavior.

How you structure the day for your children will determine in part how and what they learn. You will want to develop your daily schedule with attention and care.

PRESCHOOL QUALITY INDICATORS

Today, quality is a major goal for preschool programs. Quality is often elusive, so it helps to have some standards to guide planning and decision making. The following guidelines in the form of questions will help you assure a high-quality program for all children:

1. What are the physical accommodations like? Is the facility pleasant, light, clean, and airy? Is it a physical setting you would want to spend time in? (If not, children will not want to, either.) Are plenty of materials available for the children to use?
2. Do the children seem happy and involved, or passive? Is television used as a substitute for a good curriculum and quality professionals?
3. What kinds of materials are available for play and learning? Is there variety and an abundance of materials? Are there materials (like puzzles) that help children learn concepts and think?
4. Is there a balance of activity and quiet play and of individual, small-group, and group activities? child-directed and professional-directed activities? indoor and outdoor play?
5. Is the physical setting safe and healthy?
6. Does the school have a written philosophy, objectives, and curriculum? Does the program philosophy agree with the parents' personal philosophy of how children should be reared and educated? Are the philosophy and goals age appropriate for the children being served?
7. Is there an emphasis on early literacy development? Do teachers read to children throughout the day? A general rule of thumb is that teachers should read to children at least twenty minutes a day. Are there books and other materials that support literacy development? Another rule of thumb is that preschool children should be familiar with seventy-five to one hundred books by the time they enter kindergarten.
8. Is there a written curriculum designed to help children learn skills for literacy, math, and science? Does the curriculum provide for skills in self-help; readiness for learning; and cognitive, language, physical, and social-emotional development?

9. Does the staff have written plans? Is there a smooth flow of activities, or do children wait for long periods "getting ready" for another activity? Lack of planning indicates lack of direction. Although a program whose staff does not plan is not necessarily a poor program, planning is one indicator of a good program.

10. What is the adult:child ratio? How much time do teachers spend with children one to one or in small groups? Do teachers take time to give children individual attention? Do children have an opportunity to be independent and do things for themselves?

11. How does the staff relate to children? Are the relationships loving and caring?

12. How do staff members handle typical discipline problems, such as disputes between children? Are positive guidance techniques used? Are indirect guidance techniques used (e.g., through room arrangement, scheduling, and appropriate activity planning)? Is there a written discipline philosophy that agrees with the parents' philosophy?

13. Are staff personnel sensitive to the gender and cultural needs and backgrounds of children and families? Are the cultures of all children respected and supported?

14. Are there opportunities for outdoor activities?

15. How is lunchtime handled? Are children allowed to talk while eating? Do staff members eat with the children? Is lunchtime a happy and learning time?

16. Is there a low turnover rate for teachers and staff? Programs that have high and constant turnovers of staff are not providing the continuity of care and education children need.

17. What kind of education or training does the staff have? The staff should have training on how to develop the curriculum and teach young children.

18. Is the director well trained? The director should have at least a bachelor's degree in childhood education or child development (refer to chapter 1, Figure 1.1). Can the director explain the program? Describing a typical day can be helpful. Is she or he actively involved in the program?

19. How does the staff treat adults, including parents? Does the program address the needs of children's families? As I have indicated previously, staff should provide for the needs of families as well as children.

20. Is the program affordable? If a program is too expensive for the family budget, parents may be unhappy in the long run. Parents should inquire about scholarships, reduced fees, fees adjusted to income level, fees paid in monthly installments, and sibling discounts.

21. Are parents of children enrolled in the program satisfied? One of the best ways to learn about a program is to talk to other parents.

22. Do the program's hours and services match parents' needs? Too often, parents have to patch together care and education to cover their work hours.

23. What are the provisions for emergency care and treatment?

24. What procedures are there for taking care of ill children?

MAKING SUCCESSFUL TRANSITIONS

A transition is a passage from one learning setting, grade, program, or experience to another. Young children face many such transitions in their lives. You can help ensure that preschool children make transitions from home to preschool to kindergarten happy and rewarding experiences.

The transition from home to preschool to kindergarten influences positively or negatively children's attitudes toward school and learning. Children with special needs who are making a transition from a special program to a mainstreamed classroom need extra attention and support, as we will discuss in chapter 16. Parents and preschool professionals can help preschool children make transitions easily and confidently in several ways:

- Educate and prepare children ahead of time for any new situation. For example, children and teachers can visit the kindergarten program the children will attend. Also, as time to enter the kindergarten approaches, children can practice certain routines as they will do them when they enter their new school or grade.
- Alert parents to new and different standards, dress, behavior, and parent–teacher interactions. Preschool professionals, in cooperation with kindergarten teachers, should share curriculum materials with parents so they can be familiar with what their children will learn.
- Let parents know ahead of time what their children will need in the new program (e.g., lunch box, change of clothing).
- Provide parents of special needs children and bilingual parents with additional help and support during the transition.
- Offer parents and children an opportunity to visit programs. Children will better understand the physical, curricular, and affective climates of the new programs if they visit in advance. Professionals can then incorporate methods into their own program that will help children adjust to new settings.
- Cooperate with the staff of any program the children will attend, to work out a transitional plan. Continuity between programs is important for social, emotional, and educational reasons. Children should see their new setting as an exciting place where they will be happy and successful.
- Additionally, what happens to children before they come to preschool influences the nature and success of their transitions to kindergarten. Three areas are particularly important in influencing the success of transitional experiences: children's skills and prior school-related experiences; children's home lives; and preschool classroom characteristics. Research demonstrates the following in relation to these three areas:
  - Children who are socially adjusted have better transitions. For example, preschool children whose parents initiate social opportunities for them are better adjusted socially.
  - Rejected children have difficulty with transitions.
  - Children with more preschool experiences have fewer transition adjustments to make.
  - Children whose parents expect them to do well in preschool and kindergarten do better than children whose parents have low expectations for them.
  - Developmentally appropriate classrooms and practices promote easier and smoother transitions for children.
- Exchange class visits between preschool and kindergarten programs. Class visits such as these are an excellent way to have preschool children learn about the classrooms they will attend as kindergartners. Having kindergarten children visit the preschool and tell the preschoolers about kindergarten provides for a sense of security and anticipation.
- Work with kindergarten teachers to make booklets about their program. These booklets can include photographs of children, letters from kindergarten children and preschoolers, and pictures of kindergarten activities. These books can be placed in the reading centers where preschool children can read about the programs they will attend.
- Hold a "kindergarten day" for preschoolers in which they attend kindergarten for a day. This program can include such things as riding the bus, having lunch, and participating in kindergarten activities.

The nature, extent, creativity, and effectiveness of transitional experiences for children, parents, and staff will be limited only by the commitment of all involved. If professionals are interested in providing good preschools, kindergartens, and primary schools, then we will include transitional experiences in the curricula of all these programs.

In addition to the issues we included in our previous discussion, a number of other issues face preschool children, families, and society.

"PUSHING" CHILDREN

Growing numbers of preschool programs are academic in nature; the curriculum consists of many activities, concepts, and skills traditionally associated with kindergarten. Critics think this kind of program puts too much pressure on children because they are not developmentally ready. A persistent and long-standing issue in early childhood education, "pushing" children usually revolves around overemphasis on learning basic skills and other skills associated with school success. The issue is complex. First, we need a precise understanding of what it means to "push" children. Some children are able to do more than others at earlier ages; some respond better to certain kinds of learning situations than others. Some parents and children are able to be involved in more activities than are others. So, we must always relate the topic of pushing to individual children and their family contexts.

ACCESS TO QUALITY PRESCHOOLS

Access to preschool is another issue facing children, families, and society. Currently, many children do not have access to preschools because there are not enough public preschools available. Many parents cannot afford to pay the tuition at private preschools. Rather than a comprehensive national program of preschools, children and families are confronted with a patchwork of fragmented public and private services that meet the needs of only some children. Additionally, available good programs are not equitably distributed.

UNIVERSAL PRESCHOOL

Universal preschool is a program whose time has come. We can identify 2002 as the year in which universal preschool officially became a permanent part of the American public school education system. We now have to refer to public schooling as beginning in preschool. Of course, it will take many more years before every four-year-old in every state has the opportunity of a public preschool education. The event that tipped the scales toward universal preschool was when, in 2002, the voters of Florida approved a constitutional amendment requiring public schools to offer prekindergarten to all four-year-old children. However, parents are not required to enroll their children. Therein lies one of the issues: whether universal preschool should be compulsory. Many parents do not support compulsory attendance for their young children because of their age and because they would rather have them at home. A second issue revolves around the cost of universal preschool. This cost includes new classrooms and teachers. One way some states and districts have responded to the facilities and teacher issues is to contract with private schools to offer state-supported services. These issues will remain, but universal preschool will continue to expand.

For more information about early intervention, go to the Companion Website at **http://www. prenhall.com/morrison**, select any chapter, then choose Topic 9 of the ECE Supersite module.

PRESCHOOL PROGRAM FUNDING AND EFFECTIVENESS

One of the ongoing issues of federal, state, and local government is what they are and are not going to fund. When there is not enough money to fund all priorities, which is always the case, different constituencies compete for funding. Questions of priorities abound. Do you fund juvenile justice programs, jails, senior health care, or preschools? Figure 10.8 shows the educational and monetary benefits of investing in high-quality preschool programs. You can use this data as you advocate for investing in young children.

To take an online self-test on this chapter's contents, go Companion at **http://mc prenhall.com/mc** select chapter 10 the Self-Test mo

300

FIGURE 10.8 What Research Says About Investing in Preschool

PROGRAM	RESULTS AND BENEFITS
Perry Preschool Project • Children are educated through child-planned activities. • Parents are involved through weekly home visits. • Teachers are trained, supervised, and assessed.	• For every dollar spent, $7.16 was saved in tax dollars. • 66% of the program group graduated from high school on time, compared to 45% of the control group. • The control group suffered twice as many arrests as the program group.
Chicago Child–Parent Center Program • Parents are required to participate in Parent Room or Classroom activities at least twice a month. • Parent education on nutrition, literacy, development, etc., is provided in the Parent Room. • Instructional approaches suit children's learning styles.	• For every dollar invested in the program, $7.10 was returned. • Participants had 51% reduction in child maltreatment. • Participants had a 41% reduction in special education placement.
Abecedarian Project • Primary medical care is provided on site. • Each child has individualized educational activities. • Activities promote cognitive, emotional, and social development, but focus on language.	• 35% attended a four-year college, compared to 13% of the control group. • 47% had skilled jobs, compared to 27% of the control group. • Participants had significantly higher reading and math skills.

Often the public thinks that money invested in preschool programs does not have the impact that money invested in other programs has. But, that is wrong. Consider what the research about three well-known early childhood interventions reveals about spending taxpayer money in the early years.

Sources: High/Scope Educational Research Foundation. The Perry Preschool Project. Available at http://www.highscope.org/Research/ PerryProject/perrymain.htm; The Child-Parent Center and Expansion Program. Available at http://www.waisman.wisc.edu/cls/Program.htm; and The Carolina Abecedarian Project. Available at http://www.fpg.unc.edu/~abc/.

For additional Internet resources or to complete an online activity for this chapter, go to the Companion Website at **http://www. prenhall.com/morrison**, select chapter 10, then choose the Linking to Learning or ʾʾking Connections module.

THE FUTURE OF PRESCHOOL EDUCATION

The further growth of public preschools for three- and four-year-old children is inevitable. This growth, to the point where all children are included, will take decades, but it will happen. Most likely, the public schools will focus more on programs for four-year-old children and then, over time, include three-year-olds. A logical outgrowth of this long-term trend will be for the public schools to provide services for even younger children and their families. One thing is certain: preschool as it was known a decade ago is not the same today, and ten years from now it will again be different. Your challenge is to develop your professional skills so that you may assume a leadership role in the development of quality universal preschool programs.

ACTIVITIES FOR FURTHER ENRICHMENT

APPLICATIONS

1. Visit preschool programs in your area. Determine their philosophies and find out what goes on in a typical day. Which would you recommend? Why?
2. Tell how you would promote learning through a specific preschool activity. For example, what learning outcomes would you have for a sand/water area? What, specifically, would be your role in helping children learn?
3. Develop a detailed daily schedule as you would use in your preschool.

FIELD EXPERIENCES

1. Collect examples of preschool curricula standards and activities from textbook publishers, teachers, school districts, and state departments of education. Place these in your files for future reference and use.
2. Interview preschool teachers to determine specific ways they believe preschool has changed over the last five years. What implications do these changes have for your teaching?

RESEARCH

1. Observe children's play and give examples of how children learn through play, and what they learn.
2. Survey preschool parents to learn what they expect from a preschool program. How do parents' expectations compare with the goals of preschool programs you visited?
3. Read and review five articles that relate to today's trend in establishing quality preschool programs. What are the basic issues discussed? Do you agree with these issues?

READINGS FOR FURTHER ENRICHMENT

Beaty, J. *Skills for Preschool Teachers*, 6th ed. Upper Saddle River, NJ: Merrill/Prentice Hall, 2001.
This text presents both theoretical background and ideas for practical applications in working with young children and their families. The content is built around the thirteen functional areas of the Child Development Associate (CDA) credential.

Catron, C.E., and Allen, J. *Early Childhood Curriculum: A Creative Play Model*, 3rd ed. Upper Saddle River, NJ: Merrill/Prentice Hall, 2003.
Provides information on planning programs with a play-based, developmental curriculum for children from birth to five years of age and covers basic principles and current research in early childhood curricula.

Eliason, C., and Jenkins, L. *A Practical Guide to Early Childhood Curriculum,* 7th ed. Upper Saddle River, NJ: Merrill/Prentice Hall, 2003.
Focuses on creating a child-centered curriculum that addresses children's needs in all developmental areas. Provides a wealth of meaningful teaching strategies, accompanied by lesson plans and activities.

Hendrick, J. *Total Learning: Developmental Curriculum for the Young Child*, 6th ed. Upper Saddle River, NJ: Merrill/Prentice Hall, 2003.

Advocates constructing curriculum based on emerging interests within a practical, flexible, thoughtful, teacher-made plan. Focuses on the developmental needs of children rather than on specific subject areas.

Sandall, S.R., and Schwartz, I.S. *Building Blocks for Teaching Preschoolers with Special Needs.* Baltimore, MD: Paul H. Brookes, 2002.

This set of educational practices emphasizes a quality early childhood program for all children and includes strategies and methods teachers can use to supplement the curriculum they currently use.

Tompkins, G. *Literacy for the Twenty-first Century: A Balanced Approach,* 2nd ed. Upper Saddle River, NJ: Merrill/Prentice Hall, 2001.

Literacy for the Twenty-first Century offers a readable, field-tested, and practical approach based on four contemporary theories of literacy learning—constructivist, sociolinguistic, interactive, and reader response. The text demonstrates how to implement a literature-based reading program with skills and strategies taught using a whole-part-whole approach.

U.S. Department of Education and U.S. Department of Health and Human Services, Early Childhood-Head Start Task Force. *Teaching our Youngest.* Washington D.C.: U.S. Government Printing Office, 2002.

This booklet draws from scientifically based research about what can be done to help children develop their language abilities, increase their knowledge, become familiar with books and other printed materials, learn letters and sounds, recognize numbers, and learn to count.

LINKING TO LEARNING

The Perpetual Preschool
http://www.perpetualpreschool.com

This site was built to celebrate the creativity and dedication of all those who contribute to the perpetual education of young children. It includes ideas for different kind of plays and other activities.

Preschool Teacher
http://www.preschoolbystormie.com

This website is dedicated to pre-K teachers. It is not necessarily for an expert in early childhood education, but the goal is to share ideas, used in the classrooms, and to provide a place where peers can share theirs.

Center for Environmental Education
http://www.cee-ane.org

This site contains numerous resources and links, including Nature's Course, *a newsletter dedicated to using children's books to teach environmental themes.*

International Association for the Child's Right to Play
http://www.ipausa.org

An interdisciplinary organization affiliated with IPA (founded in Denmark in 1961), with membership open to all professionals working for or with children. This site includes a position statement on the need for recess in elementary schools and resources on playground games and activities.

Teaching Strategies, Inc.
http://www.head-start.lane.or.us/education/curriculum/creative-curriculum/

This site provides readable letters to parents on outdoor play and sand and water play that can be used or adapted for families.

ENDNOTES

[1] Occasional Paper No. 3, Erikson Institute, Herr Research Center. *Child Assessment at the Preprimary Level: Expert Opinion and State Trends.* Carol Horton and Barbara T. Bowman. September, 2002, 3.

[2] Bowman, B., Donovan, M.S., and Burns, M.S. *Eager to Learn: Educating our Preschoolers* (Washington, DC: National Academy Press, 2001), 25–28.

[3] Shonkoff, J.P., and Phillips, D.A. (eds.). *From Neurons to Neighborhoods* (Washington, D.C.: National Academy Press, 2000), 5.

[4] Burns, M.S., Griffin, P., and Snow, C.E. (eds.). *Starting Out Right* (Washington D.C.: National Academy Press, 1999), 5.

[5] Piaget, Jean. *Play, Dreams, and Imitations in Childhood* (London: Routledge & Kegan Paul, 1967), 162.

Chapter 11

Children are like tiny flowers; they are varied and need care, but each is beautiful alone and glorious when seen in the community of peers.

FRIEDRICH FROEBEL

Kindergarten Education
Learning All You Need to Know

Focus Questions

- What is the history of kindergarten from Froebel to the present?

- What are appropriate goals, objectives, and curriculum for kindergarten programs?

- How has kindergarten changed in the last decade?

- What issues confront kindergarten education today?

AS we begin our discussion of kindergarten children and programs, perhaps you are thinking back to your kindergarten or pre-first-grade school experiences. I am sure that you have many pleasant memories and they include your teachers and classmates, what you learned, and how you learned it. It is good that you have fond memories of your kindergarten and/or other preschool experiences. However, we can't use just memories to build our understanding of what today's high-quality kindergartens are or should be like. If you have not visited a kindergarten program lately, now would be a good time to do so. You will discover that kindergarten education is undergoing a dramatic change. Compare the following changes that are transforming the kindergarten to your kindergarten observations:

- Today's kindergarten is decidedly more academic than the kindergarten of twenty years ago.
- Kindergarten programs emphasize the basic skills of reading, math, and science while meeting children's needs in all areas of development.
- More public and private schools and for-profit agencies are providing kindergarten programs. In this regard, kindergarten is becoming more universal, or more available to kindergarten children.
- More states are requiring school districts to provide kindergarten programs.
- More kindergarten programs are full-day.
- Kindergarten enrollment is exploding.
- Kindergarten for all children, or **universal kindergarten**, is now a permanent part of the American education system.
- Kindergarten programs are more challenging, and children are being asked to do and learn at higher levels.

As a result of these and other changes we discuss in this chapter, the contemporary kindergarten is a place of high expectations and achievement for all children. Figure 11.1 identifies the state requirements for kindergarten.

To review the chapter focus questions online, go to the Companion Website at **http://www.prenhall.com/morrison** and select chapter 11.

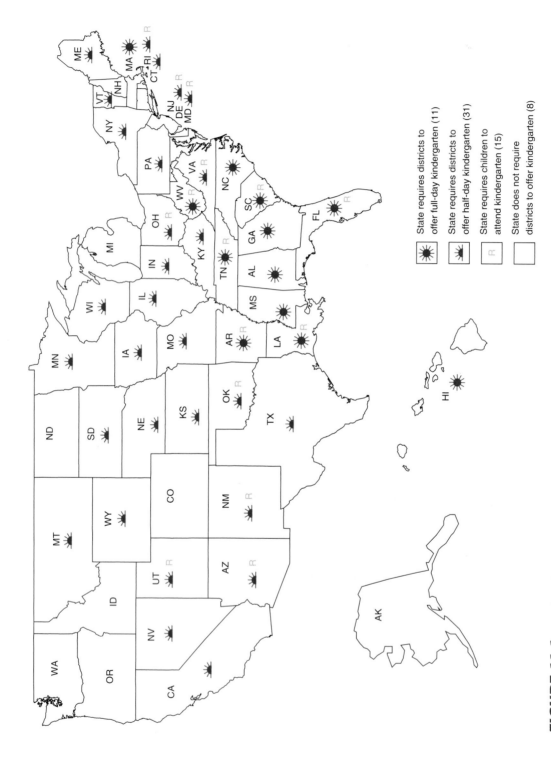

FIGURE 11.1 State Requirements for Kindergarten

Source: Indiana Department of Education Legislative Agenda Appendix B, Indianapolis, 2001.

THE HISTORY OF KINDERGARTEN EDUCATION

Froebel's educational concepts and kindergarten program were imported into the United States in the nineteenth century, virtually intact, by individuals who believed in his ideas and methods. Froebelian influence remained dominant for almost half a century, until John Dewey and his followers challenged it in the early 1900s. While Froebel's ideas still seem perfectly acceptable today, they were not acceptable to those in the mid-nineteenth century who subscribed to the notion of early education. Especially innovative and hard to accept was that learning could be based on play and children's interests—in other words, that it could be child centered. Most European and American schools were subject oriented and emphasized teaching basic skills. In addition, Froebel was the first to advocate a communal education for young children outside the home. Until Froebel, young children were educated in the home, by their mothers. Froebel's ideas for educating children as a group in a special place outside the home were revolutionary.

Margarethe Schurz established the first kindergarten in the United States. After attending lectures on Froebelian principles in Germany, she returned to the United States and in 1856 opened her kindergarten at Watertown, Wisconsin. Schurz's program was conducted in German, as were many of the new kindergarten programs of the time, since Froebel's ideas of education appealed especially to bilingual parents. Schurz influenced Elizabeth Peabody, the sister-in-law of Horace Mann, when, at the home of a mutual friend, Schurz explained the Froebelian system. Peabody was not only fascinated but converted.

Peabody opened her kindergarten in Boston in 1860. She and her sister, Mary Mann, also published *Kindergarten Guide*. Peabody almost immediately realized that she lacked the necessary theoretical grounding to adequately implement Froebel's ideas. She visited kindergartens in Germany, then returned to the United States to popularize Froebel's methods. Peabody is generally credited as kindergarten's main promoter in the United States.

One element that also helped advance the kindergarten movement was the appearance of appropriate materials. In 1860, Milton Bradley, the toy manufacturer, attended a lecture by Peabody, became a convert to the concept of kindergarten, and began to manufacture Froebel's gifts and occupations (refer to chapter 4, especially Figure 4.1). In 1869 Bradley published Froebel's *Paradise of Childhood,* America's first book on the kindergarten.

The first public kindergarten was founded in St. Louis, Missouri, in 1873 by Susan E. Blow, with the cooperation of the St. Louis superintendent of schools, William T. Harris. Elizabeth Peabody had corresponded for several years with Harris, and the combination of her prodding and Blow's enthusiasm and knowledge convinced Harris to open a public kindergarten on an experimental basis. Endorsement of the kindergarten program by a public school system did much to increase its popularity and spread the Froebelian influence within early childhood education. In addition, Harris, who later became the U.S. Commissioner of Education, encouraged support for Froebel's ideas and methods.

Training for kindergarten teachers has figured prominently in the development of higher education. The Chicago Kindergarten College was founded in 1886 to teach mothers and train kindergarten teachers. In 1930, the Chicago Kindergarten College became the National College of Education. In 1888, Lucy Wheelock opened a kindergarten training program in Boston. Known as the Wheelock School, it became Wheelock College in 1949.

The kindergarten movement in the United States was not without growing pains. Over a period of time, the kindergarten program, at first ahead of its time, became rigid and teacher centered rather than child centered. By the turn of the twentieth century, many kindergarten leaders thought that programs and training should be open to experimentation and innovation rather than rigidly following Froebel's ideas. Susan Blow was the chief defender of the Froebelian approach. In the more moderate camp was Patty Smith Hill, who thought that while the kindergarten should remain faithful to Froebel's ideas, it should nevertheless be open to innovation. She believed that the kindergarten movement, to survive, had to move into the twentieth century, and was able to convince many of her colleagues. More than anyone else, Hill is responsible for kindergarten as we know it today.

 To check your understanding of this chapter with the online Study Guide, go to the Companion Website at **http://www. prenhall.com/morrison**, select chapter 11, then choose the Study Guide module.

PORTRAITS OF KINDERGARTNERS

Lina

Introduce yourself to Lina, a 5-year-old Hispanic female. Lina weighs 39 pounds and is 3 feet 11 inches tall. She is petite and fragile. Lina speaks Spanish and English. She did not attend preschool, but is quickly learning preliteracy skills in kindergarten. Lina is a quiet learner. She listens carefully, but must be encouraged to participate verbally.

Social-Emotional	Cognitive	Motor	Adaptive (Daily Living)
Is shy and quiet. Is a good listener. Prefers to interact with one or two classmates in play situations.	Recites poems and sings in front of classmates. Names all the letters of the alphabet and knows their sounds. Sometimes confuses the pronouns "he" and "she" when retelling a story. Recalls many facts from stories Knows the parts of the story (beginning, middle, end).	Is graceful. Enjoys dancing to music. Can hop on one foot.	Knows her address. Knows her phone number. Asks adults for help when needed.

Ganali

Introduce yourself to Ganali, a 5-year-old Ghanian male. Ganali weighs 60 pounds and is 4 feet 4 inches tall. He is physically mature and looks older than his peers. Ganali is a bright, popular boy who enjoys school. He expresses his creativity through drawing and telling stories. Because he is detail-oriented, tasks sometimes take him longer to complete.

Social-Emotional	Cognitive	Motor	Adaptive (Daily Living)
Enjoys sharing about visits to Africa. Knows that his actions have consequences. Is a reliable helper in the classroom. Is a leader. Is popular and well-liked by peers.	Reads early beginner books. Is eager to learn. Has an excellent memory and recalls many details from stories. Is bright and artistic. Adds simple numbers and understands first and last.	Is well coordinated. Can stand on one foot with his eyes closed. Likes to draw; draws very detailed and creative pictures. Has excellent fine-motor coordination. Can throw a ball to a target with 95 percent accuracy.	Knows his phone numbers. Knows the city and state that he lives in. Does not know his address.

Questions about five-year-old kindergartners:

- Lina did not attend preschool. Does this appear to affect her overall development? In what ways should preschool and kindergarten programs contribute to children's development and readiness for the first grade?
- Lina is described as shy and quiet. What factors might be influencing these traits? How might temperament traits influence social-emotional and intellectual development?
- How can you respond to Lina's temperament traits?

- How could you integrate Ganali's storytelling about Africa into the classroom curriculum?
- How are Lina and Ganali similar to and different from kindergarten children you are familiar with?
- How can children's differences become assets in the classroom?
- Why is it important for you to know about children's developmental characteristics? How do you plan to respond to children's developmental characteristics in your teaching?

Jamal

Introduce yourself to Jamal, a 6-year-old African-American male. Jamal weighs 53 pounds and is 4 feet tall. He is quiet and plays with small groups of boys. Jamal is eager to assert his independence, but needs help with tasks requiring fine motor skills. Jamal will pay attention during large-group activities, but does not like to actively participate.

Social-Emotional	Cognitive	Motor	Adaptive (Daily Living)
Is quiet—talks and plays with only a few other boys. Gives yes/no responses to teacher during large-group activities. Does not ask questions or share. Is very reserved and easygoing.	Enjoys books about cars, trucks, and machinery. Does not like singing or clapping; will stay in his seat during these activities. Enjoys listening to stories. Does not like to write.	Cannot color in lines. Likes to play football. Moves slowly in halls and classroom.	Is very neat—puts things away where they belong. Wants to learn how to do things so he does not have to ask for help. Cannot tie his shoes.

Tameka

Introduce yourself to Tameka, a 6-year-old African-American female. Tameka weighs 42 pounds and is 3 feet, 8 inches tall. Tameka is an assertive kindergartner. She likes to be in control of activities and classmates. Tameka has a strong desire to learn how to read and write and asks many questions during class.

Social-Emotional	Cognitive	Motor	Adaptive (Daily Living)
Displays impulsive behavior. Bosses friends. Enjoys talking to any adult. Tattles to the teacher.	Enjoys "reading" to friends and class, using pictures as cues. Uses puppets to retell stories. Likes writing letters of the alphabet. Needs help making the connection between letters and real words. Knows the values of different coins.	Well developed gross motor skills allow her to jump rope and run gracefully. Likes to dance. Enjoys cutting and pasting—can cut on a line.	Expresses needs, wants, and dislikes. Opens own milk carton—helps friends open theirs. Enjoys responsibilities such as taking class roll to the office. Has a strong desire for class to stay on a schedule.

Questions about 6-year-old kindergartners:

- How might Jamal's motor skills interfere with his desire to learn? Brainstorm some activities that would make writing more enjoyable for children like Jamal, who need to develop fine motor skills.
- What do you think are some reasons why Jamal cannot tie his shoes?
- How can you, as an early childhood teacher, encourage all members of your class to participate without discouraging children like Tameka, who tend to dominate activities?
- Do you think Jamal is learning less because he is not actively participating in group time?
- List some ways, other than copying words, you can help Tameka make the connection between letters and real words.
- Do you think Jamal and Tameka are meeting kindergarten standards? List some academic tasks not mentioned in the portraits that you think are important for kindergartners to master.

Hill's influence is evident in the format of many present-day preschools and kindergartens. Free, creative play, in which children can use materials as they wish, was Hill's idea and represented a sharp break with Froebelian philosophy. She also introduced large blocks and centers where children could engage in housekeeping, sand and water play, and other activities.

Froebel would probably not recognize today's kindergarten programs. Many kindergarten programs are subject centered rather than child centered as Froebel envisioned them. Furthermore, he did not see his program as a "school" but a place where children could develop through play. Although kindergartens are evolving to meet the needs of society and families, we must nonetheless acknowledge the philosophy and ideals on which the first kindergartens were based.

WHAT ARE KINDERGARTEN CHILDREN LIKE?

For more information about kindergartners' development, go to the Companion Website at **http:// www.prenhall.com/ morrison**, select any chapter, then choose Topic 2 of the ECE Supersite module.

Kindergarten children are like other children in many ways. They have developmental, physical, and behavioral characteristics that are the same and characterize them as kindergartners—children ages five to six. Yet, at the same time, they have characteristics that make them the unique individuals they are.

Review now the portrait of the four kindergarten children, and respond to the accompanying questions. You can also develop your own portraits of kindergarten children.

Most kindergarten children, especially those who have been to preschool, are very confident, are eager to be involved, and want to and can accept a great deal of responsibility. They like going places and doing things, such as working on projects, experimenting, and working with others. Socially, kindergarten children are at the same time solitary and independent workers and growing in their ability and desire to work cooperatively with others. Their combination of a "can do" attitude and their cooperation and responsibility make them a delight to teach and work with.

Kindergarten children are energetic. They have a lot of energy, and they want to use it in physical activities such as running, climbing, and jumping. Their desire to be involved in physical activity makes kindergarten an ideal time to involve children in projects of building—for example, making **learning centers** to resemble a store, post office, or veterinary office.

Learning centers   Places in a classroom where children are free to move to explore, manipulate, create, and work where their interests take them. Different centers may include a writing center, a dramatic play center, an art center, and a math center, for example.

Kindergarten children are in a period of rapid intellectual and language growth. They have a tremendous capacity to learn words and like the challenge of learning new words. This helps explain kindergarten children's love of big words and their ability to say and use them. This is nowhere more apparent than in their fondness for dinosaurs and words such as *brontosaur.* Kindergarten children like and need to be involved in many language activities.

Additionally, kindergartners like to talk. Their desire to be verbal should be encouraged and supported, with many opportunities to engage in various language activities such as singing, telling stories, being involved in drama, and reciting poetry.

From ages five to seven, children's average weight and height approximate each other. For example, at six years, boys, on average, weigh forty-six pounds and are forty-six inches tall, while girls, on average, weigh about forty-four pounds and are forty-five inches tall. At age seven, boys weigh on average fifty pounds and are about forty-eight inches tall; girls weigh on average fifty pounds and are about forty-eight inches tall (see Table 11.1).

WHO ATTENDS KINDERGARTEN?

Froebel's kindergarten was for children three to seven years of age. In the United States, kindergarten is for five- and six-year-old children before they enter first grade. Since the age at which children enter first grade varies, the ages at which they enter kindergarten also differ. Many parents and professionals support an older rather than a younger kindergarten entrance age because they think older children are more "ready" for kindergarten and will learn better. Consequently, it is not uncommon to have children in kindergarten who are

TABLE 11.1 Average Height and Weight for Kindergarten Children

Age	Males		Females	
	Height (inches)	Weight (pounds)	Height (inches)	Weight (pounds)
5 years	43.0	41.0	42.5	40.0
5 1/2 years	44.0	43.0	44.0	42.0
6 years	45.5	46.0	45.5	44.5
6 1/2 years	47.0	48.0	46.5	47.0
7 years	48.0	50.0	48.0	50.0

Source: National Center for Health Statistics in collaboration with the National Center for Chronic Disease Prevention and Health Promotion (2000). http://www.cdc.gov/growthcharts.

seven by the end of the year. Whereas in the past children had to be five years of age prior to December 31 for kindergarten admission, today the trend is toward an older admission age; many school districts require that children be five years old by September 1 of the school year.

SHOULD KINDERGARTEN BE COMPULSORY?

There is wide public support for compulsory and tax-supported public kindergarten. On one recent Gallup poll, 80 percent of respondents favored "making kindergarten available for all those who wish it as part of the public school system," 71 percent favored compulsory kindergarten attendance, and 70 percent thought children should start school at ages four or five (29 percent favored age four and 41 percent favored age five).[1] In keeping with this national sentiment, most children attend kindergarten (see Figure 11.1).

Universal Kindergarten has rapidly become a reality for the majority of the nation's five-year-olds. Today, kindergarten is either *a whole- or half-day program* and within the reach of most of the nation's children. The number of children attending kindergarten has risen steadily.

FULL- OR HALF-DAY KINDERGARTEN?

Both half- and full-day kindergarten programs are available. A school district that operates a half-day program usually offers one session in the morning and one in the afternoon, so that one teacher can teach two classes. Although many kindergartens are half-day programs, there is no general agreement that this system is best. Those who argue for it say that this is all the schooling the five-year-old child is ready to experience and that it provides an ideal transition to the all-day first grade. Those in favor of full-day sessions generally feel that not only is the child ready for and capable of a program of this length, but also that such an approach allows for a more comprehensive program.

The general trend is toward full-day kindergarten programs for all five-year-old children. However, essentially two factors stand in the way of a more rapid transition to full-day programs: tradition and money. Kindergartens have been historically and traditionally half-day programs, although there is ample evidence of full-day programs for four- and five-year-old children. As time passes and society's needs begin to point to full-day programs to prepare children for living in an increasingly complex world, more kindergarten programs will become full-day.

Today, kindergarten is a universal part of schooling, enrolling children from different cultures and socioeconomic backgrounds and, subsequently, different life experiences. How can professionals help ensure that kindergarten experiences meet the unique needs of each child?

Universal kindergarten The availability of kindergarten to all children. The public supports universal kindergarten.

Improving Practice Through Research

Teaching is indeed a social career. We spend our days in continual interaction and communication with others. We debate, discuss, explain, analyze, reiterate, and illuminate for hours on end with children and, for some of us, very young children. The reality of teaching is that there are few opportunities for professional reflection and fewer opportunities still for professional feedback from others. Yet, reflection is a necessary component of shaping or reshaping the way we think, act, and evolve into better teachers. Engaging in the process of teacher research provides an arena for educators to have opportunities to reflect, react, re-create, and evolve into more effective and more energized professionals.

I became a teacher researcher because I know that there are aspects of my teaching that needed improvement and fresh ideas. Although I routinely attend in-services and various seminars to stay current on philosophical and practical aspects of teaching, the results are often the same. I leave the sessions hoping that I will find the time to institute something from the day's experience that will enhance the children's learning. Sometimes I do. Many times, however, the folder full of ideas is filed for another day for consideration and further planning. I am drawn, again, into the constant rush of an early childhood world.

Teacher research groups, by their design, set apart time for reflection, create a forum for collaboration, and initiate expansion of ideas and concepts that are practical to the teacher's daily lessons. A benefit of teacher research is that the teacher researcher chooses the area to engage in reflective research. The topic is drawn from something that the teacher identifies as a puzzlement—not the district, the curriculum committee, or the principal. In my school, our teacher research group is comprised of teachers from different grade levels, specialty areas, and research interests. This provides a diverse and resourceful group of professionals with whom to interact. Usually six to twelve individuals form a teacher research team at my school. We are provided with one half day per month during which the school district provides funds for a substitute teacher to teach our children, while we meet to share and discuss our research.

In teacher research, the teacher takes on many roles as an observer of children and learning patterns, a seeker of meaningful impacts on learning, a problem solver, a discoverer, and ultimately a sharer of knowledge. Key elements of the research process include reflective journaling, observation of students' behaviors, professional reading, and data collection, collaborative discussions with fellow teacher researchers that we call critical friends, and all of

Money is the most important obstacle to the growth of full-day kindergarten programs. Without a doubt, it takes twice as many teachers to operate full-day programs as half-day programs. But as society continues to recognize the benefits of early education and as kindergartens and early childhood programs are seen as one means for solving societal problems, more funding will be forthcoming.

Research supports the attendance of children in full-day kindergarten programs. For example, a study of 17,600 schoolchildren:

> . . . suggests that full-day kindergarten programs may have both academic and financial payoffs. The study found that, by the time they reached the third and fourth grades, former full-day kindergartners were more than twice as likely as children without any kindergarten experiences—and 26 percent more likely than graduates of half-day programs—to have made it there without having repeated a grade. . . .
> "A lot of research suggests that how students are doing those first few years is very telling of what they'll do later on," said Andrea del Gaudio Weiss, the lead researcher on the study. . . .[2]

this often results in systematic, practical, and *timely* changes in classroom teaching and planning.

As the research reveals patterns of learning, immediate changes can be made in a teacher's method or materials to create immediate results and an immediate opportunity to make a difference in what teachers and students need. This knowledge impacts the researcher's students, but is also shared with the other members of the teacher research team and the teachers in the school and throughout the school system's Teacher Research Network. Additionally, Teacher Research often leads teachers to resources such as various grants that are available through school districts, governments, or private/commercial businesses. In turn, the teacher's findings are published to a wider audience through the grant submissions and publications and this research can impact many other educators as well.

Each year, our principal designates the last faculty meeting of the year to the Teacher Research roundtables. At this meeting, the teacher researchers informally present their research projects, including their reflections and findings from the year to the whole staff. After attending one such presentation, I began to consider how I could effectively and expediently modify my teaching practices to impact the children's literacy growth in my classroom. I attended a colleague's discussion on how she enhanced her K-1 classroom's writing performance by using shared writing during her free-choice/center time. This prompted me to consider that the children in my classroom did not choose literacy activities during Choice Time. Many children were active in the hands-on math, science, art, and writing centers. . . but not the reading center. It was then that my research began, because it was then that I identified the area of need for reflective research.

The following September, I joined the Teacher Research Committee. Through my participation, I was taking the theory of all my training and making it come alive, utilizing philosophies that I had not acted on since my Masters training. Now these strategies and philosophies moved me from theory to practice to make significant yet manageable changes in my literacy program. By providing my students with hands-on retelling props to prompt literacy growth, I rediscovered many of the theoretical teachings from my training: how significantly teaching the use of props enhanced the children's retelling success, how stories with predictable text, strong structure, and background knowledge supported success, how motivation is linked to success. . . and the list goes on. The most significant finding in my research is that, ultimately, it is the children who benefit. I have watched children who speak no English work through the motions of our favorite fairy tales demonstrating understanding without the use of one word of English. I have seen many children cheerfully break from the building blocks, puzzles, or drama centers to retell a story with a friend, and I have listened to the enhanced story language and comprehension as the students engage in storytelling with props. Mostly I have watched the joy of a great story come alive by my students. So significant were my findings that I pursued my next research topic—sharing this knowledge with the parents through an at-home story retelling program.

Teacher research provides meaningful, designated time and resources for classroom teachers to seek knowledge for specific professional development. It provides teacher researchers with the opportunity to put their findings into practice through collaboration, reevaluation and reflection, and the privilege to share it through publishing research papers, and presenting at schools as well as Teacher Research Conferences. It creates an on-going reflective nature that changes teaching forever.

Contributed by Deborah Q. Seidel, Ed. M., Kindergarten Teacher, Deer Park Elementary, Centreville, Virginia.

READINESS AND PLACEMENT OF KINDERGARTEN CHILDREN

THE ESCALATED CURRICULUM

By now you may be amazed about how kindergartens are changing. After your visit to kindergarten programs, you might have left thinking, "Wow, a lot of what they're doing in kindergarten I did in first grade!" Many early childhood professionals would agree. More is expected of kindergarten children today than ever before, and this trend will continue.

A number of reasons account for the "escalated" curriculum. First, beginning in the 1980s there has been a decided emphasis on "academics" in U.S. education, particularly early childhood education, as discussed in chapter 2. Second, some parents believe an academic approach to learning is the best way to succeed in school and the work world. They might also see academics as one of the ways to compensate for the lack of experiences and opportunities prior to their children's entry into school. Third, some first grade teachers are demanding children who are grounded in academics. And fourth, the standards, testing,

A Gift of Time for Nicholas

The plaque on the classroom door read "Mrs. Parker—Kindergarten." Nicholas reached for the brass doorknob and turned it enough to open it a crack. Mrs. Parker, standing nearby, pushed it open wide and said "Good Morning, Nicholas."

Nicholas could feel his face flush hot and pink as he wrinkled his nose and gave his teacher his best smile. He walked five steps and slid his backpack straps off his shoulders. The backpack fell to the floor with a thud just below the terrarium table next to the cubbies. He unbuttoned his yellow jacket, unzipped his backpack, and tidied his socks. Out came his shiny red lunch box which he placed on the shelf above the cubbies. Struggling with the sleeve of his jacket, Mrs. Parker pulled the jacket off one arm as she passed by on her way to the sink. Nicholas glanced her way with a shy smile as the other sleeve slipped off easily. Once his jacket was hung he let out a big sigh of relief and walked ten steps to his table. He was the first one today. He loved being first. He loved his teacher and his best friend Billy who hadn't arrived yet.

He turned his head toward the long windows and there it was, still standing—the skyscraper that he and Billy had made the day before at Center Time. Center Time was his favorite. You got to choose what you wanted to do. Mrs. Parker had been so proud of how tall the skyscraper was, that she brought the big black marker over, along with a long white strip, and helped the boys sound out the letters, "S-K-Y-S-C-R-A-P-E-R." She laid the newly printed word at the base of the building for all the class to see. Everyone gathered around and Chelsea clapped.

Chelsea is the silly girl who sits beside Nicholas and makes funny faces at him. Nicholas closes his eyes tight to avoid her funny faces, but she makes them anyway. Here comes that funny-face Chelsea right now.

Mrs. Parker gently touched Chelsea's shoulder as she passed by and knelt down next to Nicholas. "Nicholas, did you bring back that important paper I sent home yesterday for Mommy and Daddy to sign?" Nicholas jumped to his feet and ran back to his cubby to find the white paper. His mom had put it in the pocket with the secret zipper. She had told him all about it. It said he needed more time . . .

more time to run and jump and play and let nature take its course.

Dad had said "Yes, Bud! Just think of this year as practice for the 'Big Game'."

So Nicholas would be going to TK-1 next year. So would his friend Billy and silly funny-face Chelsea. Billy's parents came to school on the same night Nicholas' parents came to watch a movie about TK-1. Everyone already knew the TK-1 teacher, Mrs. Shaw. She was really nice and she let her class play kick ball.

"Yeah, when you got to go to TK-1 you got to play kick ball and you learned to read too!" Nicholas had told his parents. He had already read some things like the stop sign and the word Cheerios on his cereal box. He loved to listen to stories at the rug, but those stories were just a little too long.

"Time is a gift," his Grandma had said. "You don't get time back." So he was off to TK-1 right after summer vacation. But first, he got to play and swim all summer and celebrate his birthday, too.

Nicholas is not ready for a formal first grade setting. He needs additional time before he enters the first grade classroom. Brevard Public Schools recognize that children grow at different rates and this process should not be rushed or altered. Transitional Kindergarten-First Grade (TK-1) is designed for children who are developmentally younger than six.

The Brevard County, Florida, TK-1 Program, in effect for over twenty years, upholds a developmental philosophy backed by research concerning the manner in which young children learn:

- Children need a smooth transition from the home environment to the school environment. A working partnership between home and school should be encouraged and fostered for the benefit of the children.
- Children go through predictable stages of development at individual rates of growth that cannot be altered, hurried, or remediated. Activities, materials, and methods of working with children should be differentiated to meet their emotional, social, physical, and intellectual needs.

- Children will develop a positive self-image in a setting where there is total acceptance of individual needs and strengths.
- Children learn to accept and understand their own feelings and those of others through sharing and cooperating in group activities.
- Children learn and grow through active involvement. Opportunities to hop, skip, jump, stretch, balance, climb, catch, and run will enhance physical skills and motor coordination.
- Children learn through concrete experiences and play. Play is the work of children, and manipulative objects are the tools.
- Children learn by using their senses. Experiences must emphasize a multisensory approach to encompass hearing, seeing, touching, tasting, and smelling.
- Children should be taught how to think rather than what to think, thus giving them strong foundations upon which to build later experiences.
- Children should be taught to read through a balanced approach involving integrated reading, writing, and language experiences.

QUESTIONS MOST FREQUENTLY ASKED ABOUT OUR TK-1 PROGRAM ARE

Who is the TK-1 Program designed for?

The Transitional Kindergarten-First Grade Program (TK-1) is designed for children who are not ready for the formal first grade program. These children have already attended kindergarten and are developmentally younger than six.

What is the goal of the program?

The TK-1 year gives children the gift of time to develop physical, social/emotional, language, and cognitive potential. This developmental philosophy, along with research, tells us that children go through predictable stages of development at individual rates of growth that cannot be hurried or altered. The goal of the program is to help children develop a positive self-image in a setting where there is total acceptance of each child's individual needs and strengths.

How are the children chosen for the program?

The Gesell Test (a school readiness screening test) is one instrument used for screening children for placement in the developmental program. The results of this test indicate a child's developmental age, which is differentiated from chronological age. The Gesell Test is an individual test given by a trained, qualified examiner, which takes about 25 minutes.

The test is given in the spring of the kindergarten year. Recommended placement in TK-1 is also based on chronological age, teacher observation, parent input, and skill mastery as demonstrated on the Literacy Survey and other teacher checklists.

How do parents feel about this placement?

The classroom teacher hosts individual conferences regarding the recommended placement. It is the Gesell Institute's recommendation and district policy that parents have the final decision in the placement of their children in the TK-1 program. More than one parent-teacher conference may be necessary before a decision is finalized. The school also has an informational meeting for all parents considering TK-1 where they learn more about the program and meet the TK-1 teacher if possible. Parents who accept and go through the program are overwhelmingly glad that they gave their child the gift of time. The school will often have a parent speak at the meeting who has been through the program. Parents feel better when they talk to other parents who have been through the program. This gift of time is invaluable not only now, but also for the student's future as a lifelong learner.

Is this considered a retention on the child's school records?

The student's grade level assignment for the next school year is written under "Attendance" in the child's records. The term "assigned" rather than "retained" or "promoted" is used to indicate placement for the next year. TK-1 is not considered a retention.

Does the program have its own curriculum and grade level expectations?

Yes, TK-1 children have their own curriculum and grade level expectations which are chosen just for them. They are also given a different report card than in kindergarten and first grade.

How do the children adjust to the TK-1 class?

They adjust very well as they have an excellent program and have already had one year in kindergarten. They already know their way around the building and most faces are familiar to them. Parent volunteers are often used in the program, and the children get used to being comfortable with their new class family.

Would you say your program has been successful?

You would only need to walk through our TK-1 classes to see the answer. Brevard County has been committed to this developmental philosophy for over twenty years and has helped thousands of children make their early years successful.

Contributed by Linda Ridgley, Brevard (Florida) Public Schools Resource Teacher for Early Childhood, and Lynn Spadaccini, Director of Early Childhood Education and Title I Programs.

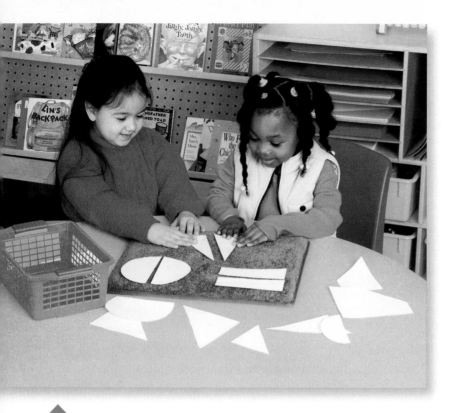

and high-quality education reform movement encourages—indeed, demands—greater emphasis on academics.

These higher expectations for kindergarten children are not necessarily bad. For several decades, in many kindergarten programs, kindergarten children did not learn the skills needed for success in the primary grades. This is especially true of minority children and children from low socioeconomic backgrounds. What many early childhood professionals are realizing is that we can no longer fail to teach children what they need in order to be ready to learn. How to achieve this goal in a developmentally appropriate way is one of the major challenges facing early childhood professionals.

ALTERNATIVE KINDERGARTEN PROGRAMS

It is not surprising, given the changing kindergarten curriculum, that some children may not be ready for many of the demands that will be placed on them. As a result, professionals have developed alternative kinds of kindergarten programs.

Children are born to learn. Learning is not something children "get ready for" but is a continuous process. What factors do you think are critical to support children's readiness to learn?

To complete a Program in Action activity, visit the Companion Website at **http://www. prenhall.com/morrison**, select chapter 11, then choose the Program in Action module.

Developmental Kindergarten.   The developmental kindergarten is a pre-kindergarten for developmentally or behaviorally delayed kindergarten children. It is seen as one means of helping at-risk children succeed in school. There is a specific procedure and rationale for placing children in such a program. Although the process may differ from program to program, the following are some of the ways placements are made in these developmental programs:

- Test kindergarten-eligible children prior to their entrance to kindergarten to determine which children are at risk (developmentally delayed).
- Give at-risk children an extra year to develop by placing them in a less cognitively oriented kindergarten classroom in which developmental needs can be addressed.
- Promote children to a regular kindergarten classroom the following year.
- As a result of having had an extra year to mature in the developmental kindergarten, a reduction in later school failure will be achieved.[3]

Transition Kindergarten.   A transition kindergarten is designed to give children the time they need to achieve what is required for entry into first grade. Children are really getting two years to achieve what they normally would achieve in one. A transition class is different from a nongraded program in that the transition class consists of children of the same age, whereas the nongraded classroom has multiage children.

The concept and practice of transition classes implies and should involve linear progression. Children are placed in a transition kindergarten so that they can continue to progress at their own pace. The curriculum, materials, and teaching practices should be appropriate for each child's developmental age or level.

Proponents of transitional programs believe they offer the following advantages:

- Placement in a transition program promotes success, whereas retention is a regressive practice that promotes failure.

- The program provides for children's developmental abilities.
- Children are with other children of the same developmental age.
- The program provides children with an appropriate learning environment.
- The program puts children's needs ahead of the need to place a child in a particular grade.
- The program provides time for children to integrate learning. This extra time is often referred to as "the gift of time."

Mixed Age/Multiage Grouping. Multiage grouping provides another approach to meeting the individual and collective needs of children. In a mixed-age group there is a diversity of abilities; at least a two-year span in children's ages; and the same teacher. The context of multiage groups provides a number of benefits and functions:

- Provides materials and activities for a wider range of children's abilities.
- Creates a feeling of community and belonging. Most mixed-age groups have a feeling of family, and this is supported because children spend at least two years in the mixed-age group.
- Supports children's social development by providing a broader range of children to associate with than they would in a same-age classroom. Children have more and less socially and academically advanced peers to interact with. Also, the mixed-age classroom provides a sustained and close relationship with children and teachers. In the mixed-age classroom, the teacher encourages and supports cross-age academic and social interactions. Furthermore, older children act as teachers, tutors, and mentors. Younger children are able to model the academic and social skills of their older class members.
- Supports the scaffolding of learning.
- Provides for a continuous progression of learning.

Looping. Looping occurs when a teacher spends two or more years with the same group of same-age children. In other words, a teacher involved in looping would begin teaching a group in kindergarten and then teach the same group as first graders and perhaps second graders. Another teacher might do the same with second, third, and fourth graders. Advantages of looping include the following:

- Looping provides freedom to expand the curriculum vertically and horizontally over a two-year period.
- The teacher has the opportunity to monitor a child's progress more closely over a two-year period before seeking child study team input.
- A teacher's familiarity with his or her children contributes to fostering a family-like atmosphere in the classroom.
- Teachers can get into the curriculum earlier in the school year because the children know what is expected of them.
- Looping allows for individualized instruction because teachers are more familiar with the strengths and weaknesses of each child in the class.
- Looping provides children with stability.
- Looping grants teachers an opportunity to stay fresh and grow professionally by changing their grade-level assignments every year.[4]

Retention. Along with the benefits of early education and universal kindergarten come political issues as well. One of these is the issue of retention. Retained children, instead of participating in kindergarten graduation ceremonies with their classmates, are destined to spend another year in kindergarten. Many of these children are retained or failed because teachers judge them to be immature, or they fail to measure up to districts' or teachers' standards for promotion to first grade. Children are usually retained in the elementary years because of

Team-Looping

Our first-to-second-grade team-looping classroom is innovative and unique because as teachers, we live by and teach by the creed, "effort creates ability." Our beliefs about learning and daily practice are clearly focused. We teach our students in the ways in which we would want our own children to be taught. In one large classroom, we have taught the same forty children for the past two years as their first and second grade teachers. This environment is extremely beneficial because it has helped us to develop meaningful relationships with students, understand how they learn, and determine how to best provide instruction. By having the same children for two years, we gain about six weeks of instructional time. We already know our students' strengths and weaknesses, and at the beginning of the second year we simply continue the previous year's work. Some of our students just need extra time; not an extra year in the same grade and our team loop is an alternative to retention. Our parents gain a greater understanding of their children's academic and social needs and become more active participants in their education. By planning picnics, potluck dinners, dessert socials, in-class luncheon dates with family members, and pool parties, we form a bond of trust and confidence with our parents. Forming that bond provides us with the necessary insight to further improve our teaching methods and student learning.

Because we share a classroom, we must also share the responsibility of sharing strategies and processes that help us to identify student needs and create an innovative approach to team teaching in a looping classroom. We use various methods to identify student needs. These methods include

verbal and written assessments, running records and portfolios, rubrics, writing samples, diagnostic testing, and teacher observation. Once our student needs are identified, we seek assistance from our school and community. Title 1 Reading and Mathematics programs assist our students who need more reinforcement and review to secure necessary skills. Our program for gifted students provides enrichment and acceleration. Our Instructional Support Team consists of a principal, guidance counselor, classroom teacher, parent, and special support personnel (if applicable). They provide additional learning strategies and alternatives to be engaged both at home and at school to help the student achieve successful encounters in the curriculum. Our comprehensive counseling therapists help children resolve issues that hinder their learning, and our after-school programs provide maintenance of skills in most subject areas.

We have utilized videoconferencing with doctoral students from the University of Pittsburgh. We have videotaped various teaching interactions within our classroom, and through live on-air discussions, they have made suggestions to help us better meet the needs of our students. We subscribe to various educational magazines, attend conferences and seminars, and take advantage of Internet services to help children reach their full potential. We encourage our students to "shoot for the moon." Even if they miss, they'll still land among the stars.

Because of our team approach, we can pool our efforts and make optimum use of our expertise within a subject level. It allows us the flexibility to vary our teaching methods to reach more students. As teachers, we complement each other, bringing our own strengths, interests, and personalities to the team. Because we work as a team, flexibility is our hallmark.

We have also included many in-school programs to keep our students motivated and actively involved in the learning process. For example, for our thematic unit on the "Polar Regions," a docent from the Carnegie Museum of Natural History visited our classroom with a program about Inuit children, customs, and traditions. For our "Pennsylvania" thematic unit, we invited a speaker from the Pennsylvania Game Commission. For our "Earth Day Celebration," we invited a county agent from the Penn State Cooperative Extension Service, a park naturalist from Twin Lakes County Park, an environmental coordinator from St. Vincent College, a resource person from the Pennsylvania Cleanways and Master Gardeners, a local beekeeper, the game commissioner from the Pennsylvania Game Commission, and a park ranger from Keystone State Park as guest speakers for the day. We have formed a special partnership with the Central Westmoreland Career and Technology Center (CWCTC). We have toured the school and have actively participated with their students in the construction of miniature sleighs that were given as Christmas gifts from our students to their parents. The cooking school from CWCTC has visited our school with a cake-decorating lesson. Their students have also helped our students to make stepping-stones for our butterfly garden and have built reading benches to be placed near our butterfly garden in the front courtyard of our school.

To help our students become involved and interested in the topics we teach, we realized that we must become role models of lifelong learners to our students. When teachers show enthusiasm for the curricula, it ignites the natural curiosity in their students. They become eager to learn and master new skills. In our classroom, we have dressed as Johnny Appleseed, Thing One and Thing Two, Hansel and Gretel, Mayzie, a Sneetch, and one-hundred-year-old teachers to motivate our students to embrace the curricula.

We have promoted student engagement, ownership, and understanding by active participation. Our most successful method of active participation has been the teaching of thematic units. These units have made vital connections across our grade-level subject matter. For example, when teaching a thematic unit on "Germany," our students learned the geography of the country, plus important historical facts (social studies). We learned to count and recite familiar phrases in German (foreign language). We read and discussed fairytales that originated in the Black Forest and used those fairytales as writing prompts (language arts and process writing). We compared and contrasted U.S. and German currency, time, size, and population (mathematics). We created gingerbread houses (art) and as a culminating activity, we celebrated Oktoberfest with authentic food and music (the

arts). We have researched and compiled information to create and teach numerous thematic units. Topics include:

- Johnny Appleseed
- Butterflies
- Zoo animals
- Dinosaurs
- Polar regions
- Toys of long ago
- Camp-outs and jamborees
- Our bodies
- Animals in nature
- Earth Day
- Our five senses in nature
- Pennsylvania
- Germany
- France
- Read Across America
- Acid mine drainage

Because children come to school with their own strengths and interests, we have integrated the process of compacting into the curricula. Compacting is a process that involves preassessing students, giving them credit for what they already know, and allowing them to move ahead in the curricula. In spelling, our students are given a pretest at the beginning of each five-day week. If the students achieve 100 percent accuracy, they are permitted to choose their own list of words to be studied for the week.

Our lessons include many hands-on projects and activities. For our "Dr. Seuss" unit, students dressed as their favorite Dr. Seuss character, made ooblek, and cooked green eggs and ham. With the help of our public library, we read fifty books, one story from each of our fifty states, for a "Read Across America" project. We reenacted the story *The Cat in the Hat Comes Back* and made our own report cards for "The Cat." When celebrating the one-hundredth day of school, students came dressed as if they were one-hundred years old. We completed one-hundred-piece puzzles, listed one hundred words that began with C (because C is the Roman numeral for 100), and answered the writing prompt, "If I told you once, I told you one hundred times. . . ." We brought one hundred given items from home and estimated the weights of those items from lightest to heaviest. We used a pan balance scale to verify our results. When investigating the weather, we e-mailed The Weather Channel, friends, and family throughout the world for weather updates.

To encourage ownership, we required students to keep a writing journal, and we also scheduled times of independent study. This provided students with the opportunity to work independently to investigate topics of interest to them. We provided supervised Internet access to pursue their studies and encouraged them to reflect on their learning in their journals. We encouraged active participation in our school's annual spelling bee, science fair, school newspaper, and reflections competition.

One of our best strategies has been the implementation of a mentorship program of parents, grandparents, high school students, community members, and school board members. These volunteers have become our companions in learning. Numerous volunteers work in our classroom each and every day. They tutor students in all subject areas and provide our students with a variety of frameworks from simple to complex.

By far, the best advantage to our team-loop approach has been the building of significant relationships with our students. Whether it was a gifted child, an overachiever, an average student, or one who required many repetitions, learning evolved in our classroom according to the student's personal continuum, not by a rigid agenda. No child was left behind.

Each and every day, as we stood in front of our team-looping classroom, we witnessed a glimpse of the future in action; and our creed of "effort creates ability" took on new meaning. An old Chinese proverb states, "Give a man a fish and he eats for a day. Teach a man to fish and he eats for a lifetime." We couldn't agree more!

As you can see, teaching is our passion! We genuinely love what we do! As teachers, we value and respect each other's teaching styles and methods. Although our personalities are quite different, we celebrate our uniqueness and use our talents to help every child feel special and loved. Not only do we teach with our minds, we teach with our hearts. We believe that no matter what you do in life, make it beautiful!

Contributed by Vicki Sheffler and Christa Pehrson, 2002 *USA Today's* First Team Teachers, Amos K. Hutchinson Elementary School, Greensburg, Pennsylvania. Photos courtesy of Diane Rus and Elaine Haley.

To complete a Program in Action activity, visit the Companion Website at **http://www.prenhall.com/morrison**, select chapter 11, then choose the Program in Action module.

low academic achievement or low IQ. (In comparison, reasons for retention are different at the junior high level, at which students are generally retained because of behavior problems or excessive absences.)

When well-meaning early childhood education professionals fail children, they do so in the belief that they are doing them and their families a favor. These professionals feel that children who have an opportunity to spend an extra year in the same grade will do better the second time around. Teachers' hopes, and consequently parents' hopes, are that these failed children will go on to do as well as (many teachers hold out the promise that they will do even better than) their nonretained classmates. But is this true? Do children do better the second time around?

Despite our intuitive feelings that children who are retained will do better, the research evidence is unequivocally to the contrary: children do not do better the second time around. In addition, parents report that retained children have a more pessimistic attitude toward school, with a consequently negative impact on their social-emotional development.[5]

The ultimate issue of retention is how to prevent failure and promote success. To achieve those goals, professionals will have to change their views about what practices are best for children and how to prevent the risk factors that create a climate for unsuccessful school experiences.

WHAT SHOULD KINDERGARTEN BE LIKE?

For more information about kindergarten curricula and teaching strategies, go to the Companion Website at **http://www.prenhall.com/morrison**, select any chapter, then choose Topic 6 of the ECE Supersite module.

All early childhood teachers have to make decisions regarding what curriculum and activities they will provide for their children. When making decisions about what kindergarten should be like, you can consider and compare the ideas and philosophies of the historic figures discussed in chapter 4 with contemporary practice. Consider Froebel, for example:

The Kindergarten is an institution which treats the child according to its nature; compares it with a flower in a garden; recognizes its threefold relation to God, man and nature; supplies the means for the development of its faculties, for the training of the senses, and for the strengthening of its physical powers. It is the institution where a child plays with children.[6]

By comparing Froebel's vision of the kindergarten with today's kindergartens, we see that many of today's kindergartens are much different than what Froebel envisioned. This situation is entirely appropriate in many ways, for society is vastly different today than it was in Froebel's time. What this means is that you have to develop your own vision of what your kindergarten will be like.

This book has emphasized that in all things early childhood professionals do for and with children, their efforts should be **developmentally appropriate.** Developmentally ap-

Developmentally appropriate Teaching based on how children grow and develop.

VIDEO VIEWPOINT

Playgrounds

One of NAEYC's guidelines for developmentally appropriate practice is that children have ample opportunities to play safely. Unsupervised playground areas and improperly maintained equipment can put children at risk.

REFLECTIVE DISCUSSION QUESTIONS

How can you create an environment that is conducive to safe and meaningful outdoor play? What kinds of play ideas and equipment can you provide to create an optimum play environment?

REFLECTIVE DECISION MAKING

Visit the website of the Consumer Product Safety Commission (http://www.cpsc.gov/cpscpub/pubs/327.html) to review its guidelines for safe playgrounds. Then visit a nearby schoolyard or park playground and examine the equipment and the play environment. What did you find out about the safety level of the playground you visited? Share your observations with your classmates.

---

propriate practice—that is, teaching and caring for young children—facilitates learning that is in accordance with children's physical, cognitive, social, and linguistic development. Understanding professionals will help children learn and develop in ways that are compatible with how old they are and who they are as individuals (e.g., their background of experiences, culture). Those early childhood professionals who embody the qualities of good kindergarten teachers will tend to be those who teach in developmentally appropriate ways.

For more information about Developmentally Appropriate Practice, go to the Companion Website at **http://www.prenhall. com/morrison**, select any chapter, then choose Topic 4 of the ECE Supersite module.

Talking about developmentally appropriate practice is one thing; putting it into practice is another. Here are some of the implications of such practice for kindergarten programs (indeed, all programs involving young children):

- Learning must be meaningful to children and related to what they already know. Children find things meaningful when they are interesting to them and they can relate to them.
- Children do not learn in the same way, nor are they interested in learning the same thing as everyone else all the time. Thus, teachers must individualize their curriculum as much as possible.
- Learning should be physically and mentally active; that is, children should be actively involved in learning activities by building, making, experimenting, investigating, and working collaboratively with their peers.
- Children should be involved in *hands-on* activities with concrete objects and manipulatives. Emphasis is on real-life activities as opposed to workbook and worksheet activities.

LITERACY EDUCATION AND KINDERGARTEN CHILDREN

Literacy education is an important and highly visible topic today. Literacy is discussed in virtually all educational circles, and early childhood educators are talking about how to promote it. If they are not, they should be. Literacy has replaced reading readiness as the main objective of many kindergarten and primary programs. *Literacy* means the ability to read, write, speak, and listen, with emphasis on reading and writing well. To be literate also means reading, writing, speaking, and listening within the context of one's cultural and social setting.

FIGURE 11.2 Twelve Essential Components of Research-Based Programs for Beginning Reading Instruction

1. Children have opportunities to expand their use and appreciation of oral language.

2. Children have opportunities to expand their use and appreciation of printed language.

3. Children have opportunities to hear good stories and informational books read aloud daily.

4. Children have opportunities to understand and manipulate the building blocks of spoken language.

5. Children have opportunities to learn about and manipulate the building blocks of written language.

6. Children have opportunities to learn the relationship between the sounds of spoken language and the letters of written language.

7. Children have opportunities to learn decoding strategies.

8. Children have opportunities to write and relate their writing to spelling and reading.

9. Children have opportunities to practice accurate and fluent reading in decodable stories.

10. Children have opportunities to read and comprehend a wide assortment of books and other texts.

11. Children have opportunities to develop and comprehend new vocabulary through wide reading and direct vocabulary instruction.

12. Children have opportunities to learn and apply comprehension strategies as they reflect upon and think critically about what they read.

Source: Texas Reading Initiative, *Beginning Reading Instruction.* Austin, TX: Texas Education Agency Publications Division, 2002.

Literacy education is a hot topic in educational circles for a number of reasons. First, the National Adult Literacy Survey estimates that over 50 million Americans are functionally illiterate—at or below a fifth grade reading level. Furthermore, when we compare the U.S. literacy rate with that of other countries, we do not fare too well—many industrialized countries have higher literacy rates.[7] Consequently, educators and social policy planners are always concerned about the inability of the schools to teach all children to read at more than a functional level. As we have discussed, how to get all children to read is a major national concern. Figure 11.2 outlines twelve essential components of research-based programs designed to promote reading.

Second, businesses and industry are concerned about how unprepared the nation's workforce is to meet the demands of the workplace. Critics of the educational establishment maintain that many high school graduates do not have the basic literacy skills required for today's high-tech jobs. Therefore, schools, especially at the early grades, are feeling the pressure to adopt measures that will give future citizens the skills they will need for productive work and meaningful living.

Third, state governments are in the forefront of making sure that all children learn to read well and that they read on level by third grade. For example, the State of Texas conducted Kindergarten Teacher Reading Academies designed to provide teachers with knowledge and skills that promote early reading success. All kindergarten teachers attended four days of training and were paid $150 a day. These academies focused on research-based approaches to early literacy and reading. What all of this means is that the goals for kindergarten learning are higher than they have been in the past (see Figure 11.3).

FIGURE 11.3 What Should a Kindergarten Child Know?

Kindergarten Accomplishments

- Knows the parts of a book and their functions.
- Begins to track print when listening to a familiar text being read or when rereading own writing.
- "Reads" familiar text emergently (i.e., not necessarily verbatim from the print alone).
- Recognizes and can name all uppercase and lowercase letters.
- Understands that the sequence of letters in a written word represents the sequence of sounds (phonemes) in a spoken word (alphabetic principle).
- Learns many, though not all, one-to-one letter–sound correspondences.
- Recognizes some words by sight, including a few very common ones (the, I, my, you, is, are).
- Uses new vocabulary and grammatical constructions in own speech.
- Makes appropriate switches from oral to written language styles.
- Notices when simple sentences fail to make sense.
- Connects information and events in texts to life and life experiences to text.
- Retells, reenacts, or dramatizes stories or parts of stories.
- Listens attentively to books the teacher reads to class.
- Can name some book titles and authors.
- Demonstrates familiarity with a number of types or genres of text (e.g., storybooks, expository texts, poems, newspapers, and everyday print such as signs, notices, labels).
- Correctly answers questions about stories read aloud.
- Makes predictions based on illustrations or portions of stories.
- Demonstrates understanding that spoken words consist of phonemes.
- Given spoken sets like "dan, dan, den," can identify the first two as the same and the third as different.
- Given spoken sets like "dak, pat, zen," can identify the first two as sharing one identical sound.
- Given spoken segments, can merge them into a meaningful target word.
- Given a spoken word, can produce another word that rhymes with it.
- Independently writes many uppercase and lowercase letters.
- Uses phonemic awareness and letter knowledge to spell independently (invented or creative spelling).
- Writes (unconventionally) to express own meaning.
- Builds a repertoire of some conventionally spelled words.
- Shows awareness of distinction between "kid writing" and conventional orthography.
- Writes own name (first and last) and the first names of some friends or classmates.
- Can write most letters and some words when they are dictated.

Source: Adapted, with permission, from M. S. Burns, P. Griffin, and C. E. Snow, *Starting Out Right: A Guide to Promoting Children's Reading Success.* Copyright 1999 by the National Academy of Sciences. Courtesy of the National Academy Press, Washington, D.C.

FIGURE 11.4 Reading/Literacy Instructional Terminology

Alphabet knowledge: The knowledge that letters have names and shapes and that letters can represent sounds in language

Alphabetic principle: Awareness that each speech sound or phoneme in a language has its own distinctive graphic representation, and an understanding that letters go together in patterns to represent sounds

Comprehension: In reading, the basic understanding of the words and the content or meaning contained within printed material

Onset-rime: The onset is the part of the syllable that precedes the vowel, while the rime is the remaining part of the syllable

Orthographic awareness: Familiarity with written symbols and an understanding of the relationships between these symbols and the sounds they represent

Phoneme: The smallest unit of speech that makes a difference to meaning

Phonemic awareness: The ability to deal explicitly and segmentally with sound units smaller than the syllable

Phonological awareness: The ability to manipulate language at the levels of syllables, rhymes, and individual speech sounds

Print awareness: The recognition of conventions and characteristics of a written language

---

The nation has set a goal of having all children read and write at or above level by third grade. What are some activities and practices you can implement that will help ensure that all children achieve this national goal?

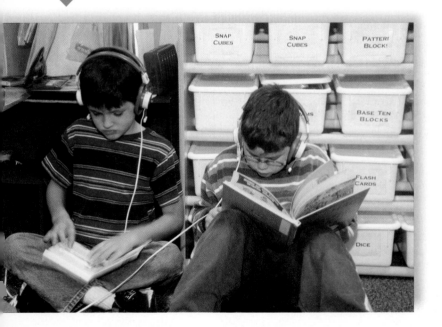

EMERGENT LITERACY AND READING

Today, early childhood professionals place a high priority on children's literacy and reading success. Literacy involves reading, writing, speaking, and listening. Professionals view literacy as a process that begins at birth (perhaps before) and continues to develop across the life span, through the school years and into adulthood. Thus, with the first cry, children are considered to begin language development (see chapter 9 for a discussion of linguistic development). Throughout our discussion about literacy, reading, and the ways to promote them, the terms in Figure 11.4 will prove useful to your study of the process.

Emergent literacy involves a range of activities and behaviors related to written language, including those undertaken by very young children who depend on the cooperation of others, and/or on creative play, to deal with the material. It involves reading- and writing-related activities and behaviors that change over time, culminating in conventional literacy during middle school.[8]

Many literacy themes emphasize using environmental and social contexts to support and extend children's reading and writing. Children want to make sense of what they read and write. The meaningful part of reading and writing occurs when children talk to each other, write letters, and read good literature or have it read to them. All of this occurs within a print-rich environment, one in which children see others read, make lists, and use language and the written word to achieve goals. Proponents of early literacy maintain that this environment is highly preferable to previous approaches to literacy development.

The process of becoming literate is also viewed as a natural process; reading and writing are processes that children participate in naturally, long before they come to school. No doubt you have participated with or know of toddlers and preschoolers who are literate in many ways. They "read" all kinds of signs (McDonald's) and labels (Campbell's soup) and scribble with and on anything and everything.

The concept of emergent literacy, then, is based on the following beliefs about literacy and about how children learn:

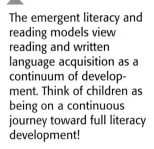

▲

The emergent literacy and reading models view reading and written language acquisition as a continuum of development. Think of children as being on a continuous journey toward full literacy development!

- Reading and writing involve cognitive and social abilities that children employ in the processes of becoming literate and gaining meaning from reading, writing, speaking, and listening.
- Most children begin processes involved in reading and writing long before they come to school; they do not wait until someone teaches them. They should not have to wait to be taught. (Remember what Montessori said about early literacy.)
- Literacy is a social process that develops within a context in which children have the opportunity to interact with and respond to printed language and to other children and adults who are using printed language. In this context, children bring meaning to and derive meaning from reading and writing. Teachers and classrooms should encourage discussing and sharing knowledge and ideas through reading and writing.
- The cultural group in which children become literate influences how literacy develops and the form it takes. Children should also have opportunities to read the literature of many cultural groups in addition to their own.

Emergent reading involves reading-related activities and behaviors, especially those prior to a child's achieving the capacity to read fluently and conventionally. This includes (a) the attentive presence of a child while another writes according to the child's intentions, (b) the execution of acts with materials related to reading (e.g., page turning, letter naming), and (c) the pretense of processing and/or comprehending written language.[9]

DEVELOPING LITERACY AND READING IN YOUNG CHILDREN

Literacy and reading are certainly worthy national and educational goals, not only for young children but for everyone. However, how best to promote literacy has always been a controversial topic.

What do children need to know to become good and skillful readers? Research identifies the following:[10]

- Knowledge of letter names
- Speed at which children can name individual letters
- Phonemic awareness (letter sound awareness)

Latino Family Literacy

This program is a two-part comprehensive bilingual family literacy project designed to increase parents' involvement in their children's literacy learning. It also addresses the growing awareness that the literacy proficiencies of children are closely tied to the adults in their family. This program recognizes that the motivation, common to many adult learners, is a desire to help their children. The program supports parents' involvement in their children's development, language and literacy development and provides a forum where parents can discuss parenting concerns, family traditions, and education. Each session is designed to establish a family reading routine and provide books, materials, and art projects, which are culturally and linguistically relevant to the lives of Latino families.

The ten-week program is designed to be presented by a trained teacher, parent center leader, or volunteer parent. Once a week, parents attend a two-hour session and are introduced to bilingual-children's books that they take home and read with their children. The books are returned the following session and parents are provided the opportunity to discuss their experiences reading with their children and how the books related to their lives.

All books are bilingual so as to include the linguistic and literacy skills of the entire family. Books are culturally reflective of Latin families, values, and traditions. This grounding in the Latin culture helps to maintain parents' interest in reading with their children. The books are also beautifully illustrated, which assists parents and children in following the story. This is especially helpful for parents and children who have lower level literacy skills.

Each book is accompanied with a writing and art activity that reflects the lives and issues of the participants and which contributes to making a family album. Parents are given a disposable camera to take home and take pictures of their children and their daily experiences. During the two-hour sessions, parents create a descriptive text of the photos to use to complete a family album.

The program has several goals:

- Strengthen parent and child interaction
- Establish and support a family reading routine
- Increase parents' confidence in their ability to assist their children's learning
- Challenge and empower parents to improve their own literacy skills
- Support English language skills of parents and children
- Promote enjoyment of reading

Basal approaches and materials used for literacy and reading development often emphasize a particular method. One of the most popular methods is the *sight word* approach (also called *whole-word* or *look-say*) in which children are presented with whole words (cat, bat, sat) and develop a "sight vocabulary" that enables them to begin reading and writing. Many early childhood professionals label objects in their classrooms (door, bookcase, etc.) as a means of teaching a sight vocabulary. Word walls are very popular in kindergarten and primary classrooms.

A second popular basal approach is based on *phonics* instruction, which stresses teaching letter–sound correspondence. By learning these connections, children are able to combine sounds into words (C-A-T). The proponents of phonics instruction argue that letter–sound correspondences enable children to make automatic connections between words and sounds and, as a result, they are able to sound out words and read them on their own. From the 1950s up until the present time (see chapter 3) there has been much debate about which of these two approaches to literacy development is best. Today, there is a decided reemphasis on the use of phonics instruction. One reason for this emphasis is that the research evidence suggests that phonics instruction enables children to become proficient readers.[11]

IMPLEMENTING A LATINO FAMILY LITERACY PROGRAM

If you want to implement your own Latino Family Literacy Program, here are some things you can include in each session:

- A discussion regarding how the reading with their children went at home.
- An introduction to this session's new book to take home, including reading the book aloud.
- A discussion of the new books using questions such as: What did you think about the book? What did you like about the book? What do you think the message of the book is? Did you like the illustrations? Why? Facilitate a discussion regarding what takes place in the story and how the characters might feel about what is taking place.
- Work on the day's activity.

Session 1 *We Are a Rainbow/Somos un arco iris* by Nancy Maria Grande Tabor
Introductions of participants
Informal assessment of home reading activities (pre-survey)

Session 2 *With My Brother/Con mi hermano* by Eileen Roe
Distribute disposable cameras
Activity: Participants identify positive words to describe their child(ren)

Session 3 *Family Pictures/Cuadros de familia* by Carmen Lomas Garza
Activity: Create a visual depiction of their Family Tree

Session 4 *A Gift from Papa Diego/Un regalo de Papá Diego* by Benjamin Alire Sáenz
Collect cameras
Activity: Write a letter to a family member

Session 5 *The Spirit of Tío Fernando/El espíritu de tío Fernando* by Janice Levy
Activity: Write a letter to their children

Session 6 *Carlos and the Squash Plant/Carlos y la planta de calabaza* by Jan Romero Stevens
Activity: Begin making family album using photos and writing about the photos

Session 7 *Angel's Kite/La estrella de angel* by Alberto Blanco
Activity: Continue making family album. Be sure to include letters and family tree created in earlier sessions.

Session 8 *The Woman Who Outshone the Sun/La mujer que brillaba aún más que el sol* by Alejandro Cruz Martinez
Activity: Continue making family album

Session 9 *Half Chicken/Medio pollito* by Alma Flor Ada
Activity: Complete the family album Informal assessment of reading activity taking place at home (post-survey)

Session 10 Review and Celebration*

*If funding permits a very popular way to end the program is to let each participant choose their favorite book to keep in their home library.

Contributed by Charlotte Castignola, Director of Parents as Learning Partners, District B, Los Angeles Unified School District.

Another method of literacy and reading development, the Language Experience Approach, follows the philosophy and suggestions inherent in progressive education philosophy (see chapter 2). This approach is child centered and maintains that literacy education should be meaningful to children and should grow out of experiences that are interesting to them. Children's own experience is a key element in such child-centered approaches. Many teachers transcribe children's dictated "experience" stories and use them as a basis for writing and for reading instruction.

Beginning about 1980, early childhood practitioners in the United States were influenced by literacy education approaches used in Australia and New Zealand as well as by approaches from Great Britain that were popular during the open education movement of the 1960s. These influences gradually developed into what is known as the **whole language approach** to literacy development. Since whole language is a philosophy rather than a method, its definition often depends on who is using the term. This approach nonetheless advocates using all aspects of language—reading, writing, listening, and speaking—as the basis for developing literacy. Children learn about reading and writing by speaking and

 To complete a Program in Action activity related to family literacy, visit the Companion Website at **http://www.prenhall. com/morrison**, select chapter 11, then choose the Program in Action module.

Whole language approach
Philosophy of literacy development that advocates the use of real literature—reading, writing, listening, and speaking—to help children become motivated to read and write.

listening; they learn to read by writing, and they learn to write by reading. Other characteristics of whole language include the following:

- It is *child centered*—children, rather than teachers, are at the center of instruction and learning. Thus, children's experiences and interests serve as the context for topics and as a basis for their intrinsic motivation to read, write, and converse. In this way, literacy learning becomes meaningful and functional for children.
- Social interaction is important and part of the process of becoming literate. Lev Vygotsky (see chapter 3) stressed the social dimensions of learning. He proposed that through interaction with others, especially with more confident peers and through interactions and conversations with teachers, children are able to develop higher cognitive learning. This process of learning through social interaction is referred to as *socially constructed knowledge*.
- Spending time on the processes of reading and writing is more important than spending time on learning skills for getting ready to read. Consequently, from the moment they enter the learning setting children are involved in literacy activities—that is, being read to; "reading" books, pamphlets, magazines, etc.; scribbling; "writing" notes; and so forth.
- Reading, writing, speaking, and listening are taught as an integrated whole, rather than in isolation.
- Writing begins early. This means that children are writing from the time they enter the program.
- Children's written documents are used as reading materials.
- Themes or units of study are used as a means of promoting interests and content. Generally, themes are selected cooperatively by children and teachers and are used as means of promoting ongoing intrinsic interest in literary processes.

Whole language dominated early childhood practice from about 1990 through 1995. However, growing numbers of critics of this approach, including parents and the public, maintain that because it is a philosophy rather than a specific approach, it does not teach children skills necessary for good reading. Additionally, some teachers have difficulty explaining the whole language approach to parents, and some find it difficult to implement as well. Further, some research has indicated that whole language approaches do not result in the high levels of reading achievement claimed by its supporters. As a result, proponents of phonics instruction are aggressively advocating a return to this approach as one which will best meet the needs of parents, children, and society.

A BALANCED APPROACH

As with most things, a balanced approach is probably the best, and many early childhood advocates are encouraging literacy approaches that provide a balance between whole language methods and phonics instruction and that meet the specific needs of individual children. One thing is clear: systematic instruction that enables children to acquire skills they need to learn to read is very much in evidence in today's early childhood classrooms. It is likely that the debate over "the best approach" will continue. At the same time, there will be increased efforts to integrate the best of all approaches into a unified whole to make literacy education a reality for all children.

SUPPORTING CHILDREN'S LEARNING TO READ

A primary goal of kindergarten education is for children to learn how to read. Teachers must instruct, support, and guide children in helping them learn what is necessary for them to be successful in school and life. Figure 11.5 lists some of the things you can do to motivate children's learning. Also, stop for a minute and reflect on what we said in chapter 5 about Vygotsky's theory of scaffolding children's learning. Figure 5.6 will help you learn how to scaffold children's literacy development.

FIGURE 11.5 Suggestions for Motivating Children to Read

- Include a variety of different types of books, such as picture books without words, fairy tales, nursery rhymes, picture storybooks, realistic literature, decodable and predictable books, information books, chapter books, biographies, big books, poetry, and joke and riddle books.
- Provide other types of print such as newspapers, magazines, and brochures.
- Introduce and discuss several books each week (may be theme-related, same authors, illustrators, types of books, etc.).
- Have multiple copies of popular books.
- Include books in children's home languages.
- Have an easy-to-use system for checking out books.
- Provide a record-keeping system for keeping track of books read (may include a picture-coding system to rate or evaluate the book).
- Showcase many books by placing them so the covers are visible, especially those that are new, shared in read-aloud sessions, or theme-related.
- Organize books on shelves by category or type (may color code).
- Provide comfortable, inviting places to read (pillows, rugs, a sofa, large cardboard boxes, etc.).
- Encourage children to read to "friends" (include stuffed animals and dolls for "pretend" reading).
- Have an Author's Table with a variety of writing supplies to encourage children to write about books.
- Have a Listening Table for recorded stories and tapes.

Source: From Lesley Mandel Morrow, *Literacy Development in the Early Years,* 4e © 2001. Published by Allyn and Bacon, Boston, MA. Copyright © 2001 by Pearson Education. Adapted by permission of the publisher.

KINDERGARTEN CHILDREN AND TRANSITIONS

A transition is a passage from one learning setting, grade, program, or experience to another. Young children face many such transitions in their lives. They are left with baby-sitters and enter child care programs, preschools, kindergarten, and first grade. Depending on how adults help children make these transitions, they can be either unsettling and traumatic or happy and rewarding experiences.

The transition from home to preschool to kindergarten influences positively or negatively children's attitudes toward school. Under no circumstances should the transition from preschool to kindergarten or from kindergarten to first grade be viewed as the beginning of "real learning." Leaving kindergarten to enter first grade is a major transition. The transition may not be too difficult for children whose kindergarten classroom is housed in the same building as the primary grades. For others whose kindergarten is separate from the primary program or who have not attended kindergarten, the experience can be unsettling. Children with special needs who are making a transition from a special program to a mainstreamed classroom need extra attention and support, as we will discuss in chapter 16.

Parents and kindergarten professionals can help children make transitions easily and confidently in several ways:

- Educate and prepare children ahead of time for any new situation. For example, children and teachers can visit the kindergarten or first grade program the children will attend. Also, toward the end of the preschool or kindergarten year or as the time to enter kindergarten or first grade approaches, children can practice certain routines as they will do them when they enter their new school or grade.

LESSON PLAN

The following lesson plan, Plentiful Penguins, was written by a kindergarten teacher in the Miami-Dade (FL) Public Schools, Sylvia McCabe, a National Board for Professional Teaching Standards (NBPTS) Certified Teacher. The lesson plan has a number of interesting elements.

- Notice how the lesson integrates many content areas.
- Make a list of the various teaching strategies Sylvia uses to teach her lesson.
- Notice how Sylvia connects classroom learning to home learning.

Plentiful Penguins
Goals and Objectives

Goal: Kindergarten children will learn about penguins and relate similarities of penguins to human family behavior.

Instructional Objectives

The students will . . .

1. Recall facts, characteristics and habits about penguins and their families.
2. Compare and contrast different species of penguins.
3. Use the paint program, KidWorks2™, to illustrate a penguin and record facts about penguins.
4. Learn the following basic word-processing skills: keyboard keys and functions, writing a sentence, saving, and printing a document.
5. Use a variety of technological and informational resources to gather and synthesize information about penguins.
6. Choose their favorite penguin of the penguins studied. As a home learning project, they will write an important fact about their favorite penguin. They will also make up a song or poem about their favorite penguin and share it with the class.

Prerequisite Skills

1. Students should be familiar with the computer—how to use the mouse, how to type on a keyboard, and how to print.
2. Students will write sentences, using inventive spelling if necessary.
3. Students will use appropriate skills to produce art projects.

Time Frame

Approximately two weeks

Lesson Activities

Activity One: I introduced my students to facts about penguins through nonfiction books.

Activity Two: My students viewed three to four Internet sites about penguins. After viewing these Internet sites and learning about the different types of penguins, they compared and contrasted penguin characteristics.

Activity Three: My students learned the song "All The Penguins" and learned poems about penguins. They made penguins using paper plates and construction paper.

Activity Four: My students gathered in groups and looked at pictures of five different penguins that they had been studying and chose their favorite penguin. As a home learning project, they wrote an important fact about their penguin and drew a picture of their penguin. They also made up a song or poem to bring to class to share with their classmates.

Activity Five: My students used the KidWorks2 Paint Program to replicate their hand drawing of the penguin and used their keyboarding skills to write a fact about the penguin.

Activity Six: Students' pictures and writings were printed to make a class book to share with others.

Introducing Penguins

I introduced the students to penguins through an integrated curriculum approach. Reading aloud from nonfiction books emphasizes language arts. We talked about the different kinds of penguins and their habitats. I checked for recalled information by asking the students to share facts they remembered about the different penguins. I wrote these facts on chart paper to post in the classroom for reference throughout the unit.

The arts were incorporated as the students learned several poems and a song about penguins, "All the Penguins." They drew pictures, wrote at least one fact about penguins, and made a penguin out of paper plates and construction paper. I provided a variety of learning experiences in order to capitalize on my students' learning styles and interests. I also used a wide range of instructional resources and strategies to integrate developmentally appropriate learning experiences across the content disciplines.

This lesson can also be introduced using KWL strategies. This technique activates students' prior knowledge by asking them to talk about what they already *know,* what they *want* to learn, and discussing what they have *learned* after the activity (Ogle, 1986). I use KWL strategies when I begin units as a discussion starter with my students and as a way to pique their curiosity, grab their attention, and activate prior knowledge. My students' questions about what they want to know helped me choose the information to present in the lessons. Writing the information on a chart helped my students remember what they knew and what their questions were. We returned to the chart frequently and reviewed it together as we progressed through the unit. This method helped my students organize their thoughts. It also helped them remember more information accurately.

Internet Research

The students viewed three or four Internet sites about penguins. We used a computer image projected onto a larger screen so that all students could see and understand the navigation and the resources present on the site. I bookmarked these and other penguin sites on the classroom computers so that the students could return to them during independent computer time, in a center, or in the lab.

During independent center time, I sat with a small group of students and demonstrated how to navigate within the penguin sites. After modeling the use of the cursor and the mouse to enhance their searches, I gave each child a turn with the mouse and let him or her practice these skills individually.

I helped the students in my class use technological resources to access information and to support and extend traditional resources.

Comparing and Contrasting Penguins

The students used the facts and knowledge they gained from their research and the class discussion to compare and contrast penguins.

I use these kinds of group activities to build on prior knowledge and foster appropriate group behavior. These group conversations in my class extend and clarify concepts. They teach the importance of listening to other classmates and increase oral language skills.

Choosing a Penguin for the Home Learning Project

The students gathered in small groups to look at pictures of the five different penguins we have been studying. Each student chose a favorite penguin. As a home learning project, each student drew a picture of the chosen penguin and wrote an important fact learned though our discussions and research. Each child made up a song or poem to share with the class. They practiced these songs and poems at home with their parents and siblings.

I provide many opportunities for choice in my class. The students have the opportunity to make independent choices as well as making choices together in a group. For example, we made class rules together, planned field trips, and developed rules for safety on those trips. I like to try different decision-making experiences to give them confidence and develop critical thinking skills. In developing a safe environment, choices allow students to take risks and try new things. Small group activities also foster developing social skills.

I am fortunate to have a parent community that supports children's learning. We work together to complete and present home learning projects that are engaging and interesting for both parents and children.

Learning to Use KidWorks2

I introduced the software program KidWorks2 to the children by showing them how to draw a penguin. The computer screen was projected onto a large TV screen so that all of the children could see what I was doing.

We experimented with the different tools in this program to outline and fill in the picture. I expanded the students' growing knowledge of shapes by asking them to describe the pictures I drew.

I have found that this projection technique and shared learning experience works well when introducing technology concepts to the whole class. I deliberately make mistakes or choose to erase my work so that the students can feel comfortable experimenting with the software. The students then have a chance to practice what they have learned from my modeling during center time or independent computer time.

I use these technology tools to facilitate the writing process and to develop creativity. Using multiple paths to learning, such as the use of drawing, writing, computer-aided drawing, and other tools, I help my students develop the literacy skills that are critical to success in later years.

Each student used this software program to make an electronic drawing of his or her penguin and type in the important fact. Each of these items was printed separately, instead of typing words directly onto the electronic picture. I found that this works better for developing writers. These drawings and facts were shared with classmates and parents through the class website, a slide show, and a book. We also e-mailed drawings as attachments to the other kindergarten class.

Source: Ogle, Donna. "K-W-L: A Teaching Model that Develops Active Reading of Expository Text," *The Reading Teacher;* Vol. 39 (February 1986), 564–70.

▲▼▲

Here are some questions to consider about Sylvia's lesson:

- How would you describe an "integrated" approach to teaching?
- What would you say to critics of technology who maintain that kindergarten children are too young to learn with technology?
- How could you apply the KWL approach to your own learning? To your classroom teaching?
- How does Sylvia assure that her children learn kindergarten state standards?

- Alert parents to new and different standards, dress, behavior, and parent–teacher interactions. Preschool professionals, in cooperation with kindergarten teachers, should share curriculum materials with parents so they can be familiar with what their children will learn. Kindergarten professionals can do the same with first grade teachers.
- Let parents know ahead of time what their children will need in the new program (e.g., lunch box, change of clothing).
- Provide parents of special needs children and bilingual parents with additional help and support during the transition.
- Offer parents and children an opportunity to visit programs. Children will better understand the physical, curricular, and affective climates of the new programs if they visit in advance. Professionals can then incorporate methods into their own program that will help children adjust to new settings.
- Cooperate with the staff of any program the children will attend, to work out a *transitional plan.* Continuity between programs is important for social, emotional, and educational reasons. Children should see their new settings as an exciting place where they will be happy and successful.

Additionally, what happens to children *before* they come to kindergarten influences the nature and success of their transitions. Three areas are particularly important in influencing the success of transitional experiences: children's skills and prior school-related experiences; children's home lives; and preschool and kindergarten classroom characteristics. Research demonstrates the following in relation to these three areas:[12]

KINDERGARTEN ISSUES

You would think that with all that is happening in the new kindergarten, we would have discussed all the issues! Not only is kindergarten education a fascinating topic, but coming as it does almost at the beginning of formal education, there are a number of issues that relate to beginnings.

DIVERSITY TIE-IN

Is Poverty Linked to Kindergarten Achievement?

The answer to our question is a resounding "yes!" The graph illustrates how poverty is linked to the math and reading achievement of kindergarten children. As you will observe, the link is not good in terms of children's school and life outcomes.

Data that show a link of poverty to achievement in kindergarten children are not intended to convey a sense of determinism and lead to the conclusion that all poor, minority children are destined to fail. We know that this is not true. Rather, such data should create a sense of urgency and encourage us to advocate for policies that will help poor children and their families be successful in school and life. Some things you can advocate for and support are these:

- Development of and access to high-quality preschool and kindergarten programs for all children to assure minority and poor children have equal opportunity to achieve
- Family literacy programs and other programs that will enable families to help their children learn
- Public awareness of the importance of early learning and how early learning or the lack of it shapes children's futures
- Entrance of all poor and minority children into early education programs
- Early education programs that assure that all children will learn the knowledge and skills necessary to achieve in school

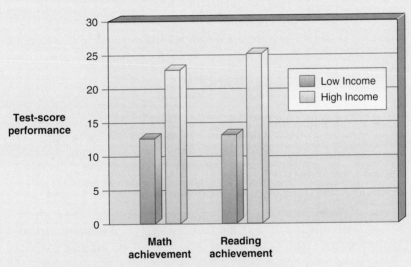

Source: V. E. Lee & D. T. Burkham (2002). *Inequality at the Starting Gate: Social Background Differences in Achievement as Children Begin School.* Economic Policy Institute. Available at http://www.epinet.org/books/ starting_gate.html.

REDSHIRTING

You may have head of the practice of redshirting college football players. This is the practice of holding a player out a year for them to grow and mature. The theory is that the extra year will make them better football players. The same practice applies to kindergarten children. The U.S. Department of Education estimates that about 10 percent of entering kindergarten children are *redshirted*—held out of school for a year.[13] Parents and administrators who practice red-shirting think that the extra year will give children an opportunity to mature intellectually, socially, and physically. On the one hand, redshirting

To complete an activity related to this diversity topic, go to the Companion Website at **http:// www.prenhall.com/ morrison**, select chapter 11 then choose the Diversity Tie-In module.

might have some benefit for children who are immature and whose birth dates fall close to the school entrance date cut-off. On the other hand, some affluent parents redshirt their children, their sons in particular, because they want them to be the oldest members of the kindergarten class. They reason that their children will be class leaders, will get more attention from the teachers, and will have another year under their belt, all the better to handle the increasing demands of the kindergarten curriculum.

HIGH-STAKES KINDERGARTEN TESTING

Children at all grade levels are being subjected to more testing. For kindergarten children, this testing not only includes achievement testing but also developmental and readiness screening. Developmental screening is, as the term implies, designed to assess current developmental status and identify children's language, cognitive, and social-emotional delays. Traditionally, this information is used to modify existing curriculum and/or provide specific learning activities and programs designed to help children learn. This is what developmental practice is all about. However, increasing numbers of kindergarten children and their parents are confronting readiness screening, designed to determine if children have the cognitive and behavioral skills necessary for kindergarten success. Unfortunately, many children may be "screened-out" of kindergarten rather than have a school experience that will help them succeed. Many of the children who are screened out of programs are the children who need a high-quality school program.

There are a number of other issues with readiness tests:

- Many lack validity; that is, they don't measure what they say they are measuring.
- Many readiness tests measure things that require teaching, such as colors, letters, and shapes. Consequently, children who would benefit most from a kindergarten program are judged not ready.
- There is a mismatch between what readiness tests measure and what kindergarten teachers say is important for school success (see Figure 10.2).[14]

KINDERGARTEN ENTRANCE AGE

Undoubtedly, there will be ongoing debates and discussions about the appropriate age for kindergarten entrance. Current legislative practices indicate that states and school districts will continue to push back the kindergarten entrance age. For example, Maryland recently raised the age at which children can be admitted to kindergarten. Now children must be five by September 1 rather than the previous date of December 31. The state's superintendent of schools said the change was necessary because of the increased academic focus in today's kindergartens.[15]

Rather than the constant juggling of entrance ages, what is needed are early childood programs designed to meet and serve the needs of all children, regardless of the ages at which they enter school. At the heart of this issue of age and time is whether maturation or school is the more potent factor in children's achievement. Research studies comparing age and school effects suggest educational intervention contributes more to children's cognitive competence than does maturation.[16]

These and other issues will continue to fuel the educational debates and will make learning about and teaching in kindergarten even more fascinating as the years go by.

- Children who are socially adjusted have better transitions. For example, kindergarten children whose parents initiate social opportunities for them are better adjusted socially.
- Rejected children have difficulty with transitions.
- Children with more preschool experiences have fewer transition adjustments to make.
- Children whose parents expect them to do well in kindergarten do better than children whose parents have low expectations for them.
- Developmentally appropriate classrooms and practices promote easier and smoother transitions for children.

The nature, extent, creativity, and effectiveness of transitional experiences for children, parents, and staff will be limited only by the commitment of all involved. If we are interested in providing good preschools, kindergartens, and primary schools, then we will include transitional experiences in the curricula of all these programs.

THE FUTURE OF KINDERGARTEN

From our discussions in this chapter, you may have several ideas about how kindergarten programs will evolve in the next decade. Add your ideas to the ones cited here:

- The trend in kindergarten education is toward full-day, cognitive-based programs. Kindergartens give public schools an opportunity to provide children with the help they need for later success in school and life. Children come to kindergarten programs knowing more than their counterparts of twenty years ago. Children with different abilities and a society with different needs require that kindergarten programs change accordingly.
- Kindergarten curricula will include more writing and reading. This literacy emphasis is appropriate and flows naturally out of the realization that reading success plays a major role in school success. The challenge for all professionals is to keep literacy development from becoming a rigid, basic skills approach.
- Technology (see chapter 13) will be included more in both preschool and kindergarten programs. This technology inclusion is in keeping with the current growth of technology in all grade levels. However, as with many things, we think that earlier is better, so introducing technology early is seen as one way of making children in the United States computer literate. The Program in Action in chapter 13 that describes the kindergarten instructional program at the Alexander D. Henderson University School illustrates and emphasizes the following points: (1) technology as an instructional model exists in growing numbers of early childhood programs, (2) technology is no longer something that can be feared or ignored by early childhood professionals, and (3) children are and can be very comfortable with, and adept at, technological applications to their lives and learning.

ACTIVITIES FOR FURTHER ENRICHMENT

APPLICATIONS

1. For each of the changes in kindergarten education we have discussed in this chapter, identify how they will influence how and what you will teach. What professional development and/or other help might you need to professionally prepare yourself to meet these new changes in the kindergarten?
2. As a teacher, would you support an earlier or later entrance age to kindergarten? If your local legislator wanted specific reasons, what would you tell him or her? Ask other teachers and compare their viewpoints.
3. Compare the curriculum of a for-profit kindergarten, a parochial school kindergarten, and a public school kindergarten. What are the similarities and differences? Which would you send your child to? Why?
4. You have been asked to speak to a parent group about the pros and cons of contemporary approaches to literacy development in kindergarten. What major topics would you include?

FIELD EXPERIENCES

1. Give examples from your observations of kindergarten programs to support one of these opinions: (1) Society is pushing kindergarten children. (2) Many kindergartens are not teaching children enough.

To take an online self-test on this chapter's contents, go to the Companion Website at **http://www. prenhall.com/morrison**, select chapter 11, then choose the Self-Test module.

For additional Internet resources or to complete an online activity for this chapter, go to the Companion Website at **http://www. prenhall.com/morrison**, select chapter 11, then choose the Linking to Learning or Making Connections module.

2. Develop a list of suggestions for how parents can promote literacy in the home.
3. Use the format of the portraits of Lina and Ganali to develop portraits of two other kindergarten children. Then compare your portraits to Lina and Ganali using the portrait questions as a basis.

RESEARCH

1. Interview parents to determine what they think children should learn in kindergarten. How do their ideas compare with the ideas in this chapter? With your ideas?
2. State the pros and cons for why you think kindergarten should be mandatory for all five-year-old children. At what age should it be mandatory?

READINGS FOR FURTHER ENRICHMENT

Moomaw, S., and Hieronymus, B. *More than Letters: Literacy Activities for Preschool, Kindergarten, and First Grade.* St. Paul, MN: Redleaf Press, 2001.

Filled with dozens of fun and engaging activities designed to make literacy adventurous and meaningful for children. Contains an extensive whole-language curriculum that creates classroom environments that surround children with meaningful print. Activities are accompanied by a photograph and a detailed explanation of how to set up the activity and construct materials.

Morrow, L. M. *Literacy Development in the Early Years: Helping Children Read and Write.* Boston and New York: Allyn & Bacon and Longman, 2000.

Presents a research-based rationale as well as practical applications based on theory. It embraces integrated language arts and an interdisciplinary approach to literacy development as it addresses developing writing, reading, and oral language in the home and school curriculum.

Seefeldt, C., and Wasik, B. A. *Kindergarten: Fours and Fives Go to School.* Upper Saddle River, NJ: Merrill/Prentice Hall, 2002.

Focuses on issues of readiness, the current state of kindergarten, the growth and development needs of kindergarten students, and the demands these place on schools and the creation of an integrated curriculum.

LINKING TO LEARNING

Connect for Kids
http://www.connectforkids.org/

Provides virtual information for adults who want to make their communities better places for kids; links to pertinent books, websites, and resources related to early child care.

Early Childhood Education Online
http://www.ume.maine.edu/ECEOL-L/

The community offers support and opportunities for information exchange to all educators: families, teachers, caregivers, and others interested in providing quality care and learning situations for young children.

Experts: Kindergarten
http://www.parentsoup.com/elementary

A forum of experts who explain about types of schools and programs, discipline, social and cognitive development, and behavior.

Family Education Network
http://familyeducation.com/topic/front/0,1156,27-2247,00.html

Tips, activities, and expert advice you need to keep your kindergartner on the path to academic success.

Inside Kindergarten
http://www.geocities.com/Athens/Aegean/2221

The personal homepage of kindergarten teacher Addie Gaines of the nationally renowned Seneca Elementary, MO.

KIDS Inc.
http://www.kidsinc.com

KIDS, Inc. is committed to quality products and resources for early childhood educators and parents of preschool and kindergarten-age children.

Kindergarten Connection
http://www.kconnect.com

The Kindergarten Connection is dedicated to providing valuable resources to primary teachers. Each week they offer new hints, tips, and information.

National Kindergarten Alliance
http://www.kconnect.com/nka.html

The National Kindergarten Alliance is the result of a summit of leaders from various kindergarten associations, organizations, and interest groups from across the nation that met in January 2000. It is a national organization that serves kindergarten teachers throughout the United States.

Parent Education Resources
http://www.parent-education.com

An online handbook to surviving the kindergarten years, for both children and parents. It includes a forum of links, workshops, and a question-and-answer feature.

Susan Elizabeth Blow and History of the Kindergarten
http://www.froebelweb.org/images/blow.html

Outlines Blow's contributions to the development of the kindergarten and provides many links to Froebel and interesting kindergarten topics.

ENDNOTES

[1] Gallup, Alec M. "The 18th Annual Gallup Poll of the Public's Attitudes Toward Public Schools," *Phi Delta Kappan* 68 (1), 55–56.

[2] Viadero, D. "Study: Full-Day Kindergarten Boosts Academic Performance," *Education Week* (April 17, 2002), 14.

[3] Burkart, Jeffrey. "Developmental Kindergarten—In the Child's Best Interest?" *National Association of Early Childhood Teacher Educators* 10 (1989), 9–10.

[4] Bellis, Marilyn. "Look Before You Loop," *Young Children* (May 1999), 72.

[5] Mantzicopoulos, P. and Morrison, D. "Kindergarten Retention: Academics and Behavioral Outcomes through the End of Second Grade," *American Educational Research Journal* 29 (1), 182–198.

[6] Froebel, Friedrich. *Mother's Songs, Games and Stories* (New York: Arno, 1976), 136.

[7] Literacy Volunteers of America, *Facts on Literacy* (Syracuse, NY: Author, 1994).

[8] National Research Council, *Starting Out Right: A Guide to Promoting Children's Reading Success* (Washington, DC: National Academy Press, 1999), 148.

[9] Ibid.

[10] Adams, Marilyn Jager. *Beginning to Read: Thinking and Learning about Print* (Urbana, IL: The Reading Research and Education Center, 1990), 36–38.

[11] Ibid., 8.

[12] Maxwell, K. L. and Elder, S. K. "Children's Transition to Kindergarten," *Young Children* 49 no.6 (1994), 56–63.

[13] Education Statistics Quarterly, 2001. http://nces.ed.gov/pubs2001/quarterly/fall/elm_kindergarten.html

[14] Stipek, D. "At What Age Should Children Enter Kindergarten? A Question for Policy Makers and Parents," *Social Policy Report*, XVI, no. 2 (2002), 10–11.

[15] Starr, L. "Kindergarten Is for Kids" *Education World* (June 4, 2002). http://www.education-world.com/a_issues/issues325.shtml

[16] Stipek, p. 11.

Chapter 12

The Early Elementary Grades
Preparation for Lifelong Success

Focus Questions

- What are the physical, cognitive, language, psychosocial, and moral developmental characteristics of children in grades 1 to 3?

- What are the political and social forces contributing to changes in elementary education?

- How are grades being restructured?

- How is the curriculum of the early elementary grades changing?

TEACHING IN GRADES 1 TO 3

As this text has indicated a number of times, reform is sweeping across the educational landscape. Nowhere is this more evident than in grades 1 to 3. The curriculum and instructional practices in these grades *are* changing. Grassroots efforts led by parents, teachers, and building- or program-level administrators are aimed at changing how schools operate and are organized, how teachers teach, how children are taught and evaluated, and how schools involve and relate to parents and the community. At the same time, the top-down process is also at work. State governments are specifying the curriculum and testing agendas. Accountability and collaboration are in; schooling as usual in the primary grades is out.

As we begin our discussion of living and learning in grades 1 to 3, it will be helpful to keep several realities in mind.

- First, contemporary American society is undergoing dramatic change. Added to normal societal change have been events associated with and following September 11, 2001.
- Societal and political events have, in turn, impacted the schools and have caused a major rethinking about what to teach and how to teach it.
- As society changes, so do its children. The children of today are not the same as the children of yesterday, and the children of tomorrow will be different from the children of today.

For these and other reasons that we have discussed and will discuss, you and other early childhood professionals must look at the education of children in grades 1 to 3 with new eyes and with a fresh approach to teaching them. We begin our new look at the new education in grades 1 to 3 with the children you will teach.

To review the chapter focus questions online, go to the Companion Website at **http://www.prenhall.com/morrison** and select chapter 12.

Companion
Website

To check your understanding of this chapter with the online Study Guide, go to the Companion Website at **http://www. prenhall.com/morrison**, select chapter 12, then choose the Study Guide module.

WHAT ARE CHILDREN IN GRADES 1 TO 3 LIKE?

Throughout this text, we stress the uniqueness and individuality of children who also share common characteristics. The common characteristics of children guide our practice of teaching them. However, we must always account for the individual needs of children. All children are unique in many ways.

Why are children of today different than the children of yesterday? We can look to several factors:

- Children of today are "smarter" than children of previous generations. Average intelligence test scores have increased about 10 points over each generation. There are a number of reasons for this: better health and nutrition; better educated parents; better schooling; access to and involvement with technology such as computers, electronic games, and learning systems, and television.
- Many children bring to school a vast background of experiences that contribute to their knowledge and ability to learn.
- However many children do not have a rich background separate from school experiences. As I indicated in chapter 2, many children live in poverty and come to school unprepared for the schoolhouse and its lessons.
- More children are "minority" children, although in many communities and schools, minority children make up the majority. Many children of minority populations come to school with health, home, and learning challenges.

For more information about the development of children in the primary grades, go to the Companion Website at **http://www. prenhall.com/morrison**, select any chapter, then choose Topic 2 of the ECE Supersite module.

Let's take a look at six "typical" children in classrooms today so you can see up-close and personal what they are like. As you review and reflect on the Portraits of First, Second, and Third Graders, answer the questions that accompany them.

PHYSICAL DEVELOPMENT

Two words describe the physical growth of primary age children: *slow* and *steady*. Children at this age do not make the rapid and obvious height and weight gains of infants, toddlers, and preschoolers. Instead, they experience continual growth, develop increasing control over their bodies, and explore the things they are able to do. Primary children are building on the development of the earlier years.

From ages seven to eight, children's average weight and height approximate each other, as shown in Table 12.1. The weight of boys and girls tends to be the same until after age nine, when girls begin to pull ahead of boys in both height and weight. Wide variations appear in both individual rates of growth and development and among the sizes of children in each classroom. These differences in physical appearance result from genetic and cultural factors, nutritional intake and habits, health care, and experiential background.

TABLE 12.1   Average Height and Weight for First- to Third-Grade Children

Age	Males		Females	
	Height (inches)	Weight (pounds)	Height (inches)	Weight (pounds)
7 years	48.0	50.0	48.0	50.0
7 1/2 years	49.5	52.5	49.0	52.5
8 years	50.5	56.0	50.5	56.0
8 1/2 years	51.5	60.0	51.5	60.0
9 years	52.5	62.5	52.5	64.0

Source: National Center for Health Statistics in collaboration with the National Center for Chronic Disease Prevention and Health Promotion (2000). http://www.cdc.gov/growthcharts.

PORTRAITS OF FIRST, SECOND, AND THIRD GRADERS

Kevin

Introduce yourself to Kevin, a 7-year-old Hispanic male. Kevin weighs 47 pounds and is 3 feet 10 inches tall. He is a very talkative first grader and enjoys sharing facts about science with others. Although he is sometimes excitable and distracted, Kevin tries to pay attention and is eager to answer questions during class.

Social-Emotional	Cognitive	Motor	Adaptive (Daily Living)
Tries hard to fit in with other boys. Seeks approval from adults and does not like to disappoint. Is very competitive; doesn't like to lose. Is easily embarassed.	Eagerly volunteers to read aloud to class. Memorizes short poems. Enjoys learning about insects and animals. Adds and subtracts numbers to 10.	Needs extra time to write neatly. Enjoys aggressive activities, such as wrestling. Runs swiftly; rarely trips.	Has his address and telephone number memorized. Knows which family friends to call in an emergency. Organizes his personal belongings.

Mei Lei

Introduce yourself to Mei Lei, a 7-year-old Asian female. Mei Lei weighs 44 pounds and is 3 feet 8 inches tall. She is very sensitive and emotional. Although Mei Lei does well in first grade, she is often caught whispering to her best friend during lessons. Mei Lei learns new concepts easily and enjoys doing school projects that involve creativity. She is very talented in science and math.

Social-Emotional	Cognitive	Motor	Adaptive (Daily Living)
Gets her feelings hurt and cries easily. Likes to tell riddles and jokes. Has one female best friend. Prefers to spend time with siblings outside of school.	Understands basic sentence structure. Likes to read books to herself. Writes short, fictional stories. Can count in 10s to 100.	Enjoys drawing detailed pictures. Likes to climb on the jungle gym. Loves to ride her bicycle. Creates dance routines with her friends.	Does household chores such as sweeping and dusting. Can fix herself a drink and snack. Does not like to go places (bathroom, office) alone.

- Do you think Kevin and Mei Lei are going to achieve well and be successful in school? What is the basis for your opinion?
- Do you think that Kevin and Mei Lei are "at risk" in any way? If yes, in what ways? If no, why not?
- Notice that Kevin tries hard to fit in with other boys. Is "fitting in" important for school achievement? How would you help Kevin and other children fit in?

- What are some major differences between Kevin and Mei Lei? How will these influence their learning in years to come?
- What effect might Mei Lei's relationship with her siblings have on her development? List some ways her sibling relationships can be used to encourage academic success.

PORTRAITS OF FIRST, SECOND, AND THIRD GRADERS (continued)

Cameron

Introduce yourself to second grader Cameron, a 7-year-old Caucasian female. Cameron weighs 55 pounds and is 4 feet 2 inches tall. Cameron needs time to adjust to new situations. She enjoys encouraging and supporting her peers. Cameron's attention to detail helps her to be successful in writing and math.

Social-Emotional	Cognitive	Motor	Adaptive (Daily Living)
Is emotionally attached to everything. Is shy in new situations. Is hesitant to ask questions. Is chatty once comfortable.	Uses periods and questions marks appropriately when writing. Writes two-paragraph stories on one subject. Has concrete math concepts. Is interested in details.	Fine-motor skills more developed than others, especially boys. Can shoot a basketball while jumping. Likes to cheer on teammates when playing games.	Attention span is limited to around thirty minutes. Knows how to cross a street safely. Needs down-time to rest between activities.

Peter

Introduce yourself to Peter, a 7-year-old Caucasian male who is in the second grade. Peter weighs 52 pounds and is 4 feet 1 inch tall. Peter is competitive; he wants to be the best and gets frustrated when he makes mistakes. Peter has a difficult time attending to classroom lessons that do not include active participation.

Social-Emotional	Cognitive	Motor	Adaptive (Daily Living)
Shows off in new situations. Needs to stand at least every ten minutes. Is more aggressive than peers. Gets frustrated easily.	Has beginning writing skills. Is confident with individual sounds. Is inquisitive, but impatient. Likes to learn about and track weather.	Has limited fine-motor skills. Takes turns when playing games at recess. Is action oriented, rather than verbal.	Is becoming more independent. Earns and manages his allowance at home. Knows how to "stop, drop, and roll." Sometimes engages in risky activities at recess.

- What could be some reasons that Peter needs a "break" every ten minutes?
- How can you structure your class schedule to meet the needs of children like Cameron, who need breaks between activities?
- How is Peter's temperament affecting his behavioral characteristics?
- What might be some reasons for Peter's aggressiveness? Do you think that Peter's aggressiveness and Cameron's shyness are wholly attributable to the stereotypes that boys are aggressive and girls are shy?
- What can you do to help a shy child, such as Cameron, be more socially interactive?
- Why might Cameron's fine-motor skills be more developed than Peter's? What could you do to help bridge this gap?
- How can you encourage your students' independence while maintaining control of your classroom?

342

Chase

Introduce yourself to Chase, a 9-year-old Caucasian male who is in the third grade. Chase weighs 70 pounds and is 4 feet 7 inches tall. He is impulsive and social. He prefers to spend his time playing sports. Chase learns best by active participation. He becomes more engaged in learning activities when they directly apply to his life.

Social-Emotional	Cognitive	Motor	Adaptive (Daily Living)
Is extremely social.	Reads independently.	Is aggressive in physical play.	Has a limited attention span.
Is trying to establish himself in a group.	Is a hands-on learner.	Can dribble and shoot a basketball correctly.	Knows adults who can help in an emergency.
Does not consider how he affects others.	Can solve word problems in math.	Understands the rules to sports and games.	Gets food and drinks without assistance.
Is extremely confident.	Favorite subject is science.		

Claudia

Introduce yourself to third grader Claudia, a 9-year-old Hispanic female. Claudia weighs 69 pounds and is 4 feet 5 inches tall. Claudia prefers individual activities to group activities. She spends her free time reading or talking with a friend. Recently, she has become concerned about what her classmates and friends think of her.

Social-Emotional	Cognitive	Motor	Adaptive (Daily Living)
Talks a lot.	Reads chapter books with confidence.	Can walk on a balance beam without falling.	Is becoming more independent.
Prefers a friend over a group of peers.	Can read and write without assistance.	Can hit a baseball, but without direction.	Knows how to use 911.
Is easily influenced by others.	Is very curious.	Likes to play jump rope games.	Can prepare a snack for herself.
Is very sensitive.	Likes chapter books.	Is learning cursive writing.	

- How do Chase and Claudia differ in their social development? To what do you attribute these differences?
- What kinds of activities might encourage interaction between children such as Chase and Claudia?
- How is Chase's learning style related to his favorite subject?

- Chase and Claudia have different academic focuses. What can you do to accommodate their different interests when learning less-interesting subjects?
- What gender differences influence classroom behavior and organization at this age level?

MOTOR DEVELOPMENT

Primary children are adept at many motor skills. Six-year-old children are in the initiative stage of psychosocial development; seven- and eight-year-old children are in the industry stage. Not only are children intuitively driven to initiate activities, they are also learning to be competent and productive individuals. The primary years are thus a time to use and test developing motor skills. Children at this age should be actively involved in activities that enable them to use their bodies to learn and develop feelings of accomplishment and competence. Their growing confidence and physical skills are reflected in games involving running, chasing, and kicking. A nearly universal characteristic of children in this period is their almost constant physical activity.

Differences between boys' and girls' motor skills during the primary years are minimal—their abilities are about equal. Teachers therefore should not use gender as a basis for limiting boys' or girls' involvement in activities. On the contrary, we should promote all children's involvement in age-appropriate activities. During the primary years we see evidence of continuing refinement of fine-motor skills in children's mastery of many of the tasks they previously could not do or could do only with difficulty. They are now able to dress themselves relatively easily and attend to most of their personal needs, such as using utensils, combing their hair, and brushing their teeth. They are also more proficient at school tasks that require fine-motor skills, such as writing, making artwork, and using computers. In addition, primary children want to and are able to engage in real-life activities. They want the "real thing." This makes teaching them in many ways easier and more fun, since many activities have real-life applications, as I discuss in the school-to-work program later in the chapter.

COGNITIVE DEVELOPMENT

Children's cognitive development during the primary school years enables them to do things as first, second, and third graders that they could not do as preschoolers. A major difference between these two age groups is that older children's thinking has become less egocentric and more logical (see chapter 10). Concrete operational thought is the cognitive milestone that enables children between seven and eleven to think and act as they do. Logical operations, although more sophisticated than in preoperational children, still require concrete objects and referents in the here and now. Abstract reasoning comes later, in the formal operations stage during adolescence.

MORAL DEVELOPMENT

Today, more than any time in the last twenty years, there is much more concern about and interest in children's moral development. There are two reasons for this. One, professionals realize that you cannot separate children's cognitive learning from their moral attitudes about life and learning. Second, especially since September 11, 2001, the nation is more concerned about issues of good character and moral behavior. Let's review two theories of moral development that can inform your efforts to promote children's moral development.

Jean Piaget's Theory. Piaget identified two stages of moral thinking typical of children in the elementary grades as **heteronomy**—being governed by others regarding right and wrong—and **autonomy**—being governed by oneself regarding right and wrong.

Heteronomy is characterized by **relations of constraint.** In this stage, children's concepts of good and bad and right and wrong are determined by the judgments pronounced by adults. An act is "wrong" because a parent or teacher says it is wrong. Children's understanding of morality is based on the authority of adults and those values that "constrain" them.

Gradually, as children mature and have opportunities for experiences with peers and adults, moral thinking may change to relations of cooperation. This autonomy stage of personal morality is characterized by exchange of viewpoints among children and between

Although children in the primary grades do not grow as rapidly physically as when they were younger, the years between six and nine are important ones for cognitive growth. What role should professionals play in these formative years for children?

Heteronomy The stage of moral thinking in which children rely on being governed by others regarding matters of right and wrong.

Autonomy The stage of moral thinking in which children's actions and thoughts of what is right and wrong are governed by themselves.

Relations of constraint According to Piaget, children's ideas of right and wrong are determined by others.

children and adults as to what is right, wrong, good, or bad. Autonomy is not achieved by authority but rather by social experiences within which children may try out different ideas and discuss moral situations. Autonomous behavior does not mean that children agree with other children or adults but that autonomous people exchange opinions and try to negotiate solutions.

Recall that in chapter 4 we discussed Lev Vygotsky's zone of proximal development and the importance of having children collaborate with more competent peers and adults for cognitive and social development. According to Vygotsky, social interactions provide children opportunities for "scaffolding" to higher levels of thinking and behavior. Furthermore, Vygotsky said that part of the professional's pedagogical role was to challenge and help children move to higher levels of thinking and, in this case, moral development. In chapter 14 you will read about specific ways to use scaffolding techniques to help children govern and guide their own behavior.

The stage of relations of constraint is characteristic of children up through first and second grades, while the stage of **relations of cooperation** is characteristic for children in the middle and upper elementary grades. The real criterion for determining which developmental stage a child is operating in, however, is how that child is thinking, not how old she is.

Kohlberg's Theory.   Lawrence Kohlberg, a follower of Piaget, believed children's moral thinking occurs in developmental levels. Kohlberg conceptualized three levels of moral development: preconventional, conventional, and postconventional.[1] Children in early childhood are at the preconventional stage.

Preconventional Level.   When children are at the **preconventionel level,** morality is basically a matter of good or bad, based on a system of punishments and rewards as administered by adults in authority positions. In Stage 1, the **punishment and obedience orientation,** children operate within and respond to physical consequences of behavior. Good and bad are based on the rewards they bring, and children base judgments on whether an action will bring pleasure.

In Stage 2, the **instrumental-relativist orientation,** children's actions are motivated by satisfaction of their needs. Consequently, interpersonal relations have their basis in arrangements of mutual convenience based on need satisfaction. ("You scratch my back; I'll scratch yours.")

Just as Piaget's cognitive stages are fixed and invariant for all children, so too are Kohlberg's moral levels. All individuals move through the process of moral development beginning at level 1 and progress through each level. No level can be skipped, but each individual does not necessarily achieve every level. Just as intellectual development may become "fixed" at a particular level of development, so may an individual become fixed at any one of the moral levels. You can learn more about Kohlberg's stages of moral development by accessing www.vgernet.net/diogenes/ex/lists/moraldev.html.

Implications for Classrooms.   The theories of Piaget and Kohlberg and other programs for promoting moral and character education have the following implications for primary grade classroom practice:

- All teachers must like and respect children.
- The classroom climate must support individual values. Respect for children means respect for and acceptance of the value systems children bring to school.
- Teachers and schools must be willing to deal with issues, morals, and value systems children bring to school.
- A sense of justice must prevail in the schools, instead of the injustice that may arise from imposing arbitrary institutional values.
- Children must have opportunities to interact with peers, children of different age groups and cultures, and adults to enable them to move to the higher levels of moral functioning.

Relations of cooperation According to Piaget, children engage viewpoints with others in making decisions about good, bad, right, or wrong.

Preconventional level The first level in Kohlberg's theory of moral development. Morality is based on punishment and rewards.

Punishment and obedience orientation The first stage of preconventional moral development in which children make moral decisions based on physical consequences.

Instrumental-relativist orientation The second stage of preconventional moral development in which children's actions are motivated by satisfaction of their needs.

Teaching Character in Everything You Do

Carol Cates, 1999 North Carolina Educator of the Year

When I began my teaching career, many students received moral instruction from their home or church. However, times change over the years. I realized that there was a strong need for the teaching of values in schools. When character education was introduced into our school system, I was asked to be on the task force to develop plans for developing a curriculum. It was exciting to know that our system valued strong ethics and that we would be encouraged to integrate them into our curriculum.

SCHOOLWIDE INITIATIVES

Teaching with puppets was just one of the techniques I adopted to model concepts to my students and as a method to share character education with the entire school. By working with the school administrators, the guidance counselor, and the elementary grade teachers, I was able to organize a puppet team. We set up first- and second-semester teams to provide opportunities for more students to participate.

I write the skits using ideas from Thomas Lickona's book *Educating for Character,* William Bennett's *Book of Virtues,* and other literature that stresses morals, along with suggestions made by students and faculty. Using school puppets and ethnic-appropriate materials of my own, the skits are performed five to six times a year at our Terrific Kids assemblies, which are sponsored by the local Kiwanis Club. Each assembly emphasizes a monthly character word.

This project has also led to the start of two other programs that reinforce positive values: the Kids for Character Club, which meets monthly, and the Hillcrest Hornet TV News, a video shown to our entire school each Friday. Two Kids for Character Club representatives are chosen each semester by their teachers. A student who already models good behavior and one who may need more assistance in demonstrating good character skills consistently are selected to participate. The club activities include decorating character education bulletin boards, making cards for the Skilled Nursing Home of Burlington, and planting

- Students must have opportunities to make decisions and discuss the results of decision making. Children do not develop a value system through always being told what to do or through infrequent opportunities for making choices and decisions. Responsibility, for example, grows from being given opportunities to be responsible.

CHARACTER EDUCATION

For more information about character education curricula, go to the Companion Website at **http://www.prenhall.com/morrison**, select chapter 12, then choose the Linking to Learning module to connect to the Character Education Institute site.

Character education is rapidly becoming a part of many early childhood classrooms across the United States, for several reasons. While everyone believes children have to learn how to count, growing numbers of individuals also believe that schools have to teach children *what* counts. Character education is becoming a higher priority for everyone, and character education curricula designed to teach specific character traits will become commonplace. The early childhood curriculum now consists of the six Rs: *r*eading, *w*riting, *a*rithmetic, *r*easoning, *r*espect, and *r*esponsibility. For example, all school districts in the state of Georgia are required to implement a comprehensive character education program for all children. Some traits included in this curriculum are honesty, fairness, responsibility for others, kindness, cooperation, self-control, and self-respect.

flower bulbs on the school grounds. The club members have also encouraged their classmates to fill shoe boxes for distribution to needy children. These opportunities have provided Hillcrest students with opportunities to develop their character skills. As a result, parents and educators who visit our school have noticed the positive environment. The students are polite to each other and respectful of adults, and everyone takes care of our facility.

CHARACTER EDUCATION IN MY CLASSROOM

Although I enjoy these opportunities to promote character education throughout the school, my top priority is teaching twenty-two lively first graders. Character education is woven into all of our basic curriculum activities. Children become aware of the positive impact they have on others by demonstrating good character skills.

So children can broaden their perception of the world, I help them understand that their world is larger than their immediate neighborhood. I read books to the children that teach character traits, often referring to the list of traits adopted by our school system. We read the daily newspaper, locating cities and countries on our world and state maps. We use the special kids sections of the *Times News* (Character Counts and the Kids Scoop pages) to help students understand the importance of good character skills. Visitors and artifacts from other states and countries are used to help students compare where they live with other areas so they can appreciate the similarities and the differences. As we experience the variety of cultures and countries, we try to eliminate prejudice and accept cultural differences. We also study the traditions of other cultures and have international tasting parties with food, games, folktales, or stories about the cultures. We also write letters to soldiers for several holidays, including Veterans Day.

Students make encouragement cards and small gifts for the cafeteria workers, maintenance workers, and office staff. Children send thank-you notes and remembrance cards to parents and grandparents for sharing items or time with our class. We also write to other classes and school groups to express gratitude and encouragement when they have performed for our school.

In report cards, parents are given an update on their child's character development. I write notes to parents to keep them abreast of their children's progress. Students also write to their parents when they have disturbed the class with inappropriate behavior. The note indicates the character skill that was not demonstrated (e.g., "I did not show respect"), and the child finishes the note explaining how he or she will improve the next time that situation occurs. Students also take home "good" notes that I have made and ones we write together.

THE "MORAL" OF THE STORY

Character development is an ongoing process. It needs to be a part of each day's expectations, and children need to learn how to practice virtues and ethics at an early age. When teachers expect and stress values in their classrooms, children understand and use methods for problem solving. Students know they are to practice character skills during transition times each day, and these skills continue at home and in the community.

What is the value of teaching character skills all day every day in every way? Consistently teaching children character values interwoven with all of the curriculum areas helps children realize that character is a part of everything they do in life and that demonstrating good character is a gift they can share with others.

Contributed by Carol Cates, First grade teacher, Hillcrest Elementary School, North Carolina.

Character education programs seek to teach a set of traditional core values that will result in civic virtue and moral character, including honesty, kindness, respect, responsibility, tolerance for diversity, racial harmony, and good citizenship. Efforts to promote character qualities and values are evident in statewide efforts.

There will be a great deal more emphasis in the near future on teaching character traits because parents and society are increasingly concerned about the life direction of children and youth. As previously indicated, students not only have to know how to count but also what counts in life.

EARLY ELEMENTARY EDUCATION TODAY

Schooling in the primary years has become a serious enterprise for political, social, and economic reasons. First, educators, parents, and politicians are realizing that solutions to illiteracy, a poorly prepared work force, and many social problems begin in the first years of school or even before. Second, the public is not happy about continuing declines in educational achievement. It wants the schools to do a better job teaching children the skills that business and industry will need in the twenty-first century. Third, parents and the public in general want the schools to help solve many of society's problems (substance abuse, crime, violence, etc.) and turn around what many see as an abandonment of traditional American and family values.

A decade ago, we could say that infants, toddlers, and preschoolers received the lion's share of attention and research and that grades one through three were neglected. We can no longer say this. In the last five years, the educational spotlight has cast its beam on the early primary grades. It is in the early primary grades where the academic rubber really hits the road. Grades 1 to 3 are more academically challenging and rigorous than they have ever been. Politicians and educational reformers use the third grade as the demarcation for standards of achievement and grade promotion or retention. The federal government talks about all children being able to read on grade level by grade 3. This means that, while all teachers pre-K through 3 are responsible for assuring that all children achieve this goal, it is in the third grade where this goal is measured and decisions are made about whether children will be promoted to the fourth grade or retained in third grade. Politicians and educational reformers also are in favor of and support "the end of social promotion." This means that if, by the end of the third grade, students have not achieved the specified third-grade standards, they are retained. For example, in 2002, in Chicago's public schools, the nation's third largest school district, failed 13,308 students in grades three, six, and eight because they did not qualify for promotion to the next grade.[2]

Accordingly, one of your major challenges of teaching in grades 1 to 3 will be to assure that all your children learn and achieve so that they can be promoted with their peers. We explore in this chapter how and why the curriculum for grades 1 to 3 is changing. Some of these changes are not new to you, nor should they be new to experienced teachers. They include high standards; high-stakes tests that are used to make life-changing decisions about children; and an increased emphasis on reading, math, science, character education, and wellness and healthy living. The concepts, ideas, and lessons of this chapter will help you see how these changes are influencing what is taught and how it is taught in grades 1 to 3.

As we consider and review programs and curricula for children in grades 1, 2, and 3, these are some points for you to keep in mind and reflect on:

- Education today is standards-based. As we have discussed, **standards,** which specify what children should know and be able to do, rule the educational landscape. This means that standards are embedded in what teachers teach and how they teach it.
- Education is **outcome based** and achievement oriented. This means that teachers, administrators, and other school staff focus on helping children learn what the state standards specify and what children need to know and do.
- Assessment of student progress plays a powerful and important role in teaching and learning. Students take local and state tests in order to measure achievement and school and teacher accountability.

CHANGING SCHOOL PRACTICES

A lot of change has occurred in the primary grades, with more on the way. Single-subject teaching and learning are out; integration of subject areas is in. Curriculum leaders want to help students relate what they learn in math to what they learn in science, and they want them to know that literacy is applied across the curriculum. Helping students make sense of and apply what they learn to all areas of the curriculum and to apply it to life is one goal of contemporary curriculum reform.

Students sitting in single seats, in straight rows, solitarily doing their own work are out; learning together in small groups is in. Textbooks are used in conjunction with hands-on and active learning. Facilitation, collaboration, cooperative discipline, and coaching are in. However, **intentional teaching** is becoming more popular as teachers strive to teach children the skills they need for success. Letter grades and report cards are still very popular,

For more information about primary curricula and teaching strategies, go to the Companion Website at **http://www.prenhall. com/morrison**, select any chapter, then choose Topic 6 of the ECE Supersite module.

Standards Statements of what children should know and be able to do.

Outcome-based education Teaching that focuses on what students can actually do after they are taught, by first selecting the desired outcome and then creating the curriculum to support the intended outcome.

Intentional teaching Developing plans and selecting instructional strategies with the intention of promoting learning.

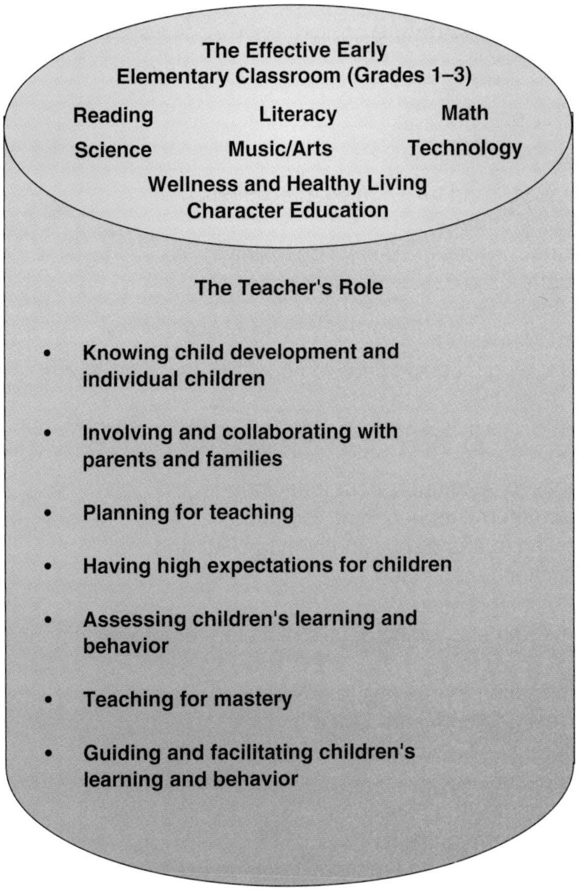

FIGURE 12.1 Features of an Effective Classroom

You will want to include all of these dimensions in your classroom to assure that you help all children learn.

The Effective Early Elementary Classroom (Grades 1–3)

Reading   Literacy   Math

Science   Music/Arts   Technology

Wellness and Healthy Living
Character Education

The Teacher's Role

- Knowing child development and individual children

- Involving and collaborating with parents and families

- Planning for teaching

- Having high expectations for children

- Assessing children's learning and behavior

- Teaching for mastery

- Guiding and facilitating children's learning and behavior

although narrative reports (in which professionals describe and report on student achievement), checklists (which describe the competencies students have demonstrated), parent conferences, portfolios containing samples of children's work, and other tools for reporting achievement are used to supplement letter grades.

While Dewey's progressive education ideas are still cultivated in the fertile ground of the hearts and minds of early childhood professionals, in many respects there is a decided back-to-basics movement in the United States today, and it is influencing the primary curriculum. The primary grades are also involved in the swinging pendulum of education change that is moving from less rigorous learning to academics. Figure 12.1 shows some of the critical features of an effective primary classroom.

STATE STANDARDS

Currently, forty-nine states have statewide academic standards, and all have some kind of test to measure how well students are learning and, in many cases, how well students and schools are meeting the set standards. Figure 12.2 shows selected state standards from Florida (first-grade language arts), California (second-grade science), and Texas (third-grade mathematics).

STANDARDS AND CHANGING TEACHER ROLES

Given our discussion so far, it should come as no surprise to you that standards have changed the art and craft of teaching. Standards and curriculum alignment have a profound impact on teachers and their teaching. Teachers have always developed their own curricula

FIGURE 12.2 **State Standards for Language Arts (Florida), Science (California), and Mathematics (Texas)**

Florida—First-Grade Language Arts

Reading

a. Uses prior knowledge, illustrations, and text to make predictions
b. Uses basic elements of phonetic analysis
c. Uses sound/symbol relationships as visual cues for decoding
d. Uses beginning letters and patterns as visual cues for decoding
e. Uses structural cues to decode words
f. Uses context clues to construct meaning
g. Cross checks visual, structural, and meaning cues to figure out unknown words
h. Knows common words from within basic categories
i. Uses knowledge of individual words in unknown compound words to predict their meaning
j. Uses resources and references to build upon word meanings
k. Uses knowledge of suffixes to determine meanings of words
l. Develops vocabulary by listening to and discussing both familiar and conceptually challenging selections read aloud
m. Uses a variety of strategies to comprehend text
n. Knows the main idea or theme and supporting details of a story or informational piece
o. Uses specific details and information from a text to answer literal questions
p. Makes inferences based on text and prior knowledge
q. Identifies similarities and differences between two texts
r. Selects material to read for pleasure
s. Reads aloud familiar stories, poems, and passages
t. Reads for information used in performing tasks
u. Uses background knowledge and supporting reasons from the text to determine whether a story or text is fact or fiction
v. Uses simple reference material to obtain information
w. Alphabetizes words according to the initial letter
x. Uses alphabetical order to locate information

Writing

a. Generates ideas before writing on self-selected topics and assigned tasks
b. Makes a plan before writing the first draft
c. Focuses on a central idea
d. Writes legibly using manuscript form
e. Knows the differences among individual letters, words, sentences, and paragraphs
f. Uses descriptive words to convey ideas in writing
g. Uses an organizational structure in writing
h. Uses strategies for narrative writing
i. Evaluates own and other's writing
j. Revises by adding or substituting text and using a caret
k. Uses spelling approximations and some conventional spelling
l. Spells commonly used, phonetically regular words at first grade or higher level
m. Uses end punctuation and capitalizes initial words of sentences, names of people, "I," days of the week, and months of the year
n. Uses complete sentences in writing
o. Writes stories about experiences, people, objects, or events
p. Contributes ideas during a group writing activity
q. Writes questions or makes notes about familiar topics, stories, or new experiences
r. Writes informal texts
s. Writes for familiar occasions, audiences, and purposes
t. Uses basic word processing skills and basic educational software for writing
u. Uses simple informational texts

FIGURE 12.2 **(Continued)**

Listening, Viewing, and Speaking

a. Follows three-step oral directions
b. Listens and responds to a variety of media
c. Knows personal preferences for listening to literature and other material
d. Uses basic conversation strategies
e. Listens for specific information in stories
f. Understands the main idea or common theme in a nonprint communication
g. Understands simple nonverbal cues
h. Speaks clearly and uses appropriate volume in a variety of settings
i. Asks questions to seek answers and further explanation of other people's ideas
j. Uses speaking vocabulary to convey a message in conversation
k. Uses eye contact and appropriate gestures to enhance oral delivery

Language

a. Uses repetition, rhyme, and rhythm in a variety of activities
b. Knows different functions of language
c. Recognizes the differences between less formal language that is used at home and more formal language that is used at school and other public settings
d. Understands that word choice can shape ideas, feelings, and actions
e. Uses repetition, rhyme, and rhythm in oral and written texts
f. Understands that the use of more than one medium increases the power to influence how one thinks and feels
g. Knows various types of mass media

Literature

a. Knows various broad literary genres
b. Knows beginning, middle, and end of a story
c. Knows main characters, setting, and simple plot in a story
d. Identifies problem(s) and solution(s) in a story
e. Relates characters and simple events in a story or biography to own life
f. Knows rhymes, rhythm, and patterned structures in children's text

California—Second-Grade Science

Physical Sciences

a. Knows the position of an object can be described by locating it in relation to another object or to the background.
b. Knows an object's motion can be described by recording the change in position of the object over time.
c. Knows the way to change how something is moving by giving it a push or a pull. The size of the change is related to the strength, or the amount of force, of the push or pull.
d. Knows tools and machines are used to apply pushes and pulls (forces) to make things move.
e. Knows that objects fall to the ground unless something holds them up.
f. Knows magnets can be used to make some objects move without being touched.
g. Knows sound is made by vibrating objects and can be described by its pitch and volume.

Life Sciences

a. Knows that organisms reproduce offspring of their own kind and that the offspring resemble their parents and one another.
b. Knows the sequential stages of life cycles are different for different animals, such as butterflies, frogs, and mice.
c. Knows many characteristics of an organism are inherited from the parents.
d. Knows characteristics are caused or influenced by the environment.
e. Knows there is variation among individuals of one kind within a population.

FIGURE 12.2 (Continued)

f. Knows light, gravity, touch, or environmental stress can affect the germination, growth, and development of plants.

g. Knows flowers and fruits are associated with reproduction in plants.

Earth Sciences

a. Knows how to compare the physical properties of different kinds of rocks and knows that rock is composed of different combinations of minerals.

b. Knows smaller rocks come from the breakage and weathering of larger rocks.

c. Knows that soil is made partly from weathered rock and partly from organic materials and that soils differ in their color, texture, capacity to retain water, and ability to support the growth of many kinds of plants.

d. Knows that fossils provide evidence about the plants and animals that lived long ago and that scientists learn about the past history of Earth by studying fossils.

e. Knows rock, water, plants, and soil provide many resources, including food fuel, and building materials, that humans use.

Investigation and Experimentation

a. Makes predictions based on observed patterns and not random guessing.

b. Measures length, weight, temperature, and liquid volume with appropriate tools and expresses those measurements in standard metric system units.

c. Compares and sorts common objects according to two or more physical attributes (e.g., color, shape, texture, size, weight).

d. Writes or draws descriptions of a sequence of steps, events, and observations.

e. Constructs bar graphs to record data, using appropriately labeled axes.

f. Uses magnifiers or microscopes to observe and draw descriptions of small objects or small features of objects.

g. Follows oral instructions for a scientific investigation.

Texas—Third-Grade Mathematics

a. Sequences numbers or words associated with the numbers when ordering a list of numbers.

b. Recognizes U.S. currency in the dollars-and-cents form or the cents-only form.

c. Matches fractions with models or models with fractions.

d. Works with comparisons using pictorial models, word phrases, or symbols.

e. Rounds numbers before performing any computations when estimating.

f. Recognizes and extends patterns with whole numbers or geometric shapes presented in lists, tables, or pictorial models.

g. Recognizes the relationship between pictures, descriptions, and formal geometric terms.

h. Works with symmetrical figures on which lines of symmetry may or may not be drawn.

i. Works with number lines that might or might not show the location of zero but will have at least two points numbered to identify the interval being used.

j. Measures with the ruler on the Mathematics Chart *only if* the item specifically instructs them to use the ruler.

k. Uses the given measurements of a figure to solve a problem.

l. Uses pictorial models of a square unit to determine the area of a figure. (Grid lines may be shown inside or outside the figure. Partial squares will be limited to half.)

m. Matches a pictorial representation of a clock with a time or with a range of times (times can be written in numerals or words and can be shown on digital or analog clocks).

FIGURE 12.2 (Continued)

n. Solves problems with temperatures given in degrees Fahrenheit (°F) or degrees Celsius (°C).

o. Converts among units within the same system.

p. Finds the amount of elapsed time or change in temperature.

q. Identifies the graph that fits a given set of data or the data that would complete a portion of the graph.

r. Reads information directly from a graph to answer a question or to interpret a graph by combining or separating some of the information from the graph.

s. Uses the information presented in written or graphic form to make a decision about the likelihood of an event (The terms *impossible* or *certain* may be used to describe that likelihood).

t. Selects the description of a mathematical situation when provided a written or pictorial prompt.

u. Identifies the information that is needed to solve a problem.

v. Selects or describes the next stop or a missing step that would be more appropriate in a problem-solving situation.

w. Identifies the question that is being asked or answered.

x. Selects the generalization of the common characteristic among examples.

y. Selects an example from among nonexamples or a nonexample from among examples based on given characteristic. (A nonexample is a counterexample or an example that shows a general statement to be false.)

Sources: Florida Department of Education "Sunshine State Standards." Available at www.firn.edu/doe/curric/prek12/frame2.htm; California State Board of Education, "Content Standards for California Public Schools." Available at www.cde.ca.gov/standards/; Texas Education Agency [online] (2002). Texas Assessment of knowledge and skills information booklet: Mathematics, Grade 3. Available at www.tea.state.tx.us/student.assessment/taks/booklets/math/gr3.pdf/

and will continue to do so, as the lesson plans in this and other chapters attest. But, standards have transformed (some would say reformed) teaching from an input model to an output model. As a result of standards, teachers are no longer able to say, "I taught Mario the use of structural cues to decode words." Now the questions are, "Is Mario able to use and apply decoding skills?" and, "Will Mario do well on decoding skills on the state test?" Good teachers have good ideas about what and how to teach, and they always will. However, the time and opportunity to do this is reduced by increasing requirements that they teach to the standards and teach so that students will master the standards.

CURRICULUM STANDARDS AND TEACHING

As we have learned by now, education is a topic full of issues, contradictions, and concerns. Standards are no different. As early childhood teachers implement standards, administer tests, and apply accountability provisions, controversies and conflicts arise. We need to examine a number of issues within the context of the early elementary grades.

Standards and Curriculum Alignment. Teaching issues are as old as teaching itself and involve frequently asked questions such as, "What should I teach?" and "How should I teach it?" As usual, the answer is, "It depends." It depends on what you and other teachers think is important and what national, state, and local standards say are important. Therein lies the issue of how to develop curriculum that is aligned with standards.

Increasing student achievement and how to accomplish this goal are at the center of the standards movement. Policymakers believe that given appropriate standards and teaching,

LESSON PLAN

The following lesson plans, How Big is Big? and 3–2–1 Pop! Rockets, were written by a 2002 *USA Today's* All-USA Teacher, Pat Smith, from Park Lane Elementary School, Broken Arrow, Oklahoma.

How Is Big?

National Science Standard D—Earth & Space: *As a result of their activities in grades K–3 (and 4), all students should develop an understanding of objects in the sky—sun, moon, stars, clouds, birds, airplanes, patterns.*

Students will demonstrate, by using models, the relative size of the Earth compared to the sun, and the distance between the Earth and the sun. Students will use skills of: observation, prediction, inferring, comparing data, and forming realistic conclusions.

Overview

This third-grade lesson demonstrates by scale models the size and distance of the Earth to the sun. Ask third graders to share some of the facts they already know about the sun. List these facts on the board.

Materials needed: 4–6 large yellow sheets of paper, 4–6 small blue sheets of paper, basketball, Nerf ball, tennis ball, jacks ball, pin, 4–6 pairs of scissors, metric rulers, pencils.

Using the basketball as a model of the sun, have students predict which other ball—Nerf, tennis, or jacks—is the size of Earth. Record the votes on the board. Then ask a student to come up to show the real Earth model; it is the head of a pin, which is pinned on your shirt. Discuss the distance from the Earth to the sun—93 million miles. It would take seventeen years on our fastest airplane to go to the sun: Does anyone want to go? Remember, you have to come home! The total trip time would be thirty-four years!

Next, to model the distance from the Earth to the sun, divide students into groups of two. One student will cut out an Earth 5 cm in diameter; the other will cut out a sun 55 cm in diameter. (You may have to show how to round the edges of the paper to simulate a circle.) If weather permits, take students outside. Have them stand in a line. Have the 'suns' walk fifty large steps (size of their sun) in one direction and the 'earths' walk fifty large steps in the opposite direction. This represents 100 times the size of the diameter of the sun. That is the correct scale distance of earth from the sun. (If weather does not permit this demonstration outside, find a long hallway in your school where students will have the ability to be 100 paces apart.)

Upon completion of this task, discuss the distance and students' opinions of it. Branch out into other discussions. How far away is our closest planet neighbor? How far is our farthest planet neighbor? Do you think we will be traveling to Pluto soon? Why? Why not? Will we be traveling to the stars? Why or why not? (FYI: There are 100 billion stars in our solar system—enough for everyone on Earth to have fifty and still leave plenty in the sky.)

Objectives

Students will demonstrate the spacing and relative size of the planets in the solar system.
Students will use modeling, predicting, measuring, ordering, inferring, and drawing reasonable conclusions skill.

Making a Toilet Paper Solar System

This third-grade classroom lesson is a Toilet Paper Scale Model Solar System. This is a simple activity to demonstrate the vast distances of the planets and emptiness of space. If you have enough room to use a scale of 1 toilet paper sheet to 1 million miles, this activity may be used outside or in a large multipurpose room and is even more dynamic. However, due to weather concerns and space and time limitations, we are using a scale of 1 toilet paper sheet to 10 million miles. Students will need two to three rolls of toilet paper (approximately 382 sheets), twenty note cards, and pens or magic marker.

Tell students 1 sheet of toilet paper equals 10 million miles is the scale we will use today, and allow them to predict how many sheets of toilet paper it will take to reach from the sun to Earth, Jupiter, Pluto, and so on. Record some of their predictions. Have one or two students make an index card with the name of the sun and other students make each planet to use as markers along the map. The sun is the size of a punch-out hole;

Mercury is the size of a pinhole; Venus is the size of a pen dot; Earth is the size of a pen dot; Mars is the size of a pinhole; Jupiter is the size of a straw end; Saturn is the size of a coffee stirrer end; Uranus is the size of a pen dot; Neptune is the size of a pen dot; and Pluto is the size of a pinhole. *Explain:* All pen dot and pinhole planets are not the same size, but we can't make them any smaller. After making the planet cards, add the distance (by toilet paper) from the sun to each card.

Mercury—3½ sheets	Mars—4½ sheets	Uranus—89½ sheets
Venus—2 sheets (additional)	Jupiter—34½ sheets	Neptune—101 sheets
Earth—4 sheets	Saturn—54 sheets	Pluto—88½ sheets

Decide on the best hallway to map out the solar system. Place the sun at one end and have the "Mercury" student place his card at the proper distance, and continue to the end of the solar system. Have the students stay with their planet until all planets are placed. Then, regroup at the sun to discuss the project and "take a walk through the solar system." How did their predictions turn out?

Q: Where are the stars?
A: Our sun is 93 million miles away and is our closest star. The farthest planet is more than 5 billion miles out in space.

Q: What else could be in the big empty space?
A. Comets or asteroids.

Q: What are comets, asteroids, and metoroids?
A: Comets, asteroids, and meteoroids are all debris remaining from the birth of our solar system. Comets are frozen gases and dust just a few miles in diameter. Asteroids are rocky bodies as large as several hundred miles in diameter. Meteoroids are small chunks of stone or stone and iron. Some are fragments of comets or asteroids. Meteoroids range in size from tiny dust particles to ten yards across. If a meteoroid enters the Earth's atmosphere, it is heated by friction and appears as a glowing streak of light called a meteor (also known as a shooting star). Most meteors burn up in the Earth's atmosphere, but those that do not and reach the Earth's surface are called meteorites.

National Science Standard B—Physical Science: As a result of the activities in grades K–3 (and 4), all students will develop an understanding of position and motion of objects.

3–2–1 POP! Rockets

Instructions

1. Wrap a tube of paper around a film canister; attach with tape. The lid end of the canister goes down.
2. Make and attach fins to the rocket.
3. Roll a cone of paper and tape it to the rocket's upper end.
4. Decorate with stickers, markers, foil, etc.
5. Put on eye protection.
6. Turn the rocket upside down and fill the canister 1/4 full of water (about 1 cm).

Work quickly on the next 4 steps.
7. Drop in 1/2 effervescent tablet.
8. Snap lid on tight.
9. Stand rocket on launch platform.
10. Stand back!
11. Have partner use altitude tracker to measure height of rocket's flight.
12. Record information on Rocket Form.

3–2–1 POP! Rocket Test Report Form

Name _____

Use your altitude tracker to measure how high it flew
Rocket 1: _____
Rocket 1: _____
Rocket 2: _____
Rocket 2: _____
Rocket 3: _____
Rocket 3: _____

Make one design change and retest. Describe change and results.
_____
_____
_____
_____
_____
_____

Discuss with your group and write below:
What do you conclude from your design changes?
What design change would you make next? Why?
Do you think the canister has an effect on the altitude? If so, what effect, and why?
Do you think the "fuel" has an effect on the altitude? If so, what effect, and why?
On the back of this paper, draw your best rocket design and point out any special details you think are the reasons it flew the best.

▲▼▲

As you review these lessons, reflect on these points:

- Pat Smith is using National Science Standards for students to plan and implement her lessons. Reflect about how you can use such National Standards in your teaching.
- The lessons are very hands-on and interactive.
- Students are working collaboratively.
- Many of the activities require students to think. Learning to think and applying thinking skills are high priorities in education today.

---

student achievement will increase. Policymakers and educators view standards, tests, and teaching alignment as a viable and practical way to help ensure student achievement. **Alignment** is the arrangement of standards, curriculum, and tests so that they complement one another. The curriculum should be based on what the standards say students should know and be able to do. Tests should measure what the standards indicate.

Florida has aligned its standards (Florida Sunshine Standards), its assessment system (Florida Comprehensive Assessment Test [FCAT]), and the Governors A+ Program, which grades schools based on how well they measure on the FCAT. This alignment of state standards with curriculum, tests, and school ranking represents a comprehensive approach to educational reform, which is influencing teaching in the elementary grades.

Curriculum alignment is the process of making sure that what is taught—the content of the curriculum—matches what the standards say students should know and be able to do. One way educators achieve alignment is through the use of **curriculum frameworks,** which specify the curriculum teachers will teach. In addition to aligning the standards and curriculum, some school districts also specify or suggest instructional activities and strategies for teachers to use so that the curriculum is implemented in ways to meet the standards.

TEACHING THINKING

We generally think of basic skills as reading, writing, and arithmetic, and many elementary schools give these subjects the major share of time and teacher emphasis. Yet some critics

Alignment   The arrangement of standards, curriculum, and tests so they are in agreement.

Curriculum alignment   The process of making sure that what is taught matches the standards.

Curriculum frameworks
Specify the curriculum and suggested teaching activities.

of education and advocates of basic education do not consider the "three Rs" the ultimate "basics" of sound education. Rather, they feel the real basic of education is **thinking.** The rationale is that if students can think, they can meaningfully engage in subject matter curriculum and the rigors and demands of the workplace and life. Increasingly, thinking and problem-solving skills are coming to be regarded as no less "basic" than math facts, spelling, knowledge of geography, and so on.

As a result, teachers are including the teaching of thinking in their daily lesson plans, using both direct and nondirect methods of instruction to teach thinking skills. A trend in curriculum and instruction today is to infuse the teaching of thinking across the curriculum and to make thinking a part of the culture of a classroom, as they are trying to do with literacy.

In classrooms that emphasize thinking, students are encouraged to use their power of analysis, and teachers ask higher-level questions. Table 12.2 shows examples of questions teachers can use following Benjamin Bloom's hierarchy of questioning levels. One teaching objective is to ask students questions across— from top to bottom—the hierarchy. Teachers are being encouraged to challenge their children to think about classroom information and learning material rather than to merely memorize acceptable responses.

Thinking To reason about or reflect on.

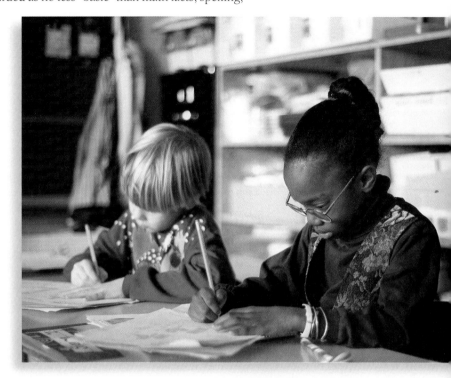

▲
Teaching about self-esteem is less important than enabling children to learn how to assume responsibility for their learning and to succeed through their own efforts. What are some things you can do to help students be more successful?

COOPERATIVE LEARNING

You can probably remember how, when you were in grade school, you competed with other kids. You probably tried to see whether you could be the first to raise your hand. You leaned out over the front of your seat, frantically waving for your teacher's attention. However, in many of today's primary classrooms, the emphasis is on cooperation, not competition. Cooperative learning is seen as a way to boost student achievement and positively enhance the climate of the classroom.

Cooperative learning is an instructional and learning strategy that focuses on instructional methods in which students are encouraged or required to work together on academic tasks. Students work in small, mixed-ability learning groups of usually four members wherein each member is responsible for learning and for helping all members learn.

Children in a cooperative learning group are assigned certain responsibilities; for example, there is a group leader, who announces the problems or task; a praiser, who praises group members for their answers and work; and a checker. Responsibilities rotate as the group engages in different tasks. Children are also encouraged to develop and use interpersonal skills, such as addressing classmates by their first names, saying "thank you," and explaining to their groupmates why they are proposing an answer.

Supporters of cooperative learning maintain that it enables children to learn how to cooperate and that children learn from each other; and because schools are usually such competitive places, it gives children an opportunity to learn cooperative skills.

Given the new approaches in the early elementary grades, it makes sense that teachers would want to use a child-centered approach that increases student achievement.

Cooperative learning A teaching strategy in which small groups of children work together using a variety of learning activities to improve their understanding of a topic. Each member of a team is responsible for learning what is taught and helping teammates learn.

TABLE 12.2 Applying Bloom's Taxonomy to Early Childhood Classrooms

Competence	Skills Demonstrated	Sample Questions
Knowledge	• Observation and recall of information • Knowledge of dates, events, places • Knowledge of major ideas • Mastery of subject matter • *Question cues:* List, define, tell, describe, identify, show, label, collect, examine, tabulate, quote, name, who, when, where, and so on	• How would you describe the size of an elephant? • Tell me three things that you can do with a soccer ball.
Comprehension	• Understanding information • Grasps meaning • Translates knowledge into new context • Interprets facts, compares, contrasts • Orders, groups, infers causes • Predicts consequences • *Question cues:* Summarize, describe, interpret, contrast, predict, associate, distinguish, estimate, differentiate, discuss, extend	• How are sounds different (contrasting)? • What is the main idea or point of the book we just read together? Explain.
Application	• Uses information • Uses methods, concepts, theories in new situations • Solves problems using required skills or knowledge • *Question cues:* Apply, demonstrate, calculate, complete, illustrate, show, solve, examine, modify, relate, change, classify, experiment, discover	• Construct two buildings in the math area, one tall building and one short building. • How would you organize your paintings to show your mother which one you painted first and which one you painted last?
Analysis	• Seeing patterns • Organization of parts • Recognition of hidden meanings • Identification of components • *Question cues:* Analyze, separate, order, explain, connect, classify, arrange, divide, compare, select, explain, infer	• What are the parts of the clarinet? Why do you think the bottom of the clarinet is bell-shaped? • If you see your friend lying down on the playground, crying, what do you suppose happened that caused your friend to do that?
Synthesis	• Uses old ideas to create new ones • Generalizes from given facts • Relates knowledge from several areas • Predicts, draws conclusions • *Question cues:* Combine, integrate, modify, rearrange, substitute, plan, create, design, invent, what if?, compose, formulate, prepare, generalize, rewrite	• Can you create a new color by mixing paints? Predict what color the new color will be most like. • Imagine yourself as a Pilgrim boy or girl. How would your life be the same as it is now? How would your life be different than it is now?
Evaluation	• Compares and discriminates between ideas • Assesses value of theories, presentations • Makes choices based on reasoned argument • Verifies value of evidence • Recognizes subjectivity • *Question cues:* Assess, decide, rank, grade, test, measure, recommend, convince, select, judge, explain, discriminate, support, conclude, compare, summarize	• Let's decide what the three most important rules of our classroom should be. • Which one of your paintings is your favorite? Why?

Source: Used with permission of Counseling Services—University of Victoria, "Learning Skills Program," http://www.coun.uvic.ca/learn/program/hndouts/bloom.html. Copyright 2002.

Furthermore, school critics say that classrooms are frequently too competitive and that students who are neither competitive nor high achievers are left behind. Cooperative learning would seem to be one of the better ways to reduce classroom competitiveness and foster "helping" attitudes.

SCHOOL TO CAREER

Today, one of the emphases in all of education is to devise ways to help students apply what they learn in school to real life and real work situations. Basic work-related skills are literacy skills—reading, writing, speaking, thinking, and working cooperatively with others.

For example, in the Western Dubuque (Iowa) Community Elementary Schools, one K–6 elementary school researched careers. Kindergartners made a video in which they described what skills they each would need to do their job and what salary they expected. They also made a computer slide show, with pictures taken. These students actually learned how to program their own photos into the computer to be included in their papers. They then typed the information on their picture pages, and these were printed out as books. Each grade had a completed career book by the end of the year. For the past three years, counselors have developed Career Portfolios on each child to build a record of the activities completed. All first graders used the new portfolios and the National Career Guidelines to track career awareness. Third graders visited area businesses and then created newspaper ads based on the information they learned about them. These were published in the local paper and paid for by each business.[3]

Critical thinking is necessary for successful participation in many life- and work-related activities. What are some ways that you will integrate critical thinking into your curriculum?

LITERACY AND READING

Just as in preschool and kindergarten, today's primary classroom decidedly emphasizes literacy development and reading. In fact, this emphasis is apparent in all the elementary grades, pre-k to 6. Society and parents want children who can speak, write, and read well.

A Holistic Approach. As discussed in chapter 11, more professionals are adopting a balanced approach to promoting children's literacy and reading development. One such approach is holistic literary education, which advocates a complete system of children's literacy development. The following are characteristic of a holistic approach:[4]

- Teachers integrate the teaching of the language arts into a single period. They recognize the interrelatedness of reading, writing, speaking, and listening . . . . Holistic teachers therefore provide children with opportunities to talk, write, listen, and speak to each other, and to the teacher.
- Teachers use children's oral language as the vehicle for helping them make the transition to the written language. Children are given opportunities to write messages, letters, and stories, using their own words and sentence patterns, even before they can accurately read, write, or spell.
- Teachers encourage students to write as soon as they enter school. Children may dictate experiences or stories for others to write, as is done in the Language Experience Approach to reading instruction; however, holistic teachers emphasize children's doing their own writing, following their belief that children's writing skills develop from scribbling to invented spellings to eventual mature writing.

Peace Corps Coverdell World Wise Schools

Mission: The Paul D. Coverdell World Wise Schools program puts Peace Corps volunteers in touch with U.S. classrooms so they can correspond. It also produces innovative educational resources that promote cross-cultural understanding and encourage public service among America's youth.

History: Since its inception in 1989 by Paul D. Coverdell, World Wise Schools has helped more than two million U.S. students communicate directly with Peace Corps volunteers all over the world. Initially set up as a correspondence "match" program between volunteers and U.S. classes, World Wise Schools has expanded its scope over the past ten years by providing a broad range of resources for educators—including award-winning videos, teacher guides, classroom speakers, an e-newsletter, and online resources.

World Wise Schools participants often find that by increasing awareness of cultural diversity around the world, students come to value the rich heritage and broad representation of peoples within their own communities.

Resources for Elementary Educators: Most programs and classroom resources are available free of charge for teachers in the United States. The resources highlighted below are those most appropriate for use with students in grades K–3 and focus on providing connections with children around the world.

Correspondence Match Program: The foundation of the World Wise Schools program, the Correspondence Match program has helped more than two million U.S. students communicate directly with Peace Corps volunteers in more than eighty countries. Through the exchange of letters, artwork, artifacts, and other educational materials, Peace Corps volunteers lead U.S. students in an exploration of the other countries and cultures of the world.

When possible, the Peace Corps volunteer selected for the correspondence match will come from the same city or state as the participating classroom. Teachers may ask to be matched with a volunteer living in a certain region of the world, or one who is working in a certain type of program (agriculture, business, education, forestry, health). Teachers may indicate preferences on the enrollment form.

To assist teachers with the correspondence, Coverdell World Wise Schools provides a handbook of ideas on how to foster an exchange that is rewarding for both students and the volunteer. However, it is up to the individ-

 To complete an activity related to this topic, go to the Companion Website at **http://www. prenhall.com/morrison**, select chapter 12, then choose the Diversity Tie-In module.

- In addition to using children's written documents as reading material, holistic teachers frequently use literature books, vocabulary-controlled and sentence-controlled stories, as well as those containing predictable language patterns. They choose the best children's literature available to read to and with children.
- Holistic teachers organize literacy instruction around themes or units of study relevant to students. Children use all of the language arts (listening, speaking, reading, and writing) as they study a particular theme. Many teachers also integrate the teaching of music, art, social studies, and other subjects into these units of study.
- Holistic teachers believe in intrinsic motivation, and when children enjoy good literature, create stories, write letters, keep personal journals, and share their written documents with others, language learning becomes intrinsically rewarding.
- Holistic teachers believe that literacy development depends on having opportunities to communicate. Since communication is not possible without social interaction, these teachers give children opportunities to read other children's compositions, and to write, listen, and speak to each other.

ual participants to develop the scope of the Coverdell World Wise Schools correspondence relationship.

The world is out there for you to discover. Teachers interested in corresponding with a Peace Corps volunteer will find information on how to enroll on the World Wise Schools website www.peacecorps.gov/wws/, or by calling 1-800-424-8580, x1450.

CyberVolunteer: Deepen students' understanding of cultural diversity. CyberVolunteer connects teachers and students in the United States with Peace Corps volunteers around the world via e-mail. Members receive an e-mail message once a month from the featured volunteers.

A schedule detailing the name and location of each featured cybervolunteer is provided so that educators can more easily integrate the cybervolunteer program into existing lessons. Letters from previous cybervolunteers are available online for review. Letters from the current school year are available only to participants.

Note that this is not a one-on-one correspondence match. The volunteers' letters are shared with a large group of classrooms through a listserv. If you are interested in signing up for a one-on-one correspondence match, visit the Correspondence Match section of the website.

Looking at Ourselves and Others: During Peace Corps service, volunteers look closely at the assumptions and values that shape their perspectives as Americans. They learn about themselves as individuals and as representatives of a multifaceted American culture. The activities contained in "Looking at Our-

selves and Others" will challenge World Wise students similarly to become more conscious of the values they share with their families, friends, and communities. The materials also provide students with analytical tools that help combat stereotypical thinking and enhance cross-cultural communication.

As your students learn about other countries and cultures, they—like Peace Corps volunteers—will begin to recognize that individuals and groups hold diverse views of the world. They will realize that this diversity often stems from the unique systems of values, beliefs, experiences, and knowledge that link people within cultural groups. In "Neighbors," returned volunteer Orin Hargraves illustrates the profound effect of looking at others from a new perspective. The activities in this guide are designed to help students develop the habit of viewing people and places from multiple points of view.

Presented in a supportive context with opportunities for reflection and application, *Looking at Ourselves and Others* and other World Wise Schools materials can help students join Peace Corps' exciting and essential mission—right in their own classrooms. It is available in print or online.

For more information on these and other Coverdell World Wise Schools resources, visit the organization's website at www.peacecorps.gov/wws.

Contributed by Donna Molinari, Marketing Specialist; Coverdell World Wise Schools, Peace Corps; 1111 20th Street, NW, Washington, DC 20526; Telephone: 202-692-1469 or 1-800-424-8580 x1469; E-mail: dmolinari@ peacecorps.gov.

- Holistic teachers give children opportunities to both teach and learn from each other. They often work collaboratively on a common interest or goal. They react to each other's written products, and they share favorite books with each other.
- Holistic teachers control literacy instruction. It may be student centered, but it is also teacher guided. . . . [H]olistic teachers recognize that direct instruction, including instruction in phonics, is not incompatible with student empowerment.
- Teachers emphasize holistic reading and writing experiences—children spend most of the classroom time available on meaningful reading and writing experiences.

LOOKING TO THE FUTURE

Although the educational system in general is slow to meet the demands and dictates of society, it is likely the dramatic changes seen in grades 1 to 3 will continue in the next decade. The direction will be determined by continual reassessment of the purpose of education

To complete a Program in Action activity, visit the Companion Website at **http://www. prenhall.com/morrison**, select chapter 12, then choose the Program in Action module.

The Montrose School-to-Career Education Partnership

THEORY

Third graders are eager to learn about the world of work, and they love field trips and classroom visitors. Teachers are eager to keep the curriculum fresh and relevant. Businesses are eager to support schools, to share their expertise and sites. Combine this energy and desire to build a dynamic relationship among elementary students, teachers, and local business: an Education Partnership with curriculum punch.

HISTORY

Montrose school district (Montrose, Colorado) prioritized development of a school-to-career component for elementary education. To ensure community support and buy-in, the district's school-to-career leadership formed a lively, mutually respectful partnership with the Montrose Chamber of Commerce.

PROCESS

The chamber's Education Committee linked with school-to-career to expand their Education Partnership program. The Education Committee guides the entire program using district input and technical assistance from the school-to-career coordinator. Third-grade teachers are invited to participate and are asked to identify what type of business or government entity would be the best match for their classroom. The committee recruits businesses based on the teachers' desires and the committee's knowledge of the community.

The committee pairs a business with one or two elementary classrooms, targeting third grade. The business partners agree to participate in a minimum of three classroom activities during the school year. They host at least one field trip, which includes a visit to the worksite. The school district assumes financial responsibility for field trip costs.

The Education Committee facilitates two yearly meetings among principals, teachers, and businesspersons. These meetings orient all participants, evaluate activities, and make program recommendations. However, the main agenda item is brainstorming, which nourishes ideas for classroom curriculum links and activities. Teachers and their business partners use the "Education Partnership Planning Guide," which formalizes activity plans for the school year.

Program emphasis for teachers is on meshing the in-place curriculum with the expertise and knowledge of their chosen partner. The emphasis for business is on bringing relevancy to the classroom by showcasing the skills, equipment, and occupations within its organizational structure. For students the emphasis is on understanding how what they are learning in school is useful and necessary in the world of work.

Teachers and business partners discover curriculum possibilities and implement them according to student ability. The bottom line, the main goal, is to expand students' knowledge and basic skills with *immediate* application in the classroom curriculum.

EXAMPLES

Banking

Norwest Bank links money management to the math curriculum and sponsors an in-depth tour of the bank, including seeing lots of money and the safe. Norwest brings tellers, the CEO, the head of security, the maintenance supervisor, and loan officers to the classroom to share their workday responsibilities. Students count and sort money, learn basic budgeting, and write practice checks. One field trip was to a bank client, Reclamation Metals, where the students observed recycling in progress and began to understand the relationship banks have to community projects.

Aerospace Industry

Scaled Technology is a partner with a class that is participating in a project involving students collecting data for the Citizen Explore Satellite. Scaled Technology engineers talk about how satellites orbit and what the word *orbit* means. Students collect data using aerosol and ultraviolet meters. The business partner helps the students learn how the instruments work and how to collect and record data. Lessons about the scientific method are also part of what employees of the company will teach. The field trip will be to the manufacturing plant where satellite parts are designed and built.

Newspapers

A journalist partners a class. She meets with students in groups of two or three, assisting with writing, editing, inspiring, and some classroom publishing. This partnership enhances language arts curriculum and the district's literacy efforts.

City Government

The City of Montrose partnership meshes perfectly with the social studies curriculum. In preparation for a tour of all departments at City Hall the students discuss job opportunities at the city level. From information provided about each employee, the students choose a job to write about. The first hour includes all departments housed at City Hall. Students meet the city manager, mayor, and department heads of Planning, Engineering, Legal, Information Technology, Human Resources, and so on. Once, the city planner explained his current assignment to study the population growth and find correct placement for a new elementary school. He provided the students with a colorful map containing all the pertinent demographic information and asked the students to formulate a recommendation to the school board on the new school site. Students leave City Hall eagerly anticipating the second field trip, which includes the City Shop, Animal Shelter, and Wastewater Treatment Plant. A third activity involves the students conducting a city council meeting by role playing city council members and staff in the actual council chambers.

Bureau of Land Management

Bureau of Land Management (BLM), like many public agencies, has a mission statement requiring interaction

with communities. The BLM leads its classroom partners into the world of environmental issues by having the students study and do experiments about soil types. Erosion and land management practices are the topics of discussion when students visit a site that illustrates soil issues.

County Government

The district judge partners with a class by linking to the social studies and health curricula. He discusses the judicial functions of government with students and encourages them to lead a drug-free and crime-free life. The students tour the criminal justice center courtroom, jail, and police headquarters.

Fire Department

The Fire Department partnership enhances the students' use of math, understanding of electricity, and health issues, while also providing a Service Learning Project. The students conducted a neighborhood survey of smoke detector use. The results were analyzed by finding the mean, median, and mode. The department provided batteries to the students to distribute to the elderly. The class also inventoried the school's use of electrical outlets and learned why overloaded circuits can start fires. As part of health study, the students learned about CPR, first aid, and the dangers of smoking. The students made fire hats and were in charge of an actual fire drill at the school. The trip to the fire station was almost anticlimactic after all this excitement!

Natural Resources Conservation Service

A specialist with the NRCS visits the class throughout the year and brings fresh ideas to parts of the science curriculum that touch on natural resources. A study of the nutrient cycle, for instance, resulted in the students building worm bins in jars, then studying how worms help decompose almost anything. Field trips to habitat reclamation projects enliven the classroom activities.

CONCLUSION

In this elementary school-to-career program, the Chamber of Commerce and school district discovered that a generous definition of the word *business* strengthens program diversity and community involvement. They actively recruit employers outside the normal school support loop. The data supports this and other strategies: participation in the first year included six schools and four businesses; participation in the second year involved sixteen classrooms and twelve businesses.

The elementary level school-to-career program energizes and provides focus for the curriculum. It generates close school and community collaboration, increases mutual understanding about the daily challenges of education, and promotes program ownership. The Montrose Education Partnership firmly believes that curriculum-linked, reality-based experiences in the world of employment successfully launches students' dreams for a productive future.

Visit the Department of Education's School-to-Work Learning Center Web site at http://stw.ed.gov/.

Text contributed by Charlie Lawhead, Coordinator, Montrose/Olathe School-to-Career Education Partnership; photos courtesy of Carol Parker.

Research shows that higher achievement results when children are engaged in learning tasks that encourage them to think. How can you include activities that help students learn to think in your classroom practices?

and attempts to match the needs of society to the goals of schools. Substance abuse, child and family abuse, violence, and illiteracy are some of the societal problems the schools are being asked to address in significant ways.

Increasingly, schools are asked to prepare children for their places in the world of tomorrow. All early childhood programs must help children and youth develop the skills necessary for life success. Even with the trend toward having children spend more time in school, we know that learning does not end with school and that children do not learn all they will need to know in an academic setting. It makes sense, therefore, to empower students with skills they can use throughout life in all kinds of interpersonal and organizational settings. Such skills include the following:

- The ability to read and to communicate with others, orally and in writing.
- The ability to work well with people of all races, cultures, and personalities.
- The ability to be responsible for directing their behavior.
- The desire and ability for success in life—measured not by earning a lot of money but by becoming a productive member of society.
- The desire and ability to continue learning throughout life.

One thing is clear about the future of the primary grades. There will be more emphasis on academics, higher achievement, and helping all students be successful.

Making Connections

First-grade teachers Marilyn McNeal and Lara Ernsting, of Kirbyville (Missouri) Elementary School, work hard at making reading meaningful and fun for their students. They utilize many techniques to strengthen the home/school and community/school connection. They find the following examples key to making reading important and fun for their students.

Each quarter they host a family reading night. Each child and family is invited to come to the classroom to read favorite titles from the classroom libraries. McNeal and Ernsting provide a snack to go along with the theme and entertainment for the evening. They discovered that entertainment is the key to family attendance. The students perform choral readings, short skits, recite poetry, and/or original works. For example, during the first quarter the students were involved in a unit on the study of fairy tales. The family reading night entertainment was a rousing rendition of the *Three Bear Rap*, followed by teddy-bear-shaped snacks.

McNeal and Ernsting continue to involve the parents with reading at home by setting goals for the number of books read outside the classroom. The students chart their progress on individual charts and are rewarded for achieving various levels. McNeal and Ernsting utilize stickers, pencils, erasers, bookmarks, gift certificates, "treasure boxes," and the Pizza Hut Book-It program. They find that by having the students chart their own progress, the students are able to see the progress they are making toward achieving the ultimate goal of reading one hundred books outside of the classroom environment.

McNeal and Ernsting use something their principal introduced at staff meetings, story-bits. The idea originated from an article by Cheryl M. Sigmon in the 4 Blocks Column on the Teachers.Net website. Story-bits give students a concrete memento to help recall particular stories. For example, the students received an acorn as a memento for the story *Chicken Little*. McNeal and Ernsting had each student create a story-bit "gift box" to store the mementos. These boxes were sent home with a letter at the beginning of the year to explain their purpose. When students bring home a memento, they retell the story to their parents, and save the memento in their story-bit box. They have found that this concrete reminder has helped their student's comprehension levels.

Volunteer readers from the community further emphasize the importance of reading. Volunteers include parents, school personnel (secretaries, janitors, bus drivers, principals, and superintendents), community leaders, DARE officers, local celebrities, and others in the community. The volunteers are encouraged to come and read often. McNeal and Ernsting find that this involvement strengthens the students' awareness of the importance of reading outside of the school community.

McNeal and Ernsting believe that no matter how you do it, students need varied exposure and many opportunities to practice their developing skills as readers. Reading should NEVER be a chore. Utilizing the resources around you, you can help students on their quest to becoming avid, excited, and life-long readers.

Contributed by first-grade teachers Marilyn McNeal and Lara Ernsting, of Kirbyville (Missouri) Elementary School, and Principal Addie Gaines.

The Giraffe Heroes Program for Character Education

The Giraffe Heroes Program for six- to eight-year-olds provides K–2 teachers with teaching assistants—Stan and Bea Tall, twin giraffes who go through the program with the class, learning character, service, active citizenship, social skills, and emotional intelligence along with the children. Stan and Bea are young friends trying, as the children are, to figure out how the world works and what their roles in it are.

Stan and Bea don't come into the classroom with lists of character traits or lectures on the importance of honesty or perseverance. They just go where the children are and help them move from there to experiences that bring forth the children's own innate compassion and their desire to contribute to their world. Stan, Bea, and the children learn together to be brave, caring, and responsible. As classroom puppets and as voices on audiotapes, Stan and Bea tell the children stories that give them models to meaningful lives. The heroes of these stories are giraffes because they stick their necks out to make the world a better place. The teacher's guide includes print, audio, and video stories of over thirty human giraffes, filling the children with stories of real heroes. The stories are from the files of the nonprofit Giraffe Project, which has been finding and commending real heroes since 1982.

Hearing these stories, kids understand what real heroism is about, despite the cultural messages that tell them that heroes are bulletproof cartoon figures, athletes, or entertainers. That's stage I of the program, Hear the Story.

In stage II, Tell the Story, the children look in their studies, in the media, and in their communities for real heroes and tell these stories to the class. Then comes putting all they've learned into action—Become the Story, Stage III. Stan and Bea guide the children through a process called Seven Neckbones (because giraffes' and humans' necks all have just seven bones).

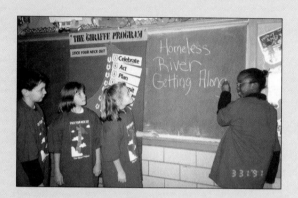

Doing Neckbones takes students from looking at problems that concern them through successfully creating and carrying out a service project that addresses one of those problems. Key to the program is the respect given to children's concerns and ideas; they drive the program. The effect on the children is powerful as they realize that their unvoiced concerns can be voiced, that their participation in their community is wanted and valued.

In contrast to the lukewarm response sometimes evoked by being directed into a service program, the enthusiasm of students is high when they invent their own programs. As in all good programs that include service learning, students experience the practical value of academic skills as they carry out their projects. An independent study of the program's contents to determine the essential learnings it contains yielded this list:

COMMUNICATIONS

1.2 Listen and observe to gain and interpret information
1.3 Check for understanding by asking questions and paraphrasing
2.1 Communicate clearly to a range of audiences

2.2   Develop content and ideas

2.3   Use effective delivery

3.1   Use language to interact effectively

3.2   Work cooperatively as a member of a group

3.3   Seek agreement and solutions through discussion

4.3   Analyze mass communications

CIVICS

1.3   Examine representative government and citizen participation

4.1   Understand individual rights and accompanying responsibilities

4.2   Identify and demonstrate rights of U.S. citizenship

4.3   Explain how citizen participation influences public policy

SOCIAL STUDIES

3.1   Identify and examine people's interactions with the environment

3.3   Examine cultural differences

MATH

5.3   Relate mathematical concepts and procedures to real-life situations

SCIENCE

1.3   Environmental and resource issues

Kids who have done the Giraffe Heroes Program know that they are more than consumers of cereal, cartoons, CDs, and sneakers—they are brave, caring young people who can make good things happen in their world.

In reviewing the Giraffe Heroes Program, Dee Dickerson, founder of New Horizons for Learning, said, "It is never too early to help children develop the character traits the world needs so urgently—altruism, compassion, gen-

erosity, and responsible citizenship. The Giraffe Heroes Program for K–2 offers an engaging, age-appropriate series of lessons that are creative, interesting, humorous, and highly motivating. This program can fit easily into any curriculum, and can facilitate the learning of reading, writing, and communication skills. What a great start for lifelong learning!"

Former teacher Paula Mirk, now of the Institute for Global Ethics, said in her review, "Every time I imagine the children who get to experience this approach I think how lucky they are and how much I'd have used something like this if I'd had it in my own classroom. I predict it will become a significant cornerstone in character education for very young children. What I like best about it is the consistent attention to respecting 'where young children are at' throughout. Text directed at the teacher constantly reminds us that young children deserve very special handling, and then the structure of the curriculum makes such care very easy and a matter of course. The layout and organization of the curriculum is very simple and easy to follow."

Teachers are given lesson plans, scheduling suggestions, ideas on using the program for standard curriculum goals, handout masters, overhead transparencies, and templates for visuals. The guide includes a video about the Giraffe Project from public television that can be used for teacher and parent orientation, and it also includes two audiotapes for the classroom. There are thirty giraffe heroes stories, each with a photograph.

Visit the Giraffe Heroes Project on the Web at http://www.giraffe.org.

Text contributed by Jennifer Sand, education director, the Giraffe Heroes Program; photos courtesy of Kathy Frazier and Charlie Lawhead.

To take an online self-test on this chapter's contents, go to the Companion Website at **http://www. prenhall.com/morrison**, select chapter 12, then choose the Self Test module.

ACTIVITIES FOR FURTHER ENRICHMENT

APPLICATIONS

1. Identify five contemporary issues or concerns facing society, and tell how teachers in grades 1 to 3 could address each of them.
2. Explain how first grade children's cognitive and physical differences make a difference in how they are taught. Give specific examples.
3. Of the three grades, 1, 2 and 3, decide which you would most like to teach, and explain your reasons.
4. What do you think are the most important subjects of grades 1, 2 and 3? Why? What would you say to a parent who thought any subjects besides reading, writing, and arithmetic were a waste of time?

FIELD EXPERIENCES

1. Gather information from the websites provided in this chapter. Organize these by topics (e.g., character education). Put these in your teaching portfolio for future use.
2. Inquire whether there are schools in your area that have character education programs, use cooperative learning, or incorporate other curricula that seek to help children be better learners, persons, and citizens. Put information from these programs in your activity file or portfolio.

RESEARCH

1. Interview parents and teachers to determine their views pro and con, of nonpromotion and the end of social promotion. Summarize your findings. What are your opinions on retention?
2. Compile a list of character traits that you believe are most important for teaching young children. Ask parents and community members what they believe are the most important traits. Compile a complete list.

 For additional Internet resources or to complete an online activity for this chapter, go to the Companion Website at **http://www. prenhall.com/morrison**, select chapter 12, then choose the Linking to Learning or Making Connections module.

READINGS FOR FURTHER ENRICHMENT

Allington, R., and Cunningham, P. *Schools That Work: Where All Children Read and Write,* 2nd ed. Boston: Allyn & Bacon, 2002.

> *Offers a clear view of how schools must change if they are to meet the increased demands of education for the twenty-first century.*

Cunningham, P. *Phonics They Use: Words for Reading and Writing,* 3rd ed. Reading, MA: Addison Wesley Longman, 2000.

> *This text offers a coherent collection of practical, hands-on activities to help students develop reading and spelling skills. Stresses a balanced reading program—incorporating a variety of strategic approaches—tied to the individual needs of children.*

Cunningham, P., and Allington, R. *Classrooms That Work: They Can All Read and Write,* 3rd ed. Boston: Allyn & Bacon, 2003.

> *Designed for courses that focus on instructional reading methods for at-risk and culturally diverse student populations, this inexpensive text assists preservice and in-service teachers in enriching the learning and reading skills of all children.*

Glazer, J. *Literature for Young Children,* 4th ed. Upper Saddle River, NJ: Merrill/Prentice Hall, 2000.

> *This broad introduction to early childhood literature focuses on literary analysis and specific techniques and methods of effective literature-based education. Includes a number of valuable methods and suggestions that are designed to enhance both understanding and enjoyment of literature.*

Hirsch, E. D. *What Your Third Grader Needs to Know: Fundamentals of a Good Third Grade Education,* rev. ed. (Core Knowledge Series). New York: Doubleday, 2002.

Useful books for parents and teachers, each book in the series covers the basic subjects: language arts, math, science, geography, world civilization, American civilization, and fine arts.

Rasinski, T., and Padak, N. D. *From Phonics to Fluency: Effective Teaching of Decoding and Reading Fluency in the Elementary School.* Boston: Allyn & Bacon, 2001.

Provides a wealth of methods, strategies, and activities for moving from early reading to fluency.

Ruddell, R. *Teaching Children to Read and Write: Becoming an Effective Literacy Teacher,* 2nd ed. Boston; London: Allyn & Bacon, 2002.

Central to this text is the real-world classroom; thus, theory and research is applied to literacy teaching through examples, instructional strategies, and illustrations—all intended to guide and support readers toward the goal of becoming an influential literacy teacher.

LINKING TO LEARNING

Baltimore County Public School
http://www.bcps.org

This program integrates the teaching of values throughout all curricular areas. Local school values committees are responsible for identifying a common core of values to be stressed for their school population. Materials include How to Establish a Values Education Program in your School: A Handbook for School Administrators.

Character Education
http://www.indiana.edu/~eric_rec/ieo/bibs/characte.html

An introductory exploration of Internet sources, journals, and books addressing the topic of character education.

A to Z Teacher Stuff
http://www.atozteacherstuff.com/

Created for teachers by a teacher, this site was designed to help teachers find online lesson plans and resources quickly and easily. It offers ideas on thematic units and lesson plans and contains a large collection of printable worksheets and pages.

CHARACTER COUNTS! National Homepage
http://www.charactercounts.org/

CHARACTER COUNTS! is a nonprofit, nonpartisan, nonsectarian coalition of schools, communities, and nonprofit organizations working to advance character education by teaching the Six Pillars of Character: trustworthiness, respect, responsibility, fairness, caring, and citizenship.

The Character Education Partnership
http://www.character.org/

The Character Education Partnership (CEP) is a nonpartisan coalition of organizations and individuals dedicated to developing moral character and civic virtue in our nation's youth as one means of creating a more compassionate and responsible society.

DiscoverySchool.com
http://school.discovery.com

DiscoverySchool.com is dedicated to making teaching and learning an exciting, rewarding adventure for students, teachers, and parents. This site provides innovative teaching materials for teachers, useful and enjoyable resources for students, and smart advice for parents about how to help their kids enjoy learning and excel in school.

The Four-Blocks
http://www.wfu.edu/~cunningh/fourblocks/index.html

This site, developed by Pat Cunningham and Dick Allington, provides information, sources, answers to common questions, and teaching ideas for teachers. The Four Blocks—Guided

Reading, Self-Selected Reading, Writing, and Words—represent four different approaches to teaching children to read.

KidBibs

http://kidbibs.com/

KidBibs is a website devoted to bringing kids and books together. It provides information and tools for strengthening reading success, such as learning tips for teachers and printable award certificates to build students motivation.

Learning Page

http://www.learningpage.com/

Learning Page is a huge collection of professionally produced instructional material for you to download and print. Lesson plans, books, worksheets, and much more can be found on this site.

Scholastic Teachers

http://teacher.scholastic.com/

The Scholastic website for teachers contains great resources for building students success, including lesson plans, activities, reproducibles, and thematic units. It also provides time-saving teacher tools, such as "Standards Match," which lets you easily locate classroom resources aligned to your state standards.

ENDNOTES

[1] Kohlberg, Lawrence. "The Claim to Moral Adequacy of a Highest Stage of Moral Judgment," *Journal of Philosophy* 70(18), 630–646.

[2] Gewertz, C. "More Chicago Pupils Flunk Grade," *Education Week* (2002), 13.

[3] School-to-Work Initiative: http://www.stw.ed.gov/expsrch.cfm.

[4] Eldredge, J. Lloyd. *Teaching Decoding in Holistic Classroom* (Upper Saddle River, NJ: Merrill/Prentice Hall, 1995), 5–6. Adapted by permission of Prentice Hall, Upper Saddle River, New Jersey.

Part 5

Meeting the Special Needs of Young Children

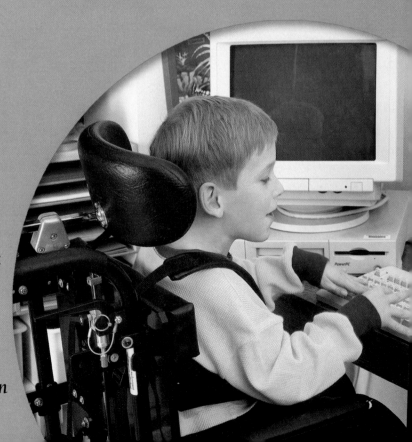

Chapter 13

Technology must be integrated into our classrooms in ways that will help increase student achievement.

ROD PAIGE, U.S. SECRETARY OF EDUCATION

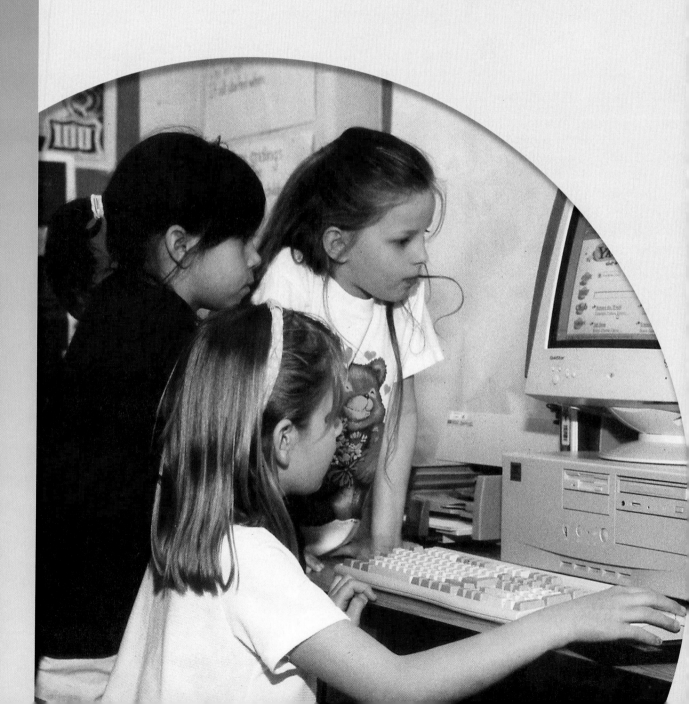

Technology and Young Children

Education for the Information Age

Focus Questions

- What does technological literacy mean for you, children, and families?

- What challenges do young children face in terms of access to technology and technological equity?

- How can technology help special populations of children, such as those with disabilities and with limited English proficiency?

- How can you and other educators integrate technology in the early childhood learning environment?

- How has technology changed parents' roles in their children's education?

You need go no farther than the daily newspaper (online, of course!) to see how technology is changing the face of education as we know it. A recent front-page headline declared: "Software for Kids a Growing Proposition." The writer of the article was acknowledging what many people think as they wander the aisles of computer software stores—the fastest growing software category is for young children under five. With names like *Jumpstart Baby* and *Reader Rabbit Playtime for Baby*, parents spend more than $41 million on young children's software annually.[1]

Curriculum-based technology such as Leapfrog teaches basic skills of reading, math, and science. These programs are a growing presence in many early childhood classrooms.

THE COMPUTER GENERATION

Perhaps you are wondering about your role as a teacher in the integration of technology into your classroom and programs. You may also wonder how you can use technology to become a better teacher. One thing is certain: Children today are technologically oriented. They are the "dot-com" generation. Their growth, development, and learning are intimately tied to large doses of television, videos, electronic games, and computers in the home and shopping center.

Every day, newspapers, television, and other forms of popular media chronicle the latest technological benefits to society. What once was exceptional is now commonplace. Computers were once huge, power-hungry machines that filled rooms the size of small houses. Today, powerful computers are small enough to sit on students' desks, and more and more students have laptop and hand-held computers they easily carry back and forth between home and school.

Home computing has grown in popularity during the past decade and will continue. A host of computer manufacturers have introduced computers targeted for the home market. Manufacturers design software to entertain and educate adults and children at home. Publishers of educational software for school use now design many of their newest titles with families in mind as well.

To review the chapter focus questions online, go to the Companion Website at **http://www.prenhall.com/morrison** and select chapter 13.

We cannot speak or think about technology as though it were separate from what goes on in the everyday world. Technology influences all of society. The production of consumer goods—from automobiles to zwieback—depend on computers and other technology. The point is that technology is all around us. In addition, many children are very savvy about technology and its use. Therefore, you and other early childhood professionals must incorporate computers and other technology into your programs and into children's lives.

TECHNOLOGY: A DEFINITION

Technology The application of tools and information to make products and solve problems.

Technology is the application of tools and information to make products and solve problems. Using this definition, technology goes beyond computers and video games. Of course, the most common use of the term technology refers to electronic and digital technology—in other words, devices that you can plug in. Such tools commonly found in early childhood programs include computers, computer programs, television, video recorders, videotapes, tape recorders, cassettes, digital cameras, and types of assistive technology. These forms of technology have many teaching applications. In addition, twelve states have online high school programs, twenty-five states allow the creation of cyber charter schools, and thirty-two states are involved in the establishment of e-learning initiatives, enabling K–12 students to take courses over the Internet.[2] Consequently, as an early childhood professional you must consider the full range of technology that is applicable to your classroom, learning centers, and activities.

To check your understanding of this chapter with the online study guide, go to the Companion Website at **http://www. prenhall.com/morrison,** select chapter 13, then choose the Study Guide module.

TECHNOLOGICAL LITERACY

Technology is changing, and in the process has changed the goals of education, what it means to be educated, and what literacy means. Literacy now has added dimensions. Students not only have to read, write, listen, and speak—skills fundamental to participation in a democratic society—they also have to learn to use technology to be truly literate. As a society, we increasingly feel that this **technological literacy,** the ability to understand and apply technology to meet personal goals, is as important as the traditional components of literacy—reading, writing, speaking, and listening.

Technological literacy The ability to understand, use, and apply technological devices to personal goals and to learning.

The following are some of the many dimensions to technological literacy:

- Understanding the language and vocabulary of the technological world. Figure 13.1 will help you achieve this goal.
- Using navigational strategies to access and find information.
- Staying literate. In the technological context, being literate is not a one-time thing, nor is it static. The challenge for today's students and teachers is in constantly keeping up—staying literate. Today's technological skills and knowledge are soon made obsolete by rapid change and innovation.
- Developing critical thinking and analytical skills necessary to assess and evaluate the information that almost anyone can publish. The abilities to sort fact from error, truth from fiction, and clarity from distortion are essential. Just because information is online doesn't mean that it is valid or true.
- Comprehending and managing the various dimensions of how information is presented (e.g., CDs, websites, digital photographs).[3]

These dimensions of the new literacy affect not only how you and your students learn but also how you and they conduct their daily lives. Empowerment, or the lack of it, may well mean the difference between achievement and failure, employment and unemployment.

For more information about how to close the gap between technology "haves" and "have nots," go to the Companion Website at **http:// www.prenhall.com/morrison**, select chapter 13, then choose the Linking to Learning module to connect to the kidzOnline site.

EQUITY AND ACCESS TO TECHNOLOGY

Many educators fear that the United States may be creating a new class of illiterates—children who do not have *access* to computers and other technology and who do not know how to use and apply technology. Table 13.1 shows the percentage of students who use the Internet based

FIGURE 13.1   Glossary of Technological and Internet Terms

Browser: A software program used to access World Wide Web (see definition) sites. Browsers can be text based (such as *Lynx*) or graphic (such as *Netscape* or *Internet Explorer*).

Bulletin Board System (BBS): A computerized meeting and announcement system that allows people to carry on discussions, upload and download files, and make announcements without the people being connected to the computer at the same time. There are many thousands of BBSs around the world; most are very small, running on a single IBM clone PC with one or two phone lines. Some are very large, and the line between a BBS and a system like CompuServe gets crossed at some point, but it is not clearly drawn.

CD-R, CD-RW (Compact Disc Recordable, Compact Disc-Rewriteable): A type of CD-ROM that may be used in a CD-R or CD-RW drive to record data or create multimedia or audio CDs. A CD-R may be written to only once, while a CD-RW can be erased and reused in similar fashion to a floppy disk.

CD-ROM (Compact Disc-Read Only Memory): A disk that looks like an audio CD that is used to store computer data (up to 650 megabytes). Many computer software packages are distributed on CD-ROM, and these programs may include color graphics, text, sound, and full-motion video.

Cookie: A collection of information, usually including a username and the current date and time, stored on the local computer of a person using the World Wide Web, used chiefly by websites to identify users who have previously registered or visited the site.

DVD (Digital Versatile Disk): A storage medium that is the same physical size as a CD-ROM but holds a much greater amount of data. The medium's most common content is motion pictures, but DVD computer games and educational software are now common.

E-mail: Messages or "mail" sent from one person to another via computer. For example, my E-mail address is morrison@unt.edu. Any person linked to the Internet (see definition) can communicate with me through E-mail. E-mail is also the standard form of communication for many mailing lists. As a result, persons can "post" notices to mailing lists, often consisting of large numbers of subscribers, and read the responses through their E-mail.

Ethernet: Common method of connecting computers in a Local Area Network (LAN). Typical ethernet data transfer rate is 10,000,000 bits per second, and ethernet will work with almost any computer, regardless of power or age.

Freenet: An organization that provides Internet access to the public for free or for a small contribution.

Hard disk drive: A sealed disk used to store data. It stores more information and runs much faster than a floppy disk. Hard drives come in many sizes, and the bigger the better, because much of today's software takes large amounts of disk space. Hard drives have become so large that their size is typically measured in gigabytes (GB).

Home page: Typically used to refer to the main page of the website of a business or organization.

Hypermedia: Software that enables the user to access or link to other media such as graphics, audio, video, animation, and so forth, through a process known as branching. For example, you could read a small biography on Mozart, click a button to hear a symphony, and click another button to read about the influence of his music on the film industry.

Hypertext: Refers to any text that, when clicked by the user, causes another document to be retrieved.

FIGURE 13.1 *(continued)*

Internet: A worldwide computer network that links the various computer systems at participating government agencies, educational institutions, and commercial and private entities. The Department of Defense started the network (then ARPANET) in 1969. Today, it is estimated that the Internet consists of well over 60,000 interconnected networks. Quite an electronic highway!

Internet Service Provider (ISP): A company that provides other companies or individuals with access to, or presence on, the Internet. Most ISPs are also Internet Access Providers; extra services include help with design, creation, and administration of World Wide Web sites, training, and administration of intranets.

Joint Photographic Experts Group (JPEG or JPG): The standard algorithm for the compression of digital images.

Local Area Network (LAN): A network (usually ethernet) that connects computers that are close to each other, usually in the same building, linked by cable.

Modem (MOdulator/DEModulator): Hardware, either internal or external, that connects to a telephone line and converts computer language to be sent over telephone lines. The modem transforms the computer's digital signal(s) (0s and 1s) to analog signals (sound). Given this conversion process, modems are inherently slower than a direct digital connection, but are still cheaper and more readily available for home users. So-called cable modems are becoming more popular and offer a performance increase of up to ten times more than the fastest analog modems.

Multimedia: The integration of still pictures, motion pictures, text, and sound with reading, writing, drawing, problem solving, searching, and creating. This definition is different from a common use of the word to mean the use of various media hardware such as television, computers, projectors, and so forth.

Netiquette: Used to refer to acceptable behavior or etiquette on the Internet. Acceptable behavior, of course, will vary greatly from one Internet site to another.

Newsgroup: Typically used to refer to a USENET (see definition) discussion group. There are thousands upon thousands of USENET discussion groups covering practically every conceivable topic.

Plug-in: A small piece of software that adds functionality to a larger piece of software. For example, to add audio and video features to a Web browser, a plug-in supporting the various media standards will need to be added to the browser. More popular formats (such as *RealAudio* and *Shockwave*) have plug-ins built into or shipped with the browser software.

Scanner: An input device that copies pictures and words into the computer by turning the visual representations (analog) into digital information. Once in the computer, the digital information may be manipulated, stored, and printed.

Spam: Refers to "junk" or bulk E-mail that the user did not request to receive. Spam typically takes the form of advertising or get-rich-quick schemes. Many E-mail software packages now have anti-Spam utilities.

Uniform Resource Locator (URL): The unique Internet address that identifies Web pages and sites. For example, the URL of my Web site is http://www.unt.edu/velma_schmidt. The inclusion of a URL has become almost ubiquitous in print and television advertising.

Virtual reality: A computer-based simulated environment that users seem to enter and that seems real for the participant.

Virus: A cracker program that searches out other programs and "infects" them by embedding a copy of itself in them, so that they become Trojan horses. When these programs are executed, the embedded virus is executed too, thus propagating the "infection." This normally happens invisibly to the user.

World Wide Web (WWW): This term has essentially two meanings. It is often used (albeit incorrectly) to refer to the Internet itself but more correctly refers specifically to the vast number of linked hypertext servers (http servers) that allow text, graphics, and streaming audio and video to be mixed together.

TABLE 13.1 Percentage of Students Using the Internet (based on socioeconomic status)

Household Income	Age 3–8	Age 9–17
Less than $15,000	5.4%	28.8%
$15,000 to $24,999	9.8%	36.3%
$25,000 to $34,999	12.7%	45.7%
$35,000 to $49,999	17.0%	54.7%
$50,000 to $74,999	19.1%	64.1%
$75,000 and above	21.8%	74.7%

Source: U.S. Department of Commerce, National Telecommunications and Information Administration (2000).
Falling through the Net: Toward Digital Inclusion. Available at http://www.ntia.doc.gov/ntiahome/fttn00/falling.htm.

DIVERSITY TIE-IN

The Internet Digital Divide

We tend to take technology for granted. We think that technology is available for and used by all. This is not the case. There is a great Internet digital divide that separates children by race, gender, and socioeconomic status. Look at the table below and Table 13.1 above.

The percentage of children between the ages of three and eight who use the Internet is small now. However, Internet usage of young children will likely increase as Internet access becomes more widespread; as Kidz Privacy [Online] becomes available; and as better filtering systems are developed. In our table, boys in the three-to-eight age group tend to use the Internet more than girls, and there is already a disparity in Internet use between whites, African Americans, and Hispanics. In the nine-to-seventeen age group, there is hardly any disparity by gender, but the disparity by race constitutes more of a chasm than a divide. As you reflect on this data, identify some actions you could take to help close the gap between the haves and have-nots of Internet access. For example, you could invite parents without Internet access to a series of family nights devoted to classes on how to use the Internet.

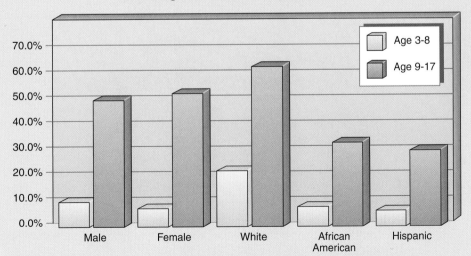

Percentage of Students Using the Internet

Source: U.S. Department of Commerce, National Telecommunications and Information Administration (2000).
Falling through the Net: Toward Digital Inclusion. Available at http://www.ntia.doc.gov/ntiahome/fttn00/falling.htm.

East Rock Magnet School's Technology Program

East Rock Magnet School (New Haven, Connecticut) is a pioneer in technology instruction for K–8 education and a forerunner for technology implementation for the twenty-first century. The school has a formal partnership with Compaq Computer (now part of HP), Microsoft Corporation, and Xerox Technologies. Recently, the school was chosen as a model for a national wireless laptop program for the Federal Education Department. Comcast Cable, Inspiration Software, Visions Technology, Enterasys, Digital Curriculum, Bytes of Learning, STOP Security, and Altiris Software are additional sponsors, contributing extensively in program development each year. The school also receives funding from the New Haven Public Schools and from various grants and sponsorships.

MISSION STATEMENT

East Rock Magnet: A Global Studies School, is dedicated to increasing the students' awareness and knowledge of their world. Its goal is to equip students with information-processing skills of accessing, analyzing, and communicating information effectively. Emphasis is directed toward improving student achievement levels through an interdisciplinary curriculum that incorporates state-of-the-art technology.

VISION STATEMENT

East Rock Magnet School recognizes that a Balanced Literacy-Based Program is the key to the future success of our students. The philosophy is integrated into the district's curriculum framework, the national standards, and the global studies/technology curriculum of East Rock. It ensures that our students learn the necessary literacy skills to compete in a global, technological, and information-driven society for the next millennium. Our new technology provides the proper tools for:

- Teachers to facilitate learning
- Students to learn higher-level thinking skills and communicate ideas
- Teachers and students to access, organize, and process information; reinforce prior learning; and solve problems more creatively, effectively, and efficiently

The sizable collection of print, audiovisual materials, and technology resources, based on the school's global studies curriculum, promotes the success of resource-based teaching/learning, and recreational reading. The Library Media Center serves as an extension of the classroom, and is the educational hub of the school. Furthermore, the library contains a Technology Media Center and a Teacher Resource Area. These added resources enhance and optimize the staff's professional development on an ongoing basis. This unique arrangement provides a utopia for the perfect educational setting.

In addition, our students, staff members, parents, and members of the community have access to our state-of-

To complete an activity related to this topic, go to the Companion Website at **http://www.prenhall.com/morrison**, select chapter 13, then choose the Diversity Tie-In module.

on socioeconomic status and by gender and culture as discussed in our Diversity Tie-In. These demographics of technological use have serious implications for children, families, and you. If one group, socioeconomic class, or gender is more comfortable with, skillful with, and proficient in technology, inequities and technological illiteracy result. We must avoid creating a generation of technology "have nots." As an early childhood educator, you should advocate for increased access to technology for you and your students.

Equity means that all students have the opportunity to become technologically literate. All students must have equitable access to technology that is appropriate for them. Although some may think it a worthy goal for all students to spend the same amount of time on a computer, all students may not need the same exposure. Some students may have to spend more time to master the objectives of their particular grade and subject.

the-art technology, which includes the automation of the Library Media Center, schoolwide accessible networking (WAN), and our abundant and diverse collection of reference and literature. The Internet, the Library Media Center's online catalog (OPAC), the New Haven Free Public Library's online catalog, and software programs can be accessed from anywhere in the school.

To plan thematic units, the staff works collaboratively with the library media specialist, who further identifies that portion of the collection and technology that will enrich their instructional programs. This is made feasible by a newly developed flex schedule and a mapping of all grades with a monthly list of all core objectives. The Library Media Center services our students, teachers, support staff, and parents throughout the regular school day, as well as during our extended school day program.

In addition, the technology facilitator/systems engineer and the two curriculum facilitators collaboratively plan with the library media specialist to promote and enhance many of the goals and objectives of the core program. A full-time technology facilitator/systems engineer executes all of the sophisticated network/software installations and maintenance, as well as the teaching and correlation of software programs. Our curriculum facilitators advance the magnet school concept by working with both the teachers and students on various thematic unit projects, including a full-scale video production studio. As a result, the students are active, curious learners who excel in the fundamentals of education: literacy, math, and science.

INFRASTRUCTURE AND DESIGN OF NETWORK

The results of the computer implementation of East Rock exemplify the recent scholarly evaluations showing that the use of technology improves teaching and learning. Integrating computers into classroom instruction is increasing student achievement dramatically each year.

East Rock is a highly connected network providing access to resources, tools, and information across discipli-

nary, institutional, national, and international boundaries. Its OC3 backbone connection (high bandwidth) for the Internet enables teachers and students to use Web-based software and digital streaming video for curriculum enhancement on a daily basis. With the advent of more than 221 wireless laptops for grades 3–5 and the installation of numerous wireless access points, East Rock will become a leader in one-to-one e-learning.

CONCLUSION

As the world shrinks, all of its people and knowledge are reachable from any point. The globe, once so vast, becomes more village-like. Any village and any learner can touch all the globe. (Marshall McLuhan)

Children around the world are growing up in a global society. Most of us were educated throughout our lifetimes in a world quite different from the one that our children now know. Children need new literacy and technology skills to function productively in this unique and culturally rich environment.

Children who grow up seeing themselves as human beings related to all other human beings have the potential for developing responsive, humane institutions and technologies to enhance the human condition throughout the world. As they explore the nature of being human, they come to see that each person depends on and is responsible for all other human beings. (Philosophy, East Rock Magnet School)

Visit East Rock Magnet School at http://www.eastrock.org on the Web.

Contributed by Domenic A. Grignano, technology facilitator and systems engineer at East Rock Magnet School in New Haven, Connecticut. He is a leading technology pioneer in K–12 education, a consultant for schools and major software companies, as well as a freelance writer for *Classroom Connect Newsletter.*

Society, parents, teachers, and policymakers must be leaders in helping ensure that there are no technological gender gaps and that all software is free of bias. As discussed in chapter 14 and elsewhere throughout this text, all professionals must take into consideration the diversity present in contemporary society. When professionals select materials, including computer software, videos, films, and other technologically based applications, they must make sure these materials include depictions of children and adults with differing abilities, ages, and ethnic backgrounds and that these materials are nonstereotypic of gender, culture, and socioeconomic class. The software industry has made progress in this regard but still has a long way to go to meet antibias criteria in their products. You must evaluate all software you purchase and continually advocate for nonbiased software.

Figure 13.2, the Software Evaluation Checklist, will help you in selecting software for young children.

 For help in choosing high-quality, appropriate software, go to the Companion Website at **http://www.prenhall. com/morrison**, select chapter 13, then choose the Linking to Learning module to connect to the SuperKids Educational Software Review site.

FIGURE 13.2 Software Evaluation Checklist

Title of Software Evaluated: _____

❏ The software offers a divergent path and choice-making opportunities.

❏ The software is open-ended and invites exploration in a non-threatening environment.

❏ The software provides problem-solving opportunities.

❏ The software allows a child to be successful.

❏ The software stimulates a child's interest.

❏ The software encourages active involvement.

❏ The software contains quality animation, graphics, sound, and color.

❏ The content reflects a diverse society.

❏ The content is developmentally appropriate.

❏ The feedback is effective and non-threatening.

❏ The responses to "incorrect" input are not demeaning.

❏ The program is easy to navigate.

❏ The program operates at an acceptable speed.

❏ The program is easy to exit.

❏ The instructions, if any, are clear and easy to follow.

❏ The software is compatible with classroom hardware.

Comments:

_____

_____

_____

_____

_____

Source: © Center for Best Practices in Early Childhood, 27 Horrabin Hall, 1 University Circle, Western Illinois University, Macomb, IL, 61455

Many children come to school familiar with computers and other technology. Other children have very limited exposure. What can you do to ensure that all children's technological needs are met?

TECHNOLOGY AND SPECIAL CHILDHOOD POPULATIONS

Technology can have a profound effect on children with special needs, including very young children, students with disabilities, and students who are bilingual or have limited English proficiency.

TECHNOLOGY AND INFANTS, TODDLERS, AND PRESCHOOLERS

Technology is a growing part of the world of very young children. Computers and other technology have a great deal to offer, and there is much that young children can learn via technology in all domains—cognitive, social, emotional, and linguistic. Software is being designed for children as young as nine months. This software is often referred to as

FIGURE 13.3 NAEYC Position Statement on Technology and Young Children

Although there is considerable research that points to the positive effects of technology on children's learning and development, the research indicates that, in practice, computers supplement and do not replace highly valued early childhood activities and materials, such as art, blocks, sand, water, books, exploration with writing materials, and dramatic play. Research indicates that computers can be used in developmentally appropriate ways beneficial to children and also can be misused, just as any tool can. Developmentally appropriate software offers opportunities for collaborative play, learning, and creation. Educators must use professional judgment in evaluating and using this learning tool appropriately, applying the same criteria they would to any other learning tool or experience. They must also weigh the costs of technology with the costs of other learning materials and program resources to arrive at an appropriate balance for their classrooms.

- In evaluating the appropriate use of technology, NAEYC applies principles of developmentally appropriate practice and appropriate curriculum and assessment. In short, NAEYC believes that in any given situation, a professional judgment by the teacher is required to determine if a specific use of technology is age appropriate, individually appropriate, and culturally appropriate.

- Used appropriately, technology can enhance children's cognitive and social abilities.

- Appropriate technology is integrated into the regular learning environment and used as one of many options to support children's learning.

- Early childhood educators should promote equitable access to technology for all children and their families. Children with special needs should have access when this is helpful.

- The power of technology to influence children's learning and development requires that attention be paid to eliminating stereotyping of any group and eliminating exposure to violence, especially as a problem-solving strategy.

- Teachers, in collaboration with parents, should advocate for more appropriate technology applications for children.

- The appropriate use of technology has many implications for early childhood professional development.

Source: "NAEYC Position Statement: Technology and Young Children, Ages 3 Through 8," *Young Children* (September 1996), pp. 11–16. Copyright © 1996 by the National Association for the Education of Young Children. Reprinted by permission.

"lapware" because children are held in their parents' laps to use it, and it is intended to be used by parents and children together.

You will find many software programs out there for the very young. For instance, *Jumpstart Baby* (www.etoys.com) and *BabyWow* (www.pctots.com) are aimed specifically at children nine months to two years. *Jumpstart Baby* leads children through eight activities, including wood-block puzzles and nursery rhyme sing-alongs. *BabyWow* has three hundred pictures and corresponding vocabulary words in eight languages.

The market for infant, toddler, and preschool software is growing, with an estimated $50 million spent each year. Programs designed for children under five represent the fastest growing educational software market. Not everyone believes that such software is developmentally appropriate, and the battle rages on in early childhood circles about how much time children should spend on computers and what kind of software they should use. Remember that not all software is good software. You must evaluate the materials you use with your children. Consult Figure 13.3, which contains highlights of NAEYC's position statement on technology and young children. How do you feel about NAEYC's position statement? Do you agree with all its statements?

TECHNOLOGY APPLIED TO LEARNING

A 4-Year-Old Child Uses Assistive Technology

Sara is a four-year-old child who has been diagnosed with cortical blindness. Despite her visual impairment, Sara is a typical preschooler who enjoys playing in the various classroom centers. To ensure her participation, Sara's teacher has adapted the environment, adding tactile and auditory components and making all materials accessible for her. Since Sara's favorite activity is listening to a story, she enjoys the reading center, which has books on tape. However, her favorite area of the classroom is the computer center. Through adaptive devices and customized software, Sara can not only listen to stories, but also interact with them and with other children at the computer.

Sara's favorite software program is *Just Me and My Dad*. When Sara wants to listen to certain parts of the program, she presses her Jellybean Switch to turn the pages. Her teacher has customized the activity by making the software switch-accessible through a software utility program, *Click It!* (IntelliTools). The teacher has also used the *IntelliPics* software to make picture overlays for the IntelliKeys, an adaptive touch sensitive tablet that serves as alternate input to the computer. Tactile material is added so that Sara can touch and identify parts of the overlay, pressing on areas to hear sounds made by objects on her favorite pages. Sara takes turns with other children, pressing areas on the overlay during small group activities. The children can also create their own version of the story through *IntelliPics* or *IntelliPics Studio*, deciding on characters, objects, actions, and words to put into their story. Sara especially enjoys this activity, since she can now tell the other children about her favorite person, her dad, through her recorded voice, sounds she has selected, and pictures from home. Technology is a tool that helps Sara develop not only emergent literacy skills, but also cognitive, social, fine motor, and communication skills.

A 7-Year-Old Child Uses Assistive Technology

Assistive technology offers young children with physical disabilities access to the same or similar developmentally appropriate, child-centered, integrated activities engaged in by typical children. With appropriate adaptations and software, young children with disabilities can participate in their own learning. James, a seven-year-old child with multiple disabilities, made images on the computer using *Kid Pix*® and adaptive peripherals. By trying different adaptations, such as a switch, a touch screen, an expanded keyboard, and a draw tablet, the teacher discovered that a draw tablet (with an overlay simulating the *Kid Pix*® draw screen) was the tool that James could use most successfully. Drawing with a draw tablet is much like drawing on a *Magna Doodle.*® A stylus is attached to the right or left side of the draw tablet, and the drawing surface is so touch sensitive that even a very light touch creates a line that appears on the monitor. James was able to make the connection between his movements with the stylus and the marks that appeared on the computer screen. As he worked, he told the teacher, "Draw." James also knew when he was successful and exclaimed, "Did it!" to let others know he was pleased with his work. When teachers integrate creative and interactive software with adaptive peripherals, all children have opportunities to gain knowledge and skills and extend their expressiveness.

© Center for Best Practices in Early Childhood, Western Illinois University, Macomb, Illinois.

The Center for Best Practices in Early Childhood

The Center for Best Practices in Early Childhood, a research and development unit at Western Illinois University, develops and promotes practices designed to improve educational opportunities for young children, including those with disabilities. Since 1975, the Center, directed by Dr. Patricia Hutinger, has implemented model development, outreach training, personnnel preparation, product development, and research projects funded through the U.S. Department of Education's Office of Special Education, the Department of Human Services, and the Illinois State Board of Education. In addition to providing training, products, and consultation to Illinois service providers and families of young children with disabilities, the Center is nationally recognized for its innovative work in assistive technology, providing services and products through 25 technology-related projects.

Since the early 1980s, computers, assistive devices, and other technologies have figured prominently in the Center's work and products. Center staff provide workshops for teachers, educational support staff, administrators, and families on such topics as selecting and using early childhood software, integrating technology into the preschool curriculum, choosing and using assistive technology, and conducting team-based technology assessments. The Center has developed four curricula focusing on the integration of technology into specialized areas, including emergent literacy, expressive arts, and math, science, and social studies to assist young children with disabilities in achieving skills. Other Center products include instructional manuals, CD-ROMs, videotapes, and a website (www.wiu.edu/thecenter/).

© Center for Best Practices in Early Childhood, Western Illinois University, Macomb, Illinois.

ASSISTIVE TECHNOLOGY AND CHILDREN WITH DISABILITIES

As an introduction to our discussion of using assistive technology with young children with disabilities, read the feature on the previous page that discusses a four-year-old and seven-year-old using assistive technology to learn. In addition, the Program in Action, "The Center for Best Practices in Early Childhood," illustrates the important work early childhood professionals and others are doing to help assure all children learn with technology.

The field of early childhood education is undergoing dramatic changes through integration with the field of special education. As a result, early childhood professionals are adopting assistive technology to help children and their families. According to Public Law 100–407, the Technology-Related Assistance for Individuals with Disabilities Act of 1988 (Tech Act), **assistive technology** is "any item, device or piece of equipment, or product system, whether acquired commercially off the shelf, modified, or customized, that is used to increase, maintain, or improve functional abilities of individuals with disabilities."[4]

Assistive technology covers a wide range of products and applications, from simple devices such as adaptive spoons and switch-adapted battery-operated toys to complex devices such as computerized environmental control systems. You will have opportunities to use many forms of assistive technology and modified educational software with all ages of students with special needs.

Assistive technology is particularly important for students with disabilities who depend on technology to help them communicate, learn, and be mobile. For example, closed-circuit

To complete a Program in Action activity, visit the Companion Website at **http://www. prenhall. com/morrison**, select chapter 13, then choose the Program in Action module.

Assistive technology Any device used to promote the learning of children with disabilities.

383

For more information about assistive technology, go to the Companion Website at **http://www. prenhall.com/morrison**, select chapter 13, then choose the Linking to Learning module to connect to the Assistive Technology, Inc. site.

Assistive technology enables children with disabilities to participate in regular classrooms and to learn skills and behaviors not previously thought possible. What are some examples of assistive technologies that would enable this child and others with disabilities to learn?

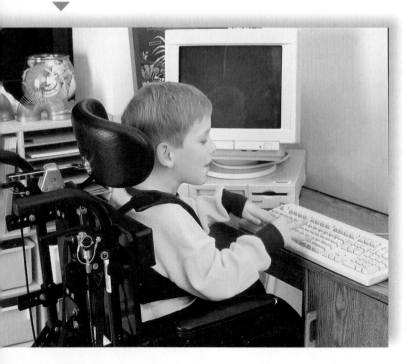

television can be used to enlarge print, a Braille printer can convert words to Braille, and audiotaped instructional materials can be provided for students with vision impairments. Closed-captioned television and FM amplification systems can assist students who are deaf or hard of hearing. Touch-screen computers, augmentative communication boards, and voice synthesizers can assist students with limited mobility or with disabilities that make communication difficult. Technology helps children with vision impairments see and children with physical disabilities read and write. Technology helps developmentally delayed children learn the skills they need to achieve at their appropriate levels and enables children with disabilities to substitute one ability for another and receive the special training they need. In addition, computer-assisted instruction provides software tools for teaching students at all ability levels, including programmed instruction for students with specific learning disabilities.

Opportunities for using many forms of assistive technology are available to even very young children, from birth to age three. Some of these include powered mobility, myoelectric prostheses, and communication devices. Infants as young as three months have interacted with computers, eighteen-month-old children have driven powered mobility devices and used myoelectric hands, and two-year-olds have talked via speech synthesizers. Children with severe physical disabilities learn how to use switches and scanning techniques.

Technology permits children with special needs to enjoy—through the process of learning—knowledge, skills, and behaviors that might otherwise be inaccessible to them. Technology empowers children with special needs; that is, it enables them to exercise control over their lives and the conditions of their learning. It enables them to do things previously thought impossible.

In addition, technology changes people's attitudes about children with disabilities. For example, some may have viewed children with disabilities as not being able to participate fully in regular classrooms; however, they may now recognize that instead of being segregated in separate programs, these children can be fully included with the assistance of technology.

Figure 13.4 will help you expand your vision of how assistive technology can support, extend, and enrich children's learning.

JUDGING APPROPRIATENESS OF ASSISTIVE TECHNOLOGY

An extremely important issue in the use of assistive technology with young children is the appropriateness of such technology. It is considered appropriate if it meets the following criteria:

1. A technology should respond to (or anticipate) specific, clearly defined goals that result in enhanced skills for the child.
2. A technology should be compatible with practical constraints such as available resources or the amount of training required to enable the child, his family, and the early childhood educator to use the technology.
3. A technology should result in desirable and sufficient outcomes. Some basic considerations for children with disabilities are related to (1) ease of training for the child and his family to use and care for the technology; (2) reasonable maintenance and repair, with regard to time and expense; and (3) monitoring of the technology's effectiveness.[5]

FIGURE 13.4 Assistive Technology

Touch Windows 17® www.riverdeep.net
- Attaches to computer monitor
- Allows children to touch screen directly, rather than using a mouse
- Can be used on a flat surface, such as a wheelchair tray
- Is scratch-resistant and resistant to breakage

BigKeys™ Keyboard www.bigkeys.com
- Keys are 4 times bigger than standard keyboard keys
- Letters are arranged in alphabetical order to assist young children
- Each key generates 1 letter regardless of how long the key is pressed
- "ASSIST MODE" accommodates children who cannot press down two or more keys simultaneously

Big Red® Switch ablenetinc.com
- Large, colorful switch to turn devices on and off
- 5-inch diameter surface is easy to see and activate
- Audible click when activated helps children make cause-effect link

Voice-in-a-Box 6 www.frame-tech.com
- Augmentative communication device allows children to communicate by pressing on pictures
- Allows for up to 36 recorded messages
- Record and re-record messages
- Preschool-friendly case is durable and appealing to young children

BookWorm™ ablenetinc.com
- Teacher or parent records worksheets and books into BookWorm
- By attaching the book to BookWorm, children can hear the story by turning pages
- A switch device can be attached for children who cannot turn pages

All-Turn-It® Spinner ablenetinc.com
- Inclusion learning tool that allows all children to participate in lessons on numbers, colors, shapes, matching, sequencing, etc.
- Spinner is controlled by a switch for easy manipulating
- Optional educational overlays, stickers, and books can be purchased

Tack-Tiles® Braille Systems www.tack-tiles.com
- Braille literacy teaching toys for all ages
- LEGO®-types blocks form Braille Codes that can be put on a board or magnetized for use on file cabinets or refrigerators
- Tolerant of sudden jarring movements
- Available in several codes, including 5 languages, mathematics, and music notation

Aurora www.aurora-systems.com
- Works with Windows to help people with learning disabilities and dyslexia write and spell better
- Helps people with physical disabilities communicate
- Aurora Prediction speeds up typing by predicting words
- Aurora Echo reads back what is typed and reads text from applications for those with reading difficulties
- Aurora Talk allows phrases to be organized into categories for quick conversation

The wonderful world of assistive technology consists of a wide variety of useful and truly amazing devices to help children with disabilities learn, develop, and achieve their fullest potential. Always keep in mind that a primary goal of assistive technology is to help children be independent learners.

The Uses of Technology for Young Children

"If schools do not become technologically sophisticated, then the technology sophisticated will not send their children to school."
—(Phil Schlecty)

Rice Creek Elementary School Technology Mission Statement

"Rice Creek Elementary School is committed to enhance learning through the use of technology. All students and staff utilize technology to research, create, and communicate within the community as well as globally. Technology is being integrated throughout the curriculum to produce lifelong learners and productive citizens of the future."

In this new millennium, students have new tools to "Navigate their Worlds." With mouse, keystrokes, and remote controls, they steer through CD-ROMs, videodiscs, channels, and Web pages. Student work displayed in the hallways should show a wide array of uses of technology. Colorful graphs, letters, and digital drawings express imaginations and creativity of students. Software aligned to the curriculum enables students to become proficient in computer skills as well as content areas. Primary students write reports and stories, create digital presentations, using Kidpix or Power Point, and use the Internet for research. Classes use the digital camera to create bulletin boards, class projects, Web pages, and presentations.

Schools with networked systems may set up student access to shared files that will enable students to use templates with instructional activities created by teachers. An entire class of students can access these on-screen worksheets simultaneously in the computer lab or classroom. This allows for practicing of skills with immediate feedback and eliminates the need for paper and pencil. Shared files are also used to save student work, reducing the usage of disks, which are easily corrupted. Teachers should make use of the shared files for student assessment, lesson plan templates, sharing ideas, and cross grade level sharing. For example, a second-grade teacher might create a digital world map that all second-grade students would access to label the continents.

All primary classrooms should be equipped with two to four computers with Internet access, tape recorders, CD players, and televisions. Overheads, LCD projectors, and VCRs should be available for checkout by the classroom teacher. Classrooms that have a computer conversion device that projects images to televisions for full class viewing make it easier for the entire class to view the computer screen while the teacher is demonstrating or explaining an activity.

Children in grades 2 and 3 should be encouraged to do research using preselected sites on the Internet. Projects work best if students this age are given one item to research with several specific questions. They will then begin to learn how to take notes and rewrite their answers in paragraph form. One example might be to assign each student an animal and have them find the answers to the following questions.

1. What is the habitat like?
2. What does it eat?
3. What does it look like?
4. What is its natural enemy?

After typing a paragraph about the animal, students may copy and paste a picture of the animal on their page. Assignments such as this should reinforce the curriculum and teach skills in research and technology, as well as provide students with the opportunity to discover and explore using different modes of learning. Children this age are not afraid to "click" and love to see the "real" pictures. It stimulates their interest in science and social studies if they are allowed to research one or two selected sites just before the teacher introduces a topic in class. For example, if second graders are getting ready to study rocks, they might want to visit sites such as http://www.fi.edu/fellows/payton/rocks/index2.html for a look at different types of rocks. Third graders studying the solar system might go to a site such as http://www.windows.ucar.edu/ to view the planets they will be studying. The main points to remember when surfing the Web with young children is to preview the websites you want them to look at to make sure that they are developmentally appropriate (most are not written for young children), and to have several questions prepared that they are to answer.

Technology assists in the assessment of young students with a variety of different programs. These include *Accelerated Reader, Accelerated Math, STAR Math, STAR Reading, STAR Early Literacy* (Advantage Learning Co.) and *Map* (Measures of Academic Progress from NWEA). Students like to use technology for assessment because it gives them instant feedback. There are several excellent technology-based, reading management systems used in elementary schools. Students are tested to find their appropriate reading level, then read books selected from specific catalogs of books that have corresponding reading tests on that level and take a computerized test on the book. The *Accelerated Reader System* is a major component of the more comprehensive *Reading Renaissance Program* carefully monitored and facilitated by teachers.

Computer programs to extend learning should be utilized regularly in all classrooms. Drawing programs such as Kidpix allow students to apply their knowledge of line, color, and shape in free-hand drawings. In order to reinforce certain academic skills, teachers may create templates. For example, a kindergarten teacher might start a pattern in Kidpix and have each student complete the pattern during his or her computer time. As long as the original template is kept, each student may use it. The Harcourt Math Series offers online math games for each grade level that align with the chapter of the book the students are studying. There are many other excellent sites that reinforce math skills on all levels on the Internet. Young students need to be guided directly to these approved sites to receive maximum curriculum benefits and not left to explore the Internet on their own. Companies are constantly developing software in all areas of the elementary curriculum. When choosing software, there are several considerations:

1. Is it compatible with your classroom computers (operating system, memory, speed and color)? Read the label on the back of the CD or in the catalog to make sure. If you still don't know, call the company and tell them what kind of machine you are using.
2. Does it match curriculum standards that you are required to teach?
3. Is it age-level appropriate?
4. Is it fun to play? Kids don't like boring software. Remember, today's students watch a lot of TV and are used to being entertained. Most companies will send you a sample disk to try in your classroom. Let the kids use it for a few days to see if they like it before you purchase it.

A click to the Rice Creek Elementary School website, www.richland2.org/rce, begins a journey into the world of Rice Creek. School policies, the weekly newsletter, *Accelerated Reader,* lists curriculum outlines, classroom news, favorite websites, and the weekly cafeteria menu provide the virtual visitor with information about all aspects of the school community. Their website is an ongoing project, created and updated by teachers, students, and community members.

E-mail should and can be a major source of communication for teachers, staff, and parents. Many teachers make a group list of all of their students' parents and keep them informed of field studies, projects, and upcoming school events using e-mail.

Technology serves as a tool for learning for all students from special education to gifted and talented. It levels the playing field by offering a wide variety of programs in different areas of the curriculum that are geared to all levels of learning. It offers students a challenging and fun environment to learn and to practice skills. Technology affords students the opportunity to visit places they will never go, and see things they will never see. It brings the world to them at an early age and can be used to spark their quest for knowledge like no other means of media has ever been able to do.

Contributed by Phyllis D. Brown, Information Technology Specialist, Rice Creek Elementary School, Columbia, South Carolina. 2000–2001 Blue Ribbon School.

Assistive technology such as the Alpha Talker II™ helps this child learn and use a basic core vocabulary. By selecting an appropriate icon, the Alpha Talker II™ enables her to talk and communicate with others. This technology is easily programmed for new words.

The mere application of technology is therefore not enough. You and other professionals have to be sensitive to the above criteria as you work with children, families, and other professionals in applying technology to learning settings and children's special needs.

IMPLEMENTING TECHNOLOGY IN EARLY CHILDHOOD EDUCATION PROGRAMS

Three challenges confront early childhood teachers in implementing an effective program of computer instruction:

1. Their own personal acceptance of computers
2. Assurance that computers have a positive influence on children
3. Decisions about how to use computers in early childhood programs and classrooms

The next few sections of this chapter will help you address these challenges, because teachers cannot afford to decide not to use computers and technology. When they do, they risk having technologically illiterate children; denying children access to skills, knowledge, and learning, and not promoting an attitude of acceptance of technology into their everyday lives. Rather, they must promote access to technology and develop creative ways to involve children with technology. Figure 13.5 provides some practical advice for infusion of technology in your teaching.

FIGURE 13.5 Recommendations for Using Technology in Early Childhood Programs

Teachers:

- Need to acknowledge that technology infusion is an evolutionary process that has fits and starts in its functionality and practicality.

- Cannot be afraid to look to others, whether it's for help infusing the curriculum with technology or for technical assistance. They need to form human networks for planning and troubleshooting. This is somewhat antithetical to teachers' experiences because they typically are alone with their students. However, the social-psychological dimension of sharing, exchanging, and helping one another is critical for success with technology. This shift in working with others also serves as a model for students as they learn to reach out to other students for assistance.

- Need to be prepared for things not to work as expected. The "Plan B" phenomenon (the need for a backup plan) is very real when working with technology, and teachers need to know how to immediately shift gears when something goes awry technologically.

- Need to be creative in allowing technology to expand their instructional plans, yet realistic in knowing what their students can handle and what their curriculum allows. This is especially important in this area of high-stakes testing.

These are some things you can do to increase your proficiency in technology use. Keep in mind that infusing technology into your professional life and practices involves risks, but at the same time offers great reward.

Source: S. B. Wepner and Liqing Tao, "From Master Teacher to Master Novice: Shifting Responsibilities in Technology-Infused Classrooms," *The Reading Teacher,* 55, *no. 7* (2002), 642–650.

SETTING A GOOD EXAMPLE: YOUR PERSONAL ACCEPTANCE OF COMPUTERS

As an early childhood educator, the first step in implementing an effective program of computer instruction is accepting technology and learning how to use it effectively and appropriately. Here are guidelines for you to keep in mind:

- Educate yourself on the potential benefits of computers and technology.
- Be willing to try new ways to use technology to help your children learn new knowledge and skills.
- Collaborate with colleagues in your school and school district to explore ways to use technology.
- Collaborate with parents and community members. Many have skills that you can use and apply.
- Advocate for and on behalf of gaining access of technology for your classroom and school.

Your confidence and comfort level with technology will set a good example for the children in your care. As you use computers to access information through the Internet, send e-mail, and keep records of children's accomplishments, children will come to understand that computers are a natural part of the process of schooling and learning. Establishing positive attitudes toward technology is an important part of fostering an appropriate and inviting classroom environment.

MAKING DECISIONS: HOW TO USE COMPUTERS IN EARLY CHILDHOOD PROGRAMS AND CLASSROOMS EFFECTIVELY

As an early childhood educator, your next responsibility is to determine how to make the most of available technologies to spark your children's learning and imagination. This implies that lectures on the history of computers or rote memorization of computer components and terminology should not be included in the curriculum. Only when meaningful concepts can be actively learned should they be considered for inclusion.

When making decisions about how to use computers and computer-based technologies in the early childhood learning environment, there are a few questions to keep in mind: Is the technology developmentally appropriate? Are you meeting learners' individual needs when using technology? Does the technology promote the kind of learning you want to promote? Is the use of technology seamlessly integrated into the curriculum?

Meeting Learners' Individual Needs with Technology One additional aspect of ensuring that technology is being used most effectively in your classroom is making sure you are meeting children's individual needs. You will want to take children's individual differences into account when making decisions about how to best involve them in learning activities with computers and other technology. Some children will need more help and encouragement than others, and some will intrinsically want to be more involved because of their learning style preference for using technology to learn.

For links to topics of interest for early childhood educators, go to the Companion Website at **http://www.prenhall.com/morrison**, select chapter 13, then choose the Linking to Learning module to connect to the ECEOL (Early Childhood Education Online) site.

Technology allows children to explore different worlds, access resources, and engage in learning activities. How can you use computers and other technology to appropriately support children's learning?

The Longfellow Links Internet Project

An Example of Technology Integration

CREATING A VISION

It is my belief that it is essential that educators should be encouraged and empowered to integrate technology in the classroom. Teachers need to see the value of technology in a nonthreatening and personal way. Bringing the technology, such as the Internet, into schools is simply not enough. Money spent on school technology will be wasted if teachers do not know how to integrate it into the curriculum. We need to look beyond the walls and move our schools as a whole by making the human connection with educators, by establishing community awareness, and by facilitating a cultural change that is curious about technology. Teachers, parents, and students need to develop an understanding that technology is a way to extend and improve the curriculum, enhance teaching strategies, and expand student and parent resources in the home.

SET YOUR GOALS

There is an ongoing need to encourage and empower teachers to use computers in the classroom. This goal can be accomplished by using the most innovative and exciting learning tool of this century, the World Wide Web. The sheer volume of places to go and things to do online can be overwhelming for any teacher. Cyberspace can also make it difficult to find the exact information that is needed. It has so much information available at your fingertips that it is extremely difficult and frustrating to make choices. In fact, some people have compared the Internet to a rich dessert that is so sweet you just have to pass it up. Educators need to simplify this technology and directly link it to the curriculum needs of each school. Remember, it is not the technology, but how it is used, that makes a difference.

What began as Internet searching to increase my curriculum resources evolved into "Longfellow Links," a website designed to simplify Internet access and directly link it, in a user-friendly way, to the curriculum needs throughout the school. The goal of this project is to provide teachers, parents, and students easy, direct access to appropriately focused and teacher reviewed online curriculum materials.

WHAT DO YOU NEED?

It is extremely important to understand what is needed for each goal. Teachers can make a list and brainstorm ideas as the plan develops. They need to carefully assess materials, time, and support necessary to integrate technology into the classroom. For this project, I recognized that I needed a computer with Internet access, software applications, training in Web page design, release time, and support from my colleagues and principal.

BUILD A PLAN

The project revolves around the current curriculum at Longfellow School, specifically around relevant curriculum grade level needs. It provides simple and direct access connecting teachers, parents, and students to valuable resources, utilizing the Internet through a curriculum resource website. Links were researched to provide entry to educational innovations that extend the curriculum and a website was then created. Adapting this tool in a personal way that meets the needs of all levels is the key to its integration into our community and life. Longfellow Links facilitates the connection.

FIND THE RESOURCES

I began by coordinating with the Brunswick Curriculum Review Team to ensure continuity across curriculum needs. I then collaborated with the teachers, parents, students, and community members to determine specific needs and locate resources. This was specifically to meet the needs of everyone who would be using the site and coordinating units with Brunswick's Curriculum Review Team. I received training in how to use HTML (HyperText Markup Language) and create Web pages from

reaching out to various community members and other educators. The school's parent group at Longfellow School purchased the software for the project.

SEEK OUT TRAINING

In order to develop this plan I took one professional day and received intense training from local technical support staff personnel in the district. It was not difficult to understand the basic concepts but practice and follow-up support were essential to the success of this project.

BE CREATIVE AND TAKE RISKS

When I implemented this project, I needed to step out of my comfort zone and accomplish a task that challenged my abilities as a teacher. What did this project entail?

1. Introduce the Internet project concept to the staff.
2. Involve teachers by requesting specific curriculum needs.
3. Research grade-level-appropriate URLs (Uniform Resource Locator) for units of interest.
4. Learn HyperText Markup Language (HTML) and create a website.
5. Provide Web training in the use of this new teaching tool.
6. Solicit feedback and share with the community.

ASSESS AND REEVALUATE

Students are highly motivated to share what they have discovered from this project with each other, their family, and the community. This has increased their ability to communicate, to cooperate, to learn, and to achieve. Each student gets involved, whether gifted, special, or average. Students work in pairs or in small groups to teach each other what they know. By restricting the website, students are free to explore in a safe environment. In addition, special needs students can produce work on the same level as anyone else. Students remain on task longer and students are more actively involved in their work.

Data collected during the past two years have provided the following information on how the Longfellow Links Project has stimulated student learning:

1. Not only are students engaged at school but also the learning carries over into the home.
2. Parents report relevant curriculum materials easily accessible from home or library. They can foster student interest at home, expanding on areas that interest their child.
3. An autistic child uses the site daily and shares research with his classmates!
4. Students' resources have expanded for "ALL" students.
5. Students donate free time to teach each other and explore.

6. Students, parents, and teachers share a common goal to learn how to use this teaching tool.
7. Use of the Internet promotes visual, auditory, and kinesthetic learning.

The overwhelming utilization of the site itself is a measure of its success: 100 percent of teachers are now using computer and Internet resources in the classroom compared to 35 percent pre-project. Students are excited about this technology! The Web page has grown to more than a thousand sites from an original seventy-five in early 1998. Parents have expressed appreciation for my giving them a valuable perspective on what is being taught at each grade level and for my providing the information for them to help their children be successful.

Community members and surrounding schools have expressed the value of having this resource available for them to use. *Educational World* magazine has recognized the site as a valuable resource to help facilitate the integration of technology into the curriculum. The article is available online at http://www.education-world.com/a_tech/tech008.shtml.

SHARE WITH OTHERS

Teachers took ownership of the project by making a determination of which units needed to be researched and by providing continuous feedback about various sites. It was well received by the staff because it met the dual needs of improving the curriculum and using technology. It provided valuable resources in a nonthreatening and comfortable way without neglecting the training necessary to utilize this new teaching tool. Training involved team teaching with colleagues during my free planning periods. This allowed teachers the opportunity to be supported using this new technology. Additionally, parents and students also provided requests for resources to be added. The strength of this project is the personal component. Parents understand clearly what is being taught at each grade level and have appropriate resources easily available to them, which make learning a fun, family endeavor. Furthermore, soliciting input from everyone creates an intergenerational approach reaching beyond the classroom and into the community in a simple but profound way. Grandparents and extended family members want to learn and explore the curriculum alongside students.

EQUIPMENT/RESOURCES

Computer with Internet access
Web editor software such as Claris Home Page,
Netscape Composer, Dream Weaver, or Front Page
Computer projector

A television and converter can be used for classroom presentations, as well.

Get started:

1. Introduce the Internet project concept. Click on my site as a model. Use the LCD panel and overhead projector for the presentation.
2. Engage teachers. Determine specific curriculum needs.
3. Begin to research grade-level appropriate URLs for units of interest. Use search engines or educational websites available to research your topics. Visit each site to determine safety and age-level appropriateness.
4. Learn HTML and create a simple website. I used Netscape Composer and took one professional day to learn the software and create the initial site.
5. Provide training for the staff in the use of this new teaching tool. This should include training on how to use a specific browser like Netscape Communicator or Internet Explorer and a computer projector.
6. Train students and parents.
7. Encourage teachers, parents, and students to submit any new URLs that might be used for additional units.
8. Seek feedback and share with the community and surrounding schools.
9. Update your site on a regular basis. I do it monthly.

SUMMARY

Using Longfellow Links provides an opportunity for collaboration and innovation. Teachers and students will be highly motivated to share what they have discovered with each other, their family, and the community. Using technology effectively will increase their ability to communicate, cooperate, learn, and achieve. Computers do make a significant difference in the way we see and experience information. This powerful technology provides the opportunity for everyone to have equal access to valuable resources. In addition, teachers can use the computers as a tool to supplement, enrich, and enhance current curriculum in an exciting new way.

A major role of the integrating technology into the classroom is to create powerful learners for the twenty-first century. Technology can be a benefit to everyone. Proper use of new technologies draws teachers, parents, students, and our community together. Using this teaching tool is essential for success in a future dominated by innovations.

The Longfellow Links include but are not limited to the following:

- Holiday resources, which include cultural traditions around the world
- Links to information about the environment
- Links to birds, plants, math fun, presidents, poetry, pumpkins, maple syrup, even dental hygiene (on the first-grade page)
- Art, art museums, and the performing arts
- Parent and teacher resources
- Math and writing for all ages
- Special education links, including sites that cover attention deficit disorder, autism, gifted and talented, and dyslexia

---

Contributed by Doug DeCamilla, M. ED., Longfellow Elementary School, Brunswick, Maine. http://www.brunswick.k12.me.us/lon/lonlinks

Individual children will have different needs, interests, and abilities and, therefore, will learn different things about computers and will use them in different ways. This should be welcomed as well as accepted; no effort should be made to force all children to "master" all aspects of computer literacy. Instead of one definition of technological literacy for all, teachers should determine what computers can do to help a particular child reach a particular goal.

Using Technology to Promote Children's Social Development. Perhaps you have heard some critics claim that computers and other technology interfere with children's social development. Let's look at this argument and consider some things you can do to ensure that your use of technology with young children supports and enhances their social development.

Social development involves interacting with and getting along with other children, siblings, parents, and teachers. Social development also includes the development of self-esteem, the feelings children have about themselves. During the early childhood years, true peer relationships begin to emerge. Children's interactions and relationships with others enlarge their views of the world and of themselves. Early childhood is also a time when children are learning self-control and self-reliance. Adults expect children to develop self-regulation, control aggression, and function without constant supervision. How children meet these expectations has tremendous implications for the development of self-concept and self-esteem. Finally, during the early childhood years children are learning about adult roles thorough play and real-life activities. As children learn about adult activities, they learn about others and themselves.

You can use computers and other technology to help children develop positive peer relationships, grow in their abilities of self-regulation and self-control, explore adult roles, and develop positive self-esteem. Here are some things you can do to accomplish these goals:

- Have children work on projects together in pairs or small groups. Several children can work on computer and other projects at the same time. Make sure that the computer has several chairs to encourage children to work together. Learning through technology is not inherently a solitary activity. You can find many ways to make it a cooperative and social learning experience.
- Provide children opportunities to talk about their technology projects. Part of social development includes learning to talk confidently, explain, and share information with others.
- Encourage children to explore adult roles related to technology, such as newscaster, weather forecaster, and photographer. Invite adults from the community to share with children how they use technology in their careers. Invite a television crew to show children how they broadcast from community locations.
- Read stories about technology and encourage children to talk about technology in their lives and the lives of their families.

As you explore other ways to promote children's social development through technology, remember that all dimensions of children's development are integrated. The cognitive, linguistic, social, emotional, and physical dimensions support and depend on each other, and technology can positively support all of these dimensions of development.

Promoting Meaningful Learning with Technology. Different educators have varying approaches to and philosophies of facilitating and promoting children's learning through computers. For some, the computer and software are seen as a central element of teachers teaching and children learning. On the other hand, some see computers as a means of providing open-ended discovery learning, problem solving, and computer competence. Different applications promote different kinds of learning experiences, and you will need to make intelligent decisions about which of these applications best suit your learners' needs and interests and your instructional objectives.

Drill Versus Discovery. A major controversy among early childhood professionals involves the purpose of computers in the classroom. On the one hand, some say that the more repetitive drill-and-practice programs have no place in the early childhood program. They say that only software that encourages learning by discovery and exploration is appropriate. On the other hand, some professionals see drill-and-practice software programs that emphasize helping children learn colors, numbers, vocabulary, phonics, and skills such as addition as a valuable means for children to learn concepts and skills they so desperately need to succeed in school.

Of course, in this case, as with so many things, a middle ground offers an appropriate solution. Many children like drill-and-practice programs and the positive feedback that often comes with them. Also, some children spend long periods of time working on such programs. However, not all children like or do well with skill-drill programs. Technology, as with other learning materials, requires you to identify and address children's learning styles. What is important is that all children have access to a variety of software and instructional and learning activities that are appropriate to them as individuals. This is what a developmentally appropriate curriculum is all about, and it applies to technology and software as well.

Higher-Order Learning. Technology can support and facilitate critical educational and cognitive processes such as cooperative learning, group and individual problem solving, critical thinking, reflective practices, analysis, inquiry, process writing, and

PROGRAM IN ACTION

A. D. Henderson University School's Emerging Technologies

A Resource for Pre-Kindergarten through University Students and Faculty

L ocated on the Boca Raton Campus of Florida Atlantic University and serving 500 children in grades K–8 as well as the university's students and researchers is a school committed to test the edges of emerging technologies. The A. D. Henderson University School is a public, demographically representative lab school affiliated with the College of Education and collaboratively engaged with other university colleges as well. This engagement includes initiatives such as expanding alternative opportunities for teacher development with the College of Education, ongoing research in bully prevention with the College of Science, developing of a solar project with the College of Engineering, and computing initiatives that extend student performance and administrative productivity.

Because it is designated as an individual Florida school district, the school is able to develop, test, and disseminate new and innovative curricula, technologies, policies, and practices designed to improve student performance that might be difficult for traditional districts. As one of only four (4) university developmental research public schools in Florida, Henderson is uniquely positioned to assist the state, the university, and various business partners in meet-

ing the K–20 educational challenges of a rapidly growing, diverse population faced with increasing global competition. (Note: Florida has a seamless system of K–20 education.) The state's desire to create additional high-wage and high-skill jobs for citizens requires industries that depend on employees' proficient use of newer technologies. Since these emerging technologies continue to proliferate with increasing rapidity and complexity, each employee's ability to quickly learn and creatively repurpose technologies constitutes a competitive requirement

public speaking. Also, technology can promote metacognition—that is, encourage children to think about their thinking. One such technological application would be the use of *LEGO/Logo*, software that links the popular LEGO construction kit with the Logo programming language. Children start by building machines out of LEGO pieces, using not only the traditional building blocks but also new pieces like gears, motors, and sensors. Then they connect their machines to a computer and write computer programs (using a modified version of Logo) to control the machines. For example, a child might build a LEGO house with lights and program them to turn on and off at particular times. Then the child might build a garage and program the door to open whenever a car approached.

LEGO/Logo engages children in thinking about their process of design and invention. Children have used this software to build and program a wide assortment of creative machines,

for the high-skill/high-wage industries. Today's learners need to develop the basic knowledge and habits of mind that promote technological familiarity and experimentation. Schools have a responsibility to support this requirement. The big traditional hurdles of expensive hardware, complicated connectivity, and endless teacher training are still large, but progress in virtually every school has been made in these areas. New low cost end-user devices like hand held computers (PDAs) are now functional enough to support smaller versions of the office suite programs that resemble their desktop originators. These PDAs can also act as server interfaces to access student or shared files or as Internet devices. They are particularly user portable and powerful when equipped with wireless access. Thanks to decreased equipment and connectivity costs and the advent of the e-rate, schools can provide Internet access at a fraction of its cost a few years ago and can experience greater reliability, throughput, and ease of use. Cabled and wireless access have various advantages, but the ability of students to electronically "carry around" developed work, generate visuals, communicate important information, gain real time access to Internet-available information and learning tools, and conceptualize new ways to leverage the technology has really begun to expand in the wireless world, including connections outside the traditional school. Simpler devices with simpler and more intuitive interfaces translate into more self-learning and less tradi-

tional teacher training. In fact, given today's technology world, all training in this area is "becoming just in time." Our colleagues (or students) become our best training source; they are more readily available, more attuned to our applications, and can target immediate concerns.

In 2003–04, the university school will expand a small pilot of handheld to include a larger cohort. Most of this work will center on the applicability of various student populations and computer applications to handhelds. Substantive work relating to appropriateness of e-books, general motivation, writing readiness, and other related instructional questions will be formulated and studies designed for initiation in 2004–05. The pilots of 2002–03 will be expanded from a few wireless access points to many, from a few teachers to many, and from a very few students to some selected groups. The software infrastructure improvements of 2002–03 provide each student with their own accounts accessible from desktop, home, or handheld. Students and faculty can access from across the university campuses a wireless network that connects to the Internet or to their own work files. Teachers, parents, and administrators perform routine tasks and communicate using the school's listservs and new student information support software. Outside network wireless access for physical education or science teachers or students supports both administrative and instructional pilots this year. Probe, video, and other opportunities await as the pilots mature. The intent is to improve student performance using all the tools and processes available given scant resources. Differentiation of instruction and the use of technologies to support improved learning by our students are key elements in our development of successful emerging learners at A. D. Henderson School; learners representing grade level students, university students, and faculty.

Contributed by Glenn Thomas, Director, Alexander D. Henderson University School, Boca Raton, Florida; photos supplied by International Business Machines Corporation.

including a programmable pop-up toaster, a "chocolate-carob factory" (inspired by the Willy Wonka children's stories), and a machine that sorts LEGO bricks according to their lengths.

The LEGO company now sells a commercial version of *LEGO/Logo* used in more than a dozen countries, including more than 15,000 elementary and middle schools in the United States. The Epistemology and Learning Group is currently involved in developing programmable bricks—LEGO bricks with tiny computers embedded inside. With these new electronic bricks, children can build computational capabilities directly into their LEGO constructions.

Technology and Curriculum Integration. Technology should be integrated as fully as possible into the early childhood curriculum and learning environment so its use can help promote learning and achieve positive outcomes for all children.

To complete a Program in Action activity, visit the Companion Website at **http://www. prenhall.com/morrison**, select chapter 13, then choose the Program in Action module.

Part of this integration involves making sure that all technology-based activities remain consistent with the beliefs, principles, and practices of your program. Another aspect of this integration is making sure technology use is not seen as a separate or add-on activity. There should not be a "computers" unit that is separate from work in social studies, science, language arts, and so on. Instead, you could create a computer/technology learning center in your classroom that children have access to as they would any other center. In this way, the technology would be used as much as possible. And, just as important, such a center should have software that enables children to work independently, with little or minimal adult supervision.

Finally, educational technology should not be something children get to use only when they have completed other tasks. It should not be used as a reward, nor should it be a supplemental activity. Technology should be an integrated part of your early childhood program.

PARENTS AND TECHNOLOGY

 To visit a website that encourages family literacy by posting original stories and articles for children, go to the Companion Website at **http://www.prenhall.com/ morrison**, select chapter 13, then choose the Linking to Learning module to connect to the Parents and Children Together Online site.

Technology has changed the way early childhood professionals teach and the way children learn, so it should come as no surprise to you that it has also changed parents' roles. With the help of technology, parents now have more resources for participating in, supervising, and directing their children's education. They also have additional responsibilities, like making sure the information their children have access to while surfing the Internet at home is developmentally appropriate. Figure 13.6 shows some interesting applications of technology to parents' many roles.

TECHNOLOGY FOR INCREASING PARENT PARTICIPATION

For most parents, parenting is a full-time proposition. In addition, many have demanding work schedules; many work two jobs to make ends meet. Juggling the demands of parenting and work causes anxiety and concern about parenting and children's school achievement. Parents' questions about and concerns for their children go well beyond the capability of teachers and school personnel to help them within the time constraints of the school day. In addition, many parents face constraints of time and mobility for getting to the school for parent conferences, programs, and assistance. Technology offers a rich assortment of ways to exchange information, gain information, and get help and assistance.

TECHNOLOGY FOR PARENTAL SUPERVISION OF CHILD CARE

Technology is also transforming how parents access information about their children in other ways. Mary Manning, human resources manager for an engineering company in Norwalk, Connecticut, engages in virtual parenting by logging on to the Internet. By typing in a special password, she is able to view a picture of her son at his preschool.[6] Growing numbers of preschools and day care programs are installing cameras and systems that enable parents to access secure websites so they can monitor how their children are doing. A special user ID and password gives parents access. Preschools and child care programs generally pay about $6,000 for systems with names such as "Watch Me Grow!" (www.watch-me.com) and "I See You" (http://www.iseeu.com).

WatchMeGrow provides products and services to help ensure a safe classroom environment. Video cameras are placed in classrooms for center and parent viewing. Footage is digitally recorded and stored. This footage can be used to discuss behavioral issues with parents, train teachers, and protect teachers from false claims. Parents are able to view live snap-shot images of classrooms over the Web. WatchMeGrow services also include Parent Link, which is a pager system that can be sent by classroom, individual, or school to parents. Messages can also be preformatted for specific situations or programmed to be sent at a specific time. Parent Link can be used for emergencies or for general announcements. The cost of WatchMeGrow in a school of one hundred or more students is about $800 per

FIGURE 13.6   Parenting and Technology

Aspire Web-Based Software http://www.aspire.com

- Internet-based tools allowing schools to communicate, teach, and report to students and parents online.
- Allows parents to track their children's grades and progress.
- Messaging keeps parents posted on news, announcements, and events.

Digital Angel http://www.digitalangel.net/

- Wireless digital safety and location system.
- Alerts parents to the exact location of their children.
- Emergency alert sends out a signal that is transferred to the parents.
- Currently available in watch form, but eventually will be small enough to implant under the skin.

TVGuardian http://www.tvguardian.com

- Filters out foul language from programs as you watch them.
- Works with television programs, DVDs, and VHS tapes.
- Foul language can be muted or replaced with other phrases and words.

WriteLinx Communicator http://www.xactcommunication.com/

- Two-way radio wristwatch.
- Allows parents and children to communicate up to 1.5 miles apart.
- Is voice activated and has an optional ear bud (single ear headset) available.

As time goes by, technology will increasingly be used not only to keep children safe, but also to enhance the parenting role. How do you react to each of the above technology applications to parenting roles? Can you think of some other ways technology can be applied to parenting? Some argue that technology is no substitute for good parenting. How do you feel about this?

month. Cost per student ranges from $4 to $10, depending on the number of students enrolled in the school.

Proponents of such access to preschool programs contend that they ease parents' minds about how their children are doing, promote communication between parents and programs, create closer bonds between parents and children, and are a safeguard against possible child abuse. On the other hand, critics say that it is another example of the intrusion of technology into the lives of children and families and that unauthorized people could get access to the system if parents are careless about their passwords or if they give them to others. What are your opinions regarding such technology? Would you want parents to have such access to your classroom? State your reasons, both pro and con.

PARENTS AND SUPERVISION OF CHILDREN'S INTERNET USE

Parents face a technological challenge in trying to screen out the good from the bad on the Internet. One way is for parents to constantly monitor what their children access. However, for most parents, this is an impractical solution and one that many don't exercise.

Another way to monitor is through the use of a *filter,* a computer program that denies access to sites parents specify as inappropriate. One such program, *Cyber Sentinel,* blocks access to chat rooms, stops instant messages, and can be programmed to stop questions such as "What is your phone number?" *Cyber Sentinel* also has built-in time management that allows parents to control when and the amount of time that their child has access to the Internet. Parents who use America Online can specify three levels of access—Kids Only (under

Virtual Preschool

For a young child, learning and discovery take place at every turn: at the water table in a classroom, in the kitchen helping to mix ingredients for dinner, or in the supermarket produce section during the weekly shopping. With this in mind, the Chicago Public Schools created Virtual Pre-K, an award-winning interactive teaching tool designed to support preschool parents as their child's first teacher. Through a series of short video lessons and a user-friendly website, Virtual Pre-K shows parents how much they can do to help their child learn, virtually anywhere. With technology, Virtual Pre-K is helping parents and teachers strengthen the educational partnership between home and school.

The goal of Virtual Pre-K is threefold: to support and encourage parents as their children's first teacher (both at home and in the community); to provide professional development for teachers; and to promote the use of educational technology by parents and teaching staff.

Virtual Pre-K has two parts (video lessons and a website) and is available in English and Spanish.

THE VIDEO LESSONS

Virtual Pre-K begins with "All About Me" available on CD-ROM and videocassette. In short video lessons, Chicago Public Schools' educators and parents demonstrate activities, lessons, and teaching techniques. Each five-minute video lesson starts with a master teacher who introduces the lesson's learning concept and shows how it is presented in the classroom. The video lesson then goes into the home, where a parent and child share a related activity using common household items. Finally, the lesson moves beyond school and home to the community, exploring fun applications of the learning concept at familiar places like the supermarket, laundromat, or the zoo.

The following lesson helps parents use children's senses to learn.

THE FIVE SENSES

IN THE CLASSROOM: Making Popcorn

Teacher Kris uses popping corn to explore all five senses with her students, causing great excitement in the classroom.

AT HOME: Hide and Sense

Senses are the key to this fun guessing game using objects found from around the house.

OUT & ABOUT: Supermarket Senses

Parents can use the sights, sounds, smells, and tastes of the grocery store to spark children's senses.

In each five-minute lesson, the parent:

- Gets a clear understanding of why the lesson topic is important for preschoolers;
- Watches teachers and parents interact with children and demonstrate activity ideas;

twelve years), Young Teen (thirteen to fifteen), and Mature Teen (sixteen and seventeen). Although many of these solutions are helpful, none can be considered 100 percent effective.

The Children's Online Privacy Act is designed to ensure privacy rights of children and protect them from unscrupulous individuals and firms. The act requires World Wide Web operators to secure parental permission before they receive children's E-mail or home addresses. In *Privacy Online: A Report to Congress,* the Federal Trade Commission reported that of 212 children's websites, 90 percent collected personal information and only 1 percent obtained parental permission.[7] Federal Trade Commission Chairman Timothy Muris believes that "none of the worries we have about privacy is greater than our concern for the privacy of our children."[8] To alleviate any privacy concerns, many businesses such as America Online use mail-in parental notifications whereby parents can fill out an information card and mail it back in to the company.[9] Congress also passed the Child Online Protection Act,

To visit a website that features an online child safety forum, go to the Companion ...://
orrison, choose module Kids

- Finds tips on ways to support learning while doing regular activities, like the weekly shopping or visiting the playground.

The final part of each video lesson is the Virtual Pre-K website.

THE WEBSITE (www.virtualpre-k.org)

Virtualpre-k.org (accessible from any computer with Internet access) provides the interactive tools parents and teachers need to build their own "virtual classroom." Each video lesson is supported with lesson plans for teachers and activity cards for parents, which can be printed and stored for quick reference. The site includes an area for parents and teachers to share ideas, questions, and concerns online through discussion boards and moderated chats. A calendar of preschool-appropriate events, all under $10 and most free, is featured each month. Virtualpre-k.org also offers choice links to other super sites on the Internet for parents, teachers, and children.

ACCESS

Copies of the video and activity cards are housed in the Virtual Pre-K Kit, a portable container that parents check out of their children's classrooms to use at home. The kits are also available for loan in local public libraries. Two of our biggest challenges with technology are access and training, particularly as the third largest school district in the nation, with approximately 84 percent of the system's students considered low-income. By offering the lessons on videocassette and CD-ROM, parents can take the low- or high-tech approach to Virtual Pre-K. Parents without much exposure to technology can get involved in Virtual Pre-K through the videocassette and activity cards (the "low-tech" approach), and then move on to the enhanced features offered on the CD-ROM and website (the "high-tech" approach) at their children's school or local public library. Parents with basic computer skills and Internet access can head straight for the high-tech approach.

TRAINING

Training begins with the classroom staff. All teachers and assistants receive hands-on computer training in use of the video and website, with a focus on ways to incorporate the lesson ideas into their classrooms, and promote parent involvement with the home and community elements. Teacher in-services are followed by workshops for parents, which provide basic Internet training as well as instruction in the Virtual Pre-K program.

ASSESSMENT

Success of the Virtual Pre-K program is assessed through traditional and online surveys and progress tracking. Registration on the website includes an anonymous demographic survey, which gives a profile of visitors to the site. The results show a significantly even distribution of users across ethnic and economic lines. The website also features a success chart, where parents and children chart their progress through the lessons, making it possible to track use of the program. In addition, traditional paper surveys are distributed to teaching staff to assess use of the program's "low-tech" approach (videocassette and activity cards), which does not appear in the website data.

COLLABORATION

As Virtual Pre-K has gained recognition, the opportunities for collaboration have increased. Working together with outside groups, such as local community-based organizations, other preschool agencies, and parents who are home-schooling their children create extensions of the program far beyond our immediate school community. Partnerships with other school districts are also being explored in an effort to build a Virtual Pre-K community throughout the country, and increase meaningful exchanges between preschool parents and teachers nationwide.

Contributed by Alicia Narvaez, Virtual Pre-K Director, Chicago Public Schools.

which calls for commercial website operators who offer "harmful" material to check the IDs of visitors. It is likely that Congress will continue to legislate ways to protect the privacy of children age twelve and under. How do you feel about such legislation? Do you believe it limits freedom of access?

YOU AND THE TECHNOLOGICAL FUTURE

Undoubtedly you have heard the saying, "You haven't seen anything yet." This remark applies to technology and its application to all school settings—especially the early childhood years from birth to age eight. The vision that each child will acquire the foundational skills and competencies to succeed as an adult in the information age should involve children in the very early years.

To take an online self-test on this chapter's contents, go to the Companion Website at **http://www.prenhall.com/morrison**, select chapter 13, then choose the Self-Test module.

What will have to happen to bring tomorrow to the classrooms today? First, you and other early childhood professionals must decide to use technology and gain the training necessary to be computer literate. Second, you must dedicate yourself to the developmentally appropriate use of technology and software. Third, you must recognize that technology and all its applications are not just add-ons to the curriculum, activities to do only when there is time, or rewards for good behavior or achievement. Technology, hardware, and software, is here to stay, and can, like text-based materials, help all children learn to their fullest potential.

When parents and children team up to search the Internet together, it provides a fun and safe way for children to learn more about computers and technology. What are some of the dangers of letting children explore the Internet unsupervised?

ACTIVITIES FOR FURTHER ENRICHMENT

APPLICATIONS

1. Select four software programs for infants and toddlers and four for grades pre-K–3 children. Evaluate the software using Figure 13.2 and these criteria:

- Is it age appropriate?
- Are the instructions clear?
- Is the software easy to use (child friendly)?
- Does the software accomplish its intended purpose?

For each software tell if you would use it with children, and explain why or why not.

2. Some teachers are not as willing as others to infuse technology into their teaching. Why is this? What are some specific things you will have to do in order to infuse technology into your teaching and work with parents and families?

3. Choose a particular theme and write a lesson plan to show how you would integrate technology relating to that theme into a subject you plan to teach.

FIELD EXPERIENCES

1. Visit classrooms in your local school districts. What evidence of the integration of technology into the curriculum can you find? What conclusions can you draw?

2. Interview grades pre-K–3 teachers in a local district. What barriers do they say they must contend with in their efforts to include technology in the curriculum? What implications do these barriers have for what you may be able to accomplish as a teacher?

3. Visit classroom programs that provide services to students with disabilities. Cite five ways technology is used to implement curriculum, help teachers teach, and promote learning.

4. Some teachers and parents think children should not be introduced to computers at an early age. List reasons why they might feel this way. Then, interview five parents and teachers. Ask them the following questions: At what age should young children use computers? Why do you feel this age to be the best?

5. Investigate whether child care centers in your community have technologically advanced programs that enable parents to contact their children to see how they are doing.

For additional Internet resources or to complete an online activity for this chapter, go to the Companion Website at **http://www. prenhall.com/morrison**, select chapter 13, then choose the Linking to Learning or Making Connections module.

RESEARCH

1. Read again the feature in this chapter called "East Rock Magnet School Technology Program." List some advantages that the program has for children. Then try to think of alternatives to this program. What do you think would be more effective in helping the students learn?

2. Write a four-paragraph report in which you explain your views of the use of technology in grades pre-K–3 programs. Present this to a center director, school principal, or similar person for feedback. Set up a conference for discussion and reaction.

3. Review with several of your classmates the NAEYC Position Statement on Technology and Young Children (Figure 13.3). Tell how and in what ways you do or do not agree with the guidelines.

4. What can you do as a teacher to help ensure that the technological gender gap between boys and girls is eliminated? What evidence of this gender gap have you experienced in your own education? What can you do to combat this?

READINGS FOR FURTHER ENRICHMENT

Casey, J. *Early Literacy: The Empowerment of Technology.* Westport, CT: Libraries Unlimited, 2000.

Helps the reader strengthen early literacy through the use of talking computers. Also, shows how to boost literacy, especially among those with learning disabilities or oral/hands-on learning styles, as well as ESL students.

Provenzo, E. F. *The Internet and the World Wide Web for Teachers.* Boston: Allyn and Bacon, 2002.

This handbook serves as an excellent resource to help beginning teachers use the Internet and the World Wide Web. By following the National Council for Accreditation of Teacher Education (NCATE) guidelines on "Technology and the New Professional Teacher," the author provides a practical and engaging introduction to using the Internet and the World Wide Web.

Roblyer, M. D., and Edwards, J. *Integrating Educational Technology into Teaching,* 2nd ed. Upper Saddle River, NJ: Merrill/Prentice Hall, 2000.

This text presents effective theory and research-based strategies for integrating technology resources and technology-based methods into everyday classroom practices.

Sharp, V., and Levine, M., et al. *The Best Web Sites for Teachers,* 5th ed. International Society for Technology in Education, 2002.

This reference text helps teachers, librarians, tech coordinators, and parents save time finding educational websites. Carefully vetted by experienced author-educators, all website URLs are verified just before press time, and each listing includes a description of the features that make the site a great classroom resource.

Thouvenelle, S. *Completing the Computer Puzzle: A Guide for Early Childhood Educators.* Boston: Allyn and Bacon, 2003.

Connects solid knowledge of early education principles with technical computer experiences, emphasizing the role of the teacher and the teacher's responsibility for meaningful integration of computer technology in the early childhood classroom.

LINKING TO LEARNING

The American Library Associations 700+ Great Sites
http://www.ala.org/parentspage/greatsites/amazing.html

A collection of sites organized by the ALA for parents, caregivers, teachers, and others who care for and about children.

Early Connections—Technology in Early Childhood Education
http://www.netc.org/earlyconnections/

This site, maintained by the Northwest Educational Technology Consortium (NETC) and the Northwest Regional Educational Laboratory's Child & Family Program, helps connect technology with the way children learn. It provides resources and information for educators and care providers in areas such as Children's Development and Technology Connections, and also answers many frequently asked questions about children and technology.

Information Technology in Childhood Education (ITCE) Annual
http://www.aace.org/pubs/child/

ITCE serves as the only scholarly journal devoted to reporting the research and applications for using information technology in the education of children—early childhood, preschool, and elementary. ITCE is a valuable resource for all educators who use computers with children.

International Society for Technology in Education
http://www.iste.org/

ISTE is a nonprofit professional organization dedicated to promoting appropriate uses of technology to support and improve learning, teaching, and administration in K–12 education and teacher education.

KidSites
http://www.kidsites.com/

"KidSites" is one of the leading guides to the best in children's websites. All websites listed at KidSites are screened for content by KidSites' staff. Also included are useful links for parents and teachers.

Reading Rockets: Launching Young Readers
http://www.pbs.org/launchingreaders/

"Reading Rockets: Launching Young Readers" is the latest in a long line of complementary educational websites from the Public Broadcasting Service (PBS). This resource, which accompanies the five-part PBS television series "Reading Rockets," provides teachers with reading strategies that are proven to work.

Technology Applications Center for Educator Development
http://www.tcet.unt.edu/START/

This site, collaboratively created by the Texas Center for Educational Technology (TCET) and the Texas Education Agency's (TEA) Educational Technology and Curriculum Divisions, provides educators with information about the TA TEKS, instruction ideas and lesson plans, assessment tools, professional development resources, and program development resources.

Technology & Young Children
http://www.techandyoungchildren.org/

The mission of the National Association for the Education of Young Children (NAEYC) Technology and Young Children Interest Forum is to lead discussions and to share research and information and best practices regarding technology, so it can be used to benefit children aged birth through eight years.

Web for Teachers
http://www.4teachers.org/

The online space for teachers integrating technology into the curriculum, "Web for Teachers" includes information on many topics, including Internet safety, lessons and WebQuests, project-based learning, activities related to state standards, and much more. Teachers can find useful tools, such as the "Assign-A-Day," with which students are able to view their teachers' calendars in order to see assignments for classes they might have missed, or to get an overview of the class.

Yahooligans!
http://www.yahooligans.com/

"Yahooligans!" is a safe Web guide for children, parents, and teachers. Children can easily find information on many topics in categories such as Around the World, School Bell, Arts and Entertainment, Science and Nature, Computers and Games, and Sports and Recreation.

Assistive Technology, Inc.
http://www.assistivetech.com

Assistive Technology was founded in 1995 to develop innovative hardware and software solutions to increase opportunities for and enhance the quality of life of people with disabilities. It provides innovative solutions to help people with learning, communication, and access difficulties lead more independent and productive lives.

ECEOL (Early Childhood Education Online)
http://www.ume.maine.edu/ECEOL-L/

This site links to places and topics of interest to early childhood educators. The address is case-specific.

Education Links
http://school.discovery.com/schrockguide

A categorized list of sites for enhancing curriculum and teacher professional growth.

Kids' Space
http://www.Kids-space.org

Children can contribute art to this site for display, as well as send in and read stories.

KidzOnline
http://www.kidzonline.org

KidzOnline is an educational organization dedicated to reducing the widening gap between the information "haves" and "have nots." They feel this can best be accomplished by having kids teach kids. The organization brings kids together electronically to share ideas, exchange viewpoints, and learn from each other.

Logo Foundation
http://el.media.mit.edu/logo-foundation/

The Logo Foundation supports a "constructivist" approach to teaching math skills and other subjects through the use of "Logo programming environments," which educators have used since the late 1970s. Includes current information and tips.

New Parent Information Network
http://npin.org

This site offers up-to-date immunization schedules, lists of recalled toys, and other important information for parents and educators.

Parents and Children Together Online
http://www.indiana.edu/~eric_rec/www/indexpcto.html

The goal of this group is to further the cause of family literacy by bringing parents and children together through the magic of reading. PCTO features original stories and articles for children, suitable for reading aloud.

Safe Kids Homepage
http://www.safekids.com

This site, for children and educators, has a Child Safety Forum and links to other websites.

SuperKids Educational Software Review
www.superkids.com

This site offers teachers and parents objective reviews of educational software. Also has on-line activities for children.

Virtual Library
http://vlib.org/overview.html

Choose from many subject categories.

ENDNOTES

[1] Addio, D. "Software for the Diaper Set," *Pittsburgh Post-Gazette*, July 12, 1998.

[2] "E-Defining Education," *Education Week* (May 9, 2002), Retrieved January 28, 2003, from http://www.edweek.com/sreports/tc02/article.cfm?slug= 35execsum.h21

[3] Healy, J. M. "The 'Meme' That Ate Childhood," *Education Week* (October 7, 1998), 56.

[4] The Technology-Related Assistance for Individuals with Disabilities Act of 1988 (PL 100–407). Available at: http://pursuit.rehab.uiuc.edu.

[5] Holder-Brown, L., and Parette, H. "Children with Disabilities Who Use Assistive Technology: Ethical Considerations," *Young Children* (September 1992), 74–75.

[6] Rabinovitz, J. "Logging on to the Baby's Day," *New York Times* (December 9, 1997), A19.

[7] Thibodeau, P. "Senate Weighs Online Privacy Rules for Tots," *Online News* (September 23, 1998). Available: www.onlinenews.com.

[8] Muris, T. J. "Protecting Consumers' Privacy: 2002 and Beyond" (2002). Available at http://www.ftc.gov/speeches/muris/privisp1002.htm.

[9] America Online Inc. "Privacy Policy," 1998. Available at www.aol.com.

Chapter 14

Consistently teaching children character values interwoven with all of the curriculum areas helps children realize that character is a part of everything they do in life and that demonstrating good character is a gift they can share with others.

CAROL CATES, 1999 NORTH CAROLINA EDUCATOR OF THE YEAR

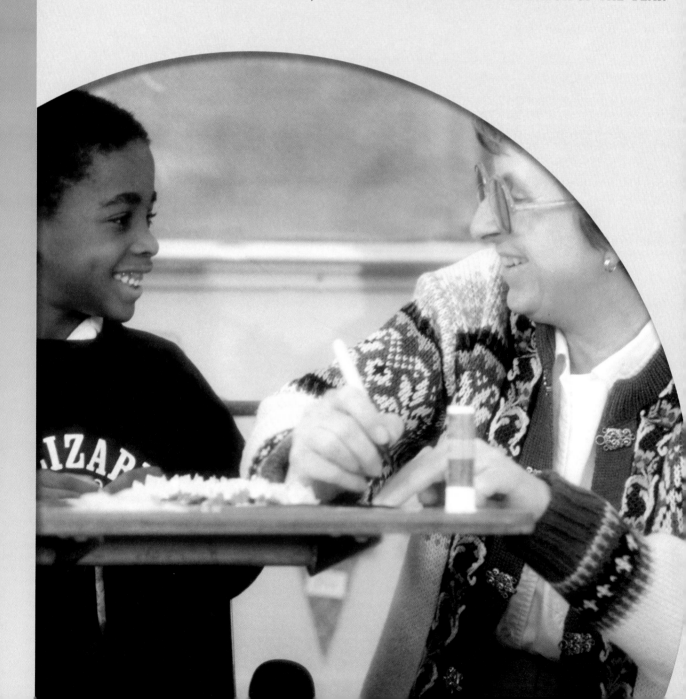

Guiding Children
Helping Children Become Responsible

Focus Questions

- Why is it important to help children guide their behavior?

- What theories of guiding children's behavior can you apply to your teaching?

- What are important elements in helping children guide their behavior?

- Why is developing a philosophy of guiding children's behavior important?

- What are important trends and issues in children's behavior guidance?

THE IMPORTANCE OF GUIDING CHILDREN'S BEHAVIOR

Why should you and other early childhood professionals want to know how to best guide children's behavior and help them become responsible? There are a number of reasons.

First, helping children learn to guide and be responsible for their own behavior is as important as helping them learn to read and write. You may think that this notion is far-fetched, but think for a moment about how many times you have said or have heard others say, "If only the children would behave, I could teach them something!" Appropriate behavior and learning go together. As the old saying goes, you can't have one without the other. One of your primary roles as an early childhood teacher is to help children learn the knowledge and skills that will help them act responsibly.

Second, helping children learn to act responsibly and guide their behavior lays the foundation for life-long responsible and productive living. As early childhood educators, we believe that the early years are the formative years. Consequently, what we teach children about responsible living; how we guide them; and the skills we help them learn will last a lifetime. Society wants educators to prepare responsible children for responsible democratic living.

Third, the roots of delinquent and deviant behavior are in the early years. From research we know what behaviors lead to future behavior problems. For example, some characteristics of preschool children that are precursors of adolescent behavior problems and delinquency include disruptive behavior, overactive, high-intensity behavior, irritability, noncompliance, and intensity in social interactions.[1]

Finally, the public is increasingly concerned about the erosion of civility, and what it perceives as a general breakdown of personal responsibility for bad behavior. One reason the public funds the public educational system at all levels is to help keep society strong and healthy. Parents and the public look to early childhood professionals for assistance in helping children learn to live cooperatively and civilly in a democratic society. Getting along with others and guiding one's behavior is a culturally and socially meaningful accomplishment.

Guiding children's behavior is a process of helping children build positive behaviors. Discipline is not about compliance and control but involves *behavior*

To review the chapter focus questions online, go to the Companion Website at **http://www. prenhall.com/morrison** and select chapter 14.

guidance, a process by which all children learn to control and direct their behavior and become independent and self-reliant. In this view, behavior guidance is a process of helping children develop skills useful over a lifetime.

As you work with young children, one of your goals will be to help them become independent and have the ability to regulate or govern their own behavior. **Self-regulation** is the "child's capacity to plan, guide, and monitor his or her behavior from within and flexibly according to changing circumstances."[2] Three teacher and parent behaviors are essential for promoting self-regulation in children:

1. The use of reasoning and verbal rationales
2. The gradual relinquishing of control
3. A combination of the two with a sense of affective nurturance and emotional warmth[3]

This chapter provides you with examples of all three of these essential elements.

Self-regulation The ability to keep track of and control one's behavior.

To check your understanding of this chapter with the online Study Guide, go to the Companion Website at **http://www.prenhall.com/morrison**, select chapter 14, then choose the Study Guide module.

USING THEORIES TO GUIDE CHILDREN

In chapter 5, "Theories Applied to Teaching and Learning," we discussed theories of learning and development and how you can use them in your teaching. Review the theories of Piaget, Vygotsky, Maslow, and Erikson so their ideas will be fresh in your mind as we now apply them to guiding children's behavior. I will also introduce you to Thomas Gordon's theory of guidance as practiced in his Teacher Effectiveness Training Program.

THE SOCIAL CONSTRUCTIVIST APPROACH: PIAGET AND VYGOTSKY

Piaget's and Vygotsky's theories support a social constructivist approach to learning and behavior. Teachers and other professionals who embrace a **social constructivist approach** believe that children construct or build their behavior as a result of learning from experiences and from making decisions that lead to responsible behavior. The teacher's primary role in the constructivist approach is to guide and help children construct or build their behavior and use it in socially appropriate and productive ways. This process begins in homes and classrooms.

In chapter 5, we also discussed Vygotsky's theories of scaffolding and the **zone of proximal development (ZPD).** We now apply these two methods for guiding children's behavior and add two additional essentials to Vygotskyian constructivist theory: **adult/child discourse** and child **self discourse** (or **private speech**). Foundational to Vygotskyian and constructivist theory are the central beliefs that the development of a child's knowledge and behaviors occurs in the context of social relations with adults and peers. This means that learning and development are socially mediated as children interact with more competent peers and adults. As children gain the ability to master language and appropriate social relations, they are able to intentionally regulate their behavior.

Social constructivist approach Approaches to teaching that emphasize the social context of learning and behavior.

Zone of proximal development (ZPD) The range of tasks that are too difficult for children to learn by themselves, but which they can learn with guidance and assistance from more competent others.

Adult/child discourse The talk between an adult and a child, which emphasizes adult suggestions for how to guide behavior and solve problems.

Private speech (self discourse) Speech that involves talking to oneself.

GUIDING BEHAVIOR IN THE ZONE OF PROXIMAL DEVELOPMENT

The ZPD is the cognitive and developmental space that is created when the child is in social interaction with a more competent person (MCP) or a more knowledgeable other (MKO). As Vygotsky explains, the ZPD is the "actual developmental level as determined by independent problem solving and the level of potential development as determined through problem solving under adult guidance or in collaboration with more capable peers."[4] Problem solving is what guiding behavior is all about. Teachers take children from the behavioral and social skills they have in their ZPD and guide them to increasingly higher levels of responsible behavior and social interactions. Also, while we often think that guiding behavior is a one-on-one activity, this is not the case. Your role in guiding behavior includes large and small groups, as well as individual children. Figure 14.1 illustrates again the ZPD and illustrates how to guide children's behavior within it.

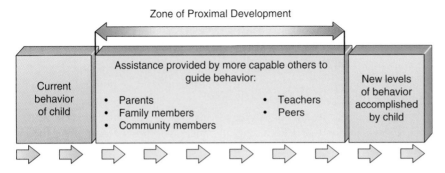

FIGURE 14.1   The Zone of Proximal Development Applied to Guiding Behavior

The zone of proximal development (ZPD) is constantly moving and changing, depending on children's behavioral accomplishments and the assistance and scaffolding provided by others. Guiding children's behavior is an ongoing process of helping children develop new behaviors.

SCAFFOLDING APPLIED TO GUIDING BEHAVIOR

Scaffolding is one of the ways teachers can guide children in the ZPD. Recall that scaffolding is the use of informal methods such as conversations, questions, modeling, guiding, and supporting to help children learn concepts, knowledge, and skills that they might not learn by themselves. When more competent others provide "help," children are able to accomplish what they would not have been able to do on their own. In the ZPD, children are capable of far more competent behavior and achievements as they receive guidance and support from teachers and parents.

ADULT/CHILD DISCOURSE

The scaffolding script that follows is illustrative of adult/child discourse. Discourse also involves talking about how children might solve problems, guide their own behavior, interact and cooperate with others, understand norms of social conduct, and learn values related to school and family living. Teachers must initiate and guide these discourses and help children learn new skills that will assist them in developing self-regulation. Here is an example of a "learning conversation" that invites student participation. This discourse centers on how student authors should act while they are sharing their stories.

> Teacher: Maybe we should now think about how to behave as the author during author's chair. What do authors do? Who can remember? Would you like to start?
>> Tina: The author sits in the author's chair and speaks loud and clear.
>> Crystal: The author should not fool around like making faces or having outside conversations.
>> Shauna: The author should not be shy and should be brave and confident.
>> The teacher continued to invite students to participate in subsequent lessons, using this type of scaffolding. A list of responsibilities was created and used in subsequent lessons.[5]

You will want to conduct similar discourses with children as you help them develop the skills and behaviors necessary to guide their own behavior.

PRIVATE SPEECH AND SELF-GUIDED BEHAVIOR

Jennifer, a four-year-old preschooler, is busily engrossed in putting a puzzle together. As she searches for a puzzle piece, she asks herself out loud, "Which piece comes next?" I'm sure you have heard children talk to themselves. More than likely, you have talked to yourself. Such conversations are commonplace in the lives of young children.

Private speech plays an important role in problem solving and self-regulation of behavior. Children learn to transfer problem-solving knowledge and responsibility from adults to themselves:

> When adults use questions and strategies to guide children and to help them discover solutions, they elevate language to the status of a primary problem-solving tool. This use of language by adults leads children to use speech to solve problems. Research reveals that the relation of private speech to children's behavior is consistent with the assumption that self-guiding utterances help bring action under the control of thought.[6]

VYGOTSKY/CONSTRUCTIVIST GUIDANCE STRATEGIES

Using our knowledge of Vygotsky's theory, we can develop some strategies to guide children's behavior. Here are some things you can do:

- Guide problem solving:
  - "Tanya, what are some things you can do to help you remember to put the books away?"
  - "Keyshawn, you and Juana want to use the easel at the same time. What are some ideas for how you can both use it?"
- Ask questions that help children arrive at their own solutions:
  - "Jesse, you can't use both toys at the same time. Which one do you want to use first?"
  - "Somer, here is an idea that might help you get to the block corner. Ask Amy, 'Would you please move over a little so I can get to the blocks?'"
- Model appropriate skills:
  - Practice social skills and manners (e.g., say "please" and "thank you").
  - Listen attentively to children and encourage listening. For example, say, "Harry has something he wants to tell us, let's listen to what he has to say."

In the short term, telling children what to do may seem like the easiest and most efficient way to manage classroom behavior. However, in the long run, it robs them of growth-producing opportunities to develop skills that will help them guide their behavior throughout their lives. This is why using strategies such as those listed above are essential and should be regularly and routinely incorporated into classroom life.

TEACHER EFFECTIVENESS TRAINING

Thomas Gordon (1918–2002) developed a child guidance program based on teacher–student relationships. Gordon developed Parent Effectiveness Training (PET) for parents and Teacher Effectiveness Training (TET) for teachers. Both programs use communication as the primary means of helping parents and teachers build positive parent/teacher–child relationships that foster self-direction, self-responsibility, self-determination, self-control, and self-evaluation.[7]

PROBLEM OWNERSHIP

The first cornerstone of the TET approach to guiding behavior is to identify who owns the behavior problem. When a problem arises, as problems inevitably do in human relationships, you, the teacher, have to determine if the child (or children) owns the problem or if you, the teacher, owns the problem. For example, preschool teacher Maria Escobar observes that several of her children are noisy and disruptive and are not following the guidelines for using the woodworking center. As Maria thought about the children's lack of self-direction, she concluded that the children owned the problem. They didn't fully understand the center directions and how to follow them.

On the other hand, Maria was becoming increasingly irritated with always having to deal with Hector's interrupting behavior during circle time. As Maria thought about Hector's behavior, she realized *she* owned the problem. She was allowing Hector's behavior to irritate her rather than work on specific ways to help Hector learn new ways of behaving and interacting.

The difference between student-owned and teacher-owned problems is essentially one of tangible and concrete (or *real*) effect. Teachers can separate their own problems from those of their students by asking themselves: "Does this behavior have any *real,* tangible, or concrete effect on me? Am I feeling unaccepting because I am being interfered with, damaged, hurt, or impaired in some way? Or am I feeling unaccepting merely because I'd like the student to act differently, not have a problem, feel the way I think he should?" If the answer is "yes" to the latter, the problem belongs to the student. If it is "yes" to the former, the teacher certainly has a real stake in the problem.[8]

ACTIVE LISTENING

Active listening is the second cornerstone of TET. Active listening will help you identify who has the problem, and it will help you communicate with children. Active listening involves interactions with a child to provide him with proof that you understand what he is talking about. This proof might come in the form of feedback.

Active listening involves seven *attitudes* or *sets:* Taken as a whole, they will help you practice and perfect active listening with the goal of helping you help children guide their behavior:

- Develop a sense of trust in students' ability to solve their own problems.
- Genuinely accept the feelings expressed by students.
- Understand that feelings are quite transitory. Many feelings exist only "of the moment."
- Want to help students with their problems and make time for them.
- Be "with" each student who is experiencing troubles, yet maintain a separate identity. Experience students' feelings as your own, but don't let them become your own.
- Understand that students are seldom able to start out by sharing the real problem.
- Respect the privacy and confidential nature of what students reveal about their lives.[9]

Determining who owns the problem is an essential part of your being able to guide children's behavior well.

I MESSAGES

Letting children know about your problem is the third cornerstone of TET. If, upon reflection, you determine you own the problem, then you will want to deliver **"I" messages.** I messages are designed to let children know that you have a problem with their behavior and that you want them to do something to change the behavior. Let's join Maria and Hector again. Maria can send an I message by responding, "Hector, when I am constantly interrupted, I can't teach what I need to, and this makes me feel like I'm not a good teacher." Notice how Maria described the behavior (interrupting), the consequences of the behavior (I can't teach), and her feelings (I'm not a good teacher). These three components constitute a good I message.

Practice makes perfect. I have briefly reviewed with you some of the major concepts associated with Vygotskyian, constructivist, and TET ideas and practices. You will want to read more about each of these and reflect how you can apply them to your teaching. Using these strategies effectively requires much determination and practice. They are worth the effort, and you will be rewarded with their beneficial results as you learn to guide children's behavior.

Active listening The practice of giving full attention to the person speaking.

I Messages A method of communication in which the speakers reflect on their true feelings about a situation or event.

WHAT DOES GUIDING BEHAVIOR INVOLVE?

The goal of most parents and early childhood professionals is to have children behave in socially acceptable and appropriate ways that contribute to and promote living in a democratic society. Teachers should view guidance of children's behavior as a process of learning by doing. Children cannot learn to develop appropriate behaviors and learn to be responsible by themselves. Just as no one learns to ride a bicycle by reading a book on the subject, children do not learn to guide themselves by being told what to do all the time. Children must be shown and taught through precept and example. They need opportunities to develop, practice, and perfect their abilities to control and guide their own behavior. They need the guidance, help, support, and encouragement of parents and early childhood professionals.

How can professionals achieve these goals? Effective guidance of children's behavior at home and in early childhood programs consists of these essential elements:

- Know and use theories for guiding behavior.
- Know child development.
- Meet children's needs in individually and culturally appropriate ways.
- Help children build new behaviors and skills of independence and responsibility.
- Establish appropriate expectations.
- Arrange and modify the environment so that appropriate, expected behavior and self-control are possible.
- Model appropriate behavior.
- Develop a partnership with parents, families, and others who are responsible for children.
- Promote empathy and prosocial behavior.

Let us take a closer look at each of these essential elements in guiding children.

Parents and early childhood professionals have an obligation to help children learn correct behaviors by guiding their actions and modeling appropriate behavior. What role does setting rules play in guiding behavior?

KNOW AND USE THEORIES FOR GUIDING BEHAVIOR

The first rule in guiding children is to know what you believe. Review again your philosophy of education you wrote in chapter 1. Unless you know your attitudes toward discipline and behavior, it will be hard to practice a positive and consistent program of guidance and consistency plays a major role in teaching and guiding. Therefore, develop a philosophy about what you believe concerning child rearing, discipline, and children. There are many child-rearing/guidance approaches available. Knowing what you want for your children at home and school helps you decide which approach to select.

Knowing yourself and what you believe also makes it easier for you to share with parents, help them guide behavior, and counsel them about discipline. Today, many parents find the challenges of child rearing overwhelming. They do not know what to do and consequently

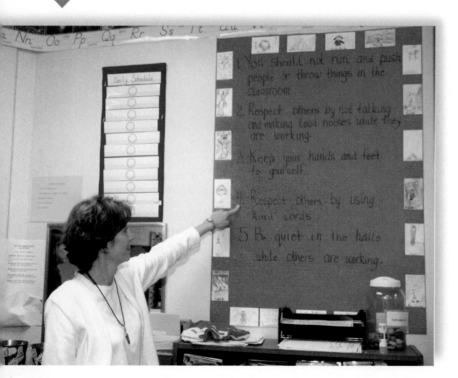

look to professionals for help. Knowing what you believe, based on sound principles of how children grow, develop, and learn, enables you to work confidently with parents.

KNOW CHILD DEVELOPMENT

The foundation for guiding all children is to know what they are like—how they grow and develop. Unfortunately, not all early childhood professionals are as knowledgeable about children as they should be. As a result, they may expect some children to behave in ways that are more appropriate for younger or older children. Here lies part of the problem of not being able to help children guide their behavior: children cannot behave well when adults expect too much or too little of them based on their development or when they expect them to behave in ways inappropriate for them as individuals. So, a key for guiding children's behavior is to *really know what they are like.*

MEET CHILDREN'S NEEDS

Part of knowing children and child development is knowing and meeting their needs. Abraham Maslow felt that human growth and development was oriented toward **self-actualization,** the striving to realize one's potential. Maslow felt that humans are internally motivated by five basic needs that constitute a hierarchy of motivating behaviors, progressing from physical needs to self-fulfillment. Maslow's hierarchy (see chapter 7 for a graphic representation of this hierarchy) moves through physical needs, safety and security needs, belonging and affection needs, and self-esteem needs, culminating in self-actualization. Let us look at an example of each of these stages and behaviors to see how we can apply them to guiding children's behavior.

Self-actualization Our inherent tendency to reach our true potential.

Physical Needs.   Children's abilities to guide their behavior depend in part on how well their physical needs are met. Children do their best in school, for example, when they are well nourished. Thus, parents should provide for their children's nutritional needs by giving them breakfast. Early childhood professionals should also stress the nutritional and health benefits of eating breakfast. Information on recent brain research provided in chapter 2 also informs us about nutrition and the brain. For example, the brain needs protein and water to function well. Many schools allow children to have water bottles at the desks and allow them to have frequent nutritional snacks.

The quality of the environment is also important. Children cannot be expected to "behave" if classrooms are dark and noisy and smell of stale air. Children also need adequate rest to do and be their best. The amount of rest is an individual matter, but many young children need eight to ten hours of sleep each day. A tired child cannot meet many of the expectations of schooling.

Safety and Security.   Children can't learn in fear. They should not have to fear parents or professionals and should feel comfortable and secure at home and at school. Asking or forcing children to do school tasks for which they do not have the skills makes them feel insecure, and children who are afraid and insecure are under a great deal of tension. Consider also the dangers many urban children face, such as crime, drugs, and homelessness, or the insecurity of children who live in an atmosphere of domestic violence. So, in addition, part of guiding children's behavior includes providing safe and secure communities, neighborhoods, homes, schools, and classrooms.

Belonging and Affection.   Children need love and affection and the sense of belonging that comes from being given jobs to do, having responsibilities, and helping make classroom and home decisions. Love and affection needs are also satisfied when parents hold, hug, and kiss their children and tell them, "I love you." Professionals meet children's affectional needs when they smile, speak pleasantly, are kind and gentle, treat children with

VOICE FROM THE FIELD

Character, Choice, and Student Behavior

Many educators have led the way to dealing with rising violence in our schools by supporting the foundations of ethical or character education in our classrooms. But we have not yet entertained those same principles of character as a guiding standard for the way in which we, the adults, respond to student behavior. We profess to want our children to be reasoned, caring humans who will contribute to the good of society while tolerating the very opposite in our school discipline procedures. We have not looked at what we model as a factor in the problem. Our response to behavior problems has been to set the rules and then set the consequences. If the rules do not work, then we set higher consequences. Or conversely, we decide that the problem is a counseling issue and that working with the student on clarifying feelings will make the difference.

More than two years ago, in a district that serves a rural population in upstate New York, we completely revamped the discipline system in the elementary schools we served. This work was undertaken by me, as supervisory principal for the district, the school psychologist, and the student counselor. We gave much thought to what we were doing before we decided what we would change, and we based that thought on the principles of moral development and in learning theory. We allowed ourselves to question all assumptions about what discipline should look like in a school, and, as happens in so many other areas of education, we discovered that much of what was done was

reflex and habit—not thought and vision. In the same way that we find ourselves proclaiming platitudes to our young that came from the mouths of our own parents ("If I've told you once, I've told you a thousand times"), in schools we react as we have always reacted, without asking ourselves whether what we are doing is working—or even if it ever did. We began with the situation before us, citing the number of children with repetitious behavior problems that were not being changed. We also discussed the fact that, whether or not we choose to label it as such, a good deal of time is devoted in a school to issues of character if we think of character in terms of the actions that reflect it. Under such a definition, all issues of student discipline are issues of character as well.

We concluded that we could start over and that we could be guided by those same characteristics of being that we so wanted in our students—attributes like respect, caring, honesty, fairness. We also concluded that we wanted real learning to result that would help the student use ethical principles in deciding what to say and do, and that we were teachers in this process, not wardens. The result was a structure that took the student out of the trouble situation if it could not be handled within the classroom, and took him or her immediately into a problem-solving process. Five adults were on call to provide one-on-one guidance through the process. These were not extra staff, but a combination of administrative, teaching, and support staff already with us.

courtesy and respect, and genuinely value each child for whom she or he is. An excellent way to show respect for children and demonstrate to them belonging and affection is to greet them personally when they come into the classroom, center, or home. A personal greeting helps children feel wanted and secure and promotes feelings of self-worth. In fact, all early childhood programs should begin with this daily validation of each child.

Self-Esteem.   Children who view themselves as worthy, responsible, and competent act in accordance with these feelings. Children's views of themselves come primarily from parents and early childhood professionals. Experiencing success gives them feelings of high

The process itself had five distinct phases: (1) describing the situation or incident; (2) defining what action the student had chosen; (3) identifying what character trait was compromised by the choice of action; (4) generating a number of alternative choices for action, ones that reflect good character; and (5) choosing an action and committing to it.

The process ended when the student had a solution that he/she could commit to and that was workable within the current situation. A "solution" was not defined as going to detention or staying out of school or doing extra schoolwork. A solution meant reflecting on what went wrong; realizing that we all have choices; and finding a choice that reflected good character. And then, and very importantly, making a personal commitment to that choice. Our underlying assumption was that children want to be people of good character and our experience consistently bore that out.

The time necessary to go through the process with a student could be anywhere from five minutes to more than one school day, depending on the problem and the student. Our approach was to take whatever time was necessary, our goal being to ensure success for the student. If the student arrived angry or unwilling to work on the problem, the adult mentor would wait until the student was ready by inviting him or her to notify of readiness. With that in mind, mentors brought their own work to the problem-solving room and were prepared to not work with the child immediately. The only condition was that the problem would be solved before the student returned to regular routine. The teacher who sent a student into problem solving also sent a referral with a brief description of the problem. Once the student had chosen a solution, the mentor and student would go back to the referring teacher and discuss the viability of the solution with the student. This step was important and handled as a meeting necessary to rejoining the group. If a student failed to use his or her chosen solution, thus resulting in a continued problem, he or she immediately returned to problem solving.

The students who experienced the greatest difficulty with the process and who thus needed more time were those for whom there was a less-developed understanding of how character looks in action or a lack of connection between ethics and personal choice. These were also the students who benefited the most from the process and where we could track the greatest growth as we reviewed our cases. Many came from homes where there was little or no modeling or support for making good choices. In such cases, we as mentors took the additional step of checking in with the student from time to time to ask how their solution was working and to give additional encouragement for good decision making.

One often-expressed objection to our plan was, "If you do not punish (i.e., impose negative consequences on) those who misbehave, then you send the wrong message to the other students," implying that the behavior of peers would deteriorate based on the degree of consequence assigned by the adult in charge. Clearly the assumption in this thinking is that the behavior of students is, and perhaps should be, dependent on fear of adult action rather than on the ability to make good choices. The secondary message is that this fear is the lesson to be valued above the lesson of learning how to make those choices.

Our results surprised even us. After two years, the decrease in problems—which we tracked through careful record keeping—was 28 percent. An unforeseen result was the effect on school climate. By maintaining the relationship of mentor and guide with the student, we remained as the support rather than the external controller of imposed behavior. Our sense of community within the school was preserved. And we could hope that we were building the basis in our children for a lifetime of good choices—choices made because they could understand how action reflects character.

Contributed by Margaret Pastor, Principal, Stedwick Elementary School, Montgomery Village, Maryland.

self-esteem, and it is up to parents and professionals to give all children opportunities for success. The foundations for self-esteem are success and achievement.

Self-Actualization.   Children want to use their talents and abilities to do things for themselves and be independent. Professionals and parents can help children become independent by helping them learn to dress themselves, go to the restroom by themselves, and take care of their environments. They can also help children set achievement and behavior goals ("Tell me what you are going to build with your blocks") and encourage them to evaluate their behavior ("Let's talk about how you cleaned up your room").

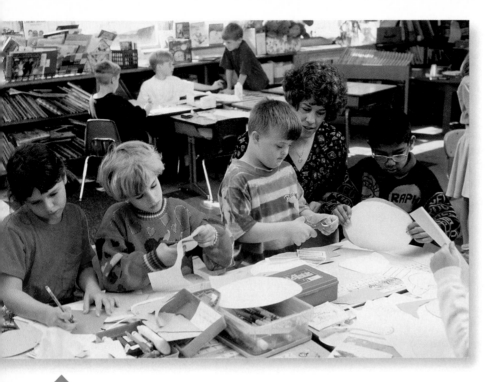

These points highlight the basic needs professionals and parents must consider when guiding children and helping them develop responsibility for their behavior.

HELP CHILDREN BUILD NEW BEHAVIORS

Helping children build new behaviors means that you help them learn that they are primarily responsible for their own behavior and that the pleasures and rewards for appropriate behavior are internal, coming from within them as opposed to always coming from outside (i.e., from the approval and praise of others). We refer to this concept as locus of control—the source or place of control. The preferred and recommended locus of control for young and old alike is internal.

Helping children become more independent by warmly supporting their efforts is one of the most effective forms of guidance. Identify some ways professionals can support children's efforts to do things for themselves.

Children are not born with this desired inner control. The process of developing an internal locus of control begins at birth, continues through the early childhood years, and is a never-ending process throughout life. We want children to control their own behavior. When their locus of control is external, children are controlled by others; they are always told what to do and how to behave. Parents and professionals must try to avoid developing an external locus of control in children.

Empower Children.   Helping children build new behaviors creates a sense of responsibility and self-confidence. As children are given responsibility, they develop greater self-direction, which means that you guide them at the next level in their Zone of Proximal Development. Some professionals and parents hesitate to let children assume responsibilities, but without responsibilities, children are bored and frustrated and become discipline problems—the very opposite of what is intended. Guidance is not a matter of adults getting children to please them by making remarks such as, "Show me how perfect you can be," "Don't embarrass me by your behavior in front of others," "I want to see nice groups," or "I'm waiting for quiet."

To reiterate, guiding behavior is not about compliance and control. Rather, it is important to instill in children a sense of independence and responsibility for their own behavior. For example, you might say, "You have really worked a long time cutting out the flower you drew. You kept working on it until you were finished. Would you like some tape to hang it up with?"

Parents and early childhood professionals can do a number of things to help children develop new behaviors that result in empowerment:

For strategies preschoolers can use to get along with others, go to the Companion Website at **http://www.prenhall. com/morrison,** select chapter 14, then choose the Linking to Learning module to connect to the National Network for Child Care site.

- *Give children responsibilities.* All children, from an early age, should have responsibilities—that is, tasks that are their job to do and for which they are responsible. Being responsible for completing tasks and doing such things as putting toys and learning materials away promote a positive sense of self-worth and convey to children that in a community people have responsibilities for making the community work well.
- *Give children choices.* Life is full of choices—some require thought and decisions; others are automatic, based on previous behavior. But every time you make a decision,

you are being responsible and exercising your right to decide. Children like to have choices, and choices help them become independent, confident, and self-disciplined. Making choices is key for children developing responsible behavior and inner control. Learning to make choices early in life lays the foundation for decision making later. Guidelines for giving children choices are as follows:

- Give children choices when there are valid choices to make. When it comes time to clean up the classroom, do not let children choose whether they want to participate, but let them pick between collecting the scissors or the crayons.
- Help children make choices. Rather than say, "What would you like to do today?" say, "Sarah, you have a choice between working in the woodworking center or the computer center. Which would you like to do?"
- When you do not want children to make a decision, do not offer them a choice.
- *Support children.* As an early childhood professional, you must support children in their efforts to be successful. Arrange the environment and make opportunities available for children to be able to do things. Successful accomplishments are a major ingredient of positive behavior.

ESTABLISH APPROPRIATE EXPECTATIONS

Expectations relate to and set the boundaries for desired behavior. They are the guideposts children use in learning to direct their own behavior.

Early childhood professionals and parents need to set appropriate expectations for children, which means they must decide what behaviors they expect of them. When children know what adults expect, they can better achieve those expectations. Up to a point, the more we expect of children, the more and better they achieve. Generally, we expect too little of most children.

However, having expectations for children is not enough. Early childhood professionals have to help children know and understand what the expectations are and help them meet these expectations. Some children will need little help in meeting expectations; others will need demonstration, explanation, encouragement, and support as they learn.

Set Limits.   Setting limits is closely associated with establishing expectations and relates to defining unacceptable behavior. For example, knocking over a block tower built by someone else and running in the classroom are generally considered unacceptable behaviors. Setting clear limits is important for three reasons:

1. It helps you clarify in your own mind what you believe is unacceptable, based on your knowledge of child development, children, their families, and their culture. When you do not set limits, inconsistency can occur.
2. Setting limits helps children act with confidence because they know which behaviors are acceptable.
3. Limits provide children with security. Children want and need limits.

As children grow and mature, the limits change and are adjusted to developmental levels, programmatic considerations, and life situations.

Classroom Rules.   Although I like to talk about and think in terms of expectations and limits, some early childhood professionals think and talk about rules. This is fine, but here are some additional guidelines about rules.

Plan classroom rules from the first day of class. As the year goes on, you can involve children in establishing classroom rules, but in the beginning, children want and need to know what they can and cannot do. For example, rules might relate to changing groups and bathroom routines. Whatever rules you establish, they should be fair, reasonable, and

For more information about guiding children's behavior, go to the Companion Website at **http://www.prenhall.com/morrison**, select chapter 14, then choose the Linking to Learning module to connect to the Virginia Cooperative Extension site.

415

appropriate to the children's age and maturity. Keep rules to a minimum; the fewer the better.

Remind children of the rules and encourage them to conform to them. Four-year-olds can realistically be expected to follow these guidelines, so there is less chance for misbehavior. Children are able to become responsible for their own behavior in a positive, accepting atmosphere where they know what the expectations are. Review the rules, and have children evaluate their behavior against the rules. You cannot have expectations without having rules. If you have activities ready for children when they enter the classroom, you establish the expectation that on arriving, they should be busy.

ARRANGE AND MODIFY THE ENVIRONMENT

Environment plays a key role in children's ability to guide their behavior. For example, if parents want a child to be responsible for taking care of his room, they should arrange the environment so he can do so, by providing shelves, hangers, and drawers at child height. Similarly, arrange your classroom so children can get and return their own papers and materials, use learning centers, and have time to work on individual projects.

In child care centers, early childhood classrooms, and family day care homes, early childhood professionals arrange the environment so that it supports the purposes of the program and makes appropriate behavior possible. Room arrangement is crucial to guiding children's behavior, and appropriate room arrangements signal to children that they are expected to guide and be responsible for their own behavior. Additionally, the appropriate environment enables teachers to observe and provide for children's interests through their selection of activities. Furthermore, it is easier to live and work in an attractive and aesthetically pleasing classroom or center. We all want a nice environment—children should have one, too. The following guidelines can be helpful to you as you think about and arrange your classroom or program area to support your efforts toward helping children guide their own behavior.

- Have an open area in which you and your children can meet as a whole group. This area is essential for story time, general class meetings, and so on. Starting and ending the day with a class meeting allows children to discuss their behavior and say how they and others can do a better job.
- Center areas should be well defined and accessible to children and have appropriate and abundant materials for children's use. Also, center boundaries should be low enough so that you and others can see over them for proper supervision and observation.
- Provide for all kinds of activities, both quiet and loud. Try to locate quiet areas together (reading area and puzzle area) and loud centers together (woodworking and blocks).
- Locate materials so that children can easily retrieve them. When children have to ask for materials, this promotes dependency and can lead to behavior problems.
- Materials should be easily stored, and children should put them away. A general rule of thumb is that there should be a place for everything and everything should be in its place when not in use.
- Provide children with guidelines for how to use centers and materials.

The Supportive Classroom.   You can arrange the physical setting of the classroom into a **supportive classroom** so that it is conducive to the behaviors you want to teach. If you want to encourage independent work, you must provide places and time for children to work alone. Disruptive behavior is often encouraged by classroom arrangements that force children to walk over other children to get to equipment and materials. You may find that your classroom actually contributes to misbehavior. The atmosphere of the classroom or the learning environment must be such that new behaviors are possible.

Supportive classroom
Arranging the physical setting of the classroom so that it is conducive to the behaviors you want to teach.

FIGURE 14.2   The Supportive Classroom

- Community and culture of caring
- Clear expectations
- High expectations
- Consistent behavior from teachers and staff
- Open communication between

   children–children

   teacher–children

   children–teacher

   teacher–parents

   parents–teacher

- Sufficient materials to support learning activities
- Efficacious teachers, those who believe children can and will learn. Efficacious teachers also believe they are good teachers.
- Routines established and maintained
- Balance between cooperation and independent learning
- Atmosphere of respect and caring
- Parent, teacher, and child partnerships

There are some basic features of classrooms that support guidance and self-regulation. As you reflect on these for your classroom, consider what other elements you could include.

The same situation applies in the home. If parents want children to keep their rooms neat and clean, they must make it possible for them to do so. Children should also be shown how to take care of their rooms. Parents may have to lower shelves or install clothes hooks. When the physical arrangement is to children's sizes, they can learn how to use a clothes hanger and where to hang certain clothes. A child's room should have a place for everything, and these places should be accessible and easy to use.

An Encouraging Environment.   The classroom should be a place where children can do their best work and be on their best behavior. It should be a rewarding place to be. The following are components of an **encouraging environment:**

- Opportunities for children to display their work
- Opportunities for freedom of movement (within guidelines)
- Opportunities for independent work
- A variety of work stations and materials based on children's interests

Figure 14.2 also identifies characteristics of classrooms that support children in their learning self-regulation and guiding their own behavior.

Time and Transitions.   Time, generally more important to adults than children, plays a major role in every program. The following guidelines relate to time and its use:

- *Do not waste children's time.* Children should be involved in interesting, meaningful activities from the moment they enter the center, classroom, or family day care home.
- *Do not make children wait.* When children have to wait for materials, their turn, and so forth, provide them with something else to do, such as listening to a story or playing in

Encouraging environment
A classroom environment that rewards student accomplishment and independence.

the block center. Problems can occur when children have to wait, because children like to be busy and involved.

- *Allow transition time.* Transitions are times when children move from one activity to another. They should be made as smoothly as possible, and as fun as possible. In one program, teachers sing, "It's Cleanup Time!" as a transition from one activity to cleanup and then to another activity.

Routines. Establish classroom routines from the beginning. Children need the confidence and security of a routine that will help them do their best. A routine also helps prevent discipline problems, because children know what to do and can learn to do it without a lot of disturbance. Parents need to establish routines in the home; a child who knows the family always eats at 5:30 P.M. can be expected to be there. As an early childhood professional, you must also be consistent. Consistency plays an important role in managing behavior in both the home and classroom. If children know what to expect in terms of routine and behavior, they will behave better.

MODEL APPROPRIATE BEHAVIOR

We have all heard the maxim, "Telling is not teaching." Nevertheless, we tend to teach by giving instructions, and, of course, children do need instructions. Professional educators soon realize, however, that actions speak louder than words.

Children see and remember how other people act. Observing another person, a child tries out a new behavior. If this new action brings a reward of some kind, she repeats it. Proponents of the modeling approach to learning believe that most behavior people exhibit is learned from the behavior of a model or models. They think children tend to model behavior that brings rewards from parents and early childhood professionals.

A model may be someone whom we respect or find interesting and whom we believe is being rewarded for the behavior he or she exhibits. Groups may also serve as models. For example, it is common to hear a teacher in an early childhood classroom comment, "I like how Cristina and Carlos are sitting quietly and listening to the story." Immediately following such a remark, you can see the group of children settle down to listen quietly to the story. Models children emulate do not necessarily have to be from real life; they can come from books and television. In addition, the modeled behavior does not have to be socially acceptable to be reinforcing.

You can use the following techniques to help children learn through modeling:

- *Show.* For example, show children where the block corner is and how and where the blocks are stored.
- *Demonstrate.* Perform a task while students watch. For example, demonstrate the proper way to put the blocks away and how to store them. Extensions of the demonstration method are to have children practice the demonstration while you supervise and to ask a child to demonstrate to other children.
- *Model.* Modeling occurs when you practice the behavior you expect of the children. Also, you can call children's attention to the desired behavior when another child models it.
- *Supervise.* Supervision is a process of reviewing, insisting, maintaining standards, and following up. If children are not performing the desired behavior, you will need to review the behavior. You must be consistent in your expectations of desired behavior. Children will soon learn they do not have to put away their blocks if you allow them not to do it even once. Remember, you are responsible for setting up the environment to enable the children's learning to take place.

As an early childhood professional, you will need to model and demonstrate social and group-living behaviors as well, including using simple courtesies (saying, "Please,"

Do Teacher–Child Relations Really Matter?

Think for a minute about your social relations with others. How others treat you affects you emotionally, physically, and cognitively. The same is true in your relationships with the children you teach. How you relate to children really matters and determines how well they achieve, as well as their present and future behavior. What are teacher behaviors that really matter in preventing children's present and future behavior problems? These include:

- Responding to children in a timely fashion
- Anticipating student needs and emotions
- Frequent teacher feedback
- Providing strong supports for children's academic and social competence in the classroom setting

Researchers have found that the extent to which children can access the instructional and socialization resources of the classroom environment may be, in part, predicated on teacher–child interactions. This provides support for the view that the classroom as a social context really matters: "[T]he association between the quality of early teacher–child relationships and later school performance can be both strong and persistent. The association is apparent in both academic and social spheres of school performance."[*]

In addition, teacher–child closeness, such as having an affectionate and warm relationship with a child, can reduce the tendency for aggressive behavior. "Closer teacher–child relationships may provide young children with resources (e.g., emotional security, guidance, and aid) that facilitate an "approach"

orientation—as opposed to an "avoidant" or "resistant" stance—toward the interpersonal and scholastic demands of the classroom and school."[†] The implication for you and other early childhood professionals is that you need to really care for your children and develop strong and affectionate relationships with them.

In one study regarding teacher–child closeness, "females tended to develop higher levels of cooperative participation, school liking, and achievement than did males."[‡] This might indicate gender differences in teacher–child relations and suggest that boys are at greater risk for not having a close teacher relationship. However, the teacher–child closeness relationship is particularly important not only for males, low-socioeconomic children, and minorities, but for all children who might not experience or have a close relationship with a caring adult.

This means that you need to provide a classroom social context that is supportive of and responsive to children's learning, social, and affectional needs. This, of course, is a challenging task, but one that is necessary, for how we relate to children helps determine their behavioral outcomes now and in the future.

---

*Hamre, B. K. and Pianta, R. C. "Early Teacher–Child Relationships and the Trajectory of Children's School Outcomes through Eighth Grade," *Child Development*, 72 (2001), 625–638.

†Ladd, G. W. and Burgess, K. B. "Do Relational Risks and Protective Factors Moderate the Linkages between Childhood Aggression and Early Psychological and School Adjustment?" *Child Development*, 72 (2001), 1579–1601.

‡Ibid.

"Thank you," "You're welcome," etc.) and practicing cooperation, sharing, and respect for others.

Parents and early childhood professionals can encourage children's misbehavior. Frequently, professionals see too much and ignore too little. Often parents expect perfection and adult behavior from children. If you focus on building responsible behavior, there will be less need to solve behavior problems.

Ignoring inappropriate behavior is probably one of the most overlooked strategies for managing an effective learning setting and guiding children's behavior. Ironically, some early childhood professionals feel guilty when they use this strategy. They believe that ignoring undesirable behaviors is not good teaching. While ignoring some inappropriate behavior can be an effective strategy, it must be combined with positive discipline and teaching.

 To complete an activity related to this topic, go to the Companion Website at **http://www.prenhall.com/morrison,** select chapter 14, then choose the Diversity Tie-In module.

Positive Guidance

Responsible, Motivated, Self-Directed Learners

The Grapevine (Texas) Elementary School staff had a vision. The vision emphasized the desire to encourage all learners to be responsible, intrinsically motivated, and self-directed in an environment of mutual respect. As we looked for a discipline management system that fit this philosophy, we recognized that we needed one that emphasized personal responsibility for behavior and cooperation instead of competition and that focused on developing a community of supportive members. We also discovered that we held several beliefs in common that should be the foundation of our discipline management plan:

1. All human beings have three basic needs—to feel connected (the ability to love and be loved), to feel capable (a sense of "I can" accomplish things), and to feel contributive (I count in the communities in which I belong).
2. Problem solving and solutions encourage responsible behavior. Punishment, by contrast, encourages rebellion and resentment.

3. Children can be creative decision makers and responsible citizens when given opportunities to direct the processes that affect the day-to-day environment in which they live.
4. Every inappropriate action does not necessitate a consequence, but rather can be used as a cornerstone of a problem-solving experience, ultimately leading to a true behavior change.

Our desire was, and is, to address the needs of the whole child as we educate our children to be responsible citizens.

ADOPTING THE PLAN

After much research, we decided to implement *Positive Discipline* as a discipline management system based on the concept of responsibilities rather than rules. Teachers established the following Grapevine Star Responsibilities:

I will be responsible for myself and my learning
I will respect others and their property

DEVELOP A PARTNERSHIP WITH PARENTS, FAMILIES, AND OTHERS

Involving parents and families is a wonderful way to gain invaluable insights about children's behavior. Furthermore, parents and early childhood professionals must be partners and work cooperatively in effectively guiding children's behaviors. In addition, involving other persons who are involved with your children is a good idea. Some of these significant others in the lives of children are other teachers, baby sitters, before- and after-school care providers, coaches, and club leaders.

Another important rule in guiding behavior is to *know your children.* A good way to learn about the children you care for and teach is through home visits. If you do not have an opportunity to visit the home, a parent conference is also valuable. Either way, you should gather information concerning the child's health history and interests; the child's attitude toward schooling; the parents' educational expectations for the child; what school support is available in the home (e.g., books, places to study); home conditions that would support or hinder school achievement (such as where the child sleeps); parents' attitudes toward schooling and discipline; parents' support of the child (e.g., encouragement to do well); parents' interests and abilities; and parents' desire to become involved in the school.

The visit or conference also offers an opportunity for you to share ideas with parents. You should, for example, express your desire for the child to do well in school; encourage

For more information about working with families, go to the Companion Website at **http://www. prenhall.com/morrison**, select any chapter, then choose Topic 10 of the ECE Supersite module.

420

I will listen and follow directions promptly

I will complete my classwork and homework in a quality manner

Furthermore, we decided that rewards—whether in the way of stickers, pencils, or award ceremonies—were not, on the whole, consistent with encouraging intrinsic motivation and the belief that all children should continuously monitor their own learning and behavior. Rather, the term *reward* should be replaced with *celebration,* and these celebrations should be based on what children find personally significant.

Teachers also discussed the understanding that they would become facilitators of decision-making sessions instead of "general in command;" and they would encourage self-evaluation by students leading to solutions.

ENGAGING STUDENTS

Throughout the course of the year, students set goals each six-week period (usually one academic goal and one behavioral goal) and conferred with their teachers at the end of the six weeks to determine the extent of their achievement toward that goal. At the end of the year, students participated in a celebration of achievement. Each student chose the goal that held the most personal significance and received a certificate that detailed the goal. The principal read each chosen goal in the grade-level celebrations as the student walked across the stage and shook hands with the principal. Teachers, parents, and students all enjoyed this ceremony, which emphasized the worth of each individual and affirmed that learning was, and is, the ultimate goal of education and school (as opposed to a grade or series of marks on a report card).

Irene Boynton, a first-grade teacher, comments that Positive Discipline allows children to experience the rewards of feeling confident and healthy about making respectful, responsible choices because it is the "right" thing to do, not because they will receive something for their choice.

THE BENEFITS

Teachers at Grapevine Elementary, when asked to comment on Positive Discipline, say such things as, "Is there any other way to teach?" and, "We would never go back to playing referee again!" Students no longer ask, "What am I going to get?" in response to a request to go the extra mile for another student or while working on a project. They are developing respect for themselves and for the rights and needs of others. The skills learned through Positive Discipline extend into academic areas, where we find that students are becoming more thoughtful, introspective, self-motivated, and effective problem solvers. We believe that we are fostering a safe, respectful community where children and adults thrive together in an atmosphere of mutual respect.

Visit Grapevine Elementary on the Web at http://www.gcisd-k12.org.schools/ges/index.html

---

For information on implementing additional components of Positive Discipline such as class meetings, "I"-messages, and role-playing, refer to *Positive Discipline in the Classroom* by Jane Nelsen, Lynn Lott, and Stephen Glenn. Contributed by Alicia King (original author: Nancy Robinson).

---

parents to take part in school and classroom programs; suggest ways parents can help children learn; describe some of the school programs; give information about school events, projects, and meetings; and explain your beliefs about discipline.

Working with and involving parents also provides early childhood professionals with opportunities to help parents with parenting skills and child-related problems. The foundation for children's behavior is built in the home, and some parents unwittingly encourage and promote children's misbehavior and antisocial behavior. In many ways, parents promote antisocial behavior in their children by using punitive, negative, and overly restrictive punishment. In particular, when children are enrolled in child care programs at an early age, professionals have an ideal opportunity to help parents learn about and use positive discipline approaches to child rearing.

In your collaborative process of working with others to help children develop self-regulation, each group has certain basic rights. Figure 14.3 lists these basic rights. Perhaps as you read them you can think of others you want to include.

 To complete a Program in Action activity, visit the Companion Website at **http://www.prenhall.com/morrison,** select chapter 14, then choose the Program in Action module.

PROMOTE PROSOCIAL BEHAVIOR

One trend in early childhood education is for professionals to focus on helping children learn how to share, care for, and assist others. We call these and similar behaviors *prosocial behaviors.*

FIGURE 14.3 Children's, Teachers', and Parents' Rights That Support Positive Behavior

Children's Rights

Children have these rights in classrooms designed to promote self-regulation:

- To be respected and treated courteously
- To be treated fairly in culturally independent and gender-appropriate ways
- To learn behaviors necessary for self-guidance
- To have teachers who have high expectations for them
- To learn and exercise independence
- To achieve to their highest levels
- To be praised and affirmed for appropriate behaviors and achievements
- To learn and practice effective social skills
- To learn and apply basic academic skills

Teachers' Rights

- To be supported by administration and parents in appropriate efforts to help children guide their behavior
- To have a partnership with parents so they can be successful
- To be treated courteously and professionally by peers and others

Parents' Rights

- To share ideas and values of child rearing and discipline with teachers
- To be involved in and informed about classroom and school discipline policies
- To receive periodic reports and information about their children's behaviors
- To be educated and informed about how to guide their children's behavior

It is easy to forget that in the home and classroom, everyone has "rights." How do you plan to honor and support these rights in your professional practice?

There is a growing feeling among early childhood professionals that the ill effects of many societal problems, including uncivil behavior and violence, can be reduced or avoided. They believe efforts to achieve this goal should begin in the primary and preschool years. Consequently, they place emphasis on prosocial behaviors—teaching children the fundamentals of peaceful living, kindness, helpfulness, and cooperation. You can do several things to foster development of prosocial skills in the classroom:

- *Be a good role model for children.* You must demonstrate in your life and relationships with children and other adults the behaviors of cooperation and kindness that you want to encourage in children. Civil behavior begins with courtesy and manners. You can model these and help children to do the same.
- *Provide positive feedback and reinforcement when children perform prosocial behaviors.* When they are rewarded for appropriate behavior, children tend to repeat that behavior. ("I like how you helped Tim get up when you accidentally ran into him. I bet that made him feel better.")
- *Provide opportunities for children to help and show kindness to others.* Cooperative programs between primary children and nursing and retirement homes are excellent opportunities to practice kind and helping behaviors.

- *Conduct classroom routines and activities so they are as free of conflict as possible.* Provide opportunities for children to work together and practice skills for cooperative living. Design learning centers and activities for children to share and work cooperatively.

- *When real conflicts occur, provide practice in conflict resolution skills.* These skills include taking turns, talking through problems, compromising, and apologizing. A word of caution regarding apologies: too often, an apology is a perfunctory response on the part of teachers and children. Rather than just saying the often empty words "I'm sorry," it is far more meaningful to help one child understand how another is feeling. Encouraging empathic behavior in children is a key to the development of prosocial behavior.

It is increasingly important for early childhood professionals to help children learn how to resolve their differences, share, and cooperate. Because of this, curricula for helping children to peaceably resolve conflict are growing in popularity.

- *Conduct classroom activities based on multicultural principles that are free from stereotyping and sexist behaviors* (see chapter 15).

- *Read stories to children that exemplify prosocial behaviors.* Provide such literature for them to read.

- *Counsel and work with parents to encourage them to limit or eliminate children's exposure to violence.* Suggest that they regulate or eliminate watching violence on television, attending R-rated movies, playing video games with violent content, and buying CDs with objectionable lyrics.

- *Help children feel good about themselves, build strong self-images, and be competent individuals.* Children who are happy, confident, and competent feel good about themselves and are more likely to behave positively toward others.

Parents and professionals want to promote the intrinsic development of empathy, a desire to engage in sympathetic behaviors, because it is the right and good thing to do. You can teach children skills for developing prosocial behavior:

- *Model resolutions.* Professionals can model resolutions for children: "Erica, please don't knock over Shantrell's building because she worked hard to build it"; "Barry, what is another way (instead of hitting) you can tell Pam that she is sitting in your chair?"

- *Do something else.* Teach children to get involved in another activity. Children can learn that they do not always have to play with a toy someone else is playing with. They can get involved in another activity with a different toy. They can do something else now and play with the toy later. Chances are, however, that by getting involved in another activity they will forget about the toy they were ready to fight for.

- *Take turns.* Taking turns is a good way for children to learn that they cannot always be first, have their own way, or do a prized activity. Taking turns brings equality and fairness to interpersonal relations.

- *Share.* Sharing is good behavior to promote in any setting. Children have to be taught how to share and how to behave when others do not share. Children can be helped to select another toy rather than hitting or grabbing. Again, keep in mind that during the early years children are egocentric, and acts of sharing are likely to be motivated by expectations of a reward or approval such as being thought of as a "good" boy or girl.

DEVELOPMENT OF AUTONOMOUS BEHAVIOR

Implicit in guiding children's behavior is the assumption that they can be, should be, and will be responsible for their own behavior. The ultimate goal of all education is to develop *autonomy* in children, which means "being governed by oneself."

Early childhood educators need to conduct programs that promote development of autonomy. One aspect of facilitating autonomy is exchanging points of view with children.

> When a child tells a lie, for example, the adult can deprive him of dessert or make him write fifty times "I will not lie." The adult can also refrain from punishing the child and, instead, look him straight in the eye with great skepticism and affection and say, "I really can't believe what you are saying because . . . " This is an example of an exchange of points of view that contributes to the development of autonomy in children. The child who can see that the adult cannot believe him can be motivated to think about what he must do to be believed. The child who is raised with many similar opportunities can, over time, construct for himself the conviction that it is best eventually for people to deal honestly with each other.[10]

The ultimate goal of developing autonomy in children is to have them regulate their own behavior and make decisions about good and bad, right and wrong (when they are mature enough to understand these concepts), and the way they will behave in relation to themselves and others. Autonomous behavior can be achieved only when children consider other people's points of view, which can occur only if they are presented with viewpoints that differ from their own and are encouraged to consider them in deciding how they will behave. The ability to take another person's point of view is largely developmental. It is not until around age eight, when children become less egocentric, that they are able to decenter and see things from other people's points of view. Autonomy is reinforced when teachers and parents allow sufficient time and opportunities for children to practice and perform tasks for themselves. Independence is also nurtured when children are allowed to use problem-solving techniques and to learn from their mistakes.

Children can be encouraged to regulate and be responsible for their own behavior through what Piaget referred to as "sanctions by reciprocity." These sanctions "are directly related to the act we want to sanction and to the adult's point of view, and have the effect of motivating the child to construct rules of conduct for himself, through the coordination of viewpoints."[11]

Examples of sanctions by reciprocity include exclusion from the group when children have a choice of staying and behaving or leaving; taking away from children the materials or privileges they have abused, while leaving open the opportunity to use them again if they express a desire to use them appropriately; and helping children fix things they have broken and clean up after themselves. A fine line separates sanctions by reciprocity and punishment. The critical ingredients that balance the scales on the side of reciprocity are your respect for children and your desire to help them develop autonomy rather than obedience.

As you read the following Program in Action, reflect on these things:

- What other theories in addition to Maslow's contribute to practices for helping children guide their behavior?
- How could you implement the three commandments of Hilltop into your classroom or program?
- How would you rate yourself on the rubrics of professional performance applied to the teachers of Hilltop school? Which of the rubrics would you need the most help in implementing?

Hilltop School

Collaborative Problem Solving

Students at Hilltop Elementary School have painted colorful M&M's candies on school windows to remind them that the only meltdowns here should be "in your mouth, not in your classroom." Operated by the Rockland Board of Cooperative Educational Services (BOCES) in West Nyack, NY, Hilltop is an alternative school that serves 44 students with severe behavior and/or academic challenges who are in kindergarten through fifth grade. Hilltop helps students learn how to regulate their behavior so they can have more success in school and in life. In 2002, Hilltop was recognized as a model for other schools when it was awarded the prestigious Magnus Award by the National School Board Association.

A combination of collaborative problem-solving and staff development training helps Hilltop succeed with even the most difficult to teach students. Staff are trained about the importance of choice making and self-reflection in acquiring two important facets of self-regulation: pattern recognition and impulse control. Students learn how to recognize the important features of an environment or task and attend to these rather than extraneous features. They learn how to bystand their own behaviors, replacing impulsive responses with ones more appropriate to the situation.

Staff and students use three school commandments to create a shared vision of the expected school climate, as well as a focus for bringing consistent expectations to daily classroom and school routines. Borrowed from Ross Greene's book *The Explosive Child,* the commandments reflect Maslow's hierarchy of needs and establish a guarantee of safety and equity as the contract made between staff and students: "all students will be safe and learn" (Commandment #1), "fair is not equal" (Commandment #2), and "everyone gets what they need" (Commandment #3) (Greene, 1998).

Collaborative problem-solving groups are used to teach students how to direct their attention to expectations implicit in the school commandments and adjust their behaviors accordingly. Behaviors corresponding to each commandment are taught and demonstrated using cooperative learning techniques (Sharan, 1994). Teachers demonstrate what the expected behaviors look and sound like. Students are encouraged to role-play prosocial behaviors and use scripts for problem-solving and group interactions. Charts describing target behaviors are posted in classrooms and are referred to by staff and students.

The number of daily collaborative problem-solving meetings varies based on student age. Kindergartners and first graders hold up to nine meetings a day, each meeting lasting approximately five minutes. Meetings are held at the beginning and end of each activity block. The older students, second through fifth grades, meet four times a day: at the beginning of the day, before lunch, after lunch, and before dismissal. The format of these meetings is always the same: Teachers and students commit to keeping agreed upon commandments. Follow-up meetings give individuals a chance to reflect on performance as well as receive feedback from the group.

The program's commitment to ongoing professional development is apparent in the rubrics used to evaluate staff performance on each of six program components: collaborative problem-solving, supervision of paraprofessional staff, ongoing training, building classroom communities, best instructional practices, and collaborative partnerships. The rubrics, shown in Figure 14.4, provide a common vision of the level of service the program is committed to. Like the commandments, they ensure consistency in responding to the needs of the children served at Hilltop.

Contributed by Susan E. Craig, Mary Jean Marsico, and Pamela Charles, with references to R. Greene, and S. Sharan (eds.) *The Explosive Child* (New York Harper Collins, 1998); *Handbook of Cooperative Learning Methods* (Westport, CT; Greenwood Press, 1994).

Rubric for Component #1: Collaborative Problem-Solving

	Level 1 (Below Expectations)	Level 2 (At Expectations)	Level 3 (Master Level)
Work with students to identify individual goals related to school commandments.	Set goals with students. Post goals. Check in randomly to ascertain progress. No charting occurs.	Set goals with students. Post goals/reviews daily. Check in once to twice daily to ascertain progress. Chart progress using color-coded system.	Set goals with students. Post goals/reviews daily. Check in three to nine times daily to ascertain progress. Chart progress using color-coded system.
Use language intended to refocus students on school commandment to cue and redirect students.	Occasionally link redirection, correction of students to school commandments. Occasionally help students identify an alternative solution/behavior.	Consistently link redirection, correction of students to school commandments. Occasionally help student identify an alternative solution/behavior.	Consistently link redirection, correction of students to school commandments. Consistently help student identify an alternative solution/behavior.

Rubric for Component #2: Supervision of Paraprofessional Staff

	Level 1 (Below Expectations)	Level 2 (At Expectations)	Level 3 (Master Level)
Plans include specific involvement of Para in preteaching/reteaching classroom activities.	Involve Para as need arises in classroom.	Preplan Para involvement. Inform at start of each activity.	Provide Para with written schedule of involvement.

Rubric for Component #3: Ongoing Training

	Level 1 (Below Expectations)	Level 2 (At Expectations)	Level 3 (Master Level)
Staff and program administrators set annual program goals to improve performance in one or more of the program components.	Staff and administrators can articulate six components of model. Staff development activities sometimes allude to, or reference, one or more of the components.	Staff and administrators select one of the model components to focus on for staff development prior to the start of the school year. At least two in-service activities are related to the component area selected.	Staff and administrators select one or more specific annual goals to work on within a selected model component. At least two in-service sessions are designed to facilitate staff acquisition of agreed upon goals.

FIGURE 14.4   Rubrics for Staff Development at Hilltop School

As you review the rubrics, think about how you could use a similar rubric in your work to promote professional development. What are your thoughts about using rubrics to promote staff development?

Rubric for Component #4: Building Classroom Communities

	Level 1 (Below Expectations)	Level 2 (At Expectations)	Level 3 (Master Level)
Students are provided with opportunities to contribute to the lives of other people.	Students contribute to community initiatives around specific issues events. Participation is not required by every classroom or every student.	Students have ongoing relationships with community social service agencies. Students perform some type of community service each week.	Students have ongoing relationships with community social service agencies and students perform some type of community service each week. Community-based problems/issues are part of project based curriculum at least once a week.

Rubric for Component #5: Best Instructional Practices

	Level 1 (Below Expectations)	Level 2 (At Expectations)	Level 3 (Master Level)
Use flexible grouping to ensure students are not tracked on the basis of a limited number of skills.	Most instruction occurs in a whole group. Students self-select who they will work with to complete group tasks.	Regrouping occurs throughout the instructional day. Groups are formed intentionally on the basis of skill to be addressed and daily opportunities for students to demonstrate competency within discipline-bound activities.	Regrouping occurs throughout the instructional day. Groups are formed intentionally on the basis of skills to be addressed and daily opportunities for students to demonstrate their competency within interdisciplinary activities.

Rubric for Component #6: Collaborative Partnerships

	Level 1 (Below Expectations)	Level 2 (At Expectations)	Level 3 (Master Level)
Parents and staff work collaboratively to promote student success.	Parent/staff contact is limited to formal quarterly meetings. Parents or staff may contact one another if a problem comes up.	Parent/staff contact occurs weekly. A menu of meetings, phone contact, notes, and so on, is made available for parents to select the type of communication that works best for them.	Parent/staff contact occurs weekly. Parents are welcome to come to school at any time. Home visits occur monthly. Other contact occurs in the manner described in Level 2.

FIGURE 14.4 (Continued)

PHYSICAL PUNISHMENT

Is it possible to guide children's behavior without physical punishment? More and more, early childhood professionals agree that it is. Whether parents and professionals should spank or paddle as a means of guiding behavior is an age-old controversy. Some parents spank their children, following a "No!" with a slap on the hand or a spank on the bottom. Some parents and religious groups base their use of physical punishment on their religious beliefs. Yet, what some parents do with their child in the home is not acceptable for others to do outside the home, where spanking is considered an inappropriate form of guidance.

For more information about alternatives to punishment, go to the Companion Website at **http://www. prenhall.com/morrison**, select chapter 14, then choose the Linking to Learning module to connect to the Center for Effective Discipline site.

In fact, in some places, such as Florida, physical punishment in child care programs is legislatively prohibited.

Several problems with spanking and other forms of physical punishment persist. First, physical punishment is generally ineffective in building behavior in children. Physical punishment does not show children what to do or provide them with alternative ways of behaving. Second, adults who use physical punishment are modeling physical aggression. They are, in effect, saying that it is permissible to use aggression in interpersonal relationships. Children who are spanked are thus more likely to use aggression with their peers. Third, spanking and physical punishment increase the risk of physical injury to the child. Spanking can be an emotionally charged situation, and the spanker can become too aggressive, overdo the punishment, and hit the child in vulnerable places. Fourth, parents, caregivers, and teachers are children's sources of security. Physical punishment takes away from and erodes the sense of security that children must have to function confidently in their daily lives. In short, the best advice regarding physical punishment is to avoid it; use nonviolent means for guiding children's behavior. (For more information on physical punishment, see the website http://www.parentsplace.com. This address links you to a community where parents can connect, communicate, and celebrate the adventures of parenting; share insights; search through extensive archives of feature articles; and pose questions to a panel of experts.)

In the long run, parents and early childhood professionals determine children's behavior. In guiding the behavior of children entrusted to their care, professionals and others must select procedures that are appropriate to their own philosophies and children's particular needs. Guiding children to help them develop their internal system of control benefits them more than a system that relies on external control and authoritarianism. Developing self-regulation in children should be a primary goal of all professionals.

TRENDS IN GUIDING CHILDREN

As we observe the field of early childhood education, we can clearly see trends in the guidance of young children. As an early childhood professional, you can expect to be involved in the following:

- *Development of democratic learning environments.* In our efforts to help prepare all children to live effectively and productively in a democracy, we are placing increasing emphasis on giving students experiences that will help promote behavior associated with democratic living. As a result, more professionals are making efforts to run their classrooms as democracies. The idea of teaching this behavior through classrooms that are miniature democracies is not new. John Dewey was an advocate of this approach and championed democratic classrooms as a way of promoting democratic living. However, running a democratic classroom is easier said than done. It requires a confident professional who believes it is worth the effort. Democratic learning environments require that students develop responsibility for their and others' behaviors and learning, that classrooms operate as communities, and that all children are respected and respectful of others.
- *The use of character education as a means of promoting responsible behavior.* In chapter 12 we discussed reasons for character education and its importance and role in the contemporary curriculum. Providing character education will continue to grow as a means of promoting fundamental behaviors that early childhood professionals and society believe are essential for living in democratic society.
- *Teaching civility.* Civil behavior and ways to promote it are of growing interest at all levels of society. The specific teaching of *civil behavior*—how to treat others well and in turn be treated well—is seen as essential for living well in contemporary society. At a minimum, civil behavior includes manners, respect, and the ability to get along with people of all races, cultures, and socioeconomic backgrounds.

To take an online self-test on this chapter's contents, go to the Companion Website at **http://www. prenhall.com/morrison**, select chapter 14, then choose the Self-Test module.

- *Early intervention.* We all know habits are hard to break and that a behavior once set is difficult to change. Early childhood professionals believe it is essential to help develop appropriate behaviors in the early years by working with parents and families to help them guide their children's behavior. Waiting to address delinquent behavior is much more costly than promoting right behavior from the beginning of children's lives.

As we have emphasized in this and other chapters, cognitive and social development and behavioral characteristics are interconnected. More early childhood professionals recognize that it does not make sense to teach children reading, writing, and arithmetic and not also teach them skills necessary for responsibly guiding their own behavior.

 For additional Internet resources or to complete an online activity for this chapter, go to the Companion Website at **http://www. prenhall.com/morrison**, select chapter 14, then choose the Linking to Learning or Making Connections module.

ACTIVITIES FOR FURTHER ENRICHMENT

APPLICATIONS

1. List five advantages of basing your teaching on theories of guiding children.
2. What is the difference between normal behavior and acceptable behavior? Give an example of when normal behavior may not be acceptable and another when acceptable behavior may not be normal.
3. Observe a primary classroom and identify aspects of the physical setting and atmosphere that could influence classroom behavior. Can you suggest improvements?
4. List five methods for guiding children's behavior. Tell why you think each is effective, and give examples.
5. Explain, with examples, why it is important for early childhood professionals and parents to agree on a philosophy of guidance.

FIELD EXPERIENCES

1. Observe an early childhood classroom. What guidance system (implicit or explicit) does the teacher use to manage the classroom? Do you think the teacher is aware of the systems in use?
2. List ten behaviors you think are desirable in toddlers, ten in preschoolers, and ten in kindergartners. For each behavior, give two examples of how you would encourage and promote development of that behavior. Place these ideas in your portfolio or idea file.

RESEARCH

1. Many levels of guidance are practiced by parents and early childhood professionals without their being aware of what they are doing or the processes they are using. Observe a mother–child relationship for examples of parental guidance. What specific strategies does she use? What was the child's resultant behavior? After further observation, answer these questions for a teacher–child relationship. In both situations, what are the ethical implications of the adult's actions?
2. Observe an early childhood classroom to see which behaviors earn the teacher's attention. Does the teacher pay more attention to positive or negative behavior? Why do you think the teacher does this?
3. Interview five parents of young children to determine what they mean when they use the word *discipline*. What implications might these definitions have for you if you were their children's teacher?

READINGS FOR FURTHER ENRICHMENT

Charles, C.M. *Building Classroom Discipline,* 7th ed. Boston: Allyn & Bacon, 2001.
For reducing types of student misbehavior that impede learning and produce stress, this text presents solutions developed by some of the most influential thinkers of the past fifty years and invites students to pick and choose from the solutions to create systems comfortable to them.

Crone, D. A., and Horner, R. H. *Building Positive Behavior Support Systems in Schools: Functional Behavioral Assessment.* New York: Guilford Publications, 2003.

Presents an up-to-date conceptual model and practical tools for systematically addressing the challenges of problem behavior in schools. Spelling out both the "why's" and "how's" of developing and implementing individuals behavior support plans, it gives particular attention to the organizational and team-based structures needed to effect change.

Goodman, J. F., and Balamore, U. *Teaching Goodness: Engaging the Moral and Academic Promise of Young Children.* Boston: Allyn & Bacon, 2003.

This text is an exploration of classroom practices that demonstrates how a teacher captures the moral and academic aspirations of young children. Takes readers into the classroom where they will see firsthand how the teacher is directive—asking leading questions, offering suggestions, and alternatives.

Janney, R., and Snell, M. *Behavioral Support.* Baltimore, MD: Paul H. Brookes Publishing Co., 2000.

Provides insight into students' behaviors and introduces fresh, proactive ideas on how to help them develop appropriate behavioral skills through forming positive relationships, communicating effectively with peers, and taking an active role in school and community. Provides the field-tested strategies that professionals need for working with students with disabilities.

Kaiser, B., and Rasminsky, J. *Challenging Behavior in Young Children: Understanding, Preventing, and Responding Effectively.* Boston: Allyn & Bacon, 2003.

Presents information and strategies to deal with the challenging behavior that teachers find more and more often in their classrooms.

Keogh, B. *Temperament in the Classroom: Understanding Individual Differences.* Baltimore, MD: Paul H. Brookes Publishing Co., 2003.

Explores the effect of temperament on educational experience, and shows readers how individual temperaments of students and teachers influence behavior and achievement.

Nelsen, J., ed. *Positive Discipline: A Teacher's A–Z Guide. Hundreds of Solutions for Every Possible Classroom Behavior Problem.* rev. 2nd ed., 2001. Rocklin, CA: Prima Publishing.

Applicable to all grade levels, this comprehensive A to Z guide addresses modern-day problems and practical solutions for establishing an effective learning environment.

Nelsen, J., Lott, L. and Glenn, S. *Positive Discipline in the Classroom: Developing Mutual Respect, Cooperation, and Responsibility in Your Classroom* (The Positive Discipline Series). Rocklin, CA: Prima Publishing, 2000.

Three parenting experts address the popular concept of class meetings, where students and teachers work together to solve problems.

Ryan, K., and Bohlin, K. *Building Character in Schools: Practical Ways to Bring Moral Instruction to Life.* Hoboken, NJ: John Wiley & Sons, 2003.

The authors outline the principles and strategies of effective character education and explain what schools must do to teach students the habits and dispositions that lead to responsible adulthood.

Siccone, F., and Lopez, L. *Educating the Heart: Lessons to Build Respect and Responsibility.* Boston: Allyn & Bacon, 2000.

Educating the Heart is specifically designed to help teachers meet two of the most demanding challenges they face—building students' respect for themselves and others, and promoting both personal and social responsibility. Provides the tools teachers need to turn their classroom into a safe and productive learning environment.

LINKING TO LEARNING

Center for Effective Discipline
http://www.stophitting.com

The Center for Effective Discipline (CED) is a nonprofit organization that provides educational information to the public on the effects of corporal punishment and on alternatives to its use.

National Network for Child Care
http://www.nncc.org

> *Preschoolers are delightful to have around but at times can be quite a challenge! This site suggests ways that a preschooler can learn to get along with others and that a caregiver can learn to guide and discipline that preschooler.*

Virginia Cooperative Extension
http://www.ext.vt.edu

> *Shows several commonsense strategies for effectively guiding the behavior of young children so they can make positive choices, learn problem-solving skills, and learn values of respect and responsibility.*

Positive Parenting.com
http://www.positiveparenting.com

> *Dedicated to providing resources and information to help make parenting more rewarding, effective, and fun.*

The Family Works
http://www.thefamilyworks.org

> *A private, nonprofit organization offering programs for families in child development, behavioral health, and social services. Integrated service designed to foster well-being in the home, school, and community.*

Parenting.com
http://www.parenting.com

> *Offers expert advice on how to deal with topics such as discipline, lying, sharing, shyness, tantrums, and more.*

International Network for Children and Families (INCAF)
http://www.incaf.com

> *Offers a variety of courses on parenting and teacher education.*

ENDNOTES

[1] Campbell, S. B., Pierce, E. W., March, C. L., Ewing, L. J., and Szumowski, E. K., "Hard-to-Manage Preschool Boys: Symptomatic Behavior across Contexts and Time," *Child Development* 65 (1994), 836–851.

[2] Diaz, R. M., Neal, C. J., and Amaya-Williams, M., *The Social Origins of Self-Regulation. Vygotsky and Education* (Cambridge: Cambridge University Press, 1996), p. 130.

[3] Ibid., p. 139.

[4] Vygotsky, L. S., *Mind in Society* (Cambridge, MA: Harvard University Press, 1978), 86.

[5] Roehler, L. R., and Cantlon, D. J., *Scaffolding: A Powerful Tool in Social Constructivist Classrooms* (1996). Available at http://edweb3.educ.msu.edu/literacy/papers/ paperlr2.html.

[6] Berk, L. E., and Winsler, A., *Scaffolding Children's Learning: Vygotsky and Early Childhood Education* (Washington, DC: National Association for the Education of Young Children, 1995), pp. 45–46.

[7] Gordon, T., *Teacher Effectiveness Training* (New York: Peter H. Hyden, 1974).

[8] Ibid., p. 40.

[9] Ibid., pp. 75–76.

[10] Constance, K., *Number in Preschool and Kindergarten* (Washington, DC: National Association for the Education of Young Children, 1982), 23.

[11] Ibid., p. 77.

Chapter 15

Getting cultural perspective is hard for students unless someone takes the time to show them the links.

SHARON M. DRAPER, 1997 NATIONAL TEACHER OF THE YEAR

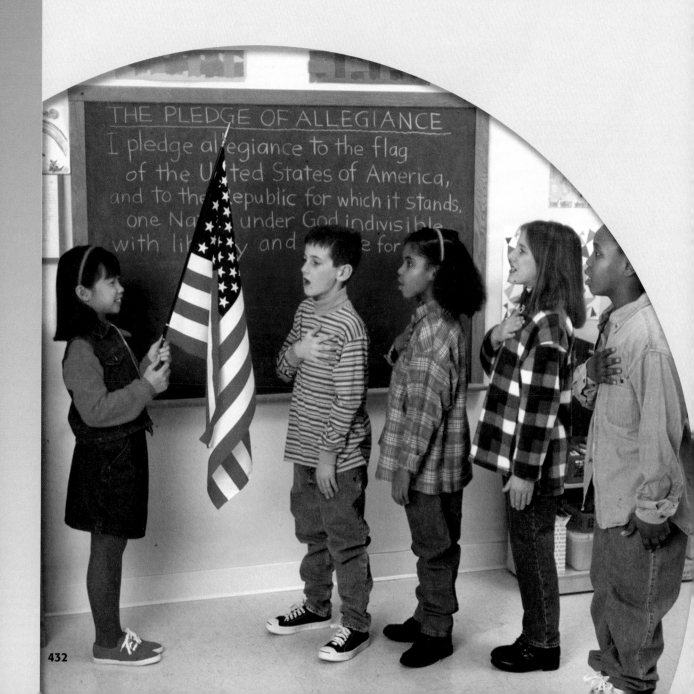

Multiculturalism
Education for Living in a Diverse Society

Focus Questions

- What is multicultural education?

- What implications does a multicultural society have for your teaching?

- How can you and other early childhood teachers infuse multicultural content in curriculum, programs, and activities?

- What contemporary issues influence the teaching of multiculturalism?

- How can you educate yourself and young children for living in a diverse society?

The population of the United States is changing and will continue to change. For example, the population will be less Caucasian. More students will be black and Hispanic. In addition, America will become even more a nation of blended races. Projections are that by 2050, 21 percent of the population will be of mixed ancestry. By 2025, almost one-fifth (20 percent) of the population will be Hispanic.

All these demographics have tremendous implications for increased multicultural education. Colleges of education must increase their efforts to recruit and educate minority teachers. As a result of changing demographics, more students will require special education, bilingual education, and other special services. Issues of culture and diversity will shape instruction and curriculum. These demographics have tremendous implications for how you teach and how your children learn. In part, how you respond to the multicultural makeup and needs of your children will determine how well they fulfill their responsibilities in the years to come. Because of the multicultural composition of society, as an early childhood educator you will want to promote multicultural awareness in your classroom.

MULTICULTURAL AWARENESS

In its simplest form, **multicultural awareness** is the appreciation for and understanding of peoples' cultures, socioeconomic status, and gender. It also includes understanding one's own culture. As you read this chapter, also refer to the glossary of terms in Figure 15.1.

Bringing multicultural awareness to the classroom does not mean teaching about certain cultures to the exclusion of the cultures represented by children in the class. Rather, multicultural awareness programs and activities focus on other cultures while making children aware of the content, nature, and richness of their own. The terms and concepts for describing multicultural education and awareness are not as important as the methods, procedures, and activities for developing meaningful early childhood programs. Learning about other cultures concurrently with their own culture enables

Multicultural awareness
Appreciation and understanding of peoples' cultures, socioeconomic status, and gender.

To review the chapter focus questions online, go to the Companion Website at **http://www. prenhall.com/morrison** and select chapter 15.

FIGURE 15.1   Glossary of Multicultural Terms

Affirmative action: First established by the Federal government in 1965, this legal mandate consists of special actions in recruitment, hiring, and other areas designed to eliminate the effects of past discrimination.

Bias-free: Curriculum, programs, materials, language, attitudes, actions, and activities that are free from biased perceptions.

Bilingual education: Education in two languages. Generally, two languages are used for the purpose of academic instruction.

Cultural diversity: Differences in race, ethnicity, language, nationality, or religion among various groups within the community, organization, or nation. A school or classroom is said to be culturally diverse if its residents include members of different groups.

Culturally fair education: Education that respects and accounts for the cultural backgrounds of all learners.

Culture: The shared values, norms, traditions, customs, arts, history, folklore, and institutions of a group of people.

Discrimination: Treatment that favors one person or group over another.

Diversity: Difference, variety, and uniqueness. Generally, diversity refers to human qualities that are different from our own and those of groups to which we belong; but that are manifested in other individuals and groups. Dimensions of diversity include but are not limited to: age, ethnicity, gender, physical abilities or qualities, race, sexual orientation, educational background, income, and religious beliefs.

English as a second language (ESL):   Instruction in which students with limited English proficiency attend a special English class.

English for speakers of other languages (ESOL):   The term that has begun to replace "ESL" for instruction in which students with limited English proficiency attend a special English class.

English language learners (ELL):   Non–English-speaking students who need support to learn the English language.

Ethnic group: Any category of people within a society who possess distinctive social or cultural traits, shared history, and a sense of their commonness.

Gender-balanced curriculum: Curriculum in which women are an integral part.

Gender-fair school: Learning environment in which male and female students participate equally and respond to similarly high expectations in all subjects.

Homophobia: Aversion to gay or homosexual people or their lifestyle, culture, or behavior, or an act based on this aversion; irrational fear of, aversion to, or discrimination against homosexuality or homosexuals.

Infusion: The process of making multiculturalism an explicit part of the curriculum throughout all the content areas.

These terms can help you in your professional development and in your work with colleagues and parents.

FIGURE 15.1 **(Continued)**

CHAPTER 15
MULTICULTURALISM

Mainstreaming: The educational and social integration of children with special needs into the school-wide instructional process, usually the regular classroom.

Maintenance bilingual programs: Transitional bilingual programs that also infuse English into content area instruction with the goal of biliteracy.

Multicultural: Of or pertaining to, or representing several different cultures or cultural elements. A *multicultural education* is a compilation of teaching and learning approaches that fosters an appreciation and respect for cultural pluralism and promotes democratic ideals of justice, equality, and democracy. *Multiculturalism* is an approach to education based on the premise that all peoples in the United States should receive proportional attention in the curriculum.

Multicultural awareness: Ability to perceive and acknowledge cultural differences among people without making value judgments about these differences.

Nonsexist education: Education that promotes attitudes and behaviors that convey that the sexes are equal.

Pluralism: A condition in which members of diverse cultural groups (a) have equal access to the resources needed for realizing their full potential; (b) obtain equal social and economic benefits; (c) have equal rights to express and nurture their cultural and linguistic heritage; and (d) are supported by official policies that express value for the diversity they contribute to the society.

Prejudice: An opinion formed without enough knowledge or thought; biased about someone or something.

Race: A group among humans that possesses inherited traits that are distinct enough to characterize its members as a unique people. Such divisions are often used by anthropologists to aid in classification. In a racially mixed society, any strict adherence to a classification scheme is limiting and problematic.

Racial profiling: This term is generally defined as wrongful and hurtful judgments about an individual or group of individuals based solely on their ethnicity or the color of their skin.

Racism: Unfair behavior whereby one race has and uses power over another. (*Note:* There is no established agreement on any scientific definition of race. Race has no biological or natural basis, but is rather a socially defined construct that is used to categorize people according to the color of their skin).

Stereotype: A generalization or oversimplification about a whole group of people. Gender stereotyping is one example. For instance, many advertisements show mothers serving meals to their families (but very few show fathers doing this). Many newspaper photographs, films, advertisements, and television programs show men engaged in physically active pastimes such as participating in sports, rock-climbing, or canoeing (but few show women doing these things).

Xenophobia: From the Greek word meaning "fear of strangers," the fear or hatred of anything that is foreign or outside of one's own group, nation, or culture.

To check your understanding of this chapter with the online Study Guide, go to the Companion Website at **http://www. prenhall.com/morrison,** select chapter 15, then choose the Study Guide module.

For more information about diversity and early childhood education, go to the Companion Website at **http://www.prenhall. com/morrison,** select any chapter, then choose Topic 8 of the ECE Supersite module.

Multiculturalism An approach to education based on the premise that all peoples in the United States should receive proportional attention in the curriculum.

Multicultural infusion Making multiculturalism an explicit part of curriculum and programs.

children to integrate commonalities and appreciate differences without inferring inferiority or superiority of one or the other.

WHO ARE MULTICULTURAL CHILDREN?

The population of young children in the United States reflects the population at large and represents a number of different cultures and ethnicities. Thus, many cities and school districts have populations that express great ethnic diversity, including Asian Americans, Native Americans, African Americans, and Hispanic Americans. For example, the Dade County, Florida, school district has children from 122 countries of the world, each with its own culture. Table 15.1 shows the proportion of minority students in the nation's ten largest school districts.

The great diversity of young children creates interesting challenges for early childhood educators. Many children speak languages other than English, behave differently based on cultural customs and values, and come from many socioeconomic backgrounds. Early childhood professionals must prepare themselves and their children to live happily and productively in this society.

Yet how to prepare children of all cultures for productive living is a major challenge for everyone. For instance, how can early childhood professionals use technology to help millions of immigrant children become literate both in their native language and English? How can professionals help ensure that multicultural children will not become technological illiterates? The answers to these questions are not easy to give or implement.

Promoting **multiculturalism** in an early childhood program has implications far beyond the program itself. Multiculturalism influences and affects work habits, interpersonal relations, and a child's general outlook on life. Early childhood professionals must take these multicultural influences into consideration when designing curriculum and instructional processes for the impressionable children they will teach. One way to accomplish the primary goal of multicultural education—to positively change the lives of children and their families—is to infuse multiculturalism into early childhood activities and practices.

WHAT IS MULTICULTURAL INFUSION?

Multicultural infusion means that multicultural education permeates the curriculum to alter or affect the way young children and teachers look at diversity issues. In a larger perspective, infusion strategies are used to ensure that multiculturalism becomes a part of the

TABLE 15.1 Proportion of Minority Students in the Ten Largest Public School Districts of the United States and Puerto Rico

Name of Reporting District	State or Commonwealth	Percentage of Minority Students
New York City Public Schools	NY	84.7
Los Angeles Unified School District	CA	90.1
Puerto Rico Department of Education	PR	100.0
City of Chicago School District	IL	90.4
Dade County School District	FL	88.7
Broward County School District	FL	58.8
Clark County School District	NV	50.1
Houston Independent School District	TX	90.0
Philadelphia City School District	PA	83.3
Hawaii Department of Education	HI	79.6

Source: U.S. Department of Education, National Center for Education Statistics. Available at: www.nces.ed.gov/pubs 2002/100_largest/table_08_1.asp

entire center, school, and home. Infusion processes used by early childhood programs encompass a range of practices that embody the following precepts:

- Foster cultural awareness
- Promote and use conflict resolution strategies
- Teach to children's learning styles
- Welcome parent and community involvement
- Encourage cooperative learning

I discuss each of these practices in detail so you may fully understand how to apply them to your life and program. Keep in mind that as an early childhood professional, you will want to be constantly developing your multicultural awareness, attitudes, knowledge, and skills.

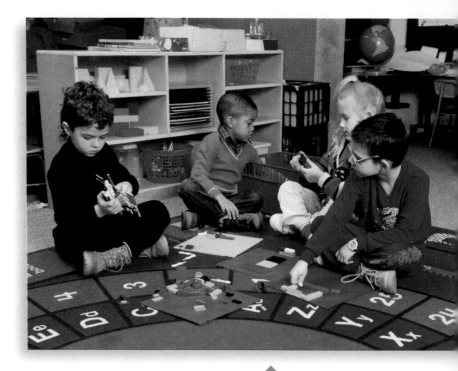

FOSTER CULTURAL AWARENESS

Assess Your Attitudes Toward Children. Before working with children to influence their multicultural awareness and education, it is important for you to first assess your own attitudes toward young children and their families to help ensure that they are multiculturally sensitive. Answer the following questions to help you assess your multicultural awareness level:

- Do you believe that all children can and will learn?
- Are you willing to spend the time and effort necessary to help all children learn?
- Are you willing to teach children individually and according to their cultural and individual learning styles?
- Do you have high expectations for all children?
- Are your expectations for children influenced by their race, socioeconomic status, or gender? If yes, why? What can you do to assure that you can teach all children fairly and equitably?
- Do you feel comfortable with all children?
- Are you familiar with the homes and the communities in which the children you teach live?
- Are you willing to work with the parents and families of children to learn more about their cultures and family educational values and preferences?
- Are you willing and able to infuse multiculturalism into your teaching and classroom?

As you reflect on and honestly answer these questions, it is doubtful that you are able to resoundingly answer yes to all of them. What is important is that you are willing to learn, change, and become the teacher all children need and deserve.

The lesson plan by Pam Johnson, beginning on page 440, provides you with some interesting opportunities to reflect on some things you might include in your teaching:

- Ms. Johnson begins with a thematic planning sheet consisting of a "web" of the topics she will include and possible teaching and learning activities.
- The goals and standards for what children will learn are clearly stated.
- The plans include a cooperative learning focus, which indicates how students will learn together and from each other.

Early childhood educators must consider the diverse needs of students—including gender, ethnicity, race, and socioeconomic factors—when planning learning opportunities for their classes. What are some ways diversity can enrich the curriculum?

For examples of multicultural education programs, go to the Companion Website at **http://www.prenhall.com/morrison**, select chapter 15, then choose the Linking to Learning module to connect to the Multicultural Education Programs site.

The Corcoran/Roberts Peace Corps Partnership Project

The Corcoran/Roberts Peace Corps Partnership Project is an activity of students at Corcoran High School and Roberts Elementary School (K–8) in Syracuse, New York. Since 1983 the students have annually funded a Peace Corps Partnership Project through the Peace Corps. Peace Corps partnerships are small-scale, finite development projects proposed by Peace Corps volunteers in the field based on their villages' needs and requests.

Corcoran High School students select the project they wish to fund and then publish student-drawn note cards, which they sell nationwide to raise the necessary funds. As part of each partnership, the Corcoran students also go to Roberts School next door and work with the youngsters there. They teach a series of lessons about the culture of the village with whom they are working. They also engage the youngsters in an exchange of pictures, stories, and letters between Roberts and the partnership village children. These lessons may include ethnic music, language, children's games, ethnic food preparation, and art projects. Another activity in which the youngsters participate is the collection of pennies for funding a particular aspect of the partnership project. For example, the Roberts students once collected 65,000 pennies and purchased a Braillewriter, which was then shipped to Bossangoa, Central African Republic. The Corcoran/Roberts project that year was funding the construction of a regional school for the blind (the first in all of Central Africa). River blindness is a common disease in Central Africa.

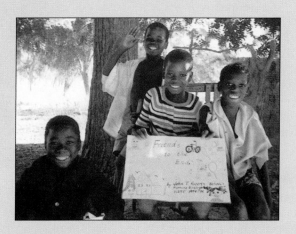

In another project, $10,000 was raised to fund construction of a primary school for nine Dogon villages in Mali. The Roberts students collected 20,000 pennies that year and purchased one dozen soccer balls for the villages that were participating in the primary school. These were the first real soccer balls any of the youngsters had ever had. The school, built of stone, was constructed at the foot of the Bandiagara cliffs. This necessitated bringing the stones down—one at a time, carried on the heads of the villagers—the 600-foot cliffs. The young men of the villages volunteered to bring them down although they were too old to attend the new school. Peace Corps volunteer Kris Hoffer organized a soccer tournament among the nine villages and awarded the new soccer balls to each village upon completion of the school

- Ms. Johnson provides for children's "multiple intelligences" based on Gardner's theory discussed in chapter 4.
- Parent involvement and participation are major parts of Ms. Johnson's planning. She is supporting education in and through family members.

Guidelines and Processes for Fostering Awareness. As an early childhood professional, you must keep in mind that you are the key to a multicultural classroom. The following guidelines can help you in teaching multiculturalism:

construction. This is an example of unexpected dividends paid through the involvement of the young people.

Corcoran students also raised $14,500 to fund construction of a community kindergarten in Mensase, Ghana. The Roberts students exchanged drawings, stories, photographs, and letters with the youngsters of Mensase. They also collected 20,000 pennies, which were used to purchase eighty children's books in Ghana. The children of Mensase sent examples of their toys to the Roberts students.

For the community kindergarten project, the students wrote a series of lesson plans revolving around the Ashanti culture. Peace Corps volunteers are eager to share their knowledge of the culture in which they are immersed, and volunteer Renee Devereux sent the students a lot of materials. There were three lessons of approximately forty-five minutes in length spread over a four-week period. Two high school students taught each class. The introductory lesson included slides of the village and villagers. Subsequent lessons included music lessons, making paper masks, making Kente cloth designs on paper, and teaching traditional dances using a cassette tape of music sent by Renee. Plantain chips (similar to potato chips) were a big hit. The youngsters also drew pictures to illustrate the stories they told (printed beneath the pictures by the teachers).

Over the years, Roberts kindergarten classes have exchanged books of their illustrated stories with each project's youngsters. These books have wallpaper covers, which make

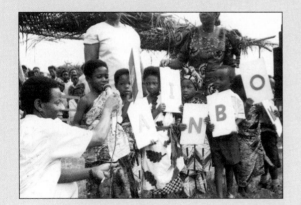

them more durable. The Peace Corps volunteer helps the village youngsters to print their illustrated stories in English.

The involvement of students, especially elementary students, in these small-scale development projects is a win–win–win situation. Schools, from administration to teachers and parents, love the positive publicity generated. The youngsters have a credible sense of accomplishment because of their involvement. They become more globally aware. Through the cross-cultural exchanges the young students begin to appreciate the lives of people from very different cultures and the values that are important to the villagers. The logistics of letter writing, penny collections, and the lessons created around the projects lend themselves to an entire school community involvement. Research projects, posters, and plays can all complement the project. Peace Corps volunteers will send pictures and cultural information throughout the partnership. Students, learning about the new culture and their new friends, can then return home and teach their own families what they have learned or teach lessons to other classes.

Peace Corps Partnership Projects are available for a commitment of as little as a few hundred dollars. The project can be accomplished within a school year, for the Peace Corps will advance the funds as soon as the commitment is received. This allows teachers to develop the cross-cultural exchange even as the project is being accomplished. For classes that don't wish to become involved in fund-raising (although events such as penny drives can easily become total-school activities), the Peace Corps World Wise Schools Program is the answer. This matches classes and schools with Peace Corps volunteers in the field primarily through the exchanges of letters.

Visit the Corcoran/Roberts Peace Corps Partnership Project on the Web at http://www.dreamscape.com/phatpc/peace; the Peace Corps Partnership Program at http://www.peacecorps.gov/contribute/partnership.html; and the World Wise Schools Program at http://www. peacecorps.gov/wws/index.html.

Text and photos contributed by Jim Miller, project adviser.

- *Recognize that all children are unique.* They all have special talents, abilities, and styles of learning and relating to others. Provide opportunities for children to be different and use their abilities.
- *Promote uniqueness and diversity as positive.*
- *Get to know, appreciate, and respect the cultural backgrounds of your children.* Visit families and community neighborhoods to learn more about cultures and religions and the ways of life they engender.
- *Infuse children's culture (and other cultures as well) in your teaching.*

To complete a Program in Action activity, visit the Companion Website at **http://www. prenhall.com/morrison**, select chapter 15, then choose the Program in Action module.

LESSON PLAN

The following lesson plan, Alaska Animals, was contributed by Pam Johnson, 2002 Disney American Teacher Award Honoree. Pam is a first-grade teacher at Koligarek School, Alabama.

Alaska Animals

Goals/Standards

The student will be able to:

- Use simple maps with symbols.
- Measure lengths.
- Estimate weight in pounds.
- Classify objects.

- Recognize ways in which animals move.
- Describe, compare, and classify animals by a variety of means.
- Recognize a variety of land forms.
- Understand interdependence between living things and their environment.
- Use science to understand and describe local environment.

- Use technical skills to compose simple nonfiction or fiction stories.
- Conduct simple research.

- Understand their own cultural traditions.
- Understand that seasonal changes affect living things.
- Know how others lived in the past and what was important to them.

- Understand food pyramid.
- Describe a balanced meal.
- Understand exercise is important to a healthy lifestyle.

- Plan art beforehand.
- Reflect on why people dance.
- Perform simple songs and dance.

Cooperative Learning Focus

- Cooperative learning groups
- Think pair share
- Team stand and share
- Jigsaw problem solving

Multiple Intelligences

- Linguistic, mathematical, spatial, musical, kinesthetic, naturalist, interpersonal, and intrapersonal

Materials and Resources (Items available from District Media Center)

Adventure of Monty the Moose	The Eye of The Needle	Little Walrus Warning
The Alaska Animal Alphabet	More Wild Critters	Denali and Friends
The Alaska Wolf	Amazing Animals	Move Like Animals
Alaska's Three Bears	A Caribou Journey	Count Alaska's colors
Arctic Animal Babies	Tundra Discoveries	Raven and River
Arctic Animals	Walrus on Location	Wild Critters
Baby Animals of the North	Alaska Cookbook	Yup'ik Stories

Deneki: An Alaskan Moose

Elders from the community: Ask elders if they would like to visit the classroom and talk about animals and their traditional uses. Ask the elders to teach native dances to the class.

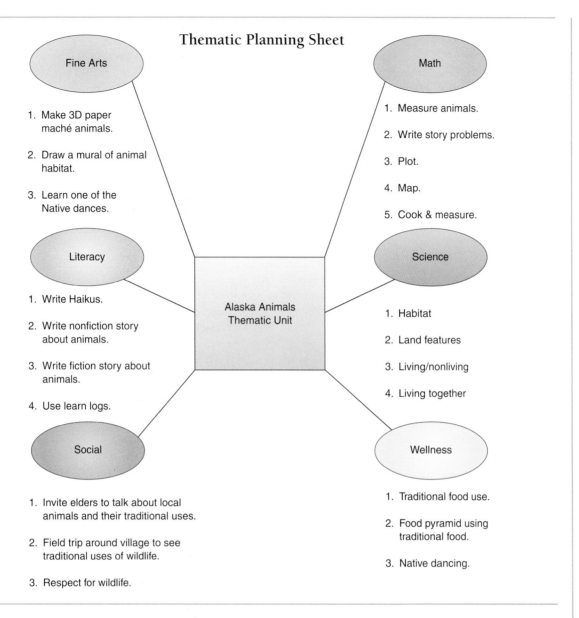

Thematic Planning Sheet

Fine Arts

1. Make 3D paper maché animals.
2. Draw a mural of animal habitat.
3. Learn one of the Native dances.

Literacy

1. Write Haikus.
2. Write nonfiction story about animals.
3. Write fiction story about animals.
4. Use learn logs.

Social

1. Invite elders to talk about local animals and their traditional uses.
2. Field trip around village to see traditional uses of wildlife.
3. Respect for wildlife.

Alaska Animals Thematic Unit

Math

1. Measure animals.
2. Write story problems.
3. Plot.
4. Map.
5. Cook & measure.

Science

1. Habitat
2. Land features
3. Living/nonliving
4. Living together

Wellness

1. Traditional food use.
2. Food pyramid using traditional food.
3. Native dancing.

Parent Presentation Ideas

Each group will present these items about their animal.

- 3D animal
- Habitat mural
- Haikus
- Stories they wrote
- Information poster about traditional uses of their animal

Whole Class Activities

- Native dancing
- Potluck (We will prepare Native Foods to share at the presentation.)
- Special thanks—Each elder that helped will get a gift made by the students and recognition for their help.

- *Use authentic situations to provide for cultural learning and understanding.* For example, a field trip to a culturally diverse neighborhood of your city or town provides children an opportunity for understanding firsthand many of the details about how people conduct their daily lives. Such an experience provides wonderful opportunities for involving children in writing, cooking, reading, and dramatic play activities. What about setting up a market in the classroom?
- *Use authentic assessment activities to assess fully children's learning and growth.* Portfolios (see chapter 11) are ideal for assessing children in nonbiased and culturally sensitive ways. The point is that early childhood professionals should use varied ways of assessing children.
- *Infuse culture into your lesson planning, teaching, and caregiving.* Use all subject areas—math, science, language arts, literacy, music, art, and social studies—to relate culture to all the children and all you do.
- *Be a role model by accepting, appreciating, and respecting other languages and cultures.*
- *Use children's interests and experiences to form a basis for planning lessons and developing activities.* This approach makes students feel good about their backgrounds, cultures, families, and experiences. Also, when children can relate what they are doing in the classroom to the rest of their daily lives, their learning is more meaningful to them.
- *Be knowledgeable about, proud of, and secure in your own culture.* Children will ask about you, and you should share your background with them.

Select Appropriate Instructional Materials.   In addition to assessing your own attitudes and instituting guidelines for infusing personal sensitivity into a multicultural classroom, you need to carefully consider and select appropriate instructional materials to support the infusion of multicultural education. The following three sections offer suggestions.

Multicultural Literature.   Choose literature that emphasizes people's habits, customs, and general living and working behaviors. This approach stresses similarities and differences regarding how children and families live their *whole* lives and avoids merely noting differences or teaching only about habits and customs. Multicultural literature today is more representative of various cultural groups than in the past and provides a more authentic language experience for young children. This literature is written by authors from particular cultures and contains more true-to-life stories and culturally authentic writing styles. The following books are representative of the rich selection now available:

For more information about teaching with multicultural materials, go to the Companion Website at **http:// www.prenhall.com/morrison**, select any chapter, then choose Topic 8 of the ECE Supersite module.

To preview existing and new multicultural education titles for educators, go to the Companion Website at **http://www.prenhall. com/morrison**, select chapter 15, then choose the Linking to Learning module to connect to the Multicultural Book Reviews site.

- *Grannie and the Jumbie: A Caribbean Tale,* by Margaret M. Hurst (HarperCollins, 2001). Emanuel's grandmother is always warning him about the evil Jumbie, a boogeyman. He bravely scoffs at her superstitious lectures until the night when he is almost spirited away. Now, when his grannie talks, Emanuel listens.
- *Quilt Alphabet,* by Lesa Cline-Ransome (Holiday House, 2001). This homespun alphabet book introduces each letter with a quilt block and clever rhyming riddle. From a basket of apples to a zigzagging country road, this ode to country living is pieced together with poetry. A quilt is defined as "A patch of you, a scrap of me, / Pieces of family history, / Common threads stitched from the heart, / Pieces of us in every part."
- *Under the Quilt of Night,* by Deborah Hopkinson (Atheneum, 2002). This historic chronicle traces the escape of a group of slaves and their eventual rescue on the Underground Railroad. Told in prose from the perspective of an adolescent girl, the story explains how quilts were used to mark safehouses. "In most quilts, center squares are red for home and earth," but a quilt with a blue center signals a house that hides runaways.
- *Round Is a Mooncake: A Book of Shapes,* by Rosanne Thong (Chronicle, 2000). A little girl's neighborhood becomes a discovery ground of things round, square, and rectangular. Many of the objects are Asian in origin, others are universal: round rice bowls and a found pebble, square dim sum and pizza boxes, rectangular Chinese lace, and

a very special pencil case. Bright art accompanies this lively introduction to shapes and short glossary explains the cultural significance of the objects featured in the book.

- *The Good Luck Cat,* by Joy Harjo (Harcourt, 2000). According to Aunt Shelly, Woogie is a good luck cat, and he certainly proves it by surviving one scrape after another. But when he doesn't come home, we wonder if this good luck cat's luck has run out. This is a light, charming celebration of a young girl's friendship with a cat. And it's a children's picture book featuring Native American characters where culture isn't the main theme.
- *Shades of Black: A Celebration of Our Children,* by Sandra L. Pinkney (Scholastic, 2000). Using simple poetic language, illuminated by brilliant photographs, this is a remarkable book of affirmation for African-American children. Photographic portraits and striking descriptions of varied skin tones, hair texture, and eye color convey a strong sense of pride in a unique heritage. *Shades of Black* is a joyous celebration of children, as well as a gracious invitation to readers of all ages and cultures to explore and embrace the rich diversity among African Americans.
- *The Three Pigs,* by David Wiesner (Clarion Books, 2001). Once upon a time, three pigs built three houses, out of straw, sticks, and bricks. Along came a wolf, who huffed and puffed. . . . So, you think you know the rest? Think again. It's never safe to assume too much. When the wolf approaches the first house, for example, and blows it in, he somehow manages to blow the pig right out of the story frame. One by one, the pigs exit the fairy tale's border and set off on an adventure of their own.

Themes.   Early childhood professionals may select and teach through thematic units that help strengthen children's understanding of themselves, their culture, and the cultures of others. Several of the lesson plans in this book are theme-based. Thematic choices from a variety of cultures can help children identify cultural similarities and encourage understanding and tolerance, as with the following suggestions:

- Getting to know myself, getting to know others
- What is special about you and me?
- Growing up in the city
- Growing up in the country
- Tell me about Africa (South America, China, etc.)

Personal Accomplishments.   Add to classroom activities, as appropriate, the accomplishments of people from different cultural groups, women of all cultures, and individuals with disabilities.

The following criteria are most important when picking materials for use in a multicultural curriculum for early childhood programs:

- Make sure people of all cultures are represented fairly and accurately.
- Make sure to represent people of color, many cultural groups, and people with exceptionalities.
- Make sure that historic information is accurate and nondiscriminatory.
- Make sure the materials do not include stereotypical roles and language.
- Make sure there is gender equity—that is, that boys and girls are represented equally and in nonstereotypical roles.

Avoid Sexism and Sex-Role Stereotyping.   Current interest in multiculturalism in general and nondiscrimination in particular has also prompted concern about sexism and sex-role stereotyping. **Sexism** is "the collection of attitudes, beliefs, and behaviors which result from the assumption that one sex is superior. *In the context of schools,* the term refers to the collection of structures, policies, practices and activities that overtly or covertly prescribe the development of girls and boys and prepare them for traditional sex roles."[1]

Title IX of the Education Amendments Acts of 1972, as amended by Public Law 93-568, prohibits such discrimination in the schools: "No person in the United States shall, on the

Sexism   Prejudice or discrimination based on sex.

Sexual harassment
Unwelcome sexual behavior
and talk.

basis of sex, be excluded from participation in, be denied the benefits of, or be subjected to discrimination under any education program or activity receiving Federal financial assistance."[2] Since Title IX prohibits sex discrimination in any educational program that receives federal money, early childhood programs as well as elementary schools, high schools, and universities cannot discriminate against males or females in enrollment policies, curriculum offerings, or activities.

You and other early childhood professionals need to be concerned about the roots of sexism and **sexual harassment** and to realize that these practices have their beginnings in practices found in children's early years in homes, centers, and preschools. Early childhood professionals must continue to examine personal and programmatic practices, evaluate materials, and work with parents for the purpose of eliminating sexism and to ensure that girls—indeed, all children—will not be shortchanged in any way.

Parents and teachers can provide children with less restrictive options and promote a more open framework in which sex roles can develop. Following are some ways for you to provide a non–sex-stereotyped environment:

- *Provide opportunities for all children to experience the activities, materials, toys, and emotions traditionally associated with both sexes.* Give boys as well as girls opportunities to experience tenderness, affection, and the warmth of close parent–child and teacher–pupil relationships. Conversely, girls as well as boys should be able to behave aggressively, get dirty, and participate in what are typically considered male activities, such as woodworking and block building.

- *Examine the classroom materials you are using and determine whether they contain obvious instances of sex-role stereotyping.* When you find examples, modify the materials or do not use them. Let publishers know your feelings, and tell other faculty members about them.

- *Examine your behavior to see whether you are encouraging sex stereotypes.* Do you tell girls they cannot empty wastebaskets but they can water the plants? Do you tell boys they should not play with dolls? Do you tell girls they cannot lift certain things in the classroom because they are too heavy for them? Do you say that "boys aren't supposed to cry"? Do you reward only females who are always passive, well behaved, and well mannered?

- *Have a colleague or parent observe you in your classroom to determine what sex-role behaviors you are encouraging.* We are often unaware of our behaviors, and self-correction begins only after someone points out the behaviors to us. Obviously, unless you begin with yourself, eliminating sex-role stereotyping practices will be next to impossible.

- *Determine what physical arrangements in the classroom promote or encourage sex-role stereotyping.* Are boys encouraged to use the block area more than girls? Are girls encouraged to use the quiet areas more than boys? Do children hang their wraps separately— a place for boys and a place for girls? All children should have equal access to all learning areas of the classroom; no area should be reserved exclusively for one sex. In addition, examine any activity and practice that promotes segregation of children by sex or culture. Cooperative learning activities and group work offer ways to ensure that children of both sexes work together.

- *Counsel with parents to show them ways to promote nonsexist child rearing.* If society is to achieve a truly nonsexist environment, parents will be the key factor, for it is in the home that many sex-stereotyping behaviors are initiated and practiced.

You can combat the development of sexist attitudes by encouraging students in your classroom to engage in activities that challenge traditional gender-role stereotypes.

- *Become conscious of words that promote sexism.* For example, in a topic on community helpers, taught in most preschool and kindergarten programs at one time or another, many words carry a sexist connotation. *Fireman, policeman,* and *mailman,* for example, are all masculine terms; nonsexist terms are *firefighter, police officer,* and *mail carrier.* You should examine all your curricular materials and teaching practices to determine how you can make them free from sexism.

- *Examine your teaching and behavior to be sure you are not limiting certain roles to either sex.* Females should not be encouraged to pursue only roles that are subservient, submissive, lacking in intellectual demands, or low paying. You can do the following specific things in your teaching:

  - Give all children a chance to respond to questions. Research consistently shows that teachers do not wait long enough after they ask a question for most children, especially girls, to respond. Therefore, quick responders—usually boys—answer all the questions. By waiting longer, you will be able to respond to more girls' answers.

  - Be an active professional. Just as we want children to engage in active learning, so too professionals should engage in active involvement in the classroom. This helps ensure that you will get to interact with and give attention to all children, not to just a few.

  - Help all children become independent and do things for themselves. Discourage behaviors and attitudes that promote helplessness and dependency. Discourage remarks such as "I can't because I'm not good at . . ."

  - Examine your classroom management and behavioral guidance techniques (see chapter 14). Are you treating both sexes and all cultures fairly and in individual and culturally appropriate ways?

  - Use portfolios, teacher observations, and other authentic means of assessing children's progress (see chapter 3) to provide bias-free assessment. Involving children in the evaluation of their own efforts also is a good way of promoting children's positive images of themselves.

- *Do not encourage children to dress in ways that lead to sex stereotyping.* Females should not be encouraged to wear frilly dresses, then forbidden to participate in an activity because they might get dirty or spoil their clothes. Children should be encouraged to dress so they will be able to participate in a range of both indoor and outdoor activities. This is an area in which you may be able to help parents if they seek your advice by discussing how dressing their child differently can contribute to more effective participation.

Implement an Antibias Curriculum and Activities.   The goal of an *antibias curriculum* is to help children learn to be accepting of others regardless of gender, race, ethnicity, socioeconomic status, and disability. Children participating in an antibias curriculum are comfortable with diversity and learn to stand up for themselves and others in the face of injustice. Additionally, in this supportive, open-minded environment, children learn to construct a knowledgeable, confident self-identity.

Young children are constantly learning about differences and need a sensitive teacher to help them form positive, unbiased perceptions about variations among people. As children color pictures of themselves, for example, you may hear a comment such as, "Your skin is white and my skin is brown." Many teachers are tempted, in the name of equality, to respond, "It doesn't matter what color we are—we are all people." While this remark does not sound harmful, it fails to help children develop positive feelings about themselves. A more appropriate response might be, "Amanda, your skin is a beautiful dark brown, which is just right for you; Christina, your skin is a beautiful light tan, which is just right for you." A comment such as this positively acknowledges each child's different skin color, which is an important step for developing a positive self-concept.

Through the sensitive guidance of caring teachers, children learn to speak up for themselves and others. By living and learning in an accepting environment, children find that

For more information about implementing an antibias curriculum, go to the Companion Website at **http://www.prenhall.com/morrison**, select any chapter, then choose Topic 8 of the ECE Supersite module.

they have the ability to change intolerable situations and can have a positive impact on the future. This is part of what empowerment is all about, and it begins in the home and in early childhood programs. It is important, then, that an antibias curriculum starts in early childhood and continues throughout the school years.

For more information about multiculturalism and content-area instruction, go to the Companion Website at **http://www.prenhall. com/morrison**, select chapter 15, then choose the Linking to Learning module to connect to the Multicultural Awareness in the Language Classroom and Multicultural Perspectives in Mathematics Education sites.

PROMOTE AND USE CONFLICT RESOLUTION STRATEGIES

We all live in a world of conflict. Television and other media bombard us with images of violence, crime, and international and personal conflict. Unfortunately, many children live in homes where conflict and disharmony are ways of life rather than exceptions. Increasingly, early childhood professionals are challenged to help children and themselves resolve conflicts in peaceful ways. For this reason, *conflict resolution strategies* seek to help children learn how to solve problems, disagree in appropriate ways, negotiate, and live in harmony with others.

Part of your goal is to have children reach mutually agreeable solutions to problems without the use of power (fighting, hitting, pushing, shoving, etc.). You may wish to adopt the following strategies for helping children resolve conflicts:

Steps in Using the "No-Lose" Method of Conflict Resolution

1. Identify and define conflict in a nonaccusatory way. ("Vinnie and Rachael, you have a problem. You both want the green paint.")
2. Invite children to participate in fixing the problem. ("Let's think of how to solve the problem.")
3. Generate possible solutions with children. Accept a variety of solutions. Avoid evaluating them. ("Yes, you could both use the same paint cup. . . . You could take turns.")
4. Examine each idea for merits and drawbacks. With children, decide which to try. Thank children for thinking of solutions. ("Jessie, that's a good idea—putting paint in the paper cups. Now both you and Amy can use the green paint at the same time.")
5. Put plan into action. ("You might have to take turns dipping your brushes into the paint. . . . Try your idea.")
6. Follow up. Evaluate how well the solution worked. (Teacher comes back in a few minutes, "Looks like your idea of how to solve your green paint problem really worked.")[3]

Not all children learn in the same way. As a result, it is important to assess each child's learning style and teach each child appropriately. What style of learning works best for you?

▼

TEACH TO CHILDREN'S LEARNING STYLES AND INTELLIGENCES

Every child has a unique learning style. Although every person's learning style is different, we can cluster learning styles for instructional purposes. It makes sense to consider these various styles and account for them in early childhood programs when organizing the environment and developing activities.

Different Children, Different Learning Styles. Learning styles are different approaches to learning. Because children are different, children have different learning styles. "Learning style is the way that students of every age are affected by their (1) immediate environment, (2) own emotionality, (3) sociological needs, (4) physical characteristics, and (5) psychological inclinations when concentrating and trying to master and remember new or difficult information or skills."[4]

Learning styles consist of the following elements:

- *Environmental*—sound, light, temperature, and design
- *Emotional*—motivation, persistence, responsibility, and the need for either structure or choice
- *Sociological*—learning alone, with others, or in a variety of ways (perhaps including media)
- *Physical*—perceptual strengths, intake, time of day or night energy levels, and mobility
- *Psychological*—global/analytic, hemispheric preference, and impulsive/reflective

There are many ways you can provide for children's learning styles while responding appropriately to diversity in your program. For example, Dunn et al. suggest the following ways to adapt the learning environment to children's individual learning styles.[5]

Noise Level.   Provide earplugs or music on earphones (to avoid distractions for those who need quiet); create conversation areas or an activity-oriented learning environment separately from children who need quiet. *Or* establish silent areas: Provide individual dens or alcoves with carpeted sections; suggest earphones without sound or earplugs to insulate against activity and noise.

Light.   Place children near windows or under adequate illumination; add table or desk lamps. *Or* create learning spaces under indirect or subdued light away from windows; use dividers or plants to block or diffuse illumination.

Authority Figures Present.   Place children near appropriate professionals and schedule periodic meetings with them; supervise and check assignments often. *Or* identify the child's sociological characteristics, and permit isolated study if self-oriented and peer groupings if peer oriented, or multiple options if learning in several ways is indicated; interact with collaborative professional.

Visual Preferences.   Use pictures, filmstrips, films, graphs, single-concept loops, transparencies, computer monitors, diagrams, drawings, books, and magazines; supply resources that require reading and seeing; use programmed learning (if student needs structure) and written assignments and evaluations. Reinforce knowledge through tactile, kinesthetic, and then auditory resources. *Or* use resources prescribed under the perceptual preferences that are strong. Use several multisensory resources such as videotapes, sound-filmstrips, television, and tactile/kinesthetic material. Introduce information through child's strongest perceptual preference.

Tactile Preferences.   Use manipulative and three-dimensional materials; resources should be touchable and movable as well as readable; allow children to plan, demonstrate, report, and evaluate with models and other real objects; encourage them to keep written or graphic records. Reinforce through kinesthetic, visual, and then auditory resources. *Or* use resources prescribed under the perceptual preferences that are strong. Use several multisensory resources such as videotapes, sound-filmstrips, television, and real-life experiences such as visits, interviewing, building, designing, and so on. Introduce information through activities such as baking, building, sewing, visiting, or acting; reinforce through visual, auditory, and kinesthetic methods. Introduce information through child's strongest perceptual preference.

Kinesthetic Preferences.   Provide opportunities for real and active experiences in planning and carrying out objectives; visits, projects, acting, and floor games are appropriate activities for such individuals. Reinforce through tactile, visual, and then auditory resources. *Or* use resources prescribed under the preferences that are strong. Use several multisensory resources such as videotapes, sound-filmstrips, television, and tactile/manipulative materials. Introduce information through real-life activities (e.g., planning a part in a play or a trip); reinforce through tactile resources such as electroboards, task cards, learning circles, and so forth; then reinforce further visual and auditory resources.

Mobility.   Provide frequent breaks, assignments that require movement to different locations, and schedules that permit mobility in the learning environment; require results, not immobility. *Or* provide a stationary desk or learning station where most of the child's responsibilities can be completed without requiring excessive movement.

WELCOME PARENT AND COMMUNITY INVOLVEMENT

As an early childhood professional, you will work with children and families of diverse cultural backgrounds. As such you will need to learn about the cultural background of children and families so that you can respond appropriately to their needs. For example, let's take a look at the Hispanic culture and its implications for parent and family involvement.

For more information about family–school relations, go to the Companion Website at **http://www. prenhall.com/morrison**, select any chapter, then choose Topic 10 of the ECE Supersite module.

Throughout Hispanic culture there is a widespread belief in the absolute authority of the school and teachers. In many Latin American countries it is considered rude for a parent to intrude into the life of the school. Parents believe that it is the school's job to educate and the parent's job to nurture and that the two jobs do not mix. A child who is well educated is one who has learned moral and ethical behavior.

Hispanics, as a whole, have strong family ties, believe in family loyalty, and have a collective orientation that supports community life; they have been found to be field dependent with a sensitivity to nonverbal indicators of feeling.[6] Culturally, this is represented by an emphasis on warm, personalized styles of interaction, a relaxed sense of time, and a need for an informal atmosphere for communication. Given these preferences, a culture clash may result when Hispanic students and parents are confronted with the typical task-oriented style of most American teachers.

Although an understanding of the general cultural characteristics of Hispanics is helpful, it is important to not overgeneralize. Each family and child is unique, and care should be taken to not assume values and beliefs just because a family speaks Spanish and is from Latin America. It is important that teachers spend the time to discover the particular values, beliefs, and practices of the families in the community.

Based on this knowledge, you can use the following guidelines to involve Hispanic parents:

- *Use a personal touch.* It is crucial to use face-to-face communication in the Hispanic parents' primary language when first making contact. Written flyers or articles sent home have proven to be ineffective even when written in Spanish. It may also take several personal meetings before the parents gain sufficient trust to actively participate. Home visits are a particularly good way to begin to develop rapport.
- *Use nonjudgmental communication.* To gain the trust and confidence of Hispanic parents, teachers must avoid making them feel they are to blame or are doing something wrong. Parents need to be supported for their strengths, not judged for perceived failings.
- *Be persistent in maintaining involvement.* To keep Hispanic parents actively engaged, activities planned by the early childhood program must respond to a real need or concern of the parents. Teachers should have a good idea about what parents will get out of each meeting and how the meeting will help them in their role as parents.
- *Provide bilingual support.* All communication with Hispanic parents, written and oral, must be provided in Spanish and English. Many programs report that having bicultural and bilingual staff helps promote trust.[7]

- *Provide strong leadership and administrative support.* Flexible policies, a welcoming environment, and a collegial atmosphere all require administrative leadership and support. As with other educational projects and practices that require innovation and adaptation, the efforts of teachers alone cannot bring success to parent involvement projects. Principals must also be committed to project goals.
- *Provide staff development focused on Hispanic culture.* All staff must understand the key features of Hispanic culture and its impact on their students' behavior and learning styles. It is the educator's obligation to learn as much about the children and their culture and background as possible.
- *Conduct community outreach.* Many Hispanic families could benefit from family literacy programs, vocational training, ESL programs, improved medical and dental services, and other community-based social services. A school or early childhood program can serve as a resource and referral agency to support the overall strength and stability of the families.

BILINGUAL EDUCATION PROGRAMS

For most people, *bilingual education* means that children (or adults, or both) will be taught a second language. Some people interpret this to mean that a child's native language (often referred to as the *home language*)—whether English, Spanish, French, Italian, Chinese, Tagalog, or any of the other 125 languages in which bilingual programs are conducted—will tend to be suppressed. For other people, bilingual education means that children will be taught in both the home language and the primary language. The Bilingual Education Act, Title VII of the Elementary and Secondary Education Act (ESEA), sets forth the federal government's policy toward bilingual education:

 For more information about bilingual education, go to the Companion Website at **http://www. prenhall.com/morrison**, select chapter 15, then choose the Linking to Learning module to connect to the National Center for Bilingual Education site.

> The Congress declares it to be the policy of the United States, in order to establish equal educational opportunity for all children and to promote educational excellence (A) to encourage the establishment and operation, where appropriate, of educational programs using bilingual educational practices, techniques, and methods, (B) to encourage the establishment of special alternative instructional programs for students of limited English proficiency in school districts where the establishment of bilingual education programs is not practicable or for other appropriate reasons, and (C) for those purposes, to provide financial assistance to local educational agencies.[8]

REASONS FOR INTEREST IN BILINGUAL EDUCATION.

Diversity is a positive aspect of U.S. society. Ethnic pride and identity have caused renewed interest in languages and a more conscious effort to preserve children's native languages. In the nineteenth and early twentieth centuries, foreign-born individuals and their children wanted to camouflage their ethnicity and unlearn their language because it seemed unpatriotic or un-American; today, however, we hold the opposite viewpoint.

A second reason for interest in bilingual education is an emphasis on civil rights. Indeed, much of the concept of providing children with an opportunity to know, value, and use their heritage and language stems from people's recognition that they have a right to them. Just as extending rights to children with disabilities is very much evident today, so it is with children and their languages, as part of the view of children as people with rights (see chapter 2).

A third reason for interest in bilingual education includes efforts to ban the use of languages other than English in state and municipal activities and prohibit the use of bilingual education to help children learn English. One attempt to curtail the implementation of bilingual programs includes the passage of "English Only" laws by state governments. What these laws mean and what they prohibit varies from state to state. Some declare English as the "official" language of the state; some limit or prohibit provision of non-English language assistance and services; others limit or prohibit bilingual education programs. Currently, 16 states

What Early Childhood Professionals Should Know About Latino Child Development

Early childhood professionals are increasingly asked to understand the needs of children and families from cultures other than their own. One group that is experiencing dramatic growth is the Latino or Hispanic population. From 1980 to 2000, the Latino population has more than doubled. Latinos or Hispanics are defined as persons whose origins are Mexican, Puerto Rican, Cuban, Central or South American, or some other Spanish origin. Mexican-origin individuals represent 64 percent of the population identified by the U.S. Census Bureau as Hispanic. Because the field of early childhood education has a professional responsibility to provide appropriate programs and services to all children, understanding the culture and value orientations of Latinos is important.

In understanding diversity, one should distinguish aspects of development that are *culturally specific* and those aspects that are *universal*, or common to all humans regardless of their cultural background. For example, toilet training will occur for all infants regardless of culture; however, the timing for the appearance of this ability is likely influenced by a culture's expectations for that behavior. Thus, we need to keep in mind both "universal" and "culturally specific" developmental processes in understanding diverse populations.

What should we know about Latinos or Hispanics that is pertinent to the provision of culturally appropriate programs and services? This is not easily answered because Latinos are, in fact, a very heterogeneous group. Latinos are often seen as having a similar family history and maintaining exactly the same set of values. However, this is a simplistic way of thinking about this population. Although Latinos may be similar in their language and possibly religious heritage, there exists other differences such as country of origin, urban/rural differences, migratory histories, and, most importantly, acculturation status. All of these factors need to be considered in understanding how culture influences individual children and families.

One of the most important factors in understanding cultural differences for Latinos is the role of socioeconomic status. Because cultural background and socioeconomic background are highly interrelated, what we think is culturally specific might be more a function of the group's adaptation to their socioeconomic conditions. Research suggests that when social class is similar, some differences between middle-income Anglos and middle-income Latinos decrease. For example, differences are found between low-income Latinos and middle-income Anglo mothers on their styles of interacting with their preschool children on a teaching task. Yet, those differences substantially decrease when comparisons are made between middle-income Latinos and middle-income Anglos. When socioeconomic status is held constant, both groups perform similarly.

Why should social class matter in understanding cultural differences? Social class standing is an important determinant for such resources as the quality of housing, employment opportunities, medical services, and most significantly, educational opportunities. Unfortunately, Latinos as a group have higher rates of poverty than many non-Latino groups. In much of the research on Latinos, low-income status is often mixed up with cultural factors making it difficult to understand the influence of culture. Some experts argue that it is not possible to separate effects of culture from socioeconomic class because they highly influence each other.

For Latinos residing in the United States, level of acculturation also plays an important role. Acculturation refers to the degree to which an individual is able to function effectively in the dominant culture. Acculturation includes the ability to speak the language of the dominant culture and have knowledge of the dominant culture's values and cultural expressions (e.g., foods, arts). These factors play a major role in determining an individual's ability to adapt to and function in the dominant society. However, it is important to note that acculturation is not a linear process where, as one becomes more acculturated, the values and attitudes of one's native culture are relinquished. It is possible that as individuals become more acculturated, they can function effectively in both their own culture and the broader dominant culture. This is referred to as biculturalism and is viewed by many as the ideal outcome of the acculturation process. Therefore, in order to effectively understand and service Latinos, the early childhood professional needs to recognize where children and families are located within the acculturation spectrum. More importantly, when working with families, it is often the case that children and their parents will differ on acculturation, creating stronger than average generational divisions.

Early childhood professionals need to consider how parental orientation may differ from the specific goals and objectives of a particular intervention program. When working with immigrant families, it is sometimes appropriate to indicate how the expectations of the school explicitly differ from the group's orientation. For many immigrant families, adaptation and innovation are a way of life, and accepting different ways of doing things is part and parcel of the immigrant experience. However, for second-generation or more acculturated groups reared in the United States, such explicit contrast might not suffice. In these instances, practitioners must become familiar with the degree of acculturation that characterizes the group and adjust their services accordingly.

Another important factor in understanding Latino child development is parental orientation to children. Specifically, early childhood professionals should ask themselves, what are the child-rearing practices that parents use, and what are parents' overall goals for their child's development? Previous research on parental beliefs suggests that cultural background is an important determinant of parental ideas. For example, in research with low-income immigrant Latino parents, expectations for their children's skill development differs from that of Latinos born in the United States. This research suggests that foreign-born Latinos perceive the behavioral capabilities of young children as developing later than do U.S.-born Latinos. It may be that foreign-born Latinos have a different perspective on children's development that is more maturational in nature. That is, non–U.S.-born Latino parents may see young children's development as occurring naturally and not requiring much direct intervention and stimulation. Thus, the early emphasis on cognitive stimulation promoted in the United States may be somewhat inconsistent with their expectations.

A maturational approach to child rearing may stem from the social and historic backgrounds of Latino groups living in the United States. In cultures in which children are expected to take part in the activities of adults, such as sibling care-taking and the economic maintenance of the family, certain parent–child patterns will emerge. Thus, in more rural, traditional cultures, parents may socialize their children by stressing observation and immediate assistance in task development rather than the explicit instruction valued by middle-class U.S. parents.

The often-referenced proposition that parents are the first teachers of their children is generally acceptable within the context of early development. Yet the role of parents as teachers of school-related tasks may vary in families of Latino heritage. The role of parents as teachers of their own children may not be congruent with a family's cultural values, perceptions of parenting, and socioeconomic reality. For example, Latino children more than Anglo children are less likely to live in nuclear families in which the mother has the exclusive responsibility for child rearing. In Latino families, siblings may play both a caretaking role and a mentoring role to younger children by helping them with their school work. Thus, the focus on the mother as the exclusive socializer of their child may overlook the important role of other family members. Early childhood professionals need to understand a family's value orientation about child development, recognize and be sensitive to parental perceptions about "teaching" young children, and see other members of the family as important contributors to a child's development.

Latinos hold certain values and beliefs that relate to childhood socialization. The following sections present an overview of important core values and beliefs that will vary in individual families depending on their acculturation level, socioeconomic standing, and ethnic loyalty. It is very important to see these core values as broad generalizations subject to adaptations to local conditions.

FAMILIALISM

This value is viewed as one of the most important culture-specific values of Latinos. Familialism refers to strong identification and connection to the immediate and extended family. Behaviors associated with familialism include strong feelings of loyalty, reciprocity, and solidarity. Familialism is manifested through the following: (1) feelings of obligation to provide both material and emotional support to the family, (2) dependence on relatives for help and support, and (3) reliance on relatives as behavioral and attitudinal role models.

RESPETO

Associated with familialism is the cultural concept of *respeto,* an extremely important underlying tenet of interpersonal interaction. Basically, *respeto* ("respect") refers to the deference ascribed to various members of the family or society because of their position. Respect is accorded to the position and not necessarily the person. For example, respect is expected toward elders, parents, older siblings within the family, and teachers, clergy, nurses, and doctors outside the family. With respect comes deference;

that is, the person will not question the individual in an authority position, will exhibit courteous behavior in front of them, and will appear to agree with information presented to them by the authority figure.

BIEN EDUCADO

A person exhibiting the characteristics associated with *respeto* is said to be *bien educado*. Important here is that the term *educado* (educated) refers not to formal education but to the acquisition of appropriate social skills and graces within the Latino cultural context. For traditional Latinos, receiving a degree from a prestigious university would not qualify one as well educated. A well-educated individual demonstrates proper social behavior as defined by core cultural values.

By both acknowledging and honoring important cultural values and beliefs the early childhood professional communicates respect towards children and families. Taken a step further, the modification of professional practice to account for cultural differences, although challenging, is even a more critical component. When working with Latino groups, it is suggested that the early childhood professional demonstrate high degrees of courtesy, understand that indirect communication on the part of the child and parent is a reflection of *respeto* to teachers as authority figures, and view the broader family configuration as an important resource for understanding Latino family dynamics. Within this general framework, the professional must accommodate individual differences and local community conditions.

Contributed by Marlene Zepeda, Ph.D., Professor, Department of Child and Family Studies, California State University, Los Angeles.

have "English Only" laws. In addition, in some states such as California (Proposition 227) and Arizona (Proposition 203) voters have passed state statues that specifically prohibit native language instruction in the public schools for most childrent with limited English proficiency.

Yet another reason for bilingual interest is the number of people who speak a language other than English. According to the Census Bureau, 47 million, or about one in five, residents of the United States speak a language other than English, with Spanish now the second most common language other than English. Table 15.2 shows the twenty most common languages (other than English) spoken in U.S. homes. Pay particular note to fastest-growing languages, such as Tagalog and Vietnamese. Taken as a group, the Asian school-age population is expected to double by the year 2020.

These data show that the chances are increasing that you will work with parents, children, and families in a language other than English. They also give you some idea what languages parents and children you work with will speak. Moreover, these increases will necessitate a need to develop culturally appropriate material and activities. As individual professionals and as a body, we cannot ignore the need for appropriate curriculum materials for children of all cultures. To do so adds to the risk of language-minority children being cut off from mainstream life and from the "American dream." Finally, there is a need to develop training programs for early childhood professionals that will enable them to work in culturally sensitive ways with parents, families, and children.

All classrooms must be places where people of all cultures, races, socioeconomic backgrounds, religions, and both genders are welcomed and accepted. If students learn to embrace diversity within the classroom, they will also embrace diversity outside of it.

PROGRAMS FOR STUDENTS WITH LIMITED ENGLISH PROFICIENCY

Early childhood programs and schools can make a number of responses to English language learning for children with limited English proficiency (LEP). Programs for the education of English language learners are shown in Figure 15.2 on page 454. Review these now. Which of these programs do you like the best? Which one of these programs would you select for your school?

ISSUES IN BILINGUAL EDUCATION

As you might expect, programs for helping children learn English are controversial. Critics of immersion programs assert that when the fo-

TABLE 15.2 The Top Twenty Languages Other than English Most Commonly Spoken at Home

Language	Total Speakers over Five Years Old
Spanish	28,101,052
Chinese	2,022,143
French	1,643,838
German	1,383,442
Tagalog	1,224,241
Vietnamese	1,009,627
Italian	1,008,370
Korean	894,063
Russian	706,242
Polish	667,414
Arabic	614,582
Portuguese / Portuguese Creole	564,630
Japanese	477,997
French Creole	453,368
Other Indic Languages	439,289
African Languages	418,505
Greek	365,436
Hindi	317,057
Persian	312,085
Urdu	262,900

Source: U.S. Census Bureau, Census 2000 Summary File 3, Matrix PCT10. Available at: http://factfinder.census.gov

cus is only on teaching English, children are at risk for losing the ability to speak and use their native language. On the other hand, proponents of immersion programs maintain that English is the language of schooling and U.S. society, and it is in children's best interests to learn English as quickly and fluently as possible. Further, they maintain that it is the parents' responsibility to help maintain native language and culture. For their part, parents want their children to be successful in both school and society. Some regret that their children have not maintained their native language because of the role it plays in culture and religion.

Critics of transitional bilingual programs maintain that it takes children too long to learn English and that it is too costly to try and maintain a child's native language. On the other hand, proponents of transitional programs say it makes sense to help children learn English while preserving native language and culture.

 To take an online self-test on this chapter's contents, go to the Companion Website at **http://www. prenhall.com/morrison**, select chapter 15, then choose the Self-Test module.

TRENDS IN MULTICULTURAL EDUCATION

As with most areas of early childhood education, we can identify trends that will affect multicultural curricula, programs, and practices. The following trends, and others to come, will affect how you teach young children:

- Multicultural curricula are becoming more pluralistic and include knowledge and information about many cultures. Children learn to look at the world through the eyes of other cultures and ethnic groups. As a result, more children will examine a full range of cultures rather than looking at only two or three, as is often the current practice.
- More early childhood teachers are recognizing that just because children are young does not mean that they cannot learn about multicultural perspectives. Consequently, multicultural activities and content are being included in curricula from the time children enter preschool programs. For example, kindergarten children might be encouraged to look at Thanksgiving through the eyes of both Native Americans and Pilgrims instead of being taught only the Pilgrims' point of view.

 To complete a Program in Action activity, visit the Companion Website at **http://www. prenhall.com/morrison**, select chapter 15, then choose Program in Action module.

Program	Description	Goal
English as a second language (ESL)	Students receive specified periods of instruction aimed at the development of English language skills, with a primary focus on grammar, vocabulary, and communication rather that academic content areas. Academic content is addressed through mainstream instruction, where no special assistance is provided.	English language fluency
Structured immersion (or "sheltered immersion")	Students are limited-English proficient, usually from different language backgrounds. Instruction is in English, with an adjustment made to the level of English so that subject matter is more easily understood. Typically, there is no native language support.	English language fluency
Transitional bilingual education	Most students are English language learners. They receive some degree of instruction through the native language. However, within the program there is a rapid shift toward using primarily English.	Transition to English as rapidly as possible
Maintenance bilingual education	Most students are English language learners and from the same language background. They receive significant amounts of instruction in the native language.	Academic proficiency in both languages
Two-way bilingual programs	About half of students are native speakers of English; the other half are English language learners from the same language group. Instruction is in both languages.	Proficiency in both languages
English language development or ESL Pull-Out	Students are usually at beginning-level proficiency. Students are integrated in mainstream, English-only classrooms in other subjects with no assistance. Students are pulled-out for instruction aimed at developing English grammar, vocabulary, and communication skills, rather than academic content.	English language fluency
Submersion with primary language support	Used when only a few students in each grade level are English language learners. Bilingual teachers tutor small groups of students by reviewing particular lessons covered in mainstream classes, using students' primary language.	English language fluency

FIGURE 15.2 Types of Programs for English Language Learners

As you can see, there are many types of programs for English language learners. Which type, or combination of types, a state or district chooses to use depends on many things, such as funding, availability of staff, and beliefs about how to best promote English language learning.

Sources: K. Hakuta, Population Characteristics, Social Goals, and Educational Treatments for English Language Learning Students, 1999. Available at http://www.stanford.edu/~hakuta/Docs/BOTAForum. PDF; R. Linquanti, Types of Instructional Program Models. WestEd, 1999. Available at http://www.wested.org/policy/pubs/fostering/originals/models.doc

The Chinese American International School of San Francisco

THE SCHOOL: DESCRIPTION AND PHILOSOPHY

The Chinese American International School (CAIS) of San Francisco was established in 1981 by a multiethnic group of parents, educators, and civic leaders. It remains the nation's only full-time school from prekindergarten through eighth grade offering instruction in English and Mandarin Chinese as equal languages in all subjects.

The school's mission emphasizes fluency in both English and Mandarin Chinese, internationalism, intellectual flexibility, and the development of character, emotional, and social maturity as a foundation for active participation and leadership in the modern world.

No prior Chinese language knowledge is necessary for children to enter the program. Children of every ethnicity are enrolled in the school, with 95 percent of the families speaking no Mandarin Chinese at home.

The program is a 50/50 "foreign language immersion" program whereby all subjects in the curriculum are taught in and through Chinese Mandarin. Chinese Mandarin is an equal language of instruction and communication with English, and not simply the object of study itself, as in traditional foreign language classes.

Parents gravitate to this program for several different reasons: Asian Americans of second, third, or fourth generation seek an education with a link to their cultural and historical heritage; international business professionals want their children to enjoy the advantage of fluency in the language and culture; families who have studied research results send their children to the school for the social and cognitive benefits of bilingual education.

THE PREKINDERGARTEN AND KINDERGARTEN CHILDREN

Entering students in prekindergarten are immediately immersed in both English and Mandarin Chinese so that by the completion of kindergarten they have developed

basic proficiency in both languages. Each class is taught by an English teacher and a Chinese teacher with the help of teaching assistants. All teachers are native speakers of the language they use for instruction.

The English kindergarten curriculum utilizes the Montessori method, allowing careful attention to each child's developmental level and individual learning style. Through lessons and everyday life skill experiences, the children develop a fine sense of order and enhanced ability to concentrate, following a complex sequence of steps. Hands-on learning materials make abstract concepts clear and concrete. Along with the opportunity to explore, it teaches them to be independent, responsible, caring individuals.

The Chinese prekindergarten and kindergarten curriculum provides similar opportunities for the children to grow and learn. It focuses on social interaction skills and respect for others as the children acquire listening and speaking skills in the foreign language. The Chinese immersion curriculum is concrete, multisensory, hands-on, and project oriented. A science class on flotation, for example, would require children to test and record flotation of real objects, enabling them to learn the objects' names as well as to express concepts related to flotation in the Chinese language.

In a typical school day, children will sing dramatized songs, produce art and craft projects, play games, listen to stories, and familiarize themselves with some written characters. The teacher uses Chinese exclusively, making use of movements, facial expressions, voice inflections, pictures, toys, and a myriad of props to ensure comprehension and participation. Children are allowed to demonstrate their understanding in multiple ways.

Together, the Chinese and English teachers in the prekindergarten programs encourage children to organize, hypothesize, explore, invent, discover, and test their experiences. An emphasis is placed on the development of each child's creativity, concentration, initiative, self-confidence, self-discipline, imagination, and love of learning. This lays the foundation for a challenging elementary school curriculum that emphasizes both oral and written communication in the two languages.

THE ELEMENTARY CURRICULUM

In elementary school, science, social studies, language arts, and mathematics share equal prominence in both the English and Chinese classes. In a fifty–fifty bilingual immersion program, students spend half a day in an English classroom, learning in much the same way as students in a monolingual school would do. Then, in the second part of the day, they will enter a different classroom, filled with Chinese writing and media. They then study subjects

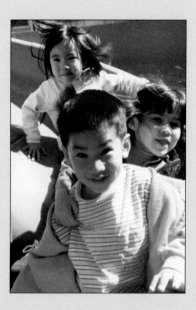

from the Chinese teacher, just as they did in the morning, but expressing themselves in Chinese. On the following day, the model repeats itself, beginning with Chinese in the morning and English in the afternoon.

Close coordination between the English and the Chinese teachers allows the development of common themes for study materials and cultural celebrations. Teachers reinforce—but do not repeat or translate—each other's activities. For instance, while the Chinese teacher assumes the responsibility for the celebration of Chinese festivals such as Chinese New Year, the English teacher leads the celebration of American holidays like Thanksgiving. In the course of the celebrations, children can learn language and content simultaneously. Besides immersion in the culture, they acquire second-language vocabulary through cooking, costume designing, and dramatization of events.

PROFESSIONAL DEVELOPMENT

Current enrollment in the new San Francisco Civic Center campus has grown to four hundred students, with most grade levels incorporating multiple sections. The earliest graduates of the Chinese American International School are now enrolled in universities throughout the United States, most continuing their Chinese studies. Alumni in high school regularly serve as counselors and aides during the school's summer session. Summer sessions also serve as training periods for new faculty who work closely with a master/mentor teacher for several years before assuming full curricular responsibility.

The growing interest in teaching Chinese language at all age levels, and in the elementary curriculum in particular, led to the development of a separate unit of the school devoted to teacher training and curricular development. The Institute for Teaching Chinese Language and Culture is supported by two national foundations in its role as the creator of a graduate training program in the CAIS immersion methodology. The elementary school serves as the laboratory practicum for teachers coming for training from throughout the United States and Asia.

Visit the Chinese American International School on the Web at http://wwww.cie-cais.org/.

Text contributed by teacher Juliana Carnes and principal Shirley Lee; photos courtesy Emily Ching.

Helping English Language Learners Succeed

My attempts to learn Spanish have given me a lot of empathy for English language learners. Perhaps you have had the same experiences of frustration with comprehension, pronunciation, and understandable communication. English language learners face these same problems and others. Many come from low socioeconomic backgrounds. Others come to this country lacking many of the early literacy and learning opportunities we take for granted.

Many school districts across the country have seen their numbers of English language learners skyrocket. For example, in the Winston-Salem/Forsyth School District in North Carolina, more than 8 percent of the 47,000 student population are English learners, representing 52 different native languages.

The chances are great that you will have English learners in your classroom wherever you choose to teach. There are a number of approaches you can use to assure that your children will learn English and that they will be academically successful.

Judith Lessow-Hurly, a bilingual expert, says, "It's important to create contexts in which kids exchange meaningful messages. Kids like to talk to other kids, and that's useful."[*] Lessow-Hurley also supports sheltered instruction (see Figure 15.2). She says, "A lot of what we call 'sheltering' is simply good instruction—all kids benefit from experiential learning, demonstrations, visuals, and routines. A lot of sheltering is also common sense—stay away from idioms, speak slowly and clearly, [and] find ways to repeat yourself."[†] Here are some other tips Lessow-Hurley offers for assisting language learners:

- *Engage cooperative groups of English language learners and English speakers in common tasks.* This gives students a meaningful context for using English.
- *Develop content around a theme.* The repetition of vocabulary and concepts reinforces language and ideas and gives ELLs better access to content.
- *Allow students nonverbal ways to demonstrate knowledge and comprehension.* For example, one teacher has early primary students hold up cardboard "lollipops" (green or red side forward) to indicate yes or no to questions.
- *Don't constantly correct students' departure from Standard English.* It's better to get students talking; they acquire accepted forms through regular use and practice. A teacher can always paraphrase a student's answer to model Standard English.
- *Consider using visual aides and hand-on activities to deliver content.* Information is better retained when a variety of senses are called upon.
- *Use routines as a way to reinforce language.* This practice increases the comfort level of second language learners; they then know what to expect and associate the routine with the language.[‡]

---

[*]Curriculum Update (Fall 2002) Acquiring English: Schools seek ways to strengthen language learning. p.6. Association for Curriculum Development.

[†] Ibid, p.6.

[‡] Ibid, p.7.

To complete an activity related to this topic, go to the Companion Website at **http://www. prenhall.com/morrison**, select chapter 15, then choose the Diversity Tie-In module.

- Many early childhood professionals are being challenged to preserve children's natural reactions to others' differences before they adopt or are taught adult stereotypical reactions. Young children are, in general, understanding and accepting of differences in others.
- Increasing amounts of materials have become available to aid in teaching multicultural education. The amount and kind of multicultural materials will continue to increase, so teachers will have ever more decisions to make regarding what kind of materials they want and can use. Because not all materials are of equal value or worth, this abundance will mean that professionals will need to be increasingly diligent when selecting appropriate materials for young children.
- There is a growing recognition that effective multicultural education is good for all. Whereas in the past some teachers and parents have resisted multicultural teaching, more and more the public is accepting and supportive of teaching multicultural education to all children.

For additional Internet resources or to complete an online activity for this chapter, go to the Companion Website at **http://www. prenhall.com/morrison**, select chapter 15, then choose the Linking to Learning or Making Connections module.

While we have a long way to go to ensure that all classrooms and curricula provide for children's multicultural needs, we are making progress. You can be at the forefront of making even greater advances by educating both yourself and young children for living in a diverse society.

ACTIVITIES FOR FURTHER ENRICHMENT

APPLICATIONS

1. The classroom environment and certain educational materials may promote sexism, and they play a powerful role in sex-role stereotyping. Examine the environment of selected classrooms and homes to determine the extent of sexist practices. Make recommendations based on your findings for minimizing or eliminating any such practices you find.
2. Effective educational programs provide children with opportunities to develop an understanding of other persons and cultures. Consider how you would accomplish the following objectives in your classroom:
   a. Provide children with firsthand, positive experiences with different cultural groups.
   b. Help children reflect on and think about their own cultural group identity.
   c. Help children learn how to obtain accurate information about other cultural groups.

FIELD EXPERIENCES

1. In addition to the books mentioned in this chapter, select ten children's books that have multicultural content. Decide how you would use these materials to promote awareness and acceptance of diversity. Read these books to children and get their reactions.
2. Survey ten teachers and your classmates, asking them what the term *multicultural* means. Ask them to share with you activities to promote multiculturalism. Put these activities in your teaching file.

RESEARCH

1. Examine children's books and textbooks to determine instances of sexism. What recommendations would you make to change such practices?
2. Stories and literature play an important role in transmitting to children information about themselves and what to expect in life.
   a. What books and literature played an important role in your growing up? In what way?

b. Identify five children's books that you think would be good to use with children and indicate why you think so.

READINGS FOR FURTHER ENRICHMENT

Bennett, C. I. *Comprehensive Multicultural Education: Theory and Practice*, 5th ed. Boston: Allyn & Bacon, 2003.

Provides teachers the historical background, basic terminology, and social science concepts of multicultural education. Also provides a curriculum model with six goals and numerous lesson plans illustrating how each goal can be implemented in the classroom.

Brown, S. C., and Kysilka, M. L. *Applying Multicultural and Global Concepts in the Classroom and Beyond.* Boston: Allyn & Bacon, 2002.

Enables teachers to apply multicultural knowledge in their classrooms, schools, and communities. Helps teachers transform their practice into culturally relevant teaching.

Colella, V., Klopfer, E. and Resnick, M. *Embracing Identities in Early Childhood Education: Diversities and Possibilities.* New York: Teachers College Press, 2001.

Drawing on the work of early childhood teachers and teacher educators, this edited volume provides examples of creative ways in which practitioners and theorists are rethinking their work. Grounded in principles of equity, difference, and the recognition of racial, ethnic, and sexual diversity, the book opens possibilities for thought and action. The contributors provide a range of thinking, theorizing, and practical applications on topical issues in the field such as equity and fairness in observing young children and gender identities in the early years.

Flor Ada, A. *A Magical Encounter: Latino Children's Literature in the Classroom*, 2nd ed. Boston: Allyn & Bacon, 2003.

Brings literature to the classroom as a vehicle for language and concept development, for creative expression, and for the development of higher thinking skills.

Howes, C. *Teaching 4- to 8-Year-Olds: Literacy, Math, Multiculturalism, and Classroom Community.* Baltimore: Paul H. Brookes Publishing, 2003.

Education professionals explain developmentally appropriate teaching practices in four crucial areas: literacy, mathematics, multiculturalism, and classroom community.

Jones, T. G., and Fuller, M. L. *Teaching Hispanic Children.* Boston: Allyn & Bacon, 2003.

This text presents information about the role of national origins and cultural backgrounds in teaching and learning and discusses why it is important for teachers to know about culture in general, and about Hispanic cultural groups in particular.

Tiedt, P. L., and Tiedt, I. M. *Multicultural Teaching: A Handbook of Activities, Information, and Resources*, 6th ed. Boston: Allyn & Bacon, 2002.

Multicultural Teaching provides activities and information designed to enable the teacher to explore the many kinds of diversity in the classroom. The authors guide readers to examine their own diversity first in order to better understand how diversity affects everyone. It presents model lesson plans, fully developed thematic units, and a variety of instructional strategies, as well as a wealth of resources that support multicultural teaching.

LINKING TO LEARNING

Culturally & Linguistically Appropriate Services (CLAS)
http://www.clas.uiuc.edu/

In collaboration with many colleagues representing diverse cultural and linguistic roots the CLAS Early Childhood Research Institute collects and describes early childhood/early intervention resources that have been developed across the United States for children with disabilities and their families and the service providers who work with them. The materials and resources available on this site reflect the intersection of culture and language, disabilities, and child development.

The Multicultural Pavilion
http://www.edchange.org/multicultural/

The Multicultural Pavilion strives to provide resources for educators, students, and activists to explore and discuss multicultural education; facilitates opportunities for educators to work toward self-awareness and development; and provides forums for educators to interact and collaborate toward a critical, transformative approach to multicultural education.

National Association for Multicultural Education
http://www.nameorg.org/

NAME is an organization that brings together individuals and groups with interests in multicultural education from all levels of education, different academic disciplines, and diverse educational institutions and occupations. There are six points of consensus regarding multicultural education that are central to NAME's philosophy, and serve as NAME's goals: to respect and appreciate cultural diversity, to promote the understanding of unique cultural and ethnic heritage, to promote the development of culturally responsible and responsive curricula, to facilitate acquisition of the attitudes, skills, and knowledge to function in various cultures, to eliminate racism and discrimination in society, and to achieve social, political, economic, and educational equity.

The National Clearinghouse for English Language Acquisition
http://www.ncela.gwu.edu/

NCELA, the National Clearinghouse for English Language Acquisition and Language Instruction Educational Programs (formerly NCBE, the National Clearinghouse for Bilingual Education) is funded by the U.S. Department of Education's Office of English Language Acquisition, Language Enhancement & Academic Achievement for Limited English Proficient Students (OELA, formerly OBEMLA) to collect, analyze, and disseminate information relating to the effective education of linguistically and culturally diverse learners in the United States.

Multicultural Awareness in the Language Classroom
http://www.wfi.fr/blair

This site contains excellent sources for language arts and English teachers.

Multicultural Book Reviews
http://www.isomedia.com/homes/jmele/homepage.html

This is a useful site for educators to preview existing and new titles in multicultural education.

Multicultural Education Programs
http://eric-web.tc.columbia.edu/families/index.html

This site provides examples of various multicultural education programs throughout the United States.

Multicultural Perspectives in Mathematics Education
http://jwilson.coe.uga.edu/DEPT/Multicultural/mathED.html

Explores multicultural dimensions of mathematics, a field often regarded as difficult to teach multiculturally.

National Multicultural Institute
http://nmci.org

This site is operated by the Washington-based National Multicultural Institute and explores many facets of diversity.

ENDNOTES

[1] *Federal Register* (August 11, 1975), 33803.

[2] *Federal Register* (June 4, 1975), 24128.

[3] Marion, Marian. *Guidance of Young Children*, 6th ed. (Upper Saddle River, NJ: Merrill/Prentice Hall, 2003), p. 58.

[4] Cabo, Marie, Dunn, Rita, and Dunn, Kenneth. *Teaching Students to Read Through Their Individual Learning Styles* (Boston: Allyn & Bacon, 1991), 2.

[5] Dunn, Rita, Dunn, Kenneth, and Price, Gary. *Learning Styles Inventory (LSI)* (Lawrence, KS: Price Systems, 1987), 14–19. Adapted by permission.

[6] Williams, N. *The Mexican American Family* (Dix Hills, NY: General Hill, 1990).

[7] Espinosa, L. *Hispanic Parent Involvement in Early Childhood Programs* (Washington, DC: Office of Educational Research and Improvement, 1995).

[8] Statute 2372, Section 703. Bilingual Education Act, Title VII of the Elementary Secondary Education Act, Statute 2268, Vol. 92 (November 1978).

Chapter 16

The education of all children, regardless of background or disability . . . must always be a national priority.

—PRESIDENT GEORGE W. BUSH

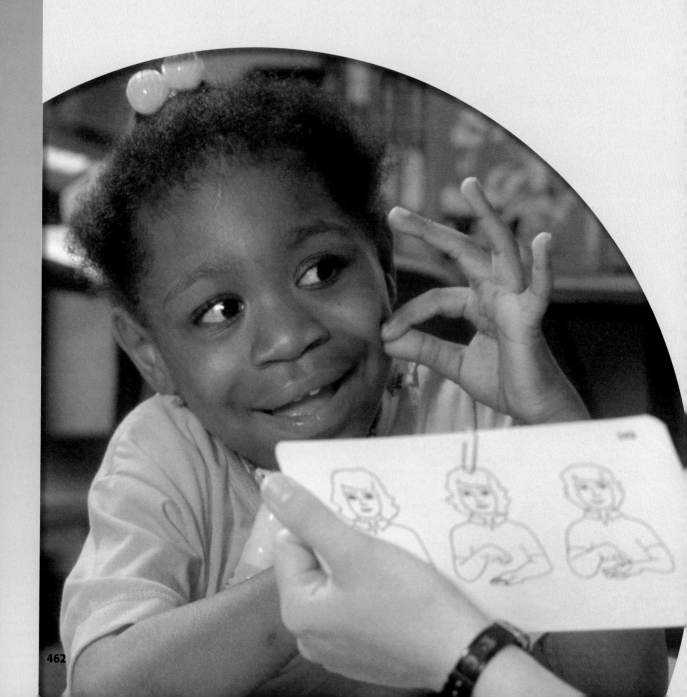

Children with Special Needs

Appropriate Education for All

Focus Questions

- What are reasons for the current interest in educating children with special needs?

- What are the legal, political, moral, and social bases for mainstreaming and full inclusion of children in early childhood programs?

- What issues relate to teaching children with special needs?

- How do programs for the gifted meet children's needs?

- What is the role of the early childhood professional in identifying and reporting child abuse?

Children with special needs are in every program, school, and classroom in the United States. As an early childhood professional, you will teach students who have a variety of special needs. They may come from low-income families or various racial and ethnic groups; they may have exceptional abilities or disabilities. Students with special needs are often discriminated against because of their disability, socioeconomic background, language, ethnicity, or gender. You and your colleagues will be challenged to provide for all students an education that is appropriate to their physical, intellectual, social, and emotional abilities and to help them achieve their best. Your challenge includes learning as much as you can about the special needs of children and collaborating with other professionals to identify and develop teaching strategies, programs, and curricula for them. Most of all, you need to be a strong advocate for meeting all children's individual needs.

As we begin our study of children with special needs, let's examine the Portraits of Kenly Marie and Jake and reflect on how providing appropriate services has helped them grow and develop. At the same time, review Figure 16.1, "A Kaleidoscope of Children With Disabilities." Also, discuss with your colleagues the questions accompanying Figure 16.1.

CHILDREN WITH DISABILITIES

Children with special needs and their families need education and services that will help them succeed. You will be a part of the process of seeing that they receive such services. Unfortunately, quite often children with disabilities are not provided appropriate services and fail to reach their full potential. This is one reason for laws to help ensure that schools and teachers will have high expectations for them and that they will have special education and related services. The federal government has passed many laws protecting and promoting the rights and needs of children with disabilities. One of the most important federal laws is PL 101-476, the Individuals With Disabilities Education Act (IDEA), passed in 1990. Congress has periodically updated IDEA, with the latest revision in 1999.

Companion Website

To review the chapter focus questions online, go to the Companion Website at **http:// www.prenhall.com/ morrison** and select chapter 16.

With Appropriate Interventions, Success Comes Naturally!

Kenly Marie of Farmington, Utah, graduated from Knowlton Elementary Preschool in the Davis School District. Kenly, age 5½, has Down syndrome and has completed her three years of preschool in an inclusive setting with a remarkably devoted teacher, Mrs. Chris Mooney.

Shortly after her birth, Kenly began receiving early intervention services through a program at Utah State University, including occupational, physical, and speech therapy. She completed her early intervention years in Davis County. Days after her third birthday, Kenly transitioned to the Davis District preschool program. Her mother was concerned that Kenly would be "in over her head" at preschool with her typical peers because of her delays. At age 3, Kenly was not walking, had limited speech, and was still in diapers.

Instead, Kenly rose to the challenge. Utilizing her talent to model others' behavior, Kenly realized she, too, should learn to walk, and did so within two months of beginning preschool. Her expressive language began blooming as she interacted with typical peers, and this progress was strengthened with speech therapy sessions within the classroom. She follows the classroom routine, sings along with all the songs, says the Pledge of Allegiance, is toilet trained, and has begun to grasp what behaviors are socially appropriate through her interaction with the other kids.

The laws under IDEA have helped Kenly build a firm foundation upon which she will build her life. Kenly is now excited about attending kindergarten in her neighborhood elementary school, Reading Elementary. Her parents are anxious to see quality special education services continued, maximizing the educational benefit to Kenly.

Parents of children with disabilities must remain involved in every single aspect of their children's lives. They must mediate, orchestrate, and advocate in order to ensure positive outcomes for their children. Added to the ordinary routines of life, this devotion can be exhausting. With all the challenges that accompany a child with disabilities (behavior issues; medical expenses; safety issues; keeping informed on current disability and legislative issues; finding qualified child care; applying for services; constant evaluations; endless appointments), parents must be able to depend on IDEA to guarantee their children's rights to free and appropriate education in the least restrictive environments, thus helping them reach their fullest future potential. Kenly's ultimate goal is to live a full and independent life in her community, which is only possible through a successful and adequately supported educational experience.

▲▼▲

Jake attends Kent City Community Schools in Kent City, Michigan. Jake is eight years old and in second grade. He no longer requires special education services. Earlier in his educational career, Jake was labeled as having an emotional impairment. Jake was in a Preprimary Impaired classroom for one year and in a self-contained kindergarten program for children who were emotionally impaired for another year. In first grade he received limited resource room assistance.

Jake had a difficult time controlling his emotions from an early age. Jake's mother worked with him on his social/emotional health but sought the help of the school system when he was only three. The school set up a behavioral plan for Jake that was carried out in the classroom and at home. This behavior plan was in accordance with the provisions of IDEA. The school staff and Jake's family worked closely together to make Jake's discipline plan as consistent as possible.

Halfway through Jake's kindergarten year a great deal of improvement was noted in his behavior. Jake's temper tantrums disappeared, his social skills grew to age level, and he was much less confrontational. Jake is an extremely intelligent child, and he worked hard at achieving his behavioral goals.

Last spring, Jake was exited from all special education services. The behavior plans and special education services helped Jake achieve his goals. The real praise for Jake's exit from special education services belongs to Jake himself for working so hard at learning to control his emotions and to his mother for supporting him in his education. A shining example of the importance and influence of early childhood intervention, Jake is a true success story.

Source: Council of Exceptional Children. Used with permission.

FIGURE 16.1 A Kaleidoscope of Children with Disabilities

- Low birth weight is found in 32 percent of children in early intervention*; African American babies are most likely to have low birth weight.

- Two-thirds of children in early intervention are described as difficult to understand; 70 percent have some trouble communicating.

- Twenty-six percent of children entering early intervention have some trouble with use of their legs or feet.

- 67 percent of children entering early intervention live in a two-adult household.

- Forty-one percent of families in the early intervention system have an annual income of less than $25,000.

- Children with disabilities comprise 5.5 percent of students enrolled in LEP (limited English proficiency) services.

- Hispanic preschoolers represent 19.3 percent of the general population but only 13.7 percent of the preschoolers with disabilities.

- African American students (age 6 through 21) represent only 14.5 percent of the general populations, but comprise 20.3 percent of students with disabilities.

- Although American Indian/Alaskan Native students represent only 1 percent of the general population, they represent 2 percent of students with deaf and/or blindness.

*Early intervention is mandated in IDEA, Part C. Early intervention services are provided to infants and toddlers with disabilities who are under the age of three. Disabilities include diagnosed developmental delays, diagnosed physical or mental conditions that have a high probability of resulting in developmental delay, and may include at-risk infants and toddlers at the state's discretion.

- Are Hispanics with disabilities underrepresented in the above data? Why might this occur?
- Why do you think African American students are overrepresented in the population of students with disabilities? What other statistic helps explain this?
- What is the primary developmental delay with children in early intervention?
- Why is early intervention important for success in school?
- What unique challenges do LEP students with disabilities face? What challenges do you face as the teacher of such students?

Source: U.S. Department of Education, Twenty-Third Annual Report to Congress on the Implementation of the Individuals with Disabilities Education Act (Washington, D.C., 2001).

The Play Bunch

INTRODUCE YOURSELF TO CORY

Cory is a young child with an orthopedic impairment who is an active member of the Play Bunch, an inclusive play group I started several years ago. Observe Cory as he moves about and interacts with the other children, as shown in these photos I've collected. What do you notice about how he is included in a variety of activities? What are the other children's relationships to Cory? How does Cory seem to relate to other children? What do you think the other children can learn from their interactions with Cory? What modifications in the learning environment might a teacher or a parent need to make in order for Cory to fully participate? How do you think the Play Bunch has contributed to Cory's confidence and independence?

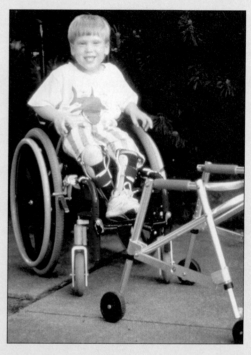

THE BEGINNING

The Play Bunch was created because a need existed for positive, guided social interaction for preschoolers in an inclusive natural play setting. As a parent, I wanted my preschool daughter to become aware of exceptionalities and learn prosocial behaviors to interact with all peers. I wanted to be the catalyst in establishing feelings of acceptance and belonging, which are critical for becoming a capable, compassionate, and productive member of the future society. By collaborating with other parents and professionals, I located a group of families who shared my belief.

The group includes children of various family structures, ethnicities, and abilities. Four families have households with two parents, a single mother heads one family, and Grandma is a part of the extended family in another home. The children are of diverse ethnic heritage, including African American, Native American, and Spanish American. Impairments of Down syndrome, spina bifida, and attention deficit are accepted by all. Our children became a play group participating and learning in developmentally appropriate and naturally inclusive environments. The children played together on a tennis court with balls and balloons, at the beach, and in a park throughout the summer and fall. These children developed friendships and learned to be aware of each other's feelings. They recognize each other with smiles when meeting outside the play setting in various travels with parents throughout the community. The Play Bunch families understand exceptionalities and celebrate the diversity of our American society.

THE PHILOSOPHY

The Play Bunch concept celebrates friendships between all children in natural play and learning environments where

ages and making community inclusion a reality. Parents can then make educated choices and be advocates for the nurturing of their young children.

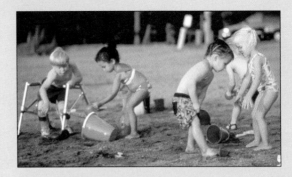

RESOURCES IN DEVELOPMENT

As an educator, I realize the importance of early reading and language stimulation with young children. I researched parent and special education resources throughout the country to locate books depicting inclusive natural play settings. There were limited color picture books for adults to read and talk about with children. Young children also just enjoy looking at books to which they can connect. Clearly such a need exists.

I am currently searching for grants that will enable me to develop The Play Bunch book and video. Parents would be empowered with an additional resource for enjoyment of reading with children and nurturing feelings. Early childhood educators would have a resource to use as language stimulation, pre-reading, and discussion of pro-social behaviors. And most of all, through looking at pictures, children would be building a foundation of acceptance of each other. For an example related to your own professional training, introduce yourself to Cory.

preschool children are nurtured and guided in the development of feelings that they are each accepted, liked, and wanted in community life. The Play Bunch offers parents a model of an inclusive lifestyle option. These connections between parents and children in outdoor play and activities can enhance the quality of family life and continue to establish the acceptance of every child's own characteristics.

Our current culture presents educators and families with a society that is developing awareness of exceptionalities and is becoming ethnically, linguistically, and culturally diverse. Families of young children serve as the catalyst for establishing social acceptance of diversities. Our basic educational belief system should also embody these values. Our society will be remembered in history by the manner in which our children are nurtured and educated.

Learning to understand the feelings of others is critical in the social development of children. This learning is fostered when children are given opportunities to interact cooperatively with peers in developmentally appropriate inclusive play activities. Educators can provide effective teaching strategies within this learning environment where children are guided in accepting their own and others' diversity and strengths. These strategies should be relevant to experiences with which young children can identify.

Another aspect of being an educator of young children is realizing the need to empower families with ideas for promoting pro-social behavior and understanding of others' feelings, thus developing social relationships outside the educational setting. Empowerment can begin by creating awareness of resources for building collaborative link-

You can learn more about and email The Play Bunch at theplaybunch@aol.com.

Text and photos contributed by Debra A. Vande Berg, The Play Bunch, Sioux Falls, South Dakota.

To complete a Program in Action activity, visit the Companion Website at **http://www. prenhall.com/morrison**, select chapter 16, then choose the Program in Action module.

To check your understanding of this chapter with the online Study Guide, go to the Companion Website at **http://www. prenhall.com/morrison**, select chapter 16, then choose the Study Guide module.

Individuals with Disabilities Education Act (IDEA) A federal act providing a free and appropriate education to youth between ages 3 and 21 with disabilities.

Students with disabilities Children with physical impairments (hearing, speech or language, visual, orthopedic) or mental/emotional impairments (mental retardation, autism, emotional disturbance, traumatic brain injury) or specific learning disabilities and who, by reason thereof, need special education and related services.

As with many special areas, the field of children with special needs has a unique vocabulary and terminology. The glossary in Figure 16.2 will help you as you read the chapter and as you work with children and families.

STUDENTS WITH DISABILITIES AND THE INDIVIDUALS WITH DISABILITIES EDUCATION ACT (IDEA)

Students with special needs and their families need education and services that will help them succeed. You will be a part of the process of seeing that they receive such services. Unfortunately, quite often students with disabilities are not provided appropriate services and fail to reach their full potential. This is one reason for laws to help ensure that schools and teachers will have high expectations for these students and that they will have special education and related services. The federal government has passed many laws protecting and promoting the rights and needs of children with disabilities. One of the most important federal laws is PL 101-476, the **Individuals with Disabilities Education Act (IDEA)**, passed in 1990. Congress has periodically updated IDEA, with the latest revision in 1999.

The purpose of the Individuals with Disabilities Education Act, as amended in 1999, is to ensure that all children with disabilities have available to them "a free appropriate public education which emphasizes special education and related services designed to meet their unique needs, to assure that the rights of the disabled children and their parents or guardians are protected, to assist states and localities to provide for the education of all disabled children, and to assess and assure the effectiveness of efforts to educate disabled children."[1]

IDEA defines **students with disabilities** as "those with mental retardation, hearing impairments (including deafness), speech or language impairments (including blindness), serious emotional disturbance, orthopedic impairments, autism, traumatic brain injury, other health impairments, or specific learning disabilities; and who, by reason thereof, need special education and related services."[2] About 10 to 12 percent of the nation's students have some type of disability. Table 16.1 lists the number of persons from six to age twenty-one with disabilities in the various categories covered under IDEA.

IDEA establishes six basic principles to follow as you provide educational and other services to children with special needs:

1. **Zero reject:** IDEA calls for educating all children and rejecting none from an education. Whereas before IDEA many children were excluded from educational programs or were denied an education, this is not the case today.

TABLE 16.1 Persons Ages 6 to 21 Years Served in Federally Supported Programs by Type of Disability

Type of Disability	Numbers Served	Percentage Served
All Disabilities	5,683,707	100.0
Specific Learning Disabilities	2,871,966	50.5
Speech or Language Impairments	1,089,964	19.2
Mental Retardation	614,433	10.8
Emotional Disturbance	470,111	8.3
Multiple Disabilities	112,993	2.0
Hearing Impairments	71,671	1.3
Orthopedic Impairments	71,422	1.3
Other Health Impairments	254,110	4.5
Visual Impairments	26,590	0.5
Autism	65,424	1.2
Deaf-Blindness	1,845	Trace
Traumatic Brain Injury	13,874	0.2
Developmental Delay	19,304	0.3

Source: U.S. Department of Education, Twenty-third annual report to Congress on the implementation of the Individuals with Disabilities Education Act, Washington, D.C., 2001. Available at http://www.ed.gov/offices/OSERS/OSEP/Products/OSEP2001AnlRpt/index.html.

FIGURE 16.2 Glossary of Terms Related to Children with Special Needs

Adaptive education: Modifying programs, environments, curricula, and activities in order to provide learning experiences that help all students achieve desired educational goals. The purpose of adaptive education is to respond effectively to student differences and to enhance each individual's ability to succeed in learning in such environments.

Children with disabilities: Replaces former terms such as *handicapped.* To avoid labeling children, do not use the reversal of these words (i.e., *disabled children*).

Co-teaching: The process by which a regular classroom professional and a special educator or a person trained in exceptional student education team teach, in the same classroom, a group of regular and mainstreamed children.

Disability: A physical or mental impairment that substantially limits one or more major life activities.

Early education and care settings: Promotes the idea that all children learn and that child care and other programs *should* be educating children birth to age eight.

Early intervention: Providing services to children and families as early in the child's life as possible in order to prevent or help with a special need or needs.

English language learners: Students with a primary language other than English.

Exceptional student education: Replaces the term *special education*; refers to the education of children with special needs.

Full inclusion: The mainstreaming or inclusion of all children with disabilities into natural environments such as playgrounds, family daycare centers, child care centers, preschool, kindergarten, and primary grades.

Individualized education program (IEP): A written plan for a child stating what will be done, how it will be done, and when it will be done.

Integration: A generic term that refers to educating children with disabilities along with typically developing children. This education can occur in mainstream, reverse mainstream, and full-inclusion programs.

Least restrictive environment (LRE): Children with disabilities are educated with children who are not disabled, and that special classes, separate schooling, or other removal of children with disabilities from the regular educational environment occurs only when the nature or severity of the disability is such that education in regular classes with the use of supplementary aids and services cannot be achieved satisfactorily.

Limited English proficiency (LEP): Describes children who have limited English skills.

Mainstreaming: The social and educational integration of children with special needs into the general instructional process; usually a regular classroom program.

Merged classroom: A classroom that includes—merges—children with special needs and children without special needs and teaches them together in one classroom.

Natural environment: Any environment it is natural for any child to be in, such as home, child care center, preschool, kindergarten, primary grades, playground, and so on.

Normalized setting: A place that is "normal" or best for the child.

Reverse mainstreaming: The process by which typically developing children are placed in programs for children with disabilities. In reverse mainstreaming, children with disabilities are in the majority.

Typically developing children: Children who are developing according to and within the boundaries of normal growth and development.

The fields of early childhood and special education are slowly integrating. This is good for the profession and for children and families. However, it also means that early childhood education must learn more about the field of early childhood special education and the terminology associated with it. This figure will help you achieve this goal.

DIVERSITY TIE-IN

Is Special Education a "Boys' Club"?

There has been much discussion lately about there being more boys than girls in special education. But, is this true? When you examine the table below, the answer is an unequivocal yes. For example, the table shows that almost 60 percent of students identified with mental retardation are male.

Some call special education a "boys' club." Why is it that more boys are in special education than girls? Some thoughts come to mind: (1) boys exhibit more behavior problems than girls, (2) boys are more aggressive than girls, and (3) there is a natural bias toward boys. However, a look behind the figures provides us with another possible explanation. This explanation is that rather than boys being *over*represented in special education, girls are *under*represented! Researchers who studied this issue of boys' overrepresentation in special education found that the boys who were admitted to

special education were appropriately placed and needed the services. However, they concluded: "We believe . . . that while there is a tendency to refer to the issue of disproportionate representation of males in special education as a problem of male overrepresentation, it may well be a viable alternative explanation for the disproportionate number of males is that females who do need some academic support and special education services but who do not exhibit concomitant behavior problems are not being referred or served in special education."

Sources: M. L. Wehmeyer and M. Schwartz, "Disproportionate Representation of Males in Special Education Services: Biology, Behavior, or Bias?" *Education and Treatment of Children, 24* (2001), 28–45; A. Vaishnav and B. Dedman, "Special Ed Gender Gap Stirs Worry," *Boston Globe* [Online]. Accessed July 8, 2002.

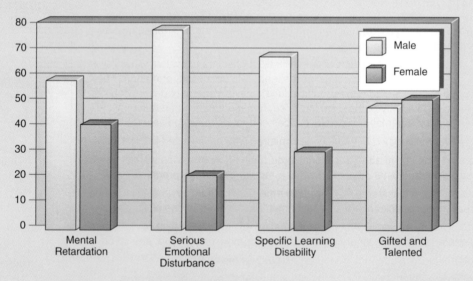

Source: U.S. Department of Education, Office for Civil Rights (1998). OCR Elementary and Secondary School Survey. OCR Reports [Online]. Available at http://205.207.175.80/ocrpublic/wds_list98p.asp.

To complete an activity related to this topic, go to the Companion Website at **http://www. prenhall.com/morrison**, select chapter 16, then choose the Diversity Tie-In module.

2. **Nondiscriminatory evaluation:** A fair evaluation to determine whether a student has a disability and, if so, what the student's education should consist of.

3. **Appropriate education:** An individualized education that benefits the student in making progress toward national policy goals. Basically, IDEA provides for a **free and appropriate education (FAPE)** for all students between the ages of 3 and 21. "Ap-

propriate" means that children must receive an education suited to their age, maturity, condition of disability, past achievements, and parental expectations.

4. **Least restrictive placement/environment:** Students with disabilities must, to the maximum extent appropriate for each one, be educated with students who do not have disabilities. The **least restrictive environment (LRE)** is not necessarily the regular classroom, although 80 percent of children with disabilities are educated in the regular classroom.

5. **Procedural due process:** IDEA provides the schools and the parents with ways to resolve their differences by mediation and, if not by that means, by having hearings before impartial hearing officers or judges.

6. **Parental and student participation:** IDEA specifies a process of shared decision making whereby educators, parents, and students collaborate in deciding the student's education plan.

ADMISSION, REVIEW, AND DISMISSAL (ARD) PROCESS

Under the provision of IDEA and other guidelines that specify the fair treatment of children with disabilities and their families, educators must follow certain procedures in developing a special plan for children with disabilities. These procedures usually occur through the admission, review, and dismissal (ARD) process. However, several steps must be taken prior to the ARD meeting. These include a referral of the student for exceptional student services by a teacher, parent, doctor, or some other professional. The referral is usually followed by a comprehensive individual assessment in order to determine if the child possesses a disability and is eligible for services. In order for testing to occur, parents or guardians must give their consent.

If the child is eligible for exceptional student services, the ARD committee meets to develop an Individualized Education Program (IEP) for the child (see Figure 16.3). Essentially, the IEP is a contract or agreement that specifies how the child will be educated and the services that will be provided in the process. The ARD committee consists of a parent or parent representa-

Free and appropriate education (FAPE) Children must receive education suited to their age, maturity, condition of disability, past achievements, and parental expectations.

Least restrictive environment (LRE) An education program that meets disabled students' needs in a manner that is identical, insofar as possible, to that provided to students in general education classrooms.

 For more information about answers to frequently asked questions about IDEA, go to the Companion Website at **http://www.prenhall.com/morrison**, select chapter 16, then choose the Linking to Learning module to connect to the IDEA Practices site.

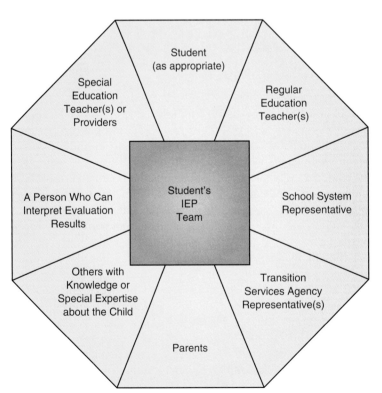

FIGURE 16.3 IEP Team Members

Certain individuals must be involved in writing a child's Individualized Education Program. An IEP team member may fill more than one of the team positions if properly qualified and designated. For example, the school system representative may also be the person who can interpret the child's evaluation results.

Source: Office of Special Education and Rehabilitative Services (2000). *A Guide to the Individualized Education Program* (Washington, DC: U.S. Department of Education). [Online: http://www.ed.gov/offices/OSERS/OSEP/Products/IEP_Guide/IEP_Guide.pdf].

FIGURE 16.4   The IEP: Purposes and Functions

- Protects children and parents by ensuring that planning will occur.

- Guarantees that children will have plans tailored to their individual strengths, weaknesses, and learning styles.

- Helps professionals and other instructional and administrative personnel focus their teaching and resources on children's specific needs, promoting the best use of everyone's time, efforts, and talents.

- Helps ensure that children with disabilities will receive a range of services from other agencies. The plan must not only include an educational component, but also specify how the child's total needs will be met.

- Helps clarify and refine decisions as to what is best for children, where they should be placed, and how they should be taught and helped.

- Ensures that children will not be categorized or labeled without discussion of their unique needs.

- Reviewed at least annually; encourages professionals to consider how and what children have learned, determine whether what was prescribed is effective, and prescribe new or modified strategies.

The IEP is one of the most important educational documents in the education of children with disabilities. It constitutes a contract between the school system, children, and parents.

tive, the student when appropriate, a special education teacher, a regular education teacher, a representative of the school district, and a principal, assistant principal, or coordinator of exceptional student services. The IEP must be reviewed annually and revised as appropriate.

The ARD committee is also responsible for dismissing students from exceptional student education services when they are able to function in a regular classroom without the services.

Individualization of instruction   Students' educations are individualized by providing for their specific needs, disabilities, and preferences.

Individualized education plan (IEP)   A plan for meeting an exceptional learner's educational needs that specifies goals, objectives, services, and procedures for evaluating progress.

Individualized family service plan (IFSP)   A plan designed to help families reach their goals, for themselves and for their children, with the following support services: special education, speech and language pathology and audiology, occupational therapy, physical therapy, psychological services, parent and family training, and counseling.

INDIVIDUALIZED EDUCATION PLANS AND INDIVIDUALIZED FAMILY SERVICE PLANS

Because IDEA requires **individualization of instruction**, schools must provide for all students' specific needs, disabilities, and preferences, as well as those of their parents. Individualization of instruction also means developing and implementing an **individualized education plan (IEP)** for each student. The IEP must specify what will be done for the child, how and when it will be done, and by whom it will be done, and this information must be in writing. Figure 16.4 outlines the purposes and functions of the IEP and Figure 16.5 shows a sample IEP. In developing the IEP, a person trained in diagnosing disabling conditions, such as a school psychologist, must be involved, as well as a classroom professional, the parent, and, when appropriate, the child.

In 1986, Congress passed PL 99-457, the Education of the Handicapped Act Amendments, which was landmark legislation relating to infants, toddlers, and preschoolers with disabilities. This law extends to children with disabilities between the ages of three and five the same rights that are extended to children with disabilities under IDEA and establishes a state grant program for infants and toddlers with disabilities. Most states participate in the infant and toddler grant program.

The process of helping young children with disabilities begins with referral and assessment and results in the development of an **individualized family service plan (IFSP)**,

INDIVIDUALIZED EDUCATION PROGRAM

Student: _Amy North_   Age: _9_   Grade: _1_   Date: _Oct 17, 2003_

1. **Unique Characteristics or Needs: Noncompliance**
   Frequently noncompliant with teacher's instructions

   Present Levels of Performance

   Complies with about 50 percent of teacher's requests/commands

   Special Education, Related Services, and Modifications

   Implemented immediately, strong reinforcement for compliance with teacher's instructions (Example: "Sure I will" plan including precision requests and reinforcer menu for points earned for compliance, as described in The Tough Kid Book by Rhode, Jenson, and Reavis, 1992); within 3 weeks, training of parents by school psychologist to use precision requests and reinforcement at home.

   Objectives (including Procedures, Criteria, and Schedule)

   Within one month, will comply with teacher's requests/commands 90 percent of the time; compliance monitored weekly by teacher

   Annual Goals

   Will become compliant with teacher's requests/commands

2. **Unique Characteristics or Needs: Reading**
   2a. Very slow reading rate
   2b. Poor comprehension
   2c. Limited phonics skills
   2d. Limited sight-word vocabulary

   1. Present Levels of Performance
      2a. Reads stories of approximately 100 words on first-grade reading level at approximately 40 words per min.
      2b. Seldom can recall factual information about stories immediately after reading them
      2c. Consistently confuses vowel sounds, often misidentifies consonants, and does not blend sounds
      2d. Has sight-word vocabulary of approximately 150 words

   2. Special Education, Related Services, and Modifications
      2a-2c. Direct instruction 30 minutes daily in vowel discrimination, consonant identification, and sound blending; begin immediately, continue throughout school year

      2a & 2d. Sight-word drill 10 minutes daily in addition to phonics instruction and daily practice; 10 minutes practice in using phonics and sight-word skills in reading story at her level; begin immediately, continue for school year

   3. Objectives (including Procedures, Criteria, and Schedule)
      2a. Within 3 months, will read stories at her level at 60 words per minute with 2 or fewer errors per story; within six months, 80 words with 2 or fewer errors, performance monitored daily by teacher or aide

      2b. Within 3 months will answer oral and written comprehension questions requiring recall of information from stories she has just read with 90 percent accuracy (e.g., Who is in the story? What happened? Why?) and be able to predict probable outcomes with 80 percent accuracy; performance monitored daily by teacher or aide

      2c. Within 3 months, will increase sight-word vocabulary to 200 words, within 6 months to 250 words, assessed by flashcard presentation

   4. Annual Goals
      2a-2c. Will read fluently and with comprehension at beginning-second-grade level

FIGURE 16.5 Sample Excerpt from an IEP

The IEP plays an important role in ensuring that children receive an individualized education through a range of services that are appropriate for them. How would an IEP help teachers work collaboratively with other professionals to guarantee that children receive the services they need?

Source: D. P. Hallahan and J. Kauffman, *Exceptional Learners: Introduction to Special Education* (7th ed.). (Boston: Allyn & Bacon, 1997). Reprinted by permission.

PROGRAM IN ACTION

Special Beginnings for Infants and Toddlers

Special Beginnings is a collaborative project between several different community agencies, including the local hospital and county health department. The emphasis of Special Beginnings, which addresses the component of Child Find (identifying children who are having difficulty in their development and providing services to them when appropriate), is to identify high-risk infants and infants with developmental delays at birth.

ALYSSA'S STORY

Alyssa was born at twenty-seven weeks gestation. She spent her first three to four months in intensive care. During that time she underwent surgery for a heart defect and hemorrhage. As Alyssa's neurological and physiological systems stabilized and she began to grow, she was transferred to Hutchinson Hospital in Hutchinson,

Kansas. Shortly after Alyssa's arrival, a Special Beginnings Infant Development Specialist visited her family and shared information about the programs and services Special Beginnings provided at the hospital and home.

WHAT IS SPECIAL BEGINNINGS?

Special Beginnings is a program that identifies infants at high risk for developmental delays at birth. Special Beginnings collaborates with the local hospital, county health department, and early childhood specialists to screen infants only a few hours old. High-risk infants are identified by the following criteria:

- Gestational age—32 weeks or less (a normal gestational time period is 38 to 42 weeks and is the term used to describe the child's developmental period in the mother's uterus).

APGAR SCORING FOR NEWBORNS

	Sign	Score 0	Score 1	Score 2
A	**Activity** (Muscle tone)	Limp	Some bending of arms, legs	Active motion
P	**Pulse** (Heart rate)	Absent	Below 100 beats/minute	Above 100 beats/minute
G	**Grimace** (Reflex irritability—baby's reaction when soles of feet are flicked)	No Response	Cries, some motion	Vigorous cry
A	**Appearance** (Skin color)	Blue-gray, pale all over	Pink body; blue hands and feet	Completely pink
R	**Respiration** (Breathing effort)	Absent	Slow, irregular	Good, crying lustily

Virginia Apgar was one of Columbia University's first female M.D.s (1933) and one of the first American women to specialize in surgery. Her research on anesthesia and childbirth led her to her greatest innovation: the Newborn Scoring System—better known as the "Apgar Score" (shown above) for assessing the health of newborn infants—which she conceived in 1949, refined, and finally published in 1953. The assessment is made at one and five minutes after birth (at fifteen minutes for babies born by Cesarean section). A perfect score of 10 is rare in practice, but a score of at least 7 virtually guarantees a newborn's health.

- *Apgar* Score (see table on p. 474)—A score of 7 to 10 is considered normal, while 4 to 7 might require some resuscitative measures, and a baby with Apgars of 3 and below requires immediate resuscitation.

- Birth trauma
  - Fetal distress, evidence indicating the baby's life is in danger.
  - Placenta previa (placenta placement is incorrect and the proper nutrients cannot be provided for the baby. This incorrect placement causes a risk of hemorrhage and can threaten the well being of the mother and baby).
  - Placenta abruption, in which the placenta separates from the uterus, requires emergency C-section (a Cesarean birth enables the delivery of the baby by means of an incision into the mother's abdominal wall and uterus).

- Small or large for gestational age—average birth weight after a normal pregnancy is 3,400 g (7 pounds, 7 ounces). Low birth weight (LBW) means birth weight less than 2,500 g (5 pounds, 7.5 ounces). Very low birth weight babies, weigh less than 1,500 g (3 pounds, 4.5 ounces) and babies with extremely low birth weight are less than 1,000 g (2 pounds, 3 ounces). LBW is not a diagnosis—it is just a convenient label to identify a group of babies with similar types of risks. About 6 percent of all births are premature and 10 percent of all births result in babies who are small for gestational age.
- Neonates with proven intracranial hemorrhages (head trauma causing bleeding or swelling).
- Blood transfusion is required.
- Born with congenital anomalies (a malformation, such as the absence of a limb or the presence of an extra toe) potentially affecting physical and/or mental development.
- Respiratory distress
- High risk for neurological impairment (having to do with the central nervous system)
- Apnea/Bradycardia (associated with cessation of breathing)
- Mother's age 17 or younger
- Infant spent time in a neonatal intensive care unit

The purpose of Special Beginnings is to do just what its title suggests—provide *Special Beginnings* to children whose normal development is at risk. The services that Special Beginnings offers are hospital contacts with the family, newborn and infant assessments, monthly follow-up clinics, family services planning, team recommendations for home activities, direct services as needed, and home visits. The Special Beginnings team includes a social worker, nurse, physical therapist, language development specialist, developmental specialist, and a physician.

ALYSSA'S STORY CONTINUED

After a three-week stay in the Hutchinson Hospital, Alyssa was able to go home on a heart-apnea monitor. Her parents left the hospital knowing that the same Special Beginnings interventionist who had helped to facilitate Alyssa's weight gain would be serving them in the home environment. The Special Beginnings coordinator (social worker) contacted the family, met with the family in their home, and collected information that facilitated contact with other needed services. Also at that time appointments were made for future developmental follow-ups/assessments.

Alyssa's family chose to meet with the developmental specialist once a month. At each appointment Alyssa's overall development appeared appropriate, given her prematurity. Developmental activities were provided to the family. Her vision and hearing were screened every six months. After participating in the program for two years Alyssa's developmental skills were age appropriate and were no longer adjusted for prematurity. Yearly screenings were recommended to monitor on-going development.

The family maintained contact with the Special Beginnings staff through Alyssa's primary school years. During this time no special education services were needed. The family is convinced that this is due to the services Alyssa received in the Special Beginnings Program.

More than 80 percent of the high-risk children seen through the Special Beginnings program are now in regular classrooms receiving no special education services. Special Beginnings has proven that by combining education, medical, and social programs into a more easily accessed system, there is less stress for families and greater probability of success for children.

Contributed by Mary Schulte, Special Beginnings Interventionist, Early Education Center, 303 East Bigger, Hutchinson, Kansas 67501.

PART 5

MEETING THE SPECIAL NEEDS OF
YOUNG CHILDREN

 To complete a Program in Action acitivity, visit the Companion Website at **http://www. prenhall.com/ morrison**, select chapter 16, then choose the Program in Action module.

 For more information about IEPs, go to the Companion Website at **http://www. prenhall.com/ morrison**, select chapter 16, then choose the Linking to Learning module to connect to the Individualized Education Plans site.

All early childhood programs should address the individual needs of children with disabilities. How can you use IEPs to ensure that those needs are being met?

which is designed to help families reach the goals they have for themselves and their children.

IDEA for Infants and Toddlers. IDEA provides funds for infants and toddlers to receive early intervention services. These services are provided through the Individualized Family Service Plan (IFSP), a written document for each infant and toddler (0–2) and their families.

The Individualized Family Service Plan. Under Part C, infants, toddlers, and their families have the right to an individualized family service plan (IFSP), which specifies what service children and their families will receive. Also, the IFSP is designed to help families reach the goals they have for themselves and their children. The IFSP provides for the following:

• Multidisciplinary assessment developed by a multidisciplinary team and the parents. Planned services must meet developmental needs and can include special education, speech and language pathology and audiology, occupational therapy, physical therapy, psychological services, parent and family training and counseling services, transition services, medical diagnostic services, and health services.
• A statement of the child's present levels of development; a statement of the family's strengths and needs in regard to enhancing the child's development; a statement of major expected outcomes for the child and family; the criteria, procedures, and timeliness for determining progress; the specific early intervention services necessary to meet the unique needs of the child and family; the projected dates for initiation of services; the name of the case manager; and transition procedures from the early intervention program into a preschool program.

Services that can be provided in the IFSP include (but are not limited to) those listed in Figure 16.6.

Benefits of Family-Centered Services. As we have discussed, family-centered services are an important component of early childhood programming, and they will only become more important. Programs that embrace and utilize family center services:

• Improve child developmental and social adjustment outcomes;
• Decrease parental stress as a result of support and assistance in accessing needed services of their child and themselves;
• Recognize the family's role as decision maker and partner in the early intervention process;
• Help families make the best choices for their children by providing comprehensive information about the full range of resources in their communities;
• Accommodate individual child, family, and community differences through creative, flexible, and collaborative approaches to services;
• Value children and families for their unique capacities, experiences, and potential;

Assistive technology devices and services

Audiology

Family training, counseling, and home visits

Health services

Medical services for diagnosis or evaluation

Nursing services

Nutrition services

Occupational therapy

Physical therapy

Psychological services

Service coordination services

Social work services

Special instruction

Speech-language pathology

Transportation and related costs

Vision services

FIGURE 16.6 **Services That Can Be Provided Under Part C of IDEA**

When we think about intervention and support services for young children, we need to think of the full range of services that can benefit them and their families. What would be some specific services provided in each of these categories? For example, what kind of nursing services might benefit young children with disabilities? Families?

Source: 34 Code of Federal Register *(CFR)* § 303.12(d).

- Seek meaningful and active family involvement in the planning and implementation of family-centered and community-based services; and
- Obtain potential health care savings due to ongoing monitoring of health status and referral for primary health care and nutritional services.[3]

Keep in mind the following ideas when striving for effective individual and family service plans:

- Methods and techniques of diagnostic and prescriptive teaching are essential as a basis for writing and implementing the IEP and the IFSP.
- Working with parents is an absolute must for every classroom professional. You should learn all you can about parent conferences and communication, parent involvement, and parents as volunteers and aides (see chapter 17).
- Working with all levels of professionals offers a unique opportunity for the classroom professional to individualize instruction. Since it is obvious that all professionals need help in individualizing instruction, it makes sense to involve them in this process.
- As individual education becomes a reality for all children and families, early childhood professionals will need skills in assessing student behavior and family background and settings.

Inclusive classrooms educate students with disabilities in the least restrictive educational environment. What would you say to a parent of a child without a disability who questions the idea of an inclusive classroom?

VOICE FROM THE FIELD

Teaching in the Inclusive Classroom

Teaching in an inclusive classroom is the result of legal litigation, changing attitudes, heated debates, and school reform. Inclusive education has been the catalyst for the necessary role change for today's regular and special education teachers. No longer should regular and special educators operate as two distinct entities, but merge into one unified system structured to meet the unique needs of all students within the classroom. This concept has promoted the partnership between the disciplines while blending the strengths of both educational systems. Teachers are now cast in roles as facilitators, co-teachers, consultants, coaches, counselors, and itinerants. In some inclusive classrooms, teachers accept a shared responsibility for providing instruction for all students in the classroom based on individual needs, regardless of their ability or disability. Inclusive classrooms assist to eliminate the stigma placed on persons with disabilities by heightening the awareness of the likenesses and differences we all possess.

An important component of an inclusive classroom is teamwork. Working together assists in identifying areas of the student's breakdown in learning. The team—composed of parents, special and regular educators, and related service providers—can share their expertise to provide an optimal learning experience for each individual student. Working with parents collaboratively can make the education of their child twice as effective.

Educational research also embraces the concept of collaboration and consultation of regular and special educators

as an integral component in providing effective instructional programs to accommodate all students. The challenges and opportunities faced by educators and students continually change in our society. During initial implementation, the inclusive classroom teachers are faced with the challenge of defining the goals of their program and then assessing the effectiveness based on student outcome and teacher satisfaction. The identification of goals should be a collaborative effort of both educators. Goals of the model may include, but are not limited to, the following:

- To form a partnership between the disciplines and define roles to blend the strengths of both professionals
- To provide appropriate instructional programs for the student with disabilities in order to maximize the students' learning potential
- To provide specialized, individualized learning instructional strategies for students experiencing difficulty within the classroom
- To modify the regular classroom curriculum to enable all students to learn in that setting
- To utilize multisensory learning centers to address the unique needs of all students
- To improve communication between the special educator, general educator, and parent

Inclusion may be an unrealistic goal for special educators who serve more than one school or for those who, because of exceptionally high caseloads, are faced with scheduling conflicts. Additionally, not every special educa-

- Professionals must know how to identify sources of, and how to order and use, a range of instructional materials, including the various media technologies. You cannot hope to individualize without a full range of materials and media. You must be concerned with students' visual, auditory, and tactile/kinesthetic learning styles. Some children in a classroom may learn best through one mode, others through another.

FULL INCLUSION

Mainstreaming and full inclusion differ in that in full inclusion the student with disabilities is assumed to be in the natural environment from the beginning. It is important to know this when planning full-inclusion programs, because full-inclusion programs do not have separate exceptional education programs. The services formerly provided in separate ex-tion students' intervention needs can be best met in an inclusive classroom. For the special educator involved in the inclusive classroom, the disadvantages may include an increase of caseload due to shared ownership of all students within the classroom, the need for additional collaborative planning time with parents and staff, and the responsibility of acquiring materials and strategies to enable all students to succeed in the general education classroom.

For the general education teacher, the disadvantages may include the need for additional planning time with the special educator, the acceptance of the added responsibility of utilizing the various instructional strategies, and additional training. The teachers are also faced with the challenge of acquiring adequate support for scheduling, adapting curriculum, peer and social acceptance of the student with disabilities, and instructional resources with specialized training.

The opportunities tend to outweigh the challenges when strong leadership, positive collaboration, supports for students and teachers, and funding are components of the inclusive classroom. An inclusive partnership breaks the pattern of teaching in isolation. Both educators establish a partnership that combines the general educator's knowledge of what to teach with the special educator's knowledge of how to teach utilizing varied instructional strategies. The classroom is then equipped to accommodate the learning and behavioral needs of all students to the maximum extent possible.

The special educator is given the opportunity to

1. Utilize the regular educator's content area expertise
2. Gain knowledge of the daily expectations of the regular education classroom
3. Spend additional time and energy assisting students in developing motivation, effort, and a sense of responsibility in their classroom
4. Acquire moral support from a colleague
5. Share specialized skills to benefit all students
6. Improve student self-esteem
7. Increase ability to communicate with families

The regular education teacher is given the opportunity to

1. Develop an awareness of specialized teaching strategies (multisensory methods of instruction)
2. Increase teaching time
3. Promote greater understanding of specific disabilities and accommodations/modifications
4. Work collaboratively with a peer
5. Increase self-esteem via classroom successes
6. Decrease the teacher/student ratio
7. Increase ability to communicate with families

The shared expertise of the regular and special educator can create instructional programs so that all children can learn in the regular classroom. An inclusive classroom allows the students and teachers to be risk takers so that all can learn within a school culture that values different outcomes for different individuals. Working together, educators can look at individual students from all different angles and concentrate on meeting their learning needs in the least restrictive environment. This collaboration creates a dynamic classroom situation that promotes increased learning and positive experiences. It is a win–win situation for both students and teachers. A successful inclusive classroom provides interactive tasks based on learning styles and individual needs through active learning. Active learning strategies (cooperative learning, peer tutoring, critical thinking groups) engage students and enhance their higher-order thinking skills necessary for success in the future while fostering lifelong learning. An inclusive classroom can produce enlightened and intellectually curious individuals with the needed practice of cooperative and appropriate social skills.

Contributed by Susan Hentz, Florida Council of Exceptional Children 2003 Teacher of the Year.

ceptional education programs are now provided in full-inclusion programs in the natural environment by special educators and other special service providers.

Full inclusion receives a lot of attention and is the subject of great national debate for several reasons:

- Court decisions and state and federal laws mandate, support, and encourage full inclusion. Many of these laws and court cases relate to extending to children and parents basic civil rights. For example, in the 1992 case of *Oberti v. Board of Education of the Borough of Clementon School District*, the judge ruled that Rafael, an eight-year-old child with Down syndrome, should not have to earn his way into an integrated classroom but that it was his right to be there from the beginning.

 For more information about inclusion, go to the Companion Website at **http://www. prenhall.com/ morrison**, select any chapter, then choose Topic 9 of the ECE Supersite module.

Inclusion . . . Yours, Mine, Ours

Alimacani Elementary School is a National Model Blue Ribbon school located in Jacksonville, Florida. The faculty, staff, and community have consistently worked together to live up to their vision that "Alimacani is a place where education is a treasure and children are inspired to reach for their dreams."

The school serves preK–5 students that originally included self-contained classes for kindergarten children with varying exceptionalities. After several years of serving the youngsters using a traditional self-contained model and mainstreaming individually as appropriate, frustration ran high. Although the children with disabilities were occasional visitors to the kindergarten classes, they were never a part of the general classroom learning and social community. As our team of kindergarten teachers looked at this model of serving children, we brainstormed ideas of how to better meet the needs of individual students. After many difficult conversations, we agreed to focus on a model that would best serve the needs of all of our children. We decided to take the entire population of children with special needs and include them in regular kindergarten classes, matching children with teacher strengths.

As our vision for inclusion was first formed, we were anxious and unsure. We would have to teach with other

teachers and give up ownership of children and space. All of our roles would change. We had read about the benefits of collaboration with our colleagues, but we knew that the reality of so intimate a bond would require trust, respect, a great deal of faith, and a strong sense of humor!

Despite our reservations and uncertainty, we were full of enthusiasm! Our expectations changed daily. Even our assignments changed, as we enrolled and identified a record number of kindergarten children with special needs. In partnership with parents of the children with disabilities and with parents of typically developing children, we stretched, bent, and broadened our ideas. In most

- Some parents of children with disabilities are dissatisfied with their children's attending separate programs. They view separate programs for their children as a form of segregation. In addition, they want their children to have the social benefits of attending classes in general education classrooms.
- Some teachers feel they do not have the training or support necessary to provide for the disabilities of children in full-inclusion classrooms. These teachers also believe they will not be able to provide for children with disabilities, even with the assistance of aides and special support services.
- Some people believe the cost of full inclusion outweighs the benefits. There is no doubt that it costs more to educate students with disabilities than students who have no disabilities. The average cost of educating a regular classroom student nationally is $6,565, compared with $12,474 (1.90 times) for educating an exceptional education student in a special education program. (This cost can be more for some individual students and can cost more in some school districts.)[4] Some professionals think that the money spent on separate special education facilities and programs can be better used for full-inclusion programs.

cases, visitors could not identify the children with disabilities in our classrooms from their typically developing peers. They also could not always identify general education teachers from special educators. Eighteen children with a variety of special needs were included in three different kindergarten classes during that initial year, including children with Down syndrome, autism, mild physical and mental disabilities, attention deficit (hyperactivity) disorder, Asperger's syndrome, fetal alcohol syndrome, learning disabilities, and developmental delays.

To say that the first year was a success is an understatement. Without exception, we felt that we had done a better job of educating exceptional children than we had ever achieved in our self-contained model. We also learned that we did not have to sacrifice the many for the few. Our typically developing population of kindergartners thrived with the new responsibilities of helping their peers. As we came together to develop alternative methods of instruction for children with special needs, we found many of those same methods reaching our typically developing children. We were extremely proud of *all* of our kindergartners at the end of the year as they marched ahead into first grade.

This is not to say that there were no roadblocks, but we tried to turn each obstacle into an opportunity. We detoured, we had traffic jams, and occasionally even head-on collisions, but we used each experience as a learning and building block. Out of one of our moments of frustration, we developed our website, http://www.rushservices.com/Inclusion, as a voice for teachers and parents to exchange information. We have logged on thousands of participants from all over the world who have willingly shared their insights and inspiration, their challenges and many successes.

Even with our own successes in K–5 inclusion classrooms, we have come to believe that inclusion is not for everyone. We believe that there must continue to be an array of services to meet individual needs. We believe that we must learn to first look at the needs of our students, and then design programs and assign personnel to make learning successful.

We have chosen as our symbol the starfish. You may be familiar with the story of the person who comes upon a beach filled with starfish washed ashore. He spots a young man throwing starfish back into the ocean one at a time. He questions the young man as to why he is taking the time to throw the starfish back into the sea. After all, there is no way he can save all of the starfish on the beach. The young man answers that his efforts do make a difference to each starfish he is able to save. Well, that is how we feel at Alimacani. We are walking that same beach, making a real difference, one "starfish" at a time.

Visit the inclusive classrooms of Kerry Rogers and Lori Medlock at http://www.rushservices.com/Inclusion.

Text contributed by Dayle Timmons, Marie Rush, Kerry Rogers, and Lori Medlock of Alimacani Elementary School, Jacksonville, Florida; photos courtesy Kerry Rogers.

A Continuum of Inclusive Services.   The policy of the Council for Exceptional Children (CEC), a professional organization of special educators, is as follows:

> CEC believes that a continuum of services must be available for all children, youth, and young adults. CEC also believes that the concept of inclusion is a meaningful goal to be pursued in our schools and communities. In addition, CEC believes children, youth, and young adults with disabilities should be served whenever possible in general education classrooms in inclusive neighborhood schools and community settings. Such settings should be strengthened and supported by an infusion of especially trained personnel and other appropriate supportive practices according to the individual needs of the child.[5]

A *continuum of services* means that a full range of services is available for individuals from the most restrictive to the least restrictive placements. This continuum implies a graduated range of services with one level of services leading directly to the next. For example, a continuum of services for students with disabilities would define institutional placement as the most restrictive and a general education classroom as the least

To complete a Program in Action acitivity, visit the Companion Website at **http://www. prenhall.com/ morrison**, select chapter 16, then choose the Program in Action module.

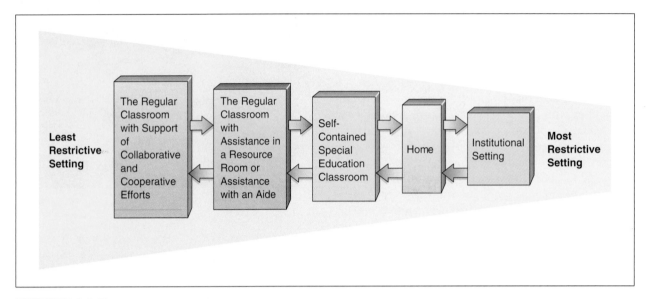

FIGURE 16.7 A Continuum of Services

Schools provide for a continuum of services in many different ways. The continuum service options range from the most physically integrated (left-hand side), in which the regular classroom teacher meets most of a child's needs with help and support, to the least integrated (right-hand side), a residential setting providing a therapeutic environment.

Source: From George S. Morrison, *Teaching in America*, 3e © 2003. Published by Allyn & Bacon, Boston, MA. Copyright © 2003 by Pearson Education. Adapted by permission of the publisher.

restrictive. (Figure 16.7 shows this continuum of services.) There is considerable debate over whether providing such a continuum is an appropriate policy. Advocates of inclusion say that the approach works against developing truly inclusive programs. Figure 16.8 presents the policy on inclusion for the Division for Early Childhood of the Council for Exceptional Children.

There are many benefits for children in inclusive classrooms. They demonstrate increased acceptance and appreciation of diversity; develop better communication and social skills; show greater development in moral and ethical principles; create warm and caring friendships; and demonstrate increased self-esteem.

Given the great amount of interest in inclusion, discussions regarding its appropriateness and how best to implement it will continue for some time. As an early childhood professional, you will have many opportunities to participate in this discussion and to help shape the policies of implementation and classroom practice. You should fully participate in such processes.

Cross-categorical classroom
A classroom or other setting of students with a variety of disabilities or delays.

Cross-Categorical Classrooms.   The **cross-categorical classroom**, which Scott Simon describes in his Program in Action on page 488, illustrates inclusion in action. Nancy King Little's Voice from the Field on page 489, which follows Scott's, gives you an up-close look at inclusion in a faith-based preschool program.

Itinerant teacher   Teacher who provides services by traveling to children, or having the children travel to the teacher.

Itinerant Teachers.   As you can see by now, teaching in an inclusion classroom provides many opportunities and challenges. Perhaps you will be fortunate enough to have help from a special education **itinerant teacher** (SEIT), who will work closely with you. A special education itinerant teacher provides services individually or to small groups. An itinerant teacher travels to the child(ren) or the child(ren) travel(s) to the teachers. The Voice from the Field, "Collaboration with an Itinerant Special Educator," on page 492, explains roles and services.

FIGURE 16.8 **The Division for Early Childhood's Position Statement on Inclusion**

Inclusion, as a value, supports the right of all children, regardless of abilities, to participate actively in natural settings within their communities. Natural settings are those in which the child would spend time had he or she not had a disability. These settings include, but are not limited to home, preschool, nursery schools, Head Start programs, kindergartens, neighborhood school classrooms, child care, places of worship, and recreational (such as community playgrounds and community events) and other settings that all children and families enjoy.

DEC supports and advocates that young children and their families have full and successful access to health, social, educational, and other support services that promote full participation in family and community life. DEC values the cultural, economic, and educational diversity of families and supports a family-guided process for identifying a program of service.

As young children participate in group settings (such as preschool, play groups, child care, kindergarten) their active participation should be guided by developmentally and individually appropriate curriculum. Access to and participation in the age appropriate general curriculum becomes central to the identification and provision of specialized support services.

To implement inclusive practices DEC supports:

(a) The continued development, implementation, evaluation, and dissemination of full inclusion supports, services, and systems that are of high quality for all children;

(b) The development of preservice and inservice training programs that prepare families, service providers, and administrators to develop and work within inclusive settings;

(c) Collaboration among key stakeholders to implement flexible fiscal and administrative procedures in support of inclusion;

(d) Research that contributes to our knowledge of recommended practice; and

(e) The restructuring and unification of social, educational, health, and intervention supports and services to make them more responsive to the needs of all children and families.

Ultimately, the implementation of inclusive practice must lead to optimal developmental benefit for each individual child and family.

The philosophy and practice of inclusion is based on the premise that children with disabilities have the right to be educated in the regular classroom. In addition, all children benefit from such inclusion in classrooms, schools, and communities. Inclusion provides lasting benefits to children, families, and teachers.
Source: Division for Early Childhood of the Council for Exceptional Children [Online], adopted December 1993, reaffirmed December 1996, revised June 2000. Used by permission.

CHILDREN WITH ATTENTION DEFICIT HYPERACTIVITY DISORDER (ADHD)

Students with **attention deficit hyperactivity disorder (ADHD)** generally display cognitive delays and have difficulties in three specific areas: attention, impulse control, and hyperactivity. To be classified as having ADHD, a student must display for a minimum of six months before age seven at least eight of the characteristics outlined in Figure 16.9, page 487.

ADHD is diagnosed more often in boys than in girls and occurs in about 20 percent of all students. About half of the cases are diagnosed before age four. Frequently, the term *attention deficit disorder (ADD)* is used to refer to ADHD, but ADD is a form of learning disorder, whereas ADHD is a behavioral disorder.

Attention deficit hyperactivity disorder (ADHD)
Children with ADHD have an unusual degree of difficulty with attention and self-control, which leads to problems with learning, social functioning, and behavior that occur in more than one situation and that have been present for a significant length of time.

Bridges for Families Early Intervention Program

The Bridges for Families Early Intervention Program (Madison, Wisconsin) is a family-centered, community-based, birth to three years, early intervention program for infants and toddlers with disabilities and their families. Bridges is contracted by Dane County to ensure that the county meets its mandated requirements for Part C of the Individuals with Disabilities Education Act (IDEA). The program is housed within the Waisman Center, University Center for Excellence in Developmental Disabilities, University of Wisconsin–Madison.

The program operates from this philosophy:

- Parents and professionals are full partners in the planning, coordination, and implementation of early intervention services.
- The overall purpose of early intervention is to support family members and other caregivers and enhance their abilities to meet the needs of children with special needs.

- Services need to be a collaborative effort among community agencies and resources that support families of infants and toddlers with special needs.
- An early intervention program needs to be flexible, have an array of services, resources, and parent involvement options, and continually adapt to the changing needs of families and the community.

The program is community based and offers services to approximately 395 families a year in a variety of natural environments, including, but not limited to, family homes, family day care homes/centers, child care centers, early childhood programs, and other community sites where children and their families spend their days. Bridges has twenty staff members, some who work part-time to accommodate individual preferences and family situations. Primary program staff include early childhood special education teachers, physical therapists, occupational therapists, speech and language pathologists, and social workers. At least two staff members have children with

STRATEGIES FOR TEACHING CHILDREN WITH DISABILITIES

Sound teaching strategies work well for all students, including those with disabilities. You must plan how to create inclusive teaching environments. The following ideas will help you teach children with disabilities and create inclusive settings that enhance the education of all students:

For more information about teaching students with disabilities, go to the Companion Website at **http://www.prenhall. com/morrison**, select any chapter, then choose Topic 9 of the ECE Supersite module.

- *Accentuate the positive.* One of the most effective strategies is to emphasize what children can do rather than what they cannot do. Children with disabilities have talents and abilities similar to other children, and by exercising professional knowledge and skills you can help these and all children reach their full academic potential.
- *Use appropriate assessment, including work samples, cumulative records, and appropriate assessment instruments.* Discussions with parents and other professionals who have worked with the individual child are sources of valuable information and contribute to making accurate and appropriate plans for children.
- *Use concrete examples and materials.*
- *Develop and use multisensory approaches to learning.*
- *Model what children are to do rather than just telling them what to do.* Have a child who has mastered a certain task or behavior model it for others. Ask each child to perform a designated skill or task with supervision. Give corrective feedback.

special needs, offering unique perspectives to families served by the program and insights to improve staff practices. Additionally two staff members are bilingual (English and Spanish) reflecting the growing Latino population in our community. Other interpreters are contracted as needed (e.g., sign language, Chinese, Russian, Hmong). Grandparents, early childhood teachers, child care providers, and other community members are brought into the team for individual children as needed. Parents, program staff, and community members work together to develop Individualized Family Service Plans (IFSPs) for each child and family. These plans summarize the goals for each child and state the types, frequency, and duration of services to be provided to each child and family and the locations where they will be provided. The plans are based on family concerns, the child's developmental needs, priorities, and resources. Service coordinators then help identify and link families with community supports and resources.

On a typical day, a teacher or therapist will make three to five different home or community visits to work directly with a child in his or her family home or child care setting. Once or twice a week, staff conduct evaluations or meet with families to develop IFSPs. Time is built into the week for team meetings focused on program development and growth, case-based problem-solving discussions, routine staff meetings, and staff supervision and support. Commitment to this time has contributed to team functioning, program outcomes, and staff morale.

The program has established and maintained collaborative relationships with other community agencies working on behalf of children and families. A recent survey of community collaborators indicated that Bridges is positively perceived in the community and that collaborators perceive that families receive quality services from the program.

Being located at the Waisman Center with Wisconsin's personnel development system for birth to age three and other related early intervention training and technical assistance projects offers mutual benefits to each entity. The daily practices of Bridges staff inform statewide training efforts in early intervention, and vice versa. Bridges staff are frequently asked to participate in planning groups and present at statewide and local trainings. In addition, Bridges serves as a training site for university students from a range of academic departments to promote exemplary early intervention services.

Parents are actively involved in many aspects of the program. They participate on advisory boards, serve as family mentors for university students, speak at local and statewide early intervention training activities, speak at university courses, and participate in local and statewide parent leadership and support sessions. Annual family surveys indicate that families are satisfied with the Bridges program and report that their child with developmental delays and their family benefited from the services they received. A survey of family mentors has indicated a high level of satisfaction from helping future providers experience family life with a young child with special needs—from the inside out.

Visit the Bridges for Families Early Intervention Program on the Web at http://www.waisman.wisc.edu/cedd/ecfr.html.

Contributed by Linda Tuchman, program director. Bridges for Families Early Intervention Program, Madison, Wisconsin.

- *Let children practice or perform a certain behavior,* involving them in their own assessment of that behavior.
- *Make the learning environment a pleasant, rewarding place to be.*
- *Create a dependable classroom schedule.* Young children develop a sense of security when daily plans follow a consistent pattern. Allowing for flexibility also is important, however.
- *Encourage parents to volunteer at school and to read to their children at home.*
- *Identify appropriate tasks children can accomplish on their own* to create in them an opportunity to become more independent of you and others.
- *Use cooperative learning.* Cooperative learning enables all students to work together to achieve common goals. Cooperative learning has five components:
  Positive interdependence. Group members establish mutual goals, divide the prerequisite tasks, share materials and resources, assume shared roles, and give joint rewards.
  Face-to-face interaction. Group members encourage and facilitate each other's efforts to complete tasks through direct communication.
  Individual accountability/personal responsibility. Individual performance is assessed, and results are reported back to both the individual and the group. The group holds each member responsible for completing his or her fair share of responsibility.

To complete a Program in Action acitivity, visit the Companion Website at **http://www. prenhall.com/morrison**, select chapter 16, then choose the Program in Action module.

Interpersonal and small-group skills. Students are responsible for getting to know and trust each other, communicating accurately and clearly, accepting and supporting each other, and resolving conflicts in a constructive manner.

Group processing. Group reflection includes describing which contributions of members are helpful or unhelpful in making decisions and which group actions should be continued or changed.

- *Use circle of friends.* This technique helps students develop friendships with their classmates. Classmates volunteer to be part of a student's circle, and the circle meets as a team on a regular basis. The teacher coordinates the circle and helps the group solve problems or concerns that arise. Students in the circle provide friendship and support so that no student is isolated or alone in the class.[6]

- *Use Classwide Peer Tutoring (CWPT) program.* CWPT involves whole classrooms of students in tutoring activities that improve achievement and student engagement, particularly for at-risk, low-income students. Having opportunities to teach peers appears to reinforce students' own learning and motivation, according to Charles R. Greenwood, the program developer.[7]

- *Develop a peer buddy system.* In a peer buddy system, classmates serve as peer buddies (friends, guides, or counselors) to students who are experiencing problems. Variations are to pair an older student with a younger one who is experiencing a problem and to pair two students who are experiencing similar problems.[8]

- *Use learning centers such as those suggested by Susan Hentz on page 497.*

Figure 16.10 on page 494 provides further information about what you will need to know and be able to do to be an effective teacher of children with disabilities.

Because they have a great deal of knowledge about their children, parents should be involved in helping plan objectives and curricula for their children with disabilities. What are some things teachers and parents might plan for children?

GIFTED AND TALENTED CHILDREN

In contrast to children with disabilities, children identified as gifted and talented are not covered under IDEA's provisions, and Congress has passed other legislation specifically to provide for these children. The Jacob K. Javits Gifted and Talented Students Education Act of 1988 defines *gifted and talented children* as those who "give evidence of high performance capabilities in areas such as intellectual, creative, artistic, or leadership capacity; or in specific academic fields, and who require services or activities not ordinarily provided by the school in order to fully develop such capabilities."[9] The definition distinguishes between *giftedness,* characterized by above-average intellectual ability, and *talented,* referring to individuals who excel in such areas as drama, art, music, athletics, and leadership. Students can have these abilities separately or in combination. A talented five-year-old may be learning disabled, and a student with orthopedic disabilities may be gifted.

Although children may not display all these signs, the presence of several of them can alert parents and early childhood professionals to make appropriate instructional, environmental, and social adjustments.

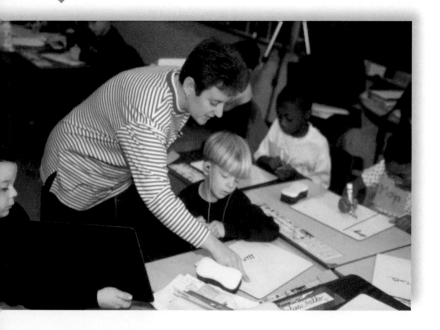

FIGURE 16.9 **Types and Characteristics of Attention Deficit Hyperactivity Disorder (ADHD)**

Attention deficit hyperactivity disorder has several types, including: (1) predominantly inattentive, (2) predominantly impulsive, or (3) combined. Individuals with this condition usually have many (but not all) of the following symptoms:

Inattention

- Often fails to finish what he starts
- Diagnosis of Attention Deficit Disorder
- Doesn't seem to listen
- Easily distracted
- Has difficulty concentrating or paying attention
- Doesn't stick with a play activity

Impulsivity

- Often acts without thinking and later feels sorry
- Shifts excessively from one activity to another
- Has difficulty organizing work
- Speaks out loud in class
- Doesn't wait to take turns in games or groups

Hyperactivity

- Runs about or climbs on things excessively
- Can't sit still and is fidgety
- Has difficulty staying in his seat and bothers classmates
- Excessive activity during sleep
- Always on the "go" and acts as if "driven"

Emotional Instability

- Angry outbursts
- Social loner
- Blames others for problems
- Fights with others quickly
- Very sensitive to criticism

Source: Reprinted with permission from the *Diagnostic and Statistical Manual of Mental Disorders,* Fourth Edition. Copyright 1994 American Psychiatric Association. Available at www.cdipage.com/adhd.htm.

Figure 16.11 on page 495 outlines characteristics displayed in each of the areas of giftedness. You can also use these to help you identify gifted children in your program.

Professionals tend to suggest special programs and sometimes schools for the gifted and talented, which would seem to be a move away from providing for these children in regular classrooms. Regular classroom professionals can provide for gifted children in their classrooms through enrichment and acceleration. *Enrichment* provides an opportunity for children to pursue topics in greater depth and in different ways than planned for in the curriculum. *Acceleration* permits children to progress academically at their own pace.

In regular classrooms, early childhood professionals can encourage gifted children to pursue special interests as a means of extending and enriching classroom learning. They can use parents and resource people to tutor and work in special ways with these children and provide opportunities for children to assume leadership responsibilities themselves.

To complete a Program in Action acitivity, visit the Companion Website at **http://www. prenhall.com/ morrison**, select chapter 16, then choose the Program in Action module.

Teaching in a Cross-Categorical Classroom

The Early Childhood Special Education Program in the Mascoutah District #19, housed at Scott Elementary School on the Scott Air Force Base in Illinois, is a program that is *cross-categorical,* which means that it serves different types of disabilities including, but not limited to, cerebral palsy, autism, Down syndrome, and delays in cognitive, language, motor, and social skills. The teachers provide each student with an Individualized Education Plan (IEP) that shows individualized goals and objectives and services provided. In addition to a certified early childhood teacher and an instructional aide, each classroom may benefit from individual care aides, social workers, speech and language pathologists, and occupational, physical, and music therapists.

Recently, the program transitioned to full day to accommodate full-day kindergartners from 8:30 A.M. to 2:45 P.M. Monday through Friday. Each classroom is carpeted, well lit, and temperature controlled—important amenities for students with health issues. In addition, computers and individual lockers are available for each student. In order to meet the individual needs of its students, the Special Education Program of Scott Elementary has integrated its educational philosophy in four specific areas: classroom environment and schedule; student, staff and peer interaction; behavior management; and special/individual needs.

Consistency is the most important aspect of classroom environment. Day to day, the classroom must be user friendly, comfortable, and able to meet as many needs as possible, and the schedule should be predictable. Teachers have learned to anticipate the reactions of students who are upset by changes in their school environment. Also, many teachers provide an open classroom that welcomes parents.

The program's philosophy on student, staff, and peer interaction centers around the teacher's ability to fill many roles: teacher, social worker, nurse, police officer, and sometimes, that of friend. Teachers do not look at their students as students with disabilities, but as students who require different approaches, attitudes, stimuli, schedules—each as an individual. Also, and more importantly, they can never become complacent—their attitude is one of looking forward,

not resting with one success on a certain day. Instead, there is a constant momentum for continued growth. At the beginning of the year, students do not act like a united class. However, at the end, they have learned how the teachers treat them, and, many times, they treat each other in the same way. Teachers lead by example.

Behavior management and guidance is aimed toward helping children learn to guide and direct their own behavior. Teachers begin with four or five classroom rules such as "keep your hands and feet to yourself." All rules are based on safety and respect. In the beginning, being directive is easier for the children to understand and gives them an immediate solution to their behavioral problem. For instance, using "stop" rather than "no" is more effective.

Students with special needs are treated as typically developing students, and teachers provide adaptive materials when necessary. Engaging students as often as possible is the primary goal. If a student is autistic and appears unresponsive, teachers persist anyway. Although a child cannot be forced to make eye contact, a teacher can go to many measures to get into the student's line of vision. What varies with each teacher and each student is the "how" and "when" techniques. Teachers must gauge how far to go with each child, when they have reached a tolerance point, how to expand an activity, and when to move on. These teaching skills are highly individualized and take time to master. There are many techniques to use to meet the special needs of each student. For instance, some teachers invite older students to assist in addressing social skills. Others will incorporate music to determine which sensory modes are most useful.

Since they work in a cross-categorical classroom, these instructors must be flexible. They are required to work on deficit areas of development but, in the end, address whatever needs attention that particular day, including toileting, feeding, writing, or interacting.

Contributed by Scott Simon, preschool teacher (cross-categorical class with students ages 5 and 6 who have a variety of disabilities and delays), Scott Elementary School, Scott Air Force Base, Illinois, *Parent and Child* Early Childhood Professional Award winner.

Inclusion in a Preschool Setting

Begin with the desired end in mind. Envision the birth of your own challenged child and the classroom in which you would wish him or her to be educated. Your answer would be this: Inclusion in the mainstream of life is always the desired path. Once the commitment to inclusion is born, any obstacles must be viewed only as opportunities to develop strategies that support the ideal, an inclusive classroom. Quite simply, the only ethical path is to develop those interventions that will support maximum inclusion for children with special needs in early care and educational settings. Anything less deprives them of a potent learning experience, of learning naturally from their peers. However, in developing best practices for challenged children, typical children must never be utilized only as facilitators for their special needs friends. Typical children must also have best practices in place to support their highest need and achievement. Each child must be served to his or her highest purpose, and the inclusive classroom should never aspire to less.

At the Palma Ceia Presbyterian Preschool, in Tampa, Florida, we are entering our twenty-second year of service to the community as a fully inclusive early childhood education program. As founder, I can attest to the changes in the community ethos that at first rejected this model, and

now embraces it by placing so many children on the waiting list that three quarters of those waiting are not ever able to be enrolled.

Our small community program began in the opposite way of most inclusive programs. It was initiated to accommodate three children with special needs who were not being served. This was pre-Public Law 94-147, and long before IDEA, so in our county, very young children were not served at that time in the public school system. However, research indicated that early intervention offered the best chance at success. As our first school year unfolded, one of the four-year-old siblings expressed a desire to come, too, and out of that most simple and natural request, inclusion was born at Palma Ceia.

Since the first staff members had expertise in special education, we had to improve our knowledge base in early childhood education, in order to teach our new "playmate." Remember, begin with the end in mind, and then figure out the strategies. Our goal was now inclusion, and we had to figure out our strategies. To meet our newest student's needs, we investigated curricular materials at her level. We had to learn to individualize so that all four of our students were challenged, and not just encourage our typical student to play a "mini-teacher" role. After all, our newest student would be starting kindergarten the next year, and her readiness was very important in her life.

The presence of typical children led to staff training by the High Scope Foundation. In turn, our new knowledge led us to a better understanding of typical early childhood development. This knowledge influenced us to see how teaching and learning could be accomplished in a more natural way with our special needs children. Many times, we found that we did not need the formal task analysis and extremely directed teaching so popular in the early 1980s.

Imagine, special needs children could be incidental learners, too. They learned from each other, not only from instructors. They did not always need extrinsic reinforcement to succeed. The presence of typical children, now increasing, kept our understanding of the developmental norms sharper, improved our assessment skills, and helped us to emphasize the quality, not only the presence, of developmental milestones for our special needs population.

In the development and current success of our school, attitude has played a role of great magnitude. As our school grew, we could have decided not to serve particular children, but we always said, "We'll try." Each diagnosis led us to new confidence as we researched and remained open to new learning. We found the answers because we looked for them. To succeed with children, begin with the goal, and then research and design specific strategies to support that child. Often, you will find a possible path to success. You will find you can do more than you think.

More recently in our history, we began to receive more referrals of children with the diagnoses of autism, Pervasive Development Delay, and with problem behaviors. Although we tried standard guidance strategies, which had in the past worked for us, we found these children to be very challenging in our community program. We were reluctant, however, to admit that we could not serve their needs. We were extremely fortunate to have in our community a nationally known researcher and author in the Department of Child and Family Studies at the University of South Florida. Dr. Lise Fox was willing to collaborate with us. We envisioned a true collaboration, in which the university helped to build our capacity to serve children with problem behaviors, and our preschool provided the university researchers with a community perspective, a site for data collection, and community home for university students. We called our collaboration First Steps Together. The collaboration did indeed build our capacity, and now our school is much more able to implement Positive Behavior Support plans for children experiencing problem behaviors. Positive Behavior Support is an approach to resolving problem behaviors that is based on person-centered values and effective procedures. PBS reduces problem behaviors through environmental enrichment, developing adaptive alternatives, and enhancing a person's competence and lifestyle. The children have responded well, and the staff takes pride in our greater professionalism. The collaboration has yielded far more than staff training, however. University and preschool staffs have presented together at local, state, and national conferences, coauthored papers for publication, and hosted two students at the school in their work toward Master's theses. Now in its sixth year, videotape of the preschool will be used in training materials produced by the university, and used nationwide.

Finally, no perspective may be ignored. Through our desire to serve the children, we grew in awareness of the perspective of teachers. Our accreditation by the National Association for the Education of Young Children and national research led us to understand that a significant part of nurturing children is in nurturing their teachers. Inclusion can be difficult, and we did not find success in browbeating teachers into teaching special needs children without the support necessary to succeed. We found success in respecting teachers and their perspectives wherever we could, in helping them understand their strengths, and in assigning children based on team perspective. In special education, few teachers have had experience or training in all the challenging conditions that may present themselves. So accommodating teachers in their understanding of their own strengths leads to a culture of trust, a culture of choice making for teachers as well as for children, and strengthening of skills needed to support children, over time.

So, concretely, what makes inclusion work for us? First of all, before inclusion can work, best practices for all children must be in place. We keep low staff-to-child ratios, at or below those recommended by the National Association for the Education of Young Children. With inclusion, a

For more information about the Gifted and Talented Students Education Act of 1999, go to the Companion Website at **http://www.prenhall.com/ morrison**, select any chapter, then choose Topic 9 of the ECE Supersite module.

For example, they may be interested in tutoring other students who need extra practice or help. Tutoring can cut across grade and age levels. Students can also help explain directions and procedures to the class. Professionals can encourage them to use their talents and abilities outside the classroom by becoming involved with other people and agencies and can foster creativity through classroom activities that require divergent thinking ("Let's think of all the different uses for a paper clip").

Professionals must challenge children to think through the use of higher-order questions that encourage them to explain, apply, analyze, rearrange, and judge. Many schools have resource rooms for gifted and talented students, in which children can spend a half day or more every week working with a professional who is interested and trained in working with them.

Of these methods, resource room pullout is the most popular.

teacher may have students with developmental ages spanning perhaps three years, instead of the more homogenous segregated classroom. Time to understand; through assessment and observation, each child's developmental level is critical, so each teacher's class load is kept low. Another strategy that has worked for us is to hire a mix of special educators and early childhood educators. The day may come when special educators have great proficiency in normal development, and early childhood educators know how to write IEPs, but for now we find the inclusion of both teaching perspectives to be important.

Our children are not differentiated by ability any more than possible adaptations require. We have speech therapists and occupational therapists working in our program, and when they are taking children out "to play," friends are always welcome. So even in that setting, challenged and typical friends are together, and the children do not view therapies as anything other than a special play setting.

We have developed key phrases to give children in their developing understanding of challenges faced by other children. Many of our key phrases start with the words "he or she needs. . . ." Typical children are able, with permission, to manipulate walkers and wheelchairs to prevent development of fear of assistive devices. As young children develop early understandings of disability, they use verbal approximations that do not always sound sensitive to adult ears. The children may say, "He is a baby." Our staff has learned to view these as early communication, and to encourage them, substituting more appropriate words such as, "She is learning to talk, and as she learns, she has some signs; let us show you what they mean."

Wherever possible, we find materials, posters, toys, and props to support our inclusion goals. The children play with dolls using wheelchairs, walkers, and other supports. We use sign language in the context of music and movement. We have access to Braille for the writing center. Challenges that are seen are handled in a matter-of-fact way, those unseen challenges are verbally addressed.

Today, our hallways are filled with awards of all kinds for our inclusive program. We deeply appreciate the validation. It is deserved wherever in this country teachers give their best to children. But the awards that live in our hearts are the tender bonds between children and teachers and parents. For each of our twenty years, we have had stories to last the ages. We got to know Jessie, who certainly is challenged, but who, while living in Italy with her family, knew the location of every piazza and could always guide her family to these treasures, every time they got lost. We got to know Rachel, who loves the Monkees, and writes to one of their famous members, who writes back. They have been pen pals for years. We watched one of our families through the death of their tiny little daughter, and rejoiced with them at the birth of their typical child. Because our program is inclusive, we taught him, too, and watched a family heal. Staff members have brought all their children to our school, special and typically special, and all the staff children belong in a special way.

In our hearts, we know what is right to do. Decide to include all children, and then figure out how. You will be able to do more than you think. You can find the help you need to succeed. If you say yes, I can promise you a wonderful and eventful journey, one that is richer and deeper than any easy ride. And you will have Jessies, Joses, Brittneys, and Nickies to fill your heart forever. Inclusion is possible, it is desirable, and it should be embraced.

Text and photo contributed by Nancy King Little, Director and Founder of Palma Ceia Presbyterian Church Preschool, Tampa, Florida, *Parent and Child* Early Childhood Professional Award winner.

ABUSED/NEGLECTED CHILDREN

Many of our views of childhood are highly romanticized. We tend to believe that parents always love their children and enjoy caring for them. We also envision family settings full of joy, happiness, and parent–child harmony. Unfortunately for children, their parents, and society, these assumptions are not always true. The extent of child abuse is far greater than we might imagine. In 2000, an estimated 3 million children were reported to Child Protective Services (CPS) agencies as alleged victims of child maltreatment (e.g., physical abuse, neglect, sexual abuse, emotional maltreatment).

Child abuse is not new, although it receives greater attention and publicity now than previously. Abuse, in the form of abandonment, infanticide, and neglect, has been docu-

Collaboration with an Itinerant Special Educator

As an early childhood educator your classes will include children with disabilities. Many school districts offer a program for preschoolers with special needs in which a special education itinerant teacher (SEIT) travels to the community setting where the child is enrolled and works collaboratively with the classroom teacher. These itinerant programs were created in response to federal laws that require school districts to serve special education students in the least restrictive environment. This means that the district must meet the children's educational needs but not remove them from a typical educational setting (with typically developing peers) anymore than necessary. If this type of itinerant program is available in your local school district, this special education teacher can be a valuable resource to you, your students, and their parents. This traveling teacher can provide information, assist you in making helpful modifications to the classroom environment, coach you in some new instructional techniques, and in some cases work directly with the child for part of each week.

As a resource person, the itinerant teacher can give you and a child's parents information about her disability and explain any jargon or medical terms that may be present in evaluation reports. Much of this will be shared during the child's Individual Education Program (IEP) conference. You will be asked to attend this meeting with the parents and special education staff where goals and short-term objectives will be developed for the child. After this conference the itinerant teacher may refer the parents to additional resources such as pertinent websites or parent support groups.

Once the child's IEP has been developed, the itinerant teacher's role unfolds even further. Most likely, she will start by watching the class in action and talking with you about how the physical environment is working for a child with a disability. Is the room fully accessible for this child,

mented throughout history. The attitude that children are property partly accounts for the history of abuse. Parents have believed, and some still do, that they own their children and can do with them as they please.

The extent to which children are abused is difficult to ascertain but is probably much greater than most people realize. Valid statistics are difficult to come by because the interest in reported child abuse is relatively new. In addition, definitions of child abuse and neglect differ from state to state and reports are categorized differently. Probably as many as one million incidents of abuse occur a year, but it is estimated that only one in four cases is reported.

Because of the increasing concern over child abuse, social agencies, hospitals, child care centers, and schools are becoming more involved in identification, treatment, and prevention of this national social problem. To do something about child abuse, those who are involved with children and parents have to know what abuse is. Public Law 93-247, the Child Abuse Prevention and Treatment Act, defines *child abuse and neglect* as the "physical or mental injury, sexual abuse, negligent treatment or maltreatment of a child under the age of eighteen by a person who is responsible for the child's welfare under circumstances which indicate that the child's health or welfare is harmed or threatened thereby as determined in accordance with regulations prescribed by the secretary."[10] In addition, all states have some kind of legal or statutory definition for child abuse and mistreatment. Many states are defining penalties for child abuse.

For information about child abuse and to link to the sites listed in this chapter, go to the Companion Website at **http://www.prenhall. com/morrison**, select chapter 16, then choose the Linking to Learning module.

is the equipment appropriate for their skill level, and does the child seem to find all areas of the room inviting? The itinerant teacher will most likely have equipment to loan to you. She might also help you provide more visual supports for the child in the classroom such as a picture-schedule or markings on the floor to indicate where children sit and line up.

Next, the itinerant teacher might study the social environment. Many children with disabilities need adult support to extend their engagement in activities and peer models in a small group setting to demonstrate slightly more advanced skills that they may strive to imitate. The itinerant teacher might ask if you feel there is enough adult attention available to this child, and if not, how might the scheduling of teacher duties be modified to help. In many instances, the itinerant teacher can help with this by working within classroom routines for at least part of each week. (This will vary from district to district.) Forming friendships is often a challenge area for children with special needs and the itinerant teacher can also work with you to improve the social environment by offering friendship activities or cooperative projects to help children interact in positive ways.

Collaborating with you on ways to **embed instruction** on specific objectives into free play activities would likely be the next type of support provided by the itinerant teacher. School districts are required to provide "specialized instruction" to students with disabilities, but this instruction can utilize **naturalistic methods**. In other words, the instruction can blend right into normal classroom routines. For example, if the child has a social ob-

jective to greet his classmates using their names, then teachers would look for natural opportunities to work on this skill. They might prompt this behavior during arrival time or during opening circle time by using a greeting-song and again when classmates enter an area where the child is working during free choice time.

Some of the child's objectives will need to be taught during teacher-directed group times such as identifying colors and shapes in the context of board games or answering questions after a story. Children with special needs can have difficulty attending and following directions in groups. The itinerant teacher can be a careful observer and help you discover ways to engage the child more effectively during group instruction. In some cases the two of you might decide that the itinerant teacher should get more directly involved by providing some direct instruction themselves. This would most likely be done in small group format with a few typically developing classmates. If this can be done at the same time the rest of the class is working in small groups, it can blend in as a natural part of the classroom routine.

Hopefully, during the course of your career you will join in a collaborative teaching experience with an itinerant special education teacher. The two of you can learn a lot from each other and together share the joy of watching young children with special needs succeed in their very own neighborhood preschool.

Contributed by Faith Haertig Sadler, M.Ed., itinerant special education teacher.

Just as debilitating as physical abuse and neglect is *emotional abuse,* which occurs when parents, teachers, and others strip children of their self-esteem and self-image. Adults take away children's self-esteem through continually criticizing, belittling, screaming and nagging, creating fear, and intentionally and severely limiting opportunities. Emotional abuse is difficult to define legally and, most certainly, difficult to document. The unfortunate consequence for emotionally abused children is that they are often left in a debilitating environment. Both abuse and neglect adversely affect children's growth and development.

Table 16.2 on page 496 will help you identify abuse and neglect. Remember that the presence of a single characteristic does not necessarily indicate abuse. You should observe the child's behavior and appearance over a period of time and should also be willing to give parents the benefit of the doubt about a child's condition.

Embedded instruction
Instruction that is included as an integral part of normal classroom routines.

Naturalistic methods
Incorporating instruction into opportunities that occur naturally or routinely in the classroom.

SEEKING HELP

What can be done about child abuse? There must be a conscious effort to educate, treat, and help abusers and potential abusers. The school is a good place to begin. Another source of help is the federal government's National Center on Child Abuse and Neglect, which helps coordinate and develop programs and policies concerning child abuse and neglect. For information, call or write to any of the following:

There is a lot to know and do when teaching in an inclusive classroom or other setting. As this figure indicates, you will need special kinds of knowledge and skills about students, the curriculum, and working with others. What are some things you can do now to prepare yourself for inclusive learning?

Knowledge of Students and Their Needs

- Learn characteristics of students with special needs.
- Learn legislation regarding students with special needs.
- Develop a willingness to teach students with special needs.
- Foster social acceptance of students with special needs.
- Use assistive and educational technologies.

Classroom Leadership and Classroom Management Skills

- Plan and manage the learning environment to accommodate students with special needs.
- Provide inclusion in varied student groupings and use peer tutoring.
- Manage the behavior of special needs students.
- Motivate all students.

EFFECTIVE TEACHING IN INCLUSIVE CLASSROOMS

Knowledge and Skills in Curriculum and Instruction

- Develop and modify instruction for students with special needs.
- Use a variety of instructional styles and media and increase the range of learning behaviors.
- Provide instruction for students of all ability levels.
- Modify assessment techniques for students with special needs.
- Individualize instruction and integrate the curriculum.

Professional Collaboration Skills

- Work closely with special educators and other specialists.
- Work with and involve parents.
- Participate in planning and implementing IEPs.

FIGURE 16.10   Knowledge and Skills for Effective Teaching in Inclusive Classrooms

Source: From George S. Morrison, *Teaching in America,* 3rd ed. © 2003. Published by Allyn and Bacon, Boston, MA. copyright © 2003 by Pearson Education. Adapted by permission of the publisher.

- The National Center on Child Abuse and Neglect, Children's Bureau, Office of Child Development, Office of Human Development, Department of Health and Human Services, 200 Independence Avenue, NW, Washington, D.C., 20201. http:// www.acf.dhhs.gov/
- Child Help USA handles crisis calls and provides information and referrals to every county in the United States. Its hotline is 1-800-422-4453. http://www.childhelpusa.org/
- The National Committee to Prevent Child Abuse (NCPCA) is a volunteer organization of concerned citizens that works with community, state, and national groups to expand and disseminate knowledge about child abuse prevention. The NCPCA has chapters in all states; the address for its national office is National Committee to Prevent Child Abuse, 332 S. Michigan Avenue, Suite 1600, Chicago, IL 60604; telephone 312-663-3520. http://www.childabuse.org/

Visual/Performing Arts
outstanding in sense of spatial relationships
unusual ability for expressing self feelings, moods, etc., through dance, music, drama
good motor coordination
exhibits creative expression
desire for producing "own product" (not content with mere copying)
observant

Leadership
assumes responsibility
high expectation for self
and others
fluent, concise self-
expression
foresees consequence
and implications of
decisions
good judgment in
decision making
likes structure
well liked by peers
self-confident
organized

Creative Thinking
independent thinker
exhibits original thinking in oral and written expression
comes up with several solutions to a given problem
possesses a sense of humor
creates and invents
challenged by creative tasks
improvises often
does not mind being different from the crowd

General Intellectual Abilities
formulates abstractions
processes information in
complex ways
observant
excited about new ideas
enjoys hypothesizing
learns rapidly
uses a large vocabulary
inquisitive
self-starter

Specific Academic Ability
good memorization ability
advanced comprehension
acquires basic-skills knowledge quickly
widely read in special-interest area
high academic success in special-interest area
pursues special interests with enthusiasm and vigor

FIGURE 16.11 Characteristics of Various Areas of Giftedness

Source: Copyright © National Association for Gifted Children (NAGC), Washington, DC. This chart may not be further reproduced without the permission of NAGC.

VIDEO VIEWPOINT

Teacher's Little Helper

As more children become more difficult for teachers to teach and control, teachers are increasingly recommending that children be placed on medication to control their behavior. This use of drugs to control children's behavior, rather than teaching children to control their own behavior, is a growing concern for many early childhood professionals. Growing numbers of professionals object to medication being part of the teacher's "bag of tricks."

REFLECTIVE DISCUSSION QUESTIONS

What are the controversies surrounding the use of Ritalin to control children's behaviors? What are some reasons why teachers would recommend that children should be placed on Ritalin? Would you as an early childhood professional consider Ritalin an appropri-

ate alternative for use with young children? Do you think the use of Ritalin is an epidemic?

REFLECTIVE DECISION MAKING

Interview parents whose children are on Ritalin. Why was the child placed on Ritalin? Do the parents believe that Ritalin is helping their child? How? What advice would you give to a parent who asked you if you thought Ritalin was an appropriate response to children's destructive/aggressive/hyperactive behavior? What would be some activities you could recommend for controlling children's behavior without medication? Interview early childhood teachers and ask their opinions regarding the use of Ritalin. Based on your discussions, do you think they are pressuring parents into having Ritalin prescribed for their children?

TABLE 16.2 Indicators of Child Abuse

Abuse Type	Physical Indicators	Behavioral Indicators
Physical Abuse	Unexplained bruises and welts • on torso, back, buttocks, thighs or face • identifiable shape of object used to inflict injury (belt, electrical cord, etc.) • appear with regularity after absence, weekend, or vacation Unexplained burns • on soles of feet, palms, back, buttocks, or head • hot water, immersion burns (glove-like, sock-like, or doughnut-shaped burn on buttocks or genitals) Unexplained fractures or dislocations Bald patches on scalp	Child states he/she "deserves" punishment Fearful when others cry Behavioral extremes • aggressive • withdrawn Frightened of parents or caretakers Afraid to go home Child reports injury by parents or caretakers Inappropriate/immature acting out Needy for affection Manipulative behaviors to get attention Tendency toward superficial relationships Unable to focus—daydreaming Self-abusive behavior or lack of concern for personal safety Wary of adult contact
Physical Neglect	Not meeting basic needs • food, shelter, clothing Failure to thrive • underweight, small for age Persistent hunger Poor hygiene Inappropriate dress for season or weather Consistent lack of supervision Unattended physical problems or medical needs Abandonment	Begging or stealing food Early arrival or late departure from school Frequent visits to the school nurse Difficulty with vision or hearing Poor coordination Often tired or falling asleep in class Takes on adult roles and responsibilities Substance abuse Acting out behavior Child verbalizes a lack of care-taking
Sexual Abuse	Difficulty walking or sitting Torn, stained, or bloody undergarments Pain, swelling, or itching in genital area Pain when urinating Bruises, bleeding, or tears around the genital area Vaginal or penile discharge Sexually transmitted diseases • herpes, crabs, vaginal warts • gonorrhea, syphilis • HIV, AIDS Excessive masturbation	Unwilling to change for gym or participate in physical education activities Sexual behavior or knowledge inappropriate to the child's age Sexual acting out on younger children Poor peer relations Delinquent or runaway behavior Report of sexual assault Drastic change in school performance Sleep disorders/nightmares Eating disorders Aggression Withdrawal, fantasy, infantile behavior Self-abusive behavior or lack of concern for personal safety Substance abuse Repetitive behaviors • hand-washing, pacing, rocking
Emotional Abuse and Neglect	Speech disorders • stuttering • baby talk • unresponsiveness Failure to thrive • underweight, small for age Hyperactivity	Learning disabilities Habits • sucking, biting, rocking Sleep disorders Poor social skills Extreme reactions to common events Unusually fearful Overly compliant behaviors • unable to set limits Suicidal thoughts or actions; self-abusive Difficulty following rules or directions Child expects to fail so does not try

Source: Childhelp USA® (2003). "Child abuse: What is it? What can you do?" Reprinted by permission.

LEARNING CENTERS IN INCLUSIVE CLASSROOMS

The following material was contributed by Susan Hentz, Florida Council of Exceptional Children 2003 Teacher of the Year.

In order to promote success in an inclusive classroom, the teachers must create an environment conducive to active learning. They must be creative, flexible, and open to new ways of teaching. The utilization of multisensory learning centers can assist in meeting the diverse needs in an inclusive classroom. Learning centers can address various instructional levels with emphasis on visual, auditory, and the kinesthetic pathways to learning.

   Basic centers can be used all year, and as the year progresses the activities within the centers can continually change based on the needs of the students. Learning center rules should be set up before your first rotation and should be consistent. Be sure to model appropriate center behaviors-role play and practice. Post procedures/visual aids at each center to be used as a reference. Examples of learning centers and materials may include, but are not limited to these:

Author's Nook/Writing Center

Various writing materials: colored pencils, crayons, markers, white boards, paper, greeting cards

Alphabet chart

Examples of good writing

Magnetic letters

Shower curtain—use for word wall or a large floor storyboard

Publishing materials

Mailbox: student letters

Alphabet stamps

Wikki sticks

Picture stamps/stickers for rebus stories

Story starters—pictures

This center should have a large, comfortable space for writing.

Listening/Sound Stage/ Auditory Center

Headphones would be useful at this center. Tapes or CDs can be commercial or teacher/parent-made.

Books on tape

Tape recorder

Spelling review tests

Following directions

Songs, poems, riddles

Language Master

Tapes of parent readers

Student-made tapes/CDs

This center can be a desktop or a corner in the classroom.

Math/Manipulative Center

A very good place for this center is near the calendar board.

Linking cubes

Scales

Stacking items

Pattern blocks

Plastic counters

Math Geo Safari

Fraction models

Play money

This center can also provide opportunities for daily graphing.

Library/Reading Center

Books can be sorted by units of study, student-made books, holidays, featured authors, journals, magazines, etc.

Puppets

Flannel board stories

Magnetic storyboards

Pocket charts: rebus, words

Books: shelves, tubs, boxes, baskets

Flashcards: letters, words

Poetry box

Encourage silent reading, buddy reading, and oral reading. This center should have comfortable seating in a secluded atmosphere.

Technology/Computer Center

Computers should have a variety of multi-level software and living books.

Learning games

Telecommunications

Cross-curricular software

Be sure to keep computers away from windows to keep the glare of sunlight off the screens.

University Primary School

MISSION AND PHILOSOPHY

University Primary School is an early childhood gifted education program serving children ages three to seven. The mission of University Primary School is to provide a site for the individuals at the College of Education of the University of Illinois at Urbana–Champaign to demonstrate, observe, study, and teach best practices in early childhood and gifted education. In this way, University Primary School is a site for research and teacher education, while at the same time providing a service to the community, especially to families with young children.

The philosophy of University Primary School is that young children are best served by teaching and curriculum practices that strengthen and support their intellectual growth and development, initiate them into basic skills, challenge them to increase their proficiency in academic tasks as well as intellectual processes, and at the same time foster the development of their social competence. University Primary School is an inclusive early childhood program that nurtures the strengths and talents of all children through its curricular and instructional approach.

INSTRUCTIONAL APPROACH AND CURRICULUM

The early childhood program adopted by University Primary School is based on principles of practice derived from the best available knowledge of how children grow, develop, and learn. These principles are generally accepted by the early childhood profession as appropriate to the age groups served. The basic assumption derived from developmental research is that in the early years, children learn best from active rather than passive experiences, from being in interactive rather than receptive roles in the learning context.

The curriculum is child-sensitive and responsive to individual patterns of growth, development, learning, and interests. Children have regular and frequent opportunities to work in informal groups on challenging tasks, and to make decisions and choices.

The child's initiative, creativity, and problem solving are encouraged in all areas of the curriculum. By incorporating the Project Approach into the curriculum, children become actively involved in research and inquiry about topics worthy of their time and energy.

Children today are subjected to many stressful situations, including community environment, home life, and television. As early childhood professionals, what can we do to reduce or eliminate stresses that imperil children's lives and learning?

HOMELESS CHILDREN

Walking down a city street, you may have encountered homeless men and women, but have you seen a homeless child? Homeless children are the neglected, forgotten, often abandoned segment of the growing homeless population in the United States. The Urban Institute estimates there are as many as 1.35 million homeless children, living either in homeless families or on their own. The National Coalition for the Homeless says children are the fastest growing population among the homeless.

UNIQUE FEATURES OF UNIVERSITY PRIMARY SCHOOL

The daily schedule provides time for in-depth study and self-selected activities as well as small-group language arts and math instruction and an individualized reading program. These areas of the curriculum are described below.

Activity Time and Project-Work

Activity time and project-work is highly valued in our curriculum. Activity time allows students to make choices about their own learning and provides important school time to work in their interest areas. During this time period, teachers facilitate students' learning by building on their ideas. Projects present learning to children in real-life contexts and integrate the acquisition and application of basic skills through inquiry modes of learning. Activity time and project-work strive to foster "the love of learning" and provide an opportunity for teachers to engage in the learning process with their students.

Numeration and Problem-Solving Skills

Math is taught with an investigative approach, with a focus on relating math to real-life situations using manipulatives and other concrete materials. Teachers facilitate learning in the following areas at the child's individual readiness level: conceptual skills, numeration, computation, measurement, problem solving, and geometry. Many of the students' projects will reflect integration of these mathematical skills.

Language Arts

This program emphasizes a whole language approach where children learn to read by reading and to write by writing. Students are actively involved in both processes throughout the day. Importance is placed on the "making sense" process. They learn within the whole context rather than parts. Early literacy involves three reading cue systems: contextual, grammatical, and phonetic. Teachers create a literacy-rich environment and model meaningful reading and writing.

Arts and Aesthetics

The arts are integral to children's learning. Teachers guide students toward meaningful experiences in the arts with examples, materials, and cultural artifacts. Students create meaningful two- and three-dimensional representations that illuminate their thinking and understanding of the topics they study and investigate. Teachers promote sensitivity to and an appreciation of the environment.

Social and Emotional Growth

Teachers take a proactive role in creating a classroom community that is open, honest, and accepting. To this end, discipline is designed around teachers structuring appropriate choices, students learning how to solve their own problems, and students sharing in the responsibility of developing a caring classroom community. Teachers encourage self-control and strive to develop both intellectual and emotional self-confidence.

University Primary School has several curricular exemplars of students engaged in projects online. Visit University Primary School on the Web at http://www.ed.uiuc.edu/ups/.

Contributed by Nancy B. Hertzog, Ph.D., director University Primary School, Urbana–Champaign, Illinois.

Homelessness has significant mental, physical, and educational consequences for children. Homelessness results in developmental delays and can produce high levels of distress. Homeless children observed in day care centers exhibit such problem behaviors as short attention spans, weak impulse control, withdrawal, aggression, speech delays, and regressive behavior. Homeless children are at greater risk than others for health problems. If they do enter school, they face many problems relating to their previous school problems (grade failure) and attendance (long trips to attend school). In addition, childhood homelessness is a strong risk factor for adult homelessness. Fortunately, more agencies are responding to the unique needs of homeless children and their families.

Public Law 107-110, the McKinney-Vento Homeless Education Act of 2001, provides that "each State educational agency shall assure that each child of a homeless individual and each homeless youth has access to the same free, appropriate public education, including a public preschool education as provided to other children and youth."[11]

 To take an online self-test on this chapter's contents, go to the Companion Website at **http://www.prenhall.com/morrison**, select chapter 16, then choose the Self-Test module.

 To complete a Program in Action activity, visit the Companion Website at **http://www.prenhall.com/morrison**, select chapter 16, then choose the Program in Action module.

Children Who Are Poor and Homeless and Their Educational Needs

Holy Family Home and Shelter, Inc., which opened on February 3, 1989, enables homeless children to attend school, the one constant in their young and troubled lives. Children living at Holy Family attend the local schools in Willimantic, Connecticut. However, if they wish to stay in their own school, *The Education of Students in Homeless Situations* in the *2001 No Child Left Behind Act* along with the *McKinney–Vento Act* that was reauthorized in 2001, has a provision that transportation must be provided to the school of origin. Keep in mind that the shelter is merely temporary housing not a change of address.

In August of 1993, Holy Family Home and Shelter began an education program called THE KEY. This program did not replace the public school curriculum, but was an enhancement in helping the children with their education needs. One problem that was prevalent among the school-age children was homework—when to do it, how to do it, and who could help them. Our plan included a preschool, toddler time, and an after-school tutoring program. Tutors, students, and professors from the University of Connecticut and Eastern Connecticut State University, have been a vital force in the after-school program. Once the children in the shelter regained their educational footing and had the additional help from the shelter, grades improved, social attitudes changed for the better, and the children became less stressed.

In order for people to free themselves from the world of poverty and homelessness they need a key to open the door to prosperity and homeownership. This key is education—thus, the name for the education program. In the evolution of the program the name changed from THE KEY to The Holy Family Home and Shelter Education Program, keeping in mind that education is still the key that unlocks the door to personal freedom.

For additional Internet resources or to complete an online activity for this chapter, go to the Companion Website at **http://www. prenhall.com/morrison**, select chapter 16, then choose the Linking to Learning or Making Connections module.

SUMMARY

Children with disabilities today face a far brighter future than did children thirty years ago who were born with disabilities. They, their parents, and their teachers have the provisions of IDEA to help assure that they will have the best possible education and as a result the best possible life outcomes and futures. As a professional you will be teaching in inclusive classrooms with children who have a wide variety of special needs. In order to achieve this goal, you will collaborate with a wide range of professionals who can help you respond to students' needs. Indeed, collaboration may well be one of your most important professional roles. As the waves of reform that we have discussed sweep over classrooms and schools, you will also need to be a strong and vocal advocate for the needs of children with disabilities. We can never lose sight of the vision that high-quality classrooms, programs, services, and teachers are for all of America's children.

ACTIVITIES FOR FURTHER ENRICHMENT

APPLICATIONS

1. Visit a center where children with special needs are included, and observe the children during play activities. Follow a particular child and note the materials available,

Although teachers at Holy Family may change from time to time, the essence of the program does not. Our newest teacher, Marja Prewitt, has a wealth of international classroom experience. As a result of teaching a variety of ethnic and indigenous children she was able to expand on the education program over the summer months. Holy Family's education program does not run on the local academic calendar, but provides for year-round learning. When there is no school, the children engage in educational hands on projects, such as making shadow puppets, or creating holiday pastries. Field trips to local historical museums or state parks help to broaden the children's educational vistas.

The children who come into homeless shelters carry a huge burden of abuse, neglect, and nightmarish experiences. Often we encounter children with behavioral problems. Sometimes these problems can be addressed between the school system and the education coordinator. At other times it is necessary to hospitalize the child for his/her general well-being and protection. In the Windham area there is an out-patient hospital program for children, called the Joshua Program. This program has counseling as well as an education component.

The creation of a safe, healthy, loving atmosphere for the families is the mission of Holy Family Home and Shelter. We try to bring out the best in our children, highlight their skills and talents, and build their self-esteem as opportunities arise.

Validating a child's existence is done with birthday parties and special holiday events. Occasionally a group will come and celebrate the day with the children. However, if that is not possible, the Shelter staff makes sure the day is recognized. Gifts are given and cake and ice cream are part of the celebration. The Education Program and celebrations all go into making the stay in the shelter less traumatic for the children.

Another component of the education program is an outreach program to neighborhoods where former families now live. This program, *Books to the Streets,* developed by Miriam Epstein, a Holy Family volunteer, brings new and gently used books, bookmarks, and book buddies (small stuffed animals) to our former resident children and other children in the neighborhoods. This program continues to grow. Volunteers inscribe each book with a positive reading message and then go out to the various neighborhoods and distribute the books to the children.

Another program, *Books to Dreams,* also started by Epstein, brings books, book buddies, and bookmarks into the soup kitchens and shelters in all of eastern Connecticut. At this time, *Books to Dreams* spans the state from the Rhode Island border to Hartford. Children who would not otherwise have their own books to read and keep now have the start of their own libraries. Each shelter and soup kitchen is provided with a book box to allow parents to choose books for their young children, and for older children to choose what interests them.

Contributed by Sister M. Peter Bernard, SCMC, director: public relations and volunteers. Holy Family Home and Shelter, Willimantic, Connecticut.

the physical arrangement of the environment, and the number of other children involved. Try to determine whether the child is really engaged in the play activity. Hypothesize about why the child is or is not engaged. Discuss your observations with your colleagues.

2. Develop a file or notebook where you can keep suggestions for adapting curricula for children with special needs.

3. Visit an early childhood special education classroom and a regular preschool classroom and compare the types of behavior management problems and techniques found in each setting.

FIELD EXPERIENCES

1. Visit several public schools to see how they are providing individualized and appropriate programs for children with disabilities. What efforts are being made to involve parents?

2. Visit agencies and programs that provide services for people with disabilities. Before you visit, list specific features, services, and facilities you will look for.

3. How is curriculum and instruction in a class for gifted and talented students different from that in other classes? Get permission to visit and observe such a class. Then compare that class with others you have observed or experienced. On the basis of your ob-

servations, describe how you might teach a student who is gifted and talented within your inclusive classroom.

4. Contact local schools in your area and ask them what activities and services they provide for students before and after school. How are these designed to meet students' special needs?

RESEARCH

1. Interview parents of children with disabilities. What do they feel are their greatest problems? What do they consider the greatest needs for their children? List specific ways they have been involved in educational agencies. How have educational agencies avoided or resisted providing for their children's needs?

2. Spend some time in mainstreamed inclusive classrooms. What specific skills would you need to become a good professional in such settings?

3. What programs does the federal government support for children with special needs in your area? Give specific information.

4. Discuss with people of another culture their culture's attitudes toward children with disabilities. How are they similar or different from your attitudes?

5. How does a teacher modify the classroom environment, classroom routines, learning activities, student groupings, teaching strategies, instructional materials, assessments, and homework assignments to meet all students' needs? What human and material resources for successful inclusion are available to teachers and to students with special needs? How do students show social acceptance for their classmates with special needs? Visit an inclusive classroom and take notes on what you observe. Compare and discuss your observations with classmates who have visited different settings across all grade levels.

6. Visit the teacher resource center of a local school district or in the district where you plan to teach. Develop a list of resources that would be available to you in teaching students with special needs in your class.

READINGS FOR FURTHER ENRICHMENT

Cimera, R.E. *The Truth About Special Education: A Guide for Parents and Teachers.* Lanham, MD: Scarecrow Press, 2002.

This text contains a step-by-step discussion of the special education process and has hundreds of additional resources for parents including professional organizations, support groups, and useful websites to help parents and students minimize the anxiety often associated with enrolling in a special education program.

Cook, R. E., Klein, M. D. Tessier, A., and Daley, S. *Adapting Early Childhood Curricula for Children in Inclusive Settings,* 6th ed. Upper Saddle River, NJ: Merrill/Prentice Hall, 2004.

Reflects the most recent developments in the field, presenting the skills necessary for teachers to assist infants, young children, and their families to meet their special challenges and to develop to their fullest potential.

Demchak, M.A., Greenfield, R., and Thomas, M. *Transition Portfolios for Students with Disabilities: How to Help Students, Teachers, and Families Handle New Settings.* Thousand Oaks, CA: Corwin Press, 2002.

This book provides state-of-the-art information on transitioning needs of a wide range of students with disabilities, including those with the most complex needs. Filled with practical ideas and strategies, it supports the efforts of teachers and families to help the student progress successfully through the educational experience.

Friend, M., and Bursuck, W. *Including Students with Special Needs,* 3rd ed. Needham Heights, MA: Allyn & Bacon, 2001.

A practical guide for classroom teachers on teaching all students in inclusive classrooms. Explains how to modify curricula, textbooks, classrooms, student groupings, assessments, and instruction to meet all students' learning needs.

Friend, M., and Cook, L. *Interactions: Collaboration Skills for School Professionals*, 4th ed. Needham Heights, MA: Allyn & Bacon, 2002.

Provides a cutting-edge look at how teams of school professionals can effectively work together to provide a necessary range of services to students with special needs.

Gargiulo, R., Kilgo, J., and Graves, S. *Young Children with Special Needs: An Introduction to Early Childhood Special Education.* Belmont, CA: Wadsworth, 2000.

Focuses on children from birth to age five who are at-risk for school success because of such factors as congenital disorders, developmental problems, and environmental factors such as poverty, abuse, and cultural and linguistic differences.

Howard, V. F., Williams, B. F., Port, P. D., and Lepper, C. *Very Young Children with Special Needs; A Formative Approach for the 21st Century,* 2nd ed. Upper Saddle River, NJ: Merrill/Prentice Hall, 2001.

Provides an introduction to early childhood professionals who plan to provide services and intervention to very young children with disabilities.

Lerner, J.W., Lowenthal, B., and Egan, R.W. *Preschool Children with Special Needs: Children At Risk, Children with Disabilities,* 2nd ed. Boston: Allyn & Bacon, 2003.

Explores ways of providing preschool children with special needs and their families with a learning environment that will help them develop and learn. Describes current models of curricula, which incorporate new features from research and practical experiences with children who have special needs.

Rothstein, L. F. *Special Education Law,* 3rd ed. Boston, MA: Addison Wesley Longman, 2000.

Provides a comprehensive and current overview of the major federal laws, and judicial interpretations of those laws, that apply to the education of children with disabilities.

Sands, D., Kozleski, E., and French, N. *Inclusive Education for the 21st Century.* Belmont, CA: Wadsworth, 2000.

The authors challenge preservice special education and regular education teachers to develop the knowledge and skills to produce and support "inclusive school communities," which is both a process and an outcome, providing all students with access to broad educational opportunities.

LINKING TO LEARNING

National Association for the Education of Homeless Children and Youth (NAEHCY)
http://www.naehcy.org/

A professional organization specifically dedicated to homeless education. Originally the National Association of State Coordinators for the Education of Homeless Children and Youth, NAEHCY was established to ensure research-based strategies for effective approaches to the problems faced by homeless children, youth, and families. The organization has created guidelines, goals, and objectives that function to outline strategies for dealing with government agencies and designing effective programs.

Council for Exceptional Children
http://www.cec.sped.org/

Publishes extremely up-to-date news regarding education-related legislation, and contains numerous links to other sites.

Council for Learning Disabilities
http://www.cldinternational.org

An international organization of and for professionals who represent diverse disciplines and who are committed to enhancing the education and lifespan development of individuals with learning disabilities. CLD establishes standards of excellence and promotes innovative strategies for research and practice through interdisciplinary collegiality, collaboration, and advocacy.

Disabilities Civil Rights
http://www.galaxy.com/galaxy/Government/Law/Constitutional-Law/Civil-Rights/
Disabilities.html

Articles and directories of information concerning legal issues related to disabilities.

DisABILITY: Consumer Law/Searchable Index
http://consumerlawpage.com/resource/ability.shtml

List of links to on-line resources and a searchable index. This site also offers the opportunity for users to submit links to be added to the directory.

Youreable.com
http://www.youreable.com

An interactive forum where questions can be posted and others' questions and responses may be viewed. Includes news, forums, daily living, etc.

Frequently Asked Questions About Access to Technology for Students with Disabilities

RESNA
http://www.resna.org/tap/aet_sfaq.htm

A list of numerous questions and detailed responses concerning technology and students with disabilities.

IDEA Practices
http://www.ideapractices.org

This site answers your questions about the Individuals with Disabilities Education Act, keeps you informed about ideas that work, and supports your efforts to help all children learn, progress, and realize their dreams.

The National Information Center for Children and Youth with Disabilities
http://www.nichcy.org/

The National Information Center for Children and Youth with Disabilities (NICHCY) is the national information and referral center that provides information on disabilities and disability-related issues for families, educators, and other professionals.

Office of Special Education and Rehabilitation Services
http://www.ed.gov/offices/OSERS/

The Office of Special Education and Rehabilitative Services (OSERS) supports programs that assist in educating children with special needs, provides for the rehabilitation of youth and adults with disabilities, and supports research to improve the lives of individuals with disabilities.

Special Child: For Parents of Children with Disabilities
http://www.specialchild.com

An online publication dedicated to parents of children with special needs, provided by the Resource Foundation for Children With Challenges (RFCC).

ENDNOTES

[1] Public Law 105–17, 1997.

[2] Ibid.

[3] National Early Childhood Technical Assistance System, *Helping Our Nation's Infants and Toddlers with Disabilities and Their Families, A Briefing Paper on Part H of the Individuals with Disabilities Education Act (IDEA)*, (Author, 1996). Available at: http://www.nectas.unc.edu.

[4] Chambers, J. G., Parrish, T. B., and Harr, J. J., "What Are We Spending on Special Education Services in the United States, 1999–2000?" American Institutes for Research, Center for Special Education Finance, Special Education Expenditure Project (2002). Available at http://www.seep.org/Docs/AdvRpt1.PDF.

[5] Council for Exceptional Children, 1996. Available at: http://www.cec.sped.org/.

[6] Burnette, J., "Including Students with Disabilities in General Education Classrooms: From Policy to Practice," *The Eric Review* 4 (1996), 2–11.

[7] Ibid.

[8] Ibid.

[9] Jacob K. Javits Gifted and Talented Students Education Act of 1988.

[10] U.S. Statutes at Large, vol. 88, pt. 1 (Washington, DC: U.S. Government Printing Office, 1976), 5.

[11] Public Law 100-77, the Stewart B. McKinney Homeless Assistance Act, Title VII-B—Subtitle B-Education for Homeless Youth, July 1987.

Chapter 17

T hirty years of research show that school, family, and community interaction makes a difference in a student's learning experience. Studies suggest that family involvement can improve student attendance, behavior, and academic achievement, while community involvement can help provide services schools alone cannot give students.

—SOUTHWEST EDUCATIONAL DEVELOPMENT LABORATORY

Parent, Family, and Community Involvement
Cooperation and Collaboration

Focus Questions

● How do changes in society and families influence children and early childhood programs?

● Why is parent, family, and community involvement important in early childhood programs?

● What are the benefits of involving parents and families in early childhood programs?

● How can you and other early childhood professionals encourage and support programs for involving families and communities?

O ne thing we can say with certainty about the educational landscape today is that parents, families, and communities are as much a part of the educational process as are children, teachers, and staff. At no time in U.S. educational history has support for family and community involvement in schools and programs been so high. All concerned view the involvement of families and communities as critical for individual student success as well as for the success of the "American dream" of providing all children with an education that will meet their needs and enable them to succeed in school and be productive members of society. In this chapter, we look at some of the reasons why parent, family, and community involvement in education is so important and how you can confidently and productively contribute to the process.

CHANGES IN SCHOOLING

Schooling used to consist mostly of teaching children social and basic academic skills. But as society has changed, so has the content of schooling. Early childhood programs have assumed many parental functions and responsibilities. Part of the broadening of the role and function of early education and schooling includes helping parents and families with educational and social issues that affect them and their children.

Political and social forces have led to the strengthening of the relationship between families and schools. The accountability and reform movements of the past and present have convinced families that they should no longer be kept out of their children's schools. Families believe they should insist on effective instruction and care from schools and child care centers. They have become more militant in their demand for quality education, and schools and other agencies have responded by seeking ways to involve families in the quest for quality. Education professionals and families realize that mutual cooperation is in everyone's best interest.

In response to the changing landscape of contemporary society, early childhood professionals are working with parents to develop programs to help them and their children develop to their fullest and lead productive lives.

To review the chapter focus questions online, go to the Companion Website at **http://www.prenhall.com/morrison** and select chapter 17.

A Message to the Teaching Profession

It Takes More Than One

In 1983 I graduated from the State University of West Georgia with a teaching degree in my hand, and I took off to set the education world on fire. I truly believed I would be the saving grace of every student I encountered. I alone would be the salvation of education in general. Little did I know that it takes more than one person to educate a child. It didn't take me long to conclude, as the African proverb says, "It takes a village to raise a child."

Parental support, by far, is the most important part of a child's education. Parental involvement begins at birth. Parents who read to their children before they enter school give them a head start toward reading success. Research has also proven that when parents are involved in their children's education, the children do better in school.

Involvement in the schools does not necessarily mean volunteering at the school. There are many times when volunteering is impossible. Involvement in the schools can mean reading to your child, checking homework on a regular basis, and discussing your child's progress with teachers.

Business involvement in schools is vital because the students of today are the employees of tomorrow. How can businesses become involved in our schools? Monetary donations are nice, but that's not the only way to become involved. Businesses can support the schools by providing personnel to serve as mentors for not only students at risk, but for all students. Mentoring is a way to help the students in and out of the school. It provides an opportunity for adults to get involved in kids' lives. The long-term relationship between students and volunteers is definitely a positive result for mentoring. Another way business can help is by allowing employees time away from their job without loss of money to attend functions at school. Many companies now allow employees a certain number of documented hours for involvement in their child's education. What a great benefit—not only for the employee, but also, most importantly, for the child!

Community involvement in schools is necessary because the schools are the heart of society. With the help of everyone involved, success in school is inevitable. It does take a village to raise a child.

Contributed by Theresa Stephens Stapler, Central Elementary School, Carrollton, Georgia, *USA Today's* 2002 All-USA Teacher Award winner.

To check your understanding of this chapter with the online Study Guide, go to the Companion Website at **http://www.prenhall.com/morrison**, select chapter 17, then choose the Study Guide module.

For more information about family–school relations, go to the Companion Website at **http://www.prenhall.com/morrison**, select any chapter, then choose Topic 10 of the ECE Supersite module.

CHANGING FAMILIES

The family of today is not the family of yesterday, nor will the family of today be the family of tomorrow. For example, households with children dropped from 45 percent in the 1970s to 33 percent in 2000. Table 17.1 shows some of the other ways families have changed over the years. In addition, more mothers are entering the workforce than ever before. This means that at an early age, often beginning at six weeks, children are spending eight hours a day or more in the care of others. Thus, working parents are turning their young children over to others for care and spending less time with their children. Parents need more help with rearing their children at earlier ages. As a result, opportunities have blossomed for child-serving agencies, such as child care centers and preschools, to assist and support parents in their child-rearing efforts. One of the major trends of the next decade is that more programs will provide more parents with child development and child-rearing information.

GRANDPARENTS AS PARENTS

Grandparents acting as parents for their grandchildren are a growing reality in the United States today. Since the new millennium, more grandparents are raising their grandchildren

TABLE 17.1 How Families Have Changed

Types of Families	1970	2000
Households with Own Children	45%	33%
Married Couple Families with Children	87%	69%
Single-Mother Families with Children	12%	26%
Single-Father Families with Children	1%	5%
Children Living with Relative	2%	3%
Children Living with Non-Relative	1%	1%

Several things are notable about these family demographics. Notice how married couples with children are decreasing; how single-mother families with children are increasing; and the increase in children living with other relatives. What implications does all of this have for your program of parent and family involvement?

Sources: United States Census Bureau. Available at http://www.census.gov/population/www/socdemo/hh-fam.html; J. Fields & L. M. Casper *America's Families and Living Arrangements:* March 2000; Current Population Reports, P20-537. (Washington, D.C.: U.S. Census Bureau, 2001). Available at http://www.census.gov/prod/2001pubs/p20-537.pdf.

Families continue to change, and, as they do, early childhood professionals must adapt and adopt new ways of involving family members and providing for their needs. For example, what can professionals do to ensure the involvement of grandparents in their programs?

than ever before in American history. Four million children, or 5.5 percent of all children under age eighteen, are living in homes maintained by 2.5 million grandparents. These numbers should come as no surprise when we realize that one in four adults are grandparents. In addition, many of these children are *skipped-generation children,* meaning that neither of their parents is living with them. Reasons for the increases in the number of children living with grandparents include drug use, divorce, mental and physical illness, abandonment, teenage pregnancy, child abuse and neglect, incarceration, and death of the parents.

Grandparent parents in these skipped-generation households have all of the parenting responsibilities of parents. This includes providing for their grandchildren's basic needs and care, as well as making sure that they do well in school. Grandparents need your support and educational assistance to achieve this goal. This is where you can help grandparent parents learn to parent all over again. Keep in mind that they are rearing their grandchildren in a whole different generation than the one in which they reared their children.

You can do some things to help, support, and involve grandparents:

- Provide "refresher" parenting courses to help grandparents understand how children and schooling have changed since they raised their children.
- Link grandparents to support groups such as Raising Our Children's Children (ROCC) and the American Association of Retired Persons (AARP) Grandparent Information Center (website—http://www.aarp.org/confacts/programs/gic.html).

IMPLICATIONS OF FAMILY PATTERNS FOR EARLY CHILDHOOD PROFESSIONALS

Given the changes in families today, there are a number of things you as an early childhood professional can do to help parents, including the following:

- *Provide support services.* Support can extend from being a "listening ear" to organizing support groups and seminars on single parenting. You can help families link up with other agencies and groups, such as Big Brothers and Big Sisters and Families without Partners. Through newsletters and fliers, you can offer families

For more information about changing families, go to the Companion Website at **http://www. prenhall.com/morrison**, select chapter 17, then choose the Linking to Learning module to connect to the Making Lemonade (run by a single mom) and Single and Custodial Father's Network site.

specific advice on how to help children become independent and how to meet the demands of living in single-parent families, stepfamilies, and other family configurations.

- *Provide child care.* As more families need child care, you and other early childhood personnel are logical advocates for establishing care where none exists, extending existing services, and helping to arrange cooperative baby-sitting services.

- *Avoid criticism.* Be careful not to criticize parents for the jobs they are doing. They may not have extra time to spend with their children or know how to discipline them. Regardless of their circumstances, families need help, not criticism.

- *Avoid being judgmental.* Similarly, you should examine and clarify your attitudes and values toward family patterns and remember that there is no "right" family pattern from which all children should come.

- *Arrange educational experiences.* You can address the issue of changing family patterns in the educational experiences you arrange. Offer experiences children might not otherwise have because of their family organization. For example, outdoor activities such as fishing trips and sports events can be interesting and enriching learning experiences for children who may not have such opportunities.

- *Adjust programs.* Adjust classroom and center activities to account for how particular children cope with their home situations. Children's needs for different kinds of activities depend on their experiences at home. For example, opportunities abound for role playing, and such activities help bring into the open situations that children need to talk about. Use program opportunities to discuss families and the roles they play. Make it a point in the classroom to model, encourage, and teach effective interpersonal skills.

- *Be sensitive.* There are specific ways to sensitively approach today's changing family patterns. For example, avoid having children make presents for both parents when it is inappropriate to do so and awarding prizes for bringing both parents to meetings. Replace such terms as *broken home* with *single-parent family.* Be sensitive to the demands of school in relation to children's home lives. For instance, when a professional sent a field trip permission form home with children and told them to have their mothers or fathers sign it, one child said, "I don't have a father. If my mother can't sign it, can the man she sleeps with sign it?" Seek guidance and clarification from families about how they would like specific situations handled; for example, ask whether they want you to send notices of school events to both parents.

- *Seek training.* Request in-service training to help you work with families. In-service programs can provide information about referral agencies, guidance techniques, ways to help families deal with their problems, and child abuse identification and prevention. Professionals need to be alert to the signs of all kinds of child abuse, including mental, physical, and sexual abuse.

- *Increase parent contacts.* Finally, encourage greater and different kinds of **parent involvement** through visiting homes; talking to families about children's needs; providing information and opportunities to parents, grandparents, and other family members; gathering information from families (such as through interest inventories); and keeping in touch with parents. Make parent contacts positive.

Parent involvement The participation of parents in all areas of their children's education and development based on the premise that parents are the primary influence in children's lives.

Parent/family involvement is a process of helping families use their abilities to benefit themselves, their children, and the early childhood program. Families, children, and the program are all part of the process; consequently, all three parties should benefit from a well-planned program of family involvement. Nonetheless, the focus in parent/child/family interactions is the family, and you must work with and through families if you want to be successful.

EDUCATION AS A FAMILY AFFAIR

Education starts in the home, and what happens there profoundly affects the trajectory of development and learning. The greater the family's involvement in children's learning, the more likely it is that students will receive a high-quality education.

The central role families play in children's education is a reality that teachers and schools must address as they make plans for how to reform schools and increase student achievement. Partnering with parents is a process whose time has come, and the benefits far outweigh any inconveniences or barriers that may stand in the way of bringing schools and parents together.

FAMILY-CENTERED PROGRAMS

Family-centered programs focus on meeting the needs of students through the family unit, whatever that unit may be. Education professionals recognize that to most effectively meet the needs of students, they must also meet the needs of family members and the family unit. **Family-centered teaching** and learning make sense for a number of reasons. First, the family unit has the major responsibility for meeting children's needs. Children's development begins in the family system, and this system is a powerful determiner of developmental processes, both for better and worse. Helping individuals in the family unit become better parents and family members benefits children and consequently promotes their success in school.

Second, it is frequently the case that to help children effectively, family issues and problems must be addressed first. For instance, helping parents gain access to adequate and affordable health care increases the chances that the whole family, including children, will be healthy.

Third, teachers can do many things concurrently with children and their families that benefit both. Literacy is a good example. Adopting a family approach to literacy means helping parents learn the importance of literacy and that reading to their children helps ensure children's literacy development.

Even Start is an example of family-centered teaching. It combines adult literacy and parenting training with early childhood education to break cycles of illiteracy that are often passed on from one generation to another. Even Start is, as we discussed in chapter 8, operated through the public school system. In particular, Even Start helps parents become full partners in the education of their children, assists children in reaching their full potential, and provides literacy training for parents. Even Start projects are designed to work cooperatively with existing community resources to provide a full range of services and to integrate early childhood education and adult education. Figure 17.1 diagrams family-centered teaching in action.

Family-centered teaching
A style of instruction that focuses on meeting the needs of students through the family unit.

For more information about involving families in children's education, go to the Companion Website at **http://www.prenhall. com/morrison**, select chapter 17, then choose the Linking to Learning module to connect to several sites with resources for working with families.

FIGURE 17.1 Family-Centered Teaching

Early Childhood Education Teachers

- Parent education
- Literacy programs
- Counseling programs
- Referrals to community agencies
- Assistance with problems of daily living

Outcomes / Benefits

- Increase knowledge, skills, and understanding of education process
- Help families and children address and solve problems
- Provide greater range of resources and more experts than school alone can provide
- Relieve families and children/youth of stress to make learning more possible

Many educational and other services are delivered to children and families through the family unit. For example, many literacy programs work with children and with parents and use this opportunity to improve literacy within the entire family. What else can be taught to children and family members at the same time?

Multigenerational Volunteerism Pays Off

The variety of volunteer programs at the Child Development Center of Central WV, Inc., creates an amazing opportunity for the "Meeting of the Generations." In our twenty-first-century mobile society, the preschool classroom environment sometimes resembles a four-generation family gathering.

By all standards, the ratio of staff to children is an essential indicator of quality in early care and education. Primarily, the value of lower staff to child ratios is the increase of interactions to stimulate thinking, language, learning, problem-solving, and social skills. Of course, the staff-to-child ratio indicator refers to paid, trained teachers and caregivers. Volunteers, while not figured in ratios, provide a very important service in a high-quality early childhood program by increasing the number of adults who directly interact with the children. The Child Development Center of Central WV, Inc., takes a unique approach to volunteerism by recruiting volunteers who have a deeper relationship to the Center and its children. Most of our volunteers are teenage alumni, college students, and members of the Americorps Foster Grandparents Program. Each of these groups brings to our Center, its children, and teachers, a different set of experiences.

The Americorps Foster Grandparents Program brings senior citizens and young children together where the program is developmentally appropriate for both. In our young transient society, many children miss the opportunity for regular contact with their own grandparents. Senior citizens whose grandchildren may live in distant states volunteer to be an extra pair of eyes, ears, and hands in the classroom. When a teacher needs help with feeding or handholding, or when little fingers need help with scissors or glue, no helping hands are more patient that those of a grandparent. More importantly, the unique relationship of the grandparent generation brings comfort to children when they need a little extra love or security. In this setting, the generation gap becomes an asset as grandparents share life experiences of growing up in a different millennium.

For its first twenty-five years, the Child Development Center of Central WV, Inc., served West Virginia Wesleyan College as a field laboratory for early childhood teachers. Then, in 1985, the Center became an independent, non-profit corporation, but remained on the college campus. Ten years later, the Center's board of directors obtained a grant to construct a new, state-of-the-art early childhood facility. The new building was built on the edge of the campus and the two educational institutions maintained their strong relationship.

The Center also serves as a training lab for West Virginia Wesleyan College students bound for careers that

To complete a Program in Action activity, visit the Companion Website at **http://www. prenhall.com/morrison**, select chapter 17, then choose the Program in Action module.

FAMILY-CENTERED CURRICULUM AND INSTRUCTION

Family-centered curriculum and instruction exist at three levels. First, programs and materials are designed to help parents be better parents and teachers of their children. To support parents in these roles, schools and teachers provide materials on parenting, conduct parenting classes, and furnish ideas about teaching their children reading and math skills through daily living activities. At a second level, instruction focuses on helping parents with everyday problems and issues of family living. For example, classes and information on tenant rights, nutritional meals, the importance of immunizations, and access to health services would be in keeping with the ideas of addressing families' daily living needs. At a third level, family-centered curriculum and instruction attempt to integrate students' classroom learning with learning in the home. For example, providing parents with books to read to their children at home would support efforts to link in-school learning with learning in the home.

will involve direct service to children. Commonly, students have younger siblings at home, or have volunteered in church nurseries or scouting programs. When they leave their home community for college, they want to find the joy of those relationships in their new communities. Preschool children benefit greatly from the role modeling that takes place in these big brother/big sister–type relationships. College students find meaningful experiences that replace some of the loss they feel in leaving home.

As a hidden bonus, the student community at WV Wesleyan represents a microcosm of the world community. A large group of students come from Korea and Japan, with a smattering of other world cultures represented. Along with students from all over the United States, these young adults share the world with preschoolers whose community has a 1 percent minority population. The Child Development Center of Central WV, Inc., has a rich, forty-two-year history of service to the early childhood community of Upshur County, West Virginia. In such a small area, this history—along with the longevity of many of the Center's teachers—has produced more than a thousand alumni, many of whom still have close ties to the Center.

High school students who attended the Center as preschoolers are very excited to return as volunteers, to renew relationships with teachers and classrooms, and to serve as role models for their younger counterparts. Kind and mannerly teen role models read to and play with very accepting preschool children. The volunteers themselves experience, often for the first time, the joy of returning service to their teachers, school, and community. The most uniquely rewarding aspect of the alumni volunteer program is the benefit to teachers who experience the success of positive relationships with their preschoolers of a dozen years ago. Teachers, especially in the preschool set-ting, rarely see the "end result" of their work with children. While providing the most direct benefit to the preschoolers, alumni and teachers reestablish very meaningful relationships.

In combination, the volunteer programs create a somewhat multigenerational extended classroom family. On some occasions, a classroom may buzz with the activity of all its family members at the same time, but generally, all of the "family" is not present all of the time. Teen alumni volunteers attend middle school or high school during regular school days, coming to the Center after school, on holidays, or during the summer. Foster grandparents volunteer about twenty hours each week, mostly during the busy morning schedule. College volunteers, with widely varying schedules, come and go from early morning to late evening.

Since the goals and objectives of an early childhood classroom are developmental and educational, the wide range of volunteer contacts is especially helpful in reaching these goals. Teachers consider many developmental domains, with specific attention devoted to physical, language, social/emotional, and cognitive development. As each child moves along a continuum in each of these areas of development, the teaching staff plans and implements curricula designed to "meet" children where they are and to take each child forward from that point.

A multigenerational volunteer program has proven to be beneficial to everyone involved. Children, youth, and adults leave having experienced each other in the most positive environment of caring and receiving care, of loving and being loved, of living and sharing life with one another.

Contributed by Chuck Loudin, executive director, Child Development Center of Central WV, Inc.

TWO-GENERATION AND INTERGENERATIONAL PROGRAMS

Two-generation programs involve parents and their children and are designed to help both generations and strengthen the family unit. Two-generation delivery of services can and should begin before children's birth because many problems relating to child health can be prevented by good prenatal care. **Intergenerational programs** involve grandparents and others as well. The preventive approach to maternal and prenatal health is reflected in the growing numbers of schools that have on-site health clinics. Services often include both health and education in which students and parents receive medical care and information that will support their efforts to lead healthy lives. It also includes programs in which young people provide services to older persons, in which older persons provide services to youth, and in which two generations work cooperatively on a project.

Two-generation programs
Programs that involve parents and their children and are designed to help both generations and strengthen the family unit.

Intergenerational programs
Programs that involve grandparents and their grandchildren and are designed to help both generations.

Avance   One example of a parenting program is AVANCE, from the Spanish word for "advance" or "progress," serves the needs of the hardest-to-reach, primarily Hispanic, families.

Six Types of Parent/Family Involvement

As you think about your role in parent and family involvement, it would be helpful to review the six types of parent involvement outlined in Figure 17.2. These six types of parent/family involvement constitute a comprehensive approach to your work with parents. A worthy professional goal would be for you to try to have some of your parents involved in all six of these types of parental involvement through the program year. Let's take a closer look at these types, with examples of each from actual practice.

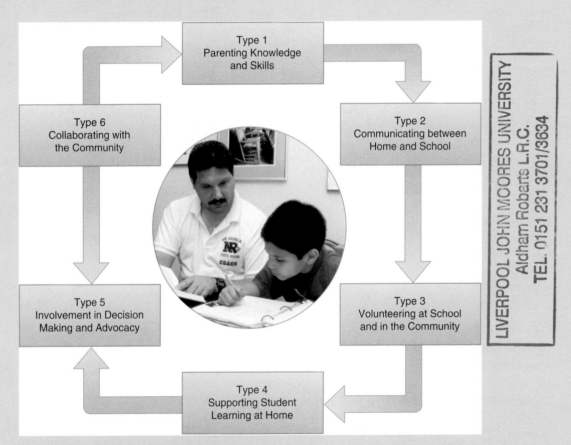

FIGURE 17.2 Types of Parent/Family Involvement

Taken as a whole, these six types of parent and family involvement constitute a comprehensive program to help assure that parents and other family members are empowered and supported in the educational process. Consider how you can implement each of these types in your present or future program.

Source: J. Epstein, *School, Family, and Community Partnerships: Preparing Educators and Improving Schools* (Boulder, Colo.: Westview Press, 2001). Photo by Shirley Zeiberg/PH College.

1. *Parenting*—Assist families with parenting and child-rearing skills, understanding child and adolescent development, and setting home conditions that support children as students at each age and grade level. Assist schools in understanding families.

Windsor Hills Elementary School
Baltimore, Maryland
The Action Team planned activities to provide Windsor Hill's grandparents with the information and resources they need to foster a positive family structure and keep children focused on their education. The two Grandparent Gatherings also supported school improvement goals of increased attendance and achievement for students in pre-K through fifth grades and improved school climate.

2. *Communicating*—Communicate with families about school programs and student progress through effective school-to-home and home-to-school communications.

Freedom Elementary School
Freedom, Wisconsin
Everyone has heard the saying, "Serve food and they will come." Freedom Elementary proved that this strategy continues to be successful. In September, the school hosted a family–school picnic supper immediately preceding open house night. Nine hundred people attended, and they all visited classrooms for open house. This rural school has 730 students enrolled in pre-K to grade 5.

3. *Volunteering*—Improve recruitment, training, work, and schedules to involve families as volunteers and audiences at the school or in other locations to support students and school programs.

Clover Street School
Windsor, Connecticut
Every year it is difficult to recruit enough parents to volunteer for the library, classrooms, and other activities. The Action Team for Partnerships (ATP) worked to solve this challenge by reaching out to an untapped source—fathers and other male relatives. The goal was to involve men in the learning community and provide opportunities for them to be role models for students. Men participating in school activities also would help break the stereotype that only mothers volunteer and monitor student progress.

4. *Learning at home*—Involve families with their children in learning activities at home, including homework and other curriculum-related activities and decisions.

Monterey Elementary School
Grove City, Ohio
The Action Team for Partnerships at Monterey Elementary throws a birthday party for Dr. Seuss to bring together families and the community during Read Across America Week. The birthday party encourages daily reading at home, models reading aloud for parents, and gives every child a new book. Monterey Elementary makes reading fun and interesting for a diverse group of people.

5. *Decision making*—Include families as participants in school decisions, governance, and advocacy through PTA/PTO, school councils, committees, and other parent organizations.

Highlands Elementary School
Naperville, Illinois
The School/Family/Community Partnership (SFCP) Team, the two parent team co-chairs and the principal hosted a lunch for all parent SFCP team members the week after school began and two weeks prior to the first full SFCP team meeting. The objectives of the parent lunch were:
- Introduce all of the parents to each other and make them feel comfortable talking to one another, the parent team co-chairs, and the principal.
- Explain the goals and procedures for the team.
- Provide an opportunity for everyone to make suggestions or present new ideas for the year.

6. *Collaborating with the community*—Coordinate resources and services for families, students, and the school with businesses, agencies, and other groups, and provide services to the community.

Mill Street Elementary School
Naperville, Illinois
The Buddy Reading Program between North Central College and Mill Street Elementary School is the partnership of approximately sixty pre-service education students and sixty fourth and fifth graders discussing a specific novel on a one-to-one basis. Communication is via a college-based WEBboard that allows students to exchange ideas and make connections using the latest computer technology.

You can learn more about these and other programs at the National Network of Partnership Schools website: http://www.csos.jhu.edu/p2000/default.htm.

Source: National Network of Partnership Schools at Johns Hopkins University (2002). Available at http://www.csos.jhu.edu/p2000/default.htm.

To complete a Program in Action activity, visit the Companion Website at **http://www. prenhall.com/morrison**, select chapter 17, then choose the Program in Action module.

FIGURE 17.3 Guidelines for Involving Parents and Families

- Get to know your children's parents and families. One good way to do this is through home visits. This approach works better in early childhood programs where the number of students is limited. However, teachers who have large numbers of students find that visiting a few homes based on special circumstances can be helpful and informative.

- Ask parents what goals they have for their children. Use these goals to help you in your planning. Encourage parents to have realistically high expectations for their children.

- Make all parents and family members feel welcome.

- Build relationships with parents so you may communicate better with them.

- Learn how to best communicate with parents based on their cultural communications preferences. Take into account cultural features that can inhibit collaboration.

- Learn how families rear children and organize themselves. Political, social, and moral values of families all have implications for parent participation and ways to teach children.

- Support parents in their roles as first teachers of their children. Support can include information, materials, and help with parenting problems.

- Provide frequent, open communication and feedback on student progress, including good news.

- Train parents as mentors, classroom aides, tutors, and homework helpers. For example, communicate guidelines for helping students study for tests.

- Support fathers in their roles as parents. By supporting and encouraging fathers, you support the whole family.

- Identify resources that individual parents and families can use to help solve family and personal problems.

- Work with and through families. Ask parents to help you in working with and involving them and other parents. Parents respond positively to parents, so it makes sense to have parents helping families.

Founded in San Antonio, Texas, the organization focuses primarily on teaching parents of children from birth though three years of age the skills they need to nurture their children to success in school and life. AVANCE provides a comprehensive parenting education program, including a twenty-seven lesson/nine-month bilingual curriculum. While parents attend the once-a-week, three-hour long parenting program, incorporating lessons in child growth and quality development, toy making, and family support, AVANCE provides transportation and quality developmental care for their children. AVANCE also includes a home visiting component with its parenting program, offers special programs for fathers, and provides literacy training. For more information about this organization, visit its website at www.avance.org.

For more information about approaches to parent and family involvement, go to the Companion Website at **http://www.prenhall. com/morrison**, select chapter 17, then choose the Linking to Learning module to connect to the National Network of Partnership-2000 Schools site.

GUIDELINES FOR INVOLVING PARENTS AND FAMILIES

As an early childhood professional, you can use the tips presented in Figure 17.3 to develop programs for parent and family involvement. In looking at and designing programs of parent and family involvement, early childhood professionals may proceed in several different ways. For example, the National PTA has developed guidelines for improving family and parent involvement, which lead to student success (see Figure 17.4).

FIGURE 17.4 The National PTA and Family Involvement

The PTA recommends that parents, educators, and community leaders work together in a cohesive way to implement effective involvement at all levels. The PTA recommends the following steps for improving and assuring parent and family involvement and success. Think about how you can apply these seven steps to your program of parent involvement:

Step 1. Create an action team

Step 2. Examine current practice

Step 3. Develop a plan of improvement

Step 4. Develop a written parent/family involvement policy

Step 5. Secure support

Step 6. Provide professional development for school/program staff

Step 7. Evaluate and revise the plan

The National PTA's National Standards for Parent/Family Involvement Programs help schools, communities, and parenting groups implement effective parent involvement programs with the aim of improving students' academic performance. Collaborating with agencies such as the National PTA is an excellent way to enhance and promote your program of parent involvement.

Source: National PTA, "National Standards for Parent/Family Involvement Programs," 2001. Used by permission.

Many programs are looking for ways to effectively integrate the care of both young children and older adults into their programs. What are some advantages of providing for the education and care of young children and older adults in the same program?

ACTIVITIES FOR INVOLVING FAMILIES

There are unlimited possibilities available for you to conduct a meaningful program of family involvement. Families can make a significant difference in their children's education, and with your assistance, they will be able to join teachers and schools in a productive partnership. The following are examples of activities that allow for significant family involvement. The activities are organized according to the six types of parent/family involvement outlined in Figure 17.2.

Type 1—Parenting Knowledge and Skills

- *Participation in workshops*—To introduce families to the school's policies, procedures, and programs. Most families want to know what is going on in the school and would do a better job of parenting and educating if they knew how.
- *Attending adult education classes*—To provide the community with opportunities to learn about a range of subjects.
- *Attending training programs*—To give parents, family members, and others skills as classroom aides, club and activity sponsors, curriculum planners, and policy decision makers. When parents, family members, and community persons are viewed as experts, empowerment results.

517

Los Niños Sunnyside Family Literacy Program

At first glance it's hard to tell the difference between the two classrooms in the portable building that is Los Niños Sunnyside Head Start in Tucson, Arizona. Both serve low-income families; both must follow federal standards of safety and cleanliness, being subject to numerous random inspections; both have state-of-the-art books, computers, and exploratory centers where children are actively engaged in learning and play; both have access to the spotless kitchen, which serves all the children two nutritious meals a day; both practice positive discipline and encourage parental involvement in their child's education. And the similarities don't end there.

The difference is that the children in one classroom, along with their parents, are students of Family Literacy. These children's parents don't go home after dropping their child off at Head Start—they head to Los Niños Elementary School for five hours of adult education (English or GED), vocational education, computers, parent time (parenting and leadership), and, perhaps most critical of all, parents and children together (PACT) time.

PACT time sets Family Literacy apart from other Head Start programs in that parents spend thirty to forty-five minutes every day in the early childhood classroom. Children plan ahead of time where they want to play and send the parent a note with this information. The goal is for parents to dedicate the entire period exclusively to their child, relinquishing control and learning to respect and understand their child's choices in play. To ease this often difficult transition, parents explore how to ask questions of their children to extend play, and they are encouraged to follow the staff's lead in using positive language and discipline.

What is the rest of the children's day like? After they arrive at Head Start, they are served a nourishing, sugar-free breakfast. They are encouraged to taste everything at least once and to drink their milk. They then do a dry brushing of their teeth. At 9:00 they go outside, and when they return forty-five minutes later they transition to group activity. At 10:00 they plan for PACT time and then sing and/or play music. Parents then arrive for PACT, which takes place between 10:30 and 11:00. During one PACT time a week, parents and children spend fifteen minutes reading together. At the end of PACT, everyone gathers in a circle for Circle Time, where we sing or read a story. Afterward, one parent stays to help set the tables and eat lunch with the children while the others go back to their room. After lunch, the children engage in a reading activity, write in their journals, and engage in "Do Time" work. At 12:55 they gather in a circle to review their day, and at 1:00 their parents come to take them home.

As mentioned above, positive guidance is a fundamental component of Head Start. Because children learn what they live, Head Start staff members guide children to make behavior decisions that are positive and safe for themselves and others. They do this by modeling positive language and actions in the classroom. For example, rules are stated in positive terms: instead of "Don't run in the classroom!" teachers say, "Ramon, remember, we walk in the classroom. We run outside." Reasons are given: "So you won't hurt yourself and others." A very important rule is "Use your words when you want something." For many children, this is the first time they've experienced a consistently positive and supportive environment.

Head Start also stresses the importance of responsibility. Children have many responsibilities, from putting toys away to setting the table for breakfast and lunch. It's fascinating to watch a four- or five-year-old child set the table! Yet they do it with ease, having no trouble remembering where things go. During lunch children serve themselves and pour their own milk. They are also responsible for bussing their dishes afterward, taking care to put the spoons in one container, the napkins in another, and the cups in another. Parents often comment that after being enrolled in Head Start, their preschoolers carry their dishes to the sink at home and are better at cleaning up after themselves in general.

For many parents, these are things that their children had heretofore been "unable" to do and so were never given the responsibility of doing. But Head Start strongly believes that we create self-esteem in our children by teaching them life skills. The ability to take care of oneself is certainly a skill that can increase a child's sense of competence. And as children become more self-confident, their self-esteem is given the chance to flower and grow.

Here at Los Niños, I have observed the effects of the Head Start/Family Literacy collaboration. Five children who were in the program last year are in kindergarten this year. Their teachers have told me how exceptionally well prepared these children were for kindergarten. Not only could they read and write, but they could also listen and follow rules. Longitudinal studies done by our office have shown that children who attend Family Literacy are consistently successful at school. And approximately 50 percent of former Family Literacy parents surveyed were still involved in their children's education by volunteering in their schools.

What makes Family Literacy stand above many preschool programs is the involvement of the whole family. This is Family Literacy's ninth year at Los Niños. Many lives have been turned around in that time, though gains are often slow. As the adult educator here, I often ask parents to share something good that's happened to them recently. Just this week one mom said she's yelling less at home now. Another said her fourth grade son, whose classroom she volunteers in two hours a week during her vocational time, told her he was proud of her. Another said that she now feels better able to help her older child with his homework. And the year just got started!

These are the small successes that add up to a program that has changed hundreds of lives. In the words of National Center for Family Literacy President Sharon Darling: "For more than ten years, the NCFL has been at the forefront of efforts to make the most important connection in education—giving parents the tools they need to be their child's first and best teacher. Recognized by academics and policymakers as invaluable to American education and multigenerational empowerment, family literacy . . . improves the lives of children and families like few other efforts." Family Literacy collaborates with other early childhood agencies besides Head Start, so see if there's a Family Literacy program in your area—and if not, start one!

Visit the National Center for Family Literacy on the Web at http://www.famlit.org/.

Contributed by Emily Creigh, adult educator at Los Niños Sunnyside Head Start, Tucson, Arizona. Photos courtesy of Emily Creigh.

 To complete a Program in Action activity, visit the Companion Website at **http://www. prenhall.com/morrison**, select chapter 17, then choose the Program in Action module.

PROGRAM IN ACTION

Ridgewood Family Night—Ready, Set, *Relax*

Ridgewood Family Night—Ready, Set, *Relax* was conceived by a committee of parents, professionals, religious leaders, and school representatives who joined together for a common cause—to examine the impact of hectic, overscheduled lives on the children and families in their community. Meeting at Family Counseling Service, the local family service agency that sponsored the initiative, the committee began by reviewing national research about overscheduling. The committee found two areas of research compelling and of concern to them as parents and professionals.

1. The potential negative effects of overscheduling on healthy child development (i.e., creativity and free thinking, decision making capabilities, capacity to manage personal time, the stress and pressures of overachievement, establishing a realistic, balanced sense of self and personal goals)

2. A national decrease in the hours families spend together (including family meals and family vacations) and the impact of this trend on family health and functioning

The committee believed that the best way to make a difference would be to share this important information with other parents in their community in a creative, nonjudgmental way. The goal would be to involve the entire community, raise awareness about overscheduling, and motivate parents to talk within their own neighborhoods and among their own friends about specific ways to slow down and reduce unnecessary pressure on families and children. The following plan of action was designed and followed.

PROGRAM OBJECTIVE

The objective of Ridgewood Family Night—Ready, Set, *Relax* is to encourage the community to reflect on their

- *Participation in classroom and center activities*—While not all families can be directly involved in classroom activities, encourage those who can. Those who are involved must have guidance, direction, and training. Involving parents and others as paid aides is also an excellent way to provide employment and training. Many programs, such as Head Start, actively support such a policy.
- *Resource libraries and materials centers*—Families benefit from books and other articles relating to parenting. Some programs furnish resource areas with comfortable chairs to encourage families to use these materials.

Type 2—Communicating Between Home and School

- *Support services such as car pools and babysitting*—This makes attendance and involvement possible.
- *Performances and plays*—These, especially ones in which children have a part, tend to bring families to school; however, the purpose of children's performances should not be solely to get families involved.
- *Telephone hotlines*—When staffed by families, they can help allay fears and provide information relating to child abuse, communicable diseases, and special events. Telephone networks are also used to help children and parents with homework and to monitor latchkey children.
- *Newsletters*—When planned with parents' help, newsletters are an excellent way to keep families informed about program events, activities, and curriculum information. Newsletters in parents' native language help keep language-minority families informed.

520

daily activities and consciously choose what matters most. We are calling for reflection about the value of family time and unscheduled time for children and parents; and for conscious decisions by families, schools, religious groups, and community organizations about the ways we can foster a balance between family time, unscheduled time, and outside enrichment activities.

PROGRAM ACTION

Ridgewood Family Night—Ready, Set, *Relax* is a one-night, communitywide awareness event held in Ridgewood, New Jersey, on March 26. With the support of our school superintendent, principals, sports officials, and religious leaders, homework, sports practices, and religious classes are cancelled for the evening. Hundreds of families in town spend time together playing board games, making special meals, watching home videos, and just relaxing together.

PROGRAM EVALUATION

The first Ridgewood Family Night was held on March 26, 2002. Following the event, evaluations were distributed to the 2,457 Ridgewood families with children in kindergarten through eighth grade, and 465 completed forms were returned. An overall assessment of the evaluations indicated that most residents felt that the night had been a good idea.

- 91 percent took part, 86 percent enjoyed it, and 89 percent hope to have another Family Night next year.

- 69 percent felt it raised awareness about the impact of overscheduling, 28 percent were not sure, and for 3 percent did not think it had any effect.
- 64 percent said they will or may make changes in their lives as a result of the event; 36 percent said they would not.

Typical comments included, "We are together as a family every night usually, but we enjoyed having no homework pressure and no running around for practices. Thanks for making us more aware of our hectic lives and focusing our lives on what's really important." Another parent shared, "The whole country is talking about Family Night. Should we be happy, or embarrassed that we needed encouragement? We are so concerned about our children getting ahead and succeeding and not being left out that we overlook the most important thing, and that's just *being* with them and allowing them to just *be.*"

The project appeared to touch a nerve nationally. Newspapers from Boston to California published articles about the event. Television networks sent camera crews to cover the evening and to interview parents and children about the special night. This suggests that the overscheduling issue is a concern in all kinds of communities across the country. In Ridgewood, based on the feedback from the community, Ridgewood Family Night will be an annual event.

For more information, contact Family Counseling Service. Phone: (201) 445-7015, Fax: (201) 652-4034. Contributed by Marcia Marra, project coordinator, Family Counseling Service Ridgewood, New Jersey.

- *Home learning materials and activities*—Putting out a monthly calendar of activities is one good way to keep families involved in their children's learning.
- *Involvement of families in writing individualized education programs (IEPs) for special needs children*—Such involvement in writing an IEP is not only a legal requirement but also an excellent learning experience.

Type 3—Volunteering at School and in the Community

- *Child care*—Families may not be able to attend programs and become involved if they do not have child care for their children. Child care makes their participation possible and more enjoyable.
- *Service exchanges*—When operated by early childhood programs and other agencies, exchanges help families in their needs for services. For example, one parent provided child care in her home in exchange for having her washing machine repaired. The possibilities for such exchanges are endless.
- *Welcoming committees*—A good way to involve families in any program is to have other families contact them when their children first join a program.

Type 4—Supporting Student Learning at Home

- *Offer books and other materials for home use*—For parents to read to their children.
- *Give suggestions to parents*—Provide parents with tips for how to help their children with homework.

 To complete a Program in Action activity, visit the Companion Website at **http://www. prenhall.com/morrison**, select chapter 17, then choose the Program in Action module.

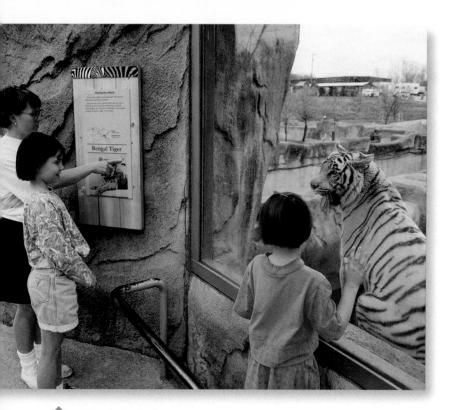

- *Develop a website for parents*—This informs them about the activities of your classroom. Give suggestions for how parents can extend and enrich classroom projects and activities at home.
- *Develop a "home learning kit"*—This can consist of activities and materials (books, activity packets, etc.). Send these kits home with children.

Type 5—Involvement in Decision Making and Advocacy

- *Fairs and bazaars*—Involve families in fund-raising.
- *Hiring and policymaking*—Parents and community members can and should serve on committees that set policy and hire staff.
- *Curriculum development and review*—Parents' involvement in curriculum planning helps them learn about and understand what constitutes a quality program and what is involved in a developmentally appropriate curriculum. When families know about the curriculum, they are more supportive of it.

Parents can be involved in early childhood programs in many ways. Here a parent accompanies children on a trip to the zoo. How could you go about determining the best way to involve parents in your programs? As you reflect on this question, review Figure 17.5 which outlines how research supports parent/family involvement.

FIGURE 17.5 **Research Support For Parent Involvement**

We have discussed many reasons for involving parents. However, one of the most compelling reasons is that research supports the positive benefits that parent involvement has for children and families. Review these research results, and as you do, reflect about how you might apply this information to your classroom or program.

- The earlier in a child's educational process parent involvement begins, the more powerful the effects.
- The most effective forms of parent involvement are those that engage parents in working directly with their children on learning activities at home.
- The most consistent predictors of children's academic achievement and social adjustment are parent expectations of the child's academic attainment and satisfaction with their child's education at school.
- Parents of high-achieving students set higher standards for their children's educational activities than parents of low-achieving students.
- The strongest and most consistent predictors of parent involvement at school and at home are the specific school programs and teacher practices that encourage parent involvement at school and guide parents in how to help their children at home.
- School-initiated activities to help parents change the home environment can have a strong influence on children's school performance.
- Parents need specific information on how to help and what to do.

Source: Michigan Department of Education, *What Research Says About Parent Involvement in Children's Education In Relation to Academic Achievement* (2001).

Type 6—Collaborating with the Community

- *Family nights, cultural dinners, carnivals, and potluck dinners*—Such events bring families and the community to the school in nonthreatening, social ways.
- *Parent support groups*—Parents need support in their roles. Support groups can provide parenting information, community agency information, and speakers.

HOME VISITS

Home visits are becoming more commonplace for early childhood professionals. In fact, California has a $15 million initiative to pay teachers overtime for visiting students' homes. Teachers who do home visiting are trained prior to going on the visits.

A home visiting program can show that the teachers, principal, and school staff are willing to "go more than halfway" to involve all parents in their children's education. Home visits help teachers demonstrate their interest in students' families and understand their students better by seeing them in their home environment. These visits should not re-

place parent–teacher conferences or be used to discuss children's progress. When done early, before any school problems can arise, they avoid putting any parents on the defensive and signal that teachers are eager to work with all parents. Teachers who have made home visits say they build stronger relationships with parents and their children, and improve attendance and achievement.

Many early childhood professionals conduct home visits to help parents learn how to support their children's learning at home. What useful information can parents provide to professionals about children's learning, experiences, and growth and development?

Planning.   Administrators and teachers must agree to participate in the program and be involved in planning it. These programs are successful when these guidelines are followed:

- Teachers' schedules are adjusted so that they have the necessary time.
- Home visits are scheduled during just one month of the school year, preferably early.
- Visits are logged so that teachers and administrators can measure their benefits.

Strategies for Successful Home Visits.   Who does the visiting? Wherever possible, teachers should visit homes of children in their classes. If this is not possible, the principal should ensure that every home that requests a visit receives one. If teachers do not speak the parents' language, translators need to accompany them.

Scheduling.   These suggestions may be helpful:

- Some schools have scheduled home visits in the afternoon right after school. Others have found that early evening is more convenient for parents. Some schedule visits right before a new school year begins. A mix of times may be needed to reach all families.
- Teachers should be given flexibility to schedule their visits during the targeted time period.

A Parent-Friendly School

Parent and community involvement makes the difference between schools being a place to go and a place to learn. "Our PTA brings the school community together and encourages student involvement in affective and academic areas," says Dr. Baker, principal of Stadium Drive Elementary School of the Arts in Lake Orion, Michigan. He cites events such as Mother–Son Dances, Daddy–Daughter Outings, Family Swim Night at the local high school, and a parent-directed Field Day as examples of parent involvement. In addition, one or two parent volunteers in a classroom is normal for most days. "When parents are welcomed and their decisions are respected, their involvement increases," says Baker.

Caring for students and their families is evident at Stadium Drive, and it sparks community involvement. Flowers, letters, telephone calls, and visits to ill children or their families show the extent of the staff commitment to welcoming parents as part of the school. Teachers stand at their classroom doors each morning and greet youngsters as they enter. A schoolwide drive collected money for a community member with a life-threatening condition. Fourth and fifth grade classes collect for UNICEF. Caring behaviors from students are rewarded through the "Caught You Being Good!" program that recognizes caring and respectful behavior. Staff pay a dollar on Fridays for the privilege of wearing blue jeans, thus creating a scholarship fund for a graduating senior alumnus of Stadium Drive.

"Communication is key to maintaining a nurturing culture between staff and families," says Marne Smith, PTA president. At Stadium Drive, named a "Parent-Friendly" school by *Parent Magazine,* a continuous school calendar of events is provided on the public access cable channel and the school's website. A weekly newsletter is published in paper and electronic form with pertinent information. A PTA quarterly newsletter offers informational articles, artwork, poetry, and prose created by PTA members, students, teachers, and the principal. "These communications, along with weekly information from individual classrooms, create and maintain a bond between each family and the school," adds Smith.

Testimony of parent comfort with school climate also comes from written comments by parents. When requesting a teacher, one parent wrote, "My daughter was in her class last year. Through the different class volunteering I did last year, I was able to see how she managed her class-

room and taught the children, and I was very impressed. Her attentiveness and compassion really helped bring out the best in children." A small excerpt from a two-page letter at the end of the year also shows parent recognition of a teacher's willingness to meet unique needs: "We were so worried about him because he had just given up as far as school was concerned. Then Mrs. X walked into his life. We talked with her before to let her know what had happened previously, but we didn't have to. She was so caring, patient, and kind, and he responded and loved going to school. She didn't let him get away with anything, but when she disciplined him it was fair and even he knew it. . . . She is like magic to kids. She treats everyone with respect and love. I cannot tell you how grateful we are that she was put into our family's life."

Stadium Drive prides itself on maintaining a positive bond among all stakeholders and school priorities result from formal and informal information gleaned from student, parent, and staff surveys. The partnership between PTA and staff supports the school's philosophy. The PTA funds assemblies in the arts that have direct connection to classroom projects and assists monetarily with field trips. PTA meetings are held in the evening or immediately after school to accommodate schedules of working parents. The PTA welcomes new families and invites parents to join specialty committees such as fund-raising, gardening, spirit week, field day, or community service.

A parent–teacher partnership exists beyond PTA activities. At Meet the Teacher Night, teachers explain grade-level curriculum and address specific issues. Fall and spring conferences are held to update parents on their children's progress. Teachers maintain contact with parents through weekly letters, work folders, and telephone calls. The high number of parent volunteers in classrooms further fosters the role that both parents and teachers have in educating children.

Partnerships beyond the Stadium Drive school walls exist with businesses and civic organizations. A local gas station donates a penny from every gallon of gasoline sold Tuesdays to the arts budget, thus increasing its business and providing needed funds. The Save for America program partners Stadium Drive students and a local bank, with students able to open and donate to their own savings account. Student artwork and written work are displayed at the credit union. Senior citizens are special guests at school activities and school recitals, concerts, and performances. During the holidays, staff and students cooperate with the Lions Club in the "Adopt a Family" program, with each classroom filling a gift basket to be delivered to a needy family. The PTA joined the community in building a playscape at a township park and founded the yearly Earth Day Celebration, an event that has grown to include other schools, local businesses, and statewide organizations.

When it comes to involving families, our teachers are pro-active, recruiting parents at the fall Meet the Teacher Night and throughout the year and then calling them to volunteer for classroom aides, special projects, and field trip chaperones. The growth in volunteerism over the past three years from 975 hours to 4,355 volunteer hours is significant. Our specialists also use parental help in the Art Room, the Media Center, and with our many dramatic productions. We also tap into students from our high school and middle school, who volunteered more than 600 hours last year. All volunteers are thanked at an end-of-the-year Volunteer Tea. Most of our parent volunteers belong to PTA, which represents 46 percent of our families. "We thrive on volunteers," says a kindergarten teacher during kindergarten information nights. "We know we are only a small part of your child's education, and we both need to learn more about your child."

Connecting parents and students to school occurs in other ways, too. In the PTA Gardening Club, parents, students, and teachers beautify the school's grounds; other parents decorate various school bulletin boards, including one that is a striking point of interest upon entering the front door. Another form of parental involvement is offered in our student placement request for a classroom teacher. Each spring, parents may request a teacher for the fall when there exists a significant academic reason that a specific teacher is preferred.

Nonacademic services for students and families include a family school coordinator, a school social worker, special education ancillary staff, and a school nurse. The Family School Coordinator counsels parents and students on issues such as child rearing, grief management, and conflict resolution, and recommends strategies for handling trauma, disruptive behavior, poor student choices, and psychological issues that interfere with learning. When child abuse, drug abuse, alcoholism, or domestic violence dictate greater attention, referrals to outside counselors, to hospitals, to community organizations (Lions, Boys and Girls Club, scouting), or to the Intermediate School District are made. Our nurse provides services, training, and information to staff, parents, and students on health issues and assists with family issues. Social work, speech therapy, occupational therapy, and psychological testing assist families, too.

Family considerations impact meeting times and decisions for parents. Scholarships aid students who would be otherwise unable to attend camp or field trips. Times of PTA meetings, parent–teacher conferences, and personal contacts are user friendly, with meetings and conferences in the evening, before school, or immediately after school, with staff willing to meet at times convenient to parents. Latchkey is available in the school before and after school. Parents and the groups to which they belong use the school's facilities after hours for scouting, martial arts training, soccer, basketball, or other sports.

Educational resources in the school and community extend learning opportunities for families in many ways. Students design Web pages to exhibit classroom activities. Our concerts and musical productions are broadcast on local cable. A parent section in the library provides materials on child growth and parenting. After school, rooms continue to hum with sounds from excited children engaged in programs such as cooking, dance, crafts, tumbling, magic, play-building, basketball, cartooning, art, scouting, sports, and computer applications. Students stay beyond school hours to rehearse for plays and construct sets.

Text and chart contributed by Dr. Jesse D. Baker, principal, Stadium Drive Elementary, Lake Orion, Michigan.

Parent-friendly schools and programs just don't happen. They require hard work and dedication by everyone involved. Here are some things you can incorporate to make your classroom and school parent friendly.

1. An active and representative parent–teacher–(student) organization
2. Student involvement in community projects
3. Student work exhibited in the community
4. Frequent mulitmedia communications to parents and community of school events and philosophy
5. Gathering of parents and community input with accompanying responsiveness to data collected
6. Flexibility in times of programs, conferences, and meetings to reflect the needs of the parents involved
7. Solicitation of parent assistance with specific tasks predetermined
8. Provision of auxiliary services to students and parents (e.g., counselors, social workers)

- Teachers of siblings may want to visit these children's homes together, but take care not to overwhelm parents.
- Some schools work with community groups (e.g., Boys and Girls Clubs, housing complexes, 4-H, Y's, and community centers) to schedule visits in neutral but convenient space.

Make Parents Feel Comfortable.   Here are some useful tips:

- Send a letter home to parents explaining the desire to have teachers make informal visits to all students' homes. Include a form that parents can mail back to accept or decline the visit.
- The letter should state clearly that the intent of this 15–30 minute visit is only to introduce the teacher and family members to each other, and not to discuss the child's progress.
- The letter might suggest that families think about special things their children would want to share with the teacher.
- The tone of the letter should try to lessen any parents' worries. One school included a note to parents that said, "No preparation is required. In fact, our homes need to be vacuumed and all of us are on diets!" This touch of humor and casualness helped to set a friendly and informal tone.
- A phone call to parents who have not responded can explain the plan for home visits and reassure parents that it is to get acquainted and not to evaluate students.
- Enlist community groups, religious organizations, and businesses to help publicize the home visits.

PARENT CONFERENCES

Parent–teacher conferences
A meeting between parents and early childhood professionals to inform the parent of the child's progress and allow the parent to actively participate in the educational process.

Significant parent involvement occurs through well-planned and well-conducted parent–early childhood professional conferences (informally referred to as **parent–teacher conferences**). Such conferences are often the first contact many families have with school. Conferences are critical both from a public relations point of view and as a vehicle for helping families and professionals accomplish their goals. The following guidelines will help you as an early childhood professional prepare for and conduct successful conferences:

- *Plan ahead.*   Be sure of the reason for the conference. What are your objectives? What do you want to accomplish? List the points you want to cover and think about what you are going to say.
- *Get to know the parents.*   This is not wasted time; the more effectively you establish rapport with a parent, the more you will accomplish in the long run.
- *Avoid an authoritative atmosphere.*   Do not sit behind your desk while the parent sits in a child's chair. Treat parents and others like the adults they are.
- *Communicate at the parent's level.*   Do not condescend or patronize. Instead, use words, phrases, and explanations the parent understands and is familiar with. Do not use jargon or complicated explanations, and speak in your natural style.
- *Accentuate the positive.*   Make every effort to show and tell the parent what the child is doing well. When you deal with problems, put them in the proper perspective: what the child is able to do, what the goals and purposes of the learning program are, what specific skill or concept you are trying to get the child to learn, and what problems the child is having in achieving. Most important, explain what you plan to do to help the child achieve and what specific role the parent can have in meeting the achievement goals.
- *Give families a chance to talk.*   You will not learn much about them if you do all the talking, nor are you likely to achieve your goals. Professionals are often accustomed

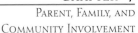

to dominating a conversation, and many parents will not be as verbal as you, so you will have to encourage families to talk.

- *Learn to listen.* An active listener holds eye contact, uses body language such as head nodding and hand gestures, does not interrupt, avoids arguing, paraphrases as a way of clarifying ideas, and keeps the conversation on track.
- *Follow up.* Ask the parent for a definite time for the next conference as you are concluding the current one. Having another conference is the best method of solidifying gains and extending support, but other acceptable means of follow-up are telephone calls, written reports, notes sent with children, and brief visits to the home. While these types of contacts may appear casual, they should be planned for and conducted as seriously as any regular parent–professional conference. No matter which approach you choose, advantages of a parent–professional conference follow-up are these:
  - Families see that you genuinely care about their children.
  - Everyone can clarify problems, issues, advice, and directions.
  - Parents, family members, and children are encouraged to continue to do their best.
  - It offers further opportunities to extend classroom learning to the home.
  - You can extend programs initiated for helping families and formulate new plans.
- *Develop an action plan.* Never leave the parent with a sense of frustration, not knowing what you are doing or what they are to do. Every communication with families should end on a positive note, so that everyone knows what can be done and how to do it.

Children and Conferences. A frequently asked question is, "Should children be present at parent–teacher conferences?" The answer is, "Yes, of course." The only caveat to this is, "if it is appropriate for them to be present," and in most instances, it is appropriate and offers a number of benefits:

- Children have much to contribute. They can talk about their progress and behavior, offer suggestions for improvement and enrichment, and discuss their interests.
- The *locus of control* is centered in the child. Children learn they have a voice and opinions and that others think this is important and are listening.
- Children's self-esteem is enhanced because they are viewed as an important part of the conference and because a major purpose of the conference is to help them and their families.
- Children become more involved in their classroom and their education. "Students take pride not only in their own accomplishments and their ability to share them, but also in the opportunity to help each other prepare for and succeed at their conferences. A team spirit—a sense of community—can emerge and this can benefit the motivation and achievement of all."[1]
- Children learn that education is a cooperative process between home and school.

Telephone Contacts. When it is impossible to arrange a face-to-face conference as a follow-up, making a telephone call is an efficient way to contact families (although, unfortunately, not all families have a telephone). The same guidelines apply as for face-to-face conferences. In addition, remember the following tips:

- Since you cannot see someone on the phone, it takes a little longer to build rapport and trust. The time you spend overcoming families' initial fears and apprehensions will pay dividends later.
- Constantly clarify what you are talking about and what you and the families have agreed to do, using such phrases as, "What I heard you say then . . . ," and, "So far, we have agreed that . . . "
- Do not act hurried. There is a limit to the amount of time you can spend on the phone, but you may be one of the few people who cares about the parent and the child. Your telephone contact may be the major part of the family's support system.

For more information about using the Web to increase communication with parents, go to the Companion Website at **http://www. prenhall.com/morrison**, select chapter 17, then choose the Linking to Learning module to connect to the nschool.com site.

INVOLVING SINGLE-PARENT FAMILIES

Many of the children you teach will be from single-parent families. Based on where you teach, as many as 50 percent of your children could be from single-parent families. Here are some things you can do to assure single-parent families are involved.

First, many adults in one-parent families are employed during school hours and may not be available for conferences or other activities during that time. You must be willing to accommodate family schedules by arranging conferences at other times, perhaps early morning (breakfast), midmorning, noon (lunch), early afternoon, late afternoon, or early evening. Some employers, sensitive to these needs, give release time to participate in school functions, but others do not. Professionals and principals need to think seriously about going to families rather than having families always come to them. Some schools have set up parent conferences to accommodate families' work schedules, while some professionals find that home visits work best.

Second, remember that single parents have a limited amount of time to spend on involvement with their children's school and with their children at home. When you talk with single-parent families, make sure that (1) the meeting starts on time, (2) you have a list of items (skills, behaviors, achievements) to discuss, (3) you have sample materials available to illustrate all points, (4) you make specific suggestions relative to one-parent environments, and (5) the meeting ends on time. One-parent families are more likely to need child care assistance to attend meetings, so child care should be planned for every parent meeting or activity.

Third, suggest some ways that single parents can make their time with their children meaningful. If a child has trouble following directions, show families how to use home situations to help in this area. Children can learn to follow directions while helping with errands, meal preparation, or housework.

Fourth, get to know families' lifestyles and living conditions. For example, you can recommend that every child have a quiet place to study, but this may be an impossible demand for some households. You need to visit some of the homes in your community before you set meeting times, decide what family involvement activities to implement, and what you will ask of families during the year. All professionals, particularly early childhood professionals, need to keep in mind the condition of the home environment when they request that children bring certain items to school or carry out certain tasks at home. When asking for parents' help, be sensitive to parents' talents and time constraints.

Fifth, help develop support groups for one-parent families within your school, such as discussion groups and classes on parenting for singles. Include the needs and abilities of one-parent families in your family involvement activities and programs. After all, single-parent families may be the majority of families represented in the program. Figure 17.6 provides some suggestions that can guide your involvement with single and working parents.

INVOLVING LANGUAGE-MINORITY PARENTS AND FAMILIES

Language-minority parents
Individuals whose English proficiency is minimal and who lack a comprehensive knowledge of the norms and social systems in the United States.

Language-minority parents are individuals whose English proficiency is minimal and who lack a comprehensive knowledge of the norms and social systems in the United States. Language-minority families often face language and cultural barriers that greatly hamper their ability to become actively involved, although many have a great desire and willingness to participate in their children's education.

Because the culture of language-minority families often differs from the majority in a community, those who seek a truly collaborative community, home, and school involvement must take into account the cultural features that can inhibit collaboration. Traditional styles of child rearing and family organization, attitudes toward schooling, organizations around which families center their lives, life goals and values, political influences, and methods of communication within the cultural group all have implications for parent participation.

FIGURE 17.6 Involving Single and Working Parents

An increasing number of children live in single-parent and step families. Many also live in foster families, and other nontraditional family forms. And in many two-parent families both parents work full days, so children come home to an empty house. Involving single and working parents presents many challenges to schools.

Communication

Communication with single-parent and other nontraditional families will be more effective if schools

- Avoid making the assumption that students live with both biological parents.
- Avoid the traditional "Dear Parents" greeting in letters and other messages, and instead use "Dear Parent," "Dear Family," "Friends," or some other form of greeting.
- Develop a system of keeping noncustodial parents informed of their children's school progress.
- Demonstrate sensitivity to the rights of noncustodial parents. Inform parents that schools may not withhold information from noncustodial parents who have the legal right to see their children's records.
- Develop a simple unobtrusive system to keep track of family changes, such as these examples:
  - ✓ At the beginning of the year ask for the names and addresses of individuals to be informed about each child and involved in school activities.
  - ✓ At mid-year send a form to each child's parents or guardians to verify that the information is still accurate. Invite the parents or guardians to indicate any changes.
- Place flyers about school events on bulletin boards of major companies in the community which are family-friendly to learning.

These approaches use different and more sensitive ways of communicating with nontraditional families, and do not require much more material resources.

Involvement

The following practices can make the involvement of single and working parents in school life more feasible:

- Hold parent–teacher conferences and other school events in the evenings.
- Welcome other children at such events, and provide organized activities or child care services.
- Provide teachers and counselors with in-service training that sensitizes them to special problems faced by children of single and working parents and the parents themselves.
- Gather information on whether joint or separate parent conferences need to be scheduled with parents.
- Sponsor evening and weekend learning activities at which parents can participate and learn with their children.
- Work with local businesses to arrange released time from work so that parents can attend conferences, volunteer or in other ways spend time at their child's school when it is in session.

Source: *Reaching All Families—Creating Family Friendly Schools,* Office of Educational Research and Improvement, U.S. Department of Education, 1996.

Language-minority families often lack information about the U.S. educational system, including basic school philosophy, practice, and structure, which can result in misconceptions, fear, and a general reluctance to respond to invitations for involvement. Furthermore, this educational system may be quite different from what these families are used to. They may have been taught to avoid active involvement in the educational process, with the result that they prefer to leave all decisions concerning their children's education to professionals and administrators.

The U.S. ideal of a community-controlled and community-supported educational system must be explained to families from cultures in which this concept is not as highly valued. Traditional roles of children, professionals, and administrators also have to be explained. Many families, especially language-minority families, are quite willing to relinquish to professionals any rights and responsibilities they have for their children's education and need to be taught to assume their roles and obligations toward schooling.

CULTURALLY SENSITIVE FAMILY INVOLVEMENT

The following suggestions for working with families are provided by Janet González-Mena.[2]

- Know what each parent in your program wants for his or her child. Find out families' goals. What are their caregiving practices? What concerns do they have about their child? Encourage them to talk about all of this. Encourage them to ask questions. Encourage the conflicts to surface—to come out in the open.
- Become clear about your own values and goals. Know what you believe in. Have a bottom line, but leave space above it to be flexible. When you are clear, you are less likely to present a defensive stance in the face of conflict. When we are ambiguous, we come on the strongest.
- Become sensitive to your own discomfort. Tune in on those times when something bothers you instead of just ignoring it and hoping it will go away. Work to identify what specific behaviors of others make you uncomfortable. Try to discover exactly what in yourself creates this discomfort. A conflict may be brewing.
- Build relationships. When you do this, you enhance your chances for conflict management or resolution. Be patient. Building relationships takes time, but it enhances communications and understandings. You'll communicate better if you have a relationship, and you'll have a relationship if you learn to communicate.
- Become effective cross-cultural communicators. It is possible to learn these communication skills. Learn about communication styles that are different from your own. Teach your own communication styles. What you think a person means may not be what he or she *really* means. Do not make assumptions. Listen carefully. Ask for clarification. Find ways to test for understanding.
- Learn how to create dialogue—how to open communication instead of shutting it down. Often, if you accept and acknowledge the other person's feelings, you encourage him or her to open up. Learn ways to let others know that you are aware of and sensitive to their feelings.
- Use a *problem-solving* rather than a *power* approach to conflicts. Be flexible—negotiate when possible. Look at your willingness to share power. Is it a control issue you are dealing with?
- Commit yourself to education—both your own and that of the families. Sometimes lack of information or understanding of each other's perspective is what keeps the conflict going.

INVOLVING TEENAGE PARENTS

At one time, most teenage parents were married, but today the majority are not. Also, most teenage families elect to keep their children rather than put them up for adoption and are

Getting Hispanic Parents Involved in Schools

As I've indicated throughout this book, parents play a powerful role in their children's educational development. Early childhood programs must make efforts to involve parents and families of all children. Unfortunately, many minority parents are not included at all or to the extent to which they should be. The urgency to involve minority parents becomes more evident when we look at the population growth for minorities. For example, the Bureau of the Census estimates that by 2025, 25 percent of all school-age children will be Hispanic.

"Historically, we know that Hispanics don't feel welcome in schools, and that's been a barrier to recruiting Hispanic parents," said Mark Townsend, Colorado's PTA president and a board member for the National PTA.[*]

In order to welcome and involve Hispanic parents, the National PTA has initiated an effort to ensure that Hispanic families are involved in their children's education. Beginning with the 2002–2003 school year, the PTA launched its Hispanic Outreach initiative in California, Florida, and Texas with its billboards and other advertisements in Spanish, such as "Los Buenos padres no nacen. Se hacen." ("Good parents are not born. They are developed.")

Across the country, as the initiative to involve Hispanic parents in the schools increases, more emphasis will be placed on how to make Hispanic and other minority parents feel welcome and involved in their children's schools. According to Delia Pompa, chair of the National PTA Hispanic Outreach Advisory Board, "Whether or not your PTA serves a community that is heavily Hispanic, this initiative is just a first step in helping all PTAs reach out to parents of many languages and cultures. Through this Hispanic outreach initiative, we hope to learn and model best practices for reaching out and including all parents in PTA."[†]

---

[*]J. Medina, "Push on to Recruit Latinos for Parent-Teacher Groups," *The New York Times* (Sept. 16, 2002), Section A, page 14.
[†]Ibid.

---

rearing them within single-parent families. Teenage families frequently live in extended families, and the child's grandmother often serves as the primary caregiver. Regardless of their living arrangements, teenage families have the following needs:

- *Support in their role as families.* Support can include information about child-rearing practices and child development. Regardless of the nature and quality of the information given to teenage families, they frequently need help in implementing the information in their interactions with their children.
- *Support in their continuing development as adolescents and young adults.* Remember that younger teenage parents are really children themselves. They need assistance in meeting their own developmental needs as well as those of their children.
- *Help with completing their own education.* Some early childhood programs provide parenting courses as well as classes designed to help teenage parent dropouts complete requirements for a high school diploma. Remember that a critical influence on children's development is the mother's education level.

As early childhood programs enroll more children of teenage families, they must be attentive to creatively and sensitively involving these families as a means of supporting the development of families and children.

To complete an activity related to this topic, go to the Companion Website at **http://www.prenhall.com/morrison**, select chapter 17, then choose the Diversity Tie-In module.

INVOLVING FATHERS

More fathers are involved in parenting responsibilities than ever before. More than one-fifth of preschool children are cared for by their fathers while their mothers work outside the home.[3] The implication is clear: early childhood professionals must make special efforts to involve all fathers in their programs.

More professionals recognize that fathering and mothering are complementary processes. Definitions of nurturing are changing to include the legitimate and positive involvement of fathers in children's lives. Many fathers are competent caregivers, directly supervising children, helping set the tone for family life, providing stability to a relationship, supporting the mother's parenting role and her career goals, and personifying a masculine role model for the children. More fathers, as they discover or rediscover these parenting roles, turn to professionals for support and advice.

There are many styles of fathering. Some fathers are at home while their wives work; some have custody of their children; some are single; some dominate home life and control everything; some are passive and exert little influence in the home; some are frequently absent because their work requires travel; some take little interest in their homes and families; some are surrogates. Regardless of the roles fathers play in their children's lives, as an early childhood professional you must make special efforts to involve them, using the methods discussed in this chapter.

Here are some father-friendly ideas you can use to assure that fathers are included in your programs of parent involvement:

- Invite fathers to your class or program. Make sure they are included in all your parent/family initiatives.
- Make fathers feel welcome in your program.
- Send a simple survey home to fathers asking them how they would like to be involved in their children's education. Keep in mind the six types of parent/family involvement.
- Provide special fatherhood and parenting classes for fathers.
- Have fathers invite other fathers to be involved. Fathers may think no other fathers are involved until they get involved with other fathers.

INVOLVING OTHER CAREGIVERS

Children of two-career families and single-parent families often are cared for by nannies, au pairs, baby-sitters, or housekeepers. Whatever their title, these adults usually play significant roles in children's lives. Many early childhood programs and schools are reaching out to involve them in activities such as professional conferences, help with field trips, and supervision of homework. This involvement should occur with families' blessings and approvals for a cooperative working relationship.

COMMUNITY INVOLVEMENT AND MORE

A comprehensive program of family involvement has, in addition to families, professionals, and schools, a fourth important component: the community. More early childhood professionals realize that neither they alone nor the limited resources of their programs are sufficient to meet the needs of many children and families. Consequently, early education professionals are seeking ways to link families to community services and resources. For example, if a child needs clothing, a professional who is aware of community resources might contact the local Salvation Army for assistance.

USING THE COMMUNITY TO TEACH

The community offers a vital and rich array of resources for helping you teach better and for helping you meet the needs of parents and their children. Schools and teachers cannot ad-

For more information about building stronger bonds between schools and communities, go to the Companion Website at **http://www.prenhall.com/ morrison**, select chapter 17, then choose the Linking to Learning module to connect to the Communities in Schools of Washington, D.C., site.

VIDEO VIEWPOINT

Feeding Hungry Children

Tired of the conditions she found in her city of Houston, Texas, Carol Porter organized an effort to feed hungry children. Her organizations started out with just her family, who spent their life savings to set up Kid Care. Now Carol and her volunteers load up vans and head for Houston's poorest neighborhoods, feeding daily lunches to those who cannot provide for themselves.

REFLECTIVE DISCUSSION QUESTIONS

What effects do hunger and undernourishment have on children's learning? Why is seeing that children are well fed becoming a part of the early childhood curriculum?

REFLECTIVE DECISION MAKING

What can you do to help ensure that the children you teach are properly fed? What community agencies can you work with to help your children receive the food they need?

---

dress the many issues facing children and youth without the partnership and collaboration of powerful sectors of society, including community agencies, businesses, and industry. Following are suggested actions you can take to learn to use your community in your teaching:

- *Know your students and their needs.* By knowing your students through observations, conferences with parents, and discussions with students, you can identify any barriers to their learning and learn what kind of help to seek.
- *Know your community.* Walk or drive around the community. Ask a parent to give you a tour to help familiarize you with agencies and individuals. Read the local newspaper and attend community events and activities.
- *Ask for help and support from parents and the community.* Keep in mind that many parents will not be involved unless you personally ask them. The only encouragement many individuals and local businesses will need is your invitation.
- *Develop a directory of community agencies.* Consult the business pages of local phone books, contact local chambers of commerce, and ask parents what agencies are helpful to them.
- *Compile a list of people who are willing to come to your classroom to speak to or work with your students.* You can start by asking parents to volunteer and for suggestions and recommendations of others.

Only by helping families meet their needs and those of their children will you create opportunities for these children to reach their full potential. For this reason alone, regardless of all the other benefits, family involvement programs and activities must be an essential part of every early childhood program. Families should expect nothing less from the profession, and we, in turn, must do our very best for them.

SCHOOL–BUSINESS INVOLVEMENT

One good way to build social capital in the community is through school–business involvement. More early childhood programs are developing this link as a means of strengthening their programs and helping children and families. For their part, businesses are

To take an online self-test on this chapter's contents, go to the Companion Website at **http://www.prenhall.com/morrison**, select chapter 17, then choose the Self-Test module.

For additional Internet resources or to complete an online activity for this chapter, go to the Companion Website at **http://www.prenhall.com/morrison**, select chapter 17, then choose the Linking to Learning or Making Connections module.

Business Builds a Future in Hartford

Business representatives work cooperatively with students, teachers, and administrators on mutually agreed upon projects to enhance education in the East Hartford, Connecticut, Public Schools. This special collaboration, known as the East Hartford School/Business Partnership, includes nonprofit as well as for-profit organizations.

Involvement with schools continues to be a good investment for organizations and for the community. Competent, successful students mean competent, successful graduates who will be the leaders and workers of tomorrow. With a stake in the product of schools, companies have found it in their best interest to commit resources to help provide the best educational environment for students. Committing their time and talents as tutors and mentors for students, volunteers are role models who provide incentive for students to develop their talents. Companies benefit from the commitment and stimulation their employees feel as part of the program. Other activities include rewards for academic improvement and achievement, classroom speakers, job shadowing, work study, intergenerational participation, parental involvement programs, instructional technology assistance, training for school personnel, and special opportunities through mini-grants.

Examples of Early Childhood Partnerships include:

- *Langford Tutorial Program*—For more than fourteen years, an average of twelve tutors have visited Langford Elementary School to tutor students for one hour per week. Tutors are an integral part of the Langford community as they provide extra support in the form of computer instruction and after-school activities.
- *Mini-Grant Program*—Monetary awards of up to $1,500 are granted to teachers and administrators for quality educational programs that demonstrate community involvement and innovation in the classroom. This is a competitive process that provides funding to programs not covered under the current Board of Education budget.
- *Hartford Jewish Coalition for Literacy*—More than 25 volunteer tutors from the Hartford Jewish Coalition for Literacy read aloud to K–3 elementary students for one hour each week at Norris School. This one-on-one reading program serves to support efforts to have children reading at grade level by the end of third grade.

Source: East Hartford, Connecticut, Public Schools, East Hartford School/Business Partnership (2001). Available at http://www.easthartford.org/business_ partnerships/.

anxious to develop the business–school connection in efforts to help schools better educate children.

NATIONAL ORGANIZATIONS

National programs dedicated to family involvement are a rich resource for information and support. Some of these are listed here:

- Institute for Responsive Education (IRE), 21 Lake Hall, Northeastern University, Boston, MA 02115; 617-373-2595; http://www.responsiveeducation.org.
- National Committee for Citizens in Education (NCCE), 900 Second St., NE, Suite 8, Washington, D.C. 20002-3557; 800-638-9675.
- The Home and School Institute, 1201 16th St., NW, Washington, D.C. 20036; 202-466-3633;. http://www.megaskillshsi.org.
- National Congress of Parents and Teachers (National PTA), 330 N. Wabash Ave., Suite 2100, Chicago, IL 60611; 312-670-6782.

Companion Website

For more information about the Institute for Responsive Education, the National Parent-Teacher Association, and other national organizations, go to the Companion Website at **http://www.prenhall.com/morrison**, select chapter 17, then choose the Linking to Learning module to connect to the IRE, PTA, and other websites.

Another organization, the Family Involvement Partnership for Learning, promotes children's learning through the development of family/school/community partnerships. The national Family Involvement Partnership for Learning began as a cooperative effort between the U.S. Department of Education and the National Coalition for Parent Involvement in Education (NCPIE). NCPIE, a coalition of more than one hundred national education and advocacy organizations, has been meeting for more than twenty years to advocate the involvement of families in their children's education and to promote relationships among home, school, and community that can enhance the education of all children and youth. NCPIE represents parents, schools, communities, religious groups, and businesses.[4]

For more information about the National Coalition for Parent Involvement in Education, go to the Companion Website at **http://www.prenhall.com/morrison**, select chapter 17, then choose the Linking to Learning module to connect to the NCPIE site.

WEBSITE CONNECTIONS

Many websites are available to help parents become more involved in their children's education. For example, the Family Education Network (http://www.familyeducation.com) and Parent Soup (http://www.parentsoup.com) offer resources and features on a wide array of educational topics. You may find other sites by entering the following keywords into one of the Internet's many available search engines:

- parent involvement
- community involvement
- school partnerships
- school/business relationships
- school/community collaboration

For more information about the Family Education Network and Parent Soup, go to the Companion Website at **http://www.prenhall.com/morrison**, select chapter 17, then choose the Linking to Learning module to connect to these sites.

The challenge to early childhood professionals is quite clear. Merely seeking ways to involve parents in school activities is no longer a sufficient program of parent involvement. Today, the challenge is to make families the focus of our involvement activities so that their lives and their children's lives are made better. Anything less will not help families and children access and benefit from the opportunities of the twenty-first century.

ACTIVITIES FOR FURTHER ENRICHMENT

APPLICATIONS

1. List the various ways early childhood professionals communicate pupils' progress to families. Which methods do you think are the most and least effective? What specific methods do you plan to use?
2. Describe the methods and techniques you would use to publicize a parent meeting about how your school plans to involve families in their children's education.
3. You have just been appointed the program director for a family involvement program in first grade. Write objectives for the program. Develop specific activities for involving families and for providing services to them.
4. Develop specific guidelines that a child care center could use to facilitate the involvement of fathers, language-minority families, and families of children with disabilities.

FIELD EXPERIENCES

1. Arrange with a local school district to be present during a parent–teacher conference. Discuss with the teacher, prior to the visit, his or her objectives and procedures. After the conference, assess its success with the teacher.

2. As discussed in this chapter, there are many ways to involve parents, family members, and the community. Some things that you can do now to help you develop a program of family education and support are these:
   a. Identify your goals for family involvement and support.
   b. Develop a plan for implementing the goals that you identified.
   c. Develop a plan for specifically involving fathers in your program.

RESEARCH

1. Visit social services agencies in your area, and list the services they offer.
   a. Describe how early childhood professionals can work with these agencies to meet the needs of children and families.
   b. Invite agency directors to meet with your class to discuss how they and early childhood professionals can work cooperatively to help families and children.
2. As families change, so, too, do the services they need. Interview families in as many settings as possible (e.g., urban, suburban, rural), from as many socioeconomic backgrounds as possible, and from as many kinds of families as possible. Determine what services they believe can help them most, then tell how you as a professional could help provide those services.

READINGS FOR FURTHER ENRICHMENT

Barbour, C., and Barbour, N. H., et al. *Families, Schools, and Communities: Building Partnerships for Educating Children* (2nd ed.). Upper Saddle River, NJ: Merrill/Prentice Hall, 2001.
   This text examines the connections between the homes, schools, and communities in which children live. The authors' vision of school improvement suggests how to arrange teaching strategies and a situation-specific curriculum that is developmentally and culturally appropriate and also emphasizes the necessity of including communities and families as equal partners with the schools.

Carnegie Task Force on Meeting the Needs of Young Children. *Starting Points: Meeting the Needs of Our Youngest Children.* New York: Carnegie Corporation of New York, 2000.
   This report focuses attention on the "quiet crisis" affecting millions of children under three and their families. It challenges professionals to create integrated programs for developing responsible parenthood, guaranteeing quality child care sources, ensuring basic health and protection, and mobilizing communities to support young children and their families.

Gonzalez-Mena, J. *The Child in the Family and the Community* (3rd ed.). Upper Saddle River, NJ: Merrill/Prentice Hall, 2002.
   Recognizing that socialization is one of the most important aspects of child development, this book examines socialization issues of young children during child rearing, in child care facilities, and in the early education system within a developmental context.

Olsen, G., and Fuller, M.L. *Home-School Relations: Working Successfully With Parents and Families* (2nd ed.). Boston: Allyn & Bacon, 2003.
   Home-School Relations examines the nature of the contemporary family and its relationship to the school and provides practical advice for developing strong home–school relationships. This text discusses the need for educators to have positive working relationships with the students that they teach and describes the techniques they must use to understand the families from which their students come.

Stegelin, D.A., and Wright, K. *Building School and Community Partnerships Through Parent Involvement* (2nd ed.). Upper Saddle River, NJ: Merrill/Prentice Hall, 2003.
   This text profiles today's American families and examines the special relationship among them, their children's schools, and their communities. Through an ecological systems approach, the authors explore the family as a child's "first teacher." Provides a wealth of strategies for involving parents and other family members in a child's education.

Family Involvement Network of Educators (FINE)
http://www.gse.harvard.edu/hfrp/projects/fine.html

> Under the leadership of the Harvard Family Research Project, FINE develops the human resource
> capacity for effective family–school–community partnerships. Through a rich and diverse offering
> of research materials and tools, FINE equips teachers to partner with families and informs
> families and communities about leading-edge approaches to full partnerships with schools.

Alliance for Parental Involvement in Education
http://www.croton.com/allpie

> A nonprofit organization that assists and encourages parental involvement in education, wherever
> that education takes place—in public schools, in private schools, at home.

Appalachia Education Laboratory
http://www.ael.org

> Offers ways to keep abreast of what's happening with school–community partnerships to address
> the pressing needs of children and their families.

Early Childhood Educators' and Family Web Corner
http://users.sgi.net/~cokids/

> Provides links to teacher pages, family pages, articles, and staff development resources.

Family Education Network
http://www.familyeducation.com

> The Family Education Network is committed to strengthening and empowering families by
> providing communities with the counseling, education, resources, information, and training
> needed to promote a positive and nurturing environment in which to raise children.

Institute for Responsive Education (IRE)
http://www.responsiveeducation.org

> The IRE is a research-based assistance and advocacy agency promoting the partnership of schools,
> families, and communities with the ultimate goal of success for all children. While the primary focus
> of IRE is on urban educational reform in the United States, its mission is enriched and informed by
> also examining, communicating, and working with rural and urban schools throughout the world.

Making Lemonade
http://makinglemonade.com

> In addition to chats, boards, and articles about forming support groups and helping children
> through divorce, this comprehensive site, run by a single mom with a sense of humor (check out
> the ever-changing department "and you thought you had it BAD . . . ?"), features links to a dating
> service and a newsletter, as well as sites for kids.

National Coalition for Parent Involvement in Education (NCPIE)
http://www.ncpie.org/

> The National Coalition for Involvement in Education (NCPIE) is dedicated to developing
> family/school partnerships throughout America. Its mission is simple: involving parents and
> families in their children's lives and fostering relationships among home, school, and community,
> which all can enhance the education of our nation's young people.

National Network of Partnership-2000 Schools
http://www.csos.jhu.edu/p2000/

> Supports the work of schools to involve families and the community and provides a research-based
> framework describing six types of involvement: parenting, communicating, volunteering, learning
> at home, decision making, and collaborating with the community.

National Parent Teacher Association (PTA)
http://www.pta.org/

> Unveiling its voluntary National Standards for Parent/Family Involvement Programs, the PTA
> calls for schools to promote partnerships that will increase parent involvement and participation
> in promoting social, emotional, and academic growth of children.

NPIN (National Parent Information Network) Homepage
http://www.npin.org

> *Identifies specific Internet sources for parents and for those who work with parents.*

Parent Soup
http://parentsoup.com

> *Offers resources and features on a wide array of educational topics.*

The Single & Custodial Father's Network
http://www.scfn.org/index.html

> *Created by a dad, the Single & Custodial Father's Network is a place for men who are primary caregivers to go. Here, you can hook up with others in the chat rooms and boards to explore everything from cooking to balancing work and family. This site also provides articles and links to more than twenty other sites.*

ENDNOTES

[1] Stiggins, Richard J. *Student-Centered Classroom Assessment,* 2nd ed. (Upper Saddle River, NJ: Merrill/Prentice Hall, 1997), p. 499.

[2] González-Mena, J. "Taking a Culturally Sensitive Approach in Infant-Toddler Programs," *Young Children* 1 (1992), pp. 8–9. Used with permission of the author.

[3] Cohen, J. S. *Parental Involvement in Education* ED 1.2:P75/6 (Washington, DC: U.S. Government Printing Office, 1991), 7.

[4] Family Involvement Partnership for Learning, *Community Update #23* (Washington, DC: Author, April 1995).

Appendix A

NAEYC Code of Ethical Conduct

PREAMBLE

NAEYC recognizes that many daily decisions required of those who work with young children are of a moral and ethical nature. The NAEYC Code of Ethical Conduct offers guidelines for responsible behavior and sets forth a common basis for resolving the principal ethical dilemmas encountered in early childhood care and education. The primary focus is on daily practice with children and their families in programs for children from birth through 8 years of age, such as infant/toddler programs, preschools, child care centers, family child care homes, kindergartens, and primary classrooms. Many of the provisions also apply to specialists who do not work directly with children, including program administrators, parent and vocational educators, college professors, and child care licensing specialists.

CORE VALUES

Standards of ethical behavior in early childhood care and education are based on commitment to core values that are deeply rooted in the history of our field. We have committed ourselves to

- Appreciating childhood as a unique and valuable stage of the human life cycle
- Basing our work with children on knowledge of child development
- Appreciating and supporting the close ties between the child and family

- Recognizing that children are best understood and supported in the context of family, culture, community, and society
- Respecting the dignity, worth, and uniqueness of each individual (child, family member, and colleague)
- Helping children and adults achieve their full potential in the context of relationships that are based on trust, respect, and positive regard

CONCEPTUAL FRAMEWORK

The Code sets forth a conception of our professional responsibilities in four sections, each addressing an arena of professional relationships: (1) children, (2) families, (3) colleagues, and (4) community and society. Each section includes an introduction to the primary responsibilities of the early childhood practitioner in that arena, a set of ideals pointing in the direction of exemplary professional practice, and a set of principles defining practices that are required, prohibited, and permitted.

The ideals reflect the aspirations of practitioners. **The principles** are intended to guide conduct and assist practitioners in resolving ethical dilemmas encountered in the field. There is not necessarily a corresponding principle for each ideal. Both ideals and principles are intended to direct practitioners to those questions which, when responsibly answered, will provide the basis for conscientious decision making. While the Code provides specific direction and suggestions for addressing some ethical dilemmas, many others will require the practitioner to combine the guidance of the Code with sound professional judgment.

The ideals and principles in this Code present a shared conception of professional responsibility that affirms our commitment to the core values of our field. The Code publicly acknowledges the responsibilities that we in the field have assumed and in so doing supports ethical behavior in our work. Practitioners who face ethical dilemmas are urged to seek guidance in the applicable parts of this Code and in the spirit that informs the whole.

ETHICAL DILEMMAS ALWAYS EXIST

Often, "the right answer"—the best ethical course of action to take—is not obvious. There may be no readily apparent, positive way to handle a situation. One important value may contradict another. When we are caught "on the horns of a dilemma," it is our professional responsibility to consult with all relevant parties in seeking the most ethical course of action to take.

SECTION I: ETHICAL RESPONSIBILITIES TO CHILDREN

Childhood is a unique and valuable stage in the life cycle. Our paramount responsibility is to provide safe, healthy, nurturing, and responsive settings for children. We are committed to support children's development, respect individual differences, help children learn to live and work cooperatively, and promote health, self-awareness, competence, self-worth, and resiliency.

IDEALS

I–1.1   To be familiar with the knowledge base of early childhood care and education and to keep current through continuing education and in-service training.

I–1.2   To base program practices upon current knowledge in the field of child development and related disciplines and upon particular knowledge of each child.

I–1.3   To recognize and respect the uniqueness and the potential of each child.

I–1.4   To appreciate the special vulnerability of children.

I–1.5   To create and maintain safe and healthy settings that foster children's social, emotional, intellectual, and physical development and that respect their dignity and their contributions.

I–1.6   To support the right of each child to play and learn in inclusive early childhood programs to the fullest extent consistent with the best interests of all involved. As with adults who are disabled in the larger community, children with disabilities are ideally served in the same settings in which they would participate if they did not have a disability.

I–1.7   To ensure that children with disabilities have access to appropriate and convenient support services and to advocate for the resources necessary to provide the most appropriate settings for all children.

PRINCIPLES

P–1.1   Above all, we shall not harm children. We shall not participate in practices that are disrespectful, degrading, dangerous, exploitative, intimidating, emotionally damaging, or physically harmful to children. This principle has precedence over all others in this Code.

P–1.2   We shall not participate in practices that discriminate against children by denying benefits, giving special advantages, or excluding them from programs or activities on the basis of their race, ethnicity, religion, sex, national origin, language, ability, or the status, behavior, or beliefs of their parents. (This principle does not apply to programs that have a lawful mandate to provide services to a particular population of children.)

P–1.3   We shall involve all of those with relevant knowledge (including staff and parents) in decisions concerning a child.

P–1.4   For every child we shall implement adaptations in teaching strategies, learning environment, and curricula, consult with the family, and seek recommendations from appropriate specialists to maximize the potential of the child to benefit from the program. If, after these efforts have been made to work with a child and family, the child does not appear to be benefiting from a program, or the child is seriously jeopardizing the ability of other children to benefit from the program, we shall communicate with the family and appropriate specialists to determine the child's current needs; identify the setting and services most suited to meeting these needs; and assist the family in placing the child in an appropriate setting.

P–1.5   We shall be familiar with the symptoms of child abuse, including physical, sexual, verbal, and emotional abuse, and neglect. We shall know and follow state laws and community procedures that protect children against abuse and neglect.

P–1.6   When we have reasonable cause to suspect child abuse or neglect, we shall report it to the appropriate community agency and follow up to ensure that appropriate action has been taken. When appropriate, parents or guardians will be informed that the referral has been made.

P–1.7   When another person tells us of a suspicion that a child is being abused or neglected, we shall assist that person in taking appropriate action to protect the child.

P–1.8 When a child protective agency fails to provide adequate protection for abused or neglected children, we acknowledge a collective ethical responsibility to work toward improvement of these services.

P–1.9 When we become aware of a practice or situation that endangers the health or safety of children, but has not been previously known to do so, we have an ethical responsibility to inform those who can remedy the situation and who can protect children from similar danger.

SECTION II: ETHICAL RESPONSIBILITIES TO FAMILIES

Families are of primary importance in children's development. (The term *family* may include others, besides parents, who are responsibly involved with the child.) Because the family and the early childhood practitioner have a common interest in the child's welfare, we acknowledge a primary responsibility to bring about collaboration between the home and school in ways that enhance the child's development.

IDEALS

I–2.1 To develop relationships of mutual trust with families we serve.

I–2.2 To acknowledge and build upon strengths and competencies as we support families in their task of nurturing children.

I–2.3 To respect the dignity of each family and its culture, language, customs, and beliefs.

I–2.4 To respect families' childrearing values and their right to make decisions for their children.

I–2.5 To interpret each child's progress to parents within the framework of a developmental perspective and to help families understand and appreciate the value of developmentally appropriate early childhood practices.

I–2.6 To help family members improve their understanding of their children and to enhance their skills as parents.

I–2.7 To participate in building support networks for families by providing them with opportunities to interact with program staff, other families, community resources, and professional services.

PRINCIPLES

P–2.1 We shall not deny family members access to their child's classroom or program setting.

P–2.2 We shall inform families of program philosophy, policies, and personnel qualifications, and explain why we teach as we do—which should be in accordance with our ethical responsibilities to children (see Section I).

P–2.3 We shall inform families of and, when appropriate, involve them in policy decisions.

P–2.4 We shall involve families in significant decisions affecting their child.

P–2.5 We shall inform the family of accidents involving their child, of risks such as exposures to contagious disease that may result in infection, and of occurrences that might result in emotional stress.

P–2.6 To improve the quality of early childhood care and education, we shall cooperate with qualified child development researchers. Families shall be fully informed of any proposed research projects involving their children and shall have the opportunity to give or withhold consent without penalty. We shall not permit or participate in research that could in any way hinder the education, development, or well being of children.

P–2.7 We shall not engage in or support exploitation of families. We shall not use our relationship with a family for private advantage or personal gain, or enter into relationships with family members that might impair our effectiveness in working with children.

P–2.8 We shall develop written policies for the protection of confidentiality and the disclosure of children's records. These policy documents shall be made available to all program personnel and families. Disclosure of children's records beyond family members, program personnel, and consultants having an obligation of confidentiality shall require familial consent (except in cases of abuse or neglect).

P–2.9 We shall maintain confidentiality and shall respect the family's right to privacy, refraining from disclosure of confidential information and intrusion into family life. However, when we have reason to believe that a child's welfare is at risk, it is permissible to share confidential information with agencies and individuals who may be able to intervene in the child's interest.

P–2.10 In cases where family members are in conflict, we shall work openly, sharing our observations of the child, to help all parties involved make informed decisions. We shall refrain from becoming an advocate for one party.

P–2.11 We shall be familiar with and appropriately use community resources and professional services that support families. After a referral has been made, we shall follow up to ensure that services have been appropriately provided.

SECTION III: ETHICAL RESPONSIBILITIES TO COLLEAGUES

In a caring, cooperative work place, human dignity is respected, professional satisfaction is promoted, and positive relationships are modeled. Based upon our core values, our primary responsibility in this arena is to establish and maintain settings and relationships that support productive work and meet professional needs. The same ideals that apply to children are inherent in our responsibilities to adults.

A—RESPONSIBILITIES TO CO-WORKERS: IDEALS

I–3A.1   To establish and maintain relationships of respect, trust, and cooperation with co-workers.

I–3A.2   To share resources and information with co-workers.

I–3A.3   To support co-workers in meeting their professional needs and in their professional development.

I–3A.4   To accord co-workers due recognition of professional achievement.

RESPONSIBILITIES TO CO-WORKERS: PRINCIPLES

P–3A.1   When we have concern about the professional behavior of a co-worker, we shall first let that person know of our concern, in a way that shows respect for personal dignity and for the diversity to be found among staff members, and then attempt to resolve the matter collegially.

P–3A.2   We shall exercise care in expressing views regarding the personal attributes or professional conduct of co-workers. Statements should be based on firsthand knowledge and relevant to the interests of children and programs.

B—RESPONSIBILITIES TO EMPLOYERS: IDEALS

I–3B.1   To assist the program in providing the highest quality of service.

I–3B.2   To do nothing that diminishes the reputation of the program in which we work unless it is violating laws and regulations designed to protect children or the provisions of this Code.

RESPONSIBILITIES TO EMPLOYERS: PRINCIPLES

P–3B.1   When we do not agree with program policies, we shall first attempt to effect change through constructive action within the organization.

P–3B.2   We shall speak or act on behalf of an organization only when authorized. We shall take care to acknowledge when we are speaking for the organization and when we are expressing a personal judgment.

P–3B.3   We shall not violate laws or regulations designed to protect children and shall take appropriate action consistent with this Code when aware of such violations.

C—RESPONSIBILITIES TO EMPLOYEES: IDEALS

I–3C.1   To promote policies and working conditions that foster mutual respect, competence, well-being, and positive self-esteem in staff members.

I–3C.2   To create a climate of trust and candor that will enable staff to speak and act in the best interests of children, families, and the field of early childhood care and education.

I–3C.3   To strive to secure equitable compensation (salary and benefits) for those who work with or on behalf of young children.

RESPONSIBILITIES TO EMPLOYEES: PRINCIPLES

P–3C.1   In decisions concerning children and programs, we shall appropriately utilize the education, training, experience, and expertise of staff members.

P–3C.2   We shall provide staff members with safe and supportive working conditions that permit them to carry out their responsibilities, timely and nonthreatening evaluation procedures, written grievance procedures, constructive feedback, and opportunities for continuing professional development and advancement.

P–3C.3   We shall develop and maintain comprehensive written personnel policies that define program standards and, when applicable, that specify the extent to which employees are accountable for their conduct outside the work place. These policies shall be given to new staff members and shall be available for review by all staff members.

P–3C.4   Employees who do not meet program standards shall be informed of areas of concern and, when possible, assisted in improving their performance.

P–3C.5   Employees who are dismissed shall be informed of the reasons for their termination. When a dismissal is for cause, justification must be based on evidence of inadequate or inappropriate behavior that is accurately documented, current, and available for the employee to review.

P–3C.6   In making evaluations and recommendations, judgments shall be based on fact and relevant to the interests of children and programs.

P–3C.7 Hiring and promotion shall be based solely on a person's record of accomplishment and ability to carry out the responsibilities of the position.

P–3C.8 In hiring, promotion, and provision of training, we shall not participate in any form of discrimination based on race, ethnicity, religion, gender, national origin, culture, disability, age, or sexual preference. We shall be familiar with and observe laws and regulations that pertain to employment discrimination.

SECTION IV: ETHICAL RESPONSIBILITIES TO COMMUNITY AND SOCIETY

Early childhood programs operate within a context of an immediate community made up of families and other institutions concerned with children's welfare. Our responsibilities to the community are to provide programs that meet its needs, to cooperate with agencies and professions that share responsibility for children, and to develop needed programs that are not currently available. Because the larger society has a measure of responsibility for the welfare and protection of children, and because of our specialized expertise in child development, we acknowledge an obligation to serve as a voice for children everywhere.

IDEALS

I–4.1 To provide the community with high-quality (age and individually appropriate, and culturally and socially sensitive) education/care programs and services.

I–4.2 To promote cooperation among agencies and interdisciplinary collaboration among professions concerned with the welfare of young children, their families, and their teachers.

I–4.3 To work, through education, research, and advocacy, toward an environmentally safe world in which all children receive adequate health care, food, and shelter, are nurtured, and live free from violence.

I–4.4 To work, through education, research, and advocacy, toward a society in which all young children have access to high-quality education/care programs.

I–4.5 To promote knowledge and understanding of young children and their needs. To work toward greater social acknowledgment of children's rights and greater social acceptance of responsibility for their well being.

I–4.6 To support policies and laws that promote the well-being of children and families, and to oppose those that impair their well-being. To participate in developing policies and laws that are needed, and to cooperate with other individuals and groups in these efforts.

I–4.7 To further the professional development of the field of early childhood care and education and to strengthen its commitment to realizing its core values as reflected in this Code.

PRINCIPLES

P–4.1 We shall communicate openly and truthfully about the nature and extent of services that we provide.

P–4.2 We shall not accept or continue to work in positions for which we are personally unsuited or professionally unqualified. We shall not offer services that we do not have the competence, qualifications, or resources to provide.

P–4.3 We shall be objective and accurate in reporting the knowledge upon which we base our program practices.

P–4.4 We shall cooperate with other professionals who work with children and their families.

P–4.5 We shall not hire or recommend for employment any person whose competence, qualifications, or character makes him or her unsuited for the position.

P–4.6 We shall report the unethical or incompetent behavior of a colleague to a supervisor when informal resolution is not effective.

P–4.7 We shall be familiar with laws and regulations that serve to protect the children in our programs.

P–4.8 We shall not participate in practices which are in violation of laws and regulations that protect the children in our programs.

P–4.9 When we have evidence that an early childhood program is violating laws or regulations protecting children, we shall report it to persons responsible for the program. If compliance is not accomplished within a reasonable time, we will report the violation to appropriate authorities who can be expected to remedy the situation.

P–4.10 When we have evidence that an agency or a professional charged with providing services to children, families, or teachers is failing to meet its obligations, we acknowledge a collective ethical responsibility to report the problem to appropriate authorities or to the public.

P–4.11 When a program violates or requires its employees to violate this Code, it is permissible, after fair assessment of the evidence, to disclose the identity of that program.

Appendix B

NAEYC Guidelines for Developmentally Appropriate Practice in Early Childhood Programs

This statement defines and describes principles of developmentally appropriate practice in early childhood programs for administrators, teachers, parents, policymakers, and others who make decisions about the care and education of young children. An early childhood program is any group program in a center, school, or other facility that serves children from birth through age 8. Early childhood programs include child care centers, family child care homes, private and public preschools, kindergartens, and primary-grade schools.

The early childhood profession is responsible for establishing and promoting standards of high-quality, professional practice in early childhood programs. These standards must reflect current knowledge and shared beliefs about what constitutes high-quality, developmentally appropriate early childhood education in the context within which services are delivered.

This position paper is organized into several components, which include the following:

1. a description of the current context in which early childhood programs operate;

2. a description of the rationale and need for NAEYC's position statement;

3. a statement of NAEYC's commitment to children;

4. the statement of the position and definition of *developmentally appropriate practice*;

5. a summary of the principles of child development and learning and the theoretical perspectives that inform decisions about early childhood practice;

6. guidelines for making decisions about developmentally appropriate practices that address the following integrated components of early childhood practice: creating a caring community of learners, teaching to enhance children's learning and development, constructing appropriate curriculum, assessing children's learning and development, and establishing reciprocal relationships with families;

7. a challenge to the field to move from *either/or* to *both/and* thinking; and

8. recommendations for policies necessary to ensure developmentally appropriate practices for all children.

This statement is designed to be used in conjunction with NAEYC's "Criteria for High Quality Early Childhood Programs," the standards for accreditation by the National Academy of Early Childhood Programs (NAEYC 1991), and with "Guidelines for Appropriate Curriculum Content and Assessment in Programs Serving Children Ages 3 through 8" (NAEYC & NAECS/SDE 1992; Bredekamp & Rosegrant 1992, 1995).

THE CURRENT CONTEXT OF EARLY CHILDHOOD PROGRAMS

The early childhood knowledge base has expanded considerably in recent years, affirming some of the profession's cherished beliefs about good practice and challenging others. In addition to gaining new knowledge, early childhood programs have experienced several important changes in recent years. The number of programs continues to increase not only in response to the growing demand for out-of-home child care but also in recognition of the critical importance of educational experiences during early years (Willer et al. 1991; NCES 1993). For example, in the late 1980s Head Start embarked on the largest expansion in its history, continuing this expansion into the 1990s with significant new services for families with infants and toddlers. The National Education Goals Panel established as an objective of Goal 1 that by the year 2000 all children will have access to high-quality, developmentally appropriate preschool programs (NEGP 1991). Welfare reform portends a greatly increased demand for child care services for even the youngest children from very-low-income families.

Some characteristics of early childhood programs have also changed in recent years. Increasingly, programs serve children and families from diverse cultural and linguistic backgrounds, requiring that all programs demonstrate understanding of and responsiveness to cultural and linguistic diversity. Because culture and language are critical components of children's development, practices cannot be developmentally appropriate unless they are responsive to cultural and linguistic diversity.

The Americans with Disabilities Act and the Individuals with Disabilities Education Act now require that all early childhood programs make reasonable accommodations to provide access for children with disabilities or developmental delays (DEC/CEC & NAEYC 1993). This legal right reflects the growing consensus that young children with disabilities are best served in the same community settings where their typically developing peers are found (DEC/CEC 1994).

The trend toward full inclusion of children with disabilities must be reflected in descriptions of recommended practices, and considerable work has been done toward converging the perspectives of early childhood and early childhood special education (Carta et al. 1991; Mallory 1992, 1994; Wolery, Strain, & Bailey 1992; Bredekamp 1993b; DEC Task Force 1993; Mallory & New 1994b; Wolery & Wilbers 1994).

Other important program characteristics include age of children and length of program day. Children are now enrolled in programs at younger ages, many from infancy. The length of the program day for all ages of children has been extended in response to the need for extended hours of care for employed families. Similarly, program sponsorship has become more diverse.

The public schools in the majority of states now provide prekindergarten programs, some for children as young as 3, and many offer before- and after-school child care (Mitchell, Seligson, & Marx 1989; Seppanen, Kaplan deVries, & Seligson 1993; Adams & Sandfort 1994).

Corporate America has become a more visible sponsor of child care programs, with several key corporations leading the way in promoting high quality programs (for example, IBM, AT&T, and the American Business Collaboration). Family child care homes have become an increasingly visible sector of the child care community, with greater emphasis on professional development and the National Association for Family Child Care taking the lead in establishing an accreditation system for high-quality family child care (Hollestelle 1993; Cohen & Modigliani 1994; Galinsky et al. 1994). Many different settings in this country provide services to young children, and it is legitimate—even beneficial—for these settings to vary in certain ways. However, since it is vital to meet children's learning and developmental needs wherever they are served, high standards of quality should apply to all settings.

The context in which early childhood programs operate today is also characterized by ongoing debates about how best to teach young children and discussions about what sort of practice is most likely to contribute to their development and learning. Perhaps the most important contribution of NAEYC's 1987 position statement on developmentally appropriate practice (Bredekamp 1987) was that it created an opportunity for increased conversation within and outside the early childhood field about practices. In revising the position statement, NAEYC's goal is not only to improve the quality of current early childhood practice but also to continue to encourage the kind of questioning and debate among early childhood professionals that are necessary for the continued growth of professional knowledge in the field. A related goal is to express NAEYC's position more clearly so that energy is not wasted in unproductive debate about apparent rather that real differences of opinion.

RATIONALE FOR THE POSITION STATEMENT

The increased demand for early childhood education services is partly due to the increased recognition of the crucial importance of experiences during the earliest years of life. Children's experiences during early childhood not only influence their later functioning in school but can have effects throughout life. For example, current research demonstrates the early and lasting effects of children's environments and experiences on brain development and cognition (Chugani, Phelps, & Mazziotta 1987; Caine & Caine 1991; Kuhl 1994). Studies show that, "From infancy through about age 10, brain cells not only form most of the connections they will maintain throughout life but during this time they retain their greatest malleability" (Dana Alliance for Brain Initiatives 1996, 7).

Positive, supportive relationships, important during the earliest years of life, appear essential not only for cognitive development but also for healthy emotional development and social attachment (Bowlby 1969; Stern 1985). The preschool years are an optimum time for development of fundamental motor skills (Gallahue 1993), language development (Dyson & Genishi

1993), and other key foundational aspects of development that have lifelong implications.

Recognition of the importance of the early years has heightened interest and support for early childhood education programs. A number of studies demonstrating long-term, positive consequences of participation in high-quality early childhood programs for children from low-income families influenced the expansion of Head Start and public school prekindergarten (Lazar & Darlington 1982; Lee, Brooks-Gunn, & Schuur 1988; Schweinhart, Barnes, & Weikart 1993; Campbell & Ramey 1995). Several decades of research clearly demonstrate that high-quality, developmentally appropriate early childhood programs produce short- and long-term positive effects on children's cognitive and social development (Barnett 1995).

From a thorough review of the research on the long-term effects of early childhood education programs, Barnett concludes that "across all studies, the findings were relatively uniform and constitute overwhelming evidence that early childhood care and education can produce sizeable improvements in school success" (1995, 40). Children from low-income families who participated in high-quality preschool programs were significantly less likely to have been assigned to special education, retained in grade, engaged in crime, or to have dropped out of school. The longitudinal studies, in general, suggest positive consequences for programs that used an approach consistent with principles of developmentally appropriate practice (Lazar & Darlington 1982; Berreuta-Clement et al. 1984; Miller & Bizzell 1984; Schweinhart, Weikart, & Larner 1986; Schweinhart, Barnes, & Weikart 1993; Frede 1995; Schweinhart & Weikart 1996).

Research on the long-term effects of early childhood programs indicates that children who attend good-quality child care programs, even at very young ages, demonstrate positive outcomes, and children who attend poor-quality programs show negative effects (Vandell & Powers 1983; Phillips, McCartney, & Scarr 1987; Fields et al. 1988; Vandell, Henderson, & Wilson 1988; Arnett 1989; Vandell & Corasanti 1990; Burchinal et al. 1996). Specifically, children who experience high-quality, stable child care engage in more complex play, demonstrate more secure attachments to adults and other children, and score higher on measures of thinking ability and language development. High-quality child care can predict academic success, adjustment to school, and reduced behavioral problems for children in first grade (Howes 1988).

While the potential positive effects of high-quality child care are well documented, several large-scale evaluations of child care find that high-quality experiences are not the norm (Whitebook, Howes, & Phillips 1989; Howes, Phillips, & Whitebook 1992; Layzer, Goodson, & Moss 1993; Galinsky et al. 1994; Cost, Quality, & Child Outcomes Study Team 1995). Each of these studies, which included observations of child care and preschool quality in several states, found that good quality that supports children's health and social and cognitive development is being provided in only about 15% of programs.

Of even greater concern was the large percentage of classrooms and family child care homes that were rated "barely adequate" or "inadequate" for quality. From 12 to 20% of the children were in settings that were considered dangerous to their health and safety and harmful to their social and cognitive development. An alarming number of infants and toddlers (35 to 40%) were found to be in unsafe settings (Cost, Quality, & Child Outcomes Study Team 1995).

Experiences during the earliest years of formal schooling are also formative. Studies demonstrate that children's success or failure during the first years of school often predicts the course of later schooling (Alexander & Entwisle 1988; Slavin, Karweit, & Madden 1989). A growing body of research indicates that more developmentally appropriate teaching in preschool and kindergarten predicts greater success in the early grades (Frede & Barnett 1992; Marcon 1992; Charlesworth et al. 1993).

As with preschool and child care, the observed quality of children's early schooling is uneven (Durkin 1987, 1990; Hiebert & Papierz 1990; Bryant, Clifford, & Peisner 1991; Carnegie Task Force 1996). For instance, in a statewide observational study of kindergarten classrooms, Durkin (1987) found that despite assessment results indicating considerable individual variation in children's literacy skills, which would call for various teaching strategies as well as individual and small-group work, teachers relied on one instructional strategy—whole-group, phonics instruction—and judged children who did not learn well with this one method as unready for first grade. Currently, too many children—especially children from low-income families and some minority groups—experience school failure, are retained in grade, get assigned to special education, and eventually drop out of school (Natriello, McDill, & Pallas 1990; Legters & Slavin 1992).

Results such as these indicate that while early childhood programs have the potential for producing positive and lasting effects on children, this potential will not be achieved unless more attention is paid to ensuring that all programs meet the highest standards of quality. As the number and type of early childhood programs increase, the need increases for a shared vision and agreed-upon standards of professional practice.

NAEYC'S COMMITMENT TO CHILDREN

It is important to acknowledge at the outset the core values that undergird all of NAEYC's work. As stated in NAEYC's Code of Ethical Conduct, standards of professional practice in early childhood programs are based on commitment to certain fundamental values that are deeply rooted in the history of the early childhood field:

- appreciating childhood as a unique and valuable stage of the human life cycle [and valuing the quality of children's lives in the present, not just as preparation for the future];
- basing our work with children on knowledge of child development [and learning];
- appreciating and supporting the close ties between the child and family;
- recognizing that children are best understood in the context of family, culture, and society;
- respecting the dignity, worth, and uniqueness of each individual (child, family member, and colleague); and
- helping children and adults achieve their full potential in the context of relationships that are based on trust, respect, and positive regard (Feeney & Kipnis 1992, 3).

Taken together, these core values define NAEYC's basic commitment to children and underlie its position on developmentally appropriate practice.

STATEMENT OF THE POSITION

Based on an enduring commitment to act on behalf of children, NAEYC's mission is to promote high-quality, developmentally appropriate programs for all children and their families. Because we define developmentally appropriate programs as programs that contribute to children's development, we must articulate our goals for children's development. The principles of practice advocated in this position statement are based on a set of goals for children: what we want for them, both in their present lives and as they develop to adulthood, and what personal characteristics should be fostered because these contribute to a peaceful, prosperous, and democratic society.

As we enter the twenty-first century, enormous changes are taking place in daily life and work. At the same time, certain human capacities will undoubtedly remain important elements in individual and societal well-being—no matter what economic or technological changes take place. With a recognition of both the continuities in human existence and the rapid changes in our world, broad agreement is emerging (e.g., Resnick 1996) that when today's children become adults they will need the ability to

- communicate well, respect others, and engage with them to work through differences of opinion, and function well as members of a team;
- analyze situations, make reasoned judgments, and solve new problems as they emerge;
- access information through various modes, including spoken and written language, and intelligently employ complex tools and technologies as they are developed; and
- continue to learn new approaches, skills, and knowledge as conditions and needs change.

Clearly, people in the decades ahead will need, more than ever, fully developed literacy and numeracy skills, and these abilities are key goals of the educational process. In science, social studies (which includes history and geography), music and the visual arts, physical education, and health, children need to acquire a body of knowledge and skills, as identified by those in the various disciplines (e.g., Bredekamp & Rosegrant 1995).

Besides acquiring a body of knowledge and skills, children must develop positive dispositions and attitudes. They need to understand that effort is necessary for achievement, for example, and they need to have curiosity and confidence in themselves as learners. Moreover, to live in a highly pluralistic society and world, young people need to develop a positive self-identity and a tolerance for others whose perspective and experience may be different from their own.

Beyond the shared goals of the early childhood field, every program for young children should establish its own goals in collaboration with families. All early childhood programs will not have identical goals; priorities may vary in some respects because programs serve a diversity of children and families. Such differences notwithstanding, NAEYC believes that all high-quality, developmentally appropriate programs will have certain attributes in common. A high-quality early childhood program is one that provides a safe and nurturing environment that promotes the physical, social, emotional, aesthetic, intellectual, and language development of each child while being sensitive to the needs and preferences of families.

Many factors influence the quality of an early childhood program, including (but not limited to) the extent to which knowledge about how children develop and learn is applied in program practices. Developmentally appropriate programs are based on what is known about how children develop and learn; such programs promote the development and enhance the learning of each individual child served.

Developmentally appropriate practices result from the process of professionals making decisions about the well-being and education of children based on at least three important kinds of information or knowledge:

1. *what is known about child development and learning*— knowledge of age-related human characteristics that permits general predictions within an age range about what activities, materials, interactions, or experiences will be safe, healthy, interesting, achievable, and also challenging to children;
2. *what is known about the strengths, interests, and needs of each individual child in the group* to be able to adapt for and be responsive to inevitable individual variation; and
3. *knowledge of the social and cultural contexts in which children live* to ensure that learning experiences are meaningful, relevant, and respectful for the participating children and their families.

Furthermore, each of these dimensions of knowledge—human development and learning, individual characteristics and experiences, and social and cultural contexts—is dynamic and changing, requiring that early childhood teachers remain learners throughout their careers.

An example illustrates the interrelatedness of these three dimensions of the decision-making process. Children all over the world acquire language at approximately the same period of the life span and in similar ways (Fernald 1992). But tremendous individual variation exists in the rate and pattern of language acquisition (Fenson et al. 1994). Also, children acquire the language or languages of the culture in which they live (Kuhl 1994). Thus, to adequately support a developmental task such as language acquisition, the teacher must draw on at least all three interrelated dimensions of knowledge to determine a developmentally appropriate strategy or intervention.

PRINCIPLES OF CHILD DEVELOPMENT AND LEARNING THAT INFORM DEVELOPMENTALLY APPROPRIATE PRACTICE

Developmentally appropriate practice is based on knowledge about how children develop and learn. As Katz states, "In a developmental approach to curriculum design, . . . [decisions] about what should be learned and how it would best be learned depend on what we know of the learner's developmental status and our understanding of the relationships between early experience and subsequent development" (1995, 109). To guide their decisions about practice, all early childhood teachers need to understand the developmental changes that typically occur in the years from birth through age 8 and beyond, variations in development that may occur, and how best to support children's learning and development during these years.

A complete discussion of the knowledge base that informs early childhood practice is beyond the scope of this document (see, for example, Seefeldt 1992; Sroufe, Cooper, & DeHart 1992; Kostelnik, Soderman, & Whiren 1993; Spodek 1993; Berk 1996). Because development and learning are so complex, no one theory is sufficient to explain these phenomena. However, a broad-based review of the literature on early childhood education generates a set of principles to inform early childhood practice. *Principles* are generalizations that are sufficiently reliable that they should be taken into account when making decisions (Katz & Chard 1989; Katz 1995). Following is a list of empirically based principles of child development and learning that inform and guide decisions about developmentally appropriate practice.

1. **Domains of children's development—physical, social, emotional, and cognitive—are closely related. Development in one domain influences and is influenced by development in other domains.**

Development in one domain can limit or facilitate development in others (Sroufe, Cooper, & DeHart 1992; Kostelnik, Soderman, & Whiren 1993). For example, when babies begin to crawl or walk, their ability to explore the world expands, and their mobility, in turn, affects their cognitive development. Likewise, children's language skill affects their ability to establish social relationships with adults and other children, just as their skill in social interaction can support or impede their language development.

Because developmental domains are interrelated, educators should be aware of and use these interrelationships to organize children's learning experiences in ways that help children develop optimally in all areas and that make meaningful connections across domains.

Recognition of the connections across developmental domains is also useful for curriculum planning with the various age groups represented in the early childhood period. Curriculum with infants and toddlers is almost solely driven by the need to support their healthy development in all domains. During the primary grades, curriculum planning attempts to help children develop conceptual understandings that apply across related subject-matter disciplines.

2. **Development occurs in a relatively orderly sequence, with later abilities, skills, and knowledge building on those already acquired.**

Human development research indicates that relatively stable, predictable sequences of growth and change occur in children during the first nine years of life (Piaget 1952; Erikson 1963; Dyson & Genishi 1993; Gallahue 1993; Case & Okamoto 1996).

Predictable changes occur in all domains of development—physical, emotional, social, language, and cognitive—although the ways that these changes are manifested and the meaning attached to them vary in different cultural contexts. Knowledge of typical development of children within the age span served by the program provides a general framework to guide how teachers prepare the learning environment and plan realistic curriculum goals and objectives and appropriate experiences.

3. **Development proceeds at varying rates from child to child as well as unevenly within different areas of each child's functioning.**

Individual variation has at least two dimensions: the inevitable variability around the average or normative course of development and the uniqueness of each person as an individual (Sroufe, Cooper, & DeHart 1992). Each child is a unique person with an individual pattern and timing of growth, as well as individual personality, temperament, learning style, and experiential and family background. All children have their own strengths, needs, and interests; for some children, special learning and developmental needs or abilities are identified. Given the enormous variation among children of the same chronological age, a child's age must be recognized as only a crude index of developmental maturity.

Recognition that individual variation is not only to be expected but also valued requires that decisions about curriculum and adults' interactions with children be as individualized as possible. Emphasis on individual appropriateness is not the same as "individualism." Rather, this recognition requires that children be considered not solely as members of an age group, expected to perform to a predetermined norm and without adaptation to individual variation of any kind. Having high expectations for all children is important, but rigid expectations of group norms do not reflect what is known about real differences in individual development and learning during the early years. Group-norm expectancy can be especially harmful for children with special learning and developmental needs (NEGP 1991; Mallory 1992; Wolery, Strain, & Bailey 1992).

4. **Early experiences have both cumulative and delayed effects on individual children's development; optimal periods exist for certain types of development and learning.**

Children's early experiences, either positive or negative, are cumulative in the sense that if an experience occurs occasionally, it may have minimal effects. If positive or negative experiences occur frequently, however, they can have powerful, lasting, even "snowballing," effects (Katz & Chard 1989; Kostelnik, Soderman, & Whiren 1993; Wieder & Greenspan 1993). For example, a child's social experiences with other children in the preschool years help him develop social skills and confidence that enable him to make friends in the early school years, and these experiences further enhance the child's social competence. Conversely, children who fail to develop minimal social competence and are neglected or rejected by peers are at significant risk to drop out of school, become delinquent, and experience mental health problems in adulthood (Asher, Hymel, & Renshaw 1984; Parker & Asher 1987).

Similar patterns can be observed in babies whose cries and other attempts at communication are regularly responded to, thus enhancing their own sense of efficacy and increasing communicative competence. Likewise, when children have or do not have early literacy experiences, such as being read to regularly, their later success in learning to read is affected accordingly. Perhaps most convincing is the growing body of research demonstrating that social and sensorimotor experiences during the first three years directly affect neurological development of the brain, with important and lasting implications for children's capacity to learn (Dana Alliance for Brain Initiatives 1996).

Early experiences can also have delayed effects, either positive or negative, on subsequent development. For instance, some evidence suggests that reliance on extrinsic rewards (such as candy or money) to shape children's behavior, a strategy that can be very effective in the short term, under certain circumstances lessens children's intrinsic motivation to engage in the rewarded behavior in the long term (Dweck 1986; Kohn 1993). For example, paying children to read books may over time undermine their desire to read for their own enjoyment and edification.

At certain points in the life span, some kinds of learning and development occur most efficiently. For example, the first three years of life appear to be an optimal period for verbal language development (Kuhl 1994). Although delays in language development due to physical or environmental deficits can be ameliorated later on, such intervention usually requires considerable effort. Similarly, the preschool years appear to be optimum for fundamental motor development (that is, fundamental motor skills are more easily and efficiently acquired at this age) (Gallahue 1995). Children who have many opportunities and adult support to practice large-motor skills (running, jumping, hopping, skipping) during this period have the cumulative benefit of being better able to acquire more sophisticated, complex motor skills (balancing on a beam or riding a two-wheel bike) in subsequent years. On the other hand, children whose early motor experiences are severely limited may struggle to acquire physical competence and may also experience delayed effects when attempting to participate in sports or personal fitness activities later in life.

5. Development proceeds in predictable directions toward greater complexity, organization, and internalization.

Learning during early childhood proceeds from behavioral knowledge to symbolic or representational knowledge (Bruner 1983). For example, children learn to navigate their homes and other familiar settings long before they can understand the words *left* and *right* or read a map of the house. Developmentally appropriate programs provide opportunities for children to broaden and deepen their behavioral knowledge by providing a variety of firsthand experiences and by helping children acquire symbolic knowledge through representing their experiences in a variety of media, such as drawing, painting, construction of models, dramatic play, verbal and written descriptions (Katz 1995).

Even very young children are able to use various media to represent their understanding of concepts. Furthermore, through representation of their knowledge, the knowledge itself is enhanced (Edwards, Gandini, & Forman 1993; Malaguzzi 1993; Forman 1994). Representational modes and media also vary with the age

of the child. For instance, most learning for infants and toddlers is sensory and motoric, but by age 2 children use one object to stand for another in play (a block for a phone or a spoon for a guitar).

6. Development and learning occur in and are influenced by multiple social and cultural contexts.

Bronfenbrenner (1979, 1989, 1993) provides an ecological model for understanding human development. He explains that children's development is best understood within the sociocultural context of the family, educational setting, community, and broader society. These various contexts are interrelated, and all have an impact on the developing child. For example, even a child in a loving, supportive family within a strong, healthy community is affected by the biases of the larger society, such as racism or sexism, and may show the effects of negative stereotyping and discrimination.

We define *culture* as the customary beliefs and patterns of and for behavior, both explicit and implicit, that are passed on to future generations by the society they live in and/or by a social, religious, or ethnic group within it. Because culture is often discussed in the context of diversity or multiculturalism, people fail to recognize the powerful role that culture plays in influencing the development of *all* children. Every culture structures and interprets children's behavior and development (Edwards & Gandini 1989; Tobin, Wu, & Davidson 1989; Rogoff et al. 1993). As Bowman states, "Rules of development are the same for all children, but social contexts shape children's development into different configurations" (1994, 220). Early childhood teachers need to understand the influence of sociocultural contexts on learning, recognize children's developing competence, and accept a variety of ways for children to express their developmental achievements (Vygotsky 1978; Wertsch 1985; Forman, Minick, & Stone 1993; New 1993, 1994; Bowman & Stott 1994; Mallory & New 1994a; Phillips 1994; Bruner 1996; Wardle 1996).

Teachers should learn about the culture of the majority of the children they serve if that culture differs from their own. However, recognizing that development and learning are influenced by social and cultural contexts does not require teachers to understand all the nuances of every cultural group they may encounter in their practice; this would be an impossible task. Rather, this fundamental recognition sensitizes teachers to the need to acknowledge how their own cultural experiences shape their perspective and to realize that multiple perspectives, in addition to their own, must be considered in decisions about children's development and learning.

Children are capable of learning to function in more than one cultural context simultaneously. However, if teachers set low expectations for children based on their home culture and language, children cannot develop and learn optimally. Education should be an additive process. For example, children whose primary language is not English should be able to learn English without being forced to give up their home language (NAEYC 1996a). Likewise, children who speak only English benefit from learning another language. The goal is that all children learn to function well in the society as a whole and move comfortably among groups of people who come from both similar and dissimilar backgrounds.

7. **Children are active learners, drawing on direct physical and social experience as well as culturally transmitted knowledge to construct their own understandings of the world around them.**

Children contribute to their own development and learning as they strive to make meaning out of their daily experiences in the home, the early childhood program, and the community. Principles of developmentally appropriate practice are based on several prominent theories that view intellectual development from a constructivist, interactive perspective (Dewey 1916; Piaget 1952; Vygotsky 1978; DeVries & Kohlberg 1990; Rogoff 1990; Gardner 1991; Kamii & Ewing 1996).

From birth, children are actively engaged in constructing their own understandings from their experiences, and these understandings are mediated by and clearly linked to the sociocultural context. Young children actively learn from observing and participating with other children and adults, including parents and teachers. Children need to form their own hypotheses and keep trying them out through social interaction, physical manipulation, and their own thought processes—observing what happens, reflecting on their findings, asking questions, and formulating answers. When objects, events, and other people challenge the working model that the child has mentally constructed, the child is forced to adjust the model or alter the mental structures to account for the new information. Throughout early childhood, the child in processing new experiences continually reshapes, expands, and reorganizes mental structures (Piaget 1952; Vygotsky 1978; Case & Okamoto 1996). When teachers and other adults use various strategies to encourage children to reflect on their experiences by planning beforehand and "revisiting" afterward, the knowledge and understanding gained from the experience is deepened (Copple, Sigel, & Saunders 1984; Edwards, Gandini, & Forman 1993; Stremmel & Fu 1993; Hohmann & Weikart 1995).

In the statement of this principle, the term "physical and social experience" is used in the broadest sense to include children's exposure to physical knowledge, learned through firsthand experience of using objects (observing that a ball thrown in the air falls down), and social knowledge, including the vast body of culturally acquired and transmitted knowledge that children need to function in the world. For example, children progressively construct their own understanding of various symbols, but the symbols they use (such as the alphabet or numerical system) are the ones used within their culture and transmitted to them by adults.

In recent years, discussions of cognitive development have at times become polarized (see Seifert 1993). Piaget's theory stressed that development of certain cognitive structures was a necessary prerequisite to learning (i.e., development precedes learning), while other research has demonstrated that instruction in specific concepts or strategies can facilitate development of more mature cognitive structures (learning precedes development) (Vygotsky 1978; Gelman & Baillargheon 1983). Current attempts to resolve this apparent dichotomy (Seifert 1993; Sameroff & McDonough 1994; Case & Okamoto 1996) acknowledge that essentially both theoretical perspectives are correct in explaining aspects of cognitive development during early childhood. Strategic teaching, of course, can enhance children's learning. Yet, direct instruction may be totally ineffective; it fails when it is not attuned to the cognitive capacities and knowledge of the child at that point in development.

8. **Development and learning result from interaction of biological maturation and the environment, which includes both the physical and social worlds that children live in.**

The simplest way to express this principle is that human beings are products of both heredity and environment and these forces are interrelated. Behaviorists focus on the environmental influences that determine learning, while maturationists emphasize the unfolding of predetermined, hereditary characteristics. Each perspective is true to some extent, and yet neither perspective is sufficient to explain learning or development. More often today, development is viewed as the result of an interactive, transactional process between the growing, changing individual and his or her experiences in the social and physical worlds (Scarr & McCartney 1983; Plomin 1994a, b). For example, a child's genetic makeup may predict healthy growth, but inadequate nutrition in the early years of life may keep this potential from being fulfilled. Or a severe disability, whether inherited or environmentally caused, may be ameliorated through systematic, appropriate intervention. Likewise, a child's inherited temperament—whether a predisposition to be wary or outgoing—shapes and is shaped by how other children and adults communicate with that child.

9. **Play is an important vehicle for children's social, emotional, and cognitive development, as well as a reflection of their development.**

Understanding that children are active constructors of knowledge and that development and learning are the result of interactive processes, early childhood teachers recognize that children's play is a highly supportive context for these developing processes (Piaget 1952; Fein 1981; Bergen 1988; Smilansky & Shefatya 1990; Fromberg 1992; Berk & Winsler 1995). Play gives children opportunities to understand the world, interact with others in social ways, express and control emotions, and develop their symbolic capabilities. Children's play gives adults insights into children's development and opportunities to support the development of new strategies. Vygotsky (1978) believed that play leads development, with written language growing out of oral language through the vehicle of symbolic play that promotes the development of symbolic representation abilities. Play provides a context for children to practice newly acquired skills and also to function on the edge of their developing capacities to take on new social roles, attempt novel or challenging tasks, and solve complex problems that they would not (or could not) otherwise do (Mallory & New 1994b).

Research demonstrates the importance of sociodramatic play as a tool for learning curriculum content with 3- through 6-year-old children. When teachers provide a thematic organization for play; offer appropriate props, space, and time; and become involved in the play by extending and elaborating on children's ideas, children's language and literacy skills can be enhanced (Levy, Schaefer, & Phelps 1986; Schrader 1989, 1990; Morrow 1990; Pramling 1991; Levy, Wolfgang, & Koorland 1992).

In addition to supporting cognitive development, play serves important functions in children's physical, emotional, and social development (Herron & Sutton-Smith 1971). Children express and represent their ideas, thoughts, and feelings when engaged in symbolic play. During play a child can learn to deal with emotions, to interact with others, to resolve conflicts, and to gain a sense of competence—all in the safety that only play affords. Through play, children also can develop their imaginations and creativity. Therefore, child-initiated, teacher-supported play is an essential component of developmentally appropriate practice (Fein & Rivkin 1986).

10. **Development advances when children have opportunities to practice newly acquired skills as well as when they experience a challenge just beyond the level of their present mastery.**

Research demonstrates that children need to be able to successfully negotiate learning tasks most of the time if they are to maintain motivation and persistence (Lary 1990; Brophy 1992). Confronted by repeated failure, most children will simply stop trying. So most of the time, teachers should give young children tasks that with effort they can accomplish and present them with content that is accessible at their level of understanding. At the same time, children continually gravitate to situations and stimuli that give them the chance to work at their "growing edge" (Berk & Winsler 1995; Bodrova & Leong 1996). Moreover, in a task just beyond the child's independent reach, the adult and more-competent peers contribute significantly to development by providing the supportive "scaffolding" that allows the child to take the next step.

Development and learning are dynamic processes requiring that adults understand the continuum, observe children closely to match curriculum and teaching to children's emerging competencies, needs, and interests, and then help children move forward by targeting educational experiences to the edge of children's changing capacities so as to challenge but not frustrate them. Human beings, especially children, are highly motivated to understand what they almost, but not quite, comprehend and to master what they can almost, but not quite, do (White 1965; Vygotsky 1978). The principle of learning is that children can do things first in a supportive context and then later independently and in a variety of contexts. Rogoff (1990) describes the process of adult-assisted learning as "guided participation" to emphasize that children actively collaborate with others to move to more complex levels of understanding and skill.

11. **Children demonstrate different modes of knowing and learning and different ways of representing what they know.**

For some time, learning theorists and developmental psychologists have recognized that human beings come to understand the world in many ways and that individuals tend to have preferred or stronger modes of learning. Studies of differences in learning modalities have contrasted visual, auditory, or tactile learners. Other work has identified learners as field-dependent or independent (Witkin 1962). Gardner (1983) expanded on this concept by theorizing that human beings possess at least seven "intelligences." In addition to having the ones traditionally emphasized in schools, linguistic and logical-mathematical, individuals are more or less proficient in at least these other areas: musical, spatial, bodily-kinesthetic, intrapersonal, and interpersonal.

Malaguzzi (1993) used the metaphor of "100 languages" to describe the diverse modalities through which children come to understand the world and represent their knowledge. The processes of representing their understanding can with the assistance of teachers help children deepen, improve, and expand their understanding (Copple, Sigel, & Saunders 1984; Forman 1994; Katz 1995). The principle of diverse modalities implies that teachers should provide not only opportunities for individual children to use their preferred modes of learning to capitalize on their strengths (Hale-Benson 1986) but also opportunities to help children develop in the modes or intelligences in which they may not be as strong.

12. **Children develop and learn best in the context of a community where they are safe and valued, their physical needs are met, and they feel psychologically secure.**

Maslow (1954) conceptualized a hierarchy of needs in which learning was not considered possible unless physical and psychological needs for safety and security were first met. Because children's physical health and safety too often are threatened today, programs for young children must not only provide adequate health, safety, and nutrition but may also need to ensure more comprehensive services, such as physical, dental, and mental health and social services (NASBE 1991; U.S. Department of Health & Human Services 1996). In addition, children's development in all areas is influenced by their ability to establish and maintain a limited number of positive, consistent primary relationships with adults and other children (Bowlby 1969; Stern 1985; Garbarino et al. 1992). These primary relationships begin in the family but extend over time to include children's teachers and members of the community; therefore, practices that are developmentally appropriate address children's physical, social, and emotional needs as well as their intellectual development.

A linear listing of principles of child development and learning, such as the above, cannot do justice to the complexity of the phenomena that it attempts to describe and explain. Just as all domains of development and learning are interrelated, so, too, there are relationships among the principles. Similarly, the following guidelines for practice do not match up one-to-one with the principles. Instead, early childhood professionals draw on all these fundamental ideas (as well as many others) when making decisions about their practice.

GUIDELINES FOR DECISIONS ABOUT DEVELOPMENTALLY APPROPRIATE PRACTICE

An understanding of the nature of development and learning during the early childhood years, from birth through age 8, generates guidelines that inform the practices of early childhood educators. Developmentally appropriate practice requires that teachers integrate the many dimensions of their knowledge base. They must know about child development and the implications of this knowledge for how to teach, the content of the curriculum—what to teach and when—how to assess what children have learned, and how to adapt curriculum and instruction to children's individual strengths, needs, and interest. Further, they must know the particular children they teach and their families and be knowledgeable as well about the social and cultural context.

The following guidelines address five interrelated dimensions of early childhood professional practice: creating a caring community of learners, teaching to enhance development and learning, constructing appropriate curriculum, assessing children's development and learning, and establishing reciprocal relationships with families. (The word *teacher* is used to refer to any adult responsible for a group of children in any early childhood program, including infant/toddler caregivers, family child care providers, and specialists in other disciplines who fulfill the role of teacher.)

Examples of appropriate and inappropriate practice in relation to each of these dimensions are given for infants and toddlers (Part 3, pp. 72–90), children 3 through 5 (Part 4, pp. 123–35), and children 6 through 8 (Part 5, pp. 161–78). In the references at the end of each part, readers will be able to find fuller discussion of the points summarized here and strategies for implementation.

1. CREATING A CARING COMMUNITY OF LEARNERS

Developmentally appropriate practices occur within a context that supports the development of relationships between adults and children, among children, among teachers, and between teachers and families. Such a community reflects what is known about the social construction of knowledge and the importance of establishing a caring, inclusive community in which all children can develop and learn.

A. The early childhood setting functions as a community of learners in which all participants consider and contribute to each other's well-being and learning.

B. Consistent, positive relationships with a limited number of adults and other children are a fundamental determinant of healthy human development and provide the context for children to learn about themselves and their world and also how to develop positive, constructive relationships with other people. The early childhood classroom is a community in which each child is valued. Children learn to respect and acknowledge differences in abilities and talents and to value each person for his or her strengths.

C. Social relationships are an important context for learning. Each child has strengths or interests that contribute to the overall functioning of the group. When children have opportunities to play together, work on projects in small groups, and talk with other children and adults, their own development and learning are enhanced. Interacting with other children in small groups provides a context for children to operate on the edge of their developing capacities. The learning environment enables children to construct understanding through interactions with adults and other children.

D. The learning environment is designed to protect children's health and safety and is supportive of children's physiological needs for activity, sensory stimulation, fresh air, rest, and nourishment. The program provides a balance of rest and active movement for children throughout the program day. Outdoor experiences are provided for children of all ages. The program protects children's psychological safety; that is, children feel secure, relaxed, and comfortable rather than disengaged, frightened, worried, or stressed.

E. Children experience an organized environment and an orderly routine that provides an overall structure in which learning takes place; the environment is dynamic and changing but predictable and comprehensible from a child's point of view. The learning environment provides a variety of materials and opportunities for children to have firsthand, meaningful experiences.

2. TEACHING TO ENHANCE DEVELOPMENT AND LEARNING

Adults are responsible for ensuring children's healthy development and learning. From birth, relationships with adults are critical determinants of children's healthy social and emotional development and serve as well as mediators of language and intellectual development. At the same time, children are active constructors of their own understanding, who benefit from initiating and regulating their own learning activities and interacting with peers. Therefore, early childhood teachers strive to achieve an optimal balance between children's self-initiated learning and adult guidance or support.

Teachers accept responsibility for actively supporting children's development and provide occasions for children to acquire important knowledge and skills. Teachers use their knowledge of child development and learning to identify the range of activities, materials, and learning experiences that are appropriate for a group or individual child. This knowledge is used in conjunction with knowledge of the context and understanding about individual children's growth patterns, strengths, needs, interests, and experiences to design the curriculum and learning environment and guide teachers' interactions with children. The following guidelines describe aspects of the teachers' role in making decisions about practice:

A. Teachers respect, value, and accept children and treat them with dignity at all times.

B. Teachers make it a priority to know each child well.

(1) Teachers establish positive, personal relationships with children to foster the child's development and keep informed about the child's needs and potentials. Teachers listen to children and adapt their responses to children's differing needs, interests, styles, and abilities.

(2) Teachers continually observe children's spontaneous play and interaction with the physical environment and with other children to learn about their interests, abilities, and developmental progress. On the basis of this information, teachers plan experiences that enhance children's learning and development.

(3) Understanding that children develop and learn in the context of their families and communities, teachers establish relationships with families that increase their knowledge of children's lives outside the classroom and their awareness of the perspectives and priorities of those individuals most significant in the child's life.

(4) Teachers are alert to signs of undue stress and traumatic events in children's lives and aware of effective strategies to reduce stress and support the development of resilience.

(5) Teachers are responsible at all times for all children under their supervision and plan for children's increasing development of self-regulation abilities.

C. Teachers create an intellectually engaging, responsive environment to promote each child's learning and development.

(1) Teachers use their knowledge about children in general and the particular children in the group as well as their familiarity with what children need to learn and develop in each curriculum area to organize the environment and plan curriculum and teaching strategies.

(2) Teachers provide children with a rich variety of experiences, projects, materials, problems, and ideas to explore and investigate, ensuring that these are worthy of children's attention.

(3) Teachers provide children with opportunities to make meaningful choices and time to explore through active involvement. Teachers offer children the choice to participate in a small-group or a solitary activity, assist and guide children who are not yet able to use and enjoy child-choice activity periods, and provide opportunities for practice of skills as a self-chosen activity.

(4) Teachers organize the daily and weekly schedule and allocate time so as to provide children with extended blocks of time in which to engage in play, projects, and/or study in integrated curriculum.

D. Teachers make plans to enable children to attain key curriculum goals across various disciplines, such as language arts, mathematics, social studies, science, art, music, physical education, and health (see "Constructing Appropriate Curriculum," p. 555).

(1) Teachers incorporate a wide variety of experiences, materials and equipment, and teaching strategies in constructing curriculum to accommodate a broad range of children's individual differences in prior experiences, maturation rates, styles of learning, needs, and interests.

(2) Teachers bring each child's home culture and language into the shared culture of the school so that the unique contributions of each group are recognized and valued by others.

(3) Teachers are prepared to meet identified special needs of individual children, including children with disabilities and those who exhibit unusual interests and skills. Teachers use all the strategies identified here, consult with appropriate specialists, and see that the child gets the specialized services he or she requires.

E. Teachers foster children's collaboration with peers on interesting, important enterprises.

(1) Teachers promote children's productive collaboration without taking over to the extent that children lose interest.

(2) Teachers use a variety of ways of flexibly grouping children for the purposes of instruction, supporting collaboration among children, and building a sense of community. At various times, children have opportunities to work individually, in small groups, and with the whole group.

F. Teachers develop, refine, and use a wide repertoire of teaching strategies to enhance children's learning and development.

(1) To help children develop their initiative, teachers encourage them to choose and plan their own learning activities.

(2) Teachers pose problems, ask questions, and make comments and suggestions that stimulate children's thinking and extend their learning.

(3) Teachers extend the range of children's interests and the scope of their thought through presenting novel experiences and introducing stimulating ideas, problems, experiences, or hypotheses.

(4) To sustain an individual child's effort or engagement in purposeful activities, teachers select from a range of strategies, including but not limited to modeling, demonstrating specific skills, and providing information, focused attention, physical proximity, verbal encouragement, reinforcement and other behavioral procedures, as well as additional structure and modification of equipment or schedules as needed.

(5) Teachers coach and/or directly guide children in the acquisition of specific skills as needed.

(6) Teachers calibrate the complexity and challenge of activities to suit children's level of skill and knowledge, increasing the challenge as children gain competence and understanding.

(7) Teachers provide cues and other forms of "scaffolding" that enable the child to succeed in a task that is just beyond his or her ability to complete alone.

(8) To strengthen children's sense of competence and confidence as learners, motivation to persist, and willingness to take risks, teachers provide experiences for children to be genuinely successful and to be challenged.

(9) To enhance children's conceptual understanding, teachers use various strategies that encourage children to reflect on and "revisit" their learning experiences.

G. Teachers facilitate the development of responsibility and self-regulation in children.

(1) Teachers set clear, consistent, and fair limits for children's behavior and hold children accountable to standards of acceptable behavior. To the extent that children are able, teachers engage them in developing rules and procedures for behavior of class members.

(2) Teachers redirect children to more acceptable behavior or activity or use children's mistakes as learning opportunities, patiently reminding children of rules and their rationale as needed.

(3) Teachers listen and acknowledge children's feelings and frustrations, respond with respect, guide children to resolve conflicts, and model skills that help children to solve their own problems.

3. CONSTRUCTING APPROPRIATE CURRICULUM

The content of the early childhood curriculum is determined by many factors, including the subject matter of the disciplines, social or cultural values, and parental input. In developmentally appropriate programs, decisions about curriculum content also take into consideration the age and experience of the learners. Achieving success for all children depends, among other essentials, on providing a challenging, interesting, developmentally appropriate curriculum. NAEYC does not endorse specific curricula. However, one purpose of these guidelines is as a framework for making decisions about developing curriculum or selecting a curriculum model. Teachers who use a validated curriculum model benefit from the evidence of its effectiveness and the accumulated wisdom and experience of others.

In some respects, the curriculum strategies of many teachers today do not demand enough of children and in other ways demand too much of the wrong thing. On the one hand, narrowing the curriculum to those basic skills that can be easily measured on multiple-choice tests diminishes the intellectual challenge for many children. Such intellectually impoverished curriculum underestimates the true competence of children, which has been demonstrated to be much higher than is often assumed (Gelman & Baillargeon 1983; Gelman & Meck 1983; Edwards, Gandini, & Forman 1993; Resnick 1996). Watered-down, oversimplified curriculum leaves many children unchallenged, bored, uninterested, or unmotivated. In such situations, children's experiences are marked by a great many missed opportunities for learning.

On the other hand, curriculum expectations in the early years of schooling sometimes are not appropriate for the age groups served. When next-grade expectations of mastery of basic skills are routinely pushed down to the previous grade and whole group and teacher-led instruction is the dominant teaching strategy, children who cannot sit still and attend to teacher lectures or who are bored and unchallenged or frustrated by doing workbook pages for long periods of time are mislabeled as immature, disruptive, or unready for school (Shepard & Smith 1988). Constructing appropriate curriculum requires attention to at least the following guidelines for practice:

A. Developmentally appropriate curriculum provides for all areas of a child's development: physical, emotional, social, linguistic, aesthetic, and cognitive.
B. Curriculum includes a broad range of content across disciplines that is socially relevant, intellectually engaging, and personally meaningful to children.
C. Curriculum builds upon what children already know and are able to do (activating prior knowledge) to consolidate their learning and to foster their acquisition of new concepts and skills.
D. Effective curriculum plans frequently integrate across traditional subject-matter divisions to help children make meaningful connections and provide opportunities for rich

conceptual development; focusing on one subject is also a valid strategy at times.
E. Curriculum promotes the development of knowledge and understanding, processes and skills, as well as the dispositions to use and apply skills and to go on learning.
F. Curriculum content has intellectual integrity, reflecting the key concepts and tools of inquiry of recognized disciplines in ways that are accessible and achievable for young children, ages 3 through 8 (e.g., Bredekamp & Rosegrant 1992, 1995). Children directly participate in study of the disciplines, for instance by conducting scientific experiments, writing, performing, solving mathematical problems, collecting and analyzing data, collecting oral history, and performing other roles of experts in the disciplines.
G. Curriculum provides opportunities to support children's home culture and language while also developing all children's abilities to participate in the shared culture of the program and the community.
H. Curriculum goals are realistic and attainable for most children in the designated age range for which they are designed.
I. When used, technology is physically and philosophically integrated in the classroom curriculum and teaching. (See "NAEYC Position Statement: Technology and Young Children—Ages Three through Eight" [NAEYC 1996b].)

4. ASSESSING CHILDREN'S LEARNING AND DEVELOPMENT

Assessment of individual children's development and learning is essential for planning and implementing appropriate curriculum. In developmentally appropriate programs, assessment and curriculum are integrated, with teachers continually engaging in observational assessment for the purpose of improving teaching and learning.

Accurate assessment of young children is difficult because their development and learning are rapid, uneven, episodic, and embedded within specific cultural and linguistic contexts. Too often, inaccurate and inappropriate assessment measures have been used to label, track, or otherwise harm young children. Developmentally appropriate assessment practices are based on the following guidelines:

A. Assessment of young children's progress and achievements is ongoing, strategic, and purposeful. The results of assessment are used to benefit children—in adapting curriculum and teaching to meet the developmental and learning needs of children, communicating with the child's family, and evaluating the program's effectiveness for the purpose of improving the program.
B. The content of assessments reflects progress toward important learning and developmental goals. The program has a systematic plan for collecting and using assessment information that is integrated with curriculum planning.
C. The methods of assessment are appropriate to the age and experiences of young children. Therefore, assessment of young children relies heavily on the results of observations

of children's development, descriptive data, collections of representative work by children, and demonstrated performance during authentic, not contrived, activities. Input from families as well as children's evaluations of their own work are part of the overall assessment strategy.

D. Assessments are tailored to a specific purpose and used only for the purpose for which they have been demonstrated to produce reliable, valid information.

E. Decisions that have a major impact on children, such as enrollment or placement, are never made on the basis of a single developmental assessment or screening device but are based on multiple sources of relevant information, particularly observations by teachers and parents.

F. To identify children who have special learning or developmental needs and to plan appropriate curriculum and teaching for them, developmental assessments and observations are used.

G. Assessment recognizes individual variation in learners and allows for differences in styles and rates of learning. Assessment takes into consideration such factors as the child's facility in English, stage of language acquisition, and whether the child has had the time and opportunity to develop proficiency in his or her home language as well as in English.

H. Assessment legitimately addresses not only what children can do independently but what they can do with assistance from other children or adults. Teachers study children as individuals as well as in relationship to groups by documenting group projects and other collaborative work.

(For a more complete discussion of principles of appropriate assessment, see the position statement *Guidelines for Appropriate Curriculum Content and Assessment for Children Ages 3 through 8* [NAEYC & NAECS/SDE 1992]; see also Shepard 1994.)

5. ESTABLISHING RECIPROCAL RELATIONSHIPS WITH FAMILIES

Developmentally appropriate practices derive from deep knowledge of individual children and the context within which they develop and learn. The younger the child, the more necessary it is for professionals to acquire this knowledge through relationships with children's families. The traditional approach to families has been a parent education orientation in which the professionals see themselves as knowing what is best for children and view parents as needing to be educated. There is also the limited view of parent involvement that sees PTA membership as the primary goal. These approaches do not adequately convey the complexity of the partnership between teachers and parents that is a fundamental element of good practice (Powell 1994).

When the parent education approach is criticized in favor of a more family-centered approach, this shift may be misunderstood to mean that parents dictate all program content and professionals abdicate responsibility, doing whatever parents want regardless of whether professionals agree that it is in children's best interest. Either of these extremes oversimplifies the importance of relationships with families and fails to provide the kind

of environment in which parents and professionals work together to achieve shared goals for children; such programs with this focus are characterized by at least the following guidelines for practice:

A. Reciprocal relationships between teachers and families require mutual respect, cooperation, shared responsibility, and negotiation of conflicts toward achievement of shared goals.

B. Early childhood teachers work in collaborative partnerships with families, establishing and maintaining regular, frequent two-way communication with children's parents.

C. Parents are welcome in the program and participate in decisions about their children's care and education. Parents observe and participate and serve in decision-making roles in the program.

D. Teachers acknowledge parents' choices and goals for children and respond with sensitivity and respect to parents' preferences and concerns without abdicating professional responsibility to children.

E. Teachers and parents share their knowledge of the child and understanding of children's development and learning as part of day-to-day communication and planned conferences. Teachers support families in ways that maximally promote family decision-making capabilities and competence.

F. To ensure more accurate and complete information, the program involves families in assessing and planning for individual children.

G. The program links families with a range of services, based on identified resources, priorities, and concerns.

H. Teachers, parents, programs, social service and health agencies, and consultants who may have educational responsibility for the child at different times should, with family participation, share developmental information about children as they pass from one level or program to another.

MOVING FROM EITHER/OR TO BOTH/AND THINKING IN EARLY CHILDHOOD PRACTICE

Some critical reactions to NAEYC's (1987) position statement on developmentally appropriate practice reflect a recurring tendency in the American discourse on education: the polarizing into *either/or* choices of many questions that are more fruitfully seen as *both/ands*. For example, heated debates have broken out about whether children in the early grades should receive whole-language or phonics instruction, when, in fact, the two approaches are quite compatible and most effective in combination.

It is true that there are practices that are clearly inappropriate for early childhood professionals—use of physical punishment or disparaging verbal comments about children, discriminating against children or their families, and many other examples that could be cited (see Parts 3, 4, and 5 for examples relevant to different age groups). However, most questions about practice require more complex responses. It is not that children need food **or** water; they need both.

To illustrate the many ways that early childhood practice draws on *both/and* thinking and to convey some of the complexity and interrelationship among the principles that guide our practice, we offer the following statements as **examples:**

- Children construct their own understanding of concepts, **and** they benefit from instruction by more competent peers and adults.
- Children benefit from opportunities to see connections across disciplines through integration of curriculum **and** from opportunities to engage in in-depth study within a content area.
- Children benefit from predictable structure and orderly routine in the learning environment **and** from the teachers' flexibility and spontaneity in responding to their emerging ideas, needs, and interests.
- Children benefit from opportunities to make meaningful choices about what they will do and learn **and** from having a clear understanding of the boundaries within which choices are permissible.
- Children benefit from situations that challenge them to work at the edge of their developing capacities **and** from ample opportunities to practice newly acquired skills and to acquire the disposition to persist.
- Children benefit from opportunities to collaborate with their peers and acquire a sense of being part of a community **and** from being treated as individuals with their own strengths, interests, and needs.
- Children need to develop a positive sense of their own self-identity **and** respect for other people whose perspectives and experiences may be different from their own.
- Children have enormous capacities to learn and almost boundless curiosity about the world, **and** they have recognized, age-related limits on their cognitive and linguistic capacities.
- Children benefit from engaging in self-initiated, spontaneous play, **and** from teacher-planned and -structured activities, projects, and experiences.

The above list is not exhaustive. Many more examples could be cited to convey the interrelationships among the principles of child development and learning or among the guidelines for early childhood practice.

POLICIES ESSENTIAL FOR ACHIEVING DEVELOPMENTALLY APPROPRIATE EARLY CHILDHOOD PROGRAMS

Early childhood professionals working in diverse situations with varying levels of funding and resources are responsible for implementing practices that are developmentally appropriate for the children they serve. Regardless of the resources available, professionals have an ethical responsibility to practice, to the best of their ability, according to the standards of their profession. Nevertheless, the kinds of practices advocated in this position statement are more likely to be implemented within an infrastructure of supportive policies and resources. NAEYC strongly recommends that policymaking groups at the state and local levels consider the following when implementing early childhood programs:

1. A comprehensive professional preparation and development system is in place to ensure that early childhood programs are staffed with qualified personnel (NAEYC 1994).
   - A system exists for early childhood professionals to acquire the knowledge and practical skills needed to practice through college-level specialized preparation in early childhood education/child development.
   - Teachers in early childhood programs are encouraged and supported to obtain and maintain, through study and participation in inservice training, current knowledge of child development and learning and its application to early childhood practice.
   - Specialists in early childhood special education are available to provide assistance and consultation in meeting the individual needs of children in the program.
   - In addition to management and supervision skills, administrators of early childhood programs have appropriate professional qualifications, including training specific to the education and development of young children, and they provide teachers time and opportunities to work collaboratively with colleagues and parents.

2. Funding is provided to ensure adequate staffing of early childhood programs and fair staff compensation that promotes continuity of relationships among adults and children (Willer 1990).
   - Funding is adequate to limit the size of the groups and provide sufficient numbers of adults to ensure individualized and appropriate care and education. Even the most well-qualified teacher cannot individualize instruction and adequately supervise too large a group of young children. An acceptable adult-child ratio for 4- and 5-year-olds is two adults with no more than 20 children. (Ruopp et al. 1979; Francis & Self 1982; Howes 1983; Taylor & Taylor 1989; Howes, Philips, & Whitebook 1992; Cost, Quality, & Child Outcomes Study Team 1995; Howes, Smith & Galinsky 1995). Younger children require much smaller groups. Group size and ratio of children to adults should increase gradually through the primary grades, but one teacher with no more than 18 children or two adults with no more than 25 children is optimum (Nye et al. 1992; Nye, Boyd-Zaharias, & Fulton 1994). Inclusion of children with disabilities may necessitate additional adults or smaller group size to ensure that all children's needs are met.
   - Programs offer staff salaries and benefits commensurate with the skills and qualifications required for specific roles to ensure the provision of quality services and the effective recruitment and retention of qualified, competent staff. (See *Compensation Guidelines for Early Childhood Professionals* [NAEYC 1993]).
   - Decisions related to how programs are staffed and how children are grouped result in increased opportunities for children to experience continuity of relationships

with teachers and other children. Such strategies include but are not limited to multiage grouping and multiyear teacher-child relationships (Katz, Evangelou, & Hartman 1990; Zero to Three 1995; Burke 1996).

3. Resources and expertise are available to provide safe, stimulating learning environments with a sufficient number and variety of appropriate materials and equipment for the age group served (Bronson 1995; Kendrick, Kaufmann, & Messenger 1995).

4. Adequate systems for regulating and monitoring the quality of early childhood programs are in place (see position on licensing [NAEYC 1987]; accreditation criteria and procedures [NAEYC 1991]).

5. Community resources are available and used to support the comprehensive needs of children and families (Kagan 1991; NASBE 1991; Kagan et al. 1995; NCSL 1995).

6. When individual children do not make expected learning progress, neither grade retention nor social promotion are used; instead, initiatives such as more focused time, individualized instruction, tutoring, or other individual strategies are used to accelerate children's learning (Shepard & Smith 1989; Ross et al. 1995).

7. Early childhood programs use multiple indicators of progress in all development domains to evaluate the effect of the program on children's development and learning and regularly report children's progress to parents. Group-administered, standardized, multiple-choice achievement tests are not used before third grade, preferably before fourth grade. When such tests are used to demonstrate public accountability, a sampling method is used (see Shepard 1994).

REFERENCES

Adams, G., & J. Sandfort. 1994. *First steps, promising futures: State prekindergarten initiatives in the early 1990s*. Washington. DC: Children's Defense Fund.

Alexander, K.L., & D.R. Entwisle. 1988. *Achievement in the first 2 years of school: Patterns and processes*. Monographs of the Society for Research in Child Development, vol. 53, no. 2, serial no. 218. Ann Arbor: University of Michigan.

Arnett, J. 1989. Caregivers in day-care centers: Does training matter? *Journal of Applied Developmental Psychology* 10 (4): 541–52.

Asher, S., S. Hymel, & P. Renshaw. 1984. Loneliness in children. *Child Development* 55: 1456–64.

Barnett, W.S. 1995. Long-term effects of early childhood programs on cognitive and school outcomes. *The Future of Children* 5 (3): 25–50.

Bergen, D. 1988. *Play as a medium for learning and development*. Portsmouth, NH: Heinemann.

Berk, L.E. 1996. *Infants and children: Prenatal through middle childhood*. 2d ed. Needham Heights, MA: Allyn & Bacon.

Berk, L., & A. Winsler. 1995. *Scaffolding children's learning: Vygotsky and early childhood education*. Washington, DC: NAEYC.

Berruetta-Clement, J.R., L.J. Schweinhart, W.S. Barnett, A.S. Epstein, & D.P. Weikart. 1984. *Changed lives: The effects of the Perry Preschool Program on youths through age 19*. Monographs of the High/Scope Educational Research Foundation, no. 8. Ypsilanti, MI: High/Scope Press.

Bodrova, E., & D. Leong. 1996. *Tools of the mind: The Vygotskian approach to early childhood education*. Englewood Cliffs, NJ: Merrill/Prentice Hall.

Bowlby, J. 1969. *Attachment and loss: Vol.1. Attachment*. New York: Basic.

Bowman, B. 1994. The challenge of diversity. *Phi Delta Kappan* 76 (3): 218–25.

Bowman, B., & F. Stott. 1994. Understanding development in a cultural context: The challenge for teachers. In *Diversity and developmentally appropriate practices: Challenges for early childhood education*, eds. B. Mallory & R. New, 119–34. New York: Teachers College Press.

Bredekamp, S., ed. 1987. *Developmentally appropriate practice in early childhood programs serving children from birth through age 8*. Exp. ed. Washington, DC: NAEYC.

Bredekamp, S. 1993a. Reflections on Reggio Emilia. *Young Children* 49 (1): 13–17.

Bredekamp, S. 1993b. The relationship between early childhood education and early childhood special education: Healthy marriage or family feud? *Topics in Early Childhood Special Education* 13 (3): 258–73.

Bredekamp, S., & T. Rosegrant, eds. 1992. *Reaching potentials: Appropriate curriculum and assessment for young children, volume 1*. Washington, DC: NAEYC.

Bredekamp, S., & T. Rosegrant, eds. 1995. *Reaching potentials: Transforming early childhood curriculum and assessment, volume 2*. Washington, DC: NAEYC.

Bronfenbrenner, U. 1979. *The ecology of human development: Experiments by nature and design*. Cambridge, MA: Harvard University Press.

Bronfenbrenner, U. 1989. Ecological systems theory. In *Annals of child development*, Vol. 6, ed. R. Vasta, 187–251. Greenwich, CT: JAI Press.

Bronfenbrenner, U. 1993. The ecology of cognitive development: Research models and fugitive findings. In *Development in context*, eds. R.H. Wozniak & K.W. Fischer, 3–44. Hillsdale, NJ: Erlbaum.

Bronson, M.B. 1995. *The right stuff for children birth to 8: Selecting play materials to support development*. Washington, DC: NAEYC.

Brophy, J. 1992. Probing the subtleties of subject matter teaching. *Educational Leadership* 49 (7): 4–8.

Bruner, J.S. 1993. *Child's talk: Learning to use language*. New York: Norton.

Bruner, J.S. 1996. *The culture of education*. Cambridge, MA: Harvard University Press.

Bryant, D.M., R. Clifford, & E.S. Peisner. 1991. Best practices for beginners: Developmental appropriateness in kindergarten. *American Educational Research Journal* 28 (4): 783–803.

Burchinal, M., J. Robert, L. Nabo, & D. Bryant. 1996. Quality of center child care and infant cognitive and language development. *Child Development* 67 (2): 606–20.

Burke, D. 1966. Multi-year teacher/student relationships are a long-overdue arrangement. *Phi Delta Kappan* 77 (5): 360–61.

Caine, R., & G. Caine. 1991. *Making connections: Teaching and the human brain*. New York: Addison-Wesley.

Campbell, F., & C. Ramey. 1995. Cognitive and school outcomes for high-risk African-American students at middle adolescence: Positive effects of early intervention. *American Educational Research Journal* 32 (4): 743–72.

Carnegie Task Force on Learning in the Primary Grades. 1996. *Years of promise: A comprehensive learning strategy for America's children*. New York: Carnegie Corporation of New York.

Carta, J., I. Schwartz, J. Atwater, & S. McConnell. 1991. Developmentally appropriate practice: Appraising its usefulness for young children with disabilities. *Topics in Early Childhood Special Education* 11 (1): 1–20.

Case, R., & Y. Okamoto. 1996. *The role of central conceptual structures in the development of children's thought*. Monographs of the Society of Research in Child Development, vol. 61, no. 2, serial no. 246. Chicago: University of Chicago Press.

Charlesworth, R., C.H. Hart, D.C. Burts, & M. DeWolf. 1993. The LSU studies: Building a research base for developmentally appropriate practice. In *Perspectives on developmentally appropriate practice*, vol. 5 of *Advances in early education and day care*, ed. S. Reifel, 3–28. Greenwich, CT: JAI Press.

Chugani, H., M.E. Phelps, & J.C. Mazziotta. 1987. Positron emission tomography study of human brain functional development. *Annals of Neurology* 22 (4): 495.

Cohen, N., & K. Modigliani. 1994. The family-to-family project: Developing family child care providers. In *The early childhood career lattice: Perspectives on professional development*, eds. J. Johnson & J.B. McCracken, 106–10. Washington, DC: NAEYC.

Copple, C., I.E. Sigel, & R. Saunders. 1984. *Educating the young thinker: Classroom strategies for cognitive growth*. Hillsdale, NJ: Erlbaum.

Cost, Quality, & Child Outcomes Study Team. 1995. *Cost, quality, and child outcomes in child care centers, public report*. 2d ed. Denver: Economics Department, University of Colorado at Denver.

Dana Alliance for Brain Initiatives. 1996. *Delivering results: A progress report on brain research*. Washington, DC: Author.

DEC/CEC (Division for Early Childhood of the Council for Exceptional Children). 1994. Position on inclusion. *Young Children* 49 (5): 78.

DEC (Division for Early Childhood) Task Force on Recommended Practices. 1993. *DEC recommended practices: Indicators of quality in programs for infants and young children with special needs and their families*. Reston, VA: Council for Exceptional Children.

DEC/CEC & NAEYC (Division for Early Childhood of the Council for Exceptional Children & the National Association for the Education of Young Children). 1993. *Understanding the ADA—The Americans with Disability Act: Information for early childhood programs*. Pittsburgh, PA, & Washington, DC: Authors.

DeVries, R., & W. Kohlberg. 1990. *Constructivist early education: Overview and comparison with other programs*. Washington, DC: NAEYC.

Dewey, J. 1916. *Democracy and education: An introduction to the philosophy of education*. New York: Macmillan.

Durkin, D. 1987. A classroom-observation study of reading instruction in kindergarten. *Early Childhood Research Quarterly* 2 (3): 275–300.

Durkin, D. 1990. Reading instruction in kindergarten: A look at some issues through the lens of new basal reader materials. *Early Children Research Quarterly* 5 (3): 299–316.

Dweck, C. 1986. Motivational processes affecting learning. *American Psychologist* 41: 1030–48.

Dyson, A.H., & C. Genishi. 1993. Visions of children as language users: Language and language education in early childhood. In *Handbook of research on the education of young children*, ed. B. Spodek, 122–36. New York: Macmillan.

Edwards, C.P., & L. Gandini. 1989. Teachers' expectations about the timing of developmental skills: A cross-cultural study. *Young Children* 44 (4): 15–19.

Edwards, C., L. Gandini, & G. Forman, eds. 1993. *The hundred languages of children: The Reggio Emilia approach to early childhood education*. Norwood, NJ: Ablex.

Erikson, E. 1963. *Childhood and society*. New York: Norton.

Feeney, S., & K. Kipnis. 1992. *Code of ethical conduct & statement of commitment*. Washington, DC: NAEYC.

Fein, G. 1981. Pretend play: An integrative review. *Child Development* 52: 1095–118.

Fein, G., & M. Rivkin, eds. *The young child at play: Reviews of research*. Washington, DC: NAEYC.

Fenson, L., P. Dale, J.S. Reznick, E. Bates, D. Thal, & S. Pethick. 1994. *Variability in early communicative development*. Monographs of the Society for Research in Child Development, vol. 59, no. 2, serial no. 242. Chicago: University of Chicago Press.

Fernald, A. 1992. Human Maternal vocalizations in infants as biologically relevant signals: An evolutionary perspective. In *The adapted mind: Evolutionary psychology and the generation of culture*, eds. J.H. Barkow, L. Cosmides, & J. Tooby, 391–428. New York: Oxford University Press.

Fields, T., W. Masi, S. Goldstein, S. Perry, & S. Parl. 1988. Infant day care facilities preschool social behavior. *Early Childhood Research Quarterly* 3 (4): 341–59.

Forman, G. 1994. Different media, different languages. In *Reflections on the Reggio Emilia approach*, eds. L. Katz & B. Cesarone, 37–46. Urbana, IL: ERIC Clearinghouse on EECE.

Forman, E.A., N. Minick, & C.A. Stone. 1993. *Contexts for learning: Sociocultural dynamics in children's development*. New York: Oxford University Press.

Francis, P., & P. Self. 1982. Imitative responsiveness of young children in day care and home settings: The importance of the child to caregiver ratio. *Child Study Journal* 12: 119–26.

Frede, E. 1995. The role of program quality in producing early childhood program benefits. *The Future of Children*, 5 (3): 115–132.

Frede, E., & W.S. Barnett. 1992. Developmentally appropriate public school preschool: A study of implementation of the High/Scope curriculum and its effects on disadvantaged children's skills at first grade. *Early Childhood Research Quarterly* 7 (4): 483–99.

Fromberg, D. 1992. Play. In *The early childhood curriculum: A review of current research*, 2d ed., ed. C. Seefeldt, 35–74. New York: Teachers College Press.

Galinsky, E., C. Howes, S. Kontos, & M. Shinn. 1994. *The study of children in family child care and relative care: Highlights of findings*. New York: Families and Work Institute.

Gallahue, D. 1993. Motor development and movement skill acquisition in early childhood education. In *Handbook of research on the education of young children*, ed. B. Spodek, 24–41. New York: Macmillan.

Gallahue, D. 1995. Transforming physical education curriculum. In *Reaching potentials: Transforming early childhood curriculum and assessment, volume 2*, eds. S. Bredekamp & T. Rosegrant, 125–44. Washington, DC: NAEYC.

Garbarino, J., N. Dubrow, K. Kostelny, & C. Pardo. 1992. *Children in danger: Coping with the consequences of community violence*. San Francisco: Jossey-Bass.

Gardner, H. 1983. *Frames of mind: The theory of multiple intelligences*. New York: Basic.

Gardner, H. 1991. *The unschooled mind: How children think and how schools should teach*. New York: Basic.

Gelman, R., & R. Baillargeon. 1983. A review of some Piagetian concepts. In *Handbook of Child Psychology*, vol. 3, ed. P.H. Mussen, 167–230. New York: Wiley.

Gelman, R., & E. Meck. 1983. Preschoolers' counting: Principles before skill. *Cognition* 13: 343–59.

Hale-Benson, J. 1986. *Black children: Their roots, cultures, and learning styles*. Rev. ed. Baltimore: Johns Hopkins University Press.

Herron, R., & B. Sutton-Smith. 1971. *Child's play*. New York: Wiley.

Hiebert, E.H., & J.M. Papierz. 1990. The emergent literacy construct and kindergarten and readiness books of basal reading series. *Early Childhood Research Quarterly* 5 (3): 317–34.

Hohmann, M., & D. Weikart. 1995. *Educating young children: Active learning practices for preschool and child care programs*. Ypsilanti, MI: High/Scope Educational Research Foundation.

Hollestelle, K. 1993. At the core: Entrepreneurial skills for family child care providers. In *The early childhood career lattice: Perspectives on professional development,* eds. J. Johnson & J.B. McCracken, 63–65. Washington, DC: NAEYC.

Howes, C. 1983. Caregiver behavior in center and family day care. *Journal of Applied Developmental Psychology* 4: 96–107.

Howes, C. 1988. Relations between early child care and schooling. *Developmental Psychology* 24 (1): 53–57.

Howes, C., D.A. Phillips, M. Whitebook. 1992. Thresholds of quality: Implications for the social development of children in center-based child care. *Child Development* 63 (2): 449–60.

Howes, C., E. Smith, & E. Galinsky. 1995. *The Florida child care quality improvement study.* New York: Families and Work Institute.

Kagan, S.L. 1991. *United we stand: Collaboration for child care and early education services.* New York: Teachers College Press.

Kagan, S., S. Goffin, S. Golub, & E. Pritchard. 1995. *Toward systematic reform: Service integration for young children and their families.* Falls Church, VA: National Center for Service Integration.

Kamil, C., & J.K. Ewing. 1996. Basing teaching on Piaget's constructivism. *Childhood Education* 72 (5): 260–64.

Katz, L. 1995. *Talks with teachers of young children: A collection.* Norwood, NJ: Ablex.

Katz, L., & S. Chard. 1989. *Engaging children minds: The project approach.* Norwood, NJ: Ablex.

Katz, L., D. Evangelou, & J. Hartman. 1990. *The case for mixed-age grouping in early education.* Washington, DC: NAEYC.

Kendrick, A., R. Kaufmann, & K. Messenger, eds. 1995. *Healthy young children: A manual for programs.* Washington, DC: NAEYC.

Kohn, A. 1993. *Punished by rewards.* Boston: Houghton Mifflin.

Kostelnik, M., A Soderman, & A. Whiren. 1993. *Developmentally appropriate programs in early childhood education.* New York: Macmillan.

Kuhl, P. 1994. Learning and representation in speech and language. *Current Opinion in Neurobiology* 4: 812–22.

Lary, R.T. 1990. Successful students. *Education Issues* 3 (2): 11–17.

Layzer, J.I., B.D. Goodson, & M. Moss. 1993. *Life in preschool: Volume one of an observational study of early childhood programs for disadvantaged four-year-olds.* Cambridge, MA: Abt Association.

Lazar, I., & R. Darlington. 1982. *Lasting effects of early education: A report from the consortium for longitudinal studies.* Monographs of the Society for Research in Child Development, vol. 47, nos. 2–3, serial no. 195. Chicago: University of Chicago Press.

Lee, V.E., J. Brooks-Gunn, & E. Schuur. 1988. Does Head Start work? A 1-year follow-up comparison of disadvantaged children attending Head Start, no preschool, and other preschool programs. *Developmental Psychology* 24 (2): 210–22.

Legters, N., & R.E. Slavin. 1992. Elementary students at risk: A status report. Paper commissioned by the Carnegie Corporation of New York for meeting on elementary-school reform. 1–2 June.

Levy, A.K., L. Schaefer, & P.C. Phelps. 1986. Increasing preschool effectiveness: Enhancing the language abilities of 3- and 4-year-old children through planned sociodramatic play. *Early Childhood Research Quarterly* 1 (2): 133–40.

Levy, A.K., C.H. Wolfgang, & M.A. Koorland. 1992. Sociodramatic play as a method for enhancing the language performance of kindergarten age students. *Early Childhood Research Quarterly* 7 (2): 245–62.

Malaguzzi, L. 1993. History, ideas, and basic philosophy. In *The hundred languages of children: The Reggio Emilia approach to early childhood education,* eds. C. Edwards, L. Gandini, & G. Forman, 41–89. Norwood, NJ: Ablex.

Mallory, B. 1992. Is it always appropriate to be developmental? Convergent models for early intervention practice. *Topics in Early Childhood Special Education* 11 (4): 1–12.

Mallory, B. 1994. Inclusive policy, practice, and theory for young children with developmental differences. In *Diversity and developmentally appropriate practices: Challenges for early childhood education,* eds. B. Mallory & R. New, 44–61. New York: Teachers College Press.

Mallory, B.L., & R.S. New. 1994a. *Diversity and developmentally appropriate practices: Challenges for early childhood education.* New York: Teachers College Press.

Mallory, B.L., & R.S. New. 1994b. Social constructivist theory and principles of inclusions: Challenges for early childhood special education. *Journal of Special Education* 28 (3): 322–37.

Marcon, R.A. 1992. Differential effects of three preschool models on inner-city 4-year-olds. *Early Childhood Research Quarterly* 7 (4): 517–30.

Maslow, A. 1954. *Motivation and personality.* New York: Harper & Row.

Miller, L.B., & R.P. Bizzell. 1984. Long-term effects of four preschool programs: Ninth and tenth-grade results. *Child Development* 55 (4): 1570–87.

Mitchell, A., M. Seligson, & F. Marx. 1989. *Early childhood programs and the public schools.* Dover, MA: Auburn House.

Morrow, L.M. 1990. Preparing the classroom environment to promote literacy during play. *Early Childhood Research Quarterly* 5 (4): 537–54.

NAEYC. 1987. *NAEYC position statement on licensing and other forms of regulation of early childhood programs in centers and family day care.* Washington, DC: Author.

NAEYC. 1991. *Accreditation criteria and procedures of the National Academy of Early Childhood Programs.* Rev. ed. Washington, DC: Author.

NAEYC. 1993. *Compensation guidelines for early childhood professionals.* Washington, DC: Author.

NAEYC. 1994. NAEYC position statement: A conceptual framework for early childhood professional development, adopted November 1993. *Young Children* 49 (3): 68–77.

NAEYC. 1996a NAEYC position statement: Responding to linguistic and cultural diversity—Recommendations for effective early childhood education. *Young Children* 51 (2): 4–12.

NAEYC. 1996b. NAEYC position statement: Technology and young children—Ages three through eight. *Young Children* 51 (6): 11–16.

NAEYC & NAECS/SDE (National Association of Early Childhood Specialists in State Departments of Education). 1992. Guidelines for appropriate curriculum content and assessment in programs serving children ages 3 through 8. In *Reaching potentials: Appropriate curriculum and assessment for young children, volume 1,* eds. S. Bredekamp & T. Rosegrant, 9–27. Washington, DC: NAEYC.

NASBE (National Association of State Boards of Education). 1991. *Caring communities: Supporting young children and families.* Alexandria, VA: Author.

Natriello, G., E. McDill, & A. Pallas. 1990. *Schooling disadvantaged children: Racing against catastrophe.* New York: Teachers College Press.

NCES (National Center for Education Statistics). 1993. *The condition of education, 1993.* Washington, DC: U.S. Department of Education.

NCSL (National Conference of State Legislatures). 1995. *Early childhood care and education: An investment that works.* Denver: Author.

NEGP (National Education Goals Panel). 1991. *National education goals report: Building a nation of learners.* Washington, DC: Author.

New, R. 1993. Cultural variations on developmentally appropriate practice: Challenges to theory and practice. In *The hundred languages of children: The Reggio Emilia approach to early childhood education,* eds. C. Edwards, L. Gandini, & G. Forman, 215–32. Norwood, NJ: Ablex.

New, R. 1994. Culture, child development, and developmentally appropriate practices: Teachers as collaborative researchers. In *Diversity and developmentally appropriate practices: Challenges for early childhood education,* eds. B. Mallory & R. New, 65–83. New York: Teachers College Press.

Nye, B.A., J. Boyd-Zaharias, & B.D. Fulton. 1994. *The lasting benefits study: A continuing analysis of the effect of small class size in kindergarten through third grade on student achievement test scores in subsequent grade levels—seventh grade (1992–93),* technical report. Nashville: Center of Excellence for Research in Basic Skills, Tennessee State University.

Nye, B.A., J. Boyd-Zaharias, B.D. Fulton, & M.P. Wallenhorst. 1992. Smaller classes really are better. *The American School Board Journal* 179 (5): 31–33.

Parker, J.G., & S.R. Asher. 1987. Peer relations and later personal adjustment: Are low-accepted children at risk? *Psychology Bulletin* 102 (3): 357–89.

Phillips, C.B. 1994. The movement of African-American children through sociocultural contexts: A case of conflict resolution. In *Diversity and developmentally appropriate practices: Challenges for early childhood education,* eds. B. Mallory & R. New, 137–54. New York: Teachers College Press.

Phillips, D.A., K. McCartney, & S. Scarr. 1987. Child care quality and children's social development. *Developmental Psychology* 23 (4): 537–43.

Piaget, J. 1952. *The origins of intelligence in children.* New York: International Universities Press.

Plomin, R. 1994a. *Genetics and experience: The interplay between nature and nurture.* Thousand Oaks, CA: Sage.

Plomin, R. 1994b. Nature, nurture, and social development. *Social Development* 3: 37–53.

Powell, D. 1994. Parents, pluralism, and the NAEYC statement on developmentally appropriate practice. In *Diversity and developmentally appropriate practices: Challenges for early childhood education,* eds. B. Mallory & R. New, 166–82. New York: Teachers College Press.

Pramling, I. 1991. Learning about "the shop": An approach to learning in preschool. *Early Children Research Quarterly* 6 (2): 151–66.

Resnick, L. 1996. Schooling and the workplace: What relationship? In *Preparing youth for the 21st century,* 21–27. Washington, DC: Aspen Institute.

Rogoff, B. 1990. *Apprenticeship in thinking: Cognitive development in social context.* New York: Oxford University Press.

Rogoff, B., J. Mistry, A. Goncu, & C. Mosier. 1993. *Guided participation in cultural activity by toddlers and caregivers.* Monographs of the Society for Research in Child Development, vol. 58, no. 8, serial no. 236. Chicago: University of Chicago Press.

Ross, S.M., L.J. Smith, J. Casey, & R.E. Slavin. 1995. Increasing the academic success of disadvantaged children: An examination of alternative early intervention programs. *American Educational Research Journal* 32 (4): 773–800.

Ruopp, R., J. Travers, F. Glantz, & C. Coelen. 1979. *Children at the center: Final report of the National Day Care Study.* Cambridge, MA: Abt Associates.

Sameroff, A., & S. McDonough. 1994. Educational implications of developmental transition: Revisiting the 5- to 7-year shift. *Phi Delta Kappan* 76 (3): 188–93.

Scarr, S., & K. McCartney. 1983. How people make their own environments: A theory of genotype–environment effects. *Child Development* 54: 425–35.

Schrader, C.T. 1989. Written language use within the context of young children's symbolic play. *Early Childhood Research Quarterly* 4 (2): 225–44.

Schrader, C.T. 1990. Symbolic play as a curricular tool for early literacy development. *Early Childhood Research Quarterly* 5 (1): 79–103.

Schweinhart, L.J., & D.P. Weikart. 1996. *Lasting differences: The High/Scope preschool curriculum comparison study through age 23.* Monographs of the High/Scope Educational Research Foundation, no 12. Ypsilanti, MI: High/Scope Press.

Schweinhart, L.J., H.V. Barnes, & D.P. Weikart. 1993. *Significant benefits: The High/Scope Perry Preschool Study through age 27.* Monographs of the High/Scope Educational Research Foundation, no. 10, Ypsilanti, MI: High/Scope Press.

Schweinhart, L.J., D.P. Weikart, & M.B. Larner. 1986. Child-initiated activities in early childhood programs may help prevent delinquency. *Early Childhood Research Quarterly* 1 (3): 303–12.

Seefeldt, C., ed. 1992. *The early childhood curriculum: A review of current research.* 2d ed. New York: Teachers College Press.

Seifert, K. 1993. Cognitive development and early childhood education. In *Handbook of research on the education of young children,* ed. B. Spodek, 9–23. New York: Macmillan.

Seppanen, P.S., D. Kaplan deVries, & M. Seligson. 1993. *National study of before and after school programs.* Portsmouth, NH: RMC Research Corp.

Shepard, L. 1994. The challenges of assessing young children appropriately. *Phi Delta Kappan* 76 (3): 206–13.

Shepard, L.A., & M.L. Smith. 1988. Escalating academic demand in kindergarten: Some nonsolutions. *Elementary School Journal* 89 (2): 135–46.

Shepard, L.A., & M.L. Smith. 1989. *Flunking grades: Research and policies on retention.* Bristol, PA: Taylor & Francis.

Slavin, R., N. Karweit, & N. Madden, eds. 1989. *Effective programs for students at-risk.* Boston: Allyn & Bacon.

Smilansky, S., & L. Shefatya. 1990. *Facilitating play: A medium for promoting cognitive, socioemotional, and academic development in young children.* Gaithersburg, MD: Psychosocial & Educational Publications.

Spodek, B., ed. 1993. *Handbook of research on the education of young children.* New York: Macmillan.

Sroufe, L.A., R.G. Cooper, & G.B. DeHart. 1992. *Child development: Its nature and course.* 2d ed. New York: Knopf.

Stern, D. 1985. *The psychological world of the human infant.* New York: Basic.

Stremmel, A.J., & V.R. Fu. 1993. Teaching in the zone of proximal development: Implications for responsive teaching practice. *Child and Youth Care Forum* 22 (5): 337–50.

Taylor, J.M., & W.S. Taylor. 1989. *Communicable diseases and young children in group settings.* Boston: Little, Brown.

Tobin, J., D. Wu, & D. Davidson. 1989. *Preschool in three cultures.* New Haven, CT: Yale University Press.

U.S. Department of Health & Human Services. 1996. *Head Start performance standards.* Washington, DC: Author.

Vandell, D.L., & M.A. Corasanti. 1990. Variations in early child care: Do they predict subsequent social, emotional, and cognitive differences? *Early Childhood Research Quarterly* 5 (4): 555–72.

Vandell, D.L., & C.D. Powers. 1983. Day care quality and children's freeplay activities. *American Journal of Orthopsychiatry* 53 (4): 493–500.

Vandell, D.L., V.K. Henderson, & K.S. Wilson. 1988. A longitudinal study of children with day-care experiences of varying quality. *Child Development* 59 (5): 1286–92.

Vygotsky, L. 1978. *Mind in society: The development of higher psychological processes.* Cambridge, MA: Harvard University Press.

Wardle, F. 1996. Proposal: An anti-bias and ecological model for multicultural education. *Childhood Education* 72 (3): 152–56.

Wertsch, J. 1985. *Culture, communication, and cognition: Vygotskian perspectives.* New York: Cambridge University Press.

White, S.H. 1965. Evidence for a hierarchical arrangement of learning processes. In *Advances in child development and behavior,* eds. L.P. Lipsitt & C.C. Spiker, 187–220. New York: Academic Press.

Whitebook, M., C. Howes, & D. Philips. 1989. *The national child care staffing study: Who cares? Child care teachers and the quality of care in America.* Final report. Oakland, CA: Child Care Employee Project.

Wieder, S., & S.I. Greenspan. 1993. The emotional basis of learning. In *Handbook of research on the education of young children,* ed. B. Spodek, 77–104. New York: Macmillan.

Willer, B. 1990. *Reaching the full cost of quality in early childhood programs.* Washington, DC: NAEYC.

Willer, B., S.L. Hofferth, E.E. Kisker, P. Divine-Hawkins, E. Farquhar, & F.B. Glantz. 1991. *The demand and supply of child care in 1990.* Washington, DC.: NAEYC.

Witkin, H. 1962. *Psychological differentiation: Studies of development.* New York: Wiley.

Wolery, M., & J. Wilbers, eds. 1994. *Including children with special needs in early childhood programs.* Washington, DC: NAEYC.

Wolery, M., P. Strain, & D. Bailey. 1992. Reaching potentials of children with special needs. In *Reaching Potentials: Appropriate curriculum and assessment for young children, volume 1,* eds. S. Bredekamp & T. Rosegrant, 92–111. Washington, DC: NAEYC.

Zero to Three: The National Center, 1995. *Caring for infants and toddlers in groups: Developmentally appropriate practice.* Arlington, VA: Author.

Index

Relations of constraint, 344
Relations of cooperation, 344–45
Relatives, child care by, 174–75
Reliability, of assessment, 57
Religions, child care and preK-12
    programs of, 83
Reporting
    observation for, 69
    by professional, 13
Representation, on behalf of children and
    families, 18
Research, 46–47
    for parent and family involvement,
        523
Resource and referral (R & R) services, of
    DoD, 189
Resource libraries, family involvement
    and, 520
Respect
    for child, 82, 141–42
    teaching of, 20
Responsibilities, to help develop new
    behaviors, 414
Restructuring, of public schools,
    Montessori and, 149
Retention, 317–20
Rice Creek Elementary School,
    technology programs at, 386–87
Ridgley, Linda, 315
Rinaldi, Carina, 163
Rivas-Chacon, Ella, 147
Roberts, Jeanne, 198, 243
Rooms, in the home, arranging to help
    children guide their behavior, 417
Rough-and-tumble play, 289
Rousseau, Jean-Jacques, 82, 84–85, 86
Routines, classroom, guiding behavior
    and use of, 418
Rubrics
    for collaborative problem solving,
        425–26
    kindergarten, 75
Running record, 63

Sadler, Faith Haertig, 493
Safe environment, quality child care and,
    186
Safety and security needs, 51
    guiding behavior and, 411
Safety awareness, infant development
    and, 243
Sand, Jennifer, 367
Scaffolding
    children's literacy development and,
        330–32
    for guiding behavior, 407
    for higher levels of thinking and
        behavior, 345
    in sociocultural theory, 121–22, 123

Schedule
    in preschool, 293–96
    for special needs children, 485
Schemes, in cognitive development, 115
Schlecty, Phil, 386
School(s)
    child-centered, 92
    City & Country School, 94
    Core Knowledge School, 99
    Dewey on, 93
    Froebel Kindergarten, 91
    infant, 87
    night schools for workers, 87
    Title I programs and, 216–17
School-age care (SAC) programs, of DoD,
    189
School-business involvement, 533–34
Schooling, changes in, 507
School readiness, 276–82
    assessment of, 58–62
    early childhood programs for, 51
    kindergarten teachers' factors for, 277
    maturation and, 277–78
    and placement of kindergarten
        children, 313–20
    ready kids and ready schools, 278
    screening measures for, 58–59
    skills for, 278–82
School-to-career education, 359–62
Schulte, Mary, 475
Schurz, Margarethe, 307
Schwartz, M., 470
Scott Elementary School (Scott Air Force
    Base), cross-categorical Early
    Childhood Special Education
    Program at, 488
Screening measures, 58–59
    instruments and observation records,
        60–62
Seamless services, 208
SECA. See Southern Early Childhood
    Association (SECA)
Secondary circular reactions, 238–39
Security, 51
Seguin, Edouard, 91–92
Seidel, Deborah Q., 313
SEIT. See Special education itinerant
    teacher (SEIT)
Self-actualization, guiding behavior and,
    411, 413–14
Self-actualization theory (Maslow), 96
    hierarchy of needs, 126, 127
    needs in, 123–26
Self-chosen projects, preschoolers and, 275
Self discourse, in Vygotskyian
    constructivist theory, 406
Self-esteem needs, guiding behavior and
    meeting, 412–13
Self-regulation, in children, 406

Sensitive period, 142
    infant learning and, 232
    for language development, 241
Sensorimotor stage
    in cognitive development, 116–18
    infants and toddlers in, 236–39
Sensory impressions, in education, 86
Sensory materials (Montessori method),
    144–46, 285
    purposes of, 146
    types of, 145
Sensory stimulation, infant development
    and, 243
Sensory training, 84
Setting limits, 415
Sexism
    avoiding, 443–45
    defined, 443
Sex-role stereotyping, avoiding,
    443–45
Sexual abuse, 492
Sexual harassment, 444
Shearing (pruning), brain and, 231
Sheffler, Vicki, 2, 36–37, 102, 320
Sheltered instruction, for English
    language learners, 457
Shonkoff, J. P., 248n
Sidney Lanier School (Dallas), 33
Sight word approach, 326
Sigmon, Cheryl M., 367
Simon, Scott, 488
Simon, Theodore, 93
Single-parent families, 38–40
    caregivers for, 532
    headed by fathers, 38, 38 (fig.)
    headed by mothers, 39 (fig.), 41, 510
    involvement of, 528, 529
    poverty among, 41
Skipped-generation children, 509
Slow-to-warm-up child, 254
Smith, Pat, 355
Snow, C. E., 323
Social behaviors, of infants, 252
Social constructivist approach, to guiding
    behavior, 406
Social development, technology and,
    392–93
Socially constructed knowledge, 328
Social play, 284–85, 286
Social policies, and children as
    investments view, 103–4
Social programs, child care and, 173
Social status, of children, 41
Sociocultural theory (Vygotsky), 95,
    121–23, 132–33
    intersubjectivity in, 122
    scaffolding in, 121–22, 123, 407
    zone of proximal development in, 121,
        122, 406, 407

Photo Credits